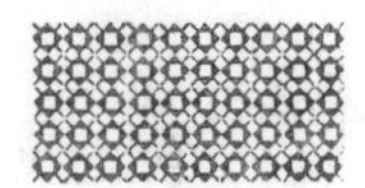

D0540723

Government Under Law

Courtesy LIFE Magazine

A galaxy of justices: Left to right, seated under a painting of Chief Justice John Marshall, are Erwin N. Griswold, Dean, Harvard Law School; Felix Frankfurter, Associate Justice, United States Supreme Court; Patrick Kerwin, Chief Justice of Canada; Earl Warren, Chief Justice of the United States; A. Van de S. Centlivres, Chief Justice of the Appellate Division of the Supreme Court of South Africa; Sir Owen Dixon, Chief Justice of the High Court of Australia; and Sir Raymond Evershed, Master of the Rolls, England.

Government Under Law

A CONFERENCE
Held at Harvard Law School
on the Occasion of the Bicentennial of

JOHN MARSHALL

Chief Justice of the United States, 1801-1835

Edited by Arthur E. Sutherland

HARVARD UNIVERSITY PRESS • CAMBRIDGE • 1956

Distributed in Great Britain by
Oxford University Press, London

Library of Congress Catalog Card Number 56-11287
PRINTED IN THE UNITED STATES OF AMERICA

FOREWORD

The two-hundredth anniversary of John Marshall's birth seems an appropriate time to consider again the ideal of government under law. Obviously great difficulties, both of theory and practice, arise in the application of this ideal to the daily business of government. But in our thinking we stubbornly return to an aspiration that was already old when John Locke wrote—

> Through the Legislative, whether placed in one or more, whether it be always in being, or only by intervals, tho' it be the Supream Power in every Commonwealth; yet . . . it is not, nor can possibly be absolutely Arbitrary over the Lives and Fortunes of the People.

In the hundred and fifty years since he became Chief Justice, John Marshall has come to symbolize for all Americans the doctrine that a written Constitution, interpreted by a Supreme Court, is the supreme law of the land, superseding all governmental action which purports to conflict with it. But this doctrine of constitutionalism seems only one instance of a more fundamental and widespread principle—that government, however organized, should strive to be just and should establish sound institutions for the correction of its own injustices.

To study anew these old ideals and difficulties, the faculty of the Harvard Law School set aside three days in September, 1955, for a conference on Government under Law. To meet with us we invited the alumni of the school and many other distinguished scholars and public men.

The Chief Justice of the United States and two associate justices joined in our deliberations. Our law and our government are part of the common law tradition, and we were aided and inspired by the counsel of representatives of other common law systems—the Chief Justice of South Africa, the Chief Justice of Australia, the Chief Justice of Canada, and the Master of the Rolls from England. We welcomed reminders that the ideal of government under law is no monopoly of common law nations—reminders given us by a distinguished French scholar and by one of our own sons who now represents his country, Costa Rica, as her ambassador to the United States. From a notable Roman Catholic scholar we heard of even older origins of this ideal. And we heard many aspects of government under law in today's troubled world discussed by other wise and learned men from our own country.

In planning for our conference four principal themes were chosen—Government as Protector of the People against the Government; Government under Law in Time of Crisis; The Meaning of Due Process; and The Value of Constitutionalism Today. In order that we might all study these matters in advance, outstanding authorities were invited to write essays on each of these subjects. These we printed and distributed four months before the conference to those expecting to attend. These essays and the addresses of our visitors from other lands were the subject-matter of the discussions during the 22nd, 23rd and 24th of September, 1955.

The conference opened with a word of welcome from the President of the University, and with an address by Mr. Justice Frankfurter on "John Marshall and the Judicial Function." At each of the four "working sessions" of the conference, held in the new James Barr Ames Courtroom in Austin Hall, we heard an address from one of our visitors from abroad; and the essays, which had been printed in advance, were discussed by their authors, by specially qualified speakers who had been invited to prepare comment, and by members of the conference who spoke from the floor. On the evening of Friday, September 23rd, the conference met with students of the Harvard Law School to hear addresses by Professor Tunc of the University of Grenoble and by the Chief Justice of South Africa. And on Saturday, September 24th, the two-hundredth anniversary of Chief Justice Marshall's birth, the conference gathered for dinner in Memorial Hall and heard the closing addresses of the President of

Harvard University and of the Chief Justice of the United States. In order to permit these papers, addresses, and discussions to be seen by a wider audience, and to provide a record of these meetings, this volume has been prepared.

It is suitable to make here a brief appraisal of the worth of this effort. Our conference did not set out to restate in detail specifications of justice in government; and indeed that task would have been impossible for us, or for any number of such gatherings, no matter how much wisdom and conscientious thought were put forth. But the eight hundred men and women who came—lawyers, political scientists, historians, philosophers, economists, churchmen, and other men of learning—did affirm by their presence that an aspiration to justice in government should and does exist, that even if we can not prescribe its precise outlines we can wish for it, and work for it according to our talents.

Three strands of thought ran notably throughout the conference. One of these was the concept that government exists as a framework for human cooperation and that men should not consider it solely with suspicion, as a force to be confined. Another was affirmation that the purpose of government and of society is the individual's good: President Pusey said, at the final gathering, "Basic to the whole discussion has been the tenet that government exists for the sake of the individual and that there is a limit to what government can do to him." The third conspicuous thread of thought was concern for the criteria of goodness in law and in government. Again and again speakers returned to the theme that fundamentally constitutionalism is a moral concept; that justice is goodness; that though it can not be defined, it can be recognized. At the final working session of the conference, John Lord O'Brian by his lofty earnestness profoundly moved all who heard him restate as his apologia his belief that in constitutional interpretation no canon can omit the element of moral conviction; that there can be no health in a democracy where there is no acceptance of the supremacy of law, where the law is not interpreted in terms of man's highest moral insights. The Bicentennial Conference was united in this statement. The significance of the affirmation could be wider than we realized.

The conference was made possible by the generous support of the Rockefeller Foundation. To that Foundation go the thanks of our School, of our University, and of all those who had the inspiration of participating in our discussion of Government under Law. It is a clear duty, and a pleasure, too, to record here the special debt of all concerned to two members of the staff of the Harvard Law School. Professor Arthur E. Sutherland, Jr., was chairman of the committee of the faculty which was in charge of the planning of the program, and carrying it out. He has also assumed the very considerable task of editing this report of the conference. Assistant Dean Russell H. Peck carried out all of the administrative arrangements for the conference, and was largely responsible for the smoothness with which the meetings were carried off. The conference was a considerable venture and many persons contributed to its success. To all of them we are much indebted for their part in this opportunity to stop in the course of current problems and consider anew the meaning and place of law as a means to man's highest aspirations.

ERWIN N. GRISWOLD

Contents

VII

The frontispiece is reproduced by courtesy of LIFE Magazine. All the other photographs are by George Woodruff.

I

I

THE OPENING OF THE CONFERENCE ON

Government Under Law

The Conference assembled at the Harvard Law School in the Ames Courtroom, Austin Hall, at eleven in the morning of Thursday, September 22, 1955. Lawyers, judges, theologians, scholars of many disciplines, and other thoughtful people from many countries filled the six hundred and more seats in the Courtroom. On the Bench with Dean Griswold were Nathan Marsh Pusey, President of Harvard, and Felix Frankfurter, long a professor at the Harvard Law School, now an Associate Justice of the United States Supreme Court. On the paneled wall behind the Bench was a portrait of John Marshall, lent to the School by the Grey family of Boston for use at the Conference. The picture came to John Chipman Grey, long Royall Professor of Law at Harvard, from the Morse family of Philadelphia, for whom it had been painted from life in 1825 by John Wesley Jarvis of that city.

Dean Griswold* opened the session with a reminder that in the stone over the portals of Langdell Hall are Bracton's words *Non sub homine sed sub Deo et lege,* words repeated by Coke on a day in the law's history which the American and English peoples think cardinal in their shared tradition. This greatest single statement of the doctrine of government under law, John Marshall made live in a Constitutional system; the Conference would rightly honor him while it considered that great inheritance.

* ERWIN NATHANIEL GRISWOLD, *Dean of the Harvard Law School.* Dean Griswold was born in Ohio in 1904. He took his A.B. and M.A. at Oberlin in 1925; his LL.B. in 1928 and his S.J.D. in 1929 at Harvard. Mr. Griswold was admitted to the Ohio Bar in 1929 and practiced law in Cleveland until he entered the office of the Solicitor-General later in that year. He remained in the Department of Justice until 1934 when he became an Assistant Professor of Law at Harvard Law School. He became a Professor in 1935 and Dean in 1946. He has served the State of Massachusetts and the United States in many different capacities and has written and published a number of books and articles in the field of taxation and conflict of laws. His most recent book is "The Fifth Amendment Today."

The Dean then introduced President Pusey.

PRESIDENT PUSEY*

Harvard University is proud indeed to be host to this distinguished gathering. We are very happy to have all of you here.

There has been a fence around Harvard Yard almost from the beginning of the history of the College. I don't know why it was put there in the first place. I suppose it was to keep the President's cow safe, and prevent stray cattle from the Common from appearing in the classroom. But the fence today serves as a useful symbol of the fact that this university, and every university, has a character and purpose peculiar to itself, and for this reason should be set off from the world outside. The fence around the Harvard Yard serves to remind us that the University must somehow be protected in its essential function.

On the other hand, it was never intended that the fence should insulate the University from the workaday world. This conference helps insure that the work of the University shall not be done in unawareness of the problems outside the University, or in any sense of irresponsibility or of social indifference. We are profoundly grateful to you for coming, and thus reminding us to do our own work with a sense of its relevance to the work in which other people are involved.

I wish that I could claim John Marshall as a Harvard man; and so I can, at least by our adoption. It is very easy to explain why John Marshall didn't come to Harvard Law School—he had been the Chief Justice, I gather, for more than fifteen years before the Harvard Law School was founded. It is a little more difficult to explain why he didn't come to Harvard College. About all I can say is that it wasn't

* NATHAN MARSH PUSEY, *President of Harvard University.* President Pusey was born in Iowa in 1907. He was a member of the class of 1928 at Harvard; took his Master's degree there in 1932 and his Ph.D. in 1937. He has been a member of the faculties of Harvard, of Lawrence, of Scripps, and of Wesleyan. He became President of Lawrence College in 1944, and President of Harvard in 1953.

President Nathan M. Pusey welcomes the conference in the Ames Courtroom of Austin Hall. At his right is Mr. Justice Frankfurter; at his left, Dean Griswold.

Harold F. Birnbaum, of the Los Angeles Bar, comments on the paper given by John Lord O'Brian.

Associate Justice Frankfurter and Chief Justice Warren.

Professor André Tunc discusses his paper.

Joseph J. Hurley, of the Boston Bar, comments on the paper given by Professor Fairman.

Left to right: Chief Justice Kerwin, Master of the Rolls Sir Raymond Evershed, and Chief Justices Warren and Centlivres.

a very usual thing for people to come from the farthest reaches of Virginia to Cambridge in the eighteenth century. But we did catch on in time, and gave John Marshall an honorary degree in 1806, so he is a Harvard man after all. The disconcerting fact is, however, that not only did John Marshall not attend Harvard, but his college experience was limited to only a few weeks at William and Mary. And actually he had very little formal education at all. The memory of this great man ought to help, I think, to keep us modest, because we had no part in his education.

We are grateful that you are here. The great perennial themes of man's history—justice, law, liberty—these all weave themselves into Marshall's works; and their present-day applications, and the difficulties connected with these great themes are the reasons why we are here. Your presence testifies to the importance of the occasion. I hope that when these days are over, every one of you will go away feeling that you have been amply repaid for coming to participate in this conference.

Dean Griswold next introduced Mr. Justice Felix Frankfurter, whose opening address to the Conference was entitled "John Marshall and the Judicial Function."

ADDRESS

John Marshall and the Judicial Function

FELIX FRANKFURTER *

Two hundred years ago a great man was born who indisputably is the "one alone" to be chosen "if American law were to be represented by a single figure." John Marshall was the chief architect "of a new body of jurisprudence, by which guiding principles are raised above the reach of statute and State, and judges are entrusted with a solemn and hitherto unheard-of authority and duty." (HOLMES, COLLECTED LEGAL PAPERS 270 (1920).) Such is the verdict of one whom so qualified a critic as Mr. Justice Cardozo deemed probably the greatest intellect in the history of the English-speaking judiciary.

Unlike other great pioneers in the law, Hardwicke in equity, Mansfield in commercial law, Stowell in prize law, Holmes in torts, the essential heritage of Marshall, because of the very nature of constitutional law, does not lie in specific precepts, definite rules more or less easy of application in new circumstances. Of his opinions it is peculiarly true that their "radiating potencies" go far beyond the actual holdings of the decisions. See *Hawks v. Hamill,* 288 U.S. 52, 58 (1933). The tendencies propelled by his opinions give him his unique place in our history; through them he belongs among the main builders of our Nation. Although he led an important diplomatic mission and was not an otiose

* FELIX FRANKFURTER, *Associate Justice of the Supreme Court of the United States.* Mr. Justice Frankfurter was born in Vienna in 1882, and came to the United States as a boy. He took degrees at the City College of New York and at the Harvard Law School. His first public service, as Assistant United States Attorney for the Southern District of New York, began in 1906, the year of his graduation from Law School. His life has included tasks performed for the United States in many different capacities, the authorship of many books, and a Professorship at Harvard in which he is gratefully remembered by students who sat in his classes and took part in his seminars. He was appointed to the Supreme Court of the United States in 1939.

Secretary of State, the decisive claim to John Marshall's distinction as a great statesman is as a judge. And he is the only judge who has that distinction. It derives from the happy conjunction of Marshall's qualities of mind and character, the opportunities afforded by the Court over which he was called to preside, the duration of his service, and the time in which he served—the formative period in the country's history.

When Jefferson heard that Hamilton was urging John Marshall to enter Congress, he wrote to Madison, on June 29, 1792: "I am told that Marshall has expressed half a mind to come. Hence I conclude that Hamilton has plyed him well with flattery & sollicitation, and I think nothing better could be done than to make him a judge." (6 THE WRITINGS OF THOMAS JEFFERSON 95-97 (Ford ed. 1895).) How ironically Fate outwitted Jefferson in his desire to sidetrack Marshall to what Jefferson conceived to be the innocuous role of a judge. (I am indebted to Professor Julian P. Boyd for calling my attention to this letter as well as for its exact phrasing, based on the recipient's copy in the Madison Papers, Library of Congress.)

When Marshall came to the Supreme Court, the Constitution was still essentially a virgin document. By a few opinions—a mere handful—he gave institutional direction to the inert ideas of a paper scheme of government. Such an achievement demanded an undimmed vision of the union of States as a Nation and the determination of an uncompromising devotion to such insight. Equally indispensable was the power to formulate views expressing this outlook with the persuasiveness of compelling simplicity.

It is shallow to deny that general ideas have influence or to minimize their importance. Marshall's ideas, diffused in all sorts of ways, especially through the influence of the legal profession, have become the presuppositions of our political institutions. He released an enduring spirit, a mode of approach for generations of judges charged with the awesome duty of subjecting the conduct of government and the claims of individual rights to the touchstone of a written document, binding the Government and safeguarding such rights. He has afforded this guidance not only for his own country. In the federalisms that have evolved out of the British Empire, Marshall's outlook in constitutional adjudications has been the lode-star. Unashamedly I recall the familiar phrase in which he expressed the core of his constitutional philosophy: "it is *a constitution* we are expounding." *M'Culloch v. Maryland,* 4 Wheat. 316, 407 (1819). It bears repeating because it is, I believe, the single most important utterance in the literature of constitutional law—most important because most comprehensive and comprehending.

I should like to follow James Bradley Thayer in believing that the conception of the Nation which Marshall derived from the Constitution and set forth in *M'Culloch v. Maryland* is his greatest single judicial performance. It *is* that, both in its persuasiveness and in its effect. As good a test as I know of the significance of an opinion is to contemplate the consequences of its opposite. The courage of *Marbury v. Madison,* 1 Cranch 137 (1803), is not minimized by suggesting that its reasoning is not impeccable and its conclusion, however wise, not inevitable. I venture to say this though fully aware that, since Marshall's time and largely, I suspect, through the momentum of the experience which he initiated, his conclusion in *Marbury v. Madison* has been deemed by great English-speaking courts an indispensable, implied characteristic of a written constitution. Holmes could say, as late as 1913: "I do not think the United States would come to an end if we lost our power to declare an Act of Congress void." But he went on to say: "I do think the Union would be imperiled if we could not make that declaration as to the laws of the several States. For one in my place sees how often a local policy prevails with those who are not trained to national views and how often action is taken that embodies what the Commerce Clause was meant to end." (HOLMES, COLLECTED LEGAL PAPERS 296 (1920).) One can, I believe, say with assurance that a failure to conceive the Constitution as Marshall conceived it in *M'Culloch v. Maryland,* to draw from it the national powers which have since been exercised and to exact deference to such powers from the States, would have been reflected by a very different United States than history knows. Marshall surely was right when he wrote, a month after he rejected the argument for Maryland: "If the principles which have been advanced on this occasion were to prevail, the Constitution would be converted into the old Confederation."

Marshall's intrinsic achievements are too solid and his personal qualities too homespun to tolerate mythical treatment. It is important not to make untouchable dogmas of the fallible reasoning of even our greatest judge, and not to attribute God-like qualities to the builders of our Nation. Does it not border on the ludicrous that by questioning whether Marshall was an original thinker Holmes nearly barred his own way to the Supreme Court? So deeply had uncritical reverence for Marshall's place in our national pantheon lodged itself in the confident judgment of President Theodore Roosevelt. (See 1 SELECTIONS FROM THE CORRESPONDENCE OF THEODORE ROOSEVELT AND HENRY CABOT LODGE 517-19 (1925).) As though one should look among even the greatest of judges for what Holmes called "originators of transforming thought." (HOLMES, COLLECTED LEGAL PAPERS 269 (1920).) I venture to suggest that had they the mind of such originators, the bench is not the place for its employment. Transforming thought implies too great a break with the past, implies too much discontinuity, to be imposed upon society by one who is entrusted with enforcing its law.

Marshall's creativeness has from time to time been discounted by attributing the ground he broke in his opinions to the arguments of the great lawyers who appeared before him, especially Webster. The latter was no mean appreciator of his own performance, but an examination of his argument in *Gibbons v. Ogden,* 9 Wheat. 1 (1824), hardly confirms his boast that Marshall's opinion "was little else than a recital of my argument." (HARVEY, REMINISCENCES AND ANECDOTES OF DANIEL WEBSTER 142 (1877).) Powerful counsel no doubt have impact upon the strongest Court, and probably never in the history of the Supreme Court has such a galaxy of talent appeared before it as in Marshall's day. Not the least distinction of a great judge is his capacity to assimilate, to modify or to reject the discursive and inevitably partisan argument of even the most persuasive counsel and to transform their raw material into a judicial judgment. So it was with Marshall.

Again, it is not to be assumed that what Marshall wrote was wholly the product of his own brain, freed from infusion of his brethren's thinking. In his day there was the closest intimacy among the judges. It is inconceivable that they did not discuss their cases in their common boarding-house. A man of Marshall's charm and power was bound to make himself deeply felt among his brethren. But the assumption that he dominated his colleagues leaves out of reckoning the strong personalities among them. Story had the deepest devotion to Marshall, but he also had views and vanity. Johnson's opinions reveal tough-mindedness, abounding intellectual energy, and a downright character. Likewise, we may be sure that Bushrod Washington was no mere echo. And so one may be confident in inferring that the novelty of the issues, the close social relations of the Justices, the ample opportunities they had for discussion among themselves, precluded Marshall's path-breaking opinions from being exclusively solo performances. Then as now, constitutional decisions are the outcome of the deliberative process, and as such, more or less, composite products. But their expression is individual. The voice of the Court cannot avoid imparting the distinction of its own accent to a Court opinion. In the leading constitutional cases Marshall spoke for the Court. But *he* spoke. The prestige of his office, the esteem which he personally aroused, the deference he evoked, enabled Marshall to formulate in his own way an agreement collectively reached. Thus, in his exposition of the Commerce

Clause, Marshall indulged in observations not only beyond the necessities of the cases but outside the demands of his own analysis.

To slight these phases of his opinions as dicta, though such they were on a technical view, is to disregard significant aspects of his labors and the ways in which constitutional law develops. There can be little doubt that Marshall saw and seized his opportunities to educate the country to a spacious view of the Constitution, to accustom the public mind to broad national powers, to counteract the commercial and political self-centeredness of States. He was on guard against every tendency to continue treating the new Union as though it were the old Confederation. He imparted such a momentum to his views that the Court and eventually the country were moved in his general direction, beyond his own time and into our own.

The role that Marshall played in the evolution of our Nation ought, I should think, to make it difficult for those who believe that history is reducible to laws, to fit him into their schemata. Surely the course of American history would have been markedly different if the Senate had not rejected the nomination of John Rutledge to succeed Jay as Chief Justice; if the benign Cushing, a Federalist of different composition from Marshall's, had not withdrawn after a week and had continued as Chief Justice till his death in 1810; if Ellsworth's resignation had come later; if John Adams had persuaded Jay to return as Chief Justice; or if some readily imaginable circumstance had delayed Ellsworth's replacement till John Adams was out of the White House so that the new Chief Justice would have been a Jeffersonian. (That it would have been Spencer Roane is an unsubstantiated tradition.) John Marshall is a conspicuous instance of Cleopatra's nose.

This does not make me an adherent of the hero theory of history. If I may quote Mr. Isaiah Berlin: "Historical movements exist, and we must be allowed to call them so. Collective acts do occur; societies do rise, flourish, decay, die.

Patterns, 'atmospheres,' complex interrelationships of men or cultures are what they are, and cannot be analysed away into atomic constituents. Nevertheless, to take such expressions so literally that it becomes natural and normal to attribute to them causal properties, active powers, transcendent properties . . . is to be fatally deceived by myths. . . . There is no formula which guarantees a successful escape from either the Scylla of populating the world with imaginary powers and dominions, or the Charybdis of reducing everything to the verifiable behavior of identifiable men and women in precisely denotable places and times." (BERLIN, HISTORICAL INEVITABILITY 16 (1954).) Certainly on this occasion it is appropriate to assert with emphasis that John Marshall was not the fated agency of inevitable economic and social forces to make his decisive contribution in the shaping of this country's destiny.

Temperament, experience and association converged to his outlook in judicial action. Even more truly than Gibbon could say of himself, "the Captain of the Hampshire grenadiers . . . has not been useless to the historian of the Roman Empire" can it be claimed that Marshall's experience at Valley Forge was not without decisive influence in the work of the great Chief Justice. (THE AUTOBIOGRAPHIES OF EDWARD GIBBON 190 (John Murray ed. 1896).) Ties of friendship and effective participation in the struggle for the Constitution confirmed his national outlook. Local government had become associated in his mind with the petty bickerings of narrow ambition and dangerous indifference to rights of property and social cohesion. This revealed the need of a strong central government to whose authority the States must be obedient. Subordination of the States to the authority of the National Government within the scope of its powers was the deepest article of his faith, political and judicial. Experience of men and affairs in the Virginia House of Burgesses, in Congress, as a diplomat, and as Secretary of State, doubtless reinforced a temperament to which abstract theorizing was never congenial. He reflected the literary tradition of his time in his partiality for abstract language to support concrete results. But he had a hardheaded appreciation of the complexities of government, particularly in a federal system. His deep instinct for the practical saved him, on the whole, from rigidities to bind the changing future. Uncompromising as was his aim to promote adequate national power, he was not dogmatic in the choice of doctrine for attaining this end. And so at times, conspicuously in *Gibbons v. Ogden,* his views appear to reflect crosscurrents of doctrine, ambiguously expressed. In one striking instance, *Willson v. The Black Bird Creek Marsh Co.,* 2 Pet. 245 (1829), he did little more than decide, stating hardly any doctrine but hinting enough to foreshadow, certainly in direction, the vitally important accommodation between national and local needs formulated more than twenty years later in *Cooley v. Board of Wardens of the Port of Philadelphia,* 12 How. 299, 319 (1851).

There is a rather supercilious tendency to speak disparagingly of Marshall's work on the Court when dealing with lawyers' law. In contrast to Jefferson's view, which continues to have echoes, of regarding Marshall's associates as his tools in the constitutional cases, praise of his judicial statecraft is sometimes used to emphasize his inferiority in nonconstitutional adjudications. Story, Bushrod Washington, William Johnson, Brockholst Livingston are counted as his superiors. Joseph Story, to be sure, carried great learning, even if not always lightly. Disregard of Bushrod Washington's judicial qualities bespeaks unfamiliarity with Judge Hopkinson's and Horace Binney's estimates of him, and Professor Donald G. Morgan's recent book on Mr. Justice Johnson ought to bring wider appreciation of one of the strongest minds in the Court's history. But none of Marshall's associates will suffer depreciation by recognizing his performance in cases that are lawyers' law. After all, this constituted nine-tenths of the Court's business during the thirty-four years of Marshall's magistracy. He was not a bookish lawyer, though he was no stranger to books. He could, as wise judges do, make them his servants. He eschewed precedents, such as were then available, in his opinions for the Court. But he showed mastery in treatment of precedents where they had been relied on for an undesirable result. By way of example, I avouch his dissent in *The Venus,* 8 Cranch 253, 288 (1814), against the strong views of Washington, J., supported by Story. Likewise, he was not overwhelmed by the parade of Story's learning in *The Nereide,* 9 Cranch 388 (1815), when such learned led to a harsh view of neutral rights. Though he respected Lord Stowell as "a very great man" he cut free from that master of prize law, deeming him to have a learning strong even if unconscious, in favor of captors.

As good an insight as any into the quality of Marshall's intellect is afforded by Francis Walker Gilmer, a brilliant Virginian contemporary of high promise. Marshall's mind, he wrote, "is not very richly stored with knowledge, but it is so creative, so well organized by nature, or disciplined by early education, and constant habits of systematick thinking, that he embraces every subject with the clearness and facility of one prepared by previous study to comprehend and explain it." GILMER, SKETCHES, ESSAYS, AND TRANSLATIONS 23-24, quoted in 2 BEVERIDGE, THE LIFE OF JOHN MARSHALL 178 (1916).)

Charged as I have been with opening a conference to commemorate the two-hundredth anniversary of the birth of John Marshall, I surely have been obedient to my duty in speaking of him. But once I leave the secure footing of that well-trodden ground, what else can be pertinent to an opening address of a three-day conference on Government Under Law, systematically planned with definite parts appropriately assigned to learned inquiriers into the perplexities of the problems summarized by this great theme?

In so far as I have not already exhausted my function, my further relation to the resplendent show to follow is like unto that of the Greek chorus. In view of the pre-occupation of this conference, of course I want to keep strictly within the law of my assignment. Accordingly, I have briefed myself on the proper task of the Greek chorus. While in early days the destiny of the chorus was "involved in that of the principal characters," when the Attic stage was at its highest perfection the chorus was "thrown much further into the background," and appears "not as a participant in the action, but merely as a sympathetic witness." The chorus was, so my authority continues, "removed from the stress and turmoil of the action into a calmer and more remote region, though it still preserves its interest in the events upon the stage." This clearly is my cue, rather than the later still more receding role of the chorus, whereby it "begins to lose even its interest in the action" and "sings odes of a mythological character, which have only the remotest connexion with the incidents of the plot." (HAIGH, THE ATTIC THEATRE 320-21 (2ed. 1898).)

There is little danger that in my remaining observations I shall be intruding on the fertile areas of inquiry that belong to the distinguished speakers whom we are to hear these three days. I hope I shall be equally successful in not straying outside my confining judicial curtilage. One brought up in the traditions of James Bradley Thayer, echoes of whom were still resounding in this very building in my student days, is committed to Thayer's statesman-like conception of the limits within which the Supreme Court should move, and I shall try to be loyal to his admonition regarding the restricted freedom of members of that Court to pursue their private views.

Marshall's significance could not be more fittingly celebrated than by scrutinizing, which is the aim of this conference, the state of "government under law," more particularly under the legal system to which Marshall so heavily contributed, a hundred and twenty years after he wrote his last opinion. Could he listen to these proceedings, nothing would be bound to strike him more than the enlarged scope of law since his day. He would, of course, think of law as legally enforceable rights. For, while he occasionally referred to "natural law," it was not much more than literary garniture, even as in our own day, and not a guiding means for adjudication. He would have sympathized, as other judges have, with Sir Frederick Pollock's remark: "In the Middle Ages natural law was regarded as the senior branch of divine law and therefore had to be treated as infallible (but there was no infallible way of knowing what it was)." (1 HOLMES-POLLOCK LETTERS 275 (Howe ed. 1941).) Marshall would be amazed by the interpenetration of law in government, because during his whole era he was concerned with the Constitution as an instrument predominantly regulating the machinery of government, and more particularly, distributing powers between the central government and the States. The Constitution was not thought of as the repository of the supreme law limiting all government, with a court wielding the deepest-cutting power of deciding whether there is any authority in government at all to do what is sought to be done.

Thus, the gravamen of the attack in the Virginia and Kentucky Resolutions against the Alien and Sedition Acts of 1798 was that they infringed on the rights of the States and were promotive of "a general consolidated government." It deserves to be recalled that even Jefferson attributed to the States the power which he denied to the Federal Government. "Nor does the opinion of the unconstitutionality and consequent nullity of that law [the Sedition Act]," he wrote to Abigail Adams, "remove all restraint from the overwhelming torrent of slander which is confounding all vice and virtue, all truth and falsehood in the US. The power to do that is fully possessed by the several state legislatures. . . . While we deny that Congress have a right to controul the freedom of the press, we have ever asserted the rights of the states, and their exclusive right, to do so." (I am indebted for the exact text of this letter, dated September 11, 1804, to the kindness of Professor Julian P. Boyd, in one of whose forthcoming volumes of "The Papers of Thomas Jefferson" it will duly appear in its entirety.)

The only two Marshallian constitutional opinions that concern individual rights as such, *Fletcher v. Peck,* 6 Cranch 87 (1810), and the *Dartmouth College Case,* 4 Wheat. 518 (1819), rather than the delimitation of power between two governments, are, in the perspective of time, not of great importance. This came to pass partly because of easy legislative correction, partly because the doctrine of strict construction devised in the *Charles River Bridge Case,* 11 Pet. 420 (1837), took the sting out of the decision of the *Dartmouth College Case.* Moreover, insofar as the latter case forbade legislative transfer of the property of the College to the Trustees, it is a safe assumption that the Due Process Clauses would condemn such an attempt. (See Chief Justice Doe's opinion in *Dow v. Northern R. Co.,* 67 N.H. 1, 27-53, 36 Atl. 510, 524-37 (1887); Doe, *A New View of the Dartmouth College Case,* 6 HARV. L. REV. 161, 213 (1892); and Jeremiah Smith in 1 PROC. N.H. BAR ASS'N 287, 302 (n.s. 1901).)

The vast change in the scope of law between Marshall's time and ours is at bottom a reflection of the vast change in the circumstances of society. The range of business covered by Marshall's Court, though operating under a written Constitution, was in the main not very different from the concerns of the English courts, except that the latter dealt much more with property settlements. The vast enveloping present-day role of law is not the design of a statesman nor attributable to the influence of some great thinker. It is a reflection of the great technological revolution which brought in its train what a quiet writer in The Economist could call "the tornado of economic and social change of the last century." Law has been an essential accompaniment of the shift from "watch-dog government"—the phrase is George Kennan's—to the service state. For government has become a service-state, whatever the tint of the party in power and whatever time-honored slogans it may use to enforce and promote measures that hardly vindicate the slogans. Profound social changes continue to be in the making, due to movements of industrialization, urbanization and permeating egalitarian ideas.

With crude accuracy I have just summarized the situation in the countries of the English-speaking world, about which alone I may speak. But when these transforming economic and social forces got under full swing in the United States, lawyers and courts found available in the Fourteenth Amendment resources for curbing legislative responses to new pressures. That Amendment was gradually invoked against the substance of legislation and not merely to support claims based on traditionally fair procedure.

I have thus reached the slippery slope of due process. But not even to take a glance at it in a reconnaissance, however sketchy, of government under law, would indeed be to play "Hamlet" without Hamlet.

It has been frequently stated that when a question arises in due course of a litigation, whether a constitutional provision has been infringed, the established courts of justice "must of necessity determine that question." (See Lord Selborne in *The Queen v. Burah,* 3 App. Cas. 889,904 (P.C. 1878), quoted approvingly by Lord Wright in *James v. Commonwealth of Australia,* [1936] A.C. 578,613 (P.C.) see also *Swart, N. O. and Nicol, N. O. v. de Kock and Garner,* [1951] 3 So. Afr. L.R. 589, 601-02 and 611).) This is only qualifieldly true regarding our Constitution. Thus, the explicit provision requiring one State to surrender to another a fugitive from justice (art. IV, § 2, cl. 2) is "merely declaratory of a moral duty" and is not, because of the subject-matter, enforceable in the courts. *Kentucky v. Dennison,* 24 How. 66 (1861). Likewise, the "guarantee to every state" of "a Republican Form of Government," must, because of the subject-matter, look elsewhere than to the courts for observance. *Pacific States Tel. & Tel. Co. v. Oregon,* 223 U.S. 118 (1912). There are not a few other instances in which judicial relief was barred because "political questions" were deemed to be involved.

It is not for me to find the common denominator of these judicial abstentions, or to give the contour and content of what questions are "political," in the sense of precluding judicial examination. But I do venture to believe that no judge charged with the duty of enforcing the Due Process Clauses of the Fifth and Fourteenth Amendments and the Equal Protection of the Laws Clause of the Fourteenth Amendment, can free himself from the disquietude that the line is often very thin between the cases in which the Court felt compelled to abstain from adjudication because of their "political" nature, and the cases that so frequently arise in applying the concepts of "liberty" and "equality."

In his First Inaugural Jefferson spoke of the "sacred principle" that "the will of the majority is in all cases to prevail."* Jefferson himself hardly meant all by "all." (See Jefferson's answers to Démeunier's first queries, reprinted in 10 THE PAPERS OF THOMAS JEFFERSON 18 (Boyd ed. 1954).) In any event, one need not give full adherence to his view to be deeply mindful of the fact that judicial review is a deliberate check upon democracy through an organ of government not subject to popular control. In relation to the judiciary's task in the type of cases I am now discussing, I am raising difficulties which I think must in all good conscience be faced, unless perchance the Court is expected to register a particular view and unless the profession that the judiciary is the disinterested guardian of our Constitution be pretense.

It may be that responsibility for decision dulls the capacity of discernment. The fact is that one sometimes envies the certitude of outsiders regarding the compulsions to be drawn from vague and admonitory constitutional provisions.

---

* The following is the sentence in which the quoted phrase occurs: "All, too, will bear in mind this sacred principle, that though the will of the majority is in all cases to prevail, that will to be rightful must be reasonable; that the minority possess their equal rights, which equal law must protect, and to violate would be oppression." A little later in that address Jefferson included in what he deemed "the essential principles of our Government," "absolute acquiescence in the decisions of the majority, the vital principle of republics, from which is no appeal but to force, the vital principle and immediate parent of despotism . . . ." 1 MESSAGES AND PAPERS OF THE PRESIDENTS 322, 323 (Richardson ed. 1899).

Only for those who have not the responsibility of decision can it be easy to decide the grave and complex problems they raise, especially in controversies that excite public interest. This is so because they too often present legal issues inextricably and deeply bound up in emotional reactions to sharply conflicting economic, social and political views. It is not the duty of judges to express their personal attitudes on such issues, deep as their individual convictions may be. The opposite is the truth; it is their duty not to act on merely personal views. But "due process," once we go beyond its strictly procedural aspect, and the "equal protection of the laws" enshrined in the Constitution, are precisely defined neither by history nor in terms. It deserves to be noted that so far as gaining light from pertinent data on the intention of Congress on specific issues in formulatng the Fourteenth Amendment, the Supreme Court found that "[a]t best, they are inconclusive." *Brown v. Board of Education,* 347 U.S. 483, 489 (1954). This finding of darkness was reached not for want of searching inquiry by Court and counsel.

No doubt, these provisions of the Constitution were not calculated to give permanent legal sanction merely to the social arrangements and beliefs of a particular epoch. Like all legal provisions without a fixed technical meaning, they are ambulant, adaptable to the changes of time. That is their strength; that also makes dubious their appropriateness for judicial enforcement. Dubious because their vagueness readily lends itself to make of the Court a third chamber with drastic veto power. This danger has been pointed out by our greatest judges too often to be dismissed as a bogey. Holding democracy in judicial tutelage is not the most promising way to foster disciplined responsibility in a people. See *AFL v. American Sash & Door Co.,* 335 U.S. 538, 555-557 (1949) (concurring opinon).

It is, of course, no longer to be questioned that claims under the Fourteenth Amendment are subject to judicial judgment. This makes it all the more important to realize what is involved in the discharge of this function of the

Court, particularly since this is probably the largest source of the Court's business. It is important, that is, fully to appreciate the intrinsic nature of the issues when the Court is called upon to determine whether the legislature or the executive has regulated "liberty" or "property" "without due process of law" or has denied "equal protection of the laws"; to appreciate the difficulties in making a judgment upon such issues, difficulties of a different order from those normally imposed upon jural tribunals; and, not least, to appreciate the qualifications requisite for those who exercise this extraordinary authority, demanding as it does a breadth of outlook and an invincible disinterestedness rooted in temperament and confirmed by discipline. Of course, individual judgment and feeling cannot be wholly shut out of the judicial process. But if they dominate, the judicial process becomes a dangerous sham. The conception by a judge of the scope and limits of his function may exert an intellectual and moral force as much as responsiveness to a particular audience or congenial environment.

We are dealing with constitutional provisions the nature of which can be best conveyed compendiously by Judge Learned Hand's phrase that they "represent a mood rather than a command, that sense of moderation, of fair play, of mutual forbearance, without which states become the prey of faction." *Daniel Reeves, Inc. v. Anderson,* 43 F. 2d 679, 682 (2d Cir. 1930). Alert search for enduring standards by which the judiciary is to exercise its duty in enforcing those provisions of the Constitution that are expressed in what Ruskin called "chameleon words," needs the indispensable counterpoise of sturdy doubt that one has found those standards. Yesterday the active area in this field was concerned with "property." Today it is "civil liberties." Tomorrow it may again be "property." Who can say that in a society with a mixed economy, like ours, these two areas are sharply separated, and that certain freedoms in relation to property may not again be deemed, as they were in the past, aspects of individual freedom?

Let me sharpen these difficulties by concreteness. In *Plessy v. Ferguson,* 163 U.S. 537, 559 (1896), Mr. Justice Harlan floated an oft-quoted epigram, but in a few short years he did not apply it, proving once more that sonorous abstractions do not solve problems with intractable variables. See *Cumming v. Richmond County Board of Education,* 175 U.S. 528 (1899), and its influence on *Gong Lum v. Rice,* 275 U.S. 78, 85 (1927). Thinking of "equality" in abstract terms led Mr. Justice Harlan to be blind to the meaning of "yellow-dog contracts" as a serious curtailment of liberty in the context of anti-union strategy, *Adair v. United States,* 208 U.S. 161 (1908); Richard Olney, *Discrimination Against Union Labor—Legal?,* 42 AM. L. REV. 161 (1908), and to be equally blind to the fact that important differences between industry and agriculture may justify differentiation in legislation. See *Connolly v. Union Sewer Pipe Co.,* 184 U.S. 540 (1902), and compare with *Tigner v. Texas,* 310 U.S. 141 (1940).

Take the other side of the medal. It is too easy to attribute judicial review resulting in condemnation of restrictions on activities pertaining to property to "economic predilection" of particular judges. The Due Process Clauses extend to triune interests—life, liberty and property—and property—and "property" cannot be deleted by judicial fiat rendering it nugatory regarding legislation touching property. Moreover, protection of property interests may, as already indicated, quite fairly be deemed, in appropriate circumstances, an aspect of liberty. Regulation of property may be struck down on the assumptions or beliefs other than narrow economic views. And so we find that Justices who were the most tolerant of legislative power dealing with economic interests have found in due process a protection even against an exercise of the so-called police power. It was true of Mr. Justice Holmes in *Pennsylvania Coal Co. v. Mahon,* 260 U.S. 393 (1922), and of Mr. Justice Brandeis in *Thompson v. Consolidated Gas Utilities Corp.,* 300 U.S. 55 (1937).

Let us turn to the much mooted "clear and present danger" doctrine. It is at least interesting that that phrase originated in one (*Schenck v. United States,* 249 U.S. 47, 52 (1919)) of a series of cases in which convictions for heavy sentences were sustained against defendants who had invoked the right of free speech in circumstances which led Mr. Justice Holmes to characterize them as "poor fools whom I should have been inclined to pass over if I could." (2 HOLMES-POLLOCK LETTERS 11 (Howe ed. 1941).) "Clear and present danger" thus had a compulsion for Mr. Justice Holmes against recognizing Debs' freedom to an utterance that in retrospect hardly seems horrendous. *Debs v. United States,* 249 U.S. 211 (1919). Would it carry equal compulsion with other judges? One can be confident, in any event, that Mr. Justice Holmes would not have deemed his doctrine a bar to the power of a state to safeguard the fair conduct of a trial for a capital offense from being thwarted by intrusion of utterances from without. See *Maryland v. Baltimore Radio Show Inc.,* 338 U.S. 912 (1950), denying certiorari to 193 Md. 300, 67 A 2d 497 (1949). There is the best of reasons for believing that Mr. Justice Brandeis would not have carried his natural devotion to the place of freedom of speech in a democracy to such a doctrinaire denial of an equally indispensable need—trial in court, not outside it—of a free society.

Concerned as I am with the evolution of social policy by way of judicial application of Delphic provisions of the Constitution, recession of judicial doctrine is as pertinent as its expansion. The history of the constitutional position of the right to strike affords an illuminating instance. After invalidating a law withdrawing the use of the injunction against strikes, *Truax v. Corrigan,* 257 U.S. 312 (1921), the Court came to conceive of the conduct of a strike as an aspect of the constitutionally protected freedom of discussion, *Thornhill v. Alabama,* 310 U.S. 88 (1940), but soon retreated from this position and recognized that picketing, as the weapons of strikes, is not merely a means of communication, *Giboney v. Empire Storage & Ice Co.,* 336 U.S. 490

(1949). No matter how often the Court insists that it is not passing on policy when determining constitutionality, the emphasis on constitutionality and its fascination for the American public seriously confound problems of constitutionality with the merits of a policy. Industrial relations are not alone in presenting problems that suffer in their solution from having public opinion too readily assume that because some measure is found to be constitutional it is wise and right, and, contrariwise, because it is found unconstitutional it is intrinsically wrong. That such miseducation of public opinion, with its effect upon action, has been an important consequence of committing to the Court the enforcement of "the mood" represented by these vague constitutional provisions, can hardly be gainsaid by any student of their history.

Much as the constitution-makers of other countries have drawn upon our experience, it is precisely because they have drawn upon it that they have, one and all, abstained from including a "due process" clause. They have rejected it in conspicuous instances after thorough consideration of our judicial history of "due process." See Wallace Mendelson, *Foreign Reactions to American Experience With "Due Process of Law"* 41 VA. L. REV. 493 (1955).) It is particularly noteworthy that such was the course of events in framing the Constitution of India. Sir B. N. Rau, one of the most penetrating legal minds of our time, had a major share in its drafting, and for the purpose he made a deep study of the workings of the Due Process Clause during an extensive stay here.

Is it the tenor of these remarks that courts should have no concern with other than material interests, that they must be unmindful of the imponderable rights and dignities of the individual which are, I am sure I shall have your agreement in saying, the ideals which the Western world holds most high? Of course not. Recognition of them should permeate the law, and it does so effectively even in courts that do not have veto power over legislation. They constitute presuppositions where parliaments have not spoken unequivocally and courts are left with the jural task of construction in its fair sense.

Thus, while the Chief Justice of Canada could say: "We have not a Bill of Rights such as is contained in the United States Constitution and decisions on that part of the latter are of no assistance," he reached the same result in *Saumur v. City of Quebec,* [1953] 2 Can. Sup. Ct. 299, as a matter of construction, that was reached under the Due Process Clause in *Lovell v. City of Griffin,* 303 U.S. 444 (1938). Again, only the other day the Supreme Court of Canada rejected the view that the mere claim of immunity by a Minister of the Crown from producing in court a document relavant to its proceeding is conclusive. It deemed such a claim "not in harmony with the basic conceptions of our polity." The reason given by Mr. Justice Rand deserves to be quoted: "What is secured by attributing to the courts this preliminary determination of possible prejudice is protection against executive encroachments upon the administration of justice; and in the present trend of government little can be more essential to the maintenance of individual security. In this important matter, to relegate the courts to such a subservience as is suggested would be to withdraw from them the confidence of independence and judicial appraisal that so far appear to have served well the organization of which we are the heirs." *Regina v. Snider,* [1954] Can. Sup. Ct. 479, 485, 486. So, likewise, the Appellate Division of the Supreme Court of South Africa ruled that when an Act conferred autocratic powers upon a Minister—it was the Suppression of Communism Act—it must, in the absence of explicit direction by Parliament, be construed with the least interference with the liberty of the subject. *Regina v. Ngwevala,* [1954] 1 So.Afr. L.R. 123.

While the subjection to Parliamentary criticism is the only remedy for much in Great Britain that with us becomes the stuff of lawsuits, the English executive is amenable to challenge in court for exceeding statutorily defined legal powers. In construing such authority, English courts enforce the right to a hearing as a presupposition of English law, unless Parliament has clearly enough indicated the contrary. (See S. A. de Smith, *The Right to a Hearing in English Administrative Law,* 68 HARV. L. REV. 569 (1955); so, likewise in Canada, *L'Alliance des Professeurs Catholiques v. Labour Relations Board,* [1953] 2 Can. Sup. Ct. 140; and in New Zealand, *New Zealand Dairy Board v. Okitu Co-operative Dairy Co.,* [1953] N.Z.L.R. 366 (1952).) The English courts have also been resourceful, through the use they make of certiorari, in setting aside executive action when based on reasons not justifiable in law. (For application of this principle in the United States see *Perkins v. Elg,* 307 U.S. 325 (1939), and *Securities and Exchange Commission v. Chenery Corp.,* 318 U.S. 80 (1943). This increasing tendency of courts to scrutinize the legal grounds given by administrative agencies for their actions may well promote greater responsibility in the agencies' exercise of authority and in their justification of that exercise.

If government under law were confined to what is judicially enforced, law in government would be very restricted, no matter how latitudianarian one's conception of what is fitting for judicial examination of governmental action. For one thing, courts have a strong tendency to abstain from constitutional controversies. *E.g., Peters v. Hobby,* 349 U.S. 331 (1955). Thereby, they may avoid conflict, at least prematurely if not permanently, with the other branches of the government and they may avoid also the determination of conflict between the nation and the states. Moreover, settlement of complicated public issues, particularly on the basis of constitutional provisions conveying indeterminate standards, is subject to the inherent limitations and contingences of the judicial process. For constitutional adjudications involve adjustment of vast and incommensurable public interests through episodic instances, upon evidence and information limited by the narrow rules of litigation, shaped and intellectually influenced by the fortuitous choice of particular counsel.

Mr. Justice Brandeis made a fair estimate in saying that

by applying its restrictive canons for adjudication, the Court has in the course of its history "avoided passing upon a large part of all the constitutional questions pressed upon it for decision." *Ashwander v. Tennessee Valley Authority,* 297 U.S. 288, 346 (1936). This is true not only of our Supreme Court, which cannot render advisory opinions however compelling the appeal for legal guidance even at times of national emergency. (See Chief Justice Jay's reply to President Washington's inquiry, conveyed by Thomas Jefferson, in 3 THE CORRESPONDENCE AND PUBLIC PAPERS OF JOHN JAY 486-89 (Johnson Ed. 1891).) Insistence on an immediate, substantial and threatening interest in raising such constitutional issues is a characteristic of all high courts with power to pass upon them. (See the recent Australian case, *Australian Boot Trade Employees' Federation v. Commonwealth of Australia,* 90 Commw. L.R. 24 (Austr. 1954); see also *Musgrove v. Chun Teeong Toy,* [1891] A.C. 272, 283, (P.C.).) But even where advisory opinions are constitutionally authorized, tribunals are reluctant to pronounce in situations that are hypothetical or abstract or otherwise not conducive to judicial disposition. (See Lord Haldane, in *Attorney General for British Columbia v. Attorney General for Canada,* [1914] A.C. 153, 162 (P.C. 1913); Lord Sankey, in *In re the Regulation and Control of Aeronautics,* [1932] A.C. 54, 66 (P.C. 1931).) It is, I believe, not inaccurate to say that most of the occasions when the Supreme Court has come into virulent conflict with public opinion were those in which the Court disregarded its settled tradition against needlessly pronouncing on constitutional issues. (The *Dred Scott Case,* 19 How. 393 (1857) does not stand alone; see the *Income Tax Cases,* 157 U.S. 429 and 158 U.S. 601 (1895), controlling until the Sixteenth Amendment of February 25, 1913; *Adkins v. Children's Hospital,* 261 U.S. 525, 543 (1923), overruled by *West Coast Hotel Co. v. Parrish,* 300 U.S. 379 (1937).)

The confining limits within which courts thus move in expounding law is not the most important reason for a conception of government under law far transcending merely law that is enforced in the courts. The day has long gone by when Austin's notions exhaust the content of law. Law is not set above the government. It defines its orbit. But government is not law except insofar as law infuses government. This is not wordplaying. Also indispensable to government is ample scope for individual insight and imaginative orgination by those entrusted with the public interest. If society is not to remain stagnant, there is need of action beyond uniformities found recurring in instances which sustain a generalization and demand its application. But law is not a code of fettering restraints, a litany of prohibitions and permissions. It is an enveloping and permeating habituation of behavior, reflecting the counsels of reason on the part of those entrusted with power in reconciling the pressures of conflicting interests. Once we conceive of "the rule of law" as embracing the whole range of presuppositions on which government is conducted and not as a technical doctrine of judicial authority, the relevant question is not, has it been achieved, but, is it conscientiously and systematically pursued.*

What matters most is whether the standards of reason and fair dealing are bred in the bones of people. Hyde Park represents a devotion to free speech far more dependable in its assurances, though unprotected by formal constitutional requirement, than reliance upon the litigious process for its enjoyment. Again, widespread popular intolerance of the third-degree, such as manifested itself in the well-known Savidge affair, reflects a more deeply grounded rule of law than is disclosed by the painful story of our continuing judicial endeavor to root out this evil through decisions in

* In what I have said of course I do not mean to give the remotest support to the notion that the law is "a brooding omnipresence in the sky." I reject it as completely as did Mr. Justice Holmes in *Southern Pacific Co. v. Jensen,* 244 U.S. 205, 222 (1917) (dissenting opinion). It might further avoid confusion to restrict the term "law," particularly in a judge's mouth, to the commands of society which it is the duty of courts to enforce, and not apply it to those decencies of conduct which should control other branches of government but are without judicial sanction. But perhaps law has so established itself as a portmanteau word that clarity does not require too pedantically restrictive a use of it so long as no doubt is left regarding the circumscribed scope of the judiciary's function.

occasional dramatic cases. (For the Savidge case, see 220 H. C. DEB (5th ser.) 805-91 (1928); *Inquiry in regard to the Interrogation by the Police of Miss Savidge,* CMD. NO. 3147 (1928). As to our experience, see *e. g.,* Chaffee, Pollak, and Stern, *Report on the Third Degree,* 4 NATIONAL COMMISSION ON LAW OBSERVANCE AND ENFORCEMENT, REPORTS 13 (1931), and the series of well-known cases in the Supreme Court Reports). Let me give another illustration. "Crichel Down" will, in its way, serve to summarize the duty of obedience to standards of fair dealing and avoidance even of the appearance of official arbitrariness. As such it will affect the future conduct of English government as much as some of the leading cases which have been important factors in the development of a democratic society. (See *Public Inquiry ordered by the Ministry of Agriculture Into the Disposal of Land at Crichel Down* CMD. NO. 9176 (1954); R. DOUGLAS BROWN, THE BATTLE OF CRICHEL DOWN (1955).) You will note that the instances I have given of manifestations of law responsive to the deep feelings of a people are drawn from a nation that does not rely on a written constitution. I need not add that the distinctive historical development in Great Britain, in the context of its progressive cultural and economic homogeneity, has made possible accommodation between stability and change, defining the powers of government and the limits within which due regard for individual rights require it to be kept, without embodying it in a single legal document enforceable in courts of law.

I hope, however, that you will not deem me unduly romantic in deriving comfort from the undertaking given the other day by the Kabaka, as a condition of his return to his people in Buganda, when he promised that he "will well and truly govern Buganda according to law." (The Times (London), Aug. 13, 1955, p. 6, col. 5.) I find reason for my comfort in the fascinating account by Professor Max Gluckman of Manchester University of the extent to which law permeates the lives of the Barotse tribes of Northern Rhodesia, law in the sense in which this Conference is discussing it and not something religious in nature. (GLUCKMAN, THE JUDICIAL PROCESS AMONG THE BAROTSE OF NORTHERN RHODESIA (1955).)

If what I have brought you, in my endeavor to give you as frankly as I may the distillation of sixteen years of reflection from within the tribunal peculiarly concerned with government under law, is charged with being an old-fashioned liberal's view of government and law, I plead guilty. For the charge implies allegiance to the humane and gradualist tradition in dealing with refractory social and political problems, recognizing them to be fractious because of their complexity and not amenable to quick and propitious solutions without resort to methods which deny law as the instrument and offspring of reason.

I have not been able to submit to you large generalizations that illumine or harmoniously assimilate discrete instances. Still less have I been able to fashion criteria for easier adjudication of the specific cases that will trouble future judges. They are bound to be troubled, whether they will be faced with variant aspects of old problems—old conflicts between liberty and authority, between the central government and its constitutent members—or new problems inevitably thrown up by the everlasting flux of life.

Believing it still important to do so, I have tried to dispel the age-old illusion that the conflicts to which the energy and ambition and imagination of the restless human spirit give rise can be subdued, even if not settled, by giving the endeavors of reason we call law a mechanical or automatic or enduring configuration. Law cannot be confined within any such mould because life cannot be so confined. Man's most piercing discernment of the future cannot see very far beyond his day, even when guided by the prophet's insight and the compassionate humility of a Lincoln. And I am the last to claim that judges are apt to be endowed with these gifts. But a fair appraisal of Anglo-American judicial history ought to leave us not without encouragement that modest goals, uncompromisingly pursued, may promote what I hope you will let me call civilized ends without the need of defining them.

In what I have been saying you have no doubt heard undertones of a judge's perplexities—particularly of a judge who has to construe, as it is called, vague and admonitory constitutional provisions. But I am very far from meaning to imply a shriveled conception of government under law. Quite the contrary. The intention of my emphasis has been not on the limited scope of judicial enforcement of laws. My concern is an affirmation—my plea is for the pervasiveness throughout the whole range of government of the spirit of law, at least in the sense of excluding arbitrary official action. But however limited the area of adjudication may be, the standards of what is fair and just set by courts in controversies appropriate for their adjudication are perhaps the single most powerful influence in promoting the spirit of law throughout government. These standards also help shape the dominant civic habits and attitudes which ultimately determine the ethos of a society.

In exercising their technical jurisdiction, courts thus release contagious consequences. Nothing is farther from my mind than to suggest that judges should exceed the professional demands of a particular decision. If judges want to be preachers, they should dedicate themselves to the pulpit; if judges want to be primary shapers of policy, the legislature is their place. Self-willed judges are the least defensible offenders against government under law. But since the grounds of decisions and their general direction suffuse the public mind and the operations of government, judges cannot free themselves from the responsibility of the inevitable effect of their opinions in constricting or promoting the force of law throughout government. Upon no functionaries is there a greater duty to promote law.

II

The Conference reassembled in the Ames Courtroom on Thursday afternoon, with Professor A. James Casner* of the Harvard Law School presiding. The session was devoted to discussion of the first of the four themes of the Conference—"Government as Protector of the People against Government"—the principle that government should establish sound institutions for the correction of its own injustices; that government, to be just, must among its officers provide champions of the governed against the governors themselves.

Because this principle is one to which the Civil Law is as deeply committed as is the Common Law, the Conference first considered the paper of Professor André Tunc of Grenoble—"Government Under Law: A Civilian View."

Next the discussion turned to the paper by Father Joseph M. Snee, S.J., "Leviathan at the Bar of Justice," with its reminders that a tradition even antecedent to that of France has insisted on the moral requirement of just governmental procedures. Both of these papers had been printed and distributed to the members of the Conference in May, 1955. They (like the other papers thus published in advance) are here reprinted preceding the report of their discussion. These essays, whose themes formed the subject-matter of the Conference, were not read aloud at the sessions; because of their earlier distribution and study they were taken as premises of the discussions by their authors and others.

* ANDREW JAMES CASNER, JR., *Professor of Law, Harvard Law School.* Professor Casner was born in Chicago in 1907. He took Arts and Law degrees at the University of Illinois, and a Doctorate of Judicial Science at Columbia in 1941. He has combined the practice of law and teaching; has been a member of the faculty of law at the Universities of Illinois, Maryland, Columbia, Michigan, Stanford, and Texas. He was a Colonel, United States Army Air Forces 1942-1945. He joined the Harvard Law School faculty in 1938, becoming a Professor of Law in 1940. He has published and edited numerous books and articles in the field of property.

Government Under Law: A Civilian View

ANDRÉ TUNC *

Nearly twenty years ago the Harvard Law School held a conference on the future of the common law.[1] Dean Roscoe Pound opened its deliberations by quoting from the psalm *De Profundis*: "Propter legem tuam sustinui te Domine"—because of thy law I abided thee, O Lord—and he felt justified in a paraphrase: "Because of thy law am I content with thee, O state." These words may be repeated today.

Government Under Law. The law should not govern only relationships between individuals. It should govern also the government itself. This is, as said by the great Chief Justice whose memory we are honoring today, "the very essence of civil liberty."[2] Only then may the individual be content with the law. Only then may he be content with the State.

The sovereignty of law, which protects us today, is the result of the long labors of our predecessors. The need for it has been felt through the centuries, alike in the common law and in the civil law worlds. Its history has, on the whole, seen it more and more widely recognized. In a still recent past, it is true, the principle has been radically rejected in certain countries. But it is now restored in most parts of Europe. Even in the Soviet Union it is regaining, at least temporarily, a place of honor.[3]

A principle is nothing, however, unless it is enforced. And no one would claim that the principle of government

---

* For biographical note see page 71.

---

1. See THE FUTURE OF THE COMMON LAW (Harvard Tercentenary Publications 1937).
2. Marbury v. Madison, 1 Cranch 137 (U.S. 1803).
3. See 1 DAVID & HAZARD, LE DROIT SOVIÉTIQUE 157-214 (1954); BERMAN, JUSTICE IN RUSSIA, AN INTERPRETATION OF SOVIET LAW 1-50 (1950); 1 GSOVSKI, SOVIET CIVIL LAW 152-92 (1948). *Cf.* Aspaturian, *The Contemporary Doctrine of the Soviet State and Its Philosophical Foundations*, 48 AM. POL. SCI. REV. 1031 (1954).

under law or, as we say in France, the principle of legality, has been always respected, even when affirmed. The history of the theoretical and practical recognition of the principle in France will be discussed on another occasion—France taken, by reason of the author's nationality, as representative of the civil law tradition. The present paper will treat only its present recognition. I propose to consider first the scope of the principle, and thereafter the techniques of its enforcement.[4]

I. The Scope of the Principle of Legality

The principle of legality, for an American audience, may appear to carry two necessary consequences: protection of the people against legislative action contrary to the constitution, and protection of the people against action of the executive branch of the government contrary either to the constitution or to a statute.[5]

A. Strange as it may appear, the French system of government failed, during the larger part of the

4. The main French treatises which will be referred to are: 1) on Constitutional Law: Duguit, Traité de droit constitutionnel (2d ed. 1921-25; 3d ed. 1927-28 for vols. 1 & 2); Laferriere, Manuel de droit constitutionnel (2d ed. 1947); Burdeau, Traité de science politique (1949-54); Vedel, Manuel élémentaire de droit constitutionnel (1949); 2) on Administrative Law: Waline, Traité élémentaire de droit administratif (6th ed. 1951); Duez & Debeyre, Traité de droit administratif (1952); de Laubadère, Traité élémentaire de droit administratif (1953). An excellent course, Odent, Contentieux administratif, is published every other year (last edition: 1954). Two excellent books in English have recently been devoted to French administrative law: Schwartz, French Administrative Law and the Common-Law World (1954); Hamson, Executive Discretion and Judicial Control, An Aspect of the French Conseil d'Etat (1954).

5. No discussion shall be devoted in this paper to the possible supremacy either of natural law or of international law over municipal law. On the last point, see the recent article by Mann, *International Delinquencies Before Municipal Courts,* 70 L.Q. Rev. 181 (1954). For recent publications on natural law, see Strauss, Natural Rights and History (1953); Proceedings of the Natural Law Institute of the University of Notre Dame (1954); Rommen, Le droit naturel, Histoire, doctrine (1945); Dabin, Théorie générale du droit 245-311 (2d ed. 1953); del Vecchio, Philosophie du Droit (1953); Darbellay, La regle juridique. Son fondement moral et social 213-36 (1945). On both problems, see also Kelsen, General Theory of Law and State (1949); Roubier, Théorie générale du droit 119-226 (2d ed. 1951).

Judge Charles E. Wyzanski, Jr., discusses his paper.

Professor Joseph M. Snee, S.J., comments on his paper.

Professor A. James Casner (right) shakes hands with Sir Raymond Evershed, Master of the Rolls. Waiting to greet Professor Casner is Chief Justice Centlivres. Associate Justice Frankfurter and Chief Justice Warren are in the background.

Ambassador Fernando Fournier comments on Professor Tunc's paper.

Chief Justice Sir Owen Dixon.

Professor Robert Braucher.

nineteenth century and the first half of the twentieth, to give to the people protection against legislative action contrary to the constitution.

The justification of judicial review of legislation given by Chief Justice Marshall in *Marbury* v. *Madison*[6] seems, it is true, to have a paramount value. His opinion establishes clearly that American courts have the power and the duty, in the normal exercise of their judicial functions, to pass on the conformity of statutes with the constitution.

> The question, whether an act, repugent to the constitution, can become the law of the land, is a question deeply interesting to the United States; but, happily, not of an intricacy proportioned to its interest. It seems only necessary to recognize certain principles, supposed to have been long and well established, to decide it.

The first of these principles, as expressed by Chief Justice Marshall, is the supremacy of the constitution over ordinary laws, supremacy without which the government would have in fact unlimited powers; the second is the duty of the courts to say what the law is and, if two laws conflict with each other, to decide on the operation of each,—an easy decision when the two laws are not on the same level. Government under law, judicial review, or judicial supremacy[7] all could be regarded as phrasings of the same idea.

These views have an intrinsic strength which make them valid anywhere. They are shared in France.[8] The reason however, why they were given very little practical recognition is a political one. The control the *Parlements* exercised by the highest courts of the Ancien Regime over royal ordinances introducing needed reforms had been so reactionary that it resulted in a great popular dissatisfaction with the courts. The revolutionary legislation thus led to the attribu-

6. 1 Cranch 137 (U.S. 1803).
7. *Cf.* Haines, The American Doctrine of Judicial Supremacy (2d ed. 1932).
8. *Cf.* 2 Duguit, *op. cit. supra* note 4, at 659-81; Burdeau, *op. cit. supra* note 4, at 346-51; Laferriere, *op. cit. supra* note 4, at 308-10, 330-31; Vedel, *op. cit. supra* note 4, at 122.

tion of a rigid meaning to the principle of separation of powers. Especially was erected a wall barring the judiciary from interference with any legislative or administrative action.[9] In the theory of the revolutionary legislation—which happily was no longer the theory of the drafters of the Code[10]—the judiciary was entrusted only with the mechanical application of a statute. The remedy given to the people against unconstitutional action on the part of the government was as logically tenable as that affirmed by Chief Justice Marshall, but, one must admit, more difficult and more dangerous to apply:

> When the government violates the rights of the people, insurrection is for the people and for each part of it the most sacred of its rights and the most necessary of its duties.[11]

Such an author as Duguit, stressing the importance of the principle of legality,[12] devotes fifteen pages to the right of the people to resist oppression,[13] considered as the *ultimum remedium* against illegality.[14]

If the French courts have always been refused the power of judicial review, a special organ has, however, sometimes been and is now charged with controlling the constitutionality of legislative acts. Twice the attempts at control proved unfortunate. A "Conservatory Senate" was vested, under the Consulate Constitution of the year VIII as well as under the Second Empire Constitution of 1852, with the duty of passing on the constitutionality of statutes, either at the request of one of the houses of the legislature or of the government (An VIII) or by spontaneous action (1852). Both experiences were failures. Since the Senate was also given the power to construe the constitution or even to promulgate

9. *Cf.* Laferriere, *La raison de la proclamation de la séparation des autorités administrative et judiciare par l'Assemblée constituante*, in MÉLANGES NÉGULESCO (1935); 3 BURDEAU, *op. cit. supra* note 4, at 366-68.

10. See the famed *Discours préliminaire* of Portalis; *cf.* Tunc, *The Grand Outlines of the Code*, in THE FRENCH CODE AND THE COMMON LAW WORLD (Schwartz ed. 1955).

11. DECLARATION OF 1793, art. 35.

12. DUGUIT, *op. cit. supra* note 4, at 681-750.

13. *id.* at 735-50.

14. See also 3 BURDEAU, *op. cit. supra* note 4, at 440-521.

regulations for its application, that body shortly became the mere instrument of the emperor and helped him to impose his will while maintaining the outward appearances of legality.[15]

The most recent attempt was made by the present constitution, promulgated on October 27, 1946, which established a special Constitutional Committee.[16] Bills passed by the National Assembly must be submitted to the Council of the Republic. Usually the Council will either give a favorable recommendation on the bill, which will enable the President to sign it, or else suggest amendments on which the National Assembly will make a final decision. The Council may, however, find the bill contrary to the constitution, in which case it must direct its President to communicate the fact to the President of the Republic, and both of them will refer the question to the Constitutional Committee provided for in Article 9.[17] This Committee has twelve members: the President of the National Assembly, the President of the Council of the Republic, seven persons chosen at the beginning of every year by the National Assembly—excluding its own membership,—representing proportionably the parties or coalitions of parties, and three members chosen by the Council of the Republic according to the same rules. The task of this Committee, as defined in Article 91, is "to consider whether the bills passed by the National Assembly imply a revision of the Constitution."[18]

The conception which explains this somewhat mysterious language is very sound and, if one thinks of it, very clear. The French people of 1955 is as sovereign as the French

---

15. *Cf.* 3 *id.* at 368-72; LAFERRIERE, MANUEL DE DROIT CONSTITUTIONNEL 311-12 (1947).

16. On the Constitutional Committee, see 3 BURDEAU, *op. cit. supra* note 4, at 375-79; LAFERRIERE, *op. cit. supra* note 15, at 951-57; VEDEL, *op. cit. supra* note 4, at 551-56; Prelot, Preface to LEMASURIER, LA CONSTITUTION DE 1946 ET LE CONTRÔLE JURIDICTIONNEL DU LÉGISLATEUR (1954).

17. Even if the Council makes a favorable recommendation, if the President of the Republic regards the bill as contrary to the Constitution he should certainly refuse to sign it, and should send it to the two Houses for reconsideration, according to the power given to him by article 36. If the bill is passed again, however, he has no choice but to sign it.

18. "Le comité constitutionnel examine si les lois votées par l'Assmblee Nationale supposent une révision de la Constitution."

people of 1946. The Constitution, it is true, must permanently be obeyed. But if the Assembly, normally vested with the sovereignty of the people, has expressed a will temporarily contrary to the Constitution, the conflict must have as a possible solution a revision of the Constitution, according to the procedural rules set forth in the Constitution itself, in order that the will of the Assembly might legally be carried out. This is the reason why the Constitutional Committee is vested with the duty "to consider whether the bills passed by the National Assembly imply a revision of the Constitution." When a bill is referred to the Committee, it must first try to bring the National Assembly and the Council of the Republic to a common view either on the bill or on a new draft. If it does not succeed, it must pronounce its decision within five days. The bills adjudged by it to be constitutional must be signed by the President. The others must be sent back to the National Assembly which may adopt a new draft, subject to the same control of the Council of the Republic and eventually the Constitutional Committee. If, however, the National Assembly fails to pass a new draft, the first one cannot be signed before a revision of the Constitution. It must be remarked that the procedure which has been described applies only in case of conflict between a statute and a provision of the constitution proper,—not the preamble. The preamble is very important, since it contains a kind of Bill of Rights. The drafters of the constitution considered, however, that many principles set forth in the preamble were too broad and too vague to be a possible check on the will of the legislature. As a matter of fact, the Constitutional Committee has been called on to give an opinion only once.[19]

Such is the only general existing control of constitutionality of the laws in France. Only in one case can we find a provision which permits or perhaps even prescribes the judicial review of some piece of legislation. On the basis of Article 28 of the Constitution, which states that the treaties

19. *Cf.* Soulier, *La délibération du comité constitutionnel du 18 juin 1948,* REVUE DU DROIT PUBLIC ET DE LA SCIENCE POLITIQUE [hereinafter R.D.P.] 195 (1949); Prelot, Preface to LEMASURIER, *op. cit. supra* note 16.

are superior in authority to statutes and that their provisions cannot be abrogated, amended or suspended, as long as the treaties are in force, a majority of text-writers and of courts of appeal seem to be of opinion that the courts should refuse to apply a law which conflicts with a treaty.[20] This is, however, the only case in which the courts may pass on the "constitutionality" of a statute. It must be added that, if the last few years have witnessed a definite increase in judicial review in European countries—its principle has been admitted by the Italian constitution and it is already in operation in Germany,[21] — the French constitutionalists remain faithful to their tradition. Everyone agrees that, theoretically, a statute contrary to the Constitution is not law and that a system of

20. Donnedieu de Vabres, *La constitution de 1946 et le droit international,* [1948] Dalloz Chronique 5; NIBOYET, COURS DE DROIT INTERNATIONAL PRIVÉ FRANÇAIS 44 (2d ed. 1949); ROUSSEAU, DROIT INTERNATIONAL PUBLIC 47-48 (1953); *cf.* 1 ROUSSEAU, PRINCIPES GÉNÉRAUX DU DROIT INTERNATIONAL PUBLIC 414-29 (1944). See also Aix, Nov. 10, 1947, [1948] Semaine Juridique [hereinafter J.C.P.] II. 4150, annotation Bencist; Paris, Jan. 30, 1948, [1948] Gazette du Palais [hereinafter Gaz. Pal.] I. 145; Paris, May 22, 1950 [1950] Dalloz Jurisprudence [hereinafter D.] 490, [1950] Gaz. Pal. II. 106; Lyon, Feb. 16, 1952, [1952] D. 801, annotation Chavrier, [1952] J.C.P. II. 7506, annotation Benoist, [1952] Gaz. Pal. I. 142. *Cf.* Cass. Crim., March 24, 1953, [1953] D. 365, annotation Savatier, [1953] J.C.P. II. 7659, annotation Weill & Leauté. According to another view, the only effect of article 28 is to oblige the Council of the Republic to stop a bill contrary to a treaty and to refer it to the Constitutional Committee in accordance with the procedure previously described. See BATIFFOL, TRAITÉ ÉLÉMENTAIRE DE DROIT INTERNATIONAL PRIVÉ 40-42 (1949).

21. A comprehensive and accurate survey of judicial review throughout the world may be found in Deener, *Judicial Review in Modern Constitutional Systems,* 46 AM. POL. SCI. REV. 1079 (1952). This excellent recent article makes it unnecessary to describe further the modern practice outside of France. Indeed it treats details of the history of the matter in France that we thought could be left out of our paper. See also 3 BURDEAU, *op. cit. supra* note 4, at 354-65; LAFERRIERE, *op. cit. Supra* note 15, at 312-15; Grant, *Judicial Control of Legislation. A Comparative Study,* 3 AM. J. COMP. L. 168 (1954); Newark, *Judicial Review of Confiscatory Legislation Under the Northern Ireland Constitution,* 3 AM. J. COMP. L. 552 (1954). On judicial review in Germany, see Von Mehren, *Constitutionalism in Germany. The First Decision of the New Constitutional Court,* 1 AM. J. COMP. L. 70 (1952); Leibholz, *The Federal Constitutional Court in Germany and the "Southwest Case,"* 46 AM. POL. SCI. REV. 723 (1952), and *Equality as a Principle in German and Swiss Constitutional Law,* 3 J. PUB. L. 156 (1954); Nagel, *Judicial Review* in Germany, 3 AM. J. COMP. L. 233 (1954). For a new development in Uruguay, see Barbagelata, *Charactéristiques générales de l'organisation constitutionnelle de l'Uruguay,* [1954] REVUE INTERNATIONALE DU DROIT COMPARÉ 455, 468, 472. For cases of judicial review in courts which have a connection with the French law sphere, see Tribunal mixte Tanger, March 10, 1939, [1939] JOURNAL DU DROIT INTERNATIONAL 670 (which refers to the American practice), and Tribunal supreme Monaco, Dec. 9 and 10, 1948, [1949] D. 353 (on the basis of an express provision of the Monaco Constitution); see also Soliman, *Le Conseil d'Etat Egyptien et le contrôle de la constitutionnalité des lois,* [1950] R.D.P. 303.

government which does not permit the courts to disregard an unconstitutional statute binds the courts to the will of the legislature and leaves the latter with powers theoretically unlimited. Most writers, however, although contrary views were held a few decades ago,[22] balk at the difficulty of organizing a satisfactory control.[23] The legislature must be deemed to obey the law. If, therefore, the courts are authorized to pass on the matter, they do so, to a certain extent, as courts of appeal from the legislature. They "review" the legislation. They assert a judicial "supremacy", which does not seem to conform to the constitution any more than a legislative unlimited power. So functioning the courts can curb the legislative will though the legislature has been vested with the exercise of popular sovereignty. Courts can be a "negative chamber"; they can establish "government by judiciary", hardly less dangerous under normal circumstances than an uncontrolled power given to the legislative body.

There is certainly no need to elaborate on the argument in this country, where the contrary views have been discussed at length.[24] Suffice it to say that the problem in a federal union is completely different from that in a unitary state. In a unitary country, the lack of judicial review does not imperil the nation.[24a] Moreover, abuses of powers by the

---

22. See 2 DUGUIT, *op. cit. supra* note 4, at 659-81; LEÇONS DE DROIT PUBLIC GÉNÉRAL 274-98, especially at 281 and 288-93.

23. See 3 BURDEAU, *op. cit. supra* note 4, at 431-39; LAFERRIERE, *op. cit. supra* note 15, at 331-40; VEDEL, *op. cit. supra* note 4, at 123-124; 2 TUNC & TUNC, LE SYSTÉME CONSTITUTIONNEL DES ETATS-UNIS D'AMÉRIQUE 278-81 (1954). *But see* ROUBIER, *op. cit. supra* note 5, at 225-26. *Cf.* BROGAN, POLITICS IN AMERICA 388-415 (1954). The attitude of the French textwriters may have been influenced to a certain extent by the famous *Le gouvernement des juges et la lutte contre la législation sociale aux Etats-Unis,* by Edouard Dambert (1921), reviewed in 37 POL. SCI. Q. 149 (L. Hand), 16 AM. POL. SCI. REV. 137 (H. White), 2 B.U.L. REV. 138 (C. Sherman), 16 ILL. L. REV. 572 (E. Freund), 70 U. PA. L. REV. 361 (W. Smithers), 11 CALIF. L. REV. 63 (M. Radin); but it is certainly based also on broader and more permanent considerations.

24. See 1 FREUND ET AL., CONSTITUTIONAL LAW. CASES AND OTHER PROBLEMS 3-20 (1954); 2 CROSSKEY, POLITICS AND THE CONSTITUTION IN THE HISTORY OF THE UNITED STATES 938-1046 (1953), and its criticism in Hart, Book Review, 67 HARV. L. REV. 1456 (1954). *Cf.* the opinions of Mr. Justice Frankfurter referred to in note 102 *infra.*

24a. *Cf.* HOLMES, COLLECTED LEGAL PAPERS 295-96 (1920): "I do not think the United States would come to an end if we lost our power to declare an Act of Congress void. I do think the Union would be imperilled if we could not make that declaration as to the laws of the several States."

legislature are much more exceptional than in a federal country since there is no partition of the powers between two entities. They are still possible, it is true. But one may feel that the dangers inherent in judicial review balance its merits, especially if public opinion may be regarded as the check of last resort against any abuse of power and if, on the other hand, proper control is exercised on executive and administrative action.

B. This is precisely the main point in the French traditional view. The French authors consider that there is a much greater need for control of executive or administrative action than for control of legislative action.[25]

In the formulation of the principle of legality as made by Duguit this appears in a striking manner: "No organ of the State may render an individual decision which would not conform to a general rule previously stated."[26] Although Duguit has previously considered, almost as a theoretical matter, the problem of unconstitutional statutes; when he comes to express the principle of legality, which is nothing else than the principle of Government under Law, he seems to think only in terms of control of executive or administrative action.[27] To the principle so understood, he gives the greatest importance. He sees in it the fundamental protection of the individual. "One can assert", he writes "that it does not, it cannot, it must not, receive any exception. A society which would not accept it or would accept it only with limitations or exceptions, would not actually live under a government of laws."[28] He specifies elsewhere that there is no government

25. *Cf.* Donnedieu de Vabres, *La protection des droits de l'homme par les jurisdictions administratives en France,* in [1949] CONSEIL D'ETAT ET DOCUMENTS 30.

26. DUGUIT, *op. cit. supra* note 4, at 681.

27. Duguit himself emphasized, however, that the legislature may not pass special laws contrary to the general laws, 3 *id.* at 682. See also a broader view of the rule of law by Maspetiol, *Le problème de la loi and et ses développements récents dans le droit public français,* in [1949] CONSEIL D'ETAT, ETUDES ET DOCUMENTS 50.

28. See also 3 DUGUIT, *op. cit. supra* note 4, at 682: "There is no principle more fundamental. If it did not exist, or if it was disregarded on certain points, there would be despotism."

of laws if the principle is not enforced by means of a high court, offering full guaranties of learning, independence and impartiality, and able to pass on any decision asserted to have been made outside the legal standards.[29] But it remains true that as there he refers only to the control of executive or administrative action he expresses the principle of legality in surprisingly narrow terms. Nevertheless the French pride themselves on their traditional review of administrative acts and feel in this review they have a sufficient safeguard for their liberties.

Is this view justified? It seems so, at least in the French system of government and in French political life. The liberties of a group of citizens may, to be sure, be threatened by the legislature. The danger is not merely theoretical. It is, however, highly exceptional in a democracy and, as said previously, French experience leads to the general opinion in that country that the remedies against the danger would be as dangerous as the danger itself. On the other hand, the powers to make either regulations or individual decisions, vested in the Premier or the members of the Cabinet, the *"Prefets"*, who represent the government in the various districts of the Nation, and the Mayors, are very important. They may be greater—although a general comparison is difficult,— or at least more often used, than the similar powers of the President, the Secretaries, the Governors, the Mayors and the City Councils in the United States. In any event, these powers are a continuous threat to individual liberties. The Parliament will not, as a matter of fact, order the deportation of an alien. The Secretary of the Interior will. The Parliament will not curb the liberties of bakers. The Mayor may, for the purpose of having a more rational distribution of bread in the city, make rules which are a burden on the bakers and may not be sufficiently justified by the public interest. He may, to avoid certain abuses, forbid the taking of pictures of passers-by by professional cameramen, which again may be too drastic a measure. *Prefet* or Mayor daily

29. LEÇONS DE DROIT PUBLIC GENERAL 274-289, especially at 280.

promulgate regulatory or individual measures which may infringe freedom of speech, freedom of religion, or freedom of assembly, either because of hostility toward certain persons or certain ideas, or even with the sole desire of protecting the peace. Freedom is threatened much more by actions of local officers or, at least, officers of the executive branch of the government, than by legislative actions. Even in the United States, the Supreme Court in the average year declares very few statutes void; while it makes such a decision for a reasonable number of other State actions or, more exceptionally, federal actions.[30]

It may be suggested, therefore, that while an American observer may be inclined to regret the lack of judicial control of constitutionality of statutes in France, he must admit that in daily life, there is no such contrast as he might have thought between the practice of Government under Law in the United States and its practice in France. A French observer considering the present attitude of the Supreme Court of the United States with respect to the acts of the Federal Government would even venture to think that it is very close to the attitude of the French *Conseil d'Etat.* [30a] Two problems, however, remain to be considered. The problem of the enforcement of the principle will be studied in the second part of this paper. But the limitations and exceptions imposed upon the principle must now be considered.

Duguit, as said previously, refused to admit any limitation or exception. Chief Justice Marshall, however, who cannot be suspected of having advocated despotism, was less absolute. In the basic case already referred to, he wrote:

> By the constitution of the United States, the President is invested with certain important political powers, in the exercise of which he is to use his own discretion, and is accountable only to his country in his political character and to his own conscience.

---

30. As far as State statutes and other State actions are concerned, see the figures given every two years by THE BOOK OF THE STATES, published by the Council on State Government, Chicago.

30a. *Cf.* SWISHER, THE GROWTH OF CONSTITUTIONAL POWER IN THE UNITED STATES 210-11 (1946).

He added:

> To aid him in the performance of these duties, he is authorized to appoint certain officers, who act by his authority, and in conformity with his orders. In such cases, their acts are his acts; and whatever opinion may be entertained of the manner in which executive discretion may be used, still there exist, and can exist, no power to control that discretion. The subjects are political.[31]

If, in the United States, the theory of "political questions" is now well settled,[32] at least in its principle, two theories seem to echo it in France.

The first one is the theory of "act of government"[33] The courts consider that they cannot pass on the legality of certain acts, as being "acts of government" and that they cannot even consider them as a basis of liability for the government. The first decisions which took this view adopted as a criterion the political motive of the act. This was certainly a very dangerous criterion, a survival of the "raison d'Etat", and it was abandoned at the end of the nineteenth century. Many legal writers adopted then a criterion very close to the one proposed by Chief Justice Marshall, the criterion of the governmental function; they draw a distinction between administrative action, which should be subject to judicial control, and governmental action, which should escape such a control. This view, although based on an idea much

---

31. See also, by Chief Justice Marshall: United States v. Palmer, 3 Wheat. 610 (U.S. 1818); Foster v. Neilson, 2 Pet. 253 (U.S. 1829).

32. See Field, *The Doctrine of Political Questions in Federal Courts,* 8 MINN. L. REV. 485 (1924); CORWIN, THE PRESIDENT. OFFICE AND POWERS 214-16 (3d ed. 1948); Mr. Justice Frankfurter in Minersvile School Dist. v. Gobitis, 310 U.S. 586 (1940), and in West Virginia State Board of Educ. v. Barnette, 319 U.S. 624, 648 (1943); Mr. Justice Jackson in *id.* at 640. Among the more recent cases, see Chicago & Southern Air Lines v. Waterman S.S. Corp. 333 U.S. 103 (1948); Eccles v. People's Bank, 333 U.S. 426 (1948); Ludecke v. Watkins, 335 U.S. 160 (1948); Harisiades v. Shaughnessy, 342 U.S. 580 (1952). *But see* Joint Anti-Fascist Refugee Comm. v. McGrath, 341 U.S. 123 (1951); Youngstown Sheet & Tube Co. v. Sawyer, 343 U.S. 579 (1952).

33. See WALINE, *op. cit. supra* note 4, at 103-108; LAUBADERE, *op. cit. supra* note 4, at 233-239; DUEZ, LES ACTES DE GOUVERNEMENT (1953); Mignon, *Une emprise nouvelle du principe de légalité: les actes de gouvernement,* [1951] Dalloz Chronique 53; Virally, *L'introuvable acte de gouvernement,* R.D.P. 317-358 (1952). For an exposition and a comparison with American law, see SCHWARTZ, *op. cit. supra* note 4, at 160-166 330-332. *Cf.* also Apelt, *L'acte de gouvernement dans la jurisprudence et la doctrine en France et en Allemagne in* LE CONSEIL D'ETAT. LIVRE JUBILAIRE 633-647 (1952).

less subject to criticism, was still considered too broad. To-day all legal writers agree that there is no general concept of "act of government", but only a certain number of acts on which the courts refuse to pass. The number of these acts has been constantly reduced. Even the presidential power to grant reprieve or pardon is no more an act of government.[34] Only two fields remain for such acts. The first one covers the relationships of the executive and the legislative branches of the government: for instance the power of the Cabinet to submit bills to the legislature, or the signing by the President of a bill passed by the legislature. The other is the field of international relations: the courts, for instance, refuse to interfere in the elaboration or denunciation of a treaty, in the official actions of a French representative abroad, in the decisions made for the conduct of a war. However, even within these comparatively narrow fields, the theory of "act of government" is under general attack from the text writers.[35] They all agree that, even if the courts are reluctant to declare certain acts to be void, they should at least be willing to consider them as a possible basis for liability of the government. They even go further. They denounce them as a shocking anomaly, an unfortunate gap in the reign of legality.[36] They recognize that a certain discretion should be left to the members of the government on some political questions. But it must be, in their opinion, a discretion within bounds, not a full discretion. They would, therefore, apply to these acts a second theory, the theory of "discretionary power."

The theory of the "discretionary power" of the adminis-

34. Gombert, Conseil d'Etat, March 28, 1947, [1947] Sirey Jurisprudence [hereinafter S.] 3. 89, with report Celier, R.D.P. 95 (1947), with annotation Waline.

35. See WALINE, *op. cit. supra* note 4, at 108; LAUBADERE, *op. cit. supra* note 4, at 234-235; DUEZ & DEBEYRE, *op. cit. supra* note 4, at 486; DUEZ, *op. cit. supra* note 33; Mignon, *supra* note 33, at 53, 60; Virally, *supra* note 33; Donnedieu de Vabres, *supra* note 25, at 44.

36. Donnedieu de Vabres takes an even more radical view of the question. In his opinion, on the basis of the existing decisions, there is no longer any executive or administrative action which would escape control. Those which might still escape control, although originating from executive organs, would not be executive in nature. *Cf.* Virally, *supra* note 33; HAMSON, *op. cit. supra* note 4, at 152-154.

trator is more supple than the previous one.[37] It may even appear somewhat vague. It is based, however, on a very sound idea,—the idea that the principle of legality, even if it should cover the entire field of administrative action, should not and cannot always bind it too strictly. The administrator should not be able to make a decision not in accord with the law; the law, however, should leave with it a certain amount of freedom, at least under certain circumstances. Administration cannot be conceived as a mere machine for the application of law. In certain cases, some discretionary power must be allowed to it.

The field of the theory of discretionary powers is very broad. Most writers seem even to admit that the administrator is strictly bound only when the statute or the regulation states the motives for which the administrator may act, or when the action of the administrator is a restraint on freedom. Only under those circumstances—very often realized, it is true—has an individual a right to a certain behavior on the part of the administrator. Otherwise, the administrator is vested with a certain discretionary power.

Discretionary powers, however, must not be conceived of as an exception to the principle of legality. They present a case where the law itself leaves the administrator with the duty to make the proper decision and, impliedly, refuses the courts the power to judge whether the decision was the proper one. The wisdom of the decision is not controlled, but this is the only control which the decision escapes. It still can be criticized and declared void for lack of power of the agent, violation of the necessary forms, or "abuse of power", abuse of power being even sometimes characterized, as will be indicated later on, by the "spirit" of the decision.[38] The theory,

37. See WALINE, *op. cit. supra* note 4, at 134-135; LAUBADERE, *op. cit. supra* note 4, at 221-228; DUEZ & DEBEYRE, *op. cit. supra* note 4, at 209-212; HAMSON, *op. cit. supra* note 4, at 160-162, 183-190; Waline, *Le pouvoir discrétionnaire de l'administration et sa limitation par le contrôle juridictionnel,* R.D.P. 197-223 (1930).

38. *Cf.* Barel, Conseil d'Etat, May 28, 1954, [1954] D. 594, with annotation Morange, R.D.P. 509-538 (1954), with report Letourneur and annotation Waline. The case is reported and discussed by HAMSON, *op. cit. supra* note 4, at 22-41, 183-204.

therefore, is not even the American theory of non-inquiry into legislative motives, expressed for the first time by Chief Justice Marshall in *Fletcher v. Peck*[39] and constantly reaffirmed by the Supreme Court.[40] It is no more than the refusal of American courts to consider the wisdom and the advisability of a statute.[41] Toleration of discretionary powers is far from condoning arbitrary decision.[42]

We felt authorized to present the two theories just discussed as an echo of the American theory of emergency. The theory of "exceptional circumstances" seems very close to it. According to this theory, actions taken beyond, or even contrary to the law may be justified if exceptional circumstances rendered them necessary.[43] The theory was created during the first world war, was then extended to circumstances considered as being consequences of war, and to "critical periods", such as a threat of general strike,[44] and it was used again during the second world war.[45]

Such a theory might be regarded as a very serious exception to the rule of law. This is true to a certain extent. It does not suffice, however, to recall the justification that Lincoln gave it. That it is applied only under exceptional circumstances should also be stressed; the courts are very conservative in recognizing circumstances as 'exceptional'. Moreover, if, when exceptional circumstances occur, administration may be justified in disregarding the written law, it does not follow that it escapes all control. Even then, administration acts under judicial control. The courts will still decide whether the administrative action was sufficiently justified by the circumstances and whether the means were appropriate. Finally, if the courts, when they pronounce the

39. Fletcher v. Peck, 6 Cranch 87 (U.S. 1810).
40. Tenney v. Brandhove, 341 U.S. 367 (1951); Brannan v. Stark, 342 U.S. 451 (1952).
41. Brannan v. Stark, 342 U.S. 451, 466 (1952); Bus Employees v. Wisconsin Board, 340 U.S. 383, 397-398 (1951); United States v. Petrillo, 332 U.S. 1 (1947).
42. Odent, Contentieux administratif 611-612 (1954).
43. See Laubadere, *op. cit. supra* note 4, at 228-233.
44. Jarrigion, Conseil d'Etat, April 18, 1947, [1948] S. 3. 33, with annotation Rivero.
45. See the cases referred to by Laubadere, *op. cit. supra,* note **4, at** 230-231.

action to have been necessary, refuse to declare it void, they will quite often grant an indemnity to the party complaining of the act. The courts may permit the administrator to forego application of the law; but they consider the parties normally entitled to its protection as being at least entitled to compensation.

It appears, therefore, that in France the principle of legality is not merely affirmed, but is basic; and that, considering the amount of freedom of decision which must necessarily be left with administration, legality does not seem dangerously qualified or limited. A comparison between American and French practices may even lead to the conclusion that the French courts, while they refuse to review legislation and while they have rarely to render such a spectacular decision as the *Steel Seizure* case,[46] exercise on executive and administrative action at least as severe a control as the American courts.

The importance of procedure is obvious; and for this reason we may well now turn to a study of the mechanics of the enforcement, under French law, of judicial control over executive and administrative action.

II. THE ENFORCEMENT OF THE PRINCIPLE OF LEGALITY

The principle of legality is enforced both administratively and judicially.

Whenever some person considers that unlawful administrative action has affected him, he is entitled to draw the attention of the government agent to the supposed illegality. It is then the agent's duty to withdraw the act, either prospectively or retrospectively, as he may deem proper.[47] Moreover, it is also the duty of the person hierarchically superior to the agent to control the legality of the latter's actions and

46. Youngstown Sheet and Tube Co. v. Sawyer, 343 U.S. 579 (1952).
47. See Suel, annotation on Dirat, Conseil d'Etat, May 26, 1950, [1951] S. 3. 69.

to cancel them, spontaneously or on demand, if he considers them illegal.[48] In operation this administrative control is quite important. We may, however, disregard it for the purpose of this paper. We are here chiefly concerned with the case where the government, including, if necessary, the highest official responsible for the action in question, upholds as lawful the action complained of for illegality.

To provide for such cases, it has been necessary to place administrative action under judicial control. But in France special courts have been instituted, which more specifically than ordinary courts, are in charge of control of the legality of executive and administrative action. They will now be dealt with. The various techniques of protection which they offer and the more exceptional protections which are offered by the judicial courts will be studied later.

A. The existence in France of special courts, called "administrative courts," has given rise, as is now well known, to considerable misunderstandings.[49] It may not be pointless to try to clarify its significance.

---

48. See Auby, annotation on Quéralt, Conseil d'Etat, June 30, 1950, [1951] S. 3. 85.

49. DICEY himself, who by his INTRODUCTION TO THE STUDY OF THE LAW OF THE CONSTITUTION (1885) is primarily responsible for the misunderstandings (see Chapters IV and XII), acknowledged his mistake in a later writing: *Droit Administratif in Modern French Law,* 17 L. Q. R. 302-318 (1901). The submission of French administration to the rule of law, as well as the significance of administrative courts in France are explained by Wade in his introduction, and chiefly in his appendix, to the 9th edition of the *Introduction* (1939) and by David in his contribution to the appendix. See also Robson, *Le droit administratif en Angleterre de 1919 à 1950, in* LE CONSEIL D'ETAT. LIVRE JUBILAIRE 649-671 (1952), and the authors referred to *supra* note 4.

The misunderstandings which spread over the United States should by now have been dispelled by such books as Professor Hamson's and Professor Schwartz's as well as by the classical books of Goodwin, Dickinson and Freund. See also ROHKAM & PRATT, STUDIES IN FRENCH ADMINISTRATIVE LAW (1947); STREET, GOVERNMENTAL LIABILITY: A COMPARATIVE STUDY (1953); Garner, *La justice administrative en France et aux Etats-Unis,* in 1 INTRODUCTION À L'ÉTUDE DU DROIT COMPARÉ (Recueil d'études en l'honneur d'Edouard Lambert), § 71, at 79-84 (1938); various studies referred to by Morstein Marx, *Quelques caracteristiques du droit administratif aux Etates-Unis,* in LE CONSEIL D'ETAT. LIVRE JUBILAIRE 673-688 (1952); Donnedieu de Vabres, *supra* note 25; Roundtable, *Les droits de l'individu et le colloque des Facultés de droit,* REVUE INTERNATIONALE DU DROIT COMPARÉ 520-525 (1954). See finally, from another point of view, ROBSON, JUSTICE AND ADMINISTRATIVE LAW (1st ed. 1928; 3d ed. 1951).

Reference has already been made to the popular dissatisfaction with the behavior of the highest courts during the Ancien Régime, and to the revolutionary desire to prevent the courts from interfering again with legislative or administrative action. A special meaning was thus given to the principle of separation of powers.[50] It was even carried so far that many legal provisions specially prohibited judges, under criminal penalties, from acting as administrators, or from interfering with administration, either by judging of the propriety of an act, by issuing injunctions or orders, or by summoning a civil servant in his official capacity. The administrator was not, of course, free to act at will. But the control of the legality of its action was entrusted to its higher officials. Hierarchical control thus was made the only guaranty of legality. This solution was considered a necessary consequence of the separation of powers—a fortunate one besides, since great respect was still paid, at the beginning of the Revolution, to the King, his Secretaries and *intendants,* while the courts remained highly unpopular.

A very important reform occurred when the Consulate Constitution of the Year VIII and a statute of the same year established special administrative courts: the *Conseil d'Etat* and the *Conseils de Prefecture.*[51] Their creation was the result of the idea that separation of administrative from judicial functions should be respected even within the administration—a sound idea which is the basis of Section 11 of the American Administrative Procedure Act of 1946. The principle remained, it is true, that the administration itself was the judge of administrative actions. The judicial power was

50. *Cf.* Laferriere, *supra* note 9; 3 BURDEAU, *op. cit. supra* note 4, Mirkine-Guetzevitch, *De l'etude du contentieux administratif du gouvernment revolutionnaire,* in LE CONSEIL D'ETAT. LIVRE JUBILAIRE 57-75 (1952).

51. *Cf.* DURANT, ETUDES SUR LE CONSEIL D'ETAT NAPOLÉONIEN (1949). —On French administrative courts, see SCHWARTZ, *op. cit. supra* note 4, at 1950; HAMSON, *op. cit. supra* note 4, at 43-90; Rohkam in ROHKAM & PRATT *op. cit. supra* note 49, at 13-20; WALINE, *op. cit. supra* note 4 at 43-97; LAUBADERE, *op. cit. supra* note 4, at 43-97, 241-293; DUEZ & DEBEYRE, *op. cit. supra* note 4 at 289-318; LE CONSEIL D'ETAT. LIVRE JUBILAIRE (1952); LETOURNEUR & MERIC, CONSEIL D'ETAT ET JURIDICTIONS ADMINISTRATIVES (1955). See also CONSEIL D'ETAT. ETUDES ET DOCUMENTS, annual, which contains articles on administrative law, reports on the work of the *Conseil d'etat,* and historical or comparative studies in administrative law.

"retained" by the administration. The *Conseil d'Etat*, either as court of first instance or as court of appeal of the *Conseil de Prefecture*, could only make recommendations to the Chief of the State. But the reform had created a court which was to become more and more independent in its attitude toward the government. By the middle of the Nineteenth Century, the *Conseil d'Etat* was already, in fact, very independent, and, nevertheless, its recommendations were nearly always followed.[52] Still, it did not guarantee a sufficient protection to the enforcement of legality.

A last improvement was made when a statute of 1872 made the *Conseil d'Etat* a fully independent court, vested with the power to pronounce final adjudications. The *Conseil d'Etat* still remains an advisory body of the Government under certain circumstances. When, however, it acts as a judge, it acts as a fully independent court.[53] The *Conseil* is even divided into administrative sections and judicial sections. The judicial decisions are made by the judicial sections; only in the most important cases do four members of the administrative sections unite with the Vice-President and nine members of the judicial sections to arrive at a decision.

If the *Conseil d'Etat* in its judicial capacity may be considered as an independent court, the question then may be asked why jurisdiction on the legality of administrative action should not be given to the normal judicial courts. If the legislator now trusts a court, why not the ordinary courts? The answer should not be found only in the weight of tradition. It is true that no one today fears political interference with administrative action by the courts. The justification for the existence of administrative courts is now different. It lies in the need for judges specially trained in administrative law and endowed with ready understanding of the special

52. See report Aucoc in Conseil d'Etat, February 26, 1869, Pinard, [1869] Dalloz Périodique [hereinafter D.P.] 3.74: " . . . you have to make a decision . . . in the exercise of and with the full independence inherent to your commission of judges, that is to say of counsellors of the supreme judge (the Emperor who see only through your eyes and, in fact, make decisions only in adopting your decisions." See also LANDON, LE RECOURS POUR EXCÈS DE POUVOIR SOUS LE RÉGIME DE LA JUSTICE RETENUE (1942).

53. See WALINE, *op. cit. supra* note 4, at 160-162.

problems which arise from administrative action. Administrative law is not only a certain field of the law, a field in which law can be properly administered only by judges who know the intricacies of the administrative machinery both in its structure and in its functioning. Fortunately or not, it has become a special law, inspired by general legal principles,[54] but adapted to the matter with which it deals and which, finally, has developed special rules. The members of the *Conseil d'Etat,* then, are traditionally appointed after an examination differing from that used for the appointment of ordinary judges, and much more difficult.[55] They come now from the young men who have gone through the three years of study of the National Administration School (*Ecole Nationale d'Administration*); they have attained an excellent knowledge of administration and an excellent preparation for their functions.[56] Moreover, there is always some exchange of personnel between "active administration" and "judicial administration": while some members of the *Conseil* will be appointed for a few years to active functions, high administrative officials who have a sufficient knowledge of law will from time to time be appointed to the *Conseil.*

No general criticism, therefore, is directed, in France against the existence of administrative courts. As long as a court is judge of the legality of administrative action and as long as this court is independent of the government, the sovereignty of the law is considered assured. As a matter of fact, it must be underlined that the *Conseil d'Etat* is very keen on maintaining its independence. It is certainly more sensitive to the normal reasonable needs of administration than judicial courts would be. But, as soon as a freedom is

---

54. *Cf. infra,* text and note 77.

55. The difficulty of the examination came in part from the small number of members of the *Conseil d'Etat* compared with the number of members of the judicial courts. Moreover, admission to the *Conseil d'Etat* was coveted by many bright young men, because of its prestige, the variety and interest of its functions, and to a certain extent, the advantage of remaining in Paris, while the young judge starts his career in the small court of a small town.

56. As a matter of fact, the *Conseil d'Etat* is usually, with the Foreign Service, the service chosen by the best of the students leaving the National Administration School.

involved, or as soon as a decision of the administration may be suspected of being a "political" one, the *Conseil d'Etat* would rather risk accusation of *"esprit de fronde"* than of unjust obedience to the government.[57] If it has sometimes been the object of unfavorable comments abroad, the action of the *Conseil d'Etat* is now usually praised.[58] It demonstrates no desire to decrease freedoms. The many countries that have, within the last decades, established similar institutions did so in no desire to decrease their liberties.[59]

The only real drawback of the institution is that in borderline cases it creates conflicts of jurisdiction between judicial and administrative courts. The institution in 1872 of a special mixed court, the *Tribunal des Conflicts* was a satisfactory solution to the problem until the second World War. During the War and after, however, so many public services were created, sometimes with functions or methods very close to those of private firms, and so many administrative decisions were taken with respect to properties, that the *Tribunal des Conflicts* was obliged to develop new rules, with the result that, too often, the normal citizen is presently,—and, it may be hoped, temporarily—unable to know in every case which court he should address.[60] It must be mentioned

57. *Cf.* Donnedieu de Vabres, *supra* note 25. See as examples of independence Barel, Conseil d'Etat, May 28, 1954, [1954] D. 594, referred to *supra* note 38; ministre de l'Agriculture, Conseil d'Etat, February 17, 1950, [1950] D. 282, discussed *infra* and referred to *infra* note 78; Société automobiles Berliet, Conseil d'Etat, December 22, 1949, [1951] S. 3. 1, with report Guionin and annotation Mathiot.

58. *Cf. supra* note 49.

59. See on the influence of the French *Conseil d'Etat* abroad, the articles published in LE CONSEIL D'ETAT. LIVRE JUBILAIRE 481-693 (1952); Lopez Rodo, *Le recours de griefs devant le Conseil d'Etat Espagnol,* REVUE INTERNATIONALE DU DROIT COMPARÉ 41-50 (1954). On the Belgian *Conseil d'Etat* and its power of control of legality, see VAUTHIER, PRÉCIS DE DROIT ADMINISTRATIF DE LA BELGIQUE 693-735 (3d ed. 1950); CAMBIER L'ANNULATION POUR EXCÈS DE POUVOIR DEVANT LE CONSEIL D'ETAT (1951); and, by the same author, *Le Conseil d'Etat et le contrôle de l'observation des formalités légales,* JOURNAL DES TRIBUNAUX 369, 390 (1953) and *Le contrôle de la légalité interne des actes de l'Administration,* JOURNAL DES TRIBUNAUX 49, 69 (1955). See also BOSCH, TRIBUNALES JUDICIALES O TRIBUNALES ADMINISTRATIVOS PARA JUZGAR A LA ADMINISTRACION PUBLICA (1951).

60. *Cf.* Delvolvé, *Une crise du principe de la séparation des autorités administratives et judiciares in* CONSEIL D'ETAT. ETUDES ET DOCUMENTS 21-41 (1950); HAMSON, *op. cit. supra* note 4, at 83-88. See among the most recent cases: Dame veuve Rezsetin, May 19, 1954, [1954] J. C. P. II. 8244, with annotation Vedel; Sté Planche, May 19, 1954, [1954] D. 785 with annotation Luchaire, [1954] J.C.P. II 8267, with annotation Vedel; Office publicitaire de France, May 19, 1954, [1954] J.C.P. II 8382 with annotation Rivero;

also that, by reason of the confidence of the citizens in the *Conseil d'Etat,* which was the normal judge of first and last instance, the number of petitions had become very high, thus making administration of justice by the *Conseil d'Etat* much too slow. [61] This is the reason why an important statute of September 30, 1953, substituted for the *Conseil d'Etat* as normal administrative courts the *Conseils de Prefecture,* henceforth called *Tribunaux administratifs.*[62] At the opposite of the old principle, the *Conseil d'Etat* is now the judge of first instance only in the cases where the law so decides. Usually, the Tribunaux administratifs are judges of first instance. The *Conseil d'Etat* remains above them as a judge to which appeal is always possible and which, therefore, will remain finally responsible for the evolution of administrative law. The selection of the judges of the *Tribunaux administratifs* is greatly improved. Most of them will prepare for their functions, as do members of the *Conseil d'Etat,* in the National Administration School and by a period of apprenticeship in the *Conseil d'Etat.*[63]

B. Three techniques cooperate to assure to the individual the application of the law against the govern-

---

Sieur Moritz, May 26, 1954, [1954] S. 3. 85 with report Letourneur, [1954] J.C.P. II 8334 with annotation Vedel. *Cf.* also, from a higher point of view, Vedel, *Les bases constitutionnelles du droit administratif* in CONSEIL D'ETAT. ETUDES ET DOCUMENTS 21-53 (1954).

61. See Mathiot, annotation on Société automobiles Berliet, Conseil d'Etat, July 22 and December 22, 1949, [1951] S. 3. 1; Liet-Veaux, *La justice administrative au ralenti,* [1948] Dalloz Chronique 133; SCHWARTZ, *op. cit. supra* note 4, at 45-48.

62. On the reform, see SCHWARTZ, *op. cit. supra* note 4, at 48-50; LAUBADERE, LES REFORMES ADMINISTRATIVES DE 1953 (1954); DUEZ & DEBEYRE, TRAITE DE DROIT ADMINISTRATIF, MISE À JOUR AU PREMIER SEPTEMBRE 1954 (1955); Gazier, *De quelques perspectives ouvertes par la récente réforme du contentieux administratif,* R. D. P. 669-683 (1954); LETOURNEUR & MERIC, *op. cit. supra* note 51. On the mission of the *Conseil d'Etat* after the reform, see Rivero, *Le Conseil d'Etat, cour regulatrice,* [1954] Dalloz Chronique 157.

63. No attempt has been made in this paper to give a complete description of the administrative courts. Besides the *Conseil d'Etat* and the *Tribunaux administratifs* which are the normal courts, there exist some special courts: See SCHWARTZ, *op. cit. supra* note 4, at 44-45; WALINE, *op. cit. supra,* note 4, at 87-97; LAUBADERE, *op. cit. supra* note 4, at 272-77; DUEZ & DEBEYRE, *op. cit. supra* note 4, at 310-18. However, it must be underlined that the *Conseil d'Etat* has asserted its power of control, at least by the *recours en cassation,* upon any administrative court: D'Aillers et Robert, Conseil d'Etat, February 7, 1947, R.D.P. 68 (1947) with report Odent and annotation Waline.

ment. The person who complains of an executive or administrative action which he considers illegal may ask the courts, according to the circumstances, either to pronounce the annulment of the act, or to adjudge him an indemnity, or to do both; or he may choose, if this is enough for his purpose, merely to disregard the act and, when sued before the courts, to raise the "exception of illegality."

1. The normal judicial action by which a person may obtain the annulment of an administrative act is the famous "*recours pour excès de pouvoir*."[64] This action is often praised as one of the best achievements of the *Conseil d'Etat*. An American observer was able to write recently that it was "amazingly simple, inexpensive, and free of technicalities."[65]

Recours pour excès de pouvoir may be regarded as a creation of the *Conseil d'Etat*. It was practised by it without any real statutory authority. Only after 1830 did the Council begin habitually to refer to a narrow statute of 1790 dealing with hierarchical control.[66] As for the statute of 1872 which, as previously explained, changed the nature of the Council, it merely states: "The *Conseil d'Etat* shall give a final judgment on petitions for annulment of *ultra vires* acts, directed against acts of the various administrative authorities."[67] On the basis of this very broad statement, the Coun-

64. *Cf.* ALIBERT, LE CONTRÔLE JURIDICTIONNEL DE L'ADMINISTRATION AU MOYEN DU RECOURS POUR EXCÈS DE POUVOIR (1926); BONNARD, LE CONTRÔLE JURIDICTIONNEL DE L'ADMINISTRATION. ETUDE DE DROIT ADMINISTRATIF COMPARÉ (1934); SCHWARTZ, *op. cit. supra* note 4, at 108-249; WALINE, *op. cit. supra* note 4, at 113-147; LAUBADERE, *op. cit. supra* note 4, at 353-401; DUEZ & DEBEYRE, *op. cit. supra*, note 4, at 336-404.

65. SCHWARTZ, *op. cit. supra* note 4, at 118.

66. *Cf.* LANDON, *op. cit. supra* note 52.

67. "*Le Conseil d'Etat statue souverainement sur les demandes d'annulation pour excès de pouvoir formées contre les actes des diverses autorités administratives.*" The translation of "*excès de pouvoir*" by "ultra vires" although being the verbatim translation, may be grossly misleading: see HAMSON, *op. cit. supra* note 4, at 7, 165, 167.

cil has been free to build and shape the *recours* as an efficient and flexible tool for the protection of the individual.[68]

The action is widely available.[69] In principle, and subject only to a few exceptions such as the theory of "acts of government," any administrative act may be attacked. The principle applies even to oral decisions or to failures to make decisions: silence of the administration during four months after a request has been presented to it is deemed a negative answer subject to review. The action is open to any person who has an interest in the annulment of the act. There is no need to give evidence of violation of a right. The mere interests of the citizen are protected as soon as legality may have been disregarded. A mere moral interest or a collective interest will be protected as much as a patrimonial and personal interest. The mere fact of being a taxpayer gives a sufficient interest for the institution of an action against a decision which will have an impact on a municipal or "departemental" (district) budget; while not deemed sufficient to authorize an action against a decision bearing on the national budget, this is only because the action would then be open to everybody.[70] The mere fact of having the necessary qualification to be appointed to a certain function authorizes criticism of the appointment of somebody else, if the appointment is illegal. The only limitation to the generality of the action consists in the "exception of parallel action." As a rule, *recours pour excès de pouvoir* cannot be used when a statute provides for a specific action before a jurisdiction other than the Council, as long as the *recours* would not give to the petitioner a result more satisfactory in any respect. The Council, however, will not bar anybody from using the

---

68. *Cf.* Waline, *Cinquante ans de jurisprudence administrative,* [1950] Dalloz Chronique 21; LE CONSEIL D'ETAT. LIVRE JUBILAIRE (1952); Donnedieu de Vabres, *supra* note 25; *Hommages à la part prise par le Président Rouchon. Mazerat dans le développement de la jurisprudence du contentieux,* a symposium in LE CONSEIL D'ETAT. ETUDES ET DOCUMENTS 49-86 (1953).

69. See SCHWARTZ, *op. cit. supra* note 4, at 150-191; Rohkam in ROHKAM & PRATT, *op. cit. supra* note 49, at 21-31; HAMSON, *op cit. supra* note 4, at 145-157; WALINE, *op. cit. supra* note 4, at 115-134; LAUBADERE, *op. cit. supra* note 4, at 358-380; DUEZ & DEBEYRE, *op. cit. supra* note 4, at 339-382.

70. *Cf.* Massachusetts v. Mellon, 262 U.S. 447 (1923).

recours, if he has an interest in using it, or if the specific action, anyhow, should have been brought to the Council.

The reasons for which an administrative act may successfully be attacked have also been decided upon by the *Conseil d'Etat* in the most liberal manner.[71] Some of them have a statutory basis. Others are nearly entirely creations of the *Conseil d'Etat*. All of them were at least broadly developed by it. While classification of these grounds for attack has been the subject-matter of discussion among textwriters,[72] these discussions do not involve any disagreement of substance.

A first ground is the lack of "jurisdiction" (*incompetence*) of the agent.[73] Under many circumstances an act is thus performed without jurisdiction: the agent may be hierarchically inferior, or superior, to the proper agent; the agent may have no authority while the proper agent is either a civil-servant exercising the same functions on another part of the territory or a civil-servant of the same rank, but with other functions. Under all those circumstances, the act will be void.

A second reason why the act may be void is the failure on the part of the agent to observe due forms or procedures for the accomplishment of the act.[74] A distinction is made, however, between forms so substantial that their omission or a serious irregularity in their accomplishment should carry with it the annulment of the act, and accessory forms, or even slight irregularities in the accomplishment of a substantial form, which do not deserve such a sanction.

An act will also be declared void by the *Conseil d'Etat* when, by its content, it violates a legal rule. Although there

71. See SCHWARTZ, *op. cit. supra* note 4, at 200-49; Rohkam in ROHKAM & PRATT, *op. cit. supra* note 49, at 32-56; WALINE, *op. cit. supra* note 4, at 134-145; LAUBADERE, *op cit. supra* note 4, at 381-399; DUEZ & DEBEYRE, *op. cit. supra* note 4, at 382-399.

72. See Gazier, *Essai de présentation nouvelles des ouvertures du recours pour excès de pouvoir en 1950* in LE CONSEIL D'ETAT. ETUDES ET DOCUMENTS 77-83 (1951).

73. *Cf.* AUBY, LA THÉORIE DE L'INEXISTENCE DES ACTES ADMINISTRATIFS (1949); HAMSON, *op. cit. supra* note 4, at 162-164.

74. See Berlia, *Le vice de forme et le contrôle de la légalité des actes administratifs,* R.D.P. 370-401 (1941); HAMSON, *op. cit. supra* note 4, at 162-164.

are some disputes on this point,[75] this cause of action may be distinguished from the previous ones by the idea that violation of the law may be found, in the case, in the content itself of the act, not in the agent who performed it nor in the procedure by which it was performed.[76] And it is, indeed, a very important cause of action. The study of the decisions reveals very clearly that the *Conseil d'Etat* considers it its duty to set aside any administrative action which would be contrary, not only to an express provision of the constitution, a statute or an administrative rule, but to a rule which might be implied from such documents, or even to the general principles of public law, derived from the past customs and the bill of rights, or implied in our conception of a civilization.[77] This kind of control is a very important one. Like the due process clauses of the Fourteenth and Fifth amendments to the United States Constitution—which, if sometimes misused, are basically fundamental guarantees of freedom,—it gives to the individual a protection which transcends mere statutory rules. The *Conseil d'Etat* is so anxious to extend its protection to everyone that it has finally come to disregard a statutory provision to the effect that a certain administrative act could not be challenged in any manner before the administration or the courts.[78] Since the Council cannot pass on the validity of statutes, it reached this decision by construction of the provision. But the provision was so absolute and so broad,[79] and its distortion by the Council is so clear, that it is hard to es-

75. See LAUBADERE, *op. cit. supra* note 4, at 382.

76. See especially DUEZ & DEBEYRE, *op. cit. supra* note 4, at 388. HAMSON, *op. cit. supra* note 4, at 164-181.

77. See LADREIT DE LACHARRIERE, LE CONTRÔLE HIÉRARCHIQUE DE L'ADMINISTRATION DANS LA FORME JURIDICTIONNELLE (1938); De Soto, annotation on Dame veuve Thompier-Graviere, Conseil d'Etat, May 5, 1944, [1945] D. 110 with report Chenot; Rivero, *Le juge administratif francais: un juge qui governe?* [1951] Dalloz Chronique 21; Letourneur, *Les "principes généraux du droit" dans la jurisprudence du Conseil d'Etat* in CONSEIL D'ETAT. ETUDES ET DOCUMENTS 19-31 (1952); JEANNEAU, LES PRINCIPES GÉNÉRAUX DU DROIT DANS LA JURISPRUDENCE ADMINISTRATIVE (1954); ODENT, CONTENTIEUX ADMINISTRATIF 583-589 (1954). See also, on a special point: DUPEYROUX, LA RÈGLE DE LA NON-RETROACTIVITÉ DES ACTES ADMINISTRATIFS (preface by Couzinet) (1954). HAMSON, *op. cit. supra* note 4, at 169-181.

78. Ministre de l'Agriculture, Conseil d'Etat, February 17, 1950, [1950] D. 282. *Cf.* HAMSON, *op. cit. supra* note 4, at 157-160.

79. *"L'octroi de la concession ne peut faire l'objet d'aucun recours administratif ou judiciaire."*

cape the feeling that, substantially, the Council disregarded the law in order to make higher principles of justice prevail.

The last two reasons which permit the annulment of an act reveal a penetrating and subtle control by the Council of administrative acts. The Council, first, passes on the justification of an act in the light of attendant circumstances. It does this in two types of cases. Sometimes, the act is within the agent's authority only under specified circumstances. The Council then asserts its duty to decide whether the circumstances were present and whether they were such as to justify the act. It passes, therefore, on both the facts[80] and the appropriateness of the measure. A measure taken by the police to safeguard the peace, for instance, is void if it is out of proportion with the danger.[81] In order to enlarge its control, the Council has enlarged the number of cases where the act could thus be within the agent's authority only under stated circumstances. The restriction on the power of the agent need not be expressed in a statutory provision; it is often imposed by the Council itself,—for instance whenever a liberty is at stake. The Council also passes on the motives of the agent whenever the agent has expressly based his decision on stated reasons, and these reasons do not appear justified either in fact or in law. Authorization to erect a building on a certain square, for instance, may be refused because the building would destroy a "monumental prospect"; the Council may deny that the square is a monumental prospect and annul the refusal of authorization.[82] A mayor, to take another example, might be removed because of certain facts; the Council might find that some of these facts did not occur and that the others were not faults: again, it annuls the removal.[83] The justification for such intervention by the

80. Consorts Barbedienne, Conseil d'Etat, January 9, 1948, [1948] S. 3. 13; Federation Nationale, Conseil d'Etat, February 4, 1950, [1950] S. 3. 57 (three cases), with report Barbet.

81. Benjamin, Conseil d'Etat, May 19, 1933, [1933] D. 3. 54, with report Michel. *Cf.* GOLDENBERG, LE CONSEIL D'ETAT JUGE DU FAIT (1932); Morange, annotations [1945] D. 164, 228; J. G., annotation [1949] D. 226.

82. Gomel, Conseil d'Etat, April 4, 1914, [1917] S. 3. 25, with annotation Hauriou.

83. Camino, Conseil d'Etat, January 14, 1916, [1922] S. 3. 10, with report Corneille.

Conseil d'Etat has given rise to interesting theoretical discussions.[84]

Finally, the *Conseil d'Etat* will declare void any act accomplished by an agent within the limits of his authority, but for an improper purpose (*detournement de pouvoir*).[85] The Council will do so wherever the agent acted for a purpose other than a desire to serve the public interest: whether because of animosity toward some person, or political party, or, on the contrary, because of favor for some person or political party. From this point of view, the Council actually appears as the guardian of administrative morals or, as it has been said, "the conscience of the administration."[86] The Council will also declare void any act done in the public interest, but not for the particular purpose for which the act was properly intended. This particular purpose for which an act is properly intended is sometimes expressed in the statute. When so or not, the Council will not hesitate to determine it from the spirit of the statute or the nature of the agent's functions. This kind of illegality may sometimes consist in the use of an improper, although apparently regular, procedure. A prefect, for instance, may prohibit bullfights on the territory of his department. But, when he does it a few days before a certain bullfight was scheduled to take place in a certain city, his decision amounts to a prohibition of the prospective bullfight. It is, therefore, an interference with the police power of the Mayor. And the *prefet* cannot take a police power which is within the authority of a Mayor without having previously sent him a formal notice Although it was only to save the Mayor the embarrassment of receiving this notice that the *prefet* had used the procedure of a general prohibi-

84. See Bonnard, *Le pouvoir discrétionnaire des autorités administratives et le recours pour excès de pouvoir,* R. D. P. 363-392 (1923); Hauriou, annotation on Lefranc, Conseil d'Etat, January 22, 1926, [1926] S. 3. 25; Vedel, Essai sur la notion de cause en drqit administratif français (1934); Charlier, *La cause dans la jurisprudence administrative récente,* [1950] J.C.P. I. 871; Lubadere, *op. cit. supra* note 4, at 397-399; the authors referred to *supra* note 81. Hamson, *op. cit. supra* note 4, at 181-183, 194-204.

85. See Alibert, *op. cit. supra* note 64, at 236-258; Hamson, *op. cit. supra* note 4, at 166-204; Rohkam in Rohkam & Pratt, *op. cit. supra* note 49, at 37-51.

86 See Welter, Le contrôle juridictionnel de la moralité administrative (1929).

tion, the *Conseil d'Etat* considered the procedure to be improper.[87]

It appears from these long developments that judicial review to annul an illegal administrative act is widely open to any person who has an interest in the annulment. It seems that the *Conseil d'Etat* has succeeded in assuring the reign of law under the highest and the most subtle aspects of legality. It may be added that the procedure to obtain annulment is extremely simple and inexpensive. It starts by the mere filing of a petition. It is simply followed by a written development of the petition on one side, an answer on the other side, and if necessary, a reply to each document. The assistance of a lawyer is not necessary. The court will, if appropriate, order the deposit of pertinent material or ask some explanations from the parties. Then, a judge will report to the court, his task being to make a recommendation, considering only the interest of justice, not the interest of the administration. The number of petitions at one time made these proceedings much too slow, but the reform of the administrative courts in 1953 should now assure prompt justice to the citizens.[88]

When the *Conseil d'Etat* considers an act as being illegal, it annuls it. In general, the decision operates retrospectively and *erga omnes*.[89] Sometimes, the Council does more than to annul the act. If it cannot, incidentally to *recours pour excès de pouvoir,* award any indemnity to the petitioner, it may refer him to an administrative service "for the proper measure to be taken," and it sometimes indicates very precisely what this should be.[90]

87. Ville de Melun, Conseil d'Etat, December 2, 1932, [1933] D.P. 3.53, with annotation Waline. — *Cf.* RAYNAUD, LE DÉTOURNEMENT DE PROCÉDURE (1950). *Cf.* HAMSON, *op. cit. supra* note 4, at 33-39, 201-204.

88. On the procedure, see SCHWARTZ, *op. cit. supra* note 4, at 131-149; HAMSON, *op. cit. supra* note 4, at 22-41, 91-142, WALINE, *op. cit. supra* note 4, at 152-160; LAUBADERE, *op. cit. supra* note 4, at 407-412; DUEZ & DEBEYRE, *op. cit. supra* note 4, at 319-332; LENOAN, LA PROCÉDURE DEVANT LE CONSEIL D'ETAT (preface by Waline) (1954).

89. See WEIL, LES CONSÉQUENCES DE L'ANNULATION D'UN ACTE ADMINISTRATIF POUR EXCÈS DE POUVOIR (1952).

90. See WALINE, *op. cit. supra* note 4, at 145-147; LAUBADERE, *op. cit supra* note 4, at 399-401; DUEZ & DEBEYRE, *op. cit. supra* note 4, at 399-403.

2. Furthermore, annulment of an act is not the only relief which may be obtained from the administrative courts against the administration.

The person who complains of the administration, for any reason, and who seeks a remedy is entitled to sue the administration before the administrative courts, not by a *recours pour excès de pouvoir,* but by a *recours de pleine juridiction.*[91]

If the *recours de pleine jurisdiction* is not favored by the law to the same extent as the *recours pour excès de pouvoir*—the assistance of a special lawyer, for instance, is necessary to the procedure,—the grounds for action and the remedies offered are as wide as possible. The petitioner may base his action, not only on an illegality, but on a violation of his personal rights or on damage caused by the administration to his person or property. He may sue the administration, for instance, not only for any disregard of the rule of law which would entitle him to *recours pour excès de pouvoir,* but for recovery of the price to be paid according to the provisions of contract entered into with the administration, if there is any disagreement between him and the administration; or for any damage suffered by him in his property when the administration performs public works, or in his person if he is injured by an administrative agent.[92] The remedies are also as diversified as may be necessary. The court will, on a proper showing, annul an administrative act. But it may also reform it—which could not certainly be done

91. See WALINE, *op. cit. supra* note 4, at 111-112; LAUBADERE, *op. cit. supra* note 4, at 349-352; DUEZ & DEBEYRE, *op. cit. supra* note 4, at 411-476.

92. *Cf.* STREET, GOVERNMENTAL LIABILITY: A COMPARATIVE STUDY (1952); SCHWARTZ, *op. cit. supra* note 4, at 250-305; Pratt in ROHKAM & PRATT, *op. cit. supra* note 49, at 61-106; DUEZ, LA RESPONSABILITE DE LA PUISSANCE PUBLIQUE (2d ed. 1938); CAMBIER, LA RESPONSABILITÉ DE LA PUISSANCE PUBLIQUE ET DE SES AGENTS (1947); CORNU, ETUDE COMPARÉE DE LA RESPONSABILITÉ DÉLICTUELLE EN DROIT PRIVÉ ET EN DROIT PUBLIC (1951); CHAPUS, RESPONSABILITÉ PUBLIQUE ET RESPONSABILITÉ PRIVÉE. LES INFLUENCES RÉCIPROQUES DES JURIDICTIONS ADMINISTRATIVE ET JUDICIARE (1953); WALINE, *op. cit. supra* note 4, at 576-608; LAUBADERE, *op. cit. supra* note 4, at 461-535; DUEZ & DEBEYRE, *op. cit. supra* note 4, at 417-476.

on the same scale by judicial courts. And it will quite often award an indemnity to the petitioner.

3. Finally, although full confidence may now be rested in the administrative courts so far as competence and independence are concerned, jurisdiction has also been given to judicial courts on certain administrative matters.

Judicial courts pass on administrative matters in two ways: in a positive or in a negative context.

Positively, some matters are in the exclusive jurisdiction of the judicial courts.[93] This may in part be the result of a tradition originating at a time when the *Conseil d'Etat* was not yet a fully independent body. In part, it may find its justification today either in cases where the administration has acted as would an ordinary person, or in cases where the protection of persons seems such an important and exclusive need that no consideration is due to the normal needs of the administration. It does not seem possible in this paper to cover completely the question of the respective powers of the administrative and judicial courts. It must be emphasized, however, that judicial courts have control of any action relating to the administration of justice—including searches, seizures and arrests[94]—that they control also those contracts which may be entered into by the administration under private law, or even those administrative services the working of which is similiar to the working of private firms;[95] that they are the only judges of the civil status of persons; that they are traditionally the protectors of persons against any important invasions of their freedoms or their properties, this principle being chiefly embodied in protection against the excess as-

93. See Waline, *op. cit. supra* note 4, at 64-69; Laubadere, *op. cit. supra* note 4, at 304-328; Duez & Debeyre, *op. cit. supra* note 4, at 248-258.

94. *Cf.* Baud, Conseil d'Etat, May 11, 1951, [1952] S. 3. 13, with report Delvolvé and annotation Drago.

95. *Cf.* Chavananon, Essai sur la notion et le régime juridique du service public industriel ou commercial (1939); Corail, La crise de la notion juridique de service public en droit administratif français (1954).

sumptions of power (*emprises*) and gross illegalities (*vois de fair*) of the administration.[96]

Judicial courts may also pass on the validity of certain administrative acts in a negative context. Even though the *recours pour excès de pouvoir,* being so simple and inexpensive, is a great instrument for the protection of the individual, it may appear that, faced with an illegal rule, the individual should be free merely to disregard it. If sued before the courts for this breach of the law, he should be authorized to justify himself on the basis of the invalidity of the rule. This prerogative, widely available to the American citizen thanks to Chief Justice Marshall, is also available, at least within some limits, to the French citizen. It is true that, for reasons previously explained, judicial courts will refuse, even in this negative context, to pass on the constitutionality of statutes. But judicial criminal courts, which usually have jurisdiction of the breach of any executive or administrative order or rule, have the power and the duty to acquit any person who has disregarded an *unconstitutional* or otherwise illegal rule. A narrow statutory provision to that effect[97] has been given such a broad scope that the power of the courts is almost entirely inclusive.[98] The only limit to this famous "*exception d'illegalité*" lies in the refusal of the courts to pass on individual decisions of the administration, as opposed to regulatory decisions,[99] unless a statutory provision gives them authority so to do.[100]

---

96. See Pinto, *La protection des droits de l'homme par les tribunaux judiciaires en France* in CONSEIL D'ETAT. ETUDES ET DOCUMENTS 21-29 (1949); Delvolvé, *supra* note 60; Vedel, *La juridiction compétente pour prévenir, faire cesser ou réparer la voie de fait administrative,* 1950 J.C.P. I. 851.

97. Penal Code, art. 471-150, punishing: "*Ceux qui* auront contrevenu *aux reglements* légalement *faits par l'autorité administrative*" (Emphasis added).

98. Tribunal des conflits, July 5, 1951, Procureur général Angers, [1952] D. 271, with annotation Blaevoet, [1952] S. 3.1, with annotation Auby, [1951] J.C.P. II 6623, with annotation Homont. See also: PELLETIER, L'APPRECIATION DE LA LÉGALITÉ DES ACTES ADMINISTRATIFS PAR LE JUGE REPRESSIF (1953); Homont, *L'appreciation de la légalité des actes administratifs individuals par les tribunaux repressifs de l'ordre judiciaire,* [1951] J.C.P. I. 956 TER.

99. See PELLETIER, *op. cit. supra* note 98, at 64-118; Homont, *supra* note 98.

100. Gerval, May 7, 1951, [1951] D. 413, with annotation A.-L.P. In the exceptional cases where a civil—as opposed to a criminal court—might be called by one of the parties to pass on the legality of an administrative act, that

CONCLUSION

As a conclusion to this survey of the French conception and practice of Government Under Law it may be interesting to venture on a tentative comparison, risky as the comparison may be, between the American and French systems.

In the beginning, we find the two systems in complete opposition. As early as 1803, and partly backed by a long tradition, Chief Justice Marshall, facing Jefferson, strikingly asserts the power of the courts to curb any illegality, whoever its author might be. His opinion, by its strength, by its clarity, by its appeal to the higher ideals of mankind, to justice and freedom, gives an illumination for the best spirits of his time, all over the world. Thirty years later, Tocqueville will testify:

> The power given to American courts to pass on the constitutionality of statutes constitutes one of the most powerful barriers which has ever been raised against tyranny of political assemblies.[101]

During the last years of the nineteenth century and the first decades of the twentieth, however, the power of the courts is certainly misused on many occasions. The highest moral authority of the American commonwealth, the Supreme Court, renders, among many wise and useful decisions, other decisions which even at the time are considered distressingly shocking, and which, today, appear as extraordinary evidences of the collective blindness which may sometime strike even people of good will. The situation has been remedied. The Supreme Court now maintains an attitude of self-restraint which is constantly urged upon it by some of its mem-

---

tribunal should, admittedly, still decline jurisdiction and refer the parties to the administrative judge: Septfonds, Tribunal des Conflicts, July 16, 1923, [1923] S. 3.49, with annotation by Hauriou. This solution has been criticized by text writers and might eventually be reversed. See Hauriou in the annotation; LAUBADERE, *op. cit. supra* note 4, at 331.

101. DE LA DÉMOCRATIE EN AMÉRIQUE (1st part, ch. VI): *"Resserré dans ses limites, le pouvoir accordé aux tribunaux américains de prononcer sur l'inconstitutionnalité des lois forme encore une des plus puissantes barrières qu'on ait jamais élevées contre la tyrannie des assemblés politiques."*

bers.[102] It may itself have been guilty, in the course of history, of disregarding the Constitution and, in effect, denying to the legislative assemblies their constitutional powers of legislating according to the popular will. The use which that Court now makes of its jurisdiction places it in the American political system as the powerful, vigilant, but reasonable, guardian of the Constitution—and moreover, as one of the greatest intellectual and moral leaders of the nation. That, under its authority, a single judge of first instance should be able to prevent a cabinet member, head of one of the departments of government, from following a Presidential order which the judge considers illegal, is a great lesson to the free world as long as the judiciary appears to be above political passions.[103] The present efforts of the Supreme Court to make actual equality prevail among all American citizens, whatever may be their race and color, are certainly another great inspiration and a great comfort for all people of ideals.

On the other hand, the complexities of modern life gave birth, by a long process, to a "fourth power": the administrative; and the problem of Administration Under Law progressively became the most important aspect of Government Under Law. Even though the rule laid down by Chief Justice Marshall applies to administrative action, the problem remained, during more than half a century, a baffling one. There was a trend in the common-law world to solve the problem, especially in its aspect of judicial review, by special courts.[104] In the United States, however, this was not the final orientation. The remarkable Administrative Procedure Act of 1946, if it does not solve all the problems, lays down the rules which the administration should follow in order to be fair toward all, and sufficient rules to permit the courts to

---

102. The most eloquent advocate of this attitude today is certainly Mr. Justice Frankfurter. See, among others, his opinions in West Virginia State Board of Education v. Barnette, 319 U.S. 624-646 (1943), in American Federation of Labor v. American Sash and Door Co. 335 U.S. 538 (1949), and in the *Steel Seizure* Case, referred to *supra* note 46.

103. Youngstown Sheet and Tube Co. v. Sawyer, 103 F. Suppl. 569 (D. C. 1952). The decision of the Supreme Court, which upheld the first decision is on 343 U. S. 579 (1952).

104. *Cf.* Robson, *supra* note 49.

exercise reasonable control over administrative actions. American administrative law may still need to be made more precise. Although one of the last born of the world's systems of administrative law—at least in its present aspect—it deserves to be carefully studied abroad.[105] It should inspire a reconsideration of the earlier systems, satisfactory as they may appear, with a view to their improvement.

Seen from the European side of the Atlantic, the American experience during the decades immediately preceding and following the year 1900 seems as though it might have occurred during the sixteenth, seventeenth and eighteenth centuries. In France the *Parlements,* which were the highest courts of justice, objected to most needed and desired reforms. As a consequence, the judiciary was distrusted and, so to say, put behind gates by the Revolutionary rulers. Public opinion long remained suspicious toward the judiciary, while heartily vesting in the legislative bodies the sovereignty of the people. As the results of the Revolution, government was, in many respects, more absolute than it had been during the Ancien Régime. Such an approach to the relationships between the three branches of the government denied to the courts permission to pass on the legality of statutes. The importance of the problem of Administration Under Law, however, was recognized much earlier than in the United States —probably because of the unitary, as opposed to federalist, nature of the French nation and of the centralized character of the administration established by Napoleon. The *Conseil d'Etat* proceeded to become, during the nineteenth century, the great court in charge of reviewing administration action.

Today, no one would challenge the complete impartiality of the *Conseil d'Etat.* Nor would anyone object to the extent of its powers. On the contrary, the remaining limitations upon its complete authority are under general attack. Thirty years ago, Dean Hauriou was still able to write:

---

105. *Cf.* SCHWARTZ LE DROIT ADMINISTRATIF AMÉRICAIN (preface by Puget) (1952); BOSCH, EL PROCEDIMIENTO ADMINISTRATIVO EN LOS ESTADOS UNIDOS DE AMERICA (1953). *Cf.* even Robson, *supra* note 49.

> It is not entirely natural, that the State, as public power, should submit to a judge those of its acts against which a petition is made, that it should agree to submit to the chance that judgment may be rendered against it, and that it should agree to comply with the decree.[106]

A contemporary scholar comments:

> We can no longer subscribe to this statement. That the State should let a judge pass on its acts and that it should comply with his decree is or should on the contrary be most natural. The executive branch of the government must obey the law if it has not the power to obtain from the legislature its amendment or abrogation. The Secretaries and their subordinates have no other duty than applying the law and serving the general interest; the public power, stripped of its majesty, is only the steward of the legal order.[107]

It must be added that, notwithstanding the respect paid to the *Conseil d'Etat* for its learning and its independence, there has been a tendency of late years to increase the power of judicial courts to review administrative actions. This tendency may be a temporary one, as principally justified by the previous slowness of administrative courts. Still it brings the French system closer to the American, at the very moment when the enlarged jurisdiction of the Court of Claims and even the assertion of control of administrative action by courts under Article 10 of the Administrative Procedure Act brings the American system closer to that traditional in France.

A foreigner may well be indulged in a little hesitation over the meaning of an English word. If by "reconcilia-

---

106. "Ce n'est pas une chose tout à fait naturelle que l'Etat puissance publique soumette à un juge ceux de ses actes contre lesquels on réclame, qu'il consente à courir le risque d'une condammation et qu'il supporte ensuite d'exécuter cette condamnation. . . ."

107. Mathiot, annotation on Sté automobiles Berliet, Conseil d'Etat, July 22 and December 22, 1949, [1951] S. 3.1, at 5: *"Nous ne pouvons plus aujourd'hui souscrire à ce judgment. Que l'Etat laisses juger ses actes administratifs et qu'il exécute ensuite la condamnation prononcée est doit être, au contraire, la chose la plus naturelle. Le Gouvernement doit respecter la loi, s'il n'a pas assez de force pour obtenir du Parlement sa modification ou son abrogation. Les ministres et leurs subordonnés n'ont d'autre rôle que d'appliquer la loi et de servir l'intérêt général et la 'puissance publique' dépouillée de sa majesté, n'est au service que de l'ordre lêgal."*

tion" you mean the end of a state of hostility, there is no possible reconciliation between the common law and the civil law, for the happy reason that between them there has never been any hostility. If, on the other hand, by "reconciliation," you mean the end of a state of mutual ignorance and of reciprocal misunderstanding, then this conclusion leads us to find such a reconciliation between the common and the civil law traditions, at least in the problem of Government Under Law. The solutions accepted in these two systems are closer than they have ever been. There is certainly no possibility of a unification of the two, nor any need for it. On the other hand, there is a need for mutual inspiration which will help in the improvement of each. Such mutual inspiration has already produced fortunate results. We shall strive toward further achievements.

COMMENT

PROFESSOR TUNC*

Dean Roscoe Pound, whom the lawyers of many countries had the good fortune to hear last year in Paris, has reminded us in a classic work that one of the basic principles of the common law is the principle of government under law. The state in its sovereignty is no more free to disregard the law than the individual as a private citizen. The law applies to the government as well as to the governed.

To what extent is this principle given recognition in the

* ANDRÉ TUNC, *Professor in the Faculty of Law and the Institute of Political Studies of the University of Grenoble.* Professor Tunc was born in Meaux, France in 1917. He graduated at the University of Paris in 1937 (LL.B.) and received his Doctorate in 1941. In 1947 Professor Tunc became a legal counselor to the International Monetary Fund. While serving with the Fund, he began, with Madame Tunc, who is also a Doctor of Law and a former assistant legal adviser to the International Monetary Fund, the study that resulted in their three books, "Le Système Constitutionel des Etats Unis d'Amérique — Histoire Constitutionelle", "Le Système Constitutionel des Etats-Unis d'Amérique — Le Système Constitutionel Actuel," and "Le Droit des Etats-Unis d'Amérique. Sources et Techniques." Beside writing these books which interpret the American legal system to French scholars and lawyers, Professor Tunc has served as visiting professor at Tulane University. He has written extensively on French law and is currently preparing a new edition of one of the leading French treatises on the law of torts and contractual liability.

civil law world? For instance to what extent is it given recognition in France? To answer this question was the purpose of my paper. As has been explained to you, I will here emphasize only a few points. For a person interested in a more thorough study I might refer not only to my paper, but also to some excellent American or English books on the subject, such as Professor Schwartz's recent book on French Administrative Law, Professor Hudson on the French *Conseil d'Etat,* and a book which we expect to see within a few months, Professor von Mehren's book on the Civil Law System.

There are two points on which I would like to give a word of explanation. First, to what extent have we judicial review? Have we any judicial review? The answer is yes and no. No as far as judicial review of legislative action is concerned: the courts cannot pass on any statute. Yes, to the extent that we have judicial review of executive and administrative action.

Why don't we have any judicial review of statutory provisions? Everybody, I think, in France, will agree with the view presented by Justice Marshall in *Marbury v. Madison.* The courts have a duty to say what is the law, and the statute which is contrary to the constitution is not actually a part of the law. It's an appearance of law—it's not actually a part of the law. Therefore, the courts should have the duty—the power and the duty—to state that a certain statute is unconstitutional and must be disregarded. Nobody, I think, in France will challenge the soundness of this view. However, we don't have any review of legislative action. Why not? I must confess that one of the main reasons is probably an historical one. The *parlements* during the sixteenth, seventeenth, and eighteenth centuries prevented the king from effecting desirable reforms—reforms desired by the people as well as by the person in charge of the kingdom. And therefore there was certainly at the time of the Revolution a general or quasi-general dissatisfaction with them. To a certain extent, the situation may be compared to the situation in the

United States, as I understand it, at the time of the elections of 1936. There was a majority in France who thought that the courts were preventing reforms which would have been desirable. Therefore, at the time of the French Revolution, a tight wall was built between the three powers. The theory of separation of powers was considered of great importance and especially the judiciary was forbidden, by many provisions, to interfere in any way with administrative or legislative action. Certainly we are still living under this tradition, although of course there is no longer any distrust of the judiciary.

But aside from these traditional and historical explanations, we have other reasons to consider that we have no great need for judicial review of legislative action.

First, we recognize the difficulty of organizing a satisfactory system of judicial review. Even if we accept the idea that judicial review is founded on reason and on law, we consider it very difficult to organize in such a way that the general will, if reasonable, will not be disregarded by a sovereign court. Secondly, we don't want our judges to be involved in any way in politics. We want them to be above any political question. We have the feeling, rightly or wrongly, that judicial review almost inevitably obliges the judge to take political positions, and we wish to avoid that as much as possible. Theoretically, of course, as some scholars have pointed out (and that has already been done here), the legislature also is deemed to obey the constitution; it is required to avoid the intentional enactment of any statute contrary to the constitution; if the courts again consider the problem, they do it to a certain extent as courts of appeal of the legislature, as being higher at least in practice, in actual operation of the mechanism, than the legislature. And of course there is no reason why the courts should be above the legislature—they should be on the same level.

Those are already two reasons. I will give you a third and last. Most of us consider that there is no real need for control of legislative action. We consider that civil liberties are much more endangered in daily life by executive or administrative action than by that of the legislature. The danger comes from rules made by a mayor or *préfet* or even individual decrees or orders so made or from orders of the central government; but in actual daily life there is extremely little danger that the legislature, the parliament, will act contrary to the constitution. I must say that I have tried to find some examples in which judicial review of legislative action would have been useful in France. I failed to see even one case where it was reasonably clear that the legislature had disregarded the constitution and where it would have been important for the courts to declare the statute inoperative.

On the other hand we feel that there is great need for control of executive and administrative action, and thus we provide a very broad possibility for the court to pass on its legality.

You may have seen in my paper some apparent exceptions but I think that I may reasonably state that any kind of executive or administrative action may be reviewed by the courts. Therefore I feel, and I know some American scholars would entirely share this opinion, that while we appear to have a very different system from yours, as a matter of actual working, we are, as far as I can see, extremely close to your practice of judicial review.

If you take the statistics of the cases decided by the Supreme Court of the United States, or by the Supreme Courts of the various states, I think that you will find that in most cases where the courts found that there was departure from constitutionality there were involved executive or administrative actions; very rarely since 1937 has either the federal Supreme Court or that of a state decided that a statute was contrary to the constitution. Therefore I think that the pictures in France and in the United States appear very far from completely different; when you come to examine them closely I think they are extremely similar.

However, there is a second point on which I would like

to give some explanation and on which the French picture is quite different from the American one. By whom is review of executive or administrative action carried out in France? First by the administrative agent himself. Anybody can go and see the administrative agent who promulgated a certain measure and explain to him why the measure is contrary to the constitution or to a statute, and ask him to cancel it. Furthermore the French administration received from Napoleon a hierarchical organization, and it is the duty of any civil servant, hierarchically superior to the agent, to can cel, to declare void, a decision made by the agent if this decision is contrary to the constitution. Between the mayor, for instance, and the government, we have the *préfet,* with the power of control of any action of the mayor, and any private person may complain first to the mayor and if the mayor refuses to change the rule, complain to the *préfet* who has the power to cancel it. I will not speak at length on this, but as a matter of fact, as a matter of practical life, the control by the superior is very important and deals with most of the cases in which some unconstitutional decision may have been made.

Now that is not, of course, a full control of the government, because it provides only for the inferior civil servant. If we turn to the control of the government itself, this is administered by administrative courts, and that was a point which raised great misunderstanding at least many decades ago. It is accomplished chiefly by the *Conseil d'Etat,* sitting as *tribunaux administratifs.* Many people have been surprised to see control of the administration entrusted to an administrative court instead of the regular courts. In part this resulted from the very strict separation of powers, and from distrust of the legislature. From the beginning of the nineteenth century, to 1872, the *Conseil d'Etat* was actually a part of the administration. Its power, its duty, was to give advice to the government on any case in which an individual complained about the administration. Cancellation of the order could be made on ly by the administration itself. It was the duty of the *Conseil d'Etat* to state to the government, "You have been right" or "You have been wrong" and "You should cancel the act" or eventually, "You should pay an indemnity." The *Conseil d'Etat* at that time was purely an advisory body. However, this body, as time went on, became more and more independent. It was trying in full fairness to state to the government what should be done, and as a matter of fact, it was always followed by the government. Therefore while it was not a court, as one understands a court to be, still it played a very important role in the defense of private rights. And ever since 1872, the *Conseil d'Etat* has been officially and actually an independent court. It has full power to say that an order made by the government is illegal, and to cancel it. Of course, this special court is fully aware that administration is a difficult enterprise, but it also tries very strongly to protect the individual against any infringement of his civil liberties. I could give you many examples.

Whenever the *Conseil d'Etat* feels that the administration has not been completely fair, has made a decision within a certain political context when it should have been fair to somebody in disregard of any political opinion, in any case of this kind, the *Conseil d'Etat* will decide against the government in full and complete independence.

Then, you may ask another question—what is the use of having a special administrative court if this court is fully independent, exactly as a Supreme Court would be? The answer is very simple. It's only a matter of division of duties. We consider that this field of law is a special one with special principles and special rules and therefore that it should be administered by special judges with special training and special learning.

The drawbacks of the system are two. First there are difficulties of jurisdiction between the special administrative courts and the normal courts. Usually that difficulty may be settled by a special court composed partly of members of the Supreme Court and partly of members of the *Conseil d'Etat*.

Traditionally, the dividing line between the jurisdiction of the two kinds of courts was not too hard to find. However, following the second World War we had an extension of administrative functions and therefore our case law had to be changed to a certain extent; and at present, I must confess, there is a certain difficulty in some cases to know whether the parties should apply to an administrative court or to the normal, judicial courts. That is unfortunate, but I hope that our law will be cleared up within a few years, as it was before the war.

Another difficulty was the backlog of cases; but since 1953 the *Conseil d'Etat* has been limited in its function in most cases to acting as a court of appeal from lower administrative courts. Henceforth, the *Conseil d'Etat* will have less work and will be able to keep up with its duty.

I cannot go into much detail, and I think that I have already exceeded the time which was allotted to me. I will only mention *recours pour excès de pouvoir,* which is the normal tool of the *Conseil d'Etat* whenever a decision has been made contrary to a statute or contrary to the constitution. This recourse is open very widely to any person who really has reason to complain of any decision of the administration. Whenever the act is not completely fair, completely reasonable, it may be challenged; it will be quashed by the *Conseil d'Etat* whenever it is not completely in accordance with the law. And when I say the law, I do not mean only statutory provisions, but I include also the general rules of law of a civilized country. Whenever the decision has not been made solely in the public interest, it will be quashed by the *Conseil d'Etat*. The *Conseil d'Etat* has been called the conscience of the administration, the guardian of its morality. Its function may be compared—with many qualifications of course—it may be compared with the traditional role of the English Chancellor. Its procedure is also extremely easy, extremely inexpensive.

I have already been too long; and still to a certain extent I am afraid that I have been too short. Being short, I may have given you too rosy a view of our review of executive and administrative acts. I don't wish you to feel that French civil servants are above every kind of human passions, —that they always act in full fairness to everybody. That would not be true at all. I would not state, either, that our administrative law is perfect—that we are fully satisfied with it. But the procedure is quite inexpensive and easy. I think the law is quite satisfactory. It is, to be sure, quite technical; sometimes it is a case law, and of course like any system of case law, you have some difficulty in reconciling certain cases. However, we feel that we have in the *Conseil d'Etat* a great institution which efficiently protects our freedoms. I think also that administrative law would be one of the fields in which common lawyers and civilians would learn the most from each other. In the United States, the Administrative Procedure Act of 1946 was a very remarkable achievement. But as our respective techniques have been completely different, I think that mutual inspiration would certainly be extremely fruitful.

PROFESSOR VON MEHREN*

It is most appropriate that the first paper to be presented at this conference takes up the problem of government under law against the background of a legal system standing outside the common law tradition. Every legal order faces the problem of government under law. Satisfactory and suggestive solutions to this problem are not by any means found only in the legal systems stemming from the English common law.

Professor Tunc's discussion of judicial review of administrative action in the French legal system gives us, at the very beginning of this conference, a deeper awareness of the

---

* ARTHUR TAYLOR VON MEHREN, *Professor of Law, Harvard Law School.* Professor von Mehren was born in Minnesota in 1922, graduated at Harvard College in 1942, at Harvard Law School in 1945, and took his Ph.D. at Harvard in 1946. Between 1946 and 1948, he studied at various European universities and was with the United States Military Government in Germany. He became a member of the Harvard Law School faculty in 1946 but was on leave in Europe until the fall of 1949 when he began his teaching career. He became a full professor in 1953. He has published numerous articles on comparative law and the conflict of laws.

universality of our problem. At the same time, his remarks broaden our perspective with respect to possible ways in which the problem can be approached. If time were available, I would have liked to discuss what has been done in various other systems outside the common law. The new German Constitutional Court, for example, represents the attempt of a society which has only recently experienced some of the most horrible manifestations of government not under law to create institutional barriers against such conditions ever returning.

A point that emerges from Professor Tunc's paper and is perhaps of particular interest to this conference is the course of development in France of the institutional devices that today insure government under law. The French Revolution swept away the *Ancien Régime*. The new governmental structure created by the Revolution provided no effective institutional restraints on legislative and administrative action. The absence of such checks is to be explained by the unsatisfactory experience that France had during the *Ancien Régime* with restraining institutions, in particular the *Parlements*. The new political forces feared, moreover, that the conservative elements were entrenched in the judiciary and would use every opportunity to frustrate the purposes of the new order.

The thinking of that period is summed up very well by Laferrière:

> Liberals applauded [the opposition of the *Parlements* to the acts of the loyal administration] when it was directed against acts of absolute power. But such opposition could not be allowed to continue under the new regime. The constant preoccupation of the constituent assembly was to see to it that in the new judicial organization that was established, no part of the political power of the old Parlements continued to exist.
>
> The various precautions that the constituent assembly took to insure this—suppression of the judicial hierarchy, election of judges, short terms of office,—were not enough to reassure the assembly. It was predictable that the new courts would be staffed in large part by members of the old judicial corps. The assembly

> was convinced that, due to their special situation, their training, their interests, these magistrates of the *Ancien Régime* were hostile to the Revolution and, as one of the most moderate members of the assembly, Thouret, said, were "the enemies of regeneration."
>
> There was only one way to avoid this danger—remove from the jurisdiction of the civil courts the disputes that might arise in connection with the operation of the administration.[1]

The regular courts were, by and large, deprived of jurisdiction to set aside governmental action. No system of administrative courts was created.

The situation was well summed up by Lucas de Pesloüan when he wrote that "although the Revolution gave the regular courts jurisdiction over certain types of litigation that had formerly been judged administratively . . . reasons, usually political in their nature, led to a continual enlargement of the domain of the administration. 'In giving power all at once to the administrative branch . . . the Revolution left, without so desiring and without suspecting that it was so doing, a formidable instrument in the hands of the government'."[2] As early as 1815, a definite reaction begins, at least as far as administrative activity is concerned, against the absence of control over governmental action.

This reaction takes the form of the regular civil courts expanding their jurisdiction. In the course of the next sixty years, largely without the aid of legislation, the regular courts assumed the right to control a considerable range of administrative action. In 1873, with the famous *Blanco* decision of the Tribunal des Conflits, a new period begins. The jurisdiction of the regular civil courts is substantially limited and that of the Council of State, which in the course of a long institutional development has become a truly judicial body, increases. The modern period of French administrative law begins with the *Blanco* decision. The fascinating story of

---

1. *Les Raisons de la Proclamation de la Règle de la Separation des Autorités Administrative et Judiciare par l'Assemblée Constituante,* in *Mélanges Paul Negulesco,* 429, at 438 (1935).

2. *Histoire de la Juridiction Administrative sous la Révolution et sous l'Empire,* 77 (*thesis, Paris,* 1907).

how the Council of State thereafter steadily expands the range and scope of its review of administrative action cannot be taken up here. Suffice it to say that the development, and this is of particular interest to us, is almost entirely a case law one. The end product has been admirably described by Professor Tunc in his paper.

The French legal system's most effective resolution of the problem of government under law was achieved through this case law development. In a sense, this entire story of institutional development and decisional law furnishes the French counterpart to Marshall's famous decision in *Marbury v. Madison.* For historical and institutional reasons, the road was a longer and more devious one in France than in the United States. Nevertheless, the results achieved offer, as Professor Tunc has pointed out, many similarities to the practices of our legal system.

One point remains upon which I would like to touch briefly. Here my analysis departs somewhat from Professor Tunc's presentation. Why has France, which has gone so far in establishing control over administrative action, not provided institutional checks upon the exercise of legislative power? Professor Tunc has described in his paper the Constitutional Committee created by the Constitution of 1946. As he points out, it is clear from the terms of the Committee's structure and powers that it can never have, and indeed was not intended to have, any effective checking power over legislation.

Professor Tunc suggests that for various reasons the French fear administrative action and do not have any particular concern about legislative action. This is a partial answer to our problem. A full answer would take us into many historical speculations. Another part of the answer certainly lies in the opposition of the judicial corps to reform during the *Ancien Régime.* The United States Supreme Court, it might be noted, is not without a certain responsibility. The constitutional barriers to social legislation that it raised during the first part of this century, and the constitutional crisis during the New Deal period, did not encourage French advocates of judicial review. The absence in France of the need for an arbiter of a federal system removes one important pressure for judicial review. It is also possible that France, as would seem to be true of England, has in its culture and the composition of its society, more effective non-institutional controls over legislative action than are found in the United States. Finally, a lack of a full understanding of the American system and of our experience played a role, as a reading of the discussion devoted by the drafters of the French Constitution of 1946 to the problem of judicial review makes all too clear.

One further element in the total French picture remains. It is this element that I should like to emphasize in concluding, because it brings out another facet of the problem of government under law. The theme of this conference is, basically, multiple. On the one hand, law, in the sense of restraints and limitations; on the other, law, in the sense of effective, positive action. A modern society engulfed by change in all departments of life, and living— it sometimes seems— from crisis to crisis, has urgent need of both. Perhaps France has not fully perceived the need of restraints upon legislation because, by and large, it has in modern times never really known effective, positive, legislative action. Modern France, with few exceptions, one of which is the Vichy regime, never learned the danger of strong government because it never had such a government. In the 1930's the United States passed through a constitutional crisis, the broader import of which was to determine the appropriate relationship for our time between these two conceptions of law. In recent generations, France has always lived with a constitutional crisis of another sort, the impossibility of strong government. Until this constitutional crisis is resolved, the basic issue in France with respect to the problem of government under law can never be judicial review of legislative action.

AMBASSADOR FOURNIER*

Even though I have been announced as an ambassador, I do not intend to talk as a diplomat today. I am a diplomat only by accident of politics; deep in my heart, I am a lawyer. I keep my association with my law firm in my country, and I intend to go back to my practice as soon as possible. I am going to talk as a regular lawyer today.

I think it is quite important to bring here the point of view of the civil law countries on this problem of government under law. We have been reading and listening; we have studied what Professor Tunc has given us from the point of view of France, and through his study we have seen a different approach to the same problem that has been under consideration by the lawyers of North America through its history—that is, government under law.

It is then important to see how a Latin American country has approached that same problem, because even though in regard to private law and administrative law our countries have all their historical roots in France and Spain, in regard to constitutional law we and you have a common parenthood. Our constitutions are daughters at the same time of the French tradition and the United States tradition. For that reason it may interest you to see how a civil law country, whose original governmental ideas were somewhat different, has tried to apply the doctrines of Chief Justice Marshall.

Chronologically, the first guarantee that we tried to build, in order to save the people from the government, from a government which perhaps might become too strong, was a *habeas corpus* writ. In a way this device has some origins

---

* FERNANDO ANTONIO FOURNIER, *Ambassador of Costa Rica to the United States.* Mr. Fournier was born in 1916 at San José, Costa Rica. He took degrees in Arts and in Laws at the University of Costa Rica in 1939 and 1940 and took his LL.M. at the Harvard Law School in 1942. He has been prominent in scholarly and official life in his own country, is a draftsman of the Constitution of Costa Rica, and has been particularly interested in its Bill of Rights. He has practiced law in Costa Rica, served as Civil Attaché of his country's diplomatic mission in Washington, 1941-1942, has been a member of the faculty of the National University of Costa Rica, and has published numerous articles on economic and political subjects in Costa Rica and abroad. He is now serving in Washington as the Ambassador of his country to the United States.

in the Middle Ages in Spain where the kingdom of Aragon used to have a similar thing. But we have had it in our countries— at least in my own—since our first Constitution of 1825.

In that same Constitution, we have also, chronologically speaking, the second guarantee that we tried to build to save the people from a too-strong government. And it was in a way a first and tentative application of the doctrines of Chief Justice Marshall. It was a declaration of the Constitution at that time saying that any law enacted against the Constitution was unjust. It did not say exactly that it was void. It was not until 1844 that the Constitution provided that any law against the Constitution was void. Still for many years the Constitution did not say which body of the government or the state was to have the authority to say when a law was unconstitutional—when a law was against the Constitution. However, the Supreme Court of my country, since the last century, has taken to itself that authority, without any written authority in the Constitution. And it applied the same doctrines of Chief Justice Marshall and declared many laws all through our history unconstitutional, without having any express authority in the constitutional text. It was not until our present Constitution of 1949 that we had an express authorization to the Supreme Court to declare it so.

The third guarantee by which we have tried to build a system of government under law is what we call the "*amparo*" writ, which may be translated as the protection writ, which is a sort of *habeas corpus* applied to all other civil rights which are not related to the personal liberties. That is to say, inviolability of the domicile, or correspondence, or freedom of speech. Any time that you have a threat from government against any of those freedoms you can go by means of a summary proceeding before the Supreme Court and ask for protection. That measure was also established in the recent Constitution of 1949.

And finally the fourth guarantee that we have is the "contentious-administrative" procedure or action. Since the

Republic has existed, it has been possible in our country, and I understand in all Latin American countries, to sue the government for damages, regarding an action of the administration which is considered unjust or illegal. But until recently there was, in my country, not exactly a prohibition against suing the government in order to obtain a declaration that an action of the administration was void, but no procedure provided to do it. Now, according to the present Constitution, it is possible not only to sue the government for pecuniary damages, but also to sue the government in order to obtain from the courts a declaration that a certain administrative act is void and should be set aside.

Finally, it might be interesting for you to know about a precedent that was recently established in my country in regard to these matters. In 1948, because of a revolution that we had against the Communists, the previous Constitution could not be enforced any more. The constitutional order had been broken. Then there was no constitution, and a *de facto* government was established. But that *de facto* government wished to limit its own authority and issued a decree declaring that the civil liberties chapter would remain in force until the new constitution was made. Then, some months after, one of the decrees of the same *de facto* government was challenged by somebody before the Supreme Court as unconstitutional. The government made the defense saying that it could not be unconstitutional because there wasn't any constitution. But the Supreme Court declared that as long as a government declares that there are certain fundamental principles of law which are superior, and that government had so declared, those principles were over any other law or decree, even though that second decree was coming from the same authority which had established its own self-limitations, and the court declared that second decree of the *de facto* government unconstitutional.

These are a few statements of our constant process, as you can see, of a civil law country trying also as you do, and as the European countries do, too, trying to build in our own country a system of government under law just as well as you do it.

DISCUSSION

Professor Casner [introducing the period of discussion from the floor]: As I understood your statement, Professor Tunc, you said that one of the reasons why you were afraid of judicial review of legislative action was the fear that the courts would get involved in political considerations in making their determinations. I wonder if you would care to comment a little further on the feeling in France about judicial review in our country. Do French authorities feel that our system has involved our courts in politics?

Professor Tunc: I think that it is true that we were, to a certain extent and at a certain time, afraid of what was happening in the United States. The struggle between the Supreme Court and the President during the New Deal was quite well known in France. I remember—I was quite young at that time, but I remember—that I was interested in the newspaper accounts of the contest between the Supreme Court and the President. I think nearly every well-informed Frenchman was aware of what was happening. Probably we did not have a very clear picture. As I told you, I am afraid that my picture of the French law would be too rosy; and similarly I would say that our picture of American law and American life at that time was very gloomy. We had the impression that something dangerous was going on—that you no longer had any normal government—that nine men were taking the place of the government and that to a certain extent you were in a state of anarchy. We certainly had a very distorted picture of what was happening here. Even some great scholars, men of complete good will, published books indicating that they were very much afraid of what was happening, very much concerned. We knew, of course, the decisions such as *Lochner v. New York* and so forth, the decisions at the beginning of the twentieth century; and we had the impression that it could be extremely dangerous to have a government of judges, according to the famous slogan. I do not think, however, that today we still fear the American example. We have learned that there can be a certain danger in judicial control, but that is certainly not the main factor in our thinking.

[*A speaker from the floor*]: Professor Tunc has stated very frankly that there was a perhaps distorted view in France of our Constitutional crisis. I wonder if we may have a distorted view of the present French situation, particularly as to what we hear about the attitude toward taxes. It may be no different, basically, from our attitude here— that we don't like them. But apparently there is more room in France not to pay them if you don't like them. Now is this perhaps in some way a reflection of the easier attitude toward administrative review or is it completely divorced from that? Do people who object to the extent of their taxes in France simply disregard them; or do they go to these administrative tribunals and exercise their rights? Could you comment on that, Professor Tunc?

Mr. Casner: Can it be that they are just carrying out Chief Justice Marshall's statement that the power to tax is the power to destroy?

Professor Tunc: I do not think that the French attitude toward taxes has any real connection with government under law—with judicial review. I think that it's a very old, traditional approach. I may give two explanations—one historical, the other psychological.

Historically during the whole *Ancien Régime* there had been a struggle between the government and the *parlements* on this problem of taxes. Many people had exemption, not only the clergy and nobility, but also many of the bourgeois holding office, members of the *parlements* and so forth, were completely exempt from taxes. As a result of that, the taxes on the ordinary people were extremely heavy at a time when the standard of living was very low. And therefore in France we have the impression that for centuries our people were burdened by heavy taxation, by unreasonable taxation, because certain favoured groups were entitled not to pay any taxes at all. Therefore we acquired habits of tax evasion. This is certainly one historical reason which may, of course (I cannot be sure) have a certain strength even now. We labor under a tradition of heavy taxation and of evasion of taxation.

And I would agree also that we are not, at least from the American point of view, a law-abiding country. That is my feeling as a Frenchman. I consider that the American people are very law-abiding and I am full of admiration for them on this point. I might say that I once had the opportunity to write that the Americans were law-abiding; and an English scholar wrote, "On, no, not at all, if you compare them to the English people, they are not at all law-abiding." That may be true; we cannot engage in a comparative discussion of the psychology of various peoples. But certainly I must confess —and I am, of course, not at all proud of this—I must confess that certainly we have a tendency to try to make our own judgments on what the law should be, and to think that if the law is unreasonable, we may disregard it to a certain extent. Those may be very bad traditions, but certainly we have them. We have certainly a great *esprit critique;* it may carry us rather far. We like to sit in judgment on our government, and that may be a source of weakness of our government. Nobody will follow the government blindly. Even the people who follow the government to a certain extent will say, "Yes, it is right up to a certain point, but I would not have done this and that," and everybody will explain what he himself would have done in the particular situation. You see there is quite a different psychological context, and sometimes they go too far. To a certain extent the taxpayer considers himself able to judge what taxation should be, and as a result, certain parts of the population do not pay the taxes which should be paid, and this makes a vicious circle. Taxation has to be heavy because many people avoid taxation; and as a result of that, many people avoid taxation. That is certainly the truth, within limits.

You see, it's an interesting comment; but I do not think that it is really connected with judicial review.

Mr. Casner: Professor Tunc, we have some ways of avoiding taxes in this country, too. Evading them is illegal, but avoiding them is all right!

Robert M. Benjamin, of the New York Bar: Professor Tunc has mentioned the French preference for judicial review by an expert tribunal, in contrast to the consensus in this country which is strongly in favor of judicial review by courts dealing with other things as well as administration. It seems to me that it might be relevant if Professor Tunc would describe for us administration below the level of the *Conseil d'Etat* and the *Tribunaux Administratifs*—that is, whether at the administrative stage, action is typically by an individual administrator or whether the lower administration includes anything of the nature of our commissions and formal administrative tribunals, which themselves deal at that stage with legal questions in a more or less formal way.

Professor Tunc: The picture may be a little difficult to give. I think that normal administration will be a decision made chiefly by individual persons. That is to say decrees, and orders, will be made by the mayor or by the *préfet,* the man who is at the appropriate point in the administrative structure. In traditional administration you find very little use of commissions, bureaus, and so forth. However, it is true that if you take the high administration, the administration in Paris, besides the traditional *ministère,* the traditional departments of the executive, you have also now many commissions of various forms, though not independent commissions. But the normal citizen feels less concern, certainly, with the independent commissions than is the case here. And usually there is very little need to review the actions of these commissions. I think the greatest danger comes from the mayor who may, for example, decide that in order to have the distribution of meat properly clean, specified measures must be taken; or he may make orders about the distribution of bread. It is on this daily level of life that there may be some danger of invasion of the various freedoms of the citizen, and therefore we feel the need to have courts, the *Conseil d'Etat* now as a court of appeal, and the *Tribunal Administratif* in each department. These tribunals will say, perhaps, that the order was a reasonable restriction of freedom, desirable in the general interest; or on the contrary that it was made from partisan political motives or as a measure of passion against somebody or in favor of somebody, or even that while it was done in the general interest, still it was not necessary to prohibit this or that means of distributing milk or bread, and it could have been better accomplished with complete freedom. Does that answer your question?

Conrad Oberdorfer, of Boston: Professor Tunc, I believe you stated that the Conseil d'Etat is guided or governed by case law. Did you mean by that that it follows the principle of binding precedent in the Anglo-American sense, or in the sense in which I believe the *Cour de Cassation* does?

Professor Tunc: You might say that there are some shades of distinction, as you would expect. The doctrine of *stare decisis* is not exactly the same as you have here. Roughly I think that we may say that the *Conseil d'Etat* follows a precedent up to the point to which they want to make distinctions, or even, sometimes, to reverse a decision. I think the picture of American law and the picture of French administrative law are very close, very similar.

Leviathan at the Bar of Justice

JOSEPH M. SNEE, S.J.* †

We Americans have long been accustomed to take for granted the merits of democracy and personal liberty and to regard the theory of limitations upon government as a matter for academic discussion. Two world wars and the recrudescence of totalitarian governments in our own "enlightened" age have startled that complacency. It is a commonplace to say that we live in an era of crisis calling for firm and incisive action. The danger, real or apparent, of internal subversion presents a particularly strong temptation to bypass the orderly procedure of law and to adopt the processes of force which seem so much more quick and effective. It is alarming to note the increasing number of citizens, some of them in high places, who believe that almost any means may be employed, provided the end is the preservation of our American institutions. Yet the principle that the end justifies the means is as fatal to a life of democratic freedom as it is to sound morality, for it implies the negation of the very principles upon which free society is based. As Walter Lippmann warns, we are in danger of keeping the form and of losing the substance:[1]

> In our time the institutions built upon the foundations of the public philosophy still stand. But they are used by a public who are not being taught, and no longer adhere to, the philosophy. Increasingly, the people are alienated from the inner principles of their institutions. . . .

The problems which we face today and the urgent need for a sound solution imperatively demand a re-examination

---

* For biographical note see page 130.

† *I wish to express my appreciation of the aid given me in the preparation of this paper by Charles M. Whelan, S.J., who checked the citations and gave me the benefit of his own keen criticism of the ideas here expressed.*—J. M. S., S.J.

1. LIPPMANN, THE PUBLIC PHILOSOPHY 102 (1955).

of the philosophical principles and the democratic methods upon which the institutions of our free society are based, and without which our tradition of freedom will inevitably perish. This Conference is concerned with one of the most fundamental of those principles—that government no less than the governed is subject to law, and that it is the function of a democratic government to protect its citizens against lawless invasion of their freedom even against governmental power itself.

There can be no question here of an adequate discussion of the many complex problems of political theory and philosophy which are inherent in any discussion of government under law or of governmental protection against government, the subject upon which I have been asked to express my thoughts today. In the limited time and space available, it will be difficult to steer a straight course between the doctrinaire and the jejune. At this risk and with this warning, I propose at least to step warily where angels fear to tread, and here merely to limn in bold outline the American solution to the perennial problem of man *versus* the state and to present the salient features of the philosophy which I believe underlies and justifies that solution.

It is only fair that at the very outset of this paper I should unmask myself for the "medievalist" that I am and confess that my own philosophy is that of natural law in the scholastic tradition.[2] Little more than a decade ago this belief would have been ridiculed as *passé,* but the far from gradual erosion of liberty in our own generation has made us skeptical of the very skepticism which denied any philosophical foundation for the freedom of man or any ultimate value in the human personality. The defenders of freedom today realize that they must have much more to defend in common than a public neutrality and a public agnosticism.[3]

2. The scholastic tradition discovers the norms of the "natural law" in the essential nature of man, unchanging and unchangeable. It has nothing in common with the bastardized forms of the "natural law" of the seventeenth and eighteenth centuries, based upon a supposed "state of nature" prior to political organization.

3. See LIPPMANN, *op. cit. supra* note 1, at 113.

I am firmly convinced that the natural-law justification of the belief in the rights of man and the ideal of freedom, equality and fraternity is the only one which is solidly based on truth. At the same time, this does not preclude agreeing on practical tenets with all those who subscribe to the democratic charter. The points of agreement and disagreement have been well stated by Maritain in speaking of the United Nations International Declaration of Rights:[4]

> . . . [I]t is doubtless not easy but it is possible to establish a common formulation of such *practical conclusions,* or in other words, of the various *rights* possessed by man in his personal and social existence. Yet it would be quite futile to look for a common *rational justification* of these practical conclusions and these rights. . . . The question raised at this point is that of the practical agreement among men who are theoretically opposed to one another.
>
> . . . Assuming they both believe in the democratic charter, a Christian and a rationalist will, nevertheless, give justifications that are incompatible with each other, . . . and about these justifications they will fight. And God keep me from saying that it is not important to know which of the two is right! That is essentially important. They remain, however, in agreement on the practical affirmation of that charter, and they can formulate together common principles of action.

It may be true that, "if men were angels, no government would be necessary."[5] The fact is that they are not. In both civilized and more primitive communities some form of government is an immemorial fact and is regarded as a perennial necessity.[6] The grounds upon which political theorists

---

4. MARITAIN, MAN AND THE STATE 76, 78-79 (1951).

5. THE FEDERALIST No. 51, at 337 (Modern Library ed., n.d.) (Hamilton or Madison). Language used by Madison a few months earlier, in a letter to Jefferson, 24 October 1787, on the necessity of controlling the government in contrast to control of the governed by government, would indicate Madison's authorship of this passage. See 2 HUNT, WRITINGS OF JAMES MADISON 32 (1901).

6. Rousseau would seem to be the exception. He described the natural status as an idyllic paradise in which autonomous individuals lived a life of perfect goodness. The formation of the *status civilis* is not necessary and hence is based upon a free compact.

have based this necessity will vary with their concept of man.[7] To cite but a few instances, Luther's doctrine of the utter corruption of human nature by sin led logically to his view of the state as God's hangman, used by the divine anger to punish and to keep the external peace.[8] The Calvinist principle of theological predestination concluded to the political predestination of the noble, wise and virtuous to govern by natural right those of servile disposition; and the ideal state is the rule of the elect over the broad masses in an aristocratic, hierarchical government.[9] Hobbes took as his *point de départ* a "Naturall condition of Mankind" in which "during the time men live without a common Power to keep them all in awe, they are in that condition which is called Warre; and such a warre, as is of every man, against every man,"[10] and the life of man is "solitary, poore, nasty, brutish, and short."[11] In our own day, the concept of man as essentially a member of a race or class has necessarily resulted in the totalitarianism of Nazism and Communism.[12]

The classical scholastic tradition, which forms the philosophical backdrop for any theories I may have on the function of government and its relation to man,[13] bases the necessity of political society squarely on human nature as that is disclosed by the total experience of man.[14] Aquinas would

7. Every political theory, especially in its treatment of the justification of legal authority and political power as against individual liberty, has as its basis a certain theory of the nature of man, even though this basic theory is seldom openly discussed. An exception is Hobbes, whose *Leviathan* duly opens with the treatise "Of Man."

8. See ROMMEN, THE STATE IN CATHOLIC THOUGHT 62-66 (1945).

9. *Id.* at 66-69.

10. HOBBES, LEVIATHAN 103 (Everyman ed. 1950).

11. *Id.* at 104.

12. See ROMMEN, *op. cit. supra* note 8, at 73-76.

13. Scholastic theories of the natural law have had a greater influence on the political theory of the West than is generally realized, although contact has been made largely through the parody of natural law offered by the rationalists of the eighteenth century. As Learned Hand once said of the Sermon on the Mount, it has been a lesson never quite learnt, yet never quite forgotten. Hand, *The Spirit of Liberty,* in THE SPIRIT OF LIBERTY 190 (Dilliard ed. 1952).

14. While it is true that the *natura humana* of the scholastics is an abstraction, it is an abstraction based upon experience. The scholastic rules of evidence prescribe that the nature of a thing shall be proved by its operations. Indeed, in scholastic jargon, *nature* is simply the name given to the ultimate dynamic principle of a being's operations. The perfection of a thing means the actual use of the total energy of its dynamic principle. The scholastic theory

brush aside as completely immaterial Hobbes' postulate of a "state of nature." His concept of the essentially political nature of man, derived from Aristotle, is thus described by d'Entrèves:[15]

> The doctrine of the political nature of man has an immediate bearing upon the treatment of political obligation. It implies that the historical origin of the State must not be confused with the problem of its rational justification. Whatever the earliest conditions of mankind, political relationship is its 'natural' condition. It is therefore quite pointless to argue about the causes of some supposed change in human conditions, and to seek in them an explanation and justification of the State and political institutions. There is no place in such doctrine for a contrast between 'nature' and 'convention.' . . . [P]olitical relationship—the *subiectio civilis* of man to man which is necessary for the attainment of the common good—is not a consequence of sin, for it is founded upon the very nature of man. Authority and obedience would still have been required even if the state of innocence had been preserved. . . . Man is unthinkable without the State, because it is only in the State and through the State that he can achieve perfection.

"No man is an island," as John Donne once said.[16] Man is a social animal requiring life in common with others. The very process of his conception requires the cooperation of two other human beings, and at birth he emerges from isolation to enter the community of men in which he will spend the rest of his life. In the modern world, even more than in the past, community life is indispensable for men simply as a means of obtaining the very necessities of life. But the same mode of living in common makes it possible to obtain much more than the bare essentials. The cuisine of Romanoff, the fashions of Dior, and the glassy monolith of the United Nations headquarters are possible only in community life. Far more important, however, than the elevation of his ma-

---

of human nature and human perfection, therefore, rests not upon some *a priori* concept of man, but on generalizations from a scientific study of what men have done, are doing, and can do.

15. D'Entrèves, Aquinas: Selected Political Writings xvi (1948).

16. Donne, Devotions upon Emergent Occasions, *Meditation 17*, reprinted in The College Survey of English Literature 340-41 (Witherspoon, shorter rev. ed. 1951).

terial standard of living is the contribution which the community makes to the development of man's knowledge and man's love.

In the scholastic concept, however, man is much more than a social animal, naturally living in community: he is a political being, because his nature demands that he live in political society[17] in order to achieve in a human way the full potentialities of his human personality. Community life is essential, but it cannot be left in a state of anarchy; and mankind knows experientially an essential need to organize politically for the attainment of the common good, unattainable by individual efforts or by private compact. Peace, order, liberty and prosperity are the purpose and the fruit of political society. Out of the raw material of the nation, which is merely a community conscious of its own unity, individuality and will to endure as a distinctive geographical, linguistic and cultural unit, men fashion the body politic, a society rationally organized for the purpose of establishing, maintaining and perfecting the conditions necessary and appropriate for community life to perform its role in the complete development of man.[18] For the most part, these conditions consist in the maintenance of external peace and order, the protection of personal liberty, the regulation of property and commerce in the common interest, and the just settlement of conflicting claims.[19]

The natural-law philosophy, therefore, conceives the function of political authority to be far more basic than the mere preservation of external order by imposing an armed truce upon Hobbes' "warre . . . of every man, against every

17. For the distinctions drawn in this article between the community, the body politic and the state, I am indebted to the penetrating analysis in MARITAIN, MAN AND THE STATE 1-27 (1951). Anyone acquainted with the writings of M. Maritain will recognize how greatly my own thinking has been influenced by his analysis of the functions of the state and its essential nature. I consider him and Rommen the outstanding modern exponents of the natural law philosophy of politics.

18. See MARITAIN, *op. cit. supra* note 17, at 4-12.

19. For a study of natural functions of the state, see MESSNER, SOCIAL ETHICS 118-40 (1949); ROMMEN, THE STATE IN CATHOLIC THOUGHT 333-34, 411-17 (1950).

man."[20] The purpose and the duty of the body politic is to provide the means necessary or conducive to the full human life, or, as Aquinas would express it, to promote the common good,[21] to provide an order of justice and liberty. Its sphere of authority extends to every external human activity which affects the common good, which strengthens or debilitates the capacity of the community and its members to play their role in the development of the truly good life. As I shall point out later, the world of commerce and property is by no means excluded; the laissez-faire concept of an untouchable and sacrosanct liberty of contract or the idea of an absolute right of private property is completely alien to the natural-law thought of St. Thomas and the scholastic tradition.[22]

Despite its necessity and pervasive character, the authority of political society is not, however, without its limitations. It is limited by the very necessity which calls it into being,—the nature of man. This fundamental concept of the intrinsic limitation of political authority was thus expressed in an early American case by Mr. Justice Chase:[23]

> . . . [T]he purposes for which men enter into Society will determine the nature and terms of the social compact; and as they are the foundation of the legislative power, they will decide what are the proper objects of it. The nature and ends of the legislative power will limit the exercise of it. . . .

It must constantly be kept in mind that the body politic is nothing but the rational self-organization of a human community for the specific purpose of promoting the common good by the establishment of optimum conditions for the perfect development of the human personality of its members. Political society as such, therefore, is not concerned directly with what a man learns or loves, but is concerned

---

20. Hobbes, Leviathan 103 (Everyman ed. 1950).
21. I Summa Theol. *q.* 90, *art.* 2, *con.*, translated in d'Entrèves, *op. cit. supra* note 15, at 111.
22. Aquinas holds that the right to acquire and dispose of property is required by the nature of man, but that the concrete title to specific property is derived solely from positive human law and must be held and used subject to the common good. II-II Summa Theol. *q.* 66, *art.* 1-2, translated in d'Entrèves, *op. cit. supra* note 15, at 167-71.
23. Calder v. Bull, 3 U.S. (3 Dall.) 386, 388 (1798).

with providing the opportunity to learn and love without fear of violence or want.[24] The development of the arts, for instance, is not an intrinsic function of political society, but the development of external conditions in which art may flourish is. The body politic is limited in its authority over men by the purpose for which it necessarily exists. It may judge a criminal, but not a poet. It may compel military service, but not murder.

In ancient and medieval times more attention was paid, in the natural-law philosophy, to the *obligations* of man than to his *rights*. The great achievement of the eighteenth century was to bring to the fore the *rights* of man as also required by natural law.[25] But the two concepts are correlative, and political society exists not only to enforce man's obligations to his neighbor and the community for the common good, but also to preserve his rights intact from all invasion for the same end. This is the primary purpose for which political society and government come into being, and the natural rights of man are an intrinsic limitation upon the exercise of all political authority. In the natural-law philosophy certain rights of man are both natural and inalienable, because they spring from his very nature as a human person. He is endowed with these rights by his Creator,[26] and political society, because it did not give them, has no moral right to infringe upon them. Man cannot achieve the full development

24. This is not meant to imply that political society may or should be wholly indifferent toward the convictions and desires of its constituents. It has the right and the duty to suppress those teachings and activities which are not in harmony with the basic public philosophy and which constitute a serious threat to the achievement of the very purposes for which the body politic was organized. See the discussion of the limits of free speech and of dissent in LIPPMANN, THE PUBLIC PHILOSOPHY 124-134 (1955). The problem, of course, is to find a norm to determine when expression of unpopular opinion, of "the thought we hate," becomes a threat to the very freedom which it enjoys. The difficulty in finding a safe norm, one which will enable the body politic to preserve its existence and fundamental structure while not making the government the final *arbiter dicendi* is illustrated by the intellectual gyrations of the Supreme Court over the past three decades, from Gitlow v. New York, 268 U.S. 652 (1925) to Dennis v. United States, 341 U.S. 494 (1951). The problem is particularly acute in situations such as that considered in Beauharnais v. Illinois, 343 U.S. 250 (1952), where the purpose of government is to protect unpopular minorities.

25. See MARITAIN, *op. cit. supra* note 17, at 94.

26. This was explicitly recognized and affirmed by the Founding Fathers in the Declaration of Independence.

and perfection of his God-given personality except in a world of ordered liberty, in which he is secure against any arbitrary or unreasonable interference with his right to life, to personal freedom of action, to the integrity of his body, to private ownership of material goods as a safeguard of his personal liberty,[27] to marry according to his choice and to raise a family, to the free intercommunication of thought with his fellows,—in a word, to all those rights which, in the phrase of Mr. Justice Cardozo, are "implicit in the concept of ordered liberty."[28] Security in the possession of these rights is required not only for the protection of the individual person, but also for the common good to which their reasonable exercise contributes in the community of men.[29] Political society exists for the protection of these rights and their regulation in the interest of the common good; their natural and inalienable character form an intrinsic limitation upon the exercise of all political authority.

Completely alien to the natural-law concept of human rights is the eighteenth-century rationalist divinization of man, which based the rights of the human person on the claim that man is subject to no law other than that of his own will and freedom. Instead of seeing God, the Creator of human nature, as the source of the moral obligations of man and therefore of his rights also, this philosophy postulated an infallible Nature (with a capital N) instructing an equally infallible Reason (with a capital R) whose sole task was to judge human acts against the norm of a Natural Law which was conceived after the pattern of a written code determining *a priori* all aspects of human activity. This philos-

---

27. Scholastic thought does not recognize an essential dichotomy between "personal" and "property" rights, but only a distinction of degree. Both are regarded as normally necessary for the full and free development of the human personality, and both are subject to limitations imposed by the requirements of the common good.

28. Palko v. Connecticut, 302 U.S. 319, 325 (1937); Wolf v. Colorado, 338 U.S. 25, 27 (1949).

29. The contribution to the common good by the preservation of individual liberty is particularly apparent in the case of freedom of speech and press; and this, I believe, underlies the favored position given to the First Amendment by the Supreme Court. See the concurring opinion of Mr. Justice Brandeis in Whitney v. California, 274 U.S. 357, 372, 375 (1927).

ophy of rights, based on the concept of the absolute autonomy of the human reason and the human will, ended up, after Rousseau and Kant, by treating the individual as a god and making all the rights ascribed to him the absolute and unlimited rights of a god.[30] The rationalist philosophy of absolute and limitless rights, untenable in theory and unworkable in practice, has had its sequel in a political philosophy which regards human rights as the gift of the state, to be granted or withdrawn as social necessity may seem to demand. It was realized with a shock that human rights cannot be unlimited, and concluded with a complete *non sequitur* that they are therefore not inalienable. Natural-law philosophy has always recognized, however, that the rights of the person are intrinsically limited by his duties to others and toward the common good, and that political authority must enforce these limitations and regulate the exercise of rights for the common good.

So far I have spoken of the body politic or political society as the rational self-organization of the community for the common good. This purpose is normally achieved by the body politic through the agency of the state. The larger the community, the more impossible it becomes for political society, although autonomous, to perform the functions of government, and the more necessary it becomes to create a specialized agency to govern and regulate the affairs of the community. Even in the small city-states of ancient Greece it was found necessary to empower officials and judges to administer the laws enacted by the *politeia*. Human experience has taught the practical necessity and advantage of committing the enactment, enforcement and interpretation of law to a specialized group within the body politic. This group is often called the *government* or the *administration*, but the word which best denotes its permanent institutional character is the *state*.[31] Since it is the state which ordinarily

30. See MARITAIN, *op. cit. supra* note 17, at 81-84.

31. It is unfortunate that writers in the field of political theory have created such a jungle of semantic confusion that it is no longer possible to use a term like *state* without defining what you mean. In this paper, *state* means the specialized, permanent institutions which carry on the actual business of government.

exercises the authority of the body politic and brings its power to bear upon the citizen, it will be useful to look briefly at its place in the scheme of things and to determine, at least summarily, its nature and functions in a democratic society.

In a democratic and free society, it is impossible to conceive the state as truly sovereign, in the classic sense of that word.[32] So far from being sovereign, it may not even be considered autonomous in a true democracy, since it derives its authority and essential structure solely from the body politic. Nor, as Maritain comments, should it be considered superior to the body politic nor an end for man:[33]

> . . . The State is only that part of the body politic especially concerned with the maintenance of law, the promotion of the common welfare and public order, and the administration of public affairs. The State is a part which *specializes* in the interests of the *whole*. . . .
>
> The State is not the supreme incarnation of the Idea, as Hegel believed; the State is not a kind of collective superman; the State is but an agency entitled to use power and coercion, and made up of experts or specialists in public order and welfare, an instrument in the service of man. Putting man at the service of that instrument is political perversion. The human person as an individual is for the body politic, and the body politic is for the human person as a person. But man is by no means for the State. The State is for man.

The state, in a democratic society, cannot be considered sovereign: it is part of the body politic, not above it or independent of it; it has authority and the right to coerce obedience to its commands, not as its own natural and inalienable prerogative, but only in accordance with the limitations imposed by the body politic in determining the basic structure of the state; it is not autonomous, but subject at all times to the final control of political society, whose instrument it is.[34]

---

32. The classic notion of sovereignty is analyzed by MARITAIN, *op. cit. supra* note 17, at 38, into these elements: (1) a right to supreme independence and supreme power, which is a *natural* and *inalienable* right; (2) a right to an independence and a power which in their proper sphere are supreme *absolutely* or *transcendently,* not *comparatively* or as *topmost part* of the whole.

33. MARITAIN, *op. cit. supra* note 17, at 12-13.

34. *Id.* at 42.

The concept of sovereignty was unknown to the Middle Ages, according to Maritain, and only took definite form at the moment when absolute monarchy was budding in Europe.[35] He lays at the door of Rousseau[36] the blame for importing the concept into the liberal democratic theory, with its inevitable conclusion in totalitarianism:[37]

> Thus Rousseau, who was not a democrat, injected in nascent modern democracies a notion of Sovereignty which was destructive of democracy, and pointed toward the totalitarian State; because, instead of getting clear of the separate and transcendent power of the absolute kings, he carried, on the contrary, that spurious power of the absolute kings to the point of an unheard-of absolutism, in order to make a present of it to the people. . . . Rousseau's State was but the Hobbesian Leviathan, crowned with the General Will instead of the crown of those whom the Jacobin vocabulary called "les rois et les tyrans."

While rejecting, therefore, the concept of a sovereign state independent of political society and possessed of supreme authority and power over it, sound political theory nonetheless recognizes the practical necessity of the state to ensure a regime of ordered liberty and justice. The body politic therefore confers upon the state its own authority, usually with certain limitations, and empowers it to act as its agent or instrument in the enactment, enforcement and interpretation of laws to regulate the activity of its members for the common good. Except in an unrealizable utopia, governmental authority thus conferred demands governmen-

35. *Id.* at 36.

36. Rousseau's concept of the sovereignty of the state, which he identified with the body politic, sounds like a forecast of modern totalitarianism. The state has absolute power over all its subjects (THE SOCIAL CONTRACT 125 (Tozer transl. 1920), Book II, c. 4); this sovereignty cannot be modified or limited (*id.* at 190, Book III, c. 16); it needs no guarantee towards its subjects, since the sovereign, for the simple reason that it is such, is always everything that it ought to be (*id.* at 113, Book I, c. 7). The "Legislator" of the *Contrat Social* gives us a preview of the modern dictator whose "great soul is the true miracle which should prove his mission" and who dares "to alter man's constitution in order to strengthen it." (Book II, c. 7). The state has the power of life and death over the citizen: "When the prince has said to him: it is expedient for the state that you should die, he must die, since it is only on this condition that he has safely lived up to that time, and since his life is no longer nature's boon only, but a conditional gift of the state." (Book II, c. 5). The logic of the reason leaves something to be desired: since the state exists to protect man's life, it acquires by the fact of such protection the right to deprive him of life!

37. MARITAIN, *op. cit. supra* note 17, at 45-46.

tal power to coerce obedience to its just commands. The crucial problem in a democracy is to find an effective means of ensuring that government's exercise of that power does not exceed its authority.

For many, this distinction between authority and power is meaningless, because it is ineradicably rooted in the natural-law concept of man as a moral being, possessed of an intellect capable of ascertaining objective truth and a will free to choose between good and evil.[38] Nevertheless, it cannot be denied that when governmental coercion is based solely upon its possession of naked power, the only limitation upon its exercise is the patience of the people; the only question is how far government may go without incurring the effective anger of the governed. When power is conceived as its own justification, the only answer is counter-power. Hobbes, to whom the state was "that great Leviathan, . . . that Mortal God,"[39] saw this clearly:[40]

> . . . And though of so unlimited a Power, men may fancy many evill consequences, yet the consequences of the want of it, which is perpetuall warre of every man against his neighbour, are much worse. The condition of man in this life shall never be without Inconveniences; but there happeneth in no Common-wealth any great Inconvenience, but what proceeds from the Subjects disobedience, and breach of those Covenants, from which the Common-wealth hath its beginning. And whosoever thinking Soveraign Power too great, will seek to make it lesse; must subject himselfe, to the Power, that can limit it; that is to say, to a greater.

The power of government is its ability to coerce compliance with its commands; it can be limited of itself only by a greater power. But where government is regarded as something more than the mere depository of power, as the possessor of authority reinforced with power, its rightful exercise of

---

38. Power politics are perhaps inevitable; but a political philosophy predicated upon power alone is neither inevitable nor desirable. Holmes once said, "I believe that force, mitigated so far as may be by good manners, is the *ultima ratio,* and between two groups that want to make inconsistent kinds of world I see no remedy except force." 2 HOLMES-POLLOCK LETTERS 36 (Howe ed. 1941). In practice, Holmes may be perfectly right; but the question still remains whether a particular exercise of power is pure might or strong right.

39. HOBBES, LEVIATHAN 143 (Everyman ed. 1950).

40. *Id.* at 176.

power is limited by that authority. If power transgresses those limitations, it is no longer right; it is only might, and justice bows before force. In a civilization where power and authority are considered to be vested in the ruler by some divine right, it is obvious that the only limitations are those imposed by the moral conscience of the ruler; and this was expressly recognized by the apologists for the divine right of kings. But when government is regarded as an agency of the body politic, where the right to political autonomy rests in the people, it becomes possible for the people to circumscribe the authority which they commit to their government and to impose legal limitations, either political or juridical in nature, upon the exercise of governmental power.

But a mere recognition of the distinction between power and authority brings the problem to the fore: it does not solve it. Any attempt on the part of political society to limit the exercise of governmental power by the concept of authority is faced with the fact that both authority and power must be entrusted into the hands of men. Government, like the common law, is not a "brooding omnipresence in the sky."[41] It is administered over men by other men, who may use the power of government, meant for the protection and the welfare of the governed, as an instrument for their oppression. The author of *The Federalist* expressed an immemorial truism of political history when he thus stated the problem:[42]

> . . . If men were angels, no government would be necessary. If angels were to govern men, neither external nor internal controls on government would be necessary. In framing a government which is to be administered by men over men, the great difficulty lies in this: you must first enable to government to control the governed; and in the next place oblige it to control itself. . . .

The problem is not whether man can exist without government: he cannot. The real question, as in the *bon mot* on the relation of the sexes, is whether he can exist *with* it. Hu-

41. The phrase is that of Holmes, dissenting in Southern Pacific Co. v. Jensen, 244 U.S. 205, 218, 222 (1917).

42. The Federalist No. 51, at 337 (Modern Library ed., n.d.). See note 5 *supra*.

man experience has taught the absolute necessity of governmental power; it has also shown the need for practical and workable limitations upon the exercise of that power. The state is but an agency entitled to use power and coercion for the maintenance of law, the promotion of the common welfare and public order, and the administration of public affairs. It is an instrument in the service of man, but it tends to regard itself as an end, as Maritain has pointed out:[43]

> . . . Power tends to increase power, the power machine tends ceaselessly to extend itself; the supreme legal and administrative machine tends toward bureaucratic self-sufficiency; it would like to consider itself an end, not a means. Those who specialize in the affairs of the whole have a propensity to take themselves for the whole; the general staffs to take themselves for the whole army, the Church authorities for the whole Church; the State for the whole body politic. By the same token, the State tends to ascribe to itself a peculiar common good—its own self-preservation and growth—distinct both from the public order and welfare which are its immediate end, and from the common good which is its final end. . . .

The story of political theory is that of a quest for effective means of limiting the exercise of governmental power and for philosophical justifications of such limitation. The problem of justification becomes particularly acute in a democratic society, where representative government is responsive to the will of the people. The American solution to that problem is bottomed upon the theory of constitutionalism, upon the principle that the actions of government as well as of the governed shall be subject to the rule of fundamental law expressed in a constitution.

It is a paradox of history that in England and America, the two countries with the longest and proudest tradition of freedom, such divergent theories have achieved the same result. The struggle for freedom in English history was largely a contest against the power of the crown. It was but natural to look to Parliament for protection against the royal power; the sequel has been the doctrine of the "absolute supremacy"

43. MARITAIN, *op. cit. supra* note 17, at 14.

of Parliament. The concept of judicial review of legislative action[44] is not an English tradition, and sporadic attempts in that direction have proved abortive.[45] Yet Mr. Justice Jackson could write that with the British "due process is a habit, if not a written constitutional dictum,"[46] and McIlwain traces the practical success of the British system to the fact that limitations upon arbitrary rule have been so fixed in the national tradition that no threats against them have seemed serious enough to warrant the adoption of a formal code.[47] No British Parliament today would dare to put into practice the statement made by Lord Chancellor Northington in 1766 during the debate on the repeal of the Stamp Act:[48]

> Every government can arbitrarily impose laws on all its subjects; there must be a supreme dominion in every state; whether monarchial, aristocratical, democratical, or mixed. And all the subjects of each state are bound by the laws made by government.

Nonetheless, the absolute supremacy of Parliament remains the orthodox doctrine of English constitutionalism, as expressed by Sir Hartley Shawcross in a speech reported in *The Times* of 13 May 1946:[49]

> Parliament is sovereign; it can make any laws. It could ordain that all blue-eyed babies shall be destroyed at birth; but it has been recognized that it is no good passing laws unless you can be reasonably sure that, in the eventualities which they contemplate, these laws will be supported and can be enforced.

---

44. Judicial remedies exist, of course, for abuse of executive action: the privilege of habeas corpus, action for false imprisonment, etc.

45. The classic example is, of course, Dr. Bonham's Case, 8 Rep. 114 (1610). See MacKay, *Coke—Parliamentary Sovereignty or the Supremacy of the Law,* 22 MICH. L. REV. 215 (1923); Plucknett, *Bonham's Case and Judicial Review,* 40 HARV. L. REV. 30 (1926). For a suggestion that Coke later abandoned this view, see Boudin, *Lord Coke and the American Doctrine of Judicial Power,* 6 N.Y.U.L. REV. 223 (1929).

46. Jackson, dissenting in Shaughnessy v. United States *ex rel.* Mezei, 345 U.S. 206, 218, 223 (1953).

47. MCILWAIN, CONSTITUTIONALISM ANCIENT AND MODERN 15 (rev. ed. 1947). The author also warns: "As the restraining influence of tradition grows weaker, the danger of a tyranny of the majority comes nearer, and the time may arrive when convention must give way to law if the rights of minorities are to be respected and safeguarded as they have been in the past." *Id.* at 20.

48. Quoted by MCILWAIN, *op. cit. supra* note 47, at 5.

49. Quoted by O'SULLIVAN, THE INHERITANCE OF THE COMMON LAW 87-88 (1950). As Richard O'Sullivan comments (*id.* at 88), this makes of parliamentary jurisprudence "a nice calculation of force."

The English, of course, with an irritating but sublime confidence in their institutions, are sure that no Parliament would so act. This confidence has been largely justified. Magna Carta and the Bill of Rights, though not a legal limitation upon the power of Parliament enforceable by the courts,[50] serve as an epitome of the English tradition of freedom which the commons is elected to safeguard and as a norm to alert a free and politically responsible democratic society against legislative encroachments upon its fundamental liberties.[51] The ultimate constitutional remedy against such encroachment by Parliament is to be found, therefore, in the polling booth and not in the courts of law; the only answer to majority approval of such action lies in the moral conscience of a free people.

American constitutional liberty, on the other hand, is juridical in nature,[52] based on the concept of a constitution as a legal rather than a merely political limitation upon governmental power, and looking to judicial review as a legal means of effectuating constitutional limitations. The government is to depend upon the constitution, and not the constitution upon the government. For Thomas Paine, foremost apologist for the American revolution, "A constitution is not the act of a government, but of a people constituting a government; and government without a constitution, is power without a right."[53] I have selected three basic principles of American constitutionalism for particular comment. (1) A constitu-

50. The fact that in the English system no legal limitations can be placed upon Parliament by a bill of rights was expressly stated in the Foreign Office Draft of an International Bill of Human Rights issued in 1947. The statement concludes, however, with this reassurance: "Therefore, the legal provisions which safeguard human rights can only have as their special safeguard the solemn International obligations undertaken in this Bill together with the firm foundation which these principles have in the deepest convictions of Parliament and the people." Quoted in O'SULLIVAN, *op. cit. supra* note 49, at 89.

51. Madison, in a letter to Jefferson dated 17 October 1788, recognized that a bill of rights incorporated into the constitution might serve these purposes even if they were legally unenforceable. 5 HUNT, WRITINGS OF JAMES MADISON 273 (1904).

52. See the distinctions made between civil liberty and constitutional liberty, and between political and judicial guarantees of constitutional liberty in CORWIN, LIBERTY AGAINST GOVERNMENT 7-8 (1948).

53. PAINE, RIGHTS OF MAN, in BASIC WRITINGS OF THOMAS PAINE 177 (1942).

tion is regarded as a fundamental law defining the authority of government, even of truly representative government, and to some extent of the body politic itself. (2) The fundamental law contained in the constitution provides a legal norm against which every exercise of power is to be adjudged. (3) Where individual rights are in question, the judiciary is the final arbiter in judging whether the test of constitutionality has been met. It will refuse to enforce unconstitutional demands of the other branches of government, and will in some cases grant affirmative relief.

A constitution, says McIlwain,[54] must be antecedent to government, since its purpose is to define the exact authority committed by the people to government. Any exercise of authority beyond those limits is an exercise of power without right.[55] Constitutionalism is meant to ensure a government based upon law instead of one based upon the arbitrary will of the ruler:[56]

> . . . [I]n all its successive phases, constitutionalism has one essential quality: it is a legal limitation on government; it is the antithesis of arbitrary rule; its opposite is despotic government, the government of will instead of law. . . . "Constitutional limitations," if not the most important part of our constitutionalism, are beyond doubt the most ancient.

The framers of the Constitution and their contemporaries saw the weakness of the Confederation and the urgent need for a strong federal government. But they also knew well the dangers to personal freedom inherent in such a government, and the even more urgent need for adequate safeguards against abuse of governmental power. The insistence upon frequent elections and the dependence of the executive on the legislative branch of the government were thought to provide a sufficient safeguard against any barefaced usurpation of power by that branch of the government; at least,

54. McIlwain, Constitutionalism Ancient and Modern 9 (rev. ed. 1947).
55. *Id.* at 9. *Cf.* Jefferson on the supremacy of constitution over government, Notes on the State of Virginia, *Query* XIII, in The Complete Jefferson 649-52 (Padover ed. 1943).
56. *Id.* at 21-22.

there is no doubt that such was their purpose.[57] But for the founders of the republic this was not enough. Their experience with the British Parliament had taught them that kings are not the only tyrants, that "legislative assemblies, born to defend the liberty of the people, have at times violated their sacred trusts and become the instruments of oppression."[58] Nor were there lacking instances even closer to home. Randolph lamented in the Virginia Ratifying Convention an instance of a bill of attainder upon one Josiah Phillips despite the prohibition in the Virginia Bill of Rights,[59] and Madison admitted in the first session of the new Congress that bills of rights had been violated in some of the states.[60] It is not surprising, therefore, to find running like a golden thread through the political debates of the day the determination to guard effectively against the possibility of an abuse of power by any part of the new government which they were creating, including the legislative branch which most clearly was to represent the popular will. John Marshall, whom we honor today, expressed the problem with his usual clarity when he asked the Virginia Ratifying Convention: "Is the power [given to the federal government] necessary, and is it guarded?"[61]

It was at least partly[62] with this purpose in mind that the architects of the new nation worked into the basic structure of the American polity a highly complex series of provisions for a "dual sovereignty" to be shared by the nation and the

---

57. See, *e.g.*, the debates in the Massachusetts Ratifying Convention, 2 ELLIOT, DEBATES ON THE FEDERAL CONSTITUTION 9, 11, 13, 15-18, 99, 114, 125, *et passim* (2d ed. 1836).

58. Black, concurring in Tenney v. Brandhove, 341 U.S. 367, 379 (1951).

59. 3 Elliott 193. Patrick Henry, whose zeal against the federal constitution sometimes carried him away, excused this bill of attainder against Phillips on the ground that the man attained was obviously guilty! *Ibid.* Must all idols have feet of clay?

60. On 8 June 1789. See 5 HUNT, WRITINGS OF JAMES MADISON 385 (1904).

61. 3 ELLIOT 227.

62. I say "partly," because there is no doubt that the primary consideration was to find an acceptable compromise to ensure some hope of adoption of the new constitution by the several states. The suggestion, however, that the dual sovereignty is, in effect at least, a safeguard for liberty is made by Madison, *Government of the United States,* National Gazette, Feb. 6, 1792, reprinted in HUNT 91-93.

states and for a "separation of powers" within the federal government. It would be a mistake to see in the federal compromise of dual sovereignty and the concept of the federal government as one of merely delegated powers only a piece of practical political expediency. That it undoubtedly was. But it was rendered necessary by more than the spirit of local pride; it was a recognition of the contemporary conviction of the people that their liberties were safer in the hands of their own legislatures, under their own state constitutions. Despite his intransigeant attitude, Patrick Henry[63] was not alone in basing his opposition to the new federal government on that ground.

The theory of separation of powers was regarded as more intimately connected with the preservation of liberty. Jefferson decried the lack of separation in the Virginia constitution, holding that "the concentration of these [legislative, executive and judicial powers] in the same hands is precisely the definition of despotic government.[64] He found small consolation in the thought that they were concentrated in the hands of the elected representatives of the people, since "an *elective despotism* was not the government we fought for, but one which should not only be founded on free principles, but in which the powers of government should be so divided and balanced among several bodies of magistracy, as that no one could transcend their legal limits, without being effectually checked and restrained by the others."[65] Madison considered the separation of powers as a fundamental principle of American constitutionalism[66] and "essential to the preservation of liberty."[67] He even found it necessary to defend the partial blending of powers in the federal constitution, on the ground that only "where the *whole* power

63. See his speeches in the Virginia Ratifying Convention, 3 ELLIOT 6, 21, 44, 56, 162, 445, 502, *et passim.*

64. Jefferson, NOTES ON THE STATE OF VIRGINIA, *Query XIII,* in THE COMPLETE JEFFERSON 648 (Padover ed. 1943).

65. *Id.* at 648-49.

66. Madison, *Spirit of Governments,* National Gazette, Feb. 20, 1792, reprinted in 5 HUNT 93-95 (1904).

67. On 17 June 1789, in the course of debate in the first session of Congress on the power of removal from office. 5 HUNT 403.

of one department is exercised by the same hands which possess the *whole* power of another department, the fundamental principles of a free constitution are subverted."[68] The theory of the separation of powers as a system of checks and balances for the prevention of arbitrary exercise of power has since been judicially recognized.[69] There can be no doubt that by this means the political theorists of the American constitutions[70] hoped to provide an added safeguard for the preservation of individual liberty.[71]

The devices of dual sovereignty and, more clearly, of the separation of powers in the federal and state governments are more than a delimitation of *authority*: they form a more or less effectual attempt to prevent the amassing of *power* in the same hands. The essential dichotomy of authority and power is more apparent and the need for an effective means of keeping power within the limits of authority more urgent, when we consider those provisions of the Constitution which enshrine the rights of the people and forbid government to infringe upon them. These are clearly restrictions upon authority. Some are already contained in the original Constitution and seem to have been the subject of little or no debate in the Convention of 1787. Specific limitations are placed upon Congress by prohibiting bills of attainder or ex post facto laws;[72] the same restrictions are imposed upon the states,[73] with the added prohibition against laws impairing the obligation of contracts.[74] Congress is restricted in its power to suspend the privilege of the writ of habeas corpus,[75] and

68. THE FEDERALIST No. 47, at 314 (Modern Library ed., n.d.) (Madison).

69. Brandeis, dissenting in Myers v. United States, 272 U.S. 52, 240, 293 (1926); cited with approval by Frankfurter, concurring in Youngstown Sheet & Tube Co. v. Sawyer, 343 U.S. 579, 593, 613-14 (1952).

70. Madison, in THE FEDERALIST No. 47, at 316-20 (Modern Library ed., n.d.), collects contemporary provisions of state constitutions providing for a separation of powers.

71. For a critique of the doctrine of separation of powers and an analysis of its limitations, see MCILWAIN, CONSTITUTIONALISM ANCIENT AND MODERN 141-42 (rev. ed. 1947).

72. U.S. CONST. art. I, § 9.

73. U.S. CONST. art. I, § 10.

74. *Ibid.*

75. U.S. CONST. art. I, § 9.

its power to declare the punishment of treason is limited by the provision that "no Attainder of Treason shall work Corruption of Blood, or Forfeiture except during the life of the Person attainted."[76] Provisions for the trial of criminal cases by a jury of the vicinage,[77] together with the definition of the crime of treason and of a constitutional quantum of proof thereof,[78] while contained in Article III of the Constitution, are without doubt restrictions upon Congressional power as well.

Despite these express limitations upon the authority of the federal government and the insistence by advocates of the new constitution that the new government was one of delegated powers, with only that authority which the Constitution conferred upon it,[79] there was widespread dissatisfaction with the lack of a more detailed bill of rights in the new Constitution. In ratifying the constitution, the states of Massachusetts,[80] New Hampshire,[81] Virginia,[82] and New York[83] recommended the adoption of more or less detailed bills of rights. North Carolina, on 1 August 1788, submitted a resolution demanding that a bill of rights be included,[84] and, together with Rhode Island, did not ratify the Constitution until after the Bill of Rights had been submitted to the states for their ratification.[85] It was this popular pressure[86] as well as his own convictions as to the value of a bill of

---

76. U.S. CONST. art. III, § 3.

77. U.S. CONST. art. III, § 2.

78. U.S. CONST. art. III, § 3.

79. This argument was made in Pennsylvania on 23 October 1787 by Mr. Wilson (2 ELLIOT 435-36) and in Massachusetts on 23 January 1788 by Mr. Bowdoin (2 *id.* at 87) and Mr. Parsons (2 *id.* at 90, 93). A similar understanding was expressed in Virginia in June 1788 by Governor Randolph (3 *id.* at 204, 469) and James Madison (3 *id.* at 330), and the following month in North Carolina by Mr. Iredell (4 *id.* at 194).

80. 1 ELLIOT 322-23.

81. *Id.* at 325-27.

82. *Id.* at 327.

83. *Id.* at 327-31.

84. *Id.* at 331-32.

85. North Carolina on 21 November 1789, and Rhode Island on 29 May 1790.

86. 1 ANNALS OF CONG. 730 (1789).

rights[87] which led Madison, on 8 June 1789, to propose its incorporation into the federal constitution.[88]

This is not a proper occasion for any comment by me on the specific guarantees of liberty contained in those amendments, together with the gloss which has been placed upon them by more than a century and a half of constitutional history, particularly since they have been made effective against the states *via* the Fourteenth Amendment. That pleasant duty will be performed, more ably than I could do it, by other contributors to this Conference. I do wish, however, to comment briefly upon two tenets of Madison's political philosophy which find concrete expression in the amendments that he fathered. They concern the *nature of the rights* which those amendments guaranteed, and the *source of the power* against which they were meant to protect.

Partially distorted though their concept of human rights may have been by the rationalism of the eighteenth century, yet the political theorists of the nascent American polity recognized clearly the transcendental nature of some of these rights. They repudiated a positivist conception of these fundamental human rights as the mere creature of the state: on the contrary, government exists primarily for their protection. Jefferson in the Declaration of Independence had declared, as a self-evident truth, that all men "are endowed by their Creator with certain unalienable Rights" and "that to secure these rights, Governments are instituted among men." Madison, in introducing his proposed amendments in the House, clearly implies an essential distinction between natural rights and those conferred by positive law,[89] and many years later commented: "If the Common Law has been called our birthright, it has been done with little regard to any precise meaning. . . . As men our birthright was from a much higher source than the common or any other human

87. See his letter of 17 October 1788 to Jefferson (5 HUNT 273), and his speech of 8 June 1789 on introducing the amendments in the House of Representatives (5 *id.* at 385).

88. 1 ANNALS OF CONG. 431-42 (1789).

89. On 8 June 1789. 5 HUNT 381 (1904).

law. . . ."[90] Mr. Justice Chase early stated the theory that political authority is intrinsically limited by the purpose for which it exists and that, even in the absence of express restrictions, there are certain rights which it may not infringe upon:[91]

> . . . I cannot subscribe to the *omnipotence* of a *State Legislature*, or that it is *absolute and without controul;* although its authority should not be *expressly* restrained by the *Constitution,* or *fundamental law,* of the State. The people of the *United States* erected their Constitutions, or forms of government, to establish justice, to promote the general welfare, to secure the blessings of liberty; and to protect their *persons* and *property* from violence. The purposes for which men enter into society will determine the *nature* and *terms* of the *social* compact; and as *they* are the foundation of the *legislative* power, *they* will decide what are the *proper* objects of it. The *nature,* and *ends* of *legislative* power will limit the *exercise* of it. . . . There are acts which the *Federal,* or *State,* Legislature cannot do, *without exceeding their authority.* There are certain *vital* principles in our *free Republican governments,* which will determine and over-rule an *apparent and flagrant* abuse of *legislative* power; as to authorize *manifest injustice by positive law;* or to take away that security for *personal liberty,* or *private property,* for the protection whereof the government was established. An ACT of the Legislature (for I cannot call it a *law*) contrary to the *great first principles* of the *social compact,* cannot be considered a *rightful exercise* of *legislative* authority. . . . A law that punished a citizen for an *innocent* action, . . .; a law that destroys, or impairs, the *lawful private* contracts of citizens; a law that makes a man *a Judge in his own cause;* or a law that takes *property* from A, and gives it to B. It is against all reason and justice, for a people to entrust Legislature with SUCH powers; . . . The *genius,* the *nature,* and the *spirit,* of our State Governments, amount to a prohibition of *such acts of legislation;* and the *general principles of law and reason* forbid them. . . . To maintain that our Federal, or State, Legislature possesses *such powers,* if they had not been *expressly* restrained, would, in my opinion, be a *political heresy,* altogether inadmissible in our *free republican governments.*

Chase's confrère, Mr. Justice Iredell, rejected natural

90. Letter to Duponceau, August 1824. 9 HUNT 200-1 (1910).
91. Calder v. Bull, 3 U.S. (3 Dall.) 386, 387-89 (1798).

justice as a judicial norm for declaring legislative acts void in the absence of express constitutional restrictions upon the legislature.[92] But, as Corwin has commented, "while Iredell's view has enjoyed in the final upshot a *formal* triumph, the *substance* of victory has gone to Chase."[93] The classic test for the police power under due process—legitimate end and reasonable means[94]—is essentially an application of the natural-law test of Chase, and the same philosophy underlies the establishment of a hierarchy of rights in the first eight amendments for the purpose of determining whether they have been made applicable to the states by the due process clause of the Fourteenth Amendment. With a bow to Iredell, the Supreme Court uses the convenient peg of that clause upon which to hang its decisions, and then proceeds to follow the view of Chase that there are *some* rights so fundamental that they must be protected in *any* free society, and therefore are part and parcel of "due process of law." It has spoken of procedures which guarantee "the very substance of individual rights to life, liberty, and property,"[95] of "a fundamental principle of liberty and justice which inheres in the very idea of a free government and is the inalienable right of a citizen of such a government,"[96] of freedoms which are "implicit in the concept of ordered liberty,"[97] of "canons of decency and fairness,"[98] of "considerations deeply rooted in reason and in the compelling traditions of the legal profession,"[99] of governmental "conduct that shocks the conscience."[100]

Mr. Justice Black, of course, is quite correct in recognizing in these decisions the language and the philosophy of natural law.[101] But the concept of a hierarchy of rights and

92. *Id.* at 398-399.
93. Corwin, Liberty Against Government 63 (1948).
94. To cite but one modern case, Nebbia v. New York, 291 U.S. 502, 525 (1934).
95. Hurtado v. California, 110 U.S. 516, 532 (1884).
96. Twining v. New Jersey, 211 U.S. 78, 106 (1908).
97. Palko v. Connecticut, 302 U.S. 319, 325 (1937); Wolf v. Colorado, 338 U.S. 25, 27 (1949).
98. Frankfurter, concurring in Adamson v. California, 332 U.S. 46, 59, 67 (1947); Rochin v. California, 342 U.S. 165, 169 (1952).
99. Rochin v. California, 342 U.S. 165, 171 (1952).
100. *Id.* at 172.
101. Black, dissenting in Adamson v. California, 332 U.S. 46, 68, 69 (1947).

freedoms was quite familiar to the thinking of the framers of the Constitution and their contemporaries. It also expresses a philosophy of common sense. A fair trial is indispensable for justice; trial by a common-law jury is not, but it is one of the fairest methods known and has met the test of centuries in the Anglo-American tradition. I have no fundamental quarrel with the attempt to incorporate the guarantees of the first eight amendments into the due process clause of the Fourteenth Amendment,[102] but I would reject the philosophy which finds such incorporation essential for the preservation of American freedom. It misses, if it does not deny, the essential distinction between fundamental rights, natural to man, which the state exists to protect, and certain other rights, positive in nature, which the body politic has freely determined to guarantee on the ground that they are apt for, but not essential to, the preservation of fundamental freedoms. In the one case, political society expressly refused to government an authority which it could not give; in the other, it placed restrictions upon government because it chose to do so.

The second point I wish to make with regard to constitutional guarantees of individual rights concerns the power against which they were meant to protect. Madison, in proposing the Bill of Rights in the House, stated that they were not so necessary as a check upon the executive, since this was the weakest branch of the government,[103] but rather against the legislative and those whom the legislature was to represent:[104]

> . . . It therefore must be levelled against the Legislative, for it is the most powerful, and most likely to be abused, because it is under the least control. . . . But I confess that I do conceive, that in a Government modified like this of the United States, the great

102. Although, unlike Mr. Justice Black, dissenting in Adamson v. California, 332 U.S. 46, 68, 71 (1947), a study of the history of the Fourteenth Amendment has not convinced me that it was the intent of the framers of the amendment to include any of the express provisions of the first eight amendments. See Fairman and Morrison, *Does the Fourteenth Amendment Incorporate the Bill of Rights?* 2 STAN. L. REV. 5, 140 (1949).

103. 5 HUNT 381.

104. *Ibid.*

danger lies rather in the abuse of the community than in the Legislative body. The prescriptions in favor of liberty ought to be levelled against that quarter where the greatest danger lies, namely, that which possesses the highest prerogative of power. But this is not found in either the Executive or Legislative departments of Government, but in the body of the people, operating by the majority against the minority.

This theme was almost an obsession with Madison. He stated that "In Virginia I have seen the bill of rights violated in every instance where it has been opposed to a popular current."[105] He had already adverted to the danger in the Federal Constitutional Convention,[106] and forty-two years later, in the Virginia Constitutional Convention of 1829, expressed his view that, "The only effectual safeguard of the rights of the minority, must be laid in such a basis and structure of the Government itself, as may afford, in a certain degree, directly or indirectly, a defensive authority in behalf of a minority having right on its side."[107] He considered the division of power between federal and state governments to be such a safeguard.[108] He thought that a bill of rights would serve to impress upon the consciousness of the majority the value of the rights they guaranteed,[109] and saw them as an encouragement to the judiciary to "consider themselves in a peculiar manner the guardians of those rights."[110] This function of a constitutional guarantee of rights has found its clearest expression in *West Virginia State Board of Education v. Barnette*:[111]

The very purpose of a Bill of Rights was to withdraw certain subjects from the vicissitudes of political controversy, to place them beyond the reach of majorities and officials and to establish them as legal principles to be applied by the courts. One's right to life, liberty, and property, to free speech, a free press, freedom

105. Letter of 17 October 1788 to Jefferson, 5 HUNT 272.
106. 3 HUNT 103. He considered this factor to be the basis of the injustice of Parliament toward America. *Id.* at 104.
107. 9 HUNT 361-62.
108. Letter of 18 December 1825 to Thomas Ritchie, 9 HUNT 232-33.
109. Speech in House, 8 June 1789, proposing the amendments, 5 HUNT 382; letter of 17 October 1788 to Jefferson, *id.* at 273.
110. Speech in House, 5 HUNT 385.
111. 319 U.S. 624, 638 (1943).

of worship and assembly, and other fundamental rights may not be submitted to vote; they depend on the outcome of no elections.

American constitutionalism represents a determination that ours shall be "a government of laws and not of men,"[112] that the Constitution shall be "a law for rulers and people,"[113] against which every exercise of power shall be adjudged. Aristotle had long since said that the rule of law is preferable to that of any individual, even the best of men,[114] and it has been stated that, "The principal foundation on which medieval political theory was built was the principle of the supremacy of law."[115] The most immediate application, of course, was to rulers and officials of government,[116] and such application has been frequent in American constitutional history.[117] But it is perhaps the most significant contribution of America to political theory to have recognized its applicability, in a polity based upon the majoritarian method, to the people themselves, and to have utilized the principle as a means of protecting the rights of a minority against the majority. The cardinal tenet of the American theory was thus expressed by an author of *The Federalist*:[118]

> . . . Though I trust the friends of the proposed Constitution will never concur with its enemies, in questioning that fundamental principle of republican government, which admits the right of the

---

112. Marbury v. Madison, 5 U.S. (1 Cranch) 137, 163 (1803). *Cf.* Truax v. Corrigan, 257 U.S. 312, 332 (1921).

113. *Ex parte* Milligan, 71 U.S. (4 Wall.) 2, 120 (1866).

114. ARISTOTLE, POLITICS, bk. III, c. 16 (Jowett transl.), in THE BASIC WORKS OF ARISTOTLE 1202 (Pégis ed. 1941).

115. 5 CARLYLE, MEDIEVAL POLITICAL THEORY IN THE WEST 457 (1928).

116. Aquinas saw this principle clearly. In I-II SUMMA THEOL. *q.* 96, *art.* 4, he discusses the question whether human laws bind in conscience. His reply is that just laws may do so, but that unjust laws cannot. Among unjust laws, contrary to the common good, he includes all regulations made by a legislator beyond the limits of the authority committed to him by the community. The passage is available in translation in 2 BASIC WRITINGS OF ST. THOMAS AQUINAS 794-95 (Pégis ed. 1945).

117. A clear expression of this application is that given by Mr. Justice Miller in United States v. Lee, 106 U.S. 196, 220 (1882): "No man in this country is so high that he is above the law. No officer of the law may set that law at defiance with impunity. All the officers of the government, from the highest to the lowest, are creatures of the law and are bound to obey it. It is the only supreme power in our system of government, and every man who by accepting office participates in its functions is only the more strongly bound to submit to that supremacy, and to observe the limitations which it imposes upon the exercise of the authority which it gives."

118. THE FEDERALIST No. 78, at 508-9 (Modern Library ed., n.d.) (Hamilton).

people to alter or abolish the established Constitution, whenever they find it inconsistent with their happiness, yet it is not to be inferred from this principle, that the representatives of the people, whenever a momentary inclination happens to lay hold of a majority of their constituents, incompatibile with the provisions in the existing Constitution, would, on that account, be justifiable in a violation of those provisions; or that the courts would be under a greater obligation to connive at infractions in this shape, than when they had proceeded wholly from the cabals of the representative body. Until the people have, by some solemn and authoritative act, annulled or changed the established form, it is binding upon themselves collectively, as well as individually; and no presumption, or even knowledge, of their sentiments, can warrant their representatives in a departure from it, prior to such an act. . . .

In a representative form of government, it is true, the state is supposed to reflect and execute the will of the people; but as Walter Lippmann has shown so clearly, the voting majority cannot be identified with the people.[119] Only in those debatable matters concerning the public good which have been selected by the people for determination by majority vote is the will of the majority reductively the will of the body politic. If the whole people, by the "solemn and authoritative act"[120] of establishing a constitution as fundamental law, have determined that certain matters are not to be subject to the will of the majority, however good or desirable may be the object of that will, then the majority have no authority to make rules and regulations in the prohibited areas. Any attempt by the majority, either directly or through their elected representatives, to do so is an attempt to exercise power without authority.

We have considered the devices of dual sovereignty and separation of powers together with express constitutional guarantees of personal freedom as efforts to minimize the danger of the private or the majority abuse of public power. These are regarded as the fundamental law under which the

---

119. LIPPMANN, THE PUBLIC PHILOSOPHY 31-36 (1955). See also Madison, Letter to Anonymous (1833) on the subject of majority governments, 9 HUNT 527.

120. THE FEDERALIST No. 78, at 509 (Modern Library ed., n.d.) (Hamilton).

operations of government are to be carried on and the public force brought to bear upon private individuals. In our complex polity, the question of whether the limits imposed by this fundamental law have been exceeded in a particular case is sure to arise. An authoritative answer is necessary: when the preservation, the peace and prosperity of the public are at stake, private interpretation is political suicide. Since these limitations are considered to be juridical, rather than merely political, in nature, it was but natural to turn to the courts of law for an authoritative interpretation. This was particular true where private rights were involved, since the adjudication of such rights has been the traditional function of courts in the common-law system.

I do not propose here to consider the many questions raised by the doctrine and practice of judicial review in the United States, but only to consider one aspect: its origin and function in the preservation of individual rights.

The framers of the Constitution, whatever their views on the broad question of judicial review of Congressional legislation, considered the judiciary a particularly apt instrument for the preservation of individual rights and saw in judicial independence and tenure a special safeguard against a tyranny of the majority. This branch of the government, because the weakest, was thought to be the least dangerous to individual freedom.[121] Hamilton, the author of *The Federalist No. 78,* stated the positive function of the judiciary unequivocally:[122]

> The complete independence of the courts of justice is peculiarly essential in a limited Constitution. By a limited Constitution, I understand one which contains certain specified exceptions to the legislative authority; such, for instance, as that it shall pass no

121. THE FEDERALIST No. 78, at 504 (Modern Library ed., n.d.) (Hamilton). And see the statement of Madison's confidence in the judiciary in the Virginia Ratifying Convention (20 June 1788). 5 HUNT 221. See also the statement of the Court of "the inherent limitations of the judicial process, arising especially from its largely negative character and limited resources of enforcement." Rescue Army v. Municipal Court of Los Angeles, 331 U.S. 549, 571 (1947).

122. THE FEDERALIST No. 78, at 505, 508-9 (Modern Library ed., n.d.) (Hamilton).

bills of attainder, no *ex-post-facto* laws, and the like. Limitations of this kind can be preserved in practice no other way than through the medium of courts of justice, whose duty it must be to declare all acts contrary to the manifest tenor of the Constitution void. Without this, all the reservations of particular rights or privileges would amount to nothing.

* * * * *

This independence of the judges is equally requisite to guard the Constitution and the rights of individuals from the effects of those ill humors, which the arts of designing men, or the influence of particular conjunctures, sometimes disseminate among the people themselves, and which, though they speedily give place to better information, and more deliberate reflection, have a tendency, in the meantime, to occasion dangerous innovations in the government, and serious oppressions of the minor party in the community. . . . But it is easy to see, that it would require an uncommon portion of fortitude in the judges to do their duty as faithful guardians of the Constitution, where legislative invasions of it had been instigated by the major voice of the community.

Jefferson wrote to Madison: "In the arguments in favor of a declaration of rights, you omit one which has great weight with me; the legal check which it puts into the hands of the judiciary."[123] Less than three months later,[124] Madison in proposing the bill of rights in the Congress urged this as a reason for the adoption of the amendments:[125]

. . . If they are incorporated into the Constitution, independent tribunals of justice will consider themselves in a peculiar manner the guardians of those rights; they will be an impenetrable bulwark against every assumption of power in the Legislative or Executive; they will naturally be led to resist every encroachment upon rights expressly stipulated for in the Constitution by the declaration of rights. . . .

Doubtless, this was one device which Madison had in mind when, forty years later, he said that the rights of a minority could be adequately safeguarded only by "such a basis and structure of the *Government itself,* as may afford, in a

123. Jefferson, Letter of 15 March 1789 to Madison, in THE COMPLETE JEFFERSON 123 (Padover ed. 1943).

124. On 8 June 1789.

125. 5 HUNT 385.

certain degree, directly or indirectly, a *defensive authority* in behalf of a minority having right on its side."[126] This clearly expresses the concept of government itself as the protector of individual rights against the abuse of governmental authority!

The judiciary, both federal and state, have been zealous in the performance of the constitutional function thus imposed upon them. The Supreme Court has declared it to be "the duty of courts to be watchful for the constitutional rights of the citizen, and against any stealthy encroachments thereon."[127] It considers its task to be "the duty our system places on this Court to say where the individual's freedom ends and the State's power begins."[128] It has thus expressed its responsibility toward unpopular minorities.[129]

> . . . Under our constitutional system, courts stand against any winds that blow as havens of refuge for those who might otherwise suffer because they are helpless, weak, outnumbered, or because they are non-conforming victims of prejudice and public excitement. . . . No higher duty, no more solemn responsibility rests upon this Court, than that of translating into living law and maintaining this constitutional shield deliberately planned and inscribed for the benefit of every human being subject to our Constitution—of whatever race, creed or persuasion.

There is merit to the contention of Madison[130] that no one department of government has the exclusive authority to declare on the constitutionality of governmental acts. Certainly it is the duty of Congress to consider the question of constitutionality in enacting legislation, and the prerogative of the President to veto legislation that he considers unconstitutional. But when individual rights are in issue, the judiciary must be the final arbiter, since it is the traditional function of the courts to adjudicate rights in accordance with law. It is this philosophy which underlies the restrictions

---

126. Speech in Virginia Constitutional Convention on 2 December 1829, 9 Hunt 361-62. (Emphasis added.)

127. Boyd v. United States, 116 U.S. 616, 635 (1886).

128. Thomas v. Collins, 323 U.S. 516, 529 (1945).

129. Chambers v. Florida, 309 U.S. 227, 241 (1940).

130. Speech in Congress, 17 June 1789, on the power of removal from office, 5 Hunt 403.

which the Court has placed upon the exercise of its jurisdiction—the requirement of a "case or controversy" involving a substantial injury to the rights of an individual which can be determined only by a constitutional decision.[131] Though the division of authority between federal and state governments and among the three branches of the federal government can be authoritatively and finally determined only by the Court, a determination made by other parts of the government will stand as constitutional, free from interference by the Court, until such time as an individual claims that his rights have been violated. In such case, the claim of the individual is not that he cannot be forced so to act, but merely that it lies without the scope of authority of the power demanding that he act.[132]

It was stated by Madison after a long political career that, "My prolonged life has made me a witness of the alternate popularity, and unpopularity of each of the great branches of the Federal Government." [133] Jefferson, who in 1789 had welcomed a bill of rights for the "legal check which it puts into the hands of the judiciary,"[134] in 1821 referred to the same judiciary as "the corps of sappers and miners, steadily working to undermine the independent rights of the States."[135] Today's defenders of the authority of the Court will be its bitterest opponents tomorrow; and yesterday's friends have become the foes of today. And in each case, disagreement with method springs from disapproval of the result of judicial decisions: it all depends on whose ox is being gored! As Professor Arthur Sutherland of Harvard Law School has remarked:[136]

---

131. See the summary of these self-imposed restrictions by Mr. Justice Brandeis, concurring in Ashwander v. Tennessee Valley Authority, 297 U.S. 288, 341, 346-48 (1936).

132. See the statement of St. Thomas, cited in note 116 *supra*.

133. Madison, Letter to Anonymous, March 1836, in 9 HUNT 609.

134. Jefferson, Letter of 15 March 1789 to Madison, in THE COMPLETE JEFFERSON 123 (Padover ed. 1943).

135. AUTOBIOGRAPHY (1821), in THE COMPLETE JEFFERSON 1119, 1173 (Padover ed. 1943).

136. Sutherland, *The Supreme Court and the General Will*, 82 PROCEEDINGS OF AMERICAN ACADEMY OF ARTS AND SCIENCES 169, 174 (1953).

> . . . The constitutionalist must construct a theory by which the Supreme Court will keep hands off the other branches of the Federal Government, and hands off the States, when aloofness is proper; and yet will act against each at proper times. . . . This is not simple, for opinions on questions of propriety are rarely unanimous.

The long struggle for judicial recognition of the right and the duty of government to promote the public welfare through economic regulation, and the attempt to enforce the concept that the rights of private property and of liberty to contract are not absolutes, is now fortunately ancient history. We need not rehearse the many battles fought in that war, nor the parallel struggle to have the Court acknowledge the unitary nature of the national economy and the need for an enlarged concept of federal jurisdiction under the commerce clause. In the days when laissez-faire was king, the liberals[137] won the battles in the legislatures and Congress, only to lose the war in the courts. It became the ordinary thing for them to damn the judicial process for thus thwarting the will of the people to secure sound economic conditions, at the same time that their adversaries were exalting the courts as the last strongholds of liberty, *viz.*, the right to an unrestricted use of private property.[138]

A more striking example of *volte face* is the contemporary change in attitude toward the phenomenon of congressional investigations. On 11 April 1924, President Coolidge in a message to the Senate protested the methods of the committee investigating Andrew Mellon, then Secretary of the Treasury. He wrote: [139]

---

137. An admirable definition of this term for present purposes is that given by Professor Sutherland, *op. cit. supra* note 136 at 170: "For the purposes of this discussion only, I take a 'liberal' to mean the sort of man who enjoyed the *New Republic* about 1923."

138. The most appalling expression of this philosophy, to my mind, is that given by Associate Justice Van Orsdel in setting aside the District of Columbia Minimum Wage Act (1918): "It should be remembered that of the three fundamental principles which underlie government, and for which government exists, the protection of life, liberty, and property, *the chief of these is property.* . . ." Children's Hospital v. Adkins, 284 Fed. 613, 622 (D.C. Cir. 1922). (Emphasis added.)

139. New York Times April 12, 1924, p. 1.

> Under a procedure of this kind, the constitutional guarantees against unwarranted search and seizure break down, the prohibition against what amounts to a Government charge of criminal action without the formal presentment of a Grand Jury is evaded, the rules of evidence which have been adopted for the protection of the innocent are ignored, the department becomes the victim of vague, unformulated and indefinite charges, and instead of a Government of law we have a Government of lawlessness.

The words have a modern ring to them in this day of congressional investigations run rampant. Yet the *New Republic* of 23 April 1924 decried the accusation made by President Coolidge. Approving wholeheartedly of the objectives of the investigation, it undertook to justify the methods employed.[140] Mr. Justice (then Professor) Felix Frankfurter wrote an article defending the value of congressional inquiries, with the significant title, "Hands Off Investigations."[141] There was no prescience of a day when more precious values would be at stake, which courts would be called upon to protect, and Mr. Justice Frankfurter would write for a unanimous Court:[142]

> Although the indispensable "informing function of Congress" [Wilson, Congressional Government 303 (1885)] is not to be minimized, determination of the "rights" which this function implies illustrates the common juristic situation thus defined for the Court by Mr. Justice Holmes: "All rights tend to declare themselves absolute to their logical extreme. Yet all in fact are limited by the neighborhood of principles of policy which are other than those on which the particular right is founded, and which become strong enough to hold their own when a certain point is reached." . . . President Wilson did not write in light of the history of events since he wrote; more particularly he did not write of the investigative power of Congress in the context of the First Amendment. And so, we would have to be that "blind" Court, against which Mr. Chief Justice Taft admonished in a famous passage, . . . that does not see what "[a]ll others can see and understand" not to know that there is wide concern, both in and

140. Both the President's protest and the reply of the *New Republic* are quoted at length by Professor Sutherland, *op. cit. supra* note 136, at 171.

141. 38 New Republic 329 (1924).

142. United States v. Rumely, 345 U.S. 41, 43-44 (1953).

out of Congress, over some aspects of the exercise of the congressional power of investigation.

The process of judicial determination of constitutional questions has been alternately praised and condemned, yet the Court has gained rather than lost in prestige.[143] The dissatisfaction has been with the result reached; the temptation has been to eliminate the process and method, judicial review, by which the undesired result was attained. Reason has fortunately prevailed over the sometimes almost irresistible impulse to throw out the baby with the bath water, and the fact that now one side and now another look to the Court for support of unpopular ideas may be the surest sign of its value in resolving the tensions inherent in our constitutional system. It may be an apt illustration of the old adage that it is impossible to fool *all* of the people *all* of the time.

Despite its inherent conservatism, perhaps because of it, I believe that the Court in placing a temporary check[144] upon the legal effectuation of the popular will, particularly in the area of human rights, fulfills and was meant to fulfil an essential function in a free and democratic society. It is an important mechanism in a popular state toward a solution of the perennial problem of law *versus* will, the most important of all practical problems. It helps to leave open the possibility of an appeal from the people drunk to the people sober, which is essential if individual and minority rights are to be safeguarded in the periods of excitement and hysteria from which we unfortunately are not immune.[145] It helps to ensure that the will even of a majority of our people shall be subject to law, in the conviction that law is in essence an *ordinatio rationis*. The Constitution is what the Supreme Court says it is. It remains within the power of the body politic to change the constitution in accordance with their will. But the concept of constitution as fundamental law enforces upon

---

143. This was evidenced by the furor caused by President Roosevelt's plan to modify the structure of the Supreme Court. The more unkind of his critics characterized it as the "court-packing plan."

144. It is temporary because of the possibility of amendment.

145. See McIlwain, CONSTITUTIONALISM ANCIENT AND MODERN 146 (1947).

an often impatient majority a long "cooling off" period, during which the afforded opportunity for discussion and debate tends to ensure that the wisest counsels will prevail, and that the result will represent the reason of our people. This function of the judiciary was considered important at the birth[146] of our constitutional era: it is no less important today. As Mr. Justice Black has said: "History indicates that individual liberty is intermittently subjected to extraordinary perils. Even countries dedicated to government by the people are not free from such cyclical dangers. . . ."[147] The attitude of so many of our citizens, which is impatient with so many of our constitutional guarantees and has converted the Fifth Amendment into an opprobrious epithet, should be convincing proof that the dangers are far from chimerical.

The independence and tenure of the judiciary provided for in the Constitution was intended to ensure that they should not be responsible to the will of the people.[148] It was not intended to make them irresponsible: their duty lies to their conscience in the faithful interpretation and guardianship of the fundamental law of the land. Nor are they to be regarded as not truly representative of the body politic which created that fundamental law, and whose instrument they are. They are, in a sense, the embodiment of its reason[149] empowered to fulfil that function by the "original and supreme will"[150] of the people which created the American polity.

It is significant that the Constitution attempts to circumscribe most carefully the authority of the two "power" branches of the government, and that the most authority is given to that branch which has the least power—the judici-

146. See THE FEDERALIST No. 78, at 503, 504, 509 (Modern Library ed. n.d.) (Hamilton); also *id.* No. 49, at 331 (Hamilton or Madison).

147. Black, concurring in Wieman v. Updegraff, 344 U.S. 183, 192 (1952).

148. See sources cited in note 146 *supra.*

149. "It [the judiciary] may truly be said to have neither FORCE nor WILL, but merely judgment; and must ultimately depend upon the aid of the executive arm even for the efficacy of its judgments." THE FEDERALIST No. 78, at 504 (Modern Library ed. n.d.) (Hamilton).

150. Marbury v. Madison, 5 U.S. (1 Cranch) 137, 176 (1803).

ary. The judges are appointed by the President with the consent of the Senate; their salaries and operating funds depend upon appropriations by the legislative; and they are powerless to enforce their decrees without the aid of the executive. Yet they have been given the authority to speak the final word on constitutionality of the exercise of governmental power by the other two branches, and have become the bastion for the preservation of individual rights against infringment by government or people. Could there be a surer indication of the American constitutional theory that power exercised without authority is might without right?

A corollary of the thesis that power must be exercised only in accordance with the limits prescribed by the fundamental law is found in an analysis of the function performed by the court when it sets aside governmental action as unauthorized. In the truest sense, it is impossible to conceive of "government as the protector of the people against government." There is only protection by government against lawless action by private individuals. When a governmental official steps beyond the limits of his authority and infringes upon the guaranteed freedom of the individual, the Court will strip from him his assumed mask of authority and fufil its traditional common-law function of protecting the rights of the citizen. It thus performs the task for which all government was instituted.

The successful working of a polity based upon the concept of authority rather than power depends ultimately upon the recognition of the moral nature of authority. Lippmann has stated this well:[151]

> . . . The laws prevail when the lawmakers and the judges and the law enforcers are attached to the laws. When they are not attached to the laws, the law of contract and the laws of the rights of man—the laws of the constitutions, of charters, of treaties—are a dead letter, like, for example, the encyclopedic bill of rights in the Soviet Constitution of 1936.
>
> . . . [T]he Habeas Corpus Act, which is a legal device to protect

151. Lippmann, The Public Philosophy 170 (1955).

the personal liberty of the individual, does that—obviously enough —only where and when it is observed and enforceable. That will be only in a country where the executive and the assembly, the judges, the jailers and the lawyers feel bound, as if by personal contract, to the principles of the Habeas Corpus Act. . . . Blackstone could not have written with such assurance that the Habeas Corpus Act prevents arbitrary detention in prison if in the England of his time the rights and duties that the Act declares had not become concrete and real, had not become matters of genuine concern.

The power mechanisms in our government have a surprising record of obedience to the limits imposed on their authority by the Constitution as interpreted by the Supreme Court. But behind the government lies the ultimate power in the community. Unless the members of the body politic are convinced of the permanent, long-term value of the constitutional guarantees of liberty and of the supremacy of law and reason over will, there is no power on earth which will serve to preserve these freedoms and the American tradition. As Madison once said: "To suppose that any form of government will secure liberty or happiness without any virtue in the people, is a chimerical idea."[152]

Unless our people are devoted to the ideal of freedom, and even more, unless they remember that their authority as a body politic is itself not without limitations, then freedom stands indeed upon shifting sands. Over and above the positive rights guaranteed in the Constitution, there exist the natural rights there enshrined. A people which wishes to remain free must remember that it is in the inviolability of these God-given rights to life, liberty, and the pursuit of happiness, and in their recognition as moral values by government and people alike, that the surest guarantee of freedom rests. The fact that our majoritarian democracy has enjoyed a freedom unparallelled in the history of mankind should not blind us to the danger of elevating a method into a principle. As Windolph has said:[153]

152. In the course of the debates during the Virginia Ratifying Convention, 20 June 1788, 3 ELLIOT 536-37.

153. WINDOLPH, LEVIATHAN AND NATURAL LAW 75 (1951).

> . . . Our history has been a fortunate one. To the extent that it has been exceptional it should not blind us to the truths that voting is not a democratic principle but a democratic method, and that unless the majority, either in obedience to a constitutional requirement or by voluntary self-restraint, is willing to tolerate the continuance of a way of life regarded by the minority as essential to the pursuit of happiness, no democracy can long endure.

Against the exercise of its power by the majority in the body politic, even in excess of its intrinsically limited authority, the only protection lies in the moral consciousness of a free people that there are rights and values which do not depend on the will of any majority, but are inherent in the dignity of the human person. The people are autonomous because they have the right to govern themselves. But they do not possess supreme and unlimited power over the members of the body politic. They are not sovereign, for only God is sovereign. Lippmann's warning is timely today:[154]

> . . . No more than the kings before them should the people be hedged with divinity. Like all princes and rulers, like all sovereigns, they are ill-served by flattery and adulation. And they are betrayed by the servile hypocrisy which tells them that what is true and what is false, what is right and what is wrong, can be determined by their votes.

COMMENT

FATHER SNEE*

Government is necessary. I think we are all agreed upon that. Some would regard it as a necessary evil. I do not

---

* JOSEPH M. SNEE, S.J., *Professor of Law, Georgetown University.* Father Snee was born in 1917, received his A.B. degree from Gonzaga University, Spokane, Washington in 1941, his Ph.L. from Gregorian University in 1942; M.A., Catholic University, Washington, D. C. in 1945; S.T.L. Pontifical Faculty of Theology, Woodstock College, Woodstock, Maryland in 1949; his LL.B., Georgetown Law School, Washington, D. C. in 1952. He studied at the Harvard Law School in 1953-1954. His writings include "Provisions on Religion in American State Constitutions and Other Organic Laws: A Documentation"; "One for the Money, Two for the Show: the Case Against Televising Congressional Investigations"; and "The Establishment Clause of the First Amendment as a Problem of Federalism." During the summer of 1955 he was on temporary duty with the United States Air Force in Germany, conducting religious services.

---

154. LIPPMANN, THE PUBLIC PHILOSOPHY 14 (1955).

subscribe to that view, being a child of the New Deal of twenty years ago. Today government has functions which are more affirmative than negative—to promote in every aspect of human life the common good, by whatever regulation of external human activity may be judged necessary for that purpose. And yet it is equally true that government and the power given to government must be restricted. And the history of mankind has been an attempt to find means of restricting the exercise of power by government, no matter what form that government may have taken. That may be done by refusing to those who hold the government the material means of exercising power; or by a dissipation of power, such as we have attempted in the United States with our concept of dual sovereignty and separation of powers. As Hobbes pointed out, so long as government is regarded merely as the possessor of bare, naked power, the only way in which the exercise of that power can be limited is by a greater power. We find ourselves in a worse situation than before.

The thing that I tried to stress in my paper was the essential dichotomy between power and authority. I discussed those two terms a great deal over in Germany with some of the legal philosophers there, with what success I don't know. I defined power as the *ability* to make a person do something, or refrain from doing something. Authority is the *right* to make him do something or refrain from doing something. We have conceded power to government. We have tried to limit that power by the means which I have already mentioned in the United States. We also regard it as being essentially limited by the concept of authority, since no matter how much power a government may have, its exercise of that power is no longer right, but mere might, when it goes beyond the authority which has been entrusted to the government possessing that power. It is that concept which underlies the whole theory of judicial review in the United States, first expressed very clearly by Thomas Paine in almost the words that I have used. It was well expressed by Madison, and by Jefferson, who in his earlier days was a great advocate of judicial review and invalidation of legislation, especially where human rights were concerned. He subsequently, as you know, changed his mind considerably as Mr. Justice Frankfurter pointed out this morning.

That, I think, is the fundamental concept—that a government must not use its power beyond the authority which has been given to it. Otherwise, it is mere might, and not right.

I do not intend to say that the American system of judicial review is necessary in order to uphold that distinction. I do not even go so far as to say it is the best way, but I did want to point out in the paper, that it is this theory which underlies the whole concept of judicial review in the United States, both as regards separation of authority between federal and state governments, between the various branches of the federal government, and against all government in the protection of certain guaranteed rights.

Another concept which I think appears very clearly in the minds of the framers of the constitution and in the minds of the judiciary in a rather continuous tradition, even to the present day, is the nature of the rights which are being protected by the constitution through this limitation of authority, and the source of power against which they are being protected. We are all aware of the discussion on our present court, especially between one of our most distinguished guests here and Mr. Justice Black, as to the character of the rights which are included in the due process clause of the Fourteenth Amendment. I think Mr. Justice Black quite correctly says that to pick out certain rights as more fundamental than others — to say that the Fourteenth Amendment "incorporates" part of the Bill of Rights, but omits part —necessarily involves a return to the natural law philosophy which he decries so much.

Mr. Justice Frankfurter seems to feel that it is not a return to the natural law philosophy; but nevertheless, from where I stand, in the natural law tradition, I must say that I find Mr. Justice Frankfurter's theory almost indistinguishable from my own. I don't know how Mr. Justice Frankfurter will care for that.

It certainly was true that Madison regarded some of the rights as fundamental, others as mere positive rights which were meant as an added protection for certain things which government could not take away. Let me make one other point. The source of power against which these rights were to be protected was not only government, not only abuse of power by government officials, but also by the so-called sovereign people themselves, by any majority. This was expressed by Madison, and by Hamilton in the Federalist Papers; it has been expressed as recently as the *Barnett* case, *Barnett v. The West Virginia Board of Education,* by the late Mr. Justice Jackson. There are certain rights which no majority can take away.

Now, I would point out the similarity, or the identity, between that view and that of the natural law view which I represent. Certain rights belong to a man as a person—they are not conferred by government, they are not conferred by political society or the body politic itself, and therefore they cannot be taken away—by that government or by the whole body politic—without an infringement of the rights of the individual, because they are natural rights which belong to him as a human person. Other rights are meant to protect those—for instance, the right to a trial by jury is not a natural law right. The right to a fair trial of some sort, is. We've decided that this is the best way to do that and therefore we have said to government you must give us trial by jury, we have said to a majority, you must give a trial by jury even against a person to whom you want to deny it, because this is the way we've decided to carry out a fair trial.

Of course, it is in times of crisis, such as we are experiencing now, that there comes a temptation to do away with these slow processes of truly democratic and liberal government. It's then more than ever that we need protection against a majority.

That brings up one further point which I want to make.

The crucial difficulty in a democracy which is supposed to have a representative form of government is in this concept of taking away from the people themselves the right to do as they please with their government. I think there's no way of explaining that under a power concept of government, or a power concept of society. It's only when we bring in the concept of authority that that can be explained. Ultimately, of course, the people possess not only their authority as a body politic, but also the ultimate source of power in the community. There is no way of protecting against that by any legal mechanism—there is no way of protecting against it by a constitution or any other juridical formula. The only protection against that lies, as I see it, in the moral conscience of a free and freedom-loving people who are convinced that there are certain rights which are so essential to human dignity and the fulfillment of the destiny of human personality that they cannot be taken away without an infringement of a right which is sacred, because it was not given by government, not given by society, but given by almighty God. In other words, a recognition that although the people are and should be autonomous, they are not completely sovereign, because only God is sovereign.

PROFESSOR WECHSLER*

To comment meaningfully on "government as protector of the people against government" in the large context of an exploration of our faith in "government under law" is not an easy task, despite the splendid papers put before us, all of which have bearing on the problem. I am comforted, however, by assurance that a commentator is supposed to func-

* HERBERT WECHSLER, *Professor of Law, Columbia University.* Professor Wechsler was born in New York City in 1909, graduated in Arts at the College of the City of New York, and took his degree in Laws at Columbia in 1931. In 1932 and 1933 he served as law secretary to Associate Justice Stone of the United States Supreme Court. He was admitted to the New York Bar in 1933. Since 1931 he has been on the faculty of the Columbia Law School. In 1945 he was appointed Professor of Law. He served on the legal staff of the New York Constitutional Convention of 1938; and has in several different capacities been a legal officer of the United States Department of Justice. He is a co-author of "Criminal Law and its Administration," and "The Federal Courts and the Federal System."

tion only as a catalytic agent, stimulating others to express their thoughts.

I shall address myself to three main points.

First: We would be less than grateful for the essay Father Snee has given us, if we ignored his thesis that the philosophic underpinnings of our constitutional position rest on the scholastic view of natural law. So many foolish things are thought and said about the great tradition Father Snee embraces that it is highly useful to have stated in these lucid terms a demonstration of how strongly that tradition affirms the fundamental rights of man. But surely we must question whether we may look to any single philosophic system for the understanding, exposition or development of our underlying premises concerning law and government. Is it not more feasible and more important that we seek to find or to maintain consensus upon ultimate conclusions with respect to matters such as the just ends of government, the scope and limits of the basic freedoms, the extent of the secular authority, than on the total system of ideas in terms of which such propositions are accepted or explained? A constitution, we might say, would be ill suited for a varied people, nursing philosophic among other factions, if it could not draw support from almost any system of ideas by which a decent man may think that he explains the moral universe and lives.

Having said this, I am obliged to add that surely Father Snee is right (and no contributor to the symposium would disagree) that this would be an idle celebration were we not united in belief in norms of right and justice that transcend positive law, yielding criteria—broad as they are—by which all government and law may properly be judged. We could not be here if we did not hold with full conviction that the interest of the stronger is not justice. This is especially the case when thought is centered on a constitution, such as ours, which embodies institutions, standards and arrangements that were not created by the generations now alive, that were deliberately made difficult to change at any time, that we collaborate in imposing on Americans as yet unborn, including the amending clause with its impressive bar to all revision. To celebrate, indeed to justify such imposition by the past upon the present and the present on the future surely calls for something more than the will or the acquiescence of a passing generation. The Constitution makes a moral claim to our allegiance, to our oaths in its support and its defense, because all things considered it serves adequately the values that we *are* prepared to call enduring, in any proper view of man, government and society and the relationships among them. If other forms might serve such values equally or better, as is urged, of course, whenever an amendment is proposed, and the proposals now are many and important, we may still justify the difficulty of revision on the ground that there is on the whole such merit in our basic charter that its sheer stability and continuity are also values serving most important human needs. If this is right it must be clear that those of us who may incline to tell the story in a somewhat different way than Father Snee has told it would differ with him more at the periphery than at the center of his thought.

Second: My second point involves the mechanisms by which government may be employed as a protector of the people against government.

In a meeting called to honor Marshall's memory, it is natural to give large attention to the courts as organs of protection and especially to the judicial function in relation to the Constitution, as defined in *Marbury v. Madison.* We may be happy, merely for the sake of truth, that the old charge against judicial review as an act of usurpation by the Supreme Court is not reflected anywhere in our volume. But granting that the Constitutional Convention contemplated that the courts should disregard an act of legislation inconsistent with a mandate of the Constitution, it is also true, and becomes truer as the passing years reduce the clarity or relevancy of the original meaning of important constitutional provisions, that this function presents to courts what are essentially political problems. They are the more political—

as Justice Jackson's last words caution and Judge Hand so forcefully admonishes and Justice Frankfurter has already said this morning—as the constitutional provisions drawn upon come closest to declaring truly fundamental rights, such as the First Amendment, due process and equal protection.

Father Snee strives manfully to reassure us on this point. He rejoices in our "concept of a constitution as a legal rather than a merely political limitation upon governmental power"; he urges that judicial review "helps to ensure that the will even of a majority of our people shall be subject to law, in the conviction that law is in essence an *ordinatio rationis;*" he pictures the judges sitting as "the embodiment" of the "reason" of "the body politic, empowered to fulfill that function by the 'original and supreme voice' of the people which [—not who but which—] created the American polity."

The question raised is whether this is a sufficient reassurance to ourselves and to the judges whom we ask to oppose their judicial reason—or perhaps their sense for what is beyond reason—to the reason of elected representatives. The French, Professor Tunc reminds us, would not think so, and regard the principles about the rights of man as both too broad and vague to check the will of legislators even through the instrument of a political committee, with the consequence that they have limited their affirmation to the preamble.

I speak as a supporter of judicial review—against even the judicious doubts of its august judicial critics—and it is interesting how far it is the judges who have doubts upon the issue—but I would put my own support upon more mundane grounds than those on which Father Snee has rested, for I think that only a prudential question is involved; that there are gains and losses either way.

The prudence of the matter, if I dare to put it in a sentence, lies for me in the belief that the judicial power, exercised with moderation, is abidingly supported as an instrument of sober second thought by the political branches which it sometimes checks, reflecting in this the opinion of the great majority among us who have an opinion on the subject; and further in the expectation that the power will be exercised with moderation in the future, notwithstanding the abuses of the past or possibly, in part at least, because of them. One of the guarantees of moderation is, of course, the striving for legality in constitutional determinations, by which I mean for that neutrality and generality of formulation which, however uncongenial to the factionalists, who can think only about winning or losing the cases in which they are interested, provides at least one major element in the distinction between law and politics. Another guarantee lies in the fact that even in the application of the Bill of Rights courts rarely interpose a really final bar to legislation; more commonly what they strike down is but one method of achieving legislative ends, while leaving other methods open. Finally, there is the point that judicial review rests very largely on the legislative formulation of the remedies that are invoked in litigation. It was Congress after all that vested an equity jurisdiction in federal courts, that defined the broad reach of the federal *habeas corpus,* that enacted the Declaratory Judgment Act, the Administrative Procedure Act, the Tucker Act and similar legislation. There would be small scope for judicial review if the media for its effective invocation were confined to the bare minimum of Marshall's times, rather than buttressed in this way.

What has developed in our polity, and happily it seems to me, is less a clear antithesis between the political process and the Constitution as a source of rights than a quite subtle form of interaction: positive legislation has facilitated invocation of the judgment of the courts and the judicial function largely serves to further fair attention in the legislative process to the reasonable claims of individuals and of minorities asserting fundamental rights. In saying this I have in mind, of course, judicial review under the Bill of Rights and the analogous Fourteenth Amendment guarantees, not the judicial function in the management of the federal system, which Justice Frankfurter so carefully distinguished this morning and where, in any case, one final word rests very largely with Congress.

Third: My third point will be brief and follows from the second. In thinking of the possibilities of using government as a protector of the people against government, meaning in practice using one organ of power or authority to check alleged abuses by another, the Constitution provides no more than minimal solutions; the real challenge is one to legislation. Even in the use of courts, despite the large improvements wrought in recent years, there is much room for fresh attention to the issues—witness, for example, the procedural problems in bringing suit against a federal official. Within the federal bureaucracy, even in the internal operations of the Congress, there are many pressing problems of this order and they cannot possibly be handled by the courts. All of these problems have their analogues within the States. Their solution by our legislators and executives, both federal and state, may have no less effect upon the long-range quality of our society, upon its rationality and justice, than the constitutional positions Father Snee has helped us to consider. Here is, indeed, much work for all of us to do for many, many years. It is a part, as Justice Frankfurter has already told us, of the enduring task of furthering just government under law.

PROFESSOR HART*

Before coming to my central point, I should like to add two footnotes to what has been said about judicial review.

The first footnote is prompted by Professor Tunc's statement of the conclusion of French jurists that judicial review is not essential as a safeguard against arbitrary action by the legislature. Reading this, I wondered, as a testing example,

* HENRY MELVIN HART, JR., *Professor of Law, Harvard Law School.* Professor Hart was born in 1904, took his Arts degree in 1926, his LL.B. in 1930 and his S.J.D. in 1931, all at Harvard. Thereafter he was law secretary for Mr. Justice Brandeis; he has been on the faculty of the Harvard Law School since 1932. He became Professor of Law in 1938. In 1937-1938 he was Head Attorney, United States Solicitor-General's office, and since that time has served the federal government in many different legal capacities. He is co-author of "The Federal Courts and the Federal System."

about the control of rents in France. I hope my information in this respect is correct. If it is, rents are being maintained there, particularly on older housing, at levels which by any standards known to American law are a denial of due process of law and of the equal protection of the laws: confiscatory, arbitrary, and unequal. And the consequences cut deep into the whole economic and political fabric of French society.

As a matter of political science, I think we can see readily enough why rents have been held so tightly in France. The Parliament is a political institution, responsive, as it has to be, to political pressures of the moment. As I understand, moreover, relief would require affirmative action by Parliament, so that all the forces of inertia, too, are on the side of existing rents. But from an institution disciplined in the effort to disregard *immediate* political expediency—*responsible* for measuring, and *expected* to measure, what is done by officials at the front line of decision against longer-run values of the society—one might expect a different result.

My other footnote is prompted by a quotation which Judge Wyzanski makes, without protest, from Judge Learned Hand. "A society so riven that the spirit of moderation is gone, no court *can* save; . . . a society where that spirit flourishes no court *need* save." I cannot help believing that Judge Hand, when he wrote that, had his attention fixed on the turning of a phrase. But if the statement is projected into a serious discussion of constitutional government, something more needs to be said. It needs to be said that the statement is an example—a particularly clear example—of the fallacy of the undistributed middle.

What the sentence assumes is that there are two kinds of societies—one kind, over here, in which the spirit of moderation flourishes, and another kind, over here, which is riven by dissension. Neither kind, Judge Hand says, can be helped very much by the courts. But, of course, that isn't what societies are like. In particular, it isn't what American society is like. A society is a something in process—in process of becoming. It has always within it, as ours does, seeds of dissension. And it has also within it forces making for moderation and mutual accommodation. The question—the relevant question—is whether the courts have a significant contribution to make in pushing American society in the direction of moderation—not by themselves; of course they can't save us by themselves; but in combination with other institutions. Once the question is put that way, the answer, it seems to me, has to be yes.

What I have said, I think, is relevant to Father Snee's paper, but let me now turn more directly to it. Father Snee's paper is one of three submitted to the conference with which I find myself in most nearly complete accord—the other two being Judge Hastie's and Professor Fairman's. I hesitate, therefore, to make my central comment one of criticism—the more so because the criticism perhaps may be more justly directed against what Father Snee was asked to do than what he did.

But Father Snee himself gives me my text for disagreement. I quote a crucial sentence which appears in his paper at the middle of page 105. "The story of political theory," the sentence says, 'is that of a quest for effective means of limiting the exercise of governmental power and for philosophical justifications of such limitation." Now on the question of what the story of political theory actually is, I am in no position to dispute with Father Snee, at least not with chapter and verse. But this much I think *can* be said—that if the sentence which I have read is true, it proves only the myopia of the political theorists. As a statement of the political *problem,* I submit, the sentence is palpably incorrect.

The political problem is *not* simply negative. It is a delusion to suppose, as so many people have, that if only you can prevent the *abuse* of governmental power everything else will be all right. The political problem is a problem also of eliciting from government officials, and from the members of the society generally, the affirmative, creative performances upon which the well-being of the society depends.

Now I hasten to add that I do not really believe that Father Snee would disagree with this. I am encouraged to believe it because I can quote him in my own support, as I am about to do. In the admirable opening part of his paper, he comes to grips with basic questions of the nature and purpose of law and of organized society. He points out the enormously important fact that man is a social being, able to realize himself as an individual only within the framework of an ordered society.

Then comes (p. 96) this excellent statement of the purpose of law: To create "a society rationally organized for the purpose of establishing, maintaining and perfecting the conditions necessary and appropriate for community life to perform its role in the complete development of man." This on its face is an *affirmative* problem. You cannot solve it by fixing your attention solely on preventing the abuse of governmental power, important though that is.

Why then do I think, as I do, that my criticism is nevertheless a fair one? Because, from page 105 on to the end of the paper, Father Snee accepts, and writes in terms of, his own statement of the problem of political theory. The analysis is essentially negative, with only occasional glimpses of the affirmative considerations involved. Dual sovereignty, the separation of powers, the express constitutional guarantees of personal freedom, and the institution of judicial review for the vindication of constitutional arrangements—all these are presented as devices, essentially, for avoiding the abuse of official power rather than as instruments also for eliciting to the full the creative potentialities both of citizens generally and of those citizens who become also officials. I have little quarrel, except in detail, with what is said. My quarrel is with what is left unsaid.

I have thought the point especially worth making because, as it seems to me, the same note of negativism runs throughout the papers submitted to the conference. In none of them separately, nor in all of them taken together, do I I find the kind of muscular statement of the reasons why constitutional government is a good thing, and of the ways in which it can be made to work at its best, which it seems to me is called for.

This failure to think affirmatively is an old failing of the legal profession. Dean Bundy, for example, puts lawyers to shame by his disclosure of what they have allowed laymen to think the law is like. At the outset of his paper he equates law with litigation, and goes ahead on that premise. But litigation represents the breakdown of law, not its essence. The essence of it is what Father Snee says it is: the job of creating "a society rationally organized for the purpose of establishing, maintaining and perfecting the conditions necessary and appropriate for community life to perform its role in the complete development of man." A large proportion of Dean Bundy's conclusions fall with his premise, including his views —views which I cannot resist describing as curious—about keeping lawyers in their proper places.

I pause only to mention Mr. Shackelford's statement at the opening of his paper that "it was never thought nor intended" that a system of separate powers "would provide the most efficient method of government." This notion that "of course we are inefficient but at least we are free" is widespread in the United States. Probably a majority of Americans thought of World War II as a struggle between the dread efficiency of totalitarianism and the pleasant wastefulness of a democratic way of life. But it isn't true that our system is inefficient—*certainly* not if you think of efficiency in government as the capacity to do the job which Father Snee has described. I think this needs to be said clearly—not only to the rest of the world, but to Americans themselves.

The title of Judge Wyzanski's paper, *Constitutionalism —Limitation and Affirmation,* seems to accentuate the positive. Yet he treats as "penetrating" many criticisms of our system which seem to me shallow. He quotes, without clear repudiation, the preposterous statement of Lord Radcliffe (pp. 477-78 that "*Mistrust* is the dominant note . . . expressed by such constitutional devices as those of the American Constitution." And when he comes to the affirmations of constitutionalism, he speaks with insight but with a strange diffidence—perhaps to be explained by his own disarming acknowledgment of the fear of sounding like a Fourth of July orator.

To be concrete, Judge Wyzanski tells us that we must not be too sure that dual federalism and the separation of powers are important because England doesn't have these arrangements, and England has done all right. The argument invites analysis. But I pass this by to reach the single sentence of his conclusion (p. 480). "Can we say more," he asks, "than that the multiplication of centers of governmental power prevents one centralized authority from stifling growth, and allows more opportunity for new or different ideas to be given a chance for development and trial?" But why is this not saying a great deal? Why is this not a point to be developed and tested and, along with others, made a central theme of the conference—instead of being relegated to a single questioning sentence? The criticism seems to me to be valid also in relation to Father Snee's paper.

As I have said, perhaps my criticism should be directed to the planning of the conference rather than to Father Snee. I do not really believe that you can discuss "government as a protector of the people against the government" without considering also government as a facility for the people. For the same institutions serve both purposes. We need to consider government, *first,* as a facility in establishing fruitful conditions under which the people can work out as many as possible of their own problems for themselves without further intervention from the government—conditions which will release to the uttermost the enormous resources of private ordering of social affairs, of private adjustment of social difficulties, of private creativity. We need to consider government, *secondly,* as a facility also in providing readily available and effective official procedures for the settlement of those problems of social living which fail of satisfactory adjustment at the primary and basic level of private decision.

DISCUSSION

Mr. Casner: All I can say is that Henry Hart had better be around to defend himself for the rest of the meeting. It seems to me that he has taken on the whole Conference rather than just Father Snee.

Father Snee, you have been taking some notes. I wonder if you would like to make any reply at this time, or hold your fire a little longer.

Father Snee: The notes are mainly question marks and exclamation points. I find myself in the very peculiar position of agreeing with all the criticisms made of my paper. I think that both Mr. Wechsler and Mr. Hart expressed things that I should have expressed, and expressed them better than I would have done. I am in complete agreement with a great deal of what was said.

One or two comments: I did not wish to give the impression that the American constitution drew its inspiration from the scholastic tradition alone. My point was that it was based upon natural law principles, which are found in many systems of philosophy. I think they are best expressed in the scholastic philosophy, but not exclusively so. As Learned Hand once remarked of the Sermon on the Mount, the natural law philosophy is a lesson never quite learnt and never quite forgotten.

Also, with regard to the question of reassurance as to the function of the judiciary in maintaining this balance between authority and power, we can't have any perfect reassurance. It's impossible to have a perfect form of government, and I am always amused somewhat by criticisms of any form of government or philosophy of government on the ground that it won't work out perfectly. I've never looked for perfection: we look for something reasonably approaching it. It's the best we can get. Another point, I think, with regard to the court as the embodiment of the reason of the people as distinguished from the will of the people—that, of course, is an oversimplification. Our judges are swayed by reasons of will, by what they want, by what they think the people want to a certain extent. Also, even though I have lived in Washington for a good while, I have not yet come to the conclusion that all legislators are completely devoid of reason. But it is true that a legislator, an elected official, is more responsive, and is supposed to be more responsive, to the will of the people as directed to what they want, whether what they want is a good thing or a bad thing. At least that is one theory of elected, representative government. A judge is supposed to be less responsive to their immediate desires and their immediate will, and in that sense can be said to be the embodiment of their reason as distinguished from their will.

In regard to Mr. Hart's comment, again I agree one hundred per cent that the function of government is not negative, but is extremely positive. I was hoping he would quote one sentence from my paper in which I did bring that out: "Its sphere of authority extends to every external human activity which affects the common good, which strengthens or debilitates the capacity of the community and its members to play their role in the development of a truly good life not excluding the so-called sacrosanct area of liberty of contract, private property and the world of commerce." I think that the function of government is positive—it is only when there has been a breakdown in the system that it becomes necessary to consider negative limitations. We are constantly experiencing such breakdowns on a minor scale.

III

This session was also held in the Ames Courtroom. Professor Robert Braucher* of the Harvard Law School acted as chairman. The proceeding consisted of two parts, the first of which was an address by Sir Raymond Evershed, Master of the Rolls, of England; the second was a discussion of the papers of Mr. Shackelford of Atlanta and Professor Fairman of the Harvard Law School, on the theme "Government Under Law in Time of Crisis."

Professor Braucher first introduced the Master of the Rolls, who spoke on the topic "Government Under Law in Post-War England."

---

* Robert Braucher, *Professor of Law, Harvard Law School.* Professor Braucher was born in New York City in 1916, took his degree in Arts at Haverford in 1936, and his LL.B. at Harvard in 1939. He practiced law in New York until 1941 when he was commissioned in the United States Army Air Forces; he served as a fighter pilot in the India-Burma theatre, and was later detailed as an intelligence officer in Washington, and as a member of the Strategic Bombing Survey in Japan. He joined the Harvard Law School faculty in 1946, becoming a Professor of Law in 1949. He has served as a consultant in the Department of the Air Force, and is a Commissioner on Uniform State Laws for the Commonwealth of Massachusetts. He has written and edited a number of books and articles in the field of banking law and other aspects of the law of commerce.

ADDRESS

Government Under Law in Post-War England

SIR RAYMOND EVERSHED *

It is natural and proper that I, whom you have honored and delighted by your invitation here to represent (in a sense) my country, should first express my humble appreciation to this great university. Among the guests from the parts of the British Commonwealth I stand alone in this: they, like the eponymous hero of the Conference, hold the rank and dignity of Chief Justice. I, coming from the country whence that office is derived and whence, also, is descended the system of law—and the faith in the law—which may fairly be said to have given the greatest significance to Anglo-American history, hold the peculiar office of Master of the Rolls, a rank and dignity whose adoption all other countries have carefully contrived to avoid.[1] It is, of course, possible that since the Master of the Rolls in England has in general had his training at the Equity Bar, and since, certainly, his office is in the direct historical line of equitable succession, you have thought that so much common law needs a little equitable leaven, or at least, according to Maitland's formula, a supplement; and though it is usual for a supplement to follow after the main substance, I am most content to be a kind of anticipatory appendix to the distinguished Chief Justices of our Commonwealth who will follow after me in point of time.

* THE RT. HON. SIR RAYMOND EVERSHED, now Baron Evershed of Stapenhill, *Master of the Rolls, England.* Lord Evershed was born in 1899 at Burton-on-Trent. He served as an officer of Royal Engineers in France in the First World War, took his degree at Balliol College, Oxford; was called to the Bar at Lincoln's Inn in 1923; became King's Counsel in 1933; Judge of the Chancery Division, the High Court of Justice in 1944; Lord Justice of Appeal in 1947; and Master of the Rolls in 1949. The list of his other public services has been a long one. He was knighted in 1944. In January 1956 he became Baron Evershed of Stapenhill in the County of Derby.

1. Save only, as the Chief Justice of Canada has since been good enough to point out to me, Prince Edward Island.—R. E.

I have, perhaps, a slight claim as an equity lawyer to special consideration here. This room is called after Dean James Barr Ames, surely one of the greatest of all teachers of equity. I like to recall his assertion that our law as a whole would have been a very imperfect instrument of justice had not the system of Common law remedies been supplemented by the system of Equitable remedies. Nor do I forget that one of my predecessors in the office of Master of the Rolls, John Singleton Copley, II, afterwards Lord Lyndhurst, was born in the city of Boston, Massachusetts, when John Marshall was learning the military skill which he shortly thereafter used to defeat the English in the field of battle.

You have given to the banner of the Conference the device "Government under Law." Mr. Justice Oliver Wendell Holmes, speaking in the Supreme Court on the day set aside to honor John Marshall, said of your national flag: "Thanks to Marshall and to the men of his generation, its red is our life blood, its stars our world, its blue our Heaven." The device you have chosen for your standard of 1955 is no less appropriate. "Government under law" is not merely an aspiration, not, indeed, so much a theme for discussion as an essential article of our faith. I assume, therefore, that the government of a free nation must *be* government under law. The question is, whether the law as we have inherited it and as we shall pass it on, the law that we as Judges try to serve, sufficiently performs its essential function.

I have referred to Dean Ames, and it is no less fitting in this place to refer, if he will allow me to do so, to Dean Roscoe Pound. I remember that I saw him first about a quarter of a century ago: and, being then only 30 years old, I was foolish enough to look upon him as a man somewhat advanced in years. I have since learned that he has one essential quality of all institutions—that of being perpetual.

Among Dean Pound's writings is the title of an essay in the form of a question—"Do we need a philosophy of law?" The question invites instinctively an affirmative answer. However much we may assert and pride ourselves upon the pragmatic character of our system of law; however much we shun, judicially, as better fitted for the university than the courts, the expounding of juristic theory; the resolution of particular contentions by the Judges must conform to principles which are not only coherent and intelligible but also generally acceptable. But to give to the sum of those principles the label and dignity of a defined philosophy is a much more difficult task. Perhaps, like many of the principles themselves, the philosophy is better unexpressed and undefined. I do not think that I am shrinking the problem. I think, indeed, that Dean Pound was much more concerned with character than definition. His fear was lest in modern conditions the law had lost a quality of spirit essential, however difficult of expression, to its continued general acceptance by a race of men who believe that freedom and the rule of law mean, in the end, much the same thing.

As an equity lawyer, let me acknowledge that I have a natural inclination to favor the undefined and undefinable in the form of principles which have never lost, by unnecessary and constricting definition, their capacity for useful growth. And I would like, here, to make the important point that these undefined principles of equity could never, so far as I can see (save to a very limited extent) be effectively or usefully comprehended, by codification, in the enacted law. At least in so far as they were comprehended, the functions of the courts in regard to them might thereby be changed—and surely not changed for the public advantage—from the more or less creative faculty of seeing whether the new relationship or the new set of facts was within or without the embrace of the principle to the narrower task of interpreting the parliamentary language. If my view is correct, then the system of equity may find, hereafter, its most valuable contribution as a supplement to the enacted law as it was formerly an appendix to the common law, with a possible reference, as some think, to those special creatures of the enacted law in my country, the executive officers of the so-called Nationalized Industries.

It may perhaps be possible to state, after a fashion, the philosophy of equity. Having regard to its insistence on personal behavior, the philosophy might be expressed in terms of a minimum standard of conscientious conduct. The former Vice Chancellor of my University of Oxford, Sir Richard Livingstone, has recently said that "There is a good deal of the spirit of the gentleman in the English temperament, and a sign of it is the importance of equity in our law." I hope that a reference to so eighteenth century a character as "an English gentleman" will not be thought to be out of place in 1955—even in Harvard. He was at any rate a man sincerely and actively aware of the validity of duty and responsibility towards his fellows for which modern democracy seems sometimes to seek in vain.

But I have digressed from the broader and more difficult question of looking for a philosophy for our system of law as a whole: and, for that, equity's ideal of the gentleman will plainly not suffice. Perhaps, in truth, the philosophy of the law must be a combination of several other philosophies all present in varying degrees in any judicial decision; and if the law is thought to fall short, it is because too little or too much attention is being paid to one component compared with the others. Benjamin Cardozo thus summed up his "Nature of the Judicial Process": "My analysis of the judicial process comes, then, to this and little more; logic and history and custom and utility and an accepted standard of right conduct are the forces which singly or in combination shape the progress of the law." "This and little more"; but it is, in all conscience, enough.

We may, of course, define the rule of law. Many have already done so, and I shall not re-state their definitions or attempt to improve upon them. But that is rather to specify the purpose to be achieved than to discern the guiding spirit which animates the process. We may also debate the nature of the sanctions upon which the law must rest. Thus, Professor Goodhart, in a series of lectures given in 1953, proclaimed his belief in the recognition of a moral obligation to obey the law as being of the essence of the law's sanction. And this is much more to my present point and, I think, to Dean Pound's question. For, after all, so far as the law depends upon the recognition of a moral obligation to obey, then it is certain that the law must not be out of line with what we may intelligibly call the social philosophy of the day. It was, I think, a fear that our law today was in danger of failure in this respect that had troubled Dean Pound. The common law, as he pointed out, had gained its power and ascendancy because in its struggle with the Royal authority it had behind it the impulse and the support of the popular will. With its great emphasis on individual rights, particularly individual proprietary rights, how does our law stand in its relation to modern social legislation? Is the law thought to be an impediment in the way of the social philosophy of the twentieth century? In that respect how have we fared in my own country?

The problem has made me think that in some respects we are more fortunate in England than you are in the United States. We are untroubled by the overriding sanctity of a written constitution. For us (and as Professor Tunc has pointed out the situation is similar in France) the pronouncements of the legislature at Westminster are unchallengeable. No question of the validity of any Act of Parliament (I am not presently concerned with questions of delegated legislation to which Mr. Justice Frankfurter referred) has yet arisen. If the theory of the moral sanction for the law is well founded, and if the theory is accepted by Parliament no less than by the general community, it is never likely to arise. We do not, for that reason, contemplate such extreme partisan measures by the legislature as, say, an indefinite prolongation of the life of a particular Parliament or the repeal of the Habeas Corpus Act. The problem has also made me wonder how you would in this country have fared—in fact, what difference in the end of all it would have made—if the

Bill of Rights and the Fourteenth Amendment had never been written into the Constitution. On that matter I believe that others may say something hereafter.

We have not, then, had your problem. Some, nevertheless, have been found to express the view that the conservatism of the law and of the Judges would threaten for a time to rob legislation of its efficacy. More violently have been stated fears of "judicial sabotage."

I do not think these fears can be treated as wholly unsubstantial. The law and its Judges no doubt tend, in common with all other professions and professional men, to be conservative. For my part I do not think that it is by any means a bad thing if they do. As Mr. Walter Lippmann has recently shown, in the book to which Father Snee has referred, modern democracy may be in some danger if the will of the people is not tempered by some restraints based on a sense of tradition and standards of value and legality. The conservatism of the law may provide a sense of stability and continuity which will in time, long or, more often, short, rob most legislation of its particular political origin. I am indebted to Mr. Justice Frankfurter again for the reminder to those who complain that the present is too much governed by the past and who wish the present to control the future, that for the future the present is the past.

Still, references to old cases provide now and then startling evidence that some of the most cherished principles which we now regard as our legal birthright—including, even, the impartiality of the judges and the assumed innocence of the prisoner at the Bar—could not always, in practice, be taken by any means for granted. Even the Habeas Corpus Act itself (according to the legend) was only passed into law by the device of counting one very fat peer as ten—a tribute, at least, to the political judgment of the teller.

In the case of our Trade Union law, a matter of high significance today, the somewhat extreme view taken by the nineteenth-century judges of the common law rules as to restraint of trade may be said to have led the courts, after the repeal of the Combination Acts in 1824, to interpret the common law crime of conspiracy and, after the Acts of 1871 and 1875, to interpret the common law of civil conspiracy, in a manner which lost touch with the social and political philosophy of the day—until the Trades Disputes Act of 1906 passed by the supreme Parliament put the matter beyond doubt. "A scope has been given to the law of Conspiracy" said the Attorney-General of the day, introducing the bill, "so loose and so wide that it is impossible to indicate beforehand what may be the legal character of those organizations and which is determined ex post facto by decisions of a legal tribunal."

To do justice to the legal profession, I have been told that the *Taff Vale* decision in the House of Lords surprised the profession (or many members of it) no less than the rest of the community—though whether it should have done so is another matter. It has been said also that the judges of the mid-nineteenth century—and let it be remembered that the judges with us, not being members of a separate profession followed from youth up, do not, as Cardozo observed "stand aloof on . . . chill and distant heights"— decided, in the case of the Scottish Judges (let it be said in fairness to them) with some reluctance, the so-called Common Employment cases at least in accordance with prevalent economic doctrine and in conformity with the classic judgment of Chief Justice Shaw of Massachusetts.

In truth, I suppose, what is later discerned as the social philosophy of the day may well at times be in conflict with the best expert opinion. That is one of the great difficulties; and, in truth also, those most affected by any trend of legal decisions may not, until too late, be sufficiently articulate to make their opinions prevail. So much can fairly be said in palliation. But as regards the Trade Union cases even so great an authority as Stephen thought that it counted for virtue in the judges that they had been "in a sense creating the offence of conspiracy."

I do not, myself, believe that criticisms of this kind could justly be made of the law and the courts of my country today in respect of the so-called social legislation of the present century, particularly those Acts which "nationalized" the hospitals, the mines, the railways, and other similar services or undertakings. On the contrary, I believe that our courts have, in regard to one notoriously difficult subject matter of legislation, namely the control of rents, found novel and useful scope for the judicial process which is for my present purpose of the greatest significance. Let me say that I am not concerned with the policy of the Acts, nor so much with the statutory limitation of rents, but with the more important right (for us) of protection against eviction. Thanks in no small measure to the judges of a generation ago—particularly, perhaps, to Lord Justice Scrutton in the Court of Appeal—something like a coherent principle has been infused by the courts into the patchwork legislation—the principle that the governing purpose of the Acts is not more but not less than to protect (subject to the conditions of the Acts) the personal occupation of his home by the sitting tenant. Our courts have thereby evolved and accepted a somewhat heretical conception, *monstrum, horrendum, informe, ingens,* the quasi-personal/quasi-proprietary right of occupation under the Statute, having many of the characteristics of a demise but without the presence of any true proprietary interest capable, as such, of transmission or disposal. The new entrant into the company of legal rights has indeed led to some difficulties and to the magnification of the idea of a license, particularly (by what may seem to be a rather far cry) in its relation to the rights of married women deserted by their husbands to the continued occupation of the matrimonial home. Upon this topic the time may well have come when a pronouncement by what have been called the "infallible voices" of the House of Lords will be useful. Sir Owen Dixon may think that we began to slide down the slippery slope forty years ago in connection with licenses to enter a cinema or go upon a racecourse. This, however, is another matter. The important thing is that the existence in a real sense of such a right, deriving its incidents substantially from the enacted law and hardly at all from the common law, but like so many things in our legal experience never precisely defined, should have been recognized and accepted by the courts. The judicial process is novel. I hope it will not be condemned as judicial escapism. The alternative process of making the statutory requirements and modifications fit into the common law proprietary scheme or of refusing them all recognition might, indeed, have led to disaster. I add here, also, that the subject has a relevance to the increased importance in modern times of personal claims as opposed to proprietary claims upon which I want to say something hereafter.

I hope you will not think that we have been in England too complacent and gone too far the other way. I emphasize again that I am keeping clear of the general subject of delegated legislation and the vexed question of administrative law. But if the courts in my country have played their part in providing an answer to Dean Pound's fears, it must also be said, and I think it of high importance, that the English Parliament has on its side been markedly conscious, even in its most ambitious social legislation, of the "standards of legality." It is impossible to read the various Nationalization Acts without discerning an emphatic recognition by Parliament, not only of the proprietary rights of the individuals affected, as understood by the law, but equally of the duty not to deny access to the courts where problems of fair assessment and the like involve questions within the province of the law. If these Acts have been considered revolutionary by some, they do not at least look, upon the face of them, like revolutionary edicts. For that, indeed, we owe a debt, I believe, greater than is generally recognized to those mute, inglorious members of our profession, the Parliamentary draftsmen who, clothing the novel legislation in the accustomed language of the law, make it instantly and naturally a part of the corpus and institution of the law; just as men clothed in academic dress become thereby a part of the institution of a University. But I think, also, that the readiness of our Courts to accept and make effective the Parliamentary will has been, in turn, rewarded by Parliamentary acceptance of the standards and judgments of the law.

There is, however, another aspect of the English Rent Control legislation which may have given rise to considerable and well-founded anxiety. For there were set up soon after the last war a number of special tribunals invested with wide discretionary powers to determine rents and governed by regulations as to their procedure far removed in many important respects from the procedure of the Queen's Courts. The reason for the establishment of these courts or tribunals was undoubtedly an impatience with the expenses, the delays, and the formalities of the ordinary courts. In other words, the mistrust of the law undoubtedly implicit in the establishment of these tribunals was in large measure a mistrust of legal procedure. Upon this matter I am perhaps unduly sensitive, having presided for six years over the work of a Committee on Supreme Court Practice and Procedure. But of this I am sure; that the importance of procedure cannot easily be exaggerated in relation to the general question of government under law, and particularly in relation to public confidence in, and support of, the law itself. But, as I have said, I think the establishment of the special rent tribunals must be a cause of real anxiety, at least to those who believe that the process of the law, if efficiently and conscientiously conducted, provides the best means of achieving a just conclusion. For, though we may sincerely so believe, we must also accept it (in England, at any rate, since the *Arlidge* case forty years ago) that natural justice does not demand the adoption of the rules of judicial procedure. Those rules must justify themselves, in the end of all, by proof that our belief in them is well founded. By way of contrast, it has been of the essence of these special rent tribunals that their proceedings should be, in an extreme degree, informal. The tribunals themselves were, by their own regulations and the terms of the Act constituting them, given the widest discretion to act upon their own notions and their own knowledge, without any limitation by reference to the evidence given (or not given) on the other side or the other. They have been charged with arriving at what they think for themselves to be "reasonable rents" by a method entirely foreign to the principles of ordinary "contentious" litigation. To those impatient of the processes of the law, they make an obvious, if (as I think) a superficial, and even irrational, appeal. So-called "People's Courts" have proved ready instruments in the hands of every modern dictator. There is no right of appeal from any of these tribunals, so that no uniformity of result is thereby secured. But the tribunals have nevertheless been subject to the restraints upon their activities imposed, upon application made, by the exercise of the prerogative processes of prohibition, mandamus, and certiorari in the Queen's Courts.

The books contain a number of Reports of proceedings of this kind, including one that went to the House of Lords: and I venture to think that such Reports are worthy of study. There cannot fail, sometimes, to have been a strong temptation for the Queen's Courts to stultify in a large measure the Parliamentary purpose in setting up the tribunals—or to attempt so to do. And the Queen's Courts have not been afraid to exercise their prerogative powers to restrain any usurpation by the tribunals of functions beyond those strictly remitted to them. But within the scope of the powers given by Parliament the Queen's Courts have scrupulously—and in the result, as I think, most fortunately—resisted the temptation. In other words, the Courts have in their decisions, as it seems to me, followed Marshall's tradition in interpreting the law(in his great cases of *Marbury v. Madison* and *McCulloch v. Maryland*) both as an instrument and as a symbol. As the present Lord Chief Justice of England observed in one of the cases; the proceedings of the tribunals and the methods whereby they reach their conclusions are entirely at variance with the accepted principles of regular trials before the Judges. But the tribunal in question had acted within the powers contemplated and conferred by the Act. It is not the function of the courts to question the wisdom of Parliamentary policy and (in the Lord Chief Justice's own words) "to bring the whole thing to a standstill."

I have said that, to my mind, this approach has been not only strictly correct, but also, in the result, most fortunate. At the time when the tribunals were set up, there was a great housing shortage as a consequence of the bombardment of our cities. It is an unfortunate fact of human experience that there will always be found those who are ready, taking advantage of the public misfortune, to make personal profits for themselves: and it is another fact of human experience that in this kind of connection, as in others, the good tend to suffer for, and be cast out by, the bad. In a more individualistic age, not only the courts, but public opinion too had been less disposed to condemn activities of the private profit seeker on moral or social grounds. In an age of press and radio publicity, the life of the social brigand is less easy. Privacy is not so much respected and moral judgments are freely passed on all deviations from recognized standards of conduct. I have no doubt that these tribunals sometimes entered upon their tasks with all the zeal of men thinking themselves "charged with the duty of leaping into the breach to relieve injustice." In the years that have passed, the housing shortage has been largely remedied. No less important, our County Courts, to which exclusively rent restriction cases under the old legislation are remitted, have shown themselves, by the quality of the present judges and the improved efficiency of their procedure, well able to dispose, without heavy costs and without any delay, of all the cases coming before them, and in doing so, to give to the parties the confidence of having received a fair hearing.

Had the Queen's Courts shown less firmness on the one hand and less restraint on the other; had they been less conscious of their strict function; there would have been a risk of serious conflict between the law and lawyers on the one hand and Parliament, claiming to represent the Will of the People, on the other. The conflict was avoided: Parliament was not able, in your phrase, to "pass the buck" of teaching moderation to the courts. On the contrary, both by their firmness and their restraint the courts have contrived to give to the tribunals an added sense of responsibility. As a result, and because of the proved efficacy of the procedure of the County Courts, the myth of the informal tribunal as a true instrument of justice, has, I think, been exposed again, as it had been exposed before. You will, I hope, acquit me not only of complacency but of over-praising the performance of the Judges of my own country. If I have seemed to do so, it has been from no excess of national vanity. I have sought only to make the point that in the different conditions of my country and in the uneasy circumstances of the immediate post-war period, we may have been able to make a contribution to the proposition that Parliament and the courts, though independent, are not thereby natural opponents of each other; but that each owes to the other an obligation of recognition and respect, and, perhaps more important still, that both owe a common obligation of recognition and respect to what I have called the standards of value and legality. Because your country and mine stand firmly together as the champions of liberal democracy, the wide differences in our systems must not be forgotten. Great Britain is a Parliamentary democracy. The United States is not. If one great menace of today lies in the possibility that under modern technical conditions, so-called mass opinions may press too much upon and enervate government, with the greater risk that the intolerance of faction may, in the end, substitute for freedom authority or power, irresponsible and uncontrolled, your Constitution, with its clear division of function between Congress and the President, may provide a better safeguard than the English. For neither, however, are the forms of the institutions enough. Professor Brogan has concluded his last written work on American politics by suggesting of the United States Supreme Court, in the language of Cardozo, that its greatest contribution may have been, in the end of all, that it has given to the ideals of the Founders of the Republic continuity of life and expression. With us, those essential but imponderable values may be, to a large extent, supplied by the continuance of the institution of the Monarchy. I do not know. But if it is so, then there may be an essential difference in the true function and therefore in the true philosophy, in our two countries, of the law and of the courts. But subject to that overriding principle, there may here be found, if not a philosophy of the law, at least the essential conditions of such a philosophy. First, a clear recognition by the courts of their duty to give effect to the Parliamentary or legislative purpose in the Acts duly passed by Parliament or the legislature, coupled with a firm rejection of all usurpations beyond the limits of the powers conferred: bringing as its own reward an increased recognition by Parliament or the legislature of what I have called "the standards of value and legality." Second (at the all important procedural level) a constant and strict review of the procedure of the courts, and of the inferior courts no less than of the superior, so as to secure a combination of the essential dignity and sense of protection in the courts (without which there can be no confidence in impartiality) and at the same time the elimination of all that is wasteful and unnecessary.

I have, I hope, given some grounds for thinking that in the more fortunate circumstances of my own country there is perhaps no pressing need for the philosophy of the law which Dean Pound thought was wanting. I think we have, as lawyers, still to get attuned to the enormous primacy in our system of the enacted law and, as Judges, to understand better the judicial process which consideration of the enacted law demands. We are, I hope, finding our feet. Parliament (of either prevailing color) seems with us, so far, content with what we have done. Parliament has, indeed (and this shall be my last observation on this part of my address) been content, rather surprisingly, in a large section of its important regulatory enactments—e.g., to take a fair assortment, in regard to factory requirements, patent agents, and bookmakers—to leave it to the courts to decide whether, above and behind the obligations to the State imposed (generally subject to penal sanctions) by those enactments, there are impliedly conferred or created civil rights and liabilities as well, i.e., whether a breach of the statutory duty, for example, by a factory occupier carries with it the right of a workman in the factory to recover in a civil action damages for injury attributable to the breach of duty. The general principle appears from the decisions to be that the question will be answered affirmatively if the courts regard the Act in question as one intended primarily for the protection of the individuals in the category affected. But, though many cases of this kind have now come before the courts, it still seems to me, I must confess, strange that Parliament should continue in enactments of this kind to leave the question *sub silentio* to the determination of the courts. It may be that this is another instance of the wisdom of avoiding definition. The phenomenon seems at least to show the acceptance by Parliament of the view that the incidents of important private rights (and personal rights, too) may find more satisfactory and coherent expression in the evolutionary process of the courts than by dependence on the inclusion of a number of separate and perhaps varying provisions in the enacted law which might, at the time, prove politically contentious.

All this leads me to a second, though brief, reference to Dean Pound. In his paper "Social Control through Law" he said: "If, therefore, the law secures property and contract more elaborately and more adequately than it secures personality, it is not because the law rates the latter less highly than the former, but because the legal machinery is intrinsically well adapted to securing the one and intrinsically ill adapted to securing the other." The criticism is not by any means confined to Dean Pound. I have seen, elsewhere, the same criticisms expressed of our own system of law in regard to what we call "personal" actions. And, if the criticism is true, it undoubtedly is a serious ground for the fear that our law has got somewhat out of step with modern social conditions. I have already stated that the emphasis is today not only very much upon the enacted law, but also upon personal, rather than proprietary, claims both under statute and otherwise. Certainly is this true in my own country, and I think the phenomenon is by no means confined to England. Mr. Justice Frankfurter, if I may return once more to the Greek chorus, pointed out not long ago the high percentage of cases now coming before the Supreme Court which are concerned with provisions of the enacted law. What is more, recent analysis has shown that, today, in England rather more than 45 per cent of the cases which come to trial in the Queen's Bench Division are personal injury actions of one kind or another, either involving the common law of negligence (in respect, particularly, of road accidents) or arising under the Factory Acts, or (commonly in the latter case) both.

Is, then, the criticism just? It is undoubtedly true that in the early days of the development of our common law the emphasis was much placed upon proprietary claims. The forms of writ, governing us, still, from their graves, prove as much. The common law would for a long time have nothing whatever to do with many forms of personal claims.

But I suggest that the difficulty is, in large measure, at any rate, due rather to the nature of the claims themselves than to the system of the law. Proprietary claims are, in their nature, more capable of certain definition. If we take the common personal action of negligence, the liability, with us, rests in the end upon the application of the standard of reasonableness: and it is not easy to see how, in any event, such cases could be otherwise than questions of degree. As regards a man's right to privacy, you have in this country been bolder than the English, who have so far found too great the difficulties of definition and limitation. Moreover, what I have already said seems at least to show a reasonable capacity in the courts to give effect to novel claims, substantially personal in character, arising out of the enacted law; and a willingness in Parliament to leave it to the courts to work out the implications, in terms of private personal rights, of a considerable body of legislation.

I have dealt briefly with this second matter, in part because I feel that this is not an occasion for entering into the detail of the procedural questions involved, and in part because the subject itself is, in truth, a corollary of the larger and more philosophical question with which I have already dealt.

And I should perhaps also add that, as regards personal claims, I have consciously omitted all reference to that distressingly large body of litigation which arises out of matrimonial disputes. I have done so because, as I conceive, those matters, involving as they do questions of status, are in a very special class of their own and because they are also now peculiarly subject to the legislative power.

But there is another aspect of our legal system to which I have earlier made a brief reference but to which I cannot think that sufficient attention has always been directed. Whereas, in other systems, the judgments of the courts (though not infrequently composed of many judges) assume a formal and wholly impersonal character, with us each individual judge must, in giving the reasons for his conclusion, publicly assume a personal responsibility which he cannot by any means avoid. The public association of his name with the judgment may sometimes be a little unfair. It is a burden which, balanced by many privileges, a judge must have the courage to assume. The first result of this native characteristic is that the judge must not only satisfy his own intelligence and his own conscience of the validity of his reasons, but must hope to satisfy, also, the critical regard of his own profession and, indeed, of a much wider public besides. The judge thereby becomes a known and, to the extent that he fulfills his capability, a respected public figure. So embedded in our way of life is the judge's personal position that it was one of the contentions of the respondent in the *Arlidge* case already mentioned that the impersonality of the Local Government Board offended against the rules of natural justice. He sought, in Lord Shaw's language, "to individualize the Board." The contention failed. But the characteristic remains. And its second and still more important consequence is that the history of our law is illustrated by the figures of men of great character and intellect, who have left the imprint of their personalities upon its pages—men who, in Miss C. V. Wedgwood's happy phrase, have started a kind of vibration in the corridors of time. It cannot be doubted that from time to time the law in important respects has been shaped and directed in the hands of those who have been its greatest servants and its greatest masters.

Of Chief Justice Marshall, Benjamin Cardozo said: "He gave to the Constitution of the United States the impress of his own mind; and the form of our Constitutional Law is what it is because he molded it while it was still plastic and malleable in the fire of his own intense convictions."

The great Chief Justice of the United States, even more, perhaps, by his faith and character than by his intellect, gave to the people of his country the assurance that his answers were right. The liberal method of interpretation which guided those answers may fairly, I suppose, be said more than any other thing to have made your Constitution work so that it has, today, easily earned the record for longevity of any written Constitution since the Christian era began; and, to quote Professor Brogan again, "If durability is not the only political virtue, still it is a virtue." In his method of interpretation Marshall followed, in fact, the principles which had been adopted in England not long before by Lord Mansfield, who saw to it that the common law was adapted to comprehend the problems of modern commerce and whose portrait in this hall hangs so close to that of Marshall. Two such shining examples seem to support the view that the secret of our law's success may in no small degree be found in its capacity to produce such exponents. Men trained in the law attain high positions in other countries. With us, great lawyers have been great public servants, though they have remained professional lawyers to the end. We have had, of late, in my country difficult and disturbing industrial problems. Members of my profession have been called upon, when the situation has become critical, to pass judgments, the justice of which the contestants and the general public alike have been content not only to accept but to assume. A recent and most serious railway strike came to an end when the parties concerned agreed to accept, unseen and what ever it might turn out to be, my brother Morris' conclusion on the outstanding issues as to figures. Whatever the shortcomings of our legal system, they must surely be set against the prestige of the men whom it is the peculiar power of the system to produce.

I have mentioned one English name—though he was, in fact, a Scotsman, so much so that Perth, the place of his origin, was, as pronounced by him, understood and entered in the books of Christ Church, Oxford, as "Bath." In the long history of our law it is not suprising, if my premise is true, that there are many notable portraits. I choose six names almost at random—six household words of what significance! Coke, Hardwicke, Blackstone, Pollock, MacNaghten, Parker.

What is, perhaps, a more remarkable source to everyone of our profession of humble pride is that in a period, short by comparison, the illustrations of American judges of worldwide eminence and prestige are hardly less numerous. Story, Kent, Shaw, Taney, Holmes, Cardozo — I choose, again, six names which come at once to my mind. I omit, of course, the living; but know that the process continues still.

And if I seek an explanation for this continued flowering of individuals in an age not notably individualistic I find it, I am sure, in no negligible degree in the influence of the law schools of this and her sister universities. In the changed circumstances of an age which has provoked Dean Pound's question, I believe that so long as our judges pursue their traditional course (as I hope they will) it is the universities which can provide, by their criticisms, their research, and their teaching, the required philosophy. There could be no better evidence of what I have said than the fact that the present distinguished holder of the office of Dean of this school should have been recently briefed as *amicus curiae* before the Supreme Court—with results which must have been eminently satisfactory to himself and gratifying to Harvard, even if the judgment of the majority involved, in the minority view, a Procrustean treatment of the Virgin Islands organic act.

But the teaching of the universities is, for my purpose, not only instruction in the law but the teaching of example. It is, I take it, the first duty of a judge to search always, without fear or favor, for the truth; and of the pursuit of truth there is no more shining example than that of the scholars of a great and free university. When a highly respected American judge, to whom I am proud to have shown a slight hospitality in my court in London, Judge Learned Hand, received his doctorate from his own university of Harvard, he expressed a moving acknowledgement of his debt to his old masters, from which I hope he will allow me now to quote. Of them he said: "Unafraid before the unknown universe, undeterred by the world's disparagements and uncorrupted by its prizes, ardent and serene in the faith by which, alone, mankind can live, they were the best lesson that I took away." So I now, using Judge Hand's language still, lay my tribute of respect before you; and bring to you the sincere congratulations and good wishes of my country, England.

Following Sir Raymond Evershed's address, the Conference turned to a discussion of Mr. Shackelford's and Professor Fairman's papers on the theme "Government Under Law in Time of Crisis."

During the first day's discussion the duty of government to establish sound institutions for the correction of its own injustices had been accepted as an aspiration of all civilized nations. But a fair question is whether this doctrine serves only in pleasant weather. Does national survival in an age of continuous crisis permit the amenities of constitutionalism, with all its connotations of debate, delay, divided powers of government, an effective system of elective legislatures, and all the individual immunities of constitutional order?

The first paper, "Separation of Powers in Time of Crisis," presented by Francis Shackelford of the Atlanta Bar, treated of a "minor" crisis, through which we had only just passed,—the crisis of the Korean War. Mr. Shackelford, with the intimate experience of a leading official in the Department of the Army, examined its impact on our constitutional system, its magnification of the executive branch; its effect on the traditional doctrine of separate powers and on the function of the Congress in devising national policy.

The second of these two papers, by Professor Fairman, bearing the title "Government Under Law in Time of Crisis," examined the possibility of constitutional government in the most startling crisis that imagination can construct—the hostile explosion of a hydrogen bomb in a crowded part of the United States.

The Separation of Powers in Time of Crisis

FRANCIS SHACKELFORD* †

I. INTRODUCTION

This paper is concerned with the practical operation of the United States system of government in the field of National defense during a time of crisis, and more particularly with the relation of this practical operation to the theoretical operation envisioned by the framers of the Constitution.

Most people think only of the serious inroads war makes on private property and the individual's civil rights. They overlook the equally serious inroads it makes on the government of this Nation. War accents so much the necessity of command and discourages so much the luxury of debate that the Constitutional system of checks and balances between the Executive and Legislative Branches undergoes a fundamental change in its practical operation at such times.

The government of the United States is built upon the doctrine of the separation of the powers of government among its three Branches—the Executive, Legislative and Judicial. Under this doctrine, the Executive is made Commander in Chief of the Armed Forces, given the power over foreign relations, and charged with the responsibility of rec-

---

* For biographical note see page 213.

† This paper would have been impossible in its present form and substance without the ideas, editing and otherwise active participation of five men who helped mold and activate the Office of Department Counselor (now Office of General Counsel) of the Department of the Army from its birth on July 25, 1950 one month after the outbreak of the Korean War, to June 1953 less than two months before the signing of the Korean Armistice on July 26, 1953—Professor Arthur E. Sutherland, Law School of Harvard University, who as Special Consultant to the Secretary of the Army advised with the Office of Army Department Counselor on numerous occasions; B. A. Monaghan of White, Bradley, Arant, All & Rose, Birmingham, Ala., Second Army Department Counselor; and three associates of the Army Department Counselor, Mac Asbill, Jr. of Sutherland, Asbill & Brennan, Washington, D. C., Melvin A. Dow of Dow & Dow, Houston, Texas, and Ernest J. Sargeant, associate of Ropes, Gray, Best, Coolidge & Rugg, Boston, Mass.

ommending military budgets to the Legislature. But deliberately split off from the Executive and assigned to the Legislature is the power to raise and support the Armed Forces and to declare war. These powers, however, although customarily regarded as separate and distinct, are not in water tight compartments and in some areas each of the Branches has the power to act on the same question.

With the impact of crisis—war, global such as World War II or localized such as the Korean War, in which United States Forces may be fighting—there is a shift in the degree of exercise of certain powers. Then the Executive, desirous of swift action, often uses one of its concurrent powers which overlap with Congressional powers, and on rare occasions in the absence of Constitutional power it impatiently encroaches upon the function of the Legislature. The Legislature in turn during such periods exercises much less vigorously than normally its controlling power over the size of the military budget, and tends to appropriate whatever sums the Executive requests. But to check the expenditure of the vast sums so appropriated for the military establishment, the Legislature sharply increases its investigation of the Defense Department. It, too, frequently exercises concurrent powers in fields where the Executive also is active and occasionally it encroaches unconstitutionally upon the powers of the Executive. While generally the Doctrine of Separation of Powers has proved to be sufficiently flexible in actual operation to accommodate satisfactorily the urgent requirements of war, in this age of supersonic speeds and almost unlimited capacity for destruction greater effectiveness of government operations is important for survival.

This paper will view the historical roots of the Doctrine of Separation of Powers as applied to the military establishment, with particular emphasis on the Army; then it will examine the relation of the theoretical concept of Separation of Powers to the practical operation of this Doctrine in time of crisis. At the close, some conclusions will be tendered and some suggestions ventured how this practical operation of government during periods of crisis may possibly be made more effective.

II. Adoption of Separation of Powers Doctrine in Constitution

The leaders who inspired, conceived, and wrote the United States Constitution were determined to distribute the powers of government among the Legislature, Judiciary and Executive and thus to prevent dictatorial rule of this Nation by any unchecked Branch of government. James Madison wrote in *The Federalist*:

> "The accumulation of all powers, legislative, executive, and judiciary, in the same hands, whether of one, a few, or many, and whether hereditary, self-appointed, or elective, may justly be pronounced the very definition of tyranny."[1]

It was intended that the system of separate powers, with its built-in checks and balances between the Branches, would guard the liberties of the people and avoid tyranny by precluding the concentration of all powers in a few hands. It was never thought nor intended that it would provide the most efficient method of government. Precisely the converse was recognized and accepted. Mr. Justice Brandeis in his dissenting opinion in *Myers v. United States,* the case which held that an appointed Postmaster could be removed by the President without the consent of the Senate, emphasized this fact:

> "The doctrine of the separation of powers was adopted by the Convention of 1787, not to promote efficiency but to preclude the exercise of arbitrary power. The purpose was, not to avoid friction, but, by means of the inevitable friction incident to the distribution of the governmental powers among three departments, to save the people from autocracy."[2]

While the powers of government were distributed

1. THE FEDERALIST, No. 47 (Madison).
2. 272 U.S. 52, 240, 293 (1926).

among the three Branches, the Branches in turn were not completely sealed off from each other. Tyranny comes "where the *whole* power of one department is exercised by the same hands which possess the *whole* power of another department".[3] But to make the United States system work, the Executive and Legislative Branches have *some* partial agency in and *some* control over the acts of each other. To take obvious examples in the field this paper is discussing, the Executive appoints the Secretary, Deputy or Under Secretary and Assistant Secretaries of Defense, Army, Navy and Air, but the Senate, except in the case of appointments made while it is in recess, must approve these appointments before any appointee may serve. The President commands the Armed Forces but the Legislature must first raise whatever Forces he commands. Every time a military budget is presented by the Executive and money is appropriated by the Legislature both Branches act on the same question.

A. *Application of Doctrine to Armed Forces*

One of the primary objectives of the Separation of Powers Doctrine was to keep a strong Executive from levying and financing an Army for his own purposes. Nevertheless, the opponents of the United States Constitution played upon the fears of the people, according to Alexander Hamilton in *The Federalist,* by claiming that the Constitution either "contained a positive injunction that standing Armies should be kept up in time of peace; or that it vested in the Executive the whole power of levying troops, without subjecting his discretion, in any shape, to the control of the Legislature".[4] The future first Secretary of the Treasury recognized the dangerously rising crescendo of these claims and met the issue squarely:

> "If he (a 'stranger to our politics, who was to read our newspapers') came afterwards to peruse the plan itself, he would be

3. THE FEDERALIST, No. 47 (Madison).
4. THE FEDERALIST, No. 24 (Hamilton).

surprised to discover, that neither the one nor the other was the case; that the whole power of raising armies was lodged in the Legislature, not in the Executive . . . "[5]

Hamilton further underscored his answer to the critics by emphasizing that even the Legislature is forbidden by the Constitution to appropriate money for the support of an Army for any period longer than two years—"a precaution which, upon a nearer view of it, will appear to be a great and real security against the keeping up of troops without evident necessity".[6] Hamilton referred, of course, to Article I of the Constitution, which provides:

> "The Congress shall have power—To raise and support armies, but no appropriation of money to that use shall be for a longer term than two years."[7]

Thus to keep the Executive from either levying or supporting troops the Constitution specifically vests both these powers in the Legislature which in turn is checked by the Constitutional limitation that no appropriation of money "shall be for a longer term than two years". Does this Constitutional theory that the major check on the Executive's control of the Armed Forces is the Congressional power of appropriation work in time of crisis? If it does not, then how does Congress compensate for its less vigorous exercise of its power to determine independently and finally the size of military appropriations?

III. Impact of Crisis on Separation of Powers Doctrine as Applied to Budgeting and Appropriations Functions

During times of global war the emphasis abruptly shifts from the problem of preserving the economic stability of the Nation over a long period to the problem of obtaining maxi-

5. THE FEDERALIST, No. 24 (Hamilton). The parenthetical phrase is transposed from the preceding paragraph in No. 24.
6. THE FEDERALIST, No. 24 (Hamilton).
7. U.S. CONST. Art. I, §8.

mum production of military equipment while raising large military forces and providing the minimum current requirements of the people who are not in unform. The pressure on both the Executive and the Legislature is to win the war at all costs whether it takes a $50 billion or a $100 billion or a $150 billion military budget. The only question is how much money can be effectively spent.

During times of localized war, on the other hand, the emphasis is dual in nature—to win the local war in which United States Forces are fighting but at the same time to preserve the national economy. The Preparedness Investigating Subcommittee of the Senate Armed Services Committee during the Korean War was troubled because it felt that in this division of emphasis the first objective—National defense—was receiving too little support. In one of its reports the Committee said:

> "Much to-do has been made about the strain of an accelerated mobilization program on our civilian economy. Civilian production and civilian expansion of industry in 1951 were far above normal. It would require only a moderate reduction of this civilian production and expansion to allow a rapid acceleration of military production. . . . we are convinced that the threat which faces our security is so grave that an overriding priority should be placed upon building our defenses."[8]

Undoubtedly the question of how much emphasis to place on the preservation of the national economy and how much to place on winning a local war will always be present at such times of crisis. Those times do not tap the national emotions nor touch directly anywhere near as many lives as do global wars. The problem of determining the proper size of a military budget when a local war is being fought in the midst of an effort to guard the national economy over the indefinite future is a far more difficult question of judgment than the determination of the size of the military budget in times of global war when the civilian economy is entirely subordinated to national survival. But during local wars as

8. Report 39 of Preparedness Investigating Subcommittee of the Committee on Armed Services, U. S. Senate, 82d Cong., 2d Sess. 7, 8 (1952).

well as during global wars the Legislature is less active than during normal years in determining the size of the military budget.

That the Legislature voluntarily decides in times of crisis not to exercise too vigorously its key control over the Armed Forces—final judgment on the amount of military appropriations—is indicated by a comparison of the sums requested by the Executive for the Army[9] during World War II, the Korean War and the more normal years in between these Wars with the sums actually appropriated by Congress in these three periods.

The vast amounts requested by the Executive in each of these Wars with the sums actually appropriated by Congress change was very slight. But it was otherwise in the normal period as shown by the following figures in dollars:

	Fiscal Year	*Army Budget Requested By Executive*	*Amount Appropriated By Congress*	*Percent of Increase or Decrease*
World War II	1942	76,473,000,000	75,463,000,000	— 1.32
	1943	42,821,000,000	42,820,000,000	— .00
	1944	59,426,000,000	59,035,000,000	— .66
	1945	15,678,000,000	15,435,000,000	— 1.55
	1946	21,963,000,000	21,497,000,000	— 2.12
Total		216,361,000,000	214,250,000,000	— .98
Normal Years	1947	7,998,000,000	6,930,000,000	—13.35
	1948	3,236,000,000	3,206,000,000	— .93
	1949	6,349,000,000	4,033,000,000	—36.48
	1950	4,637,000,000	4,405,000,000	— 5.00
Total		22,220,000,000	18,574,000,000	—16.41
Korean War	1951	19,331,000,000	19,270,000,000	— .32
	1952	23,155,000,000	21,639,000,000	— 6.55
	1953	14,200,000,000	13,608,000,000	— 4.17
Total		56,686,000,000	54,517,000,000	— 3.83

9. The figures for the Army's budget for the three periods in question illustrate much steeper reductions in the President's budget requests for the Army during normal years than do figures for Defense as a whole during these

Moreover, the foregoing bare statistics probably do not reflect the full extent of Congress' willingness to allow the Executive relatively free rein in this field during times of crisis. For instance, in Fiscal Year 1951—the first year of the Korean War—Congress, in all likelihood, would have appropriated substantially twice the budget presented by the President for the Army if he had so requested. With Congress thus giving the Executive practically a blank check in times of crisis, it becomes important to see what the Army's budgetary procedures are and to see also both why Congress relaxes its control of the purse strings and how it compensates for the less active exercise of its separate power to determine the size of the Army budget.

A. *Army's Budgetary Procedures*

There is an almost continuous discussion of present and future military budgets between responsible officials, including the Secretaries of the Army Department and the Defense Department and the Director of the Bureau of the Budget. This exchange of information is facilitated by the membership of the Secretary of Defense on the National Security Council, which takes into account intelligence reports on the world situation, military strategy in the light of this situation, and the effect of defense budgets on the economic health of the Nation. The Secretary of Defense, thus thoroughly familiar with the Government-wide point of view, meets weekly with the Armed Forces Policy Council comprising himself, the Deputy Secretary of Defense, the Secretaries of Army, Navy, and Air Force and the members of the Joint Chiefs of

same years. For the World War II years the requests of the President for Defense (Army, Navy and Air Force) were reduced 2.51%; for the Korean War years 3.69%; and for the normal years in between these two periods of crisis 4.01% (percentage of change as distinguished from percentage of reduction was 5.59% because the Legislature took the rare action of markedly increasing the President's requested Air Force budget for Fiscal Year 1950. Infra p. 157). It should be observed in this connection that cycles of feast and famine apply more sharply to the Army than they do traditionally to the Navy and to the newly-born Air Force. The Nation and the Legislature are apparently inclined to believe that in normal times the Navy and the Air Force can do more to preserve the national security and prevent war than can the Army.

Staff. The Chief of Staff of the Army is, of course, a member of the Joint Chiefs of Staff whose members are advisors to the National Security Council. The Secretary of the Army is in continuous touch with the Army Chief of Staff, and in addition is in weekly session with the Army Policy Council composed of himself, the Army's Under and Assistant Secretaries, Chief and Vice Chief of Staff, Deputy Chief of Staff, and Comptroller.

Through this system of formal meetings and informal discussions budgetary matters are under consideration at all levels of government at practically all times. The result is that the initial formal Army directions for the preparation of any given budget reflect to an important degree the conceptions which the Secretary of the Army and the Chief of Staff have developed through their contacts with each other, the Secretary of Defense, the Director of the Budget, a representative of the Bureau of the Budget assigned to work with the Army and the other members of the Joint Chiefs of Staff.

The Army's present budget procedures may be illustrated by using as an example the preparation of its budget for Fiscal Year 1956 covering the 12 months from July 1, 1955 to June 30, 1956. Early in February 1954, almost seventeen months before the start of Fiscal Year 1956, the Army began the preparation of this budget on the basis of program objectives developed by the Army's Budget Division and approved by the Secretary of the Army. These program objectives were sent to the Secretary of Defense for comment before the Budget Division distributed from the middle of March through May the numerous detailed program planning documents and late in May the Budget Directive with its technical instructions. However, the first specific written policy directions from the Secretary of Defense were fragmentary and were not received until May. Further piecemeal written directions came in July shortly before the Army Staff completed its development of the budget estimates and additional directions came in August in the midst of the review of these estimates.

After seven and one half months of preparation of the Fiscal Year 1956 budget by the Army military staff[10] the Chief of Staff reviewed the budget, made the final staff decision on its form and substance, and submitted it the first day of October to the Assistant Secretary of the Army charged with fiscal management. With any changes recommended by him, the Assistant Secretary sent the Budget quickly to the Secretary of the Army who then made any final changes and transmitted it a few days later to the Secretary of Defense for his decision.

During the crowded months of October, November and December joint hearings on the Army Budget were conducted by the Office of the Assistant Secretary of Defense (Comptroller) and a representative of the Bureau of the Budget; an analysis based on these hearings was furnished to the Army by the Assistant Secretary; the Director of the Budget conferred with the President who decided on the tentative size of all military budgets for Fiscal Year 1956; the Secretary of Defense determined the size of the Army budget after discussing the President's decision with the Deputy Secretary of Defense and the Secretaries of the Army, Navy and Air Force; the Army submitted to the Secretary of Defense its revised budget based upon the new figure; the Secretary of Defense transmitted the entire budget, including that of the Army, to the Director of the Budget who presented it in its final form to the President in the last week of December.

Because Congress in times of crisis places so much reliance on the defense budget recommended by the Executive, it is particularly important that the procedures used by the Executive in developing its defense budget be thoroughly sound. With a description of the preparation of the Army's Fiscal Year 1956 budget having now been set forth as an example of the procedures used by the Executive, a sufficient basis is perhaps established on which to make certain suggestions at the close of this paper. In any event, Congress

---

10. On page 172 is Appendix 1 setting forth in some detail the development of the Army's budget for Fiscal Year 1956.

does rely heavily on the estimates of the Executive and places much confidence in the soundness of its proposed budget. But confidence in the soundness of the budget in no sense explains fully Congress' relative failure to exercise in times of crisis its power to determine the size of the defense budget for, after all, the Executive's recommended military budget deserves the same degree of confidence in normal times when Congress more actively exercises its power over military appropriations.

B. *Explanation of Tendency by Congress Not To Exercise Its Appropriation Power in Time of Crisis*

As emphasized at the outset of this section the principal reason Congress exercises less control over budget and appropriation matters in times of crisis than in normal times is the complete shift in National emphasis during global war from preservation of the domestic economy to military production and a major though not a complete shift in the same direction during localized war. Lesser reasons, however, are also significant.

In relaxing its grip on the military purse strings in time of crisis, Congress reflects the National inclination to appropriate lavishly for defense when the Country is either in a general war, such as World War II, or a localized war, such as the Korean War. In the course of the investigation by the Senate Armed Services Committee of the ammunition shortages during the Korean War, General James A. Van Fleet, Commanding General of the Eighth Army for over 21 months from April 13, 1951 to January 22, 1953, testified that United States Forces fired six times as many shells as the Communists, but stressed that the desirable volume of fire should not be determined from any such statistical ratio. Senator Richard B. Russell, ranking Democratic minority member of the Committee at the time and now Chairman of the Committee, brought out this information in his questioning, and then stated emphatically that he opposed ammunition rationing of any kind. The testimony on this point was in part as follows:

"Senator Russell. . . . We see figures sometimes that show that they (North Korean and Chinese Communists) only fire a fraction or percentage of the number of shells against our lines that we do against theirs—I have forgotten what it was, 12, 15 percent, something like that. (Material in parentheses added.)

"General Van Fleet. Yes; it is today about a 6 to 1 ratio.

"Senator Russell. Six to one?

"General Van Fleet. But that will give you a false conclusion there. That is being quoted in the Department of Defense as a factor that we have plenty and we are doing all right, and I disagree with them on that . . . if you apply that to the Air Force, that same thought, then we should not send so many planes north. We should not send any because the enemy does not send any at us.

. . . .

"Senator Russell. I want us to have every shell over there that is necessary to be fired, and I am sure every Member of Congress shares that feeling, and it comes as a great surprise to me that there has been a shortage. . . . it is shocking to me to hear that there has been any shortage that required our units to be rationed. I do not care if it is necessary for them to fire one shell a week or a million, I want to have the rounds of ammunition there."[11]

Closely tied in with the national desire to do everything possible to win the war, protect the lives of men in uniform and provide for them the best equipment, is the wish of the Legislators to avoid any claim that they damaged the military effort or unduly risked lives by failing to appropriate whatever funds were requested by the Executive. When General Van Fleet testified that ammunition shortages cost the lives of United States soldiers in Korea, Congress at once took special pains to emphasize that from the outbreak of the Korean War it had appropriated every amount requested by the Executive for ammunition.[12] The testimony of Gen-

11. Hearings on Ammunition Supplies in the Far East, before Committee on Armed Services, U. S. Senate, 83d Cong., 1st Sess. 23 (1953).

12. In Fiscal Year 1949 the Legislature reduced the requested appropriation for ammunition from $40.9 million to $36.0 million, this being the only year between the end of World War II and the beginning of the Korean War when the President's relatively small requested appropriation for ammunition

eral Van Fleet before the Senate Committee on Armed Services and the testimony of Senator Leverett Saltonstall, Chairman of the Committee, and Senator Margaret Chase Smith, Chairman of the Subcommittee later appointed to continue the ammunition investigation, are very illuminating on this point:

> "General Van Fleet. . . . I was issuing orders to my corps commanders, 'Don't shoot the 155 howitzer; we must save the ammunition.' I have issued many such directives at times to save on certain categories, and substituting other categories where we had a better situation."[13]

. . . .

> "Chairman Saltonstall. If this is a proper question—I do not know how to phrase it—in your opinion, were lives lost because we failed to send enough ammunition or was it that you just could not advance?
>
> "General Van Fleet. The lack of ammunition means that you do not shoot as much as you wish, that you do not shoot at all the targets of opportunity . . . all our regimental, all our battalion commanders, division, corps, and myself would like to shoot more, and the more you shoot, the more enemy you kill, and the more American lives you save; that is just axiomatic."[14]

. . . .

> "Chairman Saltonstall. There never was any question of the size or amount of money appropriated by Congress."[15]

. . . .

> "Senator Smith of Maine. I am sure General Collins does not mean . . . that the Congress—or the accusation or charge that the Congress has not appropriated sufficient money go unchallenged."
>
> "General Collins. The charge has never been made. . . . I said . . . no responsible officer of the Army, to my knowledge, has ever said that Congress has never appropriated the money that was asked for by the Bureau of the Budget, or by the President's message, for the Army's account."[16]

---

was reduced by the Legislature. Until the ammunition shortage became acute the Executive neglected to emphasize adequately to the Legislature that it would require approximately 18 months after an appropriation before the first heavy rounds of ammunition could be produced.

13. Hearings, supra note 11, at 19.
14. Hearings, supra note 11, at 20.
15. Hearings, supra note 11, at 146.
16. Hearings, supra note 11, at 147.

The resolution unanimously adopted by the Senate Committee on Armed Services to have the Chairman appoint a Subcommittee to continue the ammunition investigation reached the same conclusion:

> ". . . the officials of the Army Department have unanimously testified that defense appropriations for ammunition, as promptly made by Congress upon request since the beginning of the Korean War, have been adequate: . . ."[17]

During the continued hearings before the Preparedness Subcommittee No. 2 of the Senate Committee on Armed Services, Senator Byrd in his examination of Frank Pace, Jr., Secretary of the Army from the outbreak of the Korean War on June 26, 1950 to January 20, 1953, wrote indelibly into the record the conclusion of this highest Army official that the Legislature had granted all requests by the Executive for ammunition appropriations during this War. The following colloquy between the Senator and the former Army Secretary sums it up:

> "Senator Byrd. So there is no question whatever as to the cooperation of Congress?"
>
> "Mr. Pace. None."
>
> "Senator Byrd. And that ample funds were provided?"
>
> "Mr. Pace. None."[18]

In addition to the Congressional desire to avoid the risk of, and the political accountability for, endangering the National safety, there is another factor which explains Congress' reluctance to make substantial reductions in the military budget requests of the Executive. This factor is the enormous size of wartime military budgets. It is extremely difficult, even in normal times, for the Legislature through its committees with their small staffs to determine military requirements with any degree of accuracy—either as to individual items or total budgets. In wartime, the magnitude of the task would be overwhelming.

---

17. Ammunition Shortages in the Armed Services, before Preparedness Subcommittee No. 2 of the Committee on Armed Services, U. S. Senate, 83d Cong., 1st Sess. 1 (1953).
18. Hearings, supra note 17, at 171.

The assumptions of fact and statistical data underlying the appropriation for just a single item, such as wool trousers during the Korean War, are both complex and extensive. The Legislature, in order to exercise a sound independent judgment on the proper size of appropriations for wool trousers in a given year, would have to weigh the assumptions made by the Army in setting its requirements, add to or subtract from them and compute the necessary statistical data on the basis of the assumptions finally accepted by it. This would mean taking into consideration such questions as (1) on what day will the fighting in Korea end? (2) how many soldiers is the Army to have? (3) what is the average life of wool trousers? (4) might not a new uniform be adopted before the old one was fully utilized? The answer to this last question, in turn, depends upon the evaluation of incomplete research and experimental work on several new uniform materials, including synthetics. Each such assumption is based on fallible judgments—judgments that are apt to be more fallible if the one making them is not thoroughly familiar with wool trousers, new fabrics and the life of such garments under many varying conditions.

The Legislature and its committees simply do not have either the time or the qualified staffs or the underlying basic information and experience to do such a job. While during normal times thousands of different items, each requiring its own set of assumptions and statistical data, are required, the complexity and vastness of the problem increase perceptibly in time of war.

C. *Executive Practice of Reprogramming Appropriations*

Even if the Legislature did exercise vigorously its conclusive power over the size of the military budget, the not infrequent practice by the Executive of reprogramming money for items other than those presented to Congress in its budget would nonetheless alter the decision of the Legislature to use a specific appropriation for a specific item. During periods of crisis, this practice of administrative reprogramming of funds is more extensive than in normal times. Because wartime military budgets are usually prepared in their final stages in great haste after the Secretary of Defense has determined the total budget for each military department and because the very fluidity of the military situation itself in time of war frequently dictates a change of emphasis to different items, many changes are made by the Executive in the use of specific appropriations.

The Army in its principal budget has eight major classes of appropriations[19] including Procurement and Production, Military Personnel, Research and Development, Maintenance and Operations. While the sum requested for one of these classes is justified in the budget presented to the Legislature by a detailed allocation of smaller sums to the many items falling within the class, Congress appropriates only a lump sum for the entire class without any separate appropriation for individual items. Each of the eight major classes of appropriations is subdivided into a number of Budget Programs which in turn are subdivided into Budget Projects and again into Budget Subprojects. Under the Executive's system of reprogramming, an appropriation for a specified item in one Budget Program may be switched to another Budget Program, or the appropriation for a specified item within a Budget Project may be changed, for instance, to another item in the same Budget Project. However, funds may not be reprogrammed from one major appropriation to another; thus for example, funds are not switched from Procurement and Production to Military Personnel.

A striking illustration of the practice of reprogramming was the reallocation to other items of a total appropriation of $100 million for Army overcoats granted by Congress over a period of four years from Fiscal Year 1947 to Fiscal Year 1950. Extensive hearings were held by a Subcommittee of the House Appropriations Committee on the justification of appropriating $100 million for overcoats over the 4-year peri-

19. The Army also has a ninth major class of appropriations, Military Construction, but this class has its own separate smaller budget.

od and the Army through witnesses, charts and statistical data consistently defended its need for the money. However, as events later worked out, not one penny of the $100 million was ever spent for overcoats, all of it being reprogrammed for other items not previously included in the budget as submitted to Congress or justified by the Army before the Congress as approved by the Legislature.

In the course of his examination of former Secreary of the Army Frank Pace, Jr. during the hearings on the Korean War ammunition shortages by the Preparedness Subcommittee No. 2 of the Senate Armed Services Committee, Senator Byrd brought out the fact that the Army had reprogrammed to ammunition 1.6 billion dollars originally appropriated for other purposes. The question and answer follow:

> "Senator Byrd. Mr. Pace, from your very frank statement I gather the impression—and if I am not correct I would like to be corrected—. . . that you could have transferred funds had any funds been necessary?"
>
> "Mr. Pace. We had the authority, yes, to transfer funds. In fact, a factor that I did not mention, Senator Byrd, we actually did transfer funds in the sum of approximately $1,600,000,000."[20]

1. *Implied Statutory Authority.* Such active reprogramming, long acquiesced in by the Legislature, has a probable statutory basis and some Constitutional basis. The general provisions of the United States Code concerning appropriations include a section requiring that "sums appropriated for the various branches of expenditure in the public service shall be applied solely to the objects for which they are respectively made, and for no others".[21] The eight major statutory classes of Army appropriations may be construed as the "objects" for which funds are appropriated. Given this construction it may be implied that while funds appropriated for one "object" must not be switched to another "object", they may be used for any of the many items within a particular "object" even though this means reprogramming money for

20. Hearings, supra note 17, at 171.
21. 31 U.S.C. §628 (1952).

items other than those presented to Congress by the Army in its budget.

One other section[22] of the general appropriations provisions is helpful. While it, too, falls short of affirmative statutory authority for reprogramming, it does implicitly furnish some support for the Executive practice. It requires the Executive to apportion appropriations so that they may be economically and efficiently obligated by contract and expended without any "necessity for deficiency or supplemental appropriations".[23] Any such apportionment "may be divided and subdivided administratively within the limits"[24] of the apportionment, and reserves may be established "to effect savings . . . made possible by . . . changes in requirements, greater efficiency in operations, or other developments subsequent to the date on which such appropriation was made available".[25] There is ground to infer from these several clauses that the Legislature intended to give the Executive discretionary power to vary, within any one of the eight major appropriations, the itemized budget program recommended by the President. The same inference may also be drawn from the presence in annual appropriation acts of numerous special authorizations for transfers between major appropriations and the complete absence of any similar authorizations to shift funds from one budget item to another within a single appropriation, Congress apparently recognizing that without any specific authorization the Executive normally possesses the authority to reprogram funds within a lump-sum major appropriation.[26]

The Comptroller General, who is in charge of the General Accounting Office which the Legislature especially established to audit for itself the activities of the Executive, has

22. 31 U.S.C. §665 (1952).
23. 31 U.S.C. §665(c)(1) (1952).
24. 31 U.S.C. §665(g) (1952).
25. 31 U.S.C. §665(c)(2) (1952).
26. Congress customarily inserts specific limitations in the Appropriations Act itself when it wishes to prevent a certain type of expenditure. For example, Section 718 of the Department of Defense Appropriations Act of 1955 forbids the use of appropriations to pay any person advocating "the overthrow of the United States by force or violence."

accepted in one of his Opinions the practice of reprogramming, saying:

> "The amounts of individual items in the estimates presented to the Congress on the basis of which a lump sum appropriation is enacted are not binding on administrative officers unless carried into the appropriation act itself."[27]

2. *Constitutional Authority.* Any Legislative authority for reprogramming being based upon statutory implications and not upon affirmative authorization, the President's Constitutional "executive power"[28] and his Constitutional power as Commander in Chief provide under these circumstances further support for reprogramming. When Congress authorizes a lump sum for a major military appropriation such as production and procurement without allocating to different items portions of the lump sum, the Executive in faithfully executing the law should determine on the basis of the latest available information how much of the total appropriation to spend on each of the many production and procurement items within the class. Although Congress depends on the justification for the individual items in the budget presented to it in reaching its appropriation for the entire class, it nevertheless appropriates only a lump sum for the class and leaves it to the discretion of the Executive in executing the law to weigh changing prices, altered requirements and the numerous other factors that must be taken into account. Moreover, the President as Commander in Chief has the duty to use the military appropriations to equip the forces he commands in the most effective manner. This does not mean that he can shift appropriations from one major class to another or from the Army to the Air Force, but it does mean that he can devote the appropriation for a single class to such items in such amounts as in his judgment will produce the best military force.

Reprogramming is an instance where the concurrent powers of the Legislature and the Executive permit both

27. 17 Comp. Gen. 147, 150.
28. U. S. Const. art. II, §1.

Branches to act within limitations on the same question. The presence of concurrent powers was recognized by the House Committee on Foreign Affairs in its Report on "Background Information on the Use of United States Forces in Foreign Countries":

> "In the field of foreign affairs, as in other fields of governmental activity, many powers are shared by the executive and legislative branches."[29]

Mr. Justice Jackson in his concurring opinion in *Youngstown Sheet and Tube Co. v. Sawyer,* the case which declared unconstitutional the President's seizure of the steel industry, spoke of the "concurrent authority" of the President and Congress:

> "When the President acts in absence of either a congressional grant or denial of authority, he can only rely upon his own independent powers, but there is a zone of twilight in which he and Congress may have concurrent authority, or in which its distribution is uncertain. Therefore, congressional inertia, indifference or quiescence may sometimes, at least as a practical matter, enable, if not invite, measures on independent presidential responsibility. In this area, any actual test of power is likely to depend on the imperatives of events and contemporary imponderables rather than on abstract theories of law."[30]

Regardless of the Constitutional or statutory basis for extensive reprogramming of funds, such as that in the case of the overcoats, the practice does make rather ineffective Congress' theoretical authority to decide how the government's money shall be spent. Apparently sensitive about this point, a House Subcommittee, in its report in 1954 on the reprogramming of overcoat funds, called for the inauguration of "an accounting system within the military departments which will reflect whether appropriated funds are being spent in accordance with plans presented to and approved by the Congress".[31]

---

29. H.R. Rep. No. 127, 82d Cong., 1st Sess. 10 (1951).
30. 343 U.S. 579, 637 (1951).
31. H.R. Rep. No. 1459, 83d Cong., 2d Sess. 3 (1954).

D. *Executive Decision Not to Use Appropriated Funds*

Not to be confused with reprogramming is the decision of the Executive from time to time to spend less than authorized by Congress. Such a decision, based on economic and military factors, is usually welcomed by the Legislature. However, the refusal of the President to use $736 million appropriated in a non-crisis year by the Legislature in the Fiscal Year 1950 budget was quite an exception. The Legislature, exercising vigorously indeed its power to determine the size of the Air Force budget, had added $736 million to the budget requested by the President for the express purpose of increasing the strength of the Air Force from 48 Groups to 58 Groups. This action was all the more dramatic because while Congress frequently reduces in normal times the President's requested budget for a military Department, it rarely increases one so sharply.[32]

In a public statement issued on the day the President signed the Appropriation Act for Fiscal Year 1950, H.R. 4146, he said he was "directing the Secretary of Defense to place in reserve the amounts provided by Congress in H.R. 4146 for increasing the structure of the Air Force".[33] He explained his unusual action as follows:

> "For one item . . . a sharp increase in authorizations provided by the Congress represents a major shift in the direction and emphasis of our defense program. If fully utilized, this increased authorization would result in a serious lack of balance in our defense program and would require much heavier expenditures in the future than we now contemplate."[34]

The President, in setting aside $736 million appropriated by Congress for the purpose of increasing the size of the Air Force, did not override a direction of Congress but

---

32. The outbreak of the Korean War six days before Fiscal Year 1951 began on July 1, 1950 changed the whole military situation and Congress' Air Force Appropriations for Fiscal Year 1951 authorized an increase in strength from 48 to 87 Groups.

33. Statement by the President, Press Release, Oct. 29, 1949.

34. Ibid.

merely refused to use an "authorized" expenditure. For instance, the language of the Appropriation Act covering Procurement and Production provided in part as follows:

> "The Secretary of the Air Force is authorized to enter into contracts for the foregoing purposes (including procurement of aircraft and equipment) in an amount not to exceed $1,992,755,-000."[35] (Material in parenthesis added.)

The President in his statement said that the use of the extra $736 million "would be inconsistent with a realistic and balanced security program which we can support in peacetime"[36] and that the additional appropriation must be "viewed in the light of total national policies".[37] On this basis, entirely aside from the military or political wisdom of his decision, the President was probably within his Constitutional powers in deciding not to use the $736 million to add 10 more groups to the Air Force.[38]

However, the House Appropriations Committee in its report on the Fiscal Year 1951 Appropriation Act criticised the President's action as an unconstitutional "item veto" of the 1950 Appropriation Act "thwarting . . . a major policy of Congress". Its sharp language was in part as follows:

> ". . . the President issued a statement . . . directing— '* * * the Secretary of Defense to place in reserve the amounts provided by the Congress in H.R. 4146 for increasing the structure of the Air Force', which amounted to an item veto, a power not possessed by the President."

. . . .

> "It is perfectly justifiable and proper for all possible economies to be effected and savings to be made, but there is no warrant or justification for the thwarting of a major policy of Congress by the impounding of funds. If this principle of thwarting the will of

35. 63 STAT. 787 (1950).

36. Supra note 33.

37. Ibid.

38. The President in a letter dated November 8, 1949 to the Secretary of Defense justified his action on the basis of the authority vested in him as "Commander in Chief of the Armed Forces" and pursuant to "section 202(b) of the National Security act of 1947, as amended." Section 202(b) requires the Secretary of Defense to make reports at least semi-annually to the President and Congress which set forth, among other things, "itemized statements showing the savings of public funds."

Congress by the impounding of funds should be accepted as correct, then Congress would be totally incapable of carrying out its constitutional mandate of providing for the defense of the Nation."[39]

The Air Force incident serves to show how essential it is for the oil of politics to be applied to the governmental machine if it is to run smoothly. On this subject D. W. Brogan, a distinguished British writer and professor of political science at the University of Cambridge, who knows well the Federal system and the difference between it and that of the British where the Prime Minister is both chief executive and leader of the majority in Parliament, wrote in his most recent book:

". . . the American or foreign spectator, not excessively enamoured of symmetry, or of merely smooth working, has been forced to say, with Galileo in the legend: 'it *does* move'; it does work. And it moves because the government of the United States is so deeply political, because it has never been worked as a mere instrument of power or will. It has been worked by politicians, for politicians, but also for the people of the United States."[40]

Walter Lippmann feels that the Legislature is "so deeply political" and so much more powerful today than previously that the United States Government is not working well enough. He is fearful that the Legislature, following the "pressure of the electorate . . . for the less painful alternative"[41], has become too dominant and that the balance of power between the Legislature and Executive has been damagingly upset. He attributes this in large part to the huge cost of war which has so increased the power of the Legislature, because of its appropriations authority, that the power of the Executive has been badly devitalized. This in Lippmann's

39. H.R. Rep. No. 1797, 81st Cong., 2d Sess. (1950). However, the House Armed Services Committee in its Report stated that the Department of Defense does have the "freedom" to "withhold funds appropriated by the Congress," but that it "does not consider this practice to be in harmony with the desires of the Congress." A Report of Investigation by the Committee on Armed Services, House of Representatives, on Unification and Strategy, March 1, 1950. House Document No. 600, 81st Cong., 2d Sess.

40. Brogan, An Introduction to American Politics, 267 (1st ed. 1954).

41. Lippmann, The Public Philosophy, 55 (1st ed. 1955).

opinion results in the tendency of the Executive to shrink from using its powers, express or inherent, to take a swift, decisive, and at times a painful course of action. According to his book published in 1955, *The Public Philosophy,* vastly greater appropriations constitute one of the two major causes for the present feebleness of the Executive Branch of Western Democracies generally:

> "Two great streams of evolution have converged upon the modern democracies to devitalize, to enfeeble, and to eviscerate the executive powers. One is the enormous expansion of public expenditure, chiefly for war and reconstruction; this has augmented the power of the assemblies which vote the appropriations on which the executive depends."[42]

Contrary to Mr. Lippmann's conclusion, the statistics and analyses already set forth in this paper indicate that in this Nation the Legislature's power of appropriation in time of war has certainly not been used directly to enfeeble or devitalize the power of the Executive. In fact, as shown above, the Legislature appropriates practically everything the Executive requests for defense without exercising to any great degree its separate and conclusive power to determine the size of the military budget.

The reason for this Congressional reticence, to use Mr. Lippmann's own terms, is in part "pressure of the electorate". In February, 1955, Congressman Paul J. Kilday of the House Armed Services Committee, mindful of the views of the electorate, described them thus in an address at the National War College in Washington:

> "The American people are the easiest in the world to frighten; and when frightened the military cannot be expanded rapidly enough, nothing is too good for them. No demand for numbers is ever too large. There should be no limitation of divisions of ground forces, wings for the air or naval tonnage afloat."[43]

However, the Executive is ever aware of the might of the Legislature's appropriation power which overhangs its head

---

42. Supra note 41.
43. 84 Cong. Rec. A1195 (February 24, 1955).

as a Damocles sword. Deliberately or subconsciously, it generally takes this Legislative power into careful consideration in making its decision. Congress, too, never forgets the power of its authority over appropriations and this awareness is on occasions reflected in its resolutions and Legislative acts affecting the military establishment in time of crisis. It is especially reflected in its increased number of investigations of the expenditures and operations of the Defense Department.

IV. Impact of Crisis on Separation of Powers Doctrine as Applied to Congressional Investigations

The effect of a crisis on the incidence of Congressional investigations is precisely the converse of its effect on Congress' exercise of its power over appropriations. While, as has been mentioned above, a crisis results in a decrease in Congress' exercise of its power to determine the size of appropriations, the same crisis produces a marked increase in Congressional investigating activity. The truth of this statement is strikingly apparent from a brief mention of Congressional investigations produced by a recent military crises.[44]

The greatly increased number of military investigations by Congress in time of war is illustrated by the establishment of the Special Committee Investigating the National Defense Program ("Truman Committee")[45] during World War II and the Preparedness Investigating Subcommittee ("Johnson Committee") during the Korean War. The Johnson Committee, a specially created Subcommittee of the Senate Armed Services Committee, issued 44 different reports covering its investigations of a wide variety of activities affecting

44. Principal investigations of Congressional Committees handled by the Office of Army Department Counselor from July 1950 to August 1952 are set forth in Appendix 2.

45. This Committee during the 7 years from March 1, 1941 to April 28, 1948 issued 49 majority and 2 minority reports "on every phase of procurement in connection with our national defense program." Sen. Rep. No. 440, 80th Cong., 2d Sess. 9 (1948).

the military establishment during the Korean War. Its scope extended from charges of administrative topheaviness of the Armed Forces to procurement organization, functions, and procedures; from manpower utilization at Induction Centers to the construction of the North African Air Force bases; from tungsten shortages to the comparative firepower of U. S. and Russian Divisions.[46]

With the truce talks in the Korean War begun on July 9, 1951 and the Armistice finally signed July 26, 1953 the activities of the Preparedness Investigating Subcommittee dropped off sharply.[47] From the time Senator Leverett Saltonstall became Chairman of the Armed Services Committee following the change of administrations on January 20, 1953 to the switch of the chairmanship back to Senator Richard B. Russell in January 1955 the Preparedness Subcommittee issued only 8 reports as compared to the 44 it issued under the prior chairmanship of Senator Lyndon Johnson. Instead of a single Chairman for this Subcommittee, Senator Saltonstall designated a new Chairman each time the Subcommittee investigated another major subject, the 7 Subcommittees being numbered from 1 to 7. In addition these Preparedness Subcommittees from February 27, 1953 to August 4, 1954 handled the usual stream of smaller inquiries totalling nearly 1000 during this period.

While the Preparedness Investigating Subcommittee conducted the most extensive investigations of the military establishment during the Korean War, various other Committees of both the Senate and the House were also active in this field. In fact at times two different committees could be found to be investigating the same subject. The Senate Appropriations Committee did not exhaustively explore par-

---

46. In the annual report of the Preparedness Investigating Subcommittee, dated March 20, 1952, there is a brief description of the activities of the Subcommittee from the date of its organization on July 17, 1950 through January 31, 1952, including a list in Appendix II of the Committee's first 36 reports. Annual Report of Preparedness Investigating Subcommittee of the Committee on Armed Services, U. S. Senate, 82d Cong., 2d Sess. (1952).

47. 27 of the Committee's 44 reports were issued before the truce talks began on July 9, 1951 and most of the remaining 17 reports arose out of investigations started by the Committee prior to July 9, 1951. Supra note 46, Appendix 2.

ticular subjects in the fashion of certain other Committees, but it did review generally the operations and expenditures of the Army, Navy and Air Force. The Senate Committee on Agriculture and the Senate Post Office Committee and Civil Service Committee through its Subcommittee on Federal Manpower Policies devoted some of their attention to military activities related to their work generally.

In the House, during the 81st and 82nd Congresses, the Government Operations Subcommittee of the House Committee on Expenditures in the Executive Department concerned itself with such subjects as the efficiency of the Army in using existing warehouse space, the need for new barracks and the proper number of square feet per man on which any new construction should be based, procurement policies and industry practices, the supply of spare parts for tank and automotive equipment. The Intergovernmental Relations Subcommittee of the House Committee on Expenditures in the Executive Department investigated the justification for disposing of military surplus property through a German agency and the wisdom of the Secretary of Defense's decision to establish a separate supply system for the Air Force in Europe instead of utilizing the already available Army supply system.

The House Armed Services Committee conducted few formal hearings but presented to the Defense Department a continuous flow of inquiries on various aspects of military operations, including tank production schedules, real estate purchases, allocation of strategic materials, and the organization of the Army procurement system. Through a Subcommittee on Tanks, it studied the facilities being used for tank production, the speed of production, and the comparative merits of United States and Russian tanks. Through its Subcommittee on Procurement, it investigated cataloguing and the soundness of the Executive's decision to lease a $75,000,000 ammonia plant to a particular private producer instead of to some other private producer.

A major key in explanation of the concurrent decrease

Whitney North Seymour, of the New York Bar, comments on the paper given by Judge Wyzanski.

Professor Paul A. Freund, discusses the paper delivered by Judge Hastie.

Francis Shackelford (left), of the Atlanta Bar, who delivered a paper, and Mac Asbill, Jr., who commented on Mr. Shackelford's paper, listen to further comments from the floor.

Professor W. Barton Leach comments on the paper delivered by Francis Shackelford.

Professor Arthur T. von Mehren discusses the paper given by Professor Tunc.

Roscoe Pound (left), Dean Emeritus of the Harvard Law School, and John Lord O'Brian.

in Congress' exercise of its power over the size of the military budget and the increase in its investigations lies in the complementary relation of these two functions. Congressional investigation of the Defense Department's use of the vast sums appropriated is a natural complement of the Legislature's appropriation function. This complementary relation used to be illustrated by the former names of the Committees which, under the scheme of the Legislative Reorganization Act, are intended to do the bulk of the investigation work. Until 1950 the committees, now known as the Government Operations Committee in both the Senate and the House, were called the Committees on Expenditures in the Executive Departments.

When the appropriations power goes largely unexercised because of the national insistence on generous military appropriations, the very complexity of astronomical defense budgets and the reliance of the Legislature upon the knowledge and wisdom of the Executive in making its budget recommendations, it is understandable why the Legislature's complementary power of investigation is used more actively. From the Congressional point of view, it becomes increasingly desirable to ascertain that dollars easily and freely appropriated are being prudently and effectively spent.

Extensive investigations also keep Committee Chairmen and Subcommittee Chairmen in the public eye and indicate to the electorate the alertness of their Senators and Representatives. They naturally have much appeal. They are beneficial politically to the individual investigating Congressman.[48] They involve less responsibility for failures than does independent exercise of the appropriating function as shown so aptly in the case of the ammunition shortages during the Korean War where the apprehensive Legislature was quick to show that it could not be tarred with the responsibility for appropriating less for ammunition than the Executive

48. The Chairman of the Special Committee Investigating the National Defense Program during World War II, Senator Harry S. Truman, was elected Vice President in 1944, and the Chairman of the Preparedness Investigating Subcommittee during the Korean War, Senator Lyndon B. Johnson, is now the majority leader of the Senate.

had asked. Happily for elected Congressmen, investigations are based on hindsight, not foresight. While the exercise of foresight by the Legislature in determining the proper size of the military budget would submit it to the possibility of blame for a serious mistake, hindsight "always tests 20-20", as one General wise in the ways of Congress said.

There are, however, other reasons for the increased investigations based on the finest public service and patriotic instincts. In time of crisis it is the national desire to prevent war profiteering and fraudulent use of funds appropriated for military purposes. The Legislature as the representative of the people is well qualified to help accomplish this end through its power of investigation. It moves with a giant stride toward this goal by its numerous investigations which are intended to take the profit out of war, spotlight the fraudulent, and assure the honest and aggressive execution of the laws it has enacted in the military field.

Since the great size of the military budget in time of crisis multiplies the opportunities for inefficient and corrupt use of military funds, this very multiplication increases the need for investigation on the part of the Legislature in its effort to curtail to a minimum, abuse, misuse and fraudulent use of appropriations.

A. *Encroachment by Legislature on Executive*

In its zeal during times of crisis to see that the money it appropriates is well spent by the military establishment the Legislature encroaches in various ways on the power of the Executive. Though it is the Constitutional responsibility of the Executive to "take care that the laws be faithfully executed"[49], and though the negotiation of contracts for military construction for which money has been provided is surely the Executive's responsibility, Congressional investigating committees have made deep incursions into this area. From time to time they demand authority to review proposed

49. U.S. CONST., Art. II, §3.

contract awards in advance of signing of the contract; to review plans for disposal of surplus property, including review of the list of items to be disposed of, as well as the methods of disposal (whether by formal bids or negotiation or auction). A systematic scheme for Congressional review of every proposed military acquisition or transfer of realty with an estimated value in excess of $25,000 was established during the Korean War when Congress enacted a statute which requires that the Military Departments first "come into agreement" with the House and Senate Armed Services Committees before completing any such transaction.[50]

So far has the pendulum swung that Congressman Clare Hoffman, Chairman of the House Committee on Government Operations in the 83rd Congress, was moved to append as additional views to two of his Committee's reports, statements representing most interesting declarations against interest. To the Third Intermediate Report of the Committee he added these comments:

> "These four requests[51] seem to be based upon the assumption that the subcommittee and its staff are more able, better qualified, to check and perhaps rewrite any plans which the Secretary of Defense, his Assistant Secretaries and their aides, should use to implement the supply and stock management practices of the Military Department.
>
> "If the theory of this report, as outlined in the four quoted requests, should be followed, it would permit a subcommittee of a House committee to supervise, at least on the issues here involved, the activities of the Department of Defense. . . .
>
> "Add to the foregoing request the newly claimed authority of the subcommittees of the Committee on Government Operations . . . and we approach Government by investigating committees rather than by constitutional processes. . . ."[52]

---

50. 65 STAT. 365 (1951).

51. The Committee requested (1) the Secretary of Defense to submit to the Committee a program for the improvement of supply management in all three Services, (2) the Secretary of Defense to submit a program for the use of stock funds, (3) the Secretary of the Army to report on progress of the independent accounting firm studying the problem of installing a new system in the Army for financial property accounting, (4) the Secretary of Defense and the Administrator of General Services to furnish plans for surplus property disposal. H.R. Rep. No. 857, 83d Cong., 1st Sess. (1953).

52. Supra note 51, at 54, 55.

The Chairman's comment on the Sixth Intermediate Report of the House Government Operations Committee was pointedly along the same line:

> ". . . if subcommittees are permitted to demand this type of obedience[53] on the part of executive departments, they in turn would be actually operating and directing the various executive departments. . . ."[54]

Investigations can and do serve a useful purpose but they are obviously not the mechanism for "operating and directing the various executive departments". An objective observer in the United Kingdom, *The Economist,* agrees they have gone too far:

> "Since 1792, when a special committee was appointed to investigate the failure of an expedition against the Red Indians, members of Congress have always sought to combine the functions of Solon with those of Sherlock Holmes. The process of investigation into any aspect of national life, and of open hearings, is in fact an essential part of government in America. But even by the standards of a busy detective, the last Congress went too far."[55]

V. Certain Conclusions and Suggestions

A. *Conclusions*

With today's incredibly destructive weapons, usable in surprise attack, it is far more important than at any previous time in history for the President as a leader of the Free World to be wise, strong, and capable of swift action to preserve the national security.

53. The "type of obedience" to which Congressman Hoffman referred was the Committee's request that the Secretary of Defense and the Administrator of General Services furnish plans for surplus property disposal. H.R. Rep. No. 1196, 83d Cong., 2d Sess. (1953).

54. Supra note 53, at 73.

55. The Economist, February 12, 1955, p. 543, col. 1. The "last Congress" referred to was the 83d covering the years 1953 and 1954 during which Senator Joseph R. McCarthy's investigation of the Army's installation at Ft. Monmouth took place, including its handling of the Major Peress case, and during which the Senator in turn and Secretary of the Army Robert T. Stevens, along with their chief assistants involved in the matter, were investigated in prolonged televised hearings.

The bold use by the President of the powers vested in him by the Constitution to move quickly and at times along a painful course imposes upon him certain extra responsibilities which require him, if he is to be successful under this system of government, to keep the leaders of the Legislature thoroughly informed. Otherwise the Legislature through its separate and sometimes overlapping powers can and may check the Executive by failing to appropriate the necessary funds for defense or by failing to raise the needed military forces or by investigating the leaders of the defense establishment so harshly, exhaustively and noisily that their time for administering the military departments is damagingly curtailed and the faith of the people in the Executive impaired. On the basis of his experience in Washington the writer of this paper believes there are certain things both the Executive and Legislative Branches might do to make the United States system of Government more effective under the impact of the Separation of Powers Doctrine in time of crisis. When the President makes full and courageous use of his Constitutional powers and fully informs the Legislature through its leaders before, and not simultaneously with or after major actions, this system is fundamentally strengthened, not weakened, by investigations, delay and compromise occurring even during time of crisis.

B. *Suggestions*

The military budget dominates the economy of the Nation in time of crisis, and the Executive, charged by the Constitution with the responsibility of recommending such a budget to the Legislature, must continuously strive to improve the procedures it uses in its preparation. In this regard the constant interchange of ideas, information and criticism between the leaders of the Department of Defense and the three operating Departments of Army, Navy and Air Force and between the leaders of all four of these Departments and the Bureau of the Budget should be promoted in every way possible. Formal written assumptions and directions, even though later changed as conditions may warrant, ought to be furnished by the Defense Department, which is much more capable of taking into account political and economic factors, to the three operating Departments before and not, as is now the case, during or after their tentative budgets are prepared for any given year.

The outdated system of annual budgets results in stops and starts and unsound shifts in direction of vital policies. Even medium term planning is difficult. The system should be thoroughly overhauled through the joint and cooperative action of the Executive and the Legislature. Under its responsibility to recommend "measures" the Executive should offer legislation permitting military affairs to be handled on the basis of a three year program financed not by annual military budgets but by appropriations made every two years.

The legislature is empowered under the Constitution to appropriate money to "raise and support Armies" and is admonished that "no appropriation of Monies for that Use shall be for a longer Term than two Years"; there is, however, no express constitutional restriction on the period for which money appropriated to the Navy or the Air Force may be used; and as early as 1904, Solicitor-General Hoyt wrote in an opinion:

> "The wide and unlimited power to levy and collect taxes, etc., to 'provide for the common defense and general welfare' fully authorizes Congress to provide forts, magazines, arsenals, guns, ammunition, and military stores and supplies, without reference to whether or not the appropriations therefor extend over more than two years; and, in reading this and the other clauses referred to, it is impossible to suppose that the powers thus conferred without condition or restriction were, in fact, intended to be limited and qualified by the clause here considered.
>
> "I have no hesitation in reaching the conclusion that the appropriations forbidden by Article I, section 8, clause 12 of the Constitution are those only which are to raise and support armies in the strict sense of the word 'support', and that the inhibition of that clause does not extend to appropriations for the various means which an army may use in military operations, or which are

deemed necessary for the common defense, or which may be provided as a measure of precaution irrespective of the existence or magnitude of any present army."[56]

Not only would the substitution of a 2-year budgets for 1-year budgets make sound military planning more feasible but 2-year budgets would reduce the inefficiency and instability necessarily produced by the frequency of political decisions inherent in the passage of annual military appropriations.

In furnishing to the Legislature not only recommendations for military budgets but also other information pertaining to questions of defense and foreign relations, the Executive should utilize every resource to focus the issues sharply. The consequences of recommended appropriations and other measures as well as the consequences of anticipated Executive action must be made plain—plain, for instance, that it takes three years from the day money is appropriated before the first new medium bomber is produced, 24 months before the first new medium tank rolls off the assembly line, 18 months before the first new heavy ammunition is ready. It means that the relation of present funds and future production must be laid out clearly so that the Legislature will understand the full effect of this relationship on the ability of the United States to wage war.

The Legislature on its part should improve its procedures for investigations so that the same subject will not be investigated at the same time by two or more Committees in the same House. Should two or more Committees be vitally concerned in the same investigation, they should hold a joint hearing as was done to much advantage by the Senate Foreign Relations and Armed Services Committees in the 1951 hearings on the removal of General MacArthur from his commands in the Far East, and the hearings this year on the Resolution to support the Executive in defending with force, if necessary, any Chinese Communist attacks on the Formosa Straits Area.

---

56. 25 OPS ATT'Y GEN 105, at 108 (1904).

Because each House is jealous of its powers, traditions and prerogatives, Committees of the separate Houses investigating the same subject are not inclined to hold joint hearings. However, if they would do so on major issues or else agree to the assignment of the investigation to one House or the other, the operation of government would be substantially improved.

Finally, in the vital field of military appropriations constituting over two thirds of the Federal Budget in time of crisis the Legislature might concentrate much more than it does now on the overall strategy of the Executive and the Executive's estimate of the strategy of potentially hostile nations and assess the requests of the President for major elements of the United States forces in the light of such strategy. This would mean less attention to wool trousers and more to whether this Nation should maintain 15 or 25 or 50 divisions averaging 16,000 men against Russia's 175 divisions of 10,000 men. It would mean less attention to which type of body armor to use to protect the individual soldier and more to whether in this hydrogen bomb era of potential devastation localized wars are more likely than global wars. It would mean less attention on coffee grinders and more on whether threats of massive retaliation are more effective in deterring local war than small elements of Army troops stationed on the ground at many points of danger. Increased attention to these big questions might be a more fruitful use of the Legislature's time than nibbling away too much at some of the thousands of different items needed to equip the military forces today. The determination of what quantities of these items to buy would fall easily into place once Congress decided how many divisions to raise, how many ships to activate, and how many air groups to establish. This would not affect at all the power of Congress later to investigate the expenditure of the funds appropriated, and by such investigations Congress would, of course, continue to criticise any purchase of too many or too few of a particular item, any payment of too high a price for a piece of equipment, and any failure to meet production schedules. This would make it possible for the Legislature to focus upon the really major issues at the time of considering appropriations and then after the event to investigate thoroughly the Executive's use of the appropriated funds. Knowledge that investigations were sure to follow appropriations would persuade the Executive to exercise reasonable restraint in requesting military forces of a stated strength based on its estimate of the overall strategic situation and in fixing the kind and amount of equipment for each division, ship, and air group.

APPENDIX 1

DEVELOPMENT OF ARMY'S BUDGET FOR FISCAL YEAR 1956 COVERING 12 MONTHS BEGINNING JULY 1, 1955 AND ENDING JUNE 30, 1956

February 10, 1954—Army Program Directive published by Budget Division of Army Comptroller's Office.

March 15 to June 1, 1954—Detailed Program Planning Documents completed, published and distributed by Budget Division of Army Comptroller's Office on various dates during this period.

May—Fragmentary written policy directions received from Secretary of Defense.

May 28, 1954—Budget Directive issued by Budget Division of Army Comptroller's Office.

June and July 1954—General, Special, Administrative and Technical Staffs of Army prepared Budget estimates based on (1) the Army-developed assumptions and Program Directive, (2) the Program Planning Documents, (3) the Budget Directive, (4) the experience gained from preparing the execution plans for the Fiscal Year 1955 Budget beginning on July 1, 1954, (5) current operations of the Army and its financial reports, and (6) a statement and Budget Summary from each Field Commander setting forth his appraisal of what the Program Planning Documents would mean to the programs in his command in Fiscal Year 1956 and what changes they would require in his programs for the current Fiscal Year 1955.

July—Piecemeal written policy directions received from Secretary of Defense.

August 1, 1954 to September 2, 1954—Budget estimates prepared by Army staffs, reviewed by 30 Army Budget Program Directors.

August 5, 1954 to September 3, 1954—Budget estimates reviewed by Budget Division of Army Comptroller's Office.

August—Further written policy directions received from Secretary of Defense.

August 16, 1954 to September 11, 1954—Budget estimates reviewed by Budget Advisory Committee, composed of the Chief of the Budget Division (Chairman), the Deputy Assistant Chiefs of Staff, G-1, G-2 and G-3, the Deputy Chief of Staff for Logistics, the Chief of Staff's Special Assistant for Reserve Components, the Assistant for Planning and Coordination in the Office of the Deputy Chief of Staff for Plans and Research and a representative from the Chief of Army Field Forces. Representatives of the Under Secretary and Assistant Secretaries sit with the Budget Advisory Committee as associates.

September 23, 1954—Budget sent by Budget Advisory Committee to Army Chief of Staff.

October 1, 1954—Budget sent by Army Chief of Staff to Assistant Secretary of the Army (FM).

October 1, 1954—Budget sent by Assistant Secretary of the Army (FM) to Secretary of the Army.

October 4, 1954—Budget sent by Secretary of the Army to Secretary of Defense.

October 13 to October 19, 1954—Hearings on Budget held by representatives of Office of Assistant Secretary of Defense (Comptroller) and Bureau of the Budget.

October 19, 1954—Staff analysis of Budget received by Army from Assistant Secretary of Defense (Comptroller).

November and December, 1954—Assistant Secretary of Defense (Comptroller) and representatives of Bureau of the Budget made their recommendations respectively to Secretary of Defense and Director of Budget; Director of Budget conferred with President and received from him tentative decision on amount of entire Defense Budget (Army, Navy and Air Force); Secretary of Defense conferred with Deputy Secretary of Defense and Secretaries of Army, Navy and Air Force on size of entire Defense Budget as determined by President and decided upon size of Budget for each Military Department.

December 14, 1954—Army received from Secretary of Defense revised figure for its Budget and initiated preparation of its Budget in final form.

December 20, 1954—Secretary of Army sent Budget in final form to Secretary of Defense.

December 21, 1954—Secretary of Defense sent Army Budget, together with Budgets of other Military Departments, to Director of Budget.

December 1954 (Last Week)—Director of Budget delivered entire Defense Budget in final form to President.

January 17, 1955—President presented to Congress Defense Budget for Fiscal Year 1956.

APPENDIX 2

PRINCIPAL INVESTIGATIONS OF CONGRESSIONAL COMMITTEES HANDLED BY OFFICE OF ARMY DEPARTMENT COUNSELOR JULY 1950 - AUGUST 1952

1. *Senate Preparedness Investigating Subcommittee.*

(a) *Personnel Buildup and World War II Posts, Camps and Stations.* Acting for the Army to which the Secretary of Defense had delegated responsibility for the report, the Office aided in preparing forms and tables for use by all services in compiling the requested information.

(b) *Military Induction Centers (9th Report).* A detailed study of selected basic training centers, with particular attention to the processing of new inductees and enlistees, their training, medical care, housing, food, clothing and recreation. The Army's report commented on the Committee's criticism of reception procedures and equipment shortages and described Army efforts to comply with the Committee's recommendations.

(c) *Manpower Utilization at Induction Centers (26th Report).* A criticism of the policy of maintaining I-A standards for IV-F jobs and of using combat-fit men for tasks that could be performed by civilians, either men or women. Following a Department of Defense survey of test installations, the Army reported on its plans to eliminate spaces at its test installation and to utilize WAC and civilians to replace general service military personnel.

(d) *Dependent Housing and Rent Gouging (28th and 30th Reports).* The impetus for these investigations came from the Army itself as a result of its survey of housing conditions near Army posts. Remedial steps have involved action by the Armed services, other government agencies and individual communities involved.

(e) *Procurement Organization Functions and Procedures.* In

April 1951 the Subcommittee requested from the Secretary of Defense broad information on the whole procurement system, its structure and assigned responsibilities. This Office, after conferences with Committee Counsel, worked on the formats, coordinated staff reports and edited the voluminous Army report which was transmitted to the Committee in June 1951.

(f) *Paint Procurement.* An investigation of charges that the Army had ordered enough paint to provide a four-and-a-half year supply at such early delivery dates as to cause sharp price increases. The Army's report re-evaluated present requirements and also studied the basic methods for determining them.

(g) *Tungsten Shortage (27th Report).* An investigation of the prevailing tungsten shortage and the Army's progress in developing new economical processes for using tungsten carbide in the production of ammunition cores.

(h) *Standardization of Specifications for Inspections of Agricultural Commodities (32nd Report).* An investigation that cuts across the work of several executive departments and which resulted in a joint study by Agriculture, Army, the Munitions Board and General Services Administration.

(i) *Administrative Top Heaviness of the Armed Forces (33rd Report).* This office worked with the Assistant Secretary (M&RF) and the Office of the Secretary of Defense in studying and replying to the Committee's charges and in presenting reasons justifying the retention of high ranking officers in certain positions of major responsibility.

(j) *Interim Report on Defense Mobilization (35th Report).* A critical analysis of shortcomings in the mobilization program, aimed primarily at the Munitions Board and Civil Defense agencies. This Office assisted the Munitions Board in preparing comments on behalf of the Department of Defense.

(k) *Conditions at Eight Army Training Centers (36th Report).* A study of the training of servicemen and of manpower utilization at training centers visited by Committee professional staff members. The Army's comments prepared by this Office on the basis of staff reports, won high commendation from Senator Johnson as a "model from every point of view . . . . . a pattern for future action."

(l) *North African Bases (42nd Report).* An investigation of the efficiency of construction operations, accounting procedures, personnel recruiting and other aspects of construction which involved the Air Force, the Army Engineers and a civilian contractor. The Office participated in extensive hearings and assisted in developing corrective action through an inspection trip to Morocco by the Deputy Counselor for Procurement, a complete Inspector General investigation, and an inspection by an independent civilian expert.

(m) *Greenland Bases.* A similar investigation of the reasonableness of the cost of construction of air bases.

(n) *Hawaiian Training Centers.* A study of the desirability of sending inductees to Hawaii for basic training. Army action involved a partial shutdown of the bases and allowance of leave on completion of training for inductees trained in Hawaii.

(o) *Division Fire Power (40th Report).* A report which charged that the Army division has too much fat and is surpassed 10% in man for man fire power by the Russian division. Rebutting comments were prepared by this Office and forwarded to the Committee.

2. *House Committee on Expenditures in the Executive Departments.*

(a) *Government Operations Subcommittee.*

Procurement of Spare Parts at Ordnance Tank Automotive Center. An investigation involving hearings in Washington and Detroit concerning government purchasing policies and industry practices in the supply of spare parts for tank-automotive equipment. Corrective action involved modification of the administrative organization at the Detroit Ordnance Center and initiation of Federal Trade Commission action concerning restrictive selling practices.

Construction of Barracks. An investigation of the Army's need for construction of new barracks which directed criticism at the Army's adherence to the allotment of 60 square feet per man in mobilization housing as set by the Munitions Board. The Committee position was that 50 square feet would be sufficient. The Office assisted in the presentation of medical data supporting 60 square feet, or at least 55 square feet.

Construction of Warehouses. An investigation of the Army's efficiency in using existing storage facilities, the accuracy of figures it has used to justify space requests before the Bureau of the Budget and the basic procedures used in deriving these figures. Following an executive hearing, the Committee presented a list of critical questions prepared by its professional staff. This Office arranged a series of conferences attended by a representative of this Office, G-4 experts, and the Committee's professional staff members for discussion of the technical data involved in these questions.

Army Specifications. An investigation of the complexity and cost of contract specifications now used, as well as possible methods of simplifying specifications and making them more intelligible to prospective bidders.

General Watchdog Function. The Committee investigated honesty and efficiency of the Army's Procurement operations at several Army installations, such as Rossford Ordnance Depot, Benecia Arsenal and Sierra Ordnance Depot, as well as the same problems in connection with award and administration of particular contracts such as those with the Rulon Manufacturing Company and the Hunter Fan & Ventilating Company. The Office undertook to review pertinent Inspector General reports and, on the basis of such report, to prepare replies to the Committee's inquiries.

(b) *Intergovernmental Relations Subcommittee.*

Disposal of Surplus Property in Germany. An investigation of the justification for disposing of military surplus property through the German agency, STEG, and the possibility of salvaging some property for future use. The Office's work in this area involved not only liaison with the Committee, but also processing claims resulting from reacquisition of property formerly declared to be surplus, and conferring with State Department and GAO personnel about the possibility of using surplus property to supply NATO allies. In addition the Office submitted to the State Department Army comments on a proposed draft treaty between the U. S. and the German Federal Republic which is designed to resolve all pending claims.

Army—Air Force Separate Supply Systems. An investigation of the wisdom of the Secretary of Defense's action in creating a separate supply system for the Air Force in Europe instead of utilizing the single Army Supply system for both services.

Federal Supply Management. An analysis of the comparative merits of single, joint and coordinated methods of procurement and an evaluation of the desirability of establishing central Department of Defense control over military procurement. Partially as a result of this Committee's study, Congress enacted legislation requiring Secretary of Defense to promulgate uniform procurement regulations for the three services.

3. *House Armed Services Committee.*

The full Committee, while conducting few formal investigative hearings, presented a continuous flow of inquiries on varied aspects of Army operations including "hardware" production schedules; real estate purchases, releases, and transfers, ammunition supply in Korea; allocation of strategic materials; and training of anti-aircraft maintenance personnel at Aberdeen Proving Ground. In the spring of 1951 the Office assisted in the preparation of a major study of the organization of the Army procurement system, including descriptions of the mission of each Technical Service and an illustrative description of an individual procurement.

(a) *Special Committee on Tanks.* After hearings in August 1950, the Committee criticized low tank production which had resulted from attempts to economize, and recommended immediate expansion of tank producing facilities. Army action included appearances by General Collins, Secretary Pace and Under Secretary Alexander at hearings, as well as written reports which described research and development progress, contemplated future production schedules, experience in Korea and comparative merits of U.S. and Russian tanks.

(b) *Procurement subcommittee.*

Contractor Responsibility. Investigation of several procurements in which the Committee asserted that the Army had failed to ascertain properly the contractor's plant capacity and financial ability to perform. In the case of one such investigation involving Elvair Corporation of Jackson, Mississippi, which had been awarded a three million dollar Ordnance contract for canvas goods, a representative of this Office, together with a representative from the Under Secretary's office, conducted an on the spot investigation of the Committee's charges. As to the broad problems, the Office initiated a review of Army Procurement Procedure and helped establish more comprehensive pre-award surveys.

Morgantown Ordnance Works. A 75 million dollar ammonia plant built during World War II for production of materials needed for ammunition became unnecessary after the war, but was considered worthy of retention for use in case of another emergency. The Army's objective was to lease the plant to a commercial producer whose operations would keep the facilities in good condition and at the same time provide a return on the government's investment. After advertising for bids, re-advertising, conferring with Justice Department attorneys about anti-trust problems and with West Virginia Congressmen, the Army negotiated a lease with Mathieson Chemical Company.

Cataloguing and Standardization. In addition to hearings, the Committee activity included assembly of a "Chamber of Horrors" designed to substantiate the Committee's charges that the military departments had paid different prices for the same items. The Office assisted in an attempt to present to the Committee and the public (through the medium of an appearance by Assistant Secretary on television) the full story of the complexities of military procurement—the conflicting policies, the impact of special consideration for distressed areas, small business etc. The Committee work was instrumental in enactment of a statute creating a single cataloguing agency in the Department of Defense.

4. *Senate Post Office and Civil Service Committee.*

(a) *Subcommittee on Federal Manpower Policies.* Concerned with the basic problem of utilization of civilian personnel throughout the executive branch of the government, the Committee investigated several related problems involving Army manpower practices. These included a study of the practice of sending officers to civilian law schools, use of military personnel on staff agencies where civilians could be used, and the practice of contracting out with non-government personnel where civil service employees could be used.

5. *Senate Committee on Agriculture.*

In connection with the Committee's investigation of grain shortages and the practices of contractors with the Department of Agriculture, this Office submitted information on the leasing of buildings at Camp Crowder.

6. *House Committee on Education and Labor.*

The Office assisted witnesses and aided in the preparation of the report describing the Army's Troop Information and Education projects.

7. *House Select Committee to Investigate the Katyn Massacre.*

An investigation of circumstances surrounding the massacre of Polish officers in the Katyn Forest during World War II, with the purpose of assigning guilt for the killings. The Office assisted the Committee in gathering numerous documents and in providing witnesses for hearings.

8. *House Appropriations Committee.*

   (a) *Military Construction Subcommittee of Armed Service Subcommittee.* The Subcommittee held hearings and visited some twenty Army and twenty Air Force installations in its study of construction problems. The investigation considered the comparative merits of different types of construction, space allowances, charges of waste or fraud, etc.

COMMENT

MR. SHACKELFORD*

We now come to grips with the practical operation of one of the great doctrines of our Constitution: the separation of powers between the three great branches of govern-

---

* FRANCIS SHACKELFORD *of the Atlanta, Georgia Bar.* Mr. Shackelford was born in 1909, was graduated at Princeton in 1933 and took his degree in Law at the Harvard Law School in 1936. He was admitted to the Georgia Bar in 1936 and the Bar of New York in 1938 and has practiced law both in New York City and in Atlanta. He entered the Navy in 1942 as a Lieutenant (j.g.), saw duty in the South Pacific as an Air Combat Intelligence Officer, and was released to the Reserve as a Lieutenant Commander in 1946. He was the first lawyer to hold the post of Counselor of the Department of the Army, which he occupied during the Korean War in 1950-1952. He was Assistant Secretary of the Army in 1952-53.

ment. My paper is the product of the men who were called upon to establish and man the Office of Army Department Counselor from its inception one month after the beginning of the Korean war to the signing of the Korean armistice approximately three years later.

We have devoted our time and attention to the practical operation of the doctrine of separation of powers because we feel it is so important during this post-World War II period when our nation is in a position of world responsibility and world leadership along with our other great friends in the free world. We particularly feel and we particularly emphasize that the difficulties of handling the distribution of powers between the executive branch and the legislative branch in so far as the military establishment is concerned are much greater during a time of limited war, such as the Korean war or the Indo-China war, than during a global war. The problem during such a time is more difficult, because, unlike the situation during a global war when the entire economy is devoted to winning, we have the question of dividing our national economy with the hope of preserving it over a very long period, while, at the same time, using enough of that economy to turn out sufficient weapons to win the limited war and to keep it from enlarging into a world one. I emphasize this factor because it requires great judgment on the part of the Executive Department and on the part of Congress. Likewise, it challenges us to improve the procedures of government in any way that constructive minds can improve them in order to enable us to meet our heavy burden at a time of crisis.

We read the *Federalist* papers with great interest, because, of course, it was fundamental to the framers of the Constitution that the power to raise troops and the power to appropriate the funds for those troops were intended to be the Legislature's controlling powers in preventing the Executive from misusing the military establishment. Yet in the practical operation of the separation of powers doctrine during the Korean war we found that the Executive Department's recommendations were largely accepted by the Legislature with little challenge. To a great degree, the Legislature depended upon the recommendations which were made by the Executive Department, and changed them hardly at all. The reasons for this are set forth in our paper—the reasons which we think most pertinent. The same situation has generally prevailed during every crisis of this century.

During the first year of the Korean war, fiscal year 1951, a year in which we had not only the orginal military appropriation but three supplemental appropriations, the army requested approximately $19 billion. It was our opinion that if the Executive Department in its judgment had chosen to request $40 billion, and if it had chosen to nationalize not a handful of National Guard divisions, but the great majority of them, such a request by the President would have been granted by Congress. This places great responsibility on the Executive Department because it has that difficult problem of drawing the line which will permit a limited war to be handled effectively and victoriously, and at the same time to preserve the economy over a long pull.

While Congress generally accepted the recommendations of the Executive Department in budgetary matters during the Korean war, it at the same time stepped up greatly its investigations. It investigated everything from the color of uniforms to the strength of the Communist bloc in comparison to our own strength and that of the free world. It investigated the little and the big—but very, very often the quite little.

Almost as a complement to this factor of investigation, Congress seemed seized with the importance of post review. It at times spilled over, I think, into the area of the Executive Department's responsibilities, and into the powers distributed by the Constitution to the Executive.

We found, for example, that in the 1951 defense appropriation bill, Congress tacked on a phrase in regard to real estate transactions involving sums in excess of $25,000 that required the Armed Services Committee of each House to "come into agreement" with the Executive Department before these real estate transactions were consummated. While, of course, Constitutional questions are usually subject to serious argument on both sides, it is my opinion that Congress in this instance certainly invaded the field of the Executive. It is interesting to note that exactly the same kind of invasion took place a year ago, when, in a special Act concerning Camp Blanding near Jacksonville, Florida, Congress provided that before that camp could be disposed of, the terms of the agreement would have to be approved by the Appropriations Committee of each House. The President vetoed that Act. Later it was passed without such a provision. Again this year, just in mid-July, we saw the President, when he approved the Defense Act of 1956, make the statement that he would consider invalid one section which was added on the floor of Congress, Section 638, which again dealt with the requirement that the Appropriation Committees would both have to come into agreement with intended Executive action before it was taken. The Executive action in this case is the disposal of business-like activities carried on by the defense establishment, such as the rope-making factory in Boston, or laundries, or coffee-roasting facilities. The President said that he would consider Section 638 invalid—to use his expression—while he approved the Defense Act as a whole. Thus, in its enthusiasm for post review, the Legislature does, from time to time, move into the Executive field.

The Executive, on the other hand, impatient during crisis to get the job done, has moved at times into the Legislature's field. We know that it moved into the Legislature's field, not merely in spirit, but in violation of the Constitution, in the case of the seizure of the steel industries. In less clear cases from the constitutional standpoint, we saw the Executive in 1949, after Congress had added $736 million to the budget for increasing the Air Force from forty-eight groups to fifty-eight groups, impound those funds and refuse to use that money for that purpose. We have recently, only two months ago, seen a similar situation when Secretary Wilson impounded some $46 million which the legislature had appropriated, again through action on the floor at the last minute, for the purpose of increasing the Marine establishment from 193,000 to 215,000. These acts, while they may have some constitutional basis, violated the clear intention of Congress, which, of course, is empowered by the Constitution to raise and support troops.

We have dealt first with the practical operation of the doctrine of separation of powers during times of crisis in order that we may have a foundation on which to build our suggestions for improving certain of the procedures of the Legislative and Executive branches in military matters. We want these suggestions, which are intended only as a starting point, to excite your imagination and put your minds to work. The problem is an important one. It has developed that two of our ideas are in accord with later proposals of a similar nature made by the Hoover Task Force Committee studying the national budget. In the first of these we recommend that the Executive focus the main issues much more sharply for Congress. Insofar as Congress will permit, the Executive must not allow Congress to get bogged down in detail that concerns literally thousands upon thousands of individual items. In the second place, we urge that the major policy decisions of the Secretary of Defense be presented to the operating departments—army, navy, air force—not after these departments have prepared their annual budgets but before such budgets are started. For instance, the army budget for fiscal year 1957 is now in its final throes of preparation, but the army has not yet received the formal budgetary policy decisions from Defense. The same thing happened a year ago. It is true there is elbow-to-elbow contact at all levels of government, so that the management of each military operating department understands generally what Defense is thinking and what the Director of the Budget is thinking. But the formal policy decisions of which I am talking do not come in until the budget has been prepared in a tentative form in too many cases. Totally aside from the lost hours, this makes the preparation of a sound budget still more difficult.

We have also suggested two-year budgets instead of one-year budgets for the military establishment. At least by implication it would seem that the Hoover Task Force is in disagreement with us on this point because it has urged that each military budget should be prepared and enacted within a period of twelve months instead of in a period of seventeen to eighteen months as is now the case. But we believe that two-year budgets would permit a better perspective, would permit better planning, would permit better use of man power. Whether we continue with one-year budgets or shift to two-year budgets, supplementary budgets would be necessary in either case if something unexpected developed, such as a limited or global war.

Now, let us turn to the Legislature for a moment. During its committee hearings and floor debates, it frequently spends too much time on minor items and not enough on major ones. Of course, when the Executive on its part improves its presentation of military budgets, Congress will be in a still better position to separate the wheat from chaff. At a later date, Congress would and should be able to investigate anything and everything regarding the expenditure of the funds it has appropriated. But if during the appropriation stage it concentrates on the major issues—whether to have 135 air wings, or 200 air wings, or 75; 50 army divisions, or 18—sounder decisions should be made. The smaller items would fall into place.

Also we suggest that Congress in managing its own house organize the hearings of its numerous committees in such a fashion that the duplication which now takes place is reduced if not eliminated. We saw splendid examples of the elimination of duplications during the hearings concerning the recall of General MacArthur from his Far East commands, when joint hearings were held by the Senate Foreign

Affairs Committee and the Senate Armed Services Committee. The same thing happened earlier this year when these committees, acting jointly, considered the resolutions authorizing the President to use force if necessary in the Formosan straits. We think more of this is important.

These suggestions, again I say, are only starting points. Let them spark your minds and let us together work on this problem so that this nation of ours can do a better job in formulating its national policy and in formulating its military budgets which back up that policy. Let us improve our procedures of government so that both the Legislative and Executive branches may exercise more effectively the powers given to each by our Constitution.

MR. ASBILL*

The most significant thing about Mr. Shackelford's paper is its subject matter. It seems to me to strike a dissonant note, or perhaps I should characterize it as a variation on the main theme of this conference. And I think that theme, not only in yesterday's session, but throughout the conference, and in spite of Professor Hart's dislike of this fact, is government versus the individual—the protection of the individual against government.

Now, against this background, I think Mr. Shackelford's subject may appear prosaic and rather commonplace, for it deals not with individual liberties, but with the operation of two branches of government in a time of crisis in a relatively narrow field. I think, however, that the subject is a positive one, which I hope Professor Hart likes.

That this subject was chosen seems to me to be significant because it indicates that the phrase "government under law" embraces more than civil rights and civil liberties—that it implies the operation of the branches of our gov-

* MAC ASBILL, JR., *of the Washington, D. C., Bar.* Mr. Asbill was born in 1922 in Atlanta, Georgia. He took his A.B. at Princeton in 1942. During World War II he served as a Captain of Marines. In 1948 he received his LL.B. from the Harvard Law School. During the Korean war he was a member of the staff of the Department Counselor, Department of the Army. He is practicing law in Washington.

ernment, not as may be determined from time to time by individual public servants, but within the limits, though broad and flexible, of a predetermined system. I think perhaps it will serve, also, to highlight the significance of what I consider to be the main theme of the Conference.

In that connection, I would like to say that, in my opinion, not the least danger arising from the threats of infringement of civil liberties which have created so much fear in our land, is a danger that other aspects of Constitutional study, and the study of the function of our government, tend to be neglected and overlooked, and I hope this paper will serve the purpose of reminding us that there are such other aspects worthy of our careful consideration.

I think perhaps the paper could better be described as a study of the function of two branches of the government, rather than as a study of separation of powers, or a consideration of whether or not Congress in a crisis relinquishes its separate power over the appropriations. I say that because I think that even in a time of crisis it is reasonably clear that the doctrine of separation of powers in this area works fairly well. It works differently in a time of crisis, to be sure, but I think the differences are differences in degree and I expect they are differences which were probably contemplated at the time of the adoption of the Constitution. Now in a time of crisis it is undoubtedly true that the Congress relies more than at other times on the wisdom and knowledge of the Executive Department. I think there are several reasons for that. One is that in a time of crisis, such as an all-out war —though this is not true in the case of a prolonged semicrisis—the issue is more how much can be effectively spent than it is how big a slice of the national pie should we give to the military in order to get reasonable assurance against aggression and at the same time maintain the economic vitality of the nation. I think the answer to the first question lies more within the competence of the Executive than that of the second. Another reason is that the need for speed in time of crisis is urgent, or as Mr. Shackelford puts it, a crisis accentuates so much the necessity of command, and discourages so much the luxury of debate.

Other reasons are presented in the paper. I think these reasons are not only adequate reasons, but I think that the increased reliance on the Executive, which we see in a time of crisis, does no violence to the concept of separation of powers. It seems to me that this is not the situation which may exist in another area, where as Mr. O'Brian puts it in his paper, "as the result of . . . the operations of countless administrative agencies, there has come about a definite curtailment of the judicial power of review and . . . in the broad field of activity of these agencies the original theory of the separation of powers, and of checks and balances, has become largely mythical."

I do not want to oversimplify the problem. There have been mentioned two areas where the doctrine of separation of powers may be considered to be in danger. One is a refusal by the Executive to use appropriated funds. If this is considered a threat to the doctrine, I think the situation can be remedied by more explicit and mandatory language in the appropriation acts. In that connection it is interesting to note that in a recent authorization act concerning real estate, the Congress provided for a permanent Army hospital at Fort Jackson, South Carolina. This is an item which the Army did not request and it's an item which the Army doesn't want. However, the language of the act was, if not mandatory, close to mandatory, and I understand that the Department of the Army is just now considering whether or not it must build this hospital.

The other area, of course, is exemplified by legislation which requires prior approval by Congressional committees before military installations are disposed of. I share Mr. Shackelford's feeling that that is an unwarranted attempt by Congress to run the Executive Department, and I also share his feeling that the increased tempo of Congressional investigation in the time of crisis—investigation of expenditures by the Executive Department—is a healthy exercise of Congressional authority.

Now, just two points. One is that the responsibility of the Executive increases in a time of crisis. It increases as conditions arise which make it impractical for Congress to give detailed consideration to appropriation requests. I think then, more than ever—and this point deserves emphasis—it is the duty of the Executive to present to Congress in as clear and understandable a form as possible, and concretely, the results of approval or disapproval of requested appropriations.

My other point relates to the suggestions. We all realize that the system does not work perfectly—that it can be improved. Mr. Shackelford has suggested, I think, some methods of improvement which serve as an excellent starting point. One of these is that the Congress focus more on the basic assumptions and objectives—the size of the military forces, the types of weapons to be emphasized, and so forth—leaving the details to the Executive. I think that suggestion is valid, but it seems to me that its acceptability depends upon the Executive Department's first developing better methods of internal management, costing, and the determination of requirements. Because, it seems to me, that only when Congress can be sure that the assumptions and objectives which it approves will be translated accurately into dollars will it be willing to focus on the big picture and leave the details to the Executive.

PROFESSOR LEACH*

Following the pattern of Mr. Shackelford and Mr. Asbill, I will deal with the question of separation of powers as it relates to the defense budget. I must say that for this pur-

---

* WALTER BARTON LEACH, *Professor of Law, Harvard Law School.* Professor Leach was born in Boston in 1900, took his Arts degree at Harvard in 1921 and his degree in Laws at the Harvard Law School in 1924. After service as law secretary to Associate Justice Oliver Wendell Holmes, he was admitted to the Massachusetts bar in 1925 and engaged in the general practice of law in Boston until 1930. He has been on the Harvard Law School faculty since 1929 and became a Professor of Law in 1931. He was a Visiting Professor at Oxford in 1952. Professor Leach served as a Private of Infantry in the United States

pose I would have preferred that this captive audience include those in the Department of Defense and Congress who guide our military destinies, so that we, in purporting to talk to you, could have had the luxury of lecturing at them uninterruptedly.

In this field Mr. Shackelford and I are both shirt-sleeve workers, known in the Pentagon parlance as Indians as distinguished from Chiefs. But we have been working for different things. Frank Shackelford has been working for the perpetuation of the status, mission and size of the senior service that derives its origins from Washington. Bart Leach—occupying, if I may say so, a status of less dignity and quarters of less expense to the taxpayer—has been trying to help adapt the colossal military structure of this country to the age of Air Atomic Power and the function therein that can be played by the Third Service, the United States Air Force. Generally speaking, Shackelford's job has been to seek stability and Leach's to seek change. I suggest that the ability to make rapid change is not itself a selfish objective of the Air Force, but a national necessity in times when technological advance and the shifting sands of international politics demand that rapid change be capable of attainment.

Now this difference of background between Mr. Shackelford and me produces differences of view as to the relationship between executive and legislative power. He is pretty well satisfied with things as they are, and I am not.

We are talking of times of crisis, and by that we mean now. There's no use talking about big war, atomic war, and the relationship of the executive to the legislative therein. If the H-bomb starts falling around here, there will be precious little debate about the division of powers. There will be two kinds of authority: one will be a disciplined military

---

Army in 1918, and served as Major, Lieutenant Colonel and Colonel in the Army Air Forces during World War II. He is at the present time a Brigadier-General in the United States Air Force Reserve. He has been a Consultant to the United States Air Force since 1947. He has published extensively, both books and periodicals, on the law of property. In addition to his professorship in the Harvard Law School, Mr. Leach is Director of the Harvard Defense Studies Program, and conducts a seminar on "Defense Policy and Administration."

force acting under martial law; and the other will be groups of families who are banding themselves together under what amount to frontier conditions. The times of crisis which we are talking about, the crisis has existed, though somewhat inadequately recognized, from that date when the Soviet Union decided it was not going to allow the world to live at peace. Time of crisis in my definition, and I think it also is Frank's, means a situation in which we cannot return to the minimum, peace-time armed force structure of the 1920's and 1930's. So, let us see what we can do for this time of crisis which we are now in, observe what the operations of the executive and the legislative are, and try to conduct ourselves so that the holocaust can be avoided.

In my judgment the executive has far too much power and the Congress far too little in determining the big issues,— the size and nature of the military establishment. The power of Congress is very restricted indeed; generally it is a one-way power—a power to cut down, but not a power to build up.

The principal reason why Congress has a one-way power lies in the control of information by the executive and the rather supine acquiescence of Congress in permitting this control. This is a big area where improvement is possible. I will try to take examples from periods when both political parties have been represented in the White House, for this is a matter in which both parties have equally sinned, if sinning it is.

In the spring of 1950, three months before the Korean war, the usual hearings were held on the Defense Appropriations Bill for the coming fiscal year. A student of government would be well advised to read those hearings as a case-study in misinformation and misguidance to Congress. I have recently re-read them, repressing sensations of nausea with only moderate success. The Congress was told the following things:

First, it was told by the President and the Secretary of Defense that our forces had never been so strong in peacetime and that we were buying all the defense the nation could afford. (Now, don't tell me the President doesn't testify before Congress. He does, but he does it in such a way to create maximum effect with minimum opportunity for correction of error. He makes a speech, carefully timed; and then one of the senior civilians in the Department of Defense appears before a Congressional Committee and quotes him. This gets the President's words on the record and eliminates any chance of cross-examination.)

Second, there was testimony from a senior officer (and now we get down to details rather than generalization) that certain aircraft, which he designated by name and number, could defeat in combat any aircraft operated by any other power in the world. If he had not said that, there would have been some questions as to why new and expensive aircraft were not being produced. And this in turn would have broken up Mr. Louis Johnson's plans for keeping the total military budget down to $13 billion. Three months after that testimony was given the Korean war broke out, and it proved that these aircraft could not even engage in combat with the Mig-15, a Soviet fighter available in such quantity that it could be peddled to the Chinese. Congress, in a word, was grossly misinformed.

Third, three of the four members of the Joint Chiefs of Staff testified that the then level of national defense was adequate in view of all the circumstances, particularly the need for a sound national economy. This testimony to all intents and purposes was given on order of civilian superiors. I do not know how far what these officers said was actually written for them by civilian superiors because the one member who would not buy this idea was the Chief of Staff of the Air Force whom I advised, and who refused to participate. But I do know that the first thing General Bradley did when he retired, resigned as Chairman of the Joint Chiefs of Staff, was to repudiate his statement and declare that it is improper for a military officer to express himself on balances between defense needs and economic issues.

Now, lest it be thought that I, a Republican, am simply belaboring the Democrats, I will cite one recent incident from within my own party. The National Security Act requires periodic Reports from the Secretary of Defense to the Congress on the state of the Defense establishment. Heretofor it has been the practice to have a large report covering the previous fiscal year ready and printed by December—for example, a report for the period July 1, 1951 to June 30, 1952 ready six months later in December, 1952. This practice has very recently been changed. The Report for the year ending June 30, 1954 is dated March 31, 1955 and was not in fact printed and distributed until June, 1955. What this means is that the Congress simply doesn't get this information, required by statute, in time to do it any good. By the time this Report became available, with some very significant information, the major hearings on the current military budget had so far progressed that the Report was useless to the relevant committees.

Mind, I do not say that the late appearance of the now-current although utterly obsolete report of the Secretary was intentional, but I certainly do not assert that it was not. I say only that it happened. If Congress doesn't get the information it needs, it cannot do its job, whatever the reason.

Can Congress provide a counterbalance to an administration that is neglecting defense in order to make a record at balancing budgets and reducing taxes? You bet it can.

One example is the $882 million that were appropriated in 1948 for aircraft procurement over the President's disapproval. Those $882 million produced aircraft that were available for the Korean war. Another example was the program for an Air Force of 143 wings, legislated in 1951 and 1952. The executive branch of the government which always seems to move slowly in these things, had adopted an inadequate program of 95 wings. Lifting this by over 50 per cent was the doing of the Congress, especially of Senator Henry Cabot Lodge and Chairman Carl Vinson of the House Armed Services Committee—a fine example of bicameral by-partisan cooperation in the public interest. This was not welcomed in executive circles. But it was made possible by the fact that Lodge and Vinson got the information they needed, not always through official channels.

The result of this legislative interposition was a program that has demonstrated itself as the path of wisdom. May there by much more of the same!

DISCUSSION

*Professor Gardner**: I heard it suggested in this discussion that there was something incongruous about injecting this morning's session into a discussion of government under law. I feel sure that everyone would agree that that is not so. I have had occasion to give a good deal of thought to problems of civil liberties in the last few years, and it's abundantly evident that the novelty of those problems arises essentially from the fact that a far larger proportion of the people are dependent on government disbursements than they used to be when I studied law, and the fact that they are dependent for their livelihood on government disbursements makes a consideration of the methods by which government disbursements are handled of the very essence of civil liberty itself.

Secondly I thought I noted a suggestion that there was some lack of connection between this subject and what Professor Hart said. It seems to me that the subject is extremely closely connected. He suggested that the function of government was to provide means by which free men could cooperate effectively, and that is exactly what we are discussing now.

The third thing I am going to suggest—I am going to refer to the popular press for my information, as I have no other—raises what seems to me an interesting question about the organization, both of our own policy, and that of Great Britain. I have seen it stated that nobody but the Cabinet in Great Britain is authorized to initiate proposals of spending money, and therefore that the action of our President here in

---

* George Knowles Gardner, *Professor of Law, Harvard Law School.*

refusing to spend certain funds was quite out in line with that practice; it has been suggested just now that this is wrong—that the initiative ought to come from the elected body. It may be that I am quite wrong in my information about the British practice, but as I have read what I here state, set forth in such a way as to make me believe it; and since I am in the presence of men who can correct me if I am wrong, I thought it might be worthwhile to bring that matter into the discussion at this point.

*Professor Huntington**: I was delighted to hear my friend Bart Leach come to a defense of Congress, because it seems to me that Congress has been rather getting it on the neck, so to speak, in the previous discussion. The general theme of the criticism of Congress seems to be two-fold; first of all that Congress *should not* get involved in matters of administrative detail; and secondly, that it *does not* give adequate consideration to major issues of public policy. I think there is a reverse side of the case to be presented on both points. It seems to me that the separation of powers really in a sense, has two aspects. It involves, first of all, a separation of function, in that Congress presumably is a legislative, policy-making body, and the executive is the administrative organ of the government. But it also involves a separation of power in a sense that Congress and the President derive their authority from separate clauses of the Constitution and from separate electorates. And this means that they are inherently rivals, and the separation of powers in this sense means that each branch of government has to go into the field of the authority which is assigned by the Constitution to the other branches, in terms of function. In other words, the separation of powers, the situation of natural rivalry, leads the branches to disregard the theoretical and legal and constitutional separation of function. We see this all the time, as the speakers pointed out, in that the executive makes very important ma-

---

* SAMUEL PHILLIPS HUNTINGTON, *Assistant Professor of Government, Harvard University.*

Professor Samuel H. Beer comments on the paper given by John Lord O'Brian.

Professor Charles Fairman answers Professor Leach.

Professor Herbert Wechsler discusses the paper given by Father Snee.

Left to right: Mr. Justice Frankfurter, Master of the Rolls Sir Raymond Evershed, and Dean Griswold.

Professor Benjamin Kaplan.

Sir Owen Dixon (left) and Dean Griswold.

Professor George K. Gardner comments from the floor.

jor policy decisions. It seems to me that it is quite natural and quite inevitable, and in many respects quite desirable, for Congress also to get involved in the administrative process. And it seems to me, in particular, that this is something which cannot be avoided as long as you have two entirely separate branches of government, with no real control by one over the other.

And then secondly, frequently we will play down too much the extent to which Congress gives consideration to major issues of public policy. Specifically with reference to the defense budget, for instance. I don't know what went on in the Department of Defense, in the outer ring of the Pentagon, in 1953 and 1954, but I get the feeling from everything I have read about it that very likely the major policy issue involving a cut of $5 billion in the Air Force in the '54 budget which was considered in the spring of '53, and the new look budget of fiscal '55 received at least as adequate consideration—the major policy issues, the major policy assumptions —in the hearings and discussion on the floor of the Senate and before the Senate Appropriations Committee, as it received in the Pentagon. I would say this was particularly true in the case of the '54 budget. I think you can go back (I'm a Democrat, but I won't just criticize the Republicans) and you can say that the same thing also took place in some of the Truman administration budgets.

Mr. Braucher: I think it's fair that we should give Mr. Shackelford a chance to comment on those who have commented on his work, and I think we'll close out this half of the discussion by giving him that opportunity. Anyone who is suffering from an undelivered comment, I think may be able to work it in after Professor Fairman's talk.

Mr. Shackelford: We devoutly hope that the sufferers will deliver their undelivered comment because that is very important from the standpoint of the approach we have tried to take—namely, to improve so far as the future is concerned.

I think Professor Leach and Mr. Asbill and really the speakers from the floor, in varying degrees, including myself, are all in accord. On this focus point—I want to come back to it—I want to put it into two stages. During the appropriation stage, when the budget is being considered by the appropriations committees of Congress and later debated on the floor, during that stage is when I think it is so important that the executive present the budget to the legislature and to its committees in such a fashion that it can grasp and focus upon it the really major issues of the day so far as defense is concerned. After the budget is passed, then there may well be and should be a field day of investigation of the expenditure of the funds which have been appropriated, and I think that investigation should include everything, from the small and the human, to the largest. But I think those phases are important.

Now, for the first phase. It is my opinion that when the executive department presents its positions on a major policy issue and there is a very strong minority viewpoint, as there was in the case of the Air Force before the Korean war in 1949 and '50 upon which Professor Leach has commented, I think the distilled position of the executive department should be presented as the executive department's position to the legislative branch. At the same time, I feel that it should be a matter of routine, which it very definitely now is not, for such a Chief of Staff as General Vandenberg, who then held that post, to present his minority viewpoint, which is so important to the issue at hand. For the same reason, coming down to today, when we have this great discussion of nuclear power versus the military establishments and the sizes of each, and we have General Ridgeway's viewpoint on one hand and we have the executive department's viewpoint on the other hand, there again I think the executive department should state its position and the reasons for it. But I think that that minority on a major issue of that kind should very definitely be given an opportunity and should be called upon to speak out on the issue on which it feels so strongly is of such importance to the country. As it is today, that issue has to be dug out of the Chief of Staff or the Secretary of the operating department which has a minority viewpoint. But if we do these things, and if we sharpen that focus, the legislature can and will exercise its separate powers, which are great, to the advantage of our country during these times when our responsibilities are so heavy.

Government Under Law in Time of Crisis

CHARLES FAIRMAN *

I. INTRODUCTION

The crisis that we have most to fear is, of course, a war with the Soviet Union and its allies. Lesser crises—as in an economic depression, or by reason of a stoppage of essential production—lesser crises such as these we have met before and, somehow, could meet again. We should, I suggest, concern ourselves with the great, unprecedented, crisis that would come with a sudden atomic attack upon our domestic territory.

Let us start with the assurance that ours is a Constitution "intended to endure for ages to come, and, consequently, to be adapted to the various crises of human affairs"—that in the execution of the great powers on which the welfare of the nation depends we are not hampered by immutable rules, that the choice of means is confined within no narrow limits.[1] Let us confide in the familiar proposition that the power to wage war "is a power to wage war successfully and thus it permits the harnessing of the entire energies of the people in a supreme cooperative effort to preserve the nation."[2] Let us assume that whatever, on a fair view, needs to be done *can* be done, and proceed to consider what is best to do and how best to do it.

---

* For biographical note see page 280.

---

1. Marshall, C. J., in McCulloch v. Maryland, 17 U.S. (4 Wheat.) 316, 415 (1819).

2. Hughes, C. J., in Home Building and Loan Assn. v. Blaisdell, 290 U.S. 398, 426 (1934). Supporting this point of view is Hirabayashi v. United States, 320 U.S. 81, 93 (1943).

The war that we apprehend as possible is an atomic war, striking into the body of the country and leaving death and chaos perhaps beyond our power to imagine. Let it be said briefly that current planning assumptions of the Federal Civil Defense Administration contemplate that the enemy would launch an initial air-borne attack with sufficient nuclear weapons to hit all critical target areas—(there are 92 principal cities within the "critical target areas");—that a large proportion of the bombs, perhaps 70%, would be delivered on the target;—that there would be warning time of at least one hour;—that the damage inflicted on each city hit would substantially destroy administrative, industrial and commercial facilities. The population of the critical target areas is over 67,000,000. How many would be killed, how many injured? That would depend upon the size of the bomb and where people were when it fell. Instant dispersal, rather than taking shelter, has been made the principal reliance for survival. One should think of a significant fraction, perhaps even a major fraction of 67,000,000 as the number of fatalities.

The effect of an atomic attack would be so unprecedented that we must take a fresh view of our problem of war-time government—a new view inspired by all the pertinent wisdom of the past, but not imprisoned within its precedents. *Solutions* are not to be found in a rehash of cases in the Reports; respect for the spirit of our law, however, is not only a duty but a necessity if we are to plan well.

Let us not hesitate from fear of being thought to be trouble-borrowers—or of being thought to be war-mongers. We do know that the power to launch a war against us exists, and that the holders of that power are sinister men. Thinking about the perils of such a conflict will not lead us one inch closer to it; ignoring the possibility will not avert it—the contrary is more likely. There is no need to debate how probable is another war. Enough that it appears a possibility. If we are spared that ordeal, still what we shall have done to plan our survival will have been a prudent investment. We insure against various unpleasant casualties, and do not feel regretful when at the end of the term the contract has not been invoked. We have had the solid comfort of knowing that we have prepared.

More than that: many of the adaptations that would appear needful in putting our house in order would be found to include independent advantages. In most of the States, the Civil Defense system may now be used in meeting natural disasters. This is useful in coping with those evil visitations, and also in enabling Civil Defense to learn through practice. The dispersion of industry from target areas can be made to yield more wholesome suburban living. Better highways would serve many purposes. Training for the maximum use of our human resources may improve the skill and increase the opportunities of workers, a gain to them and to the nation. Adaptation of our judicial systems to the exigencies of a war would make them more elastic and responsive to existing needs. Measures such as these would pay large incidental benefits, even though the casualty never occurred.

Still more: insofar as we really make adequate preparations, we have created a strong *deterrent* to war. This aspect is familiar in maintaining large Armed Forces in being: —we trust that by so doing we may avert a war. So too, surely, with shoring up our government and administration, our industry and finance, our community life: in preparing to withstand a blow, we make it less attractive to strike. Civil Defense has never been presented in *that* aspect. So long as one is urged merely to prepare for one's own survival in an event one never looks squarely in the face, self-consciousness and disbelief discourage compliance. If we could be brought to realize that there are things we can do now in every community actually to deter a war by making our internal strength notoriously adequate—*that* appeal should inspire willing exertions.

Indeed it is rather a matter for shame that we take so little thought for the morrow. More than mere individual self-preservation is at stake. If we believe that the Western Civilization we know is worth maintaining, if we are devoted to the conceptions of law and of justice as they have been refined in the course of our history, then surely we should be moved to make them secure. Not long ago I sat in a committee with serious and responsible men—insurance executives, men of industry, of commerce, of banking, and the like—where it was seriously urged that the great concern should be to assure the preservation of enough human stuff to regenerate the nation, after an atomic attack.

II. Presidential Leadership

Consider the face of our country as the sun rose on the morrow of an atomic attack: death, destruction, a shattering of the familiar threads of daily living. People's thoughts, I suggest, would turn toward three foci—loved ones and self, the immediate family, in concern for personal safety; their Maker and Preserver, in gratitude for life and in need of comfort; the United States Government, for direction as to what should be done. Would we not all ask, What word do we have from the Government—what does the President have to say—what are we told to do? I suggest that, with one accord, we would look to the national Government for leadership. It represents our strongest unity. We have made it the bearer of the heaviest responsibility.

The quality of the national leadership must be our major concern.

We think at once of the President, and of succession to that office. One's first reaction is that nominations for the Vice Presidency ought never to be handled with the casual unconcern that has, more often than not, marked that concluding episode of our national party conventions. This might, some evil day, prove our undoing.

Succession to the presidential office, absent both President and Vice President, is governed by the Constitution and by statute.[3] Let us look away from what has been provided to consider, what ideally should be done. Doubtless it is very well to enact, as the statute now does, that the Speaker shall succeed, and failing a Speaker, then the President pro tem. of the Senate. But should that replacement continue to the end of the normal term—or only until, in some lawful manner, an individual may be elected to the Presidency? A Speaker would certainly be experienced in politics, and distinguished as a leader. But of necessity he would be inexperienced in executive direction. We know that the Speakership has not been a station from which presidential nominees have been chosen. We know that the Presidency—most of all in time of war—calls for skill in directing tremendous administrative undertakings, capacity to deal with global strategy, and, above all, the quality of inspiring the nation's confidence. One who has been accumulating seniority in one of the Houses of Congress cannot have stood trying watches at the wheel. I suggest, then, that to make the Speaker the successor for the remainder of a term involves considerable hazard; that it would be wiser to provide simply that he act until a new President had been chosen.

We must concede at once that it would be utterly out of the question to have a special national election in the event that the President and Vice President became casualties. Our best hope, I suggest, is that the Congress, promptly convened, and sitting in joint session, choose a new President. There would be no other body in being that could so well represent the national interest, and it seems unwise to improvise. Perhaps the Speaker, already acting in the presidential

3. U. S. CONST. art. II, §1, cl. 6, and as to predecease or failure to qualify at the beginning of a term, U.S. CONST. amend. XX. The statute is 3 U.S.C. §19 (1948), which embodies the Act of July 18, 1947, 61 STAT. 380 as amended (in connection with creating the office of Secretary of Defense) by §311 of the National Security Act of July 26, 1947, 61 STAT. 509. H.R. REP. No. 817, 80th Cong. 1st Sess., reporting the bill that became the Act of July 18, 1947, includes a letter from the Acting Attorney General analysing the measure and tracing the movement for that legislation initiated by President Truman's message to Congress, dated June 19, 1945, 91 CONG. REC. 6280, recommending that the order of succession be amended to insert the Speaker and then the President pro tem. of the Senate, ahead of the Heads of Departments.

office, would be continued. Certainly the Congress would know his qualities. It might well be that a Governor or former Governor, or some other person with large executive experience, would seem the one best qualified to carry on.

If this solution is accepted—or some other solution involving a selection at large after the event—we come to the question whether it is attainable within the present terms of the fundamental law. The Constitution runs thus:

> the Congress may by Law provide for the Case of Removal, Death, Resignation or Inability, both of the President and Vice President, declaring what Officer shall then act as President, and such Officer shall act accordingly, until the Disability be removed, or a President shall be elected.[4]

Evidently this contemplates that a statute is to be enacted before the event, designating the office whose incumbent shall act as President. This is different from a power to choose a person at large, after the event.[5] Seemingly an Amendment would be needed. If this were a contingency that might arise only after an atomic attack and the passing of two lives, resort might be had simply to a statute—on the theory that for so extreme an eventuality a very free reading of the Constitution would be warranted. But the contingency might arise even in normal times, and such an Amendment would, it is believed, stand on its own merits.

Another eventuality: suppose that, by reason of the confusion and dislocation following an attack, it was impracticable to conduct national elections at the appointed time. This might be a case of obvious impossibility;—or the impracticability might appear only by the exercise of judgment. Perhaps it would be physically possible to have an election of a kind, yet impossible to attain a result that would have

---

4. Art. II, §1, cl. 6.

5. Yet it is significant that the first statute on Presidential Seccession—that of March 1, 1792, 1 Stat. 239, enacted by the Second Congress, whose members were very close to the Constitution's inception—made the line to run to the President pro tem. of the Senate and next to the Speaker, and provided that, if both of those offices were vacant, Electors should be appointed to elect a new President and Vice President. Here was a statute whose operation would have been quite inconsistent with the Constitution's synchronizing of Presidential and Congressional terms. It remained the law until 1886.

moral validity as a representative national expression. (Consider, too, a corresponding impracticability in State and local government.) Should the Constitution be amended to provide that in such an event—to be determined, say, by statute, or by joint resolution—incumbents should hold over until the impediment had been found to be at an end? I suggest, no—that the matter be left to be worked out, if the case ever arose, in the light of the moment. It seems reasonable to expect that wisdom born of the occasion would be sufficient to the need.

The foregoing discussion has run, unavoidably, into details of drafting. The essential need, however, is not mere tinkering with the machinery; it is a matter of finding the best assurance of great executive leadership. In a squad or a platoon, the natural leader may take over, spontaneously, at the moment of need, without regard to stripes and shoulder bars; but succession to the command of large units must follow the rigid rule of rank. As we now are, the Presidency descends in predetermined order—and it might fall on one who could not give strong leadership. Here is a matter that merits fresh thinking.

III. The Congress

A strong Congress is essential to maintaining the national authority.

Congress, we may apprehend, would have lost many of its members. How are the vacancies to be filled? This is not simply a matter of maintaining a quorum, a body legally competent to enact laws. It is a matter of maintaining, with adequate moral and spiritual authority, the nation's great representative body. The Constitution provides that "When vacancies happen in the representation from any State"—in the House or in the Senate—"the executive authority . . . shall issue writs of election to fill such vacancies."[6] As to vacancies

6. Art. I, §2, cl. 4; amend. XVII, cl. 2.

in the Senate, but not in the House, it adds: "That the legislature of any State may empower the executive thereof to make temporary appointments until the people fill the vacancies by election as the legislature may direct." We would need, throughout the emergency, to keep both branches of Congress renewed. It is fair to suppose that special elections could not be held—not with any promptness. It follows that provision should be made for "temporary appointments" to the House, as has been made for the Senate. On the point that elections might be impracticable, recall what vast movements of population might have taken place—the evacuation of the regular inhabitants, and perhaps the moving in of war workers. The notion of an electoral district would have lost its meaning. The individuals who once composed a Representative's constituency might now be scattered. *Representation* would have a new significance—less particular and parochial. Recall, by the way, in considering the problem of war-time renewal, that the Constitution requires only that a Representative be "an inhabitant of the State"—not necessarily of the district—wherein he is chosen. It seems reasonable to say that the Governor should have authority to fill vacancies in the House as he now does in the Senate: but every suggested expedient for renewal should be studied with care.

One might think that, whatever were done in renewing the Congress, it would still be inadequate to represent the totality of the nation in time of war. One might think that Congress reflects only the aspect of *politics,* whereas in time of total war the Government should somehow embody every significant aspect of the national effort—the economic and the social as well as "politics." One might think that Congress would prove too slender a reed—that a sturdier support could be found by uniting leaders from every major branch of the national striving, in some extraordinary body comprising our very best. Any such thinking should, I believe, be rejected. We should do nothing to discredit or minimize an established, familiar and responsible institution—the Congress. Rather, we should lean heavily upon it, and thereby emphasize its responsibility as the great central organ of our democracy. Speaking generally, it would be unwise to shift to any untested contrivance when we have at hand something that can be made to serve. Moreover, it is a merit of the Congress that it does express *politics,* that it cuts across functional lines, that it is set up to reflect us as citizens rather than as workers or owners, producers or consumers. It is greatly to be hoped that in time of total war the members would take a *more* inclusive, a *less* selective view of the national interest. Functional representation would have an important place in the direction of the war effort: as in the administration of price controls, of industrial procurement, of utilizing manpower, of agricultural production, it would be essential to *consult* with spokesmen from the various sectors of the economy. To represent the all-embracing national fellowship, however, we should look to the Congress.

Turning for a moment to a matter of lesser magnitude, it is to be noted that Congress has failed to provide facilities in a safe place to which it might repair if Washington were bombed. To do so would reduce by one the items of our unpreparedness. Moreover, Congress would thereby set an excellent example for the country.

IV. Federal-State Relationships in Civil Defense

Now we come to a really tough problem, one that involves the devising of something new in our federal system.

We need to establish means whereby the authority of the United States, transmitted to the State and local governments, may produce concerted action so far as may be needed in the national defense.

It was a classic statement in *Ex parte Siebold*[7] where Justice Bradley said for the Court,

> We hold it to be an incontrovertible principle, that the government of the United States may, by means of physical force, exercised through its official agents, execute on every foot of American soil the powers and functions that belong to it. . .

We know that, as Chief Justice White said for the Court in *Northern Pacific Ry. Co. v. North Dakota ex rel. Langer,*[8]

> The complete and undivided character of the war power of the United States is not disputable. . .

Whenever an exercise of this power reaches into a sphere where otherwise the State alone would act, "that which is paramount necessarily controls that which is subordinate."[9] The *Shreveport* Case,[10] wherein Justice Hughes wrote a great opinion for the Court, stands for the proposition that wherever federal and State concerns are so related that the government of the one involves the control of the other, it is Congress, and not the State, that is entitled to prescribe the final and dominant rule.[11]

The United States Government, being legally self-sufficient, may pursue its purposes by its own means and through its own agencies. That is its usual mode of action. Occasions when it has required that State agencies themselves carry out the federal purpose—save as expressly contemplated in the Constitution—are not numerous. We know that Congress may cast upon the State courts a duty to enforce even penal statutes of Congress: the Supremacy Clause was thought to point directly to that conclusion.[12] In Selective

7. 100 U.S. 371, 395 (1880). The opinion contains a very instructive discussion of paramount national authority as it touches the functioning of the several States.

8. 250 U.S. 135, 149 (1919).

9. *Id.* at 150.

10. Houston, East and West Texas Ry. Co. v. United States, 234 U.S. 342 (1914).

11. *Id.* Adapting language at 351-52.

12. Testa v. Katt, 330 U.S. 386 (1947). And see the remarks of Justice Frankfurter in Brown v. Allen, 344 U.S. 443, 488 at 499 (1953). Congress, if it considers that a federal purpose will be served by a requirement of full disclosure coupled with complete immunity from prosecution, may bar the use even in a State court of testimony thus obtained. Adams v. Maryland, 347 U.S. 179 (1954).

Service legislation the Congress imposed upon State officers a duty to render such services in that behalf as the President might require of them.[13] Seemingly no significant problem of Federal-State relations arose in the administration of Selective Service. What had to be done—the raising of Armed Forces—was clear and imperative, and there was no perceptible adversity of interest. Federal authority was not intruding upon any field that normally the State controlled. We encounter a novel and challenging task, however, when we consider that the Federal Government—which alone directs the war power and bears responsibility for the national defense—that this Federal Government, in order to bring us through, would have to act directly upon and through the State governments. We recall that the war power is "complete and undivided," but we ask, How in practice can this be done?

Examination will make clear, I believe, that the Federal Government must, if war came, act directly upon and through the State Governments. Its efforts must run down to the locality, providing relief and rehabilitation, leadership and direction. It could not do all this through agents exclusively its own—the thought is fantastic! In practice it would have to rely heavily upon agencies of State and municipal administration. Federal authority would have to be geared directly to the States and their subordinate units, in order that impulses imparted at the center would be conveyed efficiently throughout the country. Some looser type of transmission may suffice for less urgent matters. Control by means of strings attached to a grant in aid may suffice for road-building, school lunch programs, and so on. For

13. This was by Sec. 6 of the Act of May 18, 1917, 40 Stat. 76, 80, which authorized the President to utilize the service of any and all officers of the States or their subdivisions, and declared that persons designated "are hereby required to perform such duty as the President shall order or direct . . . "

The Act of September 16, 1940, in its §10, 54 Stat. 885, 893, provided for the appointment of local selective service boards on "recommendations made by the respective Governors . . . , " and authorized the President "to accept the services of all officers and agents of the several States . . . and subdivisions thereof . . . " Sec. 10 of the Act of June 24, 1948, 62 Stat. 604, 618, provided for the appointment upon the recommendation of the Governor of a State director "who shall represent the governor . . . ", and of local boards consisting of persons likewise recommended. The President was authorized to accept the services of officers and agents of State and local governments.

the effective exercise of the war power, however, the United States would have to be able to direct State and local agencies in all that was "necessary and proper" to that end. Examination will show that this proposition is true.

Civil Defense is the best place to start.

This new function already has a long story,[14] which merits summary for the useful lessons of experience. During World War II there was an Office of Civilian Defense, which in addition to its proper functions was called upon to sponsor bond drives, victory gardens, and other extraneous activities. After the War, in late November 1946, the War Department convened a Civil Defense Board to determine what its policies should be as to allocation within the Government of responsibilities for civil defense.[15] This resulted in the so-called Bull Board Report, released on February 15, 1948.[16] The board observed that "it is apparent, in retrospect, that the civil defense organization, in spite of the noteworthy patriotic response of the civilian volunteers, was inadequate to cope with a heavy attack."[17] Looking to the future, it pointed to the fundamental principle of self-help: every individual

---

14. Chronology prior to the Federal Civil Defense Act is set out in H.R. REP. No. 3209, 81st Cong. 2d sess., reporting that measure.

15. W. D. Memo 400-5-5 of Nov. 25, 1946, as amended by Changes No. 1, dated Dec. 30, 1946.

16. A STUDY OF CIVIL DEFENSE. A pamphlet of 24 pages, released by the Office of the Secretary of Defense. (That Office had been created by the National Security Act of 1947.)

17. P.8. The report went on to set out these findings:

Analysis points out the following in connection with activities of civil defense in this country:

a. OCD accomplished a volunteer mobilization of great magnitude, but its capabilities were untried by even a minor enemy attack.
b. Operation at local levels by augmenting existing means, was sound.
c. Regional control, sound in principle, was weak in operation due to lack of authority.
d. No clear delineation of civil defense responsibilities existed.
e. Activities in conflict with the operation of the protective services diverted effort from the primary mission of civil defense.
f. There was no advanced planning. Hasty organization became necessary.
g. There was little experienced leadership.
h. Adherence to the principle of States' rights and traditional municipal individuality blocked standardization of plans in certain instances.
i. Due to the lack of authority in the Office of Civilian Defense, State and local leaders frequently looked to the Army for command decisions.
j. Mutual aid as planned and arranged by agreements, had no backing by Federal legislation and seldom by State legislation. It is doubtful that mutual aid would have functioned under heavy and repeated air attack. Pp. 8-9.

must learn to protect to the maximum himself, his home and family, before calling for aid. The populace must learn to work in small groups under leaders. Every echelon of government must organize, train and equip for civil defense within its boundaries.

> The Federal Government must provide guidance and coordination in planning, organizing, and training for civil defense. It should direct only as necessary to insure uniform plans and action. It should employ mobile reserves, effect mutual aid activities between States and, when required, assume control.[18]

General Bull's board was clear that Civil Defense should be made a function of civil government, *not* of the Armed Forces:

> The armed forces' primary mission requires devotion of their efforts to active measures, both offensive and defensive. They must avoid diversion of effort and means to civil defense, except to meet Federal requirements and dire emergencies, beyond the capabilities of the states when the national interest is involved.[19]

Chief responsibility, the board found, should be borne by the States:

> The state government must accept the responsibility of civil defense for its people and communities. Again the problems requiring the exercise of normal functions and responsibilities of state government and utilizing largely the existing organization for their solution. Federal civil defense agencies advise, assist and secure necessary uniformity, and must have the power to direct State action when the emergency is interstate or vitally affects Federal interests.[20]

There should be "some single Federal agency" charged with making "adequate and timely plans,"[21] "an agency to determine policy at the highest level." The report continued,

> How best to organize the Federal operating agency essential to fill the gap between a national policy board and the States was more difficult to determine.[22]

18. Pp. 9-10.
19. P. 10.
20. P. 12.
21. P. 11.
22. P. 12.

Among various possibilities, its recommendation was for a single permanent civilian agency, separate from Army, Navy and Air Force, within the Department of Defense, under a civilian head reporting directly to the Secretary of Defense.[23] This military board was very clear that:

> The major civil defense problems are not appropriately military responsibilities. Such problems are civilian in nature and should be solved by civilian organization.[24]

Moving promptly to get on with the business, Mr. Forrestal, Secretary of Defense, by a directive of March 27, 1948, created the Office of Civil Defense Planning, in order to work out "an integrated national program of civil defense."[25] The late Russell J. Hopley, president of the Northwestern Bell Telephone Company, was made the director. He rendered a notable report, after a study executed with notable promptness, on October 1, 1948. He proposed

> A National Office of Civil Defense, with a small but capable staff to furnish leadership and guidance in organizing and training the people for civil defense tasks.
>
> Basic operational responsibility to be placed in States and communities, but with mutual assistance plans and mobile supporting facilities for aid in emergencies. . .[26]

Where should the Federal agency be fitted into the governmental structure?

> There are but a few places within the Executive Branch where this office could be properly placed. The two most appropriate of these would be: one, reporting directly to the President; the other, reporting directly to the Secretary of Defense. Since a very large part of the civil defense program would require continuous coordination with all agencies responsible to the Secretary of Defense, it seems reasonable that the latter would be preferable.[27]

As will be seen in a moment, the Executive and the Congress

---

23. P. 22.
24. P. 20.
25. This directive is set out as an appendix to the report, CIVIL DEFENSE FOR NATIONAL SECURITY, of Oct. 1, 1948. Government Printing Office, 1949.
26. CIVIL DEFENSE FOR NATIONAL SECURITY, p. 2.
27. P. 18.

were in accord, however, in making the Federal Civil Defense Administration an independent agency, not under the Defense roof.

President Truman placed upon the National Security Resources Board (which had been created by the National Security Act of 1947) responsibility for going forward with civil defense planning. The result was NSRB Document 128 of September 8, 1950, "The Plan," submitted by Chairman Symington. This remains the national plan. State and local organizations have been brought into line with the outlines in this document; the Civil Defense of the various States, in the main, are in accord with the Model Statute there suggested.

On September 18, 1950, the President laid the Plan before Congress. Bills were at once introduced, and extensive hearings were held before a subcommittee of the Senate Committee on Armed Services. (It was by no means a void that lay before Congress; in the years after the War, a good many States had established Civil Defense agencies, by statute or executive order. The Governors' Conference and the Council of State Governments had concerned themselves with the matter;[28] uneven progress was being made at the State level.) Out of the Congressional activity came the Federal Civil Defense Act of January 12, 1951.[29] Look at the Declaration of Policy: it was the intent of Congress to provide a plan; it was further "declared to be the policy and intent of Congress that this responsibility for civil defense shall be vested primarily in the several States and their political subdivisions;" the Federal Government would provide "necessary coordination and guidance," through an independent agency, the Federal Civil Defense Administration. Look at the functions of the Administrator: these include,

preparation of national plans and programs;

---

28. In this connection, the following publications of the Council of State Governments are pertinent: WASHINGTON LEGISLATIVE BULLETIN, No. 85, of Apr. 12, 1950, and 23 STATE GOVERNMENT, No. 11, "Civil Defense," Nov. 1950.

29. 64 Stat. 1245; 50 U.S.C. App., §§ 2251-2297.

provision for communications, dissemination of warnings;
development of protective measures;
conduct or arrangement of training programs;
dissemination of civil defense information;
encouragement of interstate mutual aid compacts;
procurement of civil defense materials;
distribution of financial aid to the States, on the basis of approved projects.

These are not strong powers; they fall far short of a power to direct. Responsibility, as the Act declares, rests primarily with the States. In the event of a "civil defense emergency" proclaimed by the President or the Congress, the Administrator may exercise additional powers—but these are in matters of procurement and assistance, not as to direction of State activities.

As a means to the advancement of State and local training, the FCDA has prepared—with elaborate consultation—administrative guides, such as *Principles of Civil Defense Operations,* and *Emergency Welfare Services,* and technical manuals, such as *Utilization and Control of Streets and Highways,* and *Organization and Operation of Casualty Services.* These are the drill and service regulations for the volunteer army of Civil Defense.

The FCDA maintains seven regional offices. Think of them as facilitating agencies, field offices whereby the FCDA moves closer to the State and local authorities and thus makes its assistance more effective. Regional offices arrange for the use of Federal personnel and resources in an emergency. They have things to give, and for that and other reasons their influence can be very important; but they do not have the power to direct State and local agencies.

The several States have recruited skeleton organizations. One finds a rather small group of permanent employees in key positions; retired officers are prominent in these cadres. Each State has its Civil Defense Plan—making assumptions as to the situation that would be presented, and outlining how the various functions should be discharged. The cities, too, have their Civil Defense organization and plans. There is a director, who often is a retired officer; the regular department chiefs of the municipal administration perform their respective functions in the Civil Defense system. I have visited a number of these State and municipal organizations as I have gone about the country: some appear to be substantial and to be getting on well with their preparations. Some, in their present state, would pretty surely buckle under an attack.

Project East River—a very elaborate survey of Civil Defense carried out at the request of the FCDA and other Government agencies—made this diagnosis in its General Report of October 1, 1952:

> The present basic civil defense organization places primary operating responsibility on state and local governments and puts the states in a position of authority that may exceed their capacity to act. The national and regional offices of the Federal Civil Defense Administration deal only with the governors and state civil defense directors. This procedure applies even with respect to the Federal responsibility of assisting in the provision of basic equipment, which was a main purpose of the civil defense law. The states are in a dominant role and can either provide or deny aid to critical target municipalities.
>
> Another feature of the present organization is an emphasis upon interstate and intermunicipal mutual-aid compacts. Such agreements are of value in that they provide for an orderly process in time of disaster when a situation does not require a governor to proclaim a state of extreme emergency. It must be recognized, however, that mutual-aid pacts are not the complete solution to mutual assistance. Their weakness lies in a situation where, because of real or anticipated local needs, a city or state would be reluctant to provide assistance even though an agreement exists. The agreements have no mandatory provisions; they contain no penalty clauses; and there is little recognition of the role that the Federal Government might have to play in a critical emergency. In the event of a severe enemy attack, they would be inadequate.
>
> Other considerations—such as the national character of the transportation system, the nature of metropolitan areas that cross state lines, and the need for effective control of mobile Federal re-

> sources—point up the need for realistic planning for greater Federal support responsibilities in a major emergency.[30]

Note the points of weakness. The States have responsibilities "that may exceed their capacity to act." They receive aid from the Federal Government, but their position is dominant and they may fail to deliver at the critical point. Mutual-aid compacts are a characteristic feature of the present scheme. Weakness lies in the possibility that these undertakings would not be honored in a critical emergency; Federal enforcement is not contemplated. Some matters are too big to be treated on less than a national basis. Evidently the machinery in operation might slip at points where it ought to hold.

One might make a serious error by designing a system wherein Federal compulsion was maximized. It is not to be assumed that in the event of war State and local authorities would be uncooperative or perverse; doubtless the national leadership would spontaneously be recognized, and the effort on every hand would be to conform. A rigid system of unitary direction, with every bit of administrative machinery driven from a central shaft, is certainly not the American pattern for getting things done. In preparing to meet an atomic war, when communications might be cut and centers of authority might be wiped out, individual initiative, local self-reliance, a willingness to take responsibility without waiting to be told —these virtues should be inculcated. So one might err by insisting too much on provision for national command, and by underestimating patriotic zeal.

One might make a very serious error by counting too much on undirected spontaneity. (The idea is reminiscent of the army of volunteers that would spring into being between sunrise and sunset, if our country were attacked.) There is more than a touch of the vigilante in the American character, and it can do great mischief in a brief moment. The Bull Board found that "[a]dherence to the principle of States' rights and traditional municipal individuality" had handicapped Civil Defense in World War II.[31] States' rights is a

30. Part I of the REPORT OF PROJECT EAST RIVER, p. 30.
31. A STUDY OF CIVIL DEFENSE, p. 9.

rationalization ever present in our thinking about politics and economics. Adequate federal authority should be clearly staked out in advance: any sudden assertion might arouse latent anti-federalism. An atomic war would be a very fast-moving affair: quick direction, not the negotiation of concurrence, must be our method. Consider the scheme of mutual aid compacts. In many instances, there is little mutuality about it. So far as can be foreseen, Maine will be a giver and not a receiver of aid. Arizona's problem consists mainly in how to handle 250,000 tourists caught in California, 500,000 migratory workers, and perhaps some panic-struck Californians—to route them along Arizona's highways, to allocate gasoline, and to provide food in a State most of whose groceries come from afar. Such one-way benefits might eventually put a strain on patriotism. It is not prudent to suppose that one State would willingly send out, say, its doctors and medical units if there was any serious fear that it might itself be imperilled. Recall that in 1942 it was purposed merely to evacuate the Japanese from the Pacific Coast; official opposition in the interior States forced an abandonment of the plan of independent movement, and the substitution of relocation centers.[32] Our present plans rely much too heavily upon the "mutual friendship . . . among the people of the different states in this union." We cannot fight an atomic war under the Articles of Confederation!

Individual initiative is entirely reconcilable with implicit obedience to central authority. One thinks of the army, which in popular conception is the model of hierarchical discipline. To be effective, the army—at any rate the American Army—must encourage the exercise of initiative in every unit, down to the individual soldier. This initiative, however, must be guided by training and discipline. Training under varied conditions will teach the soldier to be resourceful—to know how to put his initiative to good use. Discipline will

---

32. Col. Joel F. Watson, *The Japanese Evacuation and Litigation Arising Therefrom,* 22 Ore. L. Rev. 46, 53 (1942). The history is summarized, with citation to sources, in TEN BROEK, BARNHART AND MATSON, PREJUDICE, WAR AND THE CONSTITUTION (1954) at 122 et seq.

confirm him in exerting initiative toward the assigned objective. This is pertinent to Civil Defense. Of course individual citizens, officers of government, leaders of the community, directors of enterprises—all of them at all levels should exercise initiative. But it must not be the initiative of confused and unoriented men. The better they are schooled in finding the path toward safety, the better they can use their energies to attain it. If an atomic bomb fell, the survivors would have ample scope for their initiative. The question is, will they be trained to use it, not blindly in the spirit *sauve qui peut,* but in conformity to plans and signals. The ultimate word of authority must come down from the national executive; if for the moment that voice cannot be heard, then those below must use their judgment in accord with established plans.

I believe that the Federal Civil Defense Act should be amended to empower the President in time of national emergency to *direct* State and local authorities so far as appears necessary and proper to the accomplishment of the federal purpose. (This is, of course, only a general statement; such legislation would call for very careful drafting.) Included in the grant should be a power in time of peace to conduct exercises to make sure that, come an emergency, the exercise of national direction would be effective. (This is well within the principle, "Let the end be legitimate, . . . and all means which are appropriate . . . are constitutional.")[33] Power thus established would be exercisable through agents of the President's choosing—not necessarily through the Federal Civil Defense Administrator. It would not be limited to the direction of Civil Defense personnel of State and local units: it would be immaterial from the point of view of national power whether the people to be directed wore CD insignia or worked in some other part of the administrative structure.

Of course, writing a proposition into a statute does not necessarily make it true in fact. Effective working arrangements could be achieved only through practice. A clear allo-

33. McCulloch v. Maryland, 17 U.S. (4 Wheat.) 316, 421 (1819).

cation of powers and responsibilities is, however, the starting point.

A State director offered a suggestion for a more effective system of Federal-State relations in Civil Defense: that the analogy of the National Guard be followed, that State CD personnel be subject to Federal inspection to maintain Federal standards, and that they be subject to call into Federal service in event of a national emergency. The CD organization would thus remain a part of the administration of the State; it would be adapted to local needs, and available for local disasters. There would be Federal recognition where standards had been met—a matter easily managed through grants in aid. In the event of a national emergency, Federal control would come into operation: channels of direction would then run down from FCDA through the regional director to the State authorities. (Very likely the FCDA regional director would have authority to deal directly with some of the large municipal and metropolitan units—that is a matter of detail.) Federally directed training exercises would be authorized. The assumption of control in a national emergency would thus have been foreseen as a normal measure. Mutual assistance would have been put on a much firmer basis than at present. I believe that this suggestion offers the best solution to the problem of national direction of Civil Defense. The analogy of the National Guard would provide a relevant body of experience.

V. The Maintenance of Civil Administration

The General Report of the East River Project makes this observation:

> Civil defense is a part of national defense; it would hardly be in keeping with the war powers of the National Government for Federal agencies to sit idly by if some state and local governments were unable to cope with an emergency situation. *It is also inconsistent for all parties concerned to make one set of plans based*

> *on the predominant authority of the states while the same parties adhere to the unspoken premise that "when the real thing comes the Federal government (meaning the military) will have to take over." . .*[34]

The italics have been added—to focus attention on the "unspoken premise" that the East River investigators found in their inquiry, that when the "real thing" comes the Army will have to "take over." That is the matter next to be considered. But to get on with the remainder of the passage:

> In fact, in the most extreme situation, if a military theater of operations were declared, the establishment of military control over civil affairs could best be effected through the permanent machinery of Federal, state and local civil defense organizations rather than through separate machinery and disaster plans developed by the military. Even in the extreme case, the Federal Civil Defense Regional Director could possibly serve as the G-5 officer for an Army area commander if the threat of imminent invasion, for example, resulted in the declaration of a military theater of operations in continental United States.
>
> Planning for Federal-state-local action should also recognize that, although formal mechanisms may be desirable over the long term, in a critical emergency the dictates of the situation will prevail; formal channels of communication and command may be short-circuited; and a great deal of responsibility will rest upon the man on the scene. Thus, a realistic middle-ground position would provide for the greatest possible exercise of local initiative, backed up with potential Federal civilian direction and control if and when necessary. It would seem desirable, for example, that the Federal regional director of civil defense play a significant part in the development of interstate mutual-aid compacts, so that he could render a service in the determination of priorities and in the provision for Federal support when state lines have to be crossed. In the civil defense function, full emphasis should be placed upon the elements of cooperation in the Federal system; Federal, state and local governments are partners in an enterprise of mutual benefit to all. Realistic planning will be based on the principle of teamwork.[35]

---

34. P. 30. The director of the Project was Otto L. Nelson, Jr., a former officer in the Regular Army who attained the rank of major general in World War II, and who now is a vice president of the New York Life Insurance Co.

35. Pp. 30-31.

The East River investigators' perception of the "unspoken premise" in Civil Defense thinking is confirmed by some of my own conversations with CD officials as I have traveled about. One detects a belief on the part of some that in time of war we wouldn't really be carrying out the system of the Federal Civil Defense Act.

This uncertainty in official quarters is reflected in an article by Brigadier General Thomas R. Phillips, U.S.A. (Ret.), military analyst of the St. Louis Post-Dispatch, in that newspaper on Sunday, August 8, 1954.[36] The headlines are: "Decision to Establish a Joint Continental Air Command is a Long Step in Defense of U.S. But It Leaves the Problems of What to Do About Disaster Relief in Atomic Attack, Threats From Seaward and Unified Internal Security." In summary, a Continental United States Planning Group was set up by the Joint Chiefs of Staff in 1948. It produced a plan. Out of this effort has come the Joint Continental Air Command. One of the matters under study, but left unresolved, was "a unified military organization and plans for disaster relief in case of atomic attacks." The article discloses the thinking in the Planning Group:

> The United States has never suffered a disaster comparable to that which would occur if an atomic or hydrogen bomb were dropped on one or many of our great cities. The dead from a single bomb would number from hundreds of thousands to millions. The burned and injured would be in equally great numbers.
>
> Every hospital, ambulance, doctor, nurse and all available air transportation within a range of five hundred or more miles would be needed to cope with the problem. Housing and food would be problems of unrealized magnitude.
>
> *The thinking in the Continental Defense Planning Group was that a dictator in the area, backed by martial law, would be the only solution that could cope with such a disaster. The armed forces are the only agencies in the United States capable of handling the problem.*
>
> At the present time each service has disaster relief plans which are co-ordinated with the other services in the area. The plans are local. What is required, the planners believe, is a plan

36. P. 3C, cols. 1-2.

using all the resources, not actually engaged in combat or servicing combat, of all three services in a unified command. Each great city should be the subject of minutely detailed plans combining the resources of all the services, civil defense, Red Cross, police and fire departments, trucking and transportation systems and the resources of neighboring cities.

The armed forces do not like to take on these responsibilities. It detracts from their main business of war. But the fact is that it is the armed forces that are called in for every disaster, large or small. They cannot escape being forced to act in the greatest of all disasters.

To the military planners who have been living with this problem, the failure of Congress and the people to understand the danger, and the need to finance and to organize on a large scale to minimize it is incomprehensible.

(Italics supplied.)

"[A] dictator . . . backed by martial law, would be the only solution . . ." "The armed forces are the only agencies in the United States capable of handling the problem."

Such has not been the official position of the Department of Defense. When the organization of Civil Defense was being considered in hearings before a subcommittee of the Senate Armed Services Committee, in 1950, the spokesman for the Department, Colonel Barnet W. Beers, gave this testimony:

Mr. Chambers [Colonel Justice M. Chambers of the Committee Staff]: Colonel Beers, was this matter [that is, the question of putting Civil Defense in the Department of Defense] considered by the Joint Chiefs of Staff and did they advise on the final disposition?

Colonel Beers: Quite thoroughly.

Mr. Chambers: And the Joint Chiefs of Staff do agree that the administration of civil defense should not be a part of the military structure?

Colonel Beers: Yes, sir.

Senator Kefauver: Why is it they don't want it a part of the military structure, Colonel Beers?

Colonel Beers: The feeling in military circles, the military thinking, even below the level of the administrative office of the Secretary of Defense, is that they have got enough to do as it is. . .[37]

---

37. Hearings on S. 4217 and S. 4219, 81st Cong. 2d sess., 80 (1950).

At the National Civil Defense Conference in 1951, Mr. Daniel K. Edwards, then Assistant Secretary of Defense, speaking on behalf of the Department, had this to say:

> Civil defense is a program that should be carried on by civilians. In the first place, it will require the maximum effort of our armed forces to ready themselves and to conduct operations in defense of our country. They should not be burdened with a program that can be effectively carried out by the civilian population.
>
> But perhaps even more important than that, it is highly desirable that the program derive its great vitality from energies inherent in local initiative and in broad popular support.[38]

If one will re-read carefully the views attributed to the Planning Group, one will note that "The armed forces do not like to take on these responsibilities. . . They cannot escape being forced to act . . . [T]he failure of Congress and the people to understand the danger . . . is incomprehensible."

Turn to a very different quarter, and listen to Mayor Frank P. Zeidler of Milwaukee, in an address on "Restoration of Community Functions," before the American Association for the Advancement of Science, at St. Louis on December 27, 1952. It was in a section devoted to "Disaster Recovery." Mayor Zeidler said:

> While a populace is floundering under a blow, some observers think that the restoration of at least one function will serve as an orientation point for the citizenry to regain its sense of organization. Since, in disordered cities, there will be a tendency for vice and crime to mount, the protection of life and property becomes a task for early attention. Introduction of martial law usually will occur for this purpose. The forces of the military must work with the forces of the local police in protecting supplies and installations, in controlling evacuation and traffic, in the prevention of sabotage and crimes other than looting.
>
> *A properly planned restorative program may obviate the necessity for martial law, even under the most severe disaster. . . .* (Italics supplied.)

Mr. Zeidler is a mayor of outstanding ability. He has taken

38. Conference Report on meeting in Washington, 7-8 May 1951, 15.

a foremost place in seeking to make Civil Defense adequate to withstand a Soviet attack.[39] In his political philosophy he is certainly no authoritarian. Yet from his very accurate knowledge of our present situation, he foresees that there may be an "introduction of martial law" as "an orientation point for the citizenry to regain its sense of organization." Note, however, that in his judgment *"A properly planned restorative program may obviate the necessity for martial law, even under the most severe disaster."*[40]

Unless these views are misconceived, unless the "unspoken premise" is erroneous, America is inadvertently drifting into a situation where, if an atomic attack came, martial rule would follow. I think it is not a misconception to suppose that, very likely, such would be the outcome. I believe that our administrative preparations, such as they now are, would prove wholly inadequate; that in the ensuing confusion it would seem that "nobody knows what to do;" and that a cry would go up to have the Army "take over." I greatly fear that would happen; it might appear to be the only thing to do.

Such an outcome would be a catastrophe. Let's not pause just now to inveigh against the loss of civil liberty: this is not the occasion for striking attitudes. It is much more to the point to remove the danger. Let's not debate just now whether such resort to military direction would or would not be consistent with *Ex parte Milligan.*[41] If for a few moments we think concretely of the actual working of such a system, it will become apparent that this would be a very crude and awkward means toward restoration. Let us consider the practicalities.

If the Army "took over," Army channels would be the only line of communication between the stricken country and the national center of direction. The office of the Secretary of the Army would be the control point through which must

---

39. He is chairman of the Civil Defense Committee of the American Municipal Association.

40. I quote from a mimeographed copy obtained from Mayor Zeidler.

41. 4 Wall. 2 (1866).

pass all messages transmitted from the departments of Government out to the field and from the field up to the Government.[42] The Department of the Army—in addition to all its other duties in the prosecution of the war—would suddenly be made the conduit for all the impulses involved in the relief and rehabilitation of the people, the resumption of industrial production, the restoration of a shattered economy. Think, then, of the Department of the Army becoming the nation's great message center. There would be congestion, almost beyond belief.

The Army would have been made much more than a *conduit,* however; it would have been made the *director.* Let it be said at once that "the Army" does not know how to direct all the energies of the nation—in peace or, still less, after an attack. Suppose, for a moment, that this utterly stupendous new task were imposed—by what means could it be performed? Doubtless some new staff section would be created at every level—let us call it "G-5"—and possibly the operations would be directed from a nation-wide command outside the Department—(i.e., outside "the Pentagon"—but the building known by that name might have been destroyed, or at any rate abandoned). It is needless to speculate on the precise *organization;* we can see what *functions* would have to be discharged. I am seeking to convey some concrete conception of what would really be involved in the "unspoken premise".

Where could be found the personnel for the staff sections and the operating units that would be required? Doubtless the answer is, by recruiting leading civilians experienced in the many civil activities "the Army" would now have to direct—governors and mayors, legislators and public administrators, lawyers, bankers, industrialists, etc.—who, after induction and training, would be employed to conduct government at the State and local level, to administer public agencies, to enforce law, to manage finance and industry, etc. We

42. Of course I am not speaking with literal accuracy as to the routing within the Department of the Army. Dealings with other Departments would in principle go through the Secretary.

would have taken time out to play musical chairs, and presently the same group of experienced administrators would be back at the same sort of work they had left to join the Army! That would be folly. Of course, "the Army" would in the main leave the civil administrators right on the job. As the East River Report said in the passage quoted, military control "could best be effected through the permanent machinery" of government "rather than through separate machinery . . . developed by the military." It suggested, for example, that the FCDA regional director might even be made the G-5 on the staff of the Army area commander. Enough has been said to suggest that if "the Army" were called upon to direct civil administration, it would have to recruit the men to do it from the very agencies it had been called upon to direct. It has no stockpile of surplus administrators.

The Army would, it is true, be held in the bonds of discipline, when softer organizations might go to pieces. So if the very worst happened, it might be the only agency available for pulling the country together. With a municipal situation in mind, Mayor Zeidler said, that "while a populace is floundering under a blow," it may, "some observers think," be well to establish some "orientation point" to enable the citizenry "to regain its sense of organization." Martial rule, it is suggested, might be invoked as this quick restorative. Even so, the citizenry, as soon as the shock has worn off, will become restive. It will be irked by the arbitrariness of military restraints. It will resent the implication that only by external compulsion will men do their patriotic duty. Military authority, fumbling at the unfamiliar business of civil government, will do some inept things and thus expose its fallibility. All this was illustrated in Hawaii during World War II, where the military control was maintained long after any need could be shown.[43] Whatever the momentary benefit from this pick-me-up, the remedy tends to depress rather than to sustain morale. Secretary Edwards was quite right when he said that Civil Defense must "derive its great vitality from

43. Duncan v. Kahanamoku, 327 U.S. 304 (1946). As with *Ex parte* Milligan, I do not stop for an examination of the teaching of the case.

energies inherent in local initiative and in broad popular support." Those sturdy democratic values would be needed, as never before, if we were seeking to pull through a hard war. For an ordeal of blood, sweat and tears, a nation must draw upon its deepest spiritual roots. Army rule is not the sort of leadership that evokes an all-consuming popular effort—quite the contrary. The "unspoken premise" that the Army must "take over" is dangerous on spiritual as well as on administrative grounds.

The atomic attack we have to contemplate is so different from situations heretofore experienced as to make irrelevant much that we have read in the books. The attack would come from the air, and the aggressor would be gone. No hostile forces would remain on our soil; there would be no battle lines. (If land forces were brought in, say by air drop, it seems likely that this would be only after a great deal of softening.) Unlike the situation in the Civil War, there would be no opposing armies advancing and retreating over contested ground. Unlike the situation in Hawaii and on the Pacific Coast in World War II, there would probably be no immediate apprehension of invasion by land forces. Our Army, presumably, would not have to dominate threatened areas in preparation for an attack on the ground. Such conditions might arise—think, for instance, of Alaska; the general situation, however, would be quite unprecedented, and we ought to think about it very concretely. The imperative demands would be to keep the government in operation, to supply social services to the survivors, to sustain morale, to restore economic functions, and to resume production in essential industry. These are tasks for political leaders and public administrators, for social workers, for business men and industrial managers and labor leaders. Each in the field of his special competence would face demands almost impossible for his very highest skill. Our great need today is so to organize and concert our preparations that, if an attack came, the country would hold firm and carry on. The maintenance of effective civil government is at the heart of the problem. That is the objective toward which we should now bend our efforts.

VI. Judicial Review in Time of War

"It is emphatically the province and duty of the judicial department to say what the law is."[44] That is John Marshall in the *Marbury* case. Military officers no less than civil are accountable to the law as judicially determined—notwithstanding that "implicit obedience" which is "indispensably necessary to every military system."[45] That is Marshall in *Little v. Barreme.* "No man in this country is so high that he is above the law. No officer of the law may set that law at defiance with impunity. All the officers of the government, from the highest to the lowest, are creatures of the law and are bound to obey it. It is the only supreme power in our system of government . . ." That is Justice Miller in *United States v. Lee,*[46] the "Arlington Case" brought against officers holding an obedience to orders of the War Department. "The Constitution of the United States is a law for rulers and people, equally in war and in peace . . ." To suggest that its provisions can be suspended by great exigencies is "pernicious" and "false;" "the government, within the Constitution, has all the powers granted to it, which are necessary to preserve its existence . . ." That is Justice Davis, in *Ex parte Milligan.*[47] These axioms, taken together, yield a comforting assurance that the Constitution will sustain all that need be done for the national preservation, and that the judiciary will read the fundamental law with broad understanding—

44. 5 U.S. (1 Cr.) 137, 177 (1803). This was in connection with establishing the power of the judiciary to determine the validity of an act of Congress. That it is the province and duty of the judiciary to determine, if occasion arise, the validity of an executive act has far more ancient roots, running deep into the history of the common law.

45. 6 U.S. (2 Cr.) 170, 179 (1804).

46. 106 U.S. 196, 220 (1882).

47. 4 Wall. 2, 120, 121 (1866).

"not . . . with literal exactness like a mathematical formula;"[48] the courts will uphold what does not appear to have been unreasonable, but will hold bad what was clearly excessive.

Is that assurance well founded? Justice Jackson, in a dissent in *Korematsu v. United States*[49] in 1944, propounded the alarming view that the law as judicially administered cannot tolerate some expedients that may be necessary to the national safety; that those who direct the Armed Forces in time of war may have to act in excess of the Constitution, appealing for justification "to the political judgments of their contemporaries and to the moral judgments of history." Justice Frankfurter set out his own statement to counter his Brother Jackson's view. By the opposing theses the problem is neatly framed. *Korematsu,* it may be recalled, tested the validity of the exclusion of American citizens of Japanese descent from the Pacific Coast. A prosecution had been brought under the Act of March 21, 1942,[50] which makes it an offense to violate an order in a military area. The Court, per Black, J., sustained a conviction. The particular action there involved is, for present purposes, utterly irrelevant. Attention is directed toward the opposing views as to the Constitution, the judiciary, and measures of war. One might agree with Justice Frankfurter's thesis and yet think that exclusion should have been held ultra vires. One might agree with Justice Jackson as to exclusion and yet not share his views as to the role of the judiciary. Let us compare the abstract propositions: the choice to be made would be of tremendous importance in the event of another war.

Here is Justice Jackson's view:

> It would be impracticable and dangerous idealism to expect or insist that each specific military command in an area of probable operations will conform to conventional tests of constitutionality. When an area is so beset that it must be put under military

48. Hughes, C.J., in Home Building and Loan Association v. Blaisdell, 290 U.S. 398, 428 (1934).
49. 323 U.S. 214, 242.
50. 57 STAT. 173, perpetuated as 18 U.S.C. §1383 (1948).

control at all, the paramount consideration is that its measures be successful, rather than legal. The armed services must protect a society, not merely its Constitution. The very essence of the military job is to marshal physical force, to remove every obstacle to its effectiveness, to give it every strategic advantage. Defense measures will not, and often should not, be held within the limits that bind civil authority in peace. No court can require such a commander in such circumstances to act as a reasonable man; he may be unreasonably cautious and exacting. Perhaps he should be. But a commander in temporarily focusing the life of a community on defense is carrying out a military program; he is not making law in the sense the courts know the term. He issues orders, and they may have a certain authority as military commands, although they may be very bad as constitutional law.

But if we cannot confine military expedients by the Constitution, neither would I distort the Constitution to approve all that the military may deem expedient. . . .

In the very nature of things, military decisions are not susceptible of intelligent judicial appraisal. They do not pretend to rest on evidence, but are made on information that often would not be admissible and on assumptions that could not be proved. Information in support of an order could not be disclosed to courts without danger that it would reach the enemy. Neither can courts act on communications made in confidence. Hence courts can never have any real alternative to accepting the mere declaration of the authority that issued the order that it was reasonably necessary from a military viewpoint. . . .

I should hold that a civil court cannot be made to enforce an order which violates constitutional limitations even if it is a reasonable exercise of military authority. The courts can exercise only the judicial power, can apply only law, and must abide by the Constitution, or they cease to be civil courts and become instruments of military policy.

Of course the existence of a military power resting on force, so vagrant, so centralized, so necessarily heedless of the individual, is an inherent threat to liberty. But I would not lead people to rely on this Court for a review that seems to me wholly delusive. The military reasonableness of these orders can only be determined by military superiors. If the people ever let command of the war powers fall into irresponsible and unscrupulous hands, the courts wield no power equal to its restraint. The chief restraint upon those who command the physical forces of the country, in the future as in the past, must be their responsibility to the political judgments of their contemporaries and to the moral judgments of history.[51]

Now Justice Frankfurter:

The provisions of the Constitution which confer on the Congress and the President powers to enable this country to wage war are as much part of the Constitution as provisions looking to a nation at peace. And we have had recent occasion to quote approvingly the statement of former Chief Justice Hughes that the war power of the Government is "the power to wage war successfully." *Hirabayashi v. United States,* 320 U.S. 81, 93; and see *Home Building and Loan Association v. Blaisdell,* 290 U.S. 398, 426. Therefore, the validity of action under the war power must be judged wholly in the context of war. That action is not to be stigmatized as lawless because like action in times of peace would be lawless. To talk about a military order that expresses an allowable judgment of war needs by those entrusted with the duty of conducting war as "an unconstitutional order" is to suffuse a part of the Constitution with an atmosphere of unconstitutionality. The respective spheres of action of military authorities and of judges are of course very different. But within their sphere, military authorities are no more outside the bounds of obedience to the Constitution than are judges within theirs. "The war power of the United States, like its other powers . . . is subject to applicable constitutional limitations", *Hamilton* v. *Kentucky Distilleries Co.,* 251 U.S. 146, 156. To recognize that military orders are "reasonably expedient military precautions" in time of war and yet to deny them constitutional legitimacy makes of the Constitution an instrument for dialectic subleties not reasonably to be attributed to the hard-headed Framers, of whom a majority had had actual participation in war. If a military order such as that under review does not transcend the means appropriate for conducting war, such action by the military is as constitutional as would be any authorized action by the Interstate Commerce Commission within the limits of the constitutional power to regulate commerce. And being an exercise of the war power explicitly granted by the Constitution for safeguarding the national life by prosecuting war effectively, I find nothing in the Constitution which denies to Congress the power to enforce such a valid military order by making its violation an offense triable in the civil courts. Compare *Interstate Commerce Commission* v. *Brimson,* 154 U.S. 447; 155 U.S.3, and *Monongahela Bridge Co.* v.

51. 323 U.S. at 244-48.

United States, 216 U.S. 177. To find that the Constitution does not forbid the military measures now complained of does not carry with it approval of that which Congress and the Executive did. That is their business, not ours.[52]

I believe that Justice Frankfurter is right, and that Justice Jackson was wrong.[53] First, on elementary principle: it is the very beginning of wisdom, it is the greatest lesson of our constitutional experience, that the fundamental law is adequate to "the various crises of human affairs." It *must* be erroneous to say that really necessary expedients may be beyond the limits of the war power. How can executive officers, being "creatures of the law," have some political duty to "protect a society" beyond anything the law will tolerate? Ours would then be a fair-weather Constitution, deserting us in moments of extremity.

In another passage, Justice Jackson wrote, "I do not suggest that the courts should have attempted to interfere with the Army in carrying out its task."[54] This and other remarks suggest that he anticipated that the judgment of the Court might be ignored—that perhaps from the political and military viewpoint it would be necessary to ignore it. In such a case, the complainant would have no relief—the moral authority of the Executive would have been seriously impaired—the people would have been confused and their confidence shaken—by a declaration from the Court that a measure was unconstitutional, albeit perhaps necessary. Elsewhere Justice Jackson once advised his brethren to apply "a little practical wisdom," lest they "convert the constitutional Bill of Rights into a suicide pact."[55] The dissent in *Korematsu* seems itself to point toward suicide.

A commander who understands that it may be his duty to break the law, looking for justification to the political judgment of his contemporaries, is likely to be a reckless and

---

52. 323 U.S. at 224-25.
53. I hasten to record here my very great respect for Justice Jackson's work and for his character—as will be attested in a memorial article in Columbia Law Review.
54. 323 U.S. at 248.
55. Terminiello v. Chicago, 337 U.S. 1, 13 at 37 (1949) (dissenting opinion).

arbitrary man. It sounds like Caesar who, seeking to keep within the constitution while fearful of prosecution on a charge of unconstitutional acts, finally crossed the Rubicon, and looked to his contemporaries and to history. That is wholly foreign to our notions. Our democratic common-law tradition has been otherwise: a soldier should act in subordination to his civil superiors and to the law, and be confident that the law will sustain him, if question arise, so long as he does no more than appears necessary and prudent. In that sound view there lies at once assurance and restraint.

Much could be written about the problem of applying constitutional standards in time of national extremity. Here the Court's most useful discussion, I believe, is to be found in Chief Justice Hughes' opinion in *Sterling* v. *Constantin*[56]—a very great opinion about a very little emergency. There is "a permitted range of honest judgment as to the measures to be taken;" measures conceived in good faith in the face of the emergency and directly related to overcoming it fall within the Executive discretion. "What are the allowable limits of military discretion, and whether or not they have been overstepped in a particular case, are judicial questions."[57] "There is no . . . avenue of escape from the paramount authority of the Federal Constitution."[58] The principles there enunciated are of general validity, even though the occasion—trouble over limiting oil production in Texas—was minuscule as compared with an atomic war. For the measure of latitude appropriate to a matter truly of national survival, the soundest wisdom, I believe, is to be found in Lincoln's letter to A. G. Hodges, April 4, 1864:

> I did understand . . . that my oath to preserve the Constitution to the best of my ability imposed upon me the duty of preserving, by every indispensable means, that government—that nation—of which that Constitution was the organic law. Was it possible to lose the nation and yet preserve the Constitution? By general law, life and limb must be protected, yet often a limb must be

56. 287 U.S. at 399-401.
57. 287 U.S. at 399-401.
58. 287 U.S. at 398.

amputated to save a life; but a life is never wisely given to save a limb. I felt that measures, otherwise unconstitutional, might become lawful by becoming indispensable to the preservation of the Constitution through the preservation of the nation. Right or wrong, I assumed this ground, and now avow it. . . .

Lincoln's instincts were sound—often far more sound than the professional work of his legal advisers.

VII. Problems of Enforcement

It seems clear that in the event of an atomic war those in authority at every level of government must give directions to the populace—directions as to matters of immediate necessity, *e.g.*, to clear a highway, to move to a designated assembly point, to render service to stricken persons. Hoarding and profiteering are types of anti-social conduct that would at once have to be combatted. Let us hope that our people generally would show self-restraint and public spirit. Yet, surely, problems of enforcement would soon arise. What would be the sanction behind such necessary orders—how proceed against a violator? Most of the duties sought to be imposed would be such as are not required by the law of normal times, and so would not be punishable as breaches of the peace, disorderly conduct, traffic violations, or the like. How could such novel but necessary requirements be enforced?

At common law it is, very certainly, no offense to refuse obedience to an Executive order. Hear Lord Coke in the Case of Proclamations:[59]

he [the King] cannot make a thing unlawful, which was permitted by the law before: and this was well proved by the ancient and continual forms of indictments; for all indictments conclude *contra legem et consuetudinem Angliae,* or *contra leges et statuta, etc.* But never was seen any indictment to conclude *contra regiam proclamationem.*

59. 12 Co. Rep. 74 (1611).

When Star Chamber went out, there was no tribunal to enforce a mere command of the Executive.

This ancient learning was strikingly illustrated early in World War II. The President, by Executive Order No. 9066[60] of February 19, 1942, had authorized the Secretary of War or designated subordinates to prescribe military areas, as to which restrictions and even exclusion might be imposed. With this was coupled authority to take such steps as were deemed advisable to enforce compliance, "including the use of Federal troops and other Federal agencies . . ." Bold words. And if an inhabitant refused to observe, say, a curfew—what then? On March 9, 1942,[61] Secretary Stimson requested the Houses to enact a draft bill "to provide a penalty for restrictions or orders" in military areas. On March 14 he urged haste.[62] By an Act approved March 21, Congress made the violation of an order in such an area punishable by a fine up to $5,000 or imprisonment for not more than one year, or both.[63] This measure remains as 18 U.S.C. sec. 1383 (1948). The instant we became involved in another war, we would need legislation of this sort in broader form: it should support requirements imposed by competent federal authorities beside the military, and should not be limited to "military areas." Of course, the scope of the order-imposing power would need to be fixed by appropriate—albeit necessarily broad—language: it would never do to enact that the citizen must obey *any* order that is given.

Alleged offenses against the United States are, in general, prosecuted in a United States District Court. For relatively petty violations within the statute proposed above, this would be highly inconvenient. Think how far it might be to the nearest District Court. (And, by the way, where would the courts be sitting after our cities had been bombed?) 18

60. 7 F.R. 1407.

61. I have wondered at the delay from February 19 to March 9 about a measure whose necessity should have been at once apparent. Carrying out the requisite consultation within the Executive branch may, I realize, consume some days even when there is a great hurry. The mere mechanics of typing the papers and obtaining signatures is considerable.

62. H.R. Rep. No. 1906, 77th Cong. 2d sess.

63. 56 Stat. 173.

U.S.C. secs. 3401 and 3402 provides for trial before a United States commissioner for petty offenses in places where the Federal Government has exclusive or concurrent jurisdiction. Probably it would be convenient to use that device for the trial of petty offenses against war-time controls.

Testa v. *Katt*—[64] where the Court upheld the provision that actions under the Emergency Price Control Act might be brought in a State court—suggests that perhaps prosecutions under a statute similar to 18 U.S.C. sec. 1383 might also be tried in a State court. I speak of a war-time situation, where unusual expedients would have to be employed.

State and local officers, too—probably far more than federal officers— would be issuing orders and making regulations after an atomic attack. The like problem of enforceability arises. The Suggested Model State Civil Defense Act[65] declares (Sec. 7) that in the event of actual enemy attack and upon the declaration of a state of emergency, the Governor shall have power "to enforce all laws, rules, and regulations relating to civil defense . . ." Section 15, dealing with Orders, Rules, and Regulations, provides that when promulgated they shall have the force and effect of law. Section 21, Penalties, provides punishment for one violating "any rule, order, or regulation made pursuant to this Act." Legislation similar to this model may be found on the books in most of the States. A check should be made to make sure that nothing is wanting to make enforceable the controls that would immediately be needed—especially as to evacuation, hoarding, lending assistance, and the like.

This matter of enforceability is closely related to the maintenance of civil government. Even though the civil administration stood up under an attack, and at once set about directing restoration, yet if no means had been provided to make its directions enforceable in the civil courts, a demand might go up for military commissions and provost courts. Such tribunals, being of executive origin, will enforce execu-

64. 330 U.S. 386 (1947).
65. N.S.R.B. Doc. 128 (1950) at 135 et seq.

tive orders. To avoid such resort to military tribunals, adequate provision for civil enforcement should be made in advance.

VIII. The Adaptation of State and Local Government

Government in America—excepting the national system—is characterized by a very great number of self-governing units administered by officials, usually elective, who are chosen for fixed terms and whose competence is confined by territorial lines. Elections are frequent. Authority is limited. All this is in accord with our frontier heritage. Notwithstanding profound changes in the past half century to centralize power and responsibility, to substitute permanent civil servants for elected laymen, to consolidate units and to give more expert and responsive service — notwithstanding all these changes, government in America remains tied pretty rigidly to local units. Officers may function only within their respective districts. Perhaps the police or the fire department, for example, may have been authorized to act beyond the territorial boundaries, but this is not to be taken for granted. To prevent abuse, checks and limitations have been placed on official discretion. In a word, our State and local institutions are inflexible, and are based on jealousy rather than confidence in official power.

Suppose that war came, bringing the destruction of cities and the scattering of people. To cope with the resulting situation, public assistance must be mobile. Officers must be able to serve without regard to unit lines. Government must have a large discretion to act for the public safety. The present statute books should be searched to discover obstacles that should be removed now, or should be made removable in time of need. Much has been done already—as, for instance, to enable police to act extraterritorially, to enable doctors to serve in States wherein they are not licensed, etc.

But what has been done is only a small start on the task.[66] The importance of maintaining the civil courts has already been stressed. This calls for interchangeability of judges and flexibility in holding the courts. While great advances have in recent times been made, the special needs of war have not been a consideration. Broad powers to make orders for the administration of justice — quite unwarranted for normal times—would be appropriate for the contingency of hostilities.[67]

There is need for model statutes to effect adaptations in State government. If this work could be taken in hand in one or in a few quarters, and executed with distinction, many benefits would result. The models would be better than what most of the States would evolve for themselves. Enactment would be hastened. And, while each State would have to fit the drafts to its own circumstances, there would be a high measure of uniformity—which is greatly to be desired.

The need for emergency measures extends to much more than the conspicuous functions of public administration. One might easily overlook such dusty offices as the records of deeds and of probate: yet think what frustration would ensue if they were destroyed. Think how important it would be to have records and plans of a city's engineering services, in anticipation of their being hit. There is a tremendous need for requiring the preservation on microfilm, away in some safe place, of a host of public records, and of private records of public concern.

In this country, many matters of vital concern to the people are left to private, and especially to corporate enterprise. How effectively could a corporation carry on when top management had been shattered and when perhaps a competent shareholders' meeting could not be held? Pro-

---

66. "Many of the problems that people are now discovering, in preparing civil disaster plans, are legal problems involving personal injury, liability, workmen's compensation, and the right of the cities to deploy their restorative powers in new or unusual patterns. A system of claims and payments therefore must be evolved, beforehand if possible." Mayor Frank P. Zeidler, in the address on "Restoration of Community Functions," already cited note 40 *supra*.

67. Mr. Homer D. Crotty points to some of these needs in *The Administration of Justice and the A-Bomb: What Follows Disaster?* 37 A.B.A.J. 893 (1951).

fessor Cavers has led the way in pointing out what needs to be done to safeguard the legal machinery necessary to keep the nation's business running after an atomic attack.[68]

In recent times we have sought "security" in feverish ways that have undermined our confidence in our Government and in one another. Much that has been done has been silly, much has been sinister and wicked. If we had pursued the national safety in the directions mentioned above with half the zeal with which sensational inquiries have been pushed, we would today be far better prepared against our enemies.

IX. Working Relationships

Even though a unit may have developed and practiced a sound plan for its internal functions, that is not enough. *It is imperative that there be effective working relationships—the parts must work together smoothly.* Joint exercises must be conducted, followed by critiques and the indicated improvements in procedure. Such exercises, carried out realistically, would disclose weaknesses, give the assurance that comes from doing, and confirm participants in modes of action that should become habitual.[69]

---

68. David F. Cavers, *Legal Measures to Mitigate the Economic Impact of Atomic Attack.* 9 Bulletin of the Atomic Scientists 269 (1953); *Legal Planning Against the Risk of Atomic Attack,* 55 Colum. L. Rev. 127 (1955).

69. Project East River, in Part VI of its Report, Disaster Services and Operations, makes these observations on "Training Exercises for Operational Readiness:"

> The value of joint exercises cannot be over emphasized. There are some who view this joint operation as one of the weakest areas in the nation's civil defense preparedness. Many localities still do not appreciate the great complexity of the joint operations required to meet the situation resulting from a widespread disaster. . . .
>
> The remarks . . . concerning test exercises at the target area control center apply with equal force at the state and regional levels. At these higher echelons the Federal Civil Defense Administration will play an increasingly larger part. It will not be sufficient to develop an organization and then let it remain idle year after year. Hence, the Federal Civil Defense Administration must provide some motivation for keeping the civil defense forces at all levels in a high state of preparedness. Perhaps an inspection system, on which would be based each yearly contribution through Federal matching funds, might supply a competitive stimulus.
>
> Civil defense exercises should be arranged at systematic intervals and should, perhaps, be of three types:

The earlier discussion of Federal-State relations is recalled. The pattern for normal times—based upon mutual respect, comity, rendering to each its proper competence—would undergo profound modification to meet the needs of war. Men—for administration is a human process—would have to learn to work in somewhat novel association. This would take time.

Then there would be the matter of civil-military relationships: Federal civil, State civil, and Federal military (the Army) and probably State military (assuming that National Guard units were left to aid their respective States). Attaining harmonious civil-military relationships, where contact is close, may present considerable difficulty. Where different sovereigns are involved, further complexities enter. When in time of war the Armed Forces were operating all about the country, using the same communications and highways as the civil populace, competing with the civil administration for essential facilities and services, acting with the tenseness that danger inspires, the possibilities for friction and misunderstanding would be enormous. Soldiers are familiar with the relationship of command:—but it has here been argued most urgently that civil administration should *not* be brought under command. Soldiers do not readily understand a system of concurrent authorities, each competent as to its own concerns and respecting the competence of the

---

(a) Map Problems. In these exercises, a hypothetical situation is assumed for which subsequent events are programmed, including phenomena beyond the control of our forces, e.g. changing meteorological conditions or post-attack action by the enemy, as well as factors introduced by decisions and actions of the military forces or higher echelons of civil defense. Those participating in the exercise work out solutions, orally or in writing, without any reference to the limitations imposed by available personnel, equipment, and facilities.

(b) Command Post Problems. These exercises are based on the same hypothetical assumptions of events. The participants, however, work at their duty stations and follow the procedures and employ the equipment (within the control center) that would be used in an actual operation.

(c) War Game Problems. These exercises are again based on a hypothetical situation. However, stations outside as well as in the control center are manned; information comes into the control center through the actual operating channels; decisions and directions are sent out through similar channels; and the entire operation is carefully timed. These exercises are so important that the Federal Civil Defense Administration should support them, both in developing the hypothetical problem and in bearing part of the costs.

other. (They have never imbibed the spirit of *Cooley* v. *Board of Wardens.*)[70] They know how to obey and how to command—but do not readily adapt themselves to any more complicated relationship. Without going into any closer analysis here, let it be noted that much thought and practice will have to be devoted to civil-military relationships before understanding and sound practice have been attained.[71]

No amount of speculation can prescribe just what would be the best patterns of action in an atomic war. We would need to adapt promptly to the situation as it presented itself. We should become quick at perceiving where responsibility is located. Clashes of authority would cost dearly. Only by repeated practice can we learn how to work together for the common defense.

X. In Conclusion.

The obstacles to effective organization are not insuperable. The problem—so massive and unyielding at first appearance—can be broken down into manageable tasks.

First, let an analysis be made, to distinguish the major aspects of non-military defense and to assign responsibility. Professor Cavers has made a notable contribution to analysis in an article that appeared just in time for mention in the present paper. In "Legal Planning Against the Risk of Atomic War,"[72] he identifies "a series of major economic problems that must be tackled" and sets out some "examples of the precautionary measures which lawyers and business executives might now be devising . . ., including both federal and state legislation and private arrangements." Mr. Cavers has been chiefly concerned with the economic sector. The present discussion has been directed to government, and especially to the urgency of preparing for effective *civil* administration.

70. 53 U.S. (12 How.) 299 (1852).

71. Basic doctrine governing "Emergency Employment of Army Resources. Domestic Disturbances." is set out in Army Regulations No. 500-50 of Aug. 27, 1953. This is a complicated subject.

72. 55 Colum. L. Rev. 127 February (1955).

There are other important sectors. One great range of considerations looks to how people think and act in respect of the danger that confronts us, how they would think and act after an attack occurred, and what may now be done to promote sound thought and action—in preparation, and after an attack. Need it be said, this is not an invitation for uninspired questionnaires and polls of opinion? We need hard-headed studies that will yield reliable, usable, wise prescriptions—how to brace our people, in mind and spirit, for the terrible shock they may some day receive. Plans for economic survival, plans for maintaining the government, all else would utterly fail if the American people lacked the moral stamina to fight on.

The answer depends on factors that are not invariable. We may greatly improve our prospects. All that promotes civic unity counts toward success. Helping one another is an essential of civil defense. This is difficult to promote in the places most likely to be hit—for the more we dwell in congested areas, the more we live to ourselves. Whatever impedes personal communication, whatever is divisive, whatever produces tension, works against us. We need to discover and bring forward the individuals who can sustain a group in time of disaster—and many of these leaders are to be found outside the ranks of any élite. We need to foster a well-founded confidence, in our neighbors and in our national community. We need to have a reasoned understanding of our Government's purposes. All this is easy to prescribe—difficult to attain. The call is not for promoters and slogan-makers; to endure, this must be a work of insight and of intellectual integrity.

When rigorous analysis has disclosed the components of our great problem, then break it down into tasks and get on with the planning of action. Consider a war-time operation, such as moving an army overseas. The plan is made by a group of men, not supermen; then thousands of resulting actions are carried out, and finally the conception is realized, and in the appointed order men and things reach the place where they are needed. Each responsible leader has his span of control; no one mind encompasses the totality of particulars. Consider the building of a skyscraper—or the management of a railroad. Consider the plans and operations of any major industrial undertaking, or of a large mechandising establishment: by major decisions and a myriad of consequential decisions and actions, consumers' demands are foreseen and supplied in adequate quantity and on time. We accept these familiar phenomena, without stopping to appreciate our enormous capacity for planned action. Right now the challenge of organizing our non-military defense may appear so baffling that one turns away and pretends it isn't there: yet if we will face up to it, promptly and calmly, we will find that we can acquit ourselves creditably.

Mr. Cavers, when he comes to his final section on "The Organization of Planning Studies," makes this observation:

> In preparing this article, I have been oppressed by the resemblance of my role to that of the forward-looking member of the conclave of mice who proposed that a bell be tied on the cat. Advance planning and standby institutions are easy to propose, but very hard to bring about. . . [73]

He suggests the role of Government, the role of industry, and what may best be done by institutional research.

Developments are taking place, in many quarters. In government, for instance, the Civil Defense Subcommittee of the Senate Armed Services Committee, under the chairmanship of Senator Kefauver, is holding hearings on the operations and policies of the Civil Defense program.[74] (Unfortunately, the subcommittee is almost penniless. One can recall better-financed and less promising Congressional activities.) The British Government, from whose experience and planning we can profit, is also examining, in the light of

---

73. Cavers, *supra* note 72, at 155.

74. Senator Kefauver, evidently in a tentative frame of mind, has introduced S.J.RES. 8, 84th Cong. 1st sess., "To amend the Constitution to authorize governors to fill temporary vacancies in the Congress caused by a disaster." This is mentioned as a datum in the consideration of what constitutional amendments may be needed.

the thermo-nuclear bomb, what should be its policy on defense—including "home defence."[75]

Working at the local level of government, the American Municipal Association, after fresh study,[76] at its 1954 meeting adopted a revised statement of its policy on Civil Defense.[77]

---

75. I cite CMD. No. 9391, "Statement on Defence, 1955" of Feb. 1955 —the White Paper discussed by Sir Winston Churchill in opening the defense debate on March 1. The paper observes:

> These difficulties may, however, be overcome if we are patient and resolute, and these dangers avoided if we are united, vigilant and prepared. We must not be lulled into a false sense of security, nor frightened into a state of paralysis, nor provoked into hasty or ill-considered action. P.9.

Home defense is discussed in Part VIII, pp. 22-26.

76. I cite their preparatory materials, "Progress and Prospects on National Civil Defense Preparations (11 page pamphlet) and "Status of Civil Defense in America's largest Cities" (34 page pamphlet), both of November 1954. The Association's officers are at 1625 H. St. N.W., Washington 6, and 1313 E. 60th St., Chicago 37.

77. As this represents careful thought by responsible municipal officials, it merits quotation in full:

RESOLUTION NO. 8 CIVIL DEFENSE

It is apparent to everyone that the capacity for destruction inherent in atomic, biological and chemical warfare has grown enormously since our earlier policy statement on Civil Defense.

It is apparent also that a tremendous lag continues to exist in our capacity as a nation and as cities in particular to survive a hostile attack.

As a means of partially overcoming this lag we recommend a new Civil Defense and Disaster policy to be adopted by the American Municipal Association and which follows herewith.

General Policy

A-1. There should be a continuing heavy emphasis on the education of people on the effect of atomic weapons so that they can make advance personal decisions for their own safety consistent with official plans since people living in target areas are highly vulnerable.

A.-2. Since the threat of atomic attack is so enormous the Congress ought to continue thoughtful and well considered action in international affairs so that the very existence of American cities is not jeopardized. We especially recommend to the Congress again a much more complete and adequate financial program of civil defense which recognizes the urgent importance of protecting and defending our homeland.

A-3. Since certain federal agencies are advocating limited dispersal of industry over a period of time, state associations affiliated with the American Municipal Association should recommend to their state legislatures a study of the effect of federal dispersal plans as they may affect the financial, economic and political structure of cities within the target area or states themselves.

A-4. We recommend that the Congress of the United States enact such laws as may be necessary to give to all civil defense agencies a high priority in the procurement of such federal surplus properties as are necessary to the organization, maintenance and operation of an effective civil defense and disasted program.

A-5. Educators should be encouraged to include a basic course on the need for civil defense and disaster preparedness planning as a part of the course of study of every high school with emphasis on the importance of volunteer help in civil defense organizations. Civil defense and disaster preparedness appears to be a permanent part of our American way of life and acceptance of this point of view at the high school level will assure the

At various points in private business, significant studies and plans have been made. Particular reference goes to *General Aspects of Civil Defense,* the Report of the Committee on Civil Defense of the Life Insurance Association of Ameri-

---

development of a reservoir of informed adults ready to assume their responsibilities in local civil defense and disaster organizations.

A-6. We recognize that there will be difficulty in sustaining a proper level of civil defense preparedness if international tensions lessen. We also recognize that we cannot allow the preparedness to fall below a position which makes the nation vulnerable and unready for sudden emergency.

Therefore, federal, state and local governments should stress the use of trained cadres of civil defense workers for civil and natural disasters. The concept of civil defense should not neglect the primary concept of aid in civil disaster.

B. Joint Responsibilities of Federal, State and Local Government

B-1. Federal, state, county and city civil defense organizations, especially by training and education, should bring home to units of government located in the support areas the full realization of the immensity of the problems that will befall them following dispersal or evacuation of a major target area.

B-2. States must assume an even greater responsibility in coordinating and assisting development of civil defense plans and programs especially in arrangements to be made between target and support areas.

B-3. Cities, counties and other local governmental agencies should fully cooperate in making such programs effective and in providing such aid as may be required within the limits of their resources.

B-4. All levels of government especially municipalities should review their present legislation regarding civil defense and disaster preparedness in the light of present day requirements. Action should then be taken to make necessary enactments, amendments, revisions or deletions of municipal ordinances. Existing state legislation should be reviewed by affiliates of the American Municipal Association and necessary legislative action sponsored to bring Civil Defense and Disaster preparedness laws up to date.

B-5. Federal and state programs for the expending of highway funds in target areas should be increased to allow for rapid voluntary dispersal of people if the community desires it. We feel that this program will allow people to live in or near a target city and still have a means of protection. This tremendous investment made in our cities need, therefore, not be abandoned nor would it be necessary to invest additional large sums in new facilities.

B-6. State and federal policies allowing for grants-in-aid for slum clearance and urban redevelopment should be kept consistent with civil defense requirements for reduction of the richness of target areas.

B-7. Further study of a shelter program is necessary by federal, state and local officials to provide shelter in reception areas, or in areas near target areas. In this latter case, we recommend that a program of blast and radio-active-resistant shelter construction be considered for recommendation by the Federal Civil Defense Administration.

B-8. All levels of government should review the fiscal problems involved not only in the preparation of defense but involved in operating an economy after a major attack. This means that not only will there have to be an appropriation of funds for target and support areas, but it also means that a financial policy must be evolved in case the major production and financial centers are destroyed.

B-9. Federal and state governments should give particular attention to the planning for and the providing of all possible financial and all other necessary assistance to support areas, without which they will be unable to meet the burdens placed on them.

B-10. We recommend that the Federal Civil Defense Administration call a special meeting of representatives of states and local civil defense ca, of December 6, 1954.[78] This study is exceedingly informative and useful, as a starting point for any planning in business. On the basis of his study, Mr. Cavers makes special mention of the plans made by the Koppers Co., [79] the American Machine and Foundry Co., the American Telephone and Telegraph Co., and the Consolidated Edison Co. of New York.

Of institutional study, attention is invited to the work of the National Planning Association's Special Committee on Non-military Defense Planning: its Statement of National Policy is now being completed, and should be published not long after the appearance of this present paper.

It is a mistake, a resignation to intellectual laziness, to suppose that until some grand design is announced in Washington one cannot do effective planning in one's own small corner. Enough is known now to serve as a basis for any number of useful exertions—in government, in business, in private affairs. In particular, a lawyer with skill and initiative can find many worthy tasks within the field of his immediate professional concerns. As national policies are formulated from time to time, it will be a simple matter to bring subordinate planning into conformity.

---

organizations to discuss specific applications of the terms of grants-in-aid for civil defense purposes.

C. Responsibilities of Local Governments

C-1. Target cities should study methods of providing alternate water and power supplies for their own benefit.

C-2. Cities must study the problem of zoning and construction codes to reduce their own vulnerability, particularly to fire and blast hazard.

C-3. Civil defense and disaster preparedness ought to be included as a part of all municipal employees' training and civil defense and disaster assignments be made so that they may be better equipped to carry out their responsibilities.

C.4. Target cities where dispersal is considered possible should develop and maintain close liaison with suburban and rural governmental units for mutual aid and cooperative surveys and agreements on welfare, medical and evacuation problems.

78. The committee consisted of Messrs. James T. Phillips of the New York Life Insurance Co., Gerhard D. Bleicken of the John Hancock Mutual Life Insurance Co., and Samuel Milligan of the Metropolitan Life Insurance Company. It is understood that copies of this document (86 pages) may be purchased from the Association, 488 Madison Avenue, New York 22, at a charge of $2.

79. The remarks of Mr. John Redmond, Assistant Production Manager, on "Why a Plan for Emergency and Disaster," will be found useful. It appears at p. 53 in the Proceedings of Businessmen's Conference on Industrial Defense in the Atomic Age, June 15, 1954. The Chamber of Commerce of the United States convened the conference and published the proceedings.

It seems desirable that the President appoint a commission on non-military defense, to make an exact analysis of the problem and to report how to assign tasks and to organize further action. The commission should proceed forthwith in a concentrated effort.

It seems desirable, also, that a council be organized, by private initiative, to sponsor useful undertakings in aid of the national program. For instance, of special concern to lawyers, there is the need for drafting model legislation to effectuate the modifications that should be made in order that our institutions may be "adapted to the various crises of human affairs."

In many quarters, one discerns an awakening. It seems possible that by the time we convene, September 22-24, 1955, to observe John Marshall's bicentennial, preparations will have advanced significantly beyond where they are when these lines are written, in early April.

COMMENT

PROFESSOR FAIRMAN*

If we construe Professor Leach's talk as the tossing of his Air Force cap into the ring as a candidate for the office of Chief Civil Affairs Officer of the Military Government of the United States, I shall work hard for the next few minutes to keep that office from ever coming into being.

If what follows seems to be in the form of plain, bluff, paragraphs, it is in the interest of brevity. Let me say now, with diffidence and modesty, simply, I *believe* these things to be true and sound.

* CHARLES FAIRMAN, *Professor of Law, Harvard Law School.* Professor Fairman was born in Illinois in 1897, took degrees at the University of Illinois, Harvard, and the University of London, and also did graduate work at the University of Paris. He has been on the faculties of Harvard, Pomona, Williams, Stanford and Washington University, St. Louis. He served as an officer of Field Artillery in the First World War. He was on active duty as Major, Lieutenant-Colonel and Colonel, United States Army, between 1942 and 1946, serving as a legal advisor in Washington, in Algiers, in Italy, and in the European theater. He is the author of many books, and papers in legal publications. On July 1, 1955, he became Professor of Law at Harvard.

The Federal Civil Defense Act places primary responsibility in the states and their political subdivisions. That principle will have to go. Primary responsibility *must* be assumed by the United States. Such is the tenor, in part, of the Interim Report of the Subcommittee on Civil Defense of the Senate Armed Services Committee. The problem is not any want of constitutional power, but one of devising the administrative machinery whereby the authority of the United States shall be geared to the state government with its subordinate units.

In principle, the national government is entitled to do all that may be necessary in the common defense. To that extent, it may direct the state administration. But by what means can that best be done? Doubtless the President may be empowered to issue directives to the governors, but for the day-to-day conduct of post-attack administration, something less formal, more intimate, and flexible, would be required.

I believe that it will work out something like this. There would be, in each of the regions, now federal civil defense regions, a center of federal authority. Here would be found representatives of the departments—Treasury, Agriculture, Health, Education and Welfare, and so on—all working under one regional chief. This would be a powerful sub-station of the United States Government. It would impart federal direction and guidance to the state governments within the region. It would preside over the relations between the states. In formal conception, federal agencies must address themselves to the governors, who in turn would transmit the impulse to their subordinates. I doubt not, however, that straight paths would soon be beaten along functional lines, so that, for instance, representatives of the federal Department of Health, Education and Welfare and the staffs of corresponding state agencies would be dealing directly with each other. In Army language, these are technical channels, as distinguished from formal command channels.

Remember that the states would be dependent upon the

United States for grants in aid. Consider, too, the great moral authority of the presidential office—how, in time of disaster, we look spontaneously to the President, in confident expectation.

Next, we should determine, unequivocally, to maintain effective *civil* government throughout the nation from top to bottom. We should reject firmly the notion that the Army would take over—that unspoken premise to which I referred in the paper.

First, on the positive side: The system of civil government now in being has a tremendous going-concern value. It has legal competence, continuity, experience. It is familiar. I would take it as a starting point and go forward to adapt it, to build it up, so that it could bear the weight of an atomic attack. For purposes of planning, mayors, city attorneys, city engineers, the police and fire departments—the full-time working staff—guided by the civil defense director, are the people best able to concert measures. I wish I had time to speak of what has been done in perhaps the best prepared of the cities, Milwaukee, and particularly to draw attention to what the city attorney's office has done in preparing an ordinance for the maintenance of the city government, even in exile, in event of an atomic attack.

If the blow came, the experienced administrators would be the ones to put their plans in operation. Even if, say, Boston were levelled to the ground, and its survivors dispersed, still the city government as an entity should be preserved in exile as a rallying point, as a working party to prepare and execute measures for dealing with Boston. They would know best the physical features—the water mains, communications, and the like. They would know, too, the human and spiritual characteristics of Bostonians.

On the negative side, I believe the substitution of the military administration of the country would be unwise—indeed, would be an error of the first magnitude. The reasons set out in the paper were practical. First, the utter impracticability of making Army channels the conduits for reports, directions and requests flowing between the central government and the stricken country. To illustrate:—the Secretary of Agriculture wants to supply food stocks in his custody for feeding people in blasted areas. He would have to go to the Secretary of the Army to get him to pass the messages back and forth. Of course, I do not mean Secretary Benson and Secretary Brucker in person. I mean that the staff of the Department of Agriculture would have to work through the Army staff. You cannot have military administration and yet by-pass the military authorities.

Next, I pointed out that the Army would be more than a *conduit*—it would become a *director*. Now the Army is not set up to govern the country. To be sure, during World War II, we did carry on very extensive operations in military government and civil affairs in occupied and liberated countries. But as many of my colleagues here will recall, those undertakings involved tremendous preparatory work—in recruiting suitable personnel, bringing them together, in planning centers, acquiring information about the area, and perfecting operating procedures. It was a huge undertaking. The Army could not duplicate such operations here at home the day the bombs fell or for a long time thereafter.

We do have Military Government units in the Army Reserve which meet regularly and carry on their training programs. I have watched them with interest. Without going into detail, I fear that these reservists would not do nearly so well at governing American cities as would the common garden variety of mayor.

In the economic aspect, on which Professor Cavers is so much an authority, the objectives of restoring production and the like could best be performed by businessmen and their counsel, by industrial managers and labor leaders. They should be left at the jobs they know—not inducted into the Army and reassigned.

Further, I am convinced that the notion of Army rule should be rejected on *spiritual* grounds. To give leadership to a stricken people, to inspire them with zeal to carry on, to give them a feeling of full participation in the work of national survival, we should count on the leadership of *representative civil government.*

I add that if I were a responsible soldier and if there appeared some likelihood that civil government would crumble under attack, I would certainly have plans in reserve. I concede, frankly, that unprepared as we are today, martial rule might prove the best we could do; but the country should not take what would be the best in the worst extremity and accept it as the standard and approved solution. We can do far, far better, and we should go forward with firm purpose.

The paper closed with the thought that, by the time we convened for the Marshall Bicentennial, preparations would perhaps have advanced significantly beyond what they were at the time of writing, in early April. Well, there have been events. Whether we have advanced remains to be seen. First, some documentary material. There is the Report on Nonmilitary Defense by the Select Committee of the National Planning Association. It says, in part: Martial rule is a "desperate expedient" which "should be firmly rejected; but we can do so only if we prepare ourselves" (p. xxvii). The doctrine of that report is in complete accord with the paper under discussion today.

Then, in June, came the report of the Commission on Inter-Governmental Relations, under the chairmanship of Mr. Meyer Kestnbaum. The Commission recommends that Congress amend the Federal Civil Defense Act to re-allocate responsibility and place it primarily with the national government.

The Senate Subcommittee on Civil Defense—Senators Kefauver, Chairman, and Symington, Jackson, Saltonstall, and Margaret Chase Smith—continued to hold hearings, and issued a useful Interim Report.

I come now to Operation Alert. That was a nation-wide exercise wherein simulated developments over thirty days were compressed within an actual forty-eight hours. The President took an active interest. He went up to the emergency capitol. He was surrounded by a working government—Cabinet, Council of Economic Advisers, and so forth. His participation insured that all agencies should take the exercise seriously. Also, it assured a lively public attention. What was to be done there near Gettysburg was to be widely noticed and long remembered. Suddenly, there in that tent in the sun, something was evolved which, I surmise, had not been forseen by anyone—an instant decision that the way to meet an atomic attack was by a declaration of martial law and a suspension of the writ of *habeas corpus.*

I have given you the text. I forbear detailed comment. Seemingly, this action was hit upon between the President and the Attorney General on the spur of the moment. The President went on the radio to say, in part, that the liaison between the federal government and governors in the several states and the mayors of our great cities must be perfect. Certainly to interpose the Department of Defense and the six Armies as the channel between the President and the governors was not an apt way to achieve perfect cordination. "The recent blooper" is the characterization of a senior and responsible officer in the armed services writing in the confidence of private correspondence. Civil defense officials, it is fair to say, were stunned. The decision seemed to say that their work was to be scrapped—that the Army would take over. I could quote comments from some of the state and city directors. For the most part, these are retired officers, often of one or two star rank. They are not anti-Army. I say what was done was contrary to what had been firm policy. I quote from a letter of May 5, 1954, from the Assistant for Civil Defense in the Office of the Secretary of Defense. This is the senior officer in respect of Civil Defense. I had sent him a paper I was to read at the Industrial College of the Armed Forces, to make sure that its doctrine was not inconsistent with the doctrine of the Defense Department.

"There is no conceivable nation-wide apprehension of 'martial rule' as many people believe whereunder 'the military' can or will 'take over' for 'civil defense,' 'internal security' or 'military government' for the United States or its territories or possessions. Absurd as it seems to you and me there are a startling number of people who vaguely believe that that will be the case."

What had been inconceivable and absurd was what happened. The matter was raised at the President's press conference. I have given the text for that. One of the President's many splendid qualities is that he is not proud of opinion. He has asked the Attorney General to take another look—a much longer look—at this whole business. I hope that the Department of Justice will not be too proud to confess error. The very confusion into which we have been thrown has become some reason for hoping that there will soon be a clarification of official doctrine.

A great deal of studying is going on under the government roofs in Washington. I trust and I believe that these studies will conclude that we can find a much better method than the improvisation of June 16th. The House of Delegates of the American Bar Association, on the initiative of the Section on Administrative Law, has recommended the creation of a special committee to study these problems. Fortunately, Mr. Robert Benjamin is here with us today.

Finally, there is, I understand, some prospect of a Presidential commission being appointed, to proceed forthwith to make a comprehensive analysis and to recommend sound policy. That is my understanding. I have hoped all along that the Mr. Ferdinand Eberstadt, who did so much to straighten out difficulties in the Defense Department with his Task Force in 1948, might be called back. He is so astute, so intelligent, so skilful, so discerning in these matters—that, to me, would be the best promise of bringing order out of the confusion in which we now are. The creation of such a first-rate commission would, it seems to me, offer the best hope. Out of this Gettysburg nettle we might pluck the flower of national safety.

MR. HURLEY*

I stand before you as a sufferer from delivered comment: Professor Leach has neatly removed the ground on which I stand. At the outset let me say that there is another vital limitation on my comment: I stand before you as a student among scholars, and I think it will be most useful if I attempt to bring you the experience of a state, with its primary responsibility for civil defense which the Congress has so generously vested in us. Therefore my comment will present to you reflections concerning my own experience with some preparatory difficulties involved in government under law in time of crisis.

Professor Fairman has, I think, exposed for us two major groups of problems. The first are those involving what I would call the continuity of government. Here in Massachusetts, as in any other populous state, we should have problems of maintaining the governorship, and filling the ranks of the legislature; the same problems exist in connection with the Presidency and Congress. We also are concerned with the judicial reaction to some of the expected extraordinary executive authority and the orders issued in the exercise thereof. These problems are important, but we can at least begin to deal with them ourselves.

The second class of problems which Mr. Fairman laid bare I would call problems of new relations, and it is to this class that I wish to direct my attention—first, because of their intrinsic importance, and second, because these are the problems which state people are most apt to be concerned with; because these are problems about which one state acting alone can do nothing.

Our experience in Massachusetts has proved, I think,

---

* JOSEPH JAMES HURLEY, *of the Boston, Massachusetts, Bar.* Mr. Hurley was born in Boston in 1922. He took his Bachelor's degree at Boston College in 1943 and his LL.B. at the Boston College Law School in 1949. He served in the Army during World War II, has been law secretary to Mr. Justice Wilkins of the Massachusetts Supreme Judicial Court and has taught at Boston College. He has served as legal adviser to the Massachusetts Civil Defense Administration, and is now a Consultant for that organization.

that we must have uniform preparation and united action on the part of all the states, and in that term I include their lesser political subdivisions. It has been announced, for example, that a practice evacuation will be carried out in the Boston area, perhaps next year. If this evacuation were actually being carried out, it would be necessary to send upwards of 500,000 Massachusetts residents into Maine and New Hampshire, there to be cared for. It is a fact that there are not sufficient hospital beds in all of New England to care for the casualties that reasonably could be expected in a relatively minor atomic attack on the Boston area.

Now back in 1950 and '51, when the prospect was one plane, one bomb, one city, the states set out to achieve a measure of uniform preparation and united action by means of compacts, each state agreeing with the other to make certain preparations and to render mutual assistance in time of attack. And very quickly, for example, the six New England states and New York and New Jersey, just to take the northeastern area of the country, each had a compact with each of the other states; there was a total of 56 individual compacts, substantially all the same. It quickly became apparent that some central communication point was needed through which requests for assistance could be transmitted from one state to another. The Regional Office of the federal Civil Defense Administration, of which Mr. Fairman has spoken, undertook this responsibility, but as time went on, and the line of zeros behind the figure telling us of the strength of the bomb grew longer, it became equally apparent that something more than just a communications center—a message center—was needed. Someone, independent of all the states, would have to coordinate requests for assistance. Otherwise, Massachusetts in all innocence might be using fire engines from Vermont to protect a box factory in Boston when the same fire engines were needed in the State of New York to save a vital defense plant in Binghamton.

We have concluded, therefore, that there must be some agency, some power, superior to the states. I think that specific performance of an interstate civil defense contract would hardly be an adequate or appropriate remedy. We naturally look to the federal government, and it is my opinion that the same reasons which impelled us to adopt our Constitution in substitution for the Articles of Confederation lead us to look to the national government for leadership and direction in this field. It is interesting to speculate that if the Congress had the power to enact federal civil defense legislation at all it is because the Congress has the war power —because civil defense is a part of modern war. And I would suggest to you that the authority to wage war, as our United States Supreme Court has put it, is equally a responsibility to wage war successfully. This does not mean that the federal government must take over the job of running every State and local civil defense organization. We recognize our responsibilities under the police power, but we feel that this is a field of dual responsibility, and that the federal government has an equal if not primary responsibility in the field.

Finally, I would turn to the character of this federal leadership. Will it be civilian; will it be military? I would pass the question of legality of the President's recent simulated declaration of martial law. Better lawyers than I, however, seem to question it. I would pass also the effect of this declaration upon the civil defense program. It has long been felt that there is a widespread public tendency to think that if anything happens the Army will take over, and therefore we do not need civil defense, and I would suggest to you that even a simulated practice declaration of martial law strengthens, rather than weakens, this public tendency. I would pass also the fact that, in my opinion, martial law, or military rule, is a condition, a fact, not an enactment, and that these magic words do not create a complete operating disaster relief mechanism.

In conclusion, I would commend to you what I think is a salient sentence from the words of Professor Fairman: "Thinking about the perils of conflict will not lead us one inch closer to it. Ignoring the possibility will not avert it. The contrary is more likely." I suggest to you that we must plan so that fusion in the natural order will not result in fission in the social order.

DEAN CAVERS*

I believe it would be most useful in commencing my comment on Professor Fairman's notable paper, to which no summary can do justice, to stress the nature of the crisis with which he is dealing.

It is a crisis of survival, both in a very literal, physical sense and in regard to our most fundamental and cherished institutions. The crisis, as I see it, extends over two stages. The first is the stage of atomic warfare—a period that might last no more than a few days, but might continue in diminishing tempo over a period of months until one of the giant antagonists had collapsed. This would be an apocalyptic war—a war such as has never been experienced in the history of man. Though it came to an end in victory, the second stage would follow—the stage of reconstruction—and it would also have its dangers. If we had not planned well before war came, we might find that the processes of democratic civil government could not be restored, perhaps for years, perhaps for decades.

It is the very seriousness of these dangers that has led so many people in this country resolutely to close their eyes to them, or to take refuge either in a preoccupation with false problems or in seeking solutions in slogans or catchwords. I believe you will find human behavior of this sort to have preceded most of the great cataclysmic upheavals of society in the past. When, by the illumination of hind-sight, we read

* DAVID FARQUHAR CAVERS, *Associate Dean of the Harvard Law School.* Dean Cavers was born in Buffalo in 1902. He was graduated as a Bachelor of Science at the University of Pennsylvania in 1923 and as a Bachelor of Laws at Harvard in 1926. He has practiced law in New York City, has served in the Department of Justice, and has been Counsel for various government departments in Washington. He was a member of the faculty of the Duke University School of Law from 1932 to 1945 and has filled visiting professorships at Yale and Chicago. He became Professor of Law at Harvard in 1945, and Associate Dean in 1951. He has lectured on problems of economic stabilization after atomic attack at the Industrial College of the Armed Forces, and has written extensively on planning for law and government in the event of atomic war.

the stories of great civilizations overturned by war or revolution, we wonder at the impotence or the blindness of their rulers in the face of dangers that, to us, appear quite obvious. A paralysis of will seems to arise when the peril of a society is not disturbance but extinction.

In facing the present danger we in the United States have the comforting consideration that it is contingent; that honorable peace seems an increasingly real alternative to atomic war; and that we may turn this dangerous corner in our history without sustaining anything more disturbing than what we have already undergone. But the fact that we are not doomed to war should not render us jaunty or indifferent. Those, however, seem to me the only terms that adequately characterize our attitude toward those grim possibilities that we take seriously only when it comes to military appropriations.

Operation Alert, as Professor Fairman has explained, led to an abrupt resort to martial law, mock martial law. This was a means of filling the vacuum which our national leader suddenly observed to exist where our non-military defense plans should have been. The initial public response to this action—this ready solution—was relief and approval. But I believe it testifies to our deep-seated devotion to the rule of law that this first reaction was succeeded by widespread concern. It is worthy of note that one of the strongest of the questioning voices was raised by a leading publicist who drew his criticisms directly from the paper which Professor Fairman had written some months earlier for this Conference and which had been already distributed to you. This fact demonstrates, moreover, that despite the fatalism and apathy that now prevail, a forthright, responsible attack on the problem of atomic emergency can still command a hearing.

I agree with Professor Fairman completely that martial rule is not a satisfactory substitute for civil government in meeting our atomic defense problems. I am not sure, however, that recourse to the military is to be distrusted as much because the military may be untrustworthy in the use of power, as because the military would neither know what to do nor how to do it. There are certain functions that certainly the military could perform, and I believe Professor Fairman would agree with me as to this, if at least armed forces could be organized, trained and distributed with these functions in view.

Some of the problems of coping with the consequences of atomic attack would be elementary ones—how to maintain basic order and to insure the distribution of the bare essentials of life among the hoards of hungry, homeless refugees flooding into every community on the periphery of the evacuated cities. And we should remember, incidentally, that not only would those cities be evacuated which the enemy had chosen to attack but also those cities which the enemy might choose to attack the day after. Indeed, for painfully obvious reasons, the latter cities might contribute more refugees than the former.

The problem of assuring observance of the basic decencies in the administration of whatever rules might be laid down for coping with the refugee problems is something that merits careful planning. But the situation of the over-run communities would be desperate indeed, if the only planning were directed to their immediate situation. A truly crucial problem is how to maintain the social and economic vitality of the rest of the country, the areas which have been neither bombed nor evacuated in fear of bombing and which have not been contaminated by fall-outs. I think it is reasonable to suppose that those untouched areas would cover more than half the people and far more than half the territory of the United States, unless atomic war should prove more protracted than now seems likely. Physically intact, these communities would nonetheless find their activities seriously disorganized. They might, indeed, become so preoccupied with their own problems of survival as to fail to provide the succor needed by the displaced millions and the support required by our armed forces in continuing to wage war.

To enable these areas to fulfill their essential roles, we must devise procedures and instrumentalities to supplement and reinforce those that atomic attack had disrupted. Our economy is a very intricate organism in which the interdependence of the parts is comparable to that of the human body's. To assume that great cities could be laid waste, great populations up-rooted, market, supply and credit relationships disordered, transportation and communication crippled, and yet to expect the nation to be preserved as a functioning entity simply by calling on the military is to believe in magic, to use a term that I think significantly crops up in all three of these papers.

Confronting these dangers, a nation would do well to call on lawyers in advance of the event instead of on the military after it. The lawyer is the expert that society charges with foreseeing the problems that lurk in the future and with designing the procedures, the arrangements and adjustments that will enable it to achieve its objectives. There is need for such positive planning against the hazard of atomic war. The problems are many, complex, and until very recently, almost completely ignored.

There are vital problems of the inter-relationships among federal, state and local authorities, and between the civil and military authorities that Professor Fairman has emphasized. There are problems of organization within the federal government which now divides responsibility for the essentially unitary planning problem between two separate agencies, not to include the defense establishment. But beyond these problems of organization and administration there is the vast array of substantive measures necessary to preserve federal and state judiciaries, to sustain the monetary banking and credit system, to insure the flow of essential goods, to keep industries from paralysis where practicable, and to care for the sick, the homeless and the unemployed. Planning standby measures of this sort by lawyers working with experts in public administration, in business and economics, in labor relations and in social welfare, can provide the basic ingredients of an orderly, functioning, though crippled, society. Planning must provide for decentralization and for flexibility, but if we depend on improvisation after attack alone, we might see our nation disintegrate into the thousands of little Operations Survival in which the men with the guns were the rulers and the law.

Studies of these problems should not be conducted in secret, behind the curtains of classification, on the ground that the public would be frightened if they learned of them. An important step toward a more responsible approach was taken in Philadelphia when the creation of a committee of the American Bar Association to consider some of them was proposed by the initiative of the Administrative Law Section. I hope this committee when instituted may succeed in inducing the federal government to take a more positive policy toward assuring the rule of law, even in the crisis of atomic war.

DISCUSSION

Professor Braucher: Due process of Conference requires that Professor Leach—who has undoubtedly been surprised by being used as an example of the unthinking reaction and of a resort to magic—be given a moment to defend himself.

Professor Leach: Thank you for your courtesy, Professor Braucher. I should like to extract myself from this badminton game in which I seem to be playing the role of a shuttlecock. It is humiliating to me to find myself in a position of uttering an *obiter dictum* in front of Dean Pound and Justice Frankfurter, who taught me better. It was an uncalled for remark that I made about martial law being inevitable if the H-bomb falls. The only thing I had to say was that there isn't going to be any argument about separation of powers if the H-bomb falls, and it was unnecessary for me to say what I thought would happen. It's none of my business and I don't know enough to talk. I share the principles of those three fine gentlemen who have spoken; I share their hopes; I even share their activity—I, and my wife, who as a result of her own experience in the London blitz has some emotional drive behind her efforts on behalf of civilian defense. Whether I share their expectations is another thing. If their expectations are to be realized it may well be that the key to the situation lies in the heart and head of that very determined and very capable man who presides in the Department of the Treasury.

Professor Fairman: I would just like to add that if we do come to the pass of having a Chief Civil Affairs Officer I do hope he'll be as able and distinguished as Bart Leach.

Professor Braucher: Now, I think, in view of the fact that we bandied about the name of the American Bar Association a little we probably ought to ask Mr. Benjamin if he has anything to say.

Robert M. Benjamin, of the New York Bar: I should like to report on the exact status of the proposal of the Administrative Law Section of which I was chairman until a couple of weeks ago. At our instance, the House of Delegates referred that question to the Board of Governors, requesting it to consider the appointment of such a committee and authorizing it to do so, and I have very little doubt that the Board of Governors, when it meets next month, will do so. The Administrative Law Section felt that this was the kind of project that was beyond the field of its own special competence, that for that reason and also because dealing with federal officials, as we would hope this committee would do, could be better carried out by a committee than a section— it was for those reasons that we made this proposal, and it is motivated—our proposal—by the reluctance, the great reluctance, that Professor Fairman has expressed of resorting to martial law with confidence that that resort will be unnecessary if minds are put on the job now.

I should like to say in addition only that this seems to me to be one facet of the problem of government under law that is worth emphasizing—that is, the obligation of the trained citizen, and especially of the lawyer, to contribute to the formulation of the law, and to plan for operations under the law, that will make government under law possible in this field.

*Professor Elliott**: Mr. Chairman, I had hoped to recall lawyers to the fact that even lawyers have to look beyond the law, by beginning with the quotation that the Dean used yesterday, the one inscribed over Langdell Hall, a somewhat truncated quotation from Bracton through Coke: *Non sub homine sed sub deo et lege.* My impression is, from what has been said so far in this conference, that Coke's quotation, in his Sunday morning brush with James I, is quite often interpreted by lawyers as not under man, but under God and "the lawyers," rather than "the law." But I am happily set straight on that point; there is no necessity for educating our masters the lawyers, as to the primacy of policies, as Sir William Harcourt said the British would have to do for the newly enfranchised voters, the new masters, after the passage of one of the later reform acts in England in the nineteenth century. It will not be necessary, since Dean Cavers has called to the attention of this group the really salient kind of correctives—even though he relied on lawyers to save us—and Henry Hart, yesterday, set the tone that emphasized the necessity of positive action in a crisis, the dimensions of which stagger the imagination. The basic Civil Defense problem is to win a political battle—if the whole issue is not to go by default.

Now I would like to point out just two things and then ask a question. The first is that on Mr. Fairman's analysis—a very judicious, if not judicial, one I think it was—somewhat overly kind in its corrective tone toward the errors of the administration in certain respects—the President of the United States found himself confronted with a hypothetical ques-

---

* William Yandell Elliott, *Leroy B. Williams Professor of History and Political Science, Harvard University.*

tion. He was not in Gettysburg (the silliness of this is illustrated in terms of the secrecy that surrounds it, by the fact that though he was surrounded by reporters in all directions in the immediate vicinity, we can't even say where he was). He was not taking his ease at Gettysburg; he was in the mountains; not like Lee hiding out there, but still under conditions of some simulated severity. He found himself presented with a problem which, as Mr. Fairman admits, had no backing in any civil defense organization capable of dealing with a national emergency of the character and kind with which he was hypothetically presented. I am grateful to Dean Cavers for underlining this point.

Under those circumstances, I think Mr. Fairman has himself suggested that the part of wisdom was to act with what resources the President had. These were, alas, only the military services—the Defense Department—who could span a nation-wide problem immediately, in conditions where civil government could not exist because there would be no civilian authorities in some sizeable parts of the country, and where the movement of men, troops, supplies and everything else had to be done with the utmost expedition, and the control of panic and everything else that goes along with it had to be dealt with by men who believed in what they were doing as a soldier's duty.

But that does not detract from the other aspect of the matter. The record says, "the Secretary of Defense and subordinate military commanders of the respective Army areas shall enforce law and order"—that's a primary requisite—"and shall carry out determinations and decisions of federal agencies in the discharge of the regular and emergency authorities invested in them by law, and the proclamations and executive orders issued since the attack upon the United States," and so on. Now, of course, the real question that arises in this matter is: How can the civilian authorities act through military channels?

It is Mr. Fairman's assumption that they can act only through the Secretary of Defense, and that indeed is a very cumbersome method. Martial law, as he knows better than anybody (I came here as a young professor when he was just completing his initial studies, I remember, as a graduate student) is not a fixed quantity, and the decision that the President has made to have it studied in terms of its flexibility, not only in terms of its precedents, but of its possibilities, is the essential problem before us. Such a situation will exist under any kind of hypothesis that is not mere wishful dreaming and thinking or escapism. It will exist if we do not succeed in forfending it by making it improbable that it would be profitable to create that risk on the part of prospective enemies. Such a situation will, otherwise, exist as would make martial control over very large areas of the country inevitable.

But at the same time all those points that have been made about the inadequacy of mere martial control is true, and therefore the two problems I would put to you are these: How can martial law, if it is enforced in certain areas, still permit a chain of command from civilian authorities to military forces flexible enough to deal with the foreseeable problems that will come up? That's the first proposition. And the second one, I think, is: Given the necessity for creating the kind of organization of civil defense that both Professor Fairman and Dean Cavers have seen and that Bart Leach has been emphasizing for many years, national in scope, with the requisite powers—and strong *before* the possible test—how can we, under our working separation of powers, convince Congress of this necessity? Nothing in the record so far indicates the slightest recognition that we shall not proceed in the good old tradition of state-by-state action, with little possibility of real federal planning and less for real national control by a civilian setup. Until we have corrected this kind of atmosphere, the lawyers had probably better address themselves to the problem of getting the temper and tone in the country to deal with the problem rather than with setting up hypothetical solutions for which there will be no machinery whatever, unless we change the setup and the pitch that we are under. It is political education and legislative authority, including the necessary resources, that, as John Marshall saw, at the beginning of our nation, must create a new Federalist courage and temper. Without that change, one can only inveigh against martial law and military rule. The choice would fall on them by default.

Professor Fairman: Response to the first proposition calls me to shift over to the position of a staff officer—working for, I hope, as good a chief as General Leach—and trying to explain how this would appear to an Army officer cast in this situation. Suppose Professor Elliott comes in with a sheaf of papers from O.D.M., or Professor Cavers comes in from O.P.A. with a sheaf of papers, and shoves it at these Army people and says, "This is what's to be done."

Now, if my chief is to be held responsible for this operation, I'm going to say, "Wait a minute. He can't be used as a mere machine to take all sorts of directions sent in by this and that Department." I would stand in the corner with the commander and say that if he is going to be made responsible for this, his staff officers have to pass upon the measures to be taken. I can't conceive of any workable military administration where all of the civilian branches of government can come in and shove directions at the general and tell him, "Send it down the line to your people and cause them to do it: don't you talk back, your staff has no control over this, you just do it." Don't mistake: if we had so-called "martial law," officers of the Army must have a very large discretion in administering the country. So I think this whole idea of military administration is a great misconception, unless really meaning the whole thing, such as we had in Military Government abroad.

On the side of how to convince Congress of the importance of the problem, I would suggest, first, that a somewhat promising start has been made in the hearings and the reports that have come out. I think there is some feeling in some Congressional quarters, at any rate, that things need to be done. I would suggest also that I can think of no better way to persuade the country of the importance of this than to establish, as I suggested at the end, a commission of undoubted authority and of great competence and skill, to sort out this terribly confused problem and come out with something that the country can understand. And I trust that if the country understood, we could go forward with some suitable legislation. I am greatly impressed with the experience of well-led units of government such as Milwaukee. They've had excellent leadership there and they have really done a great deal. I don't know why the same kind of leadership coudn't be applied to the whole United States.

Erwin Cooper, of the Boston Bar: I have listened with a good deal of interest to what has been said about the necessity for having some type of civil defense organization do some over-all planning throughout the country. I have heard very little about what the role of the military is, what it feels that it ought to be, and what its position is with regard to this thing.

I think I have some insight into this because I have spent some time in doing one of the plans with which the military has been working relative to possibly taking over, if it had to, in such a situation as this, and I have seen the general, over-all directive, that is, in at least one Army area in which these plans are being laid.

Despite all that has been said here, the military, I gather from the directives, has no desire to enter into this situation. It would look upon it with distaste and if it got into such a situation it would want to unload it just as fast as possible. To that end, all of the plans that I have heard about and seen have calculated upon using all available civilians to enter into this situation. They have, in many cases, felt that they would look for the very people who are conducting various departments of the government, and various services of the municipal and town governments and state governments to take over similar functions under a set-up of martial law with a view to rehabilitating the situation as fast as possible and turning it back to civilian control if that were possible.

The very magnitude, however, of the task would seem to indicate that it would be some time before this could be done. There is one further difficulty with the situation which I think makes me feel that if something such as Professor Fairman is arguing for and working for could be worked out, it could be of infinite help in a plan of the sort which I have seen written and other plans which I have heard about which are similar in nature. If there could be an over-all group such as the one he illustrates, it might be that the military could make use of this quickly and then turn control back to such a group. The military has a characteristic lack of personnel to handle this type of situation, it is true. The job of the military through history has been to win a war, to hold territory, to gain territory, and to stabilize the situation. The task of Army commanders in the field is complicated by this type of situation and I do not believe that Army commanders would want to hang on in a situation such as this very long. I, however, find some difficulty in Professor Fairman's statement and his illustration of somebody's walking into a military headquarters with a sheaf of papers and throwing it upon a commander-in-chief's desk. I don't think the Military would operate that way at all. Our plan was not planned that way. We had planned, instead, to set up the commander-in-chief's staff much as any other administrative system would have to be set up, and that each member of the staff would have his liaison with his counterpart in civilian government. I think that this is the only way that a military plan could work, envisioning the type of thing that I have indicated and utilizing such people as one could find.

The only difficulty that we saw about this in the particular unit that I was with, which peculiarly enough is now defunct, is that we were always told we would take control in our own area, and we always wondered whether we'd be around to actually exercise control in the event that such a bomb should fall.

IV

This session, again held in the Ames Courtroom, consisted first of an address by Chief Justice Sir Owen Dixon of Australia, and then of a discussion of two papers, written by Judge William H. Hastie, and Dean McGeorge Bundy, both on the theme of "The Meaning of Due Process of Law." The chairman at this session was Professor Benjamin Kaplan* of the Harvard Law School. He first introduced Chief Justice Dixon, who spoke on "Marshall and the Australian Constitution."

---

* BENJAMIN KAPLAN, *Professor of Law, Harvard Law School.* Professor Kaplan was born in New York City in 1911. He took his degree in Arts at the College of the City of New York in 1929, and his LL.B. at Columbia in 1933. He practiced law in New York between 1933 and 1947, except for the war years when he served in the Army as an officer. He was discharged as Lieutenant-Colonel in 1946. He became a visiting professor at the Harvard Law School in 1947, and Professor of Law in 1948. Professor Kaplan has specialized in civil procedure and in matters of contract and copyright. He has taken especial interest in civil rights, and has written numerous articles in his chosen fields.

Marshall and the Australian Constitution

SIR OWEN DIXON *

Marshall is a name well known in Australia to all lawyers, and as I hope to show, his work had a particular influence in that country in the formative years of constitution making. As I was invited from Australia to come here, on the occasion of the celebrations of the bicentennial of his birth, I thought that it would be appropriate to speak about Marshall and the Australian Constitution, and I have so entitled my paper.

It is not always the greatest judge who feels sure of himself. But two whose greatness shines out from their judgments seem to have been very sure of themselves, Holmes and Marshall. Who else could have written of Marshall, and of Story and Kent too, as Holmes did in his closing judicial years, in the course of casual correspondence: "They were an innocent lot and didn't need caviare for luncheon."[1] It is a doubtful thesis that the early decades of the nineteenth century were, as Holmes described the period, "a God-fearing, simple time that knew nothing of your stinking twisters but had plain views of life."[2] But in the age in which it was done, the adoption of the Constitution of the United States must have appeared a bold experiment, particularly to minds

* THE RT. HON. SIR OWEN DIXON, *Chief Justice of Australia.* Sir Owen Dixon was born in 1886. He was graduated at the University of Melbourne in Australia, was called to the Bar at Victoria in 1910, became King's Counsel in 1922, Acting Judge of the Supreme Court of the state of Victoria in 1926, and Justice of the High Court of Australia in 1929. He served as Envoy Extraordinary and Minister Plenipotentiary of the Commonwealth of Australia at Washington, 1942-1944, and as the United Nations Mediator between India and Pakistan in the Kashmir dispute in 1950. He has been Chief Justice of Australia since 1952. He was knighted in 1941.

1. 2 HOLMES-LASKI LETTERS 1015, January 11, 1928.
2. *Ibid.*

moulded in the common law. If its principles were to be understood, if they were to command intelligent assent and guide the minds and thoughts of men, they must be expounded and inculcated as deep but simple truths flowing as evident consequences from the form of government that had been established and the provisions which gave it strength and coherence. Indefinite or qualified conceptions would not serve the occasion; nothing but broad sweeping doctrine simple in its certainty. It may not have been necessary that the play should please the million but it could not be caviare to the general.

A century later Australia found itself with a federal constitution new to its people. It may be that they too were an innocent lot. But they had decided to form six colonies into a nation under the British Crown and to do it by the institution of federalism. The principles of federalism had then been made familiar; familiar to those who dwelt in the North American continent, but not to those dwelling elsewhere in the English-speaking world. For elsewhere in that world, except to students of political science, federalism seems to have been beyond comprehension; and indeed even today there is reason to think that understanding of it is denied to those who pass their lives under a unitary system of government.

Australian constitution-makers turned to American sources of instruction and, according to their various propensities, studied the constitutional history and law of the United States. For example, one member[3] of the Australian Constitutional Convention of 1897-1898 long years afterwards chanced to tell me that at that time he read through the five volumes of Elliott's Debates.

But if, in the day when the six colonies of Australia were to unite in a federal Commonwealth, they had but to turn for their inspiration to the document on which the constitu-

3. Sir Isaac Isaacs, afterwards a Justice and then Chief Justice of the High Court of Australia and subsequently Governor-General of the Commonwealth.

tional system of this country rested and for their guidance to the learning and experience which had accumulated during the century of its operation, it nevertheless remained true that federalism came to Australia as an innovation embodying doctrine, and containing implications, strange to the minds of most of those then engaged in the administration of the law and the conduct of government. For the constitutions under which they lived were unitary, and there was little consciousness of the nature and consequences even of a rigid constitution.

Moreover, in an absolute sense the Australian Constitution did involve an innovation. It combined the basal conceptions of the Constitution of 1787 with the British parliamentary system under the Crown. In truth it resembles the Constitution of the United States in more than basal principles wherever it is concerned with matters arising from the federal character of the Commonwealth. In such things it follows the instrument of 1787 with remarkable fidelity. The legislative powers are more numerous and perhaps more extensive; and there are additional provisions which can be ascribed to particular considerations of Australian concern. But there are few departures in principle, and most of them find a reason in the course of judicial decision in the United States before 1900.

It is not in the legal relations of the States to the Commonwealth or in the legal separation of the functions of government that the Australian Constitution innovates upon the Constitution of the United States. It is in combining federalism of the American description with the principle which prevails in the United Kingdom and in all the Queen's self-governing dominions, the principle requiring that the Ministry should be formed of members of the legislature and should be removable by the Crown if the Ministry loses the confidence of that House of the Legislature which controls finance.

Strange as you may possibly think it, this principle has been found completely to harmonize, not only with the federal character of the Constitution, but also with a distribution of constitutional powers among the legislature, the executive, and the judiciary. It need hardly be said that a principle so deeply rooted in our political conceptions gained acceptance of its own strength. Its strength was great because it had long been seen in operation so that its working was widely understood and valued.

But it was otherwise with the supremacy of the federal authority, the limitations upon the sovereignty of the States, the conceptions of federal and State jurisdiction and other implications of federalism. These were new ideas. There was not the tendency that was encountered in Marshall's day to dispute federal authority to the point of resistance. But the new order was in need of exposition. Much of it was strange and there were many in authority to whom it was not very palatable. There was the conception of limited powers plenary within their ambit; of powers extending to all matters incidental to their exercise; of the immunity of federal agencies from State interference; of the paramountcy of federal laws over State laws; of the place occupied by the federal judicature. Upon such things Marshall had spoken. What he had said may have been simple. But it was expressed in terms of principle, broad and clear. If it be true that Marshall was not a master of the common law, nevertheless he spoke as a great common lawyer might have done. If his principles were enclosed in categories, that would not be unrecommendatory to Australian judges whose jurisprudence must then have been of the school of Austin. What could be more natural, therefore, what could be more right, than to make a grateful appropriation of Marshall's more famous judgments to Australian use?

Even before the High Court of Australia could be constituted in obedience to the Judicature chapter of the Constitution, federal officers resisted in the Supreme Court of Victoria the payment of income tax to that State. A full examination was made by the State Court of the doctrine expounded in the second part of Marshall's famous judgment in *McCulloch v. Maryland.*[4] But the doctrine was rejected by the State Court as applicable neither to the Australian Constitution nor to the case in hand, namely the case of the liability of a federal officer to State income tax in respect of his salary.[5] It is safe to neglect the distinctions which the Supreme Court of the State of Victoria then perceived between the Constitution of the United States and that of Australia. It is true that for a time the argument based upon them obtained some currency, but nowadays it would be regarded as nothing better than a misconception. On the other hand it cannot be said that the reasons were misconceived which led that Court to deny that Marshall's doctrine required that salaries of federal officers should be free of State income tax. *Dobbins v. Erie County*[6] was cited to the judges and so was *Collector v. Day,*[7] but the response of the State Court consisted in a rudimentary anticipation of *Graves v. New York.*[8]

No sooner had the High Court of Australia been constituted than it was called upon to declare itself as to the place to be accorded under the Commonwealth Constitution to that form of federal supremacy expounded in *McCulloch v. Maryland.* The case came from the Supreme Court of Tasmania where, by a divided Court, the doctrine had been rejected. By the law of Tasmania, a receipt for the payment of money must bear a duty stamp. The stamp was the smallest denomination, twopence, and it was the payee who must affix it. But federal law said that when an employee of the Commonwealth was paid his wages a receipt must be obtained from him. Was the employee under an obligation to place the State stamp on the receipt for his wages? The interference with federal functions was minute. Moreover, the question might have been answered upon the commonplace ground that State law was inconsistent with federal law if it

4. 4 Wheat. (U.S.) 316 (1819).
5. Wollaston's Case, 28 Victorian L.R. 357 (1902).
6. 16 Peters (U.S.) 435 (1842).
7. 11 Wall. (U.S.) 113 (1870).
8. 306 U.S. 466 (1939).

required the Commonwealth employee to stamp the receipt demanded in obedience to federal law. Indeed that answer was comprised in the reasons given for the decision. But the judges of the newly constituted High Court readily embraced the doctrine so grandly expressed in the second part of Marshall's famous judgment and the doctrine was received, at all events for the time being, into the law of the Commonwealth of Australia.[9]

After the decision that the receipt from salary need not be stamped, not much time was allowed to pass before the question whether federal salaries were immune from State income tax was brought to the High Court. In this day we should regard the amount of the State income tax of that time as quite negligible. But so important was the matter then thought that two cabinet ministers lent their names to the litigation which was to establish the immunity. Unfortunately, as the case made its way through the Supreme Court of Victoria to the High Court, the State Court displayed something more than reluctance to accept the principles of Marshall, notwithstanding the unreserved approval which the High Court had then so recently given to them.[10] This may have looked like an early symptom of resistance to federal supremacy and one ominously involving the judicial power of the Commonwealth. At all events the judges of the High Court were aroused to a fuller and more emphatic expression of the rationale of the doctrine and of the reasons why it was no less indispensable to the working of the Australian Constitution than to that of the United States.[11] But the general interest in the major premise appears then to have been slight compared with the interest evoked by the minor premise; for the notion that federal officers enjoyed an immunity from the only income tax then levied led the States to resort to every expedient that might be open to secure a reversal of the conclusion, and it led the Commonwealth

9. D'Emden v. Pedder, 1 Commw. L.R. 91 (1904).
10. Deakin & Lyne's Cases, 29 Victorian L.R. 748 (1904).
11. Deakin & Lyne v. Webb, 1 Commw.L.R. 585 (1904).

eventually to declare legislatively that the salaries of federal officers should be liable to State income tax. All this, however, meant no weakening in the faith of the High Court in the second part of *McCulloch v. Maryland,* and it is therefore outside the scope of this paper to trace the course of the subsequent controversy. The controversy is chiefly important as establishing the final authority of the High Court in most constitutional questions.[12]

But in the meantime there arose a claim from a new and perhaps unexpected quarter to exert a paramount federal authority. Among the enumerated legislative powers of the Commonwealth was a power to make laws with respect to conciliation and arbitration for the prevention and settlement of industrial disputes extending beyond the limits of any one State. A Court of Conciliation and Arbitration was set up and its business speedily grew. It was true that its power to make an industrial regulation depended upon the existence of a two-State dispute; but after all dispute and disagreement are indistinguishable, and those wishing to invoke the authority of the Arbitration Court did not find it difficult to ensure that the constitutional requirement was satisfied.[13]

The statute establishing this tribunal expressly included in the subject matter over which it should have jurisdiction industrial disputes upon State Government railways. It was proposed accordingly to register a union of railway servants —State railway servants—and thus to qualify it as a disputant. The States objected, and the High Court denied the validity of the provision bringing industrial disputes on State railways within the jurisdiction of the Arbitration

12. See Webb v. Outtrim, [1907] A.C. 81 (P.C. 1906) (cf. 23 LAW QUARTERLY REVIEW 373); Baxter v. Commissioners of Taxation & Flint v. Webb, 4 Commw.L.R. 1087 and 1178 (1907); Commonwealth Salaries Act (1907); N.S.W. Taxation Commissioners v. Baxter, 1908 A.C. 214; Chaplin v. Commissioner of Taxes for S.A., 12 Commw.L.R. 375 (1911); Commonwealth v. Kreglinger and Fernau Ltd., 37 Commw.L.R. 393 (1926); Commonwealth v. Limerick S.S. Co. Ltd., 35 Commw.L.R. 69 (1924); Commonwealth v. Bank of N.S.W., 79 Commw.L.R. 497 at pp. 627-8 (1949).

13. Cf. R. v. Commonwealth Court of Conciliation & Arbitration and the Australian Builders' Labourers Federation, 18 Commw.L.R. 224, at p. 256 (1914).

Court.[14] The immunity of federal agencies from state interference was found to be reciprocal. Liberal citations were made from *Collector v. Day.* Section 107 of the Commonwealth Constitution performs the office of the Tenth Amendment here, and in the citations the doctrine made its first appearance in Australia that the reserved powers of the States, like the powers affirmatively granted to the national government, carry with them implications and incidents.

For a time the High Court seemed to be less concerned with federal supremacy than with preserving the States from federal encroachment upon their immunities and legislative powers. Perhaps federal supremacy had been established too readily and too early. Strange as it may seem, it was the judges who were appointed when the Court was constituted who seemed to recede from the true principle of federal supremacy. It was they who came in the end to insist that the rule against interference by the States with federal agencies was reciprocal and operated *e converso* in favor of the States.

But when these judges had all departed, the High Court swept aside the whole doctrine as one conferring immunity on agencies and instrumentalities of the States.[15] The reasons which the Court gave combined many elements, not all of them satisfactory. But first and foremost it was insisted that you could find nothing compatible with State immunity in the principle which the High Court had adopted from *McCulloch v. Maryland* and formulated in the case concerning the twopenny duty stamp on the receipt for the federal officers' salary. Then came passages in the judgment containing protests against resort to implications; against the desertion of the golden rules of construction enshrined in English law; and against an endeavor, as the judgment described it, to find one's way through the Australian Constitution by the borrowed light of the decisions and at times of the

14. Federated Amalgamated etc. Association v. N.S.W. Railway Traffic Employees Association, 4 Commw.L.R. 488 (1906).

15. Amalgamated Society of Engineers v. Adelaide S.S. Co. Ltd., 28 Commw.L.R. 129 (1920).

dicta that American institutions and circumstances had drawn from the distinguished tribunals of the United States. We are next exhorted by the judges to bear in mind two cardinal features of our political system, namely the unity of the Crown and the principle of responsible government, and these are said radically to distinguish it from the American Constitution. And so of course they do; but in no relevant respect. For they do not touch the federal structure of the Constitution or its consequences. The warning against the use of light borrowed from the United States did not deter the judges who gave it from resorting once more to Marshall as an authority for the interpretation upon which they relied in deciding that the States are subject to the federal legislative power concerning industrial disputes. Two familiar passages are taken from what is described as "the celebrated judgment of Chief Justice Marshall in *Gibbons v. Ogden*."[16] First: "We know of no rule for construing the extent of such powers other than is given by the language of the instrument which confers them, taken in connexion with the purposes for which they are conferred." And again: "This power like all others vested in Congress is complete in itself, and acknowledges no limitations other than are prescribed in the Constitution." Finally the High Court intimated that the freedom of the Commonwealth from State interference should depend on federal legislation.

The extent to which the High Court intended that its manifesto in this case should go is not very clear. Certainly it marked the end of the notion that you should restrict federal power by reference to the reserved powers of the States.[17] But the author of the judgment, Mr. Justice Isaacs, said in an earlier judgment[18] that in *McCulloch v. Maryland* Marshall had laid down some principles and arrived at a decision

---

16. 9 Wheat. (U.S.) 1, 188, 198 (1824).

17. Based on section 107, which is analogous to the Tenth Amendment. The notion reappeared in a curious form in James v. Commonwealth, [1936] A.C. 578, at pp. 632-3 (P.C.), with which compare the uncorrected text as it appears in ARGUS L.R. (1936) at p. 344, col. 2.

18. Isaacs J. in Baxter v. Commissioners of Taxation N.S.W., 4 Commw. L.R. 1087 at p. 1157 (1907).

which are not only in consonance with the rule laid down in the case about the stamp duty on receipts for federal salary but are in strict accord with the most authoritative pronouncements of English law. Further on all questions of power the same judge invariably observed Marshall's injunction never to forget that it was a Constitution he was expounding. What was intended and what was done was to discredit the earlier doctrine protecting so-called instrumentalities of government, federal or State, from the exercise of some legislative power of the other Government on the ground that to admit that the instrumentality fell within the application of the power at all would be to admit that the one Government possessed a means of burdening or interfering with the operations of the other.

But it is one thing to discredit that doctrine; it is another, if I may speak by example, to impose judicially upon the Australian army a liability to pay municipal rates if it occupies a piece of land for a military camp. The High Court has had no difficulty in rejecting such a notion and in maintaining the principle that none of the incidents or consequences of the exercise of the executive power of the Commonwealth can ever be made the subject of special liabilities or burdens under State law.[19] The supremacy of the Commonwealth has not suffered. On the other side, a use of a general legislative power of the Commonwealth specially to control or burden the States has not been permitted. Under the powers to make laws with respect to banking the Commonwealth Parliament enacted that except with the consent of the federal Treasurer a bank should not conduct any banking business of a State or of any authority of a State. The High Court held this provision clearly invalid on that ground.[20]

In all this you must see an interesting, indeed a striking, parallel with the development in the United States. In Aus-

19. Essendon Corporation v. Criterion Theatres Ltd., 74 Commw.L.R. 1 (1947).

20. Melbourne Corporation v. The Commonwealth, 74 Commw.L.R. 31 (1947).

tralia the changes of doctrine may have appeared more abrupt, the transitional curves may have had shorter radii, but they took the same direction. The analogues to *Graves v. New York,*[21] to *New York and the Saratoga Springs Commission v. United States,*[22] and even to *Kern-Limerick Inc. v. Scurlock*[23] are clearly there. But to witness this development in Australia as it took place was to be constantly alive to the persistent influence exerted over the minds of the chief actors by Marshall's words. Holmes' description of Marshall, "loose constructionist," may be warranted; he may have been right in doubting whether Marshall's work proved more than a strong intellect, a good style, personal ascendency in his Court, courage, justice, and the convictions of his party.[24] But these are qualities of mind, and with them Marshall has been able not only to exert a prodigious influence upon the constitutional history of his own country but, as you have seen, to extend it into the judicial interpretation of the Constitution established a century later in a land unknown at his birth. The influence of his work there has by no means been confined to the second part of his judgment in *McCulloch v. Maryland.* It has covered a field almost as wide as that covered by his most famous judgments. Indeed the first part of the judgment in that celebrated case formed the foundation of quite a number of decisions of the High Court supporting a variety of exercises of the legislative power of the Commonwealth.

Perhaps it is in connection with the anomalous power to make laws with respect to conciliation and arbitration for the prevention and settlement of industrial disputes extending beyond the limits of any one State that the strongest applications have been made in Australia of the famous words "Let the end be legitimate, let it be within the scope of the Constitution, and all means which are appropriate, which are plainly adapted to that end, which are not prohibited,

21. 306 U.S. 466 (1939).
22. 326 U.S. 572 (1946).
23. 347 U.S. 110 (1954).
24. Collected Legal Papers, pp. 268-9.

but consistent with the letter and spirit of the Constitution, are constitutional."[25] It was decided many years ago by the High Court that since if you are to settle industrial disputes by arbitration you must affect large and indefinite bodies of men, it follows that the legislative power must extend to organizing, registering, and incorporating associations of employees and of employers. The two purposes were thought to be served of enabling the representation of potential disputants before the Arbitration Court and of providing a means of working out the scope and operation of industrial awards.[26] And now the High Court has upheld a provision which arms an official of the Arbitration Court, namely the Industrial Registrar, with power, in certain conditions, to undertake the conduct of an election of office-bearers of an organization—that is, a trade union, so registered.[27] This too was sustained as incidental to the main legislative power.

Strong as this application of Marshall's exposition of the incidental power may seem, the High Court had made even a stronger use of it. For at one time a federal law had prohibited strikes and lockouts, if they were on account of interstate industrial disputes. It was enacted under the same legislative power. The High Court held this suppression of the right to strike to be valid. It was done on the theory that you could not arbitrate effectively for the settlement of an industrial dispute if the alternative remedy of a strike was open, if demands could be enforced by strikes and lockouts.[28]

But the classic words of the incidental power which Marshall expounded so forcefully are not reproduced in the text of the Commonwealth Constitution. What is done results in a somewhat different provision. In the last of the enumerated powers it is provided that Parliament may make

---

25. 3 Wheat. (U.S.) 316 at p. 421 (1819).
26. Jumbunna Coal Mine v. Victorian Coal Miners' Association, 6 Commw.L.R. 309 (1908).
27. Federated Ironworkers' Association of Australia v. Commonwealth, 84 Commw.L.R. 265 (1951).
28. Stemp v. Australian Glass Manufacturers Co. Ltd., 23 Commw.L.R. 226 (1917).

laws with respect to matters incidental to the execution of any power vested by the Constitution in the Parliament or in the Government of the Commonwealth or in the federal judicature. A particular significance has been attached to the words "matters incidental to the execution of any power." They have been thought to suggest rather some particular thing that arises out of or attends the performance of a function. It would be as a matter incidental to the legislative function, for example, that a public inquiry by the examination of witnesses into some subject of proposed legislation might find its constitutional justification. The judicial function may involve a law of remedies and so on. This is somewhat different from treating the subject matter or purpose of a power as covering everything that is incidental to it. It is hardly necessary to add that every power is construed in Australia as extending to everything that is incidental to its subject or purpose. It is a construction which general principle authorizes and requires. But of course it is Marshall's principle, whether you find it in the words of the Constitution or in the common law. There is no difficulty in Australia, such is its history, in regarding the common law as antecedent to the Constitution. It supplies such principles in aid of its interpretation and operation. The common law is more real and certainly less rigid than the ether with which scientists were accustomed to fill interstellar space. But it serves all, and more than all, the purposes in surrounding and pervading the Australian system for which, in the cosmic system, that speculative medium was devised.

The constitutions conferring self-government on the Australian colonies limited the legislative powers territorially; the parliament of New South Wales might make laws for the peace, welfare, and good government of New South Wales; the parliament of Victoria, laws in and for Victoria, and so on. It was an obvious application of the common law doctrine of *ultra vires* to decide that laws of the colonies concerning extraterritorial matters were void; and the Supreme Courts of the colonies took that view as a matter of course. To the framers of the Commonwealth Constitution the thesis of *Marbury v. Madison*[29] was obvious. It did not need the reasoned eloquence of Marshall's utterance to convince them that simply because there were to be legislatures of limited powers, there must be a question of *ultra vires* for the Courts. In the course of administering the law the Courts must say whether purported legislation did or did not possess the force of law. There are few traces in the Australian Constitution of the Bill of Rights and none of the Fourteenth Amendment. Some proposals were made for the purpose of avoiding the full consequences of this application of the doctrine of *ultra vires* but they were dismissed with scant consideration. The question was therefore regarded as one arising from the distribution and demarcation of powers only. In drafting the provision stating what original jurisdiction may be conferred on the High Court the words "cases arising under this Constitution" were taken from the definition of the judicial power of the United States and transformed into "matters" arising under this Constitution or involving its interpretation. The last words impliedly acknowledge the function of the Courts.[30]

But Marshall's actual decision in *Marbury v. Madison,* the conclusion that no mandamus could go, was not accepted by the framers of the Australian Constitution. On the contrary it was felt that the High Court must be armed with authority to send mandamus to officers of the Executive Government or other functionaries of the Commonwealth. The denial of original jurisdiction to the supreme tribunal in respect of all but a special part of the subjects of judicial power found little favor with the Australian constitution-makers. Moreover the famous twenty-fifth section of the Judiciary Act of 1789 must have been considered and it is evident that great attention was given to the celebrated opinion of Mr. Justice Story in *Martin v. Hunter's Lessee*[31] and also that

29. 1 Cranch (U.S.) 137 (1803).

30. Section 76(i) of the Constitution of the Commonwealth: see also section 74.

31. 1 Wheat. (U.S.) 304 (1816).

the reasoning employed by Marshall in his historic judgment in *Cohens v. Virginia*[32] was studied. In the course of that judgment Marshall made a significant distinction in answering the objection that to hold, as the Court did, that the Supreme Court's appellate jurisdiction extended to the Courts of the States meant a complete consolidation of the States so far as respects judicial power. The Chief Justice said:

> "A complete consolidation of the States so far as respects judicial power" would authorize the legislature to confer on the federal courts appellate jurisdiction from the state courts in all cases whatsoever. The distinction between such a power and that of giving appellate jurisdiction in a few specified cases in the decision of which the nation takes an interest, is too obvious not to be perceived by all.[33]

It was resolved that this distinction should not be preserved in Australia. But the full step was not taken of entrusting the legislature with the power of conferring on federal courts appellate jurisdiction from the State Courts in all cases whatsoever. It was, however, decided to invest the High Court directly by the Constitution with a full appellate jurisdiction. It was to be an appellate jurisdiction in all cases whatsoever but the cases must come from the Supreme Courts of the States, or from other courts if exercising federal jurisdiction.[34] The High Court was thus established as a general final court of appeal in Australia and in its appellate jurisdiction the distinction between State and federal jurisdiction does not matter except for one purpose. That purpose arises from the fact that by a provision peculiar to the Australian Constitution federal jurisdiction may be vested in State Courts. The High Court is therefore empowered to entertain an appeal from any court of a State below the Supreme Court, if it is exercising federal jurisdiction by a grant from the federal Commonwealth Parliament.

But an original jurisdiction over certain matters was given to the High Court. The Constitution itself provides

32. 6 Wheat. (U.S.) 264 (1821).
33. 6 Wheat. (U.S.) 264 at p. 422 (1821).
34. Section 73 of the Constitution of the Commonwealth.

that the High Court shall have original jurisdiction in all matters in which a writ of mandamus or prohibition or an injunction is sought against an officer of the Commonwealth.[35] This provision is the outcome and of course the negative of Marshall's conclusion in *Marbury v. Madison.* The High Court has decided that although a writ of prohibition is directed to courts and judicial officers it is a remedy that belongs not to the appellate jurisdiction but to the original jurisdiction of the Court that issues it. From that it followed that under this provision the High Court has a power of which it cannot be deprived, to restrain an excess of jurisdiction on the part of any federal Court.[36] A consequence of this, perhaps an unfortunate consequence, has been that prohibitions are constantly sought from the High Court against the awards and orders of federal industrial tribunals of which the Arbitration Court is the chief. The Constitution confers original jurisdiction upon the High Court in all matters between States or beween a State and a resident of another State. In this will be recognized an attempt to resolve in advance a question of which American history gave notice to the Australian constitution-makers. Marshall's discourse in *Cohens v. Virginia* upon the Eleventh Amendment could not but awaken them to the problem, even if otherwise they were not alive to the need of dealing with it. But as will be seen from the text of the constitutional provision I have quoted they rejected the view which Marshall pressed upon the Virginia Constitutional Convention of 1788, namely, the view that no one would think that a State would be called to the bar of a federal court: that it was not rational to suppose that the sovereign power should be dragged before a court."[37] They rejected the dissenting opinion of Mr. Justice Iredell in *Chisholm v. Georgia*[38] and firmly placed the jurisdiction of the High Court to entertain a suit against

---

35. Section 75 (v).
36. R. v. Commonwealth Court of Conciliation & Arbitration and Australian Tramways Employees' Association, 18 Commw.L.R. 54 (1914).
37. 1 Beveridge, Life of Marshall, 454.
38. 2 Dallas (U.S.) 419 (1793).

a State by a resident of another State upon the footing which that decision established for a short time. The Parliament of the Commonwealth was empowered to make laws conferring rights to proceed against the Commonwealth or a State in respect of matters within the limits of judicial power,[39] and this power has been exercised so as to make States and Commonwealth liable to be sued in contract or in tort.[40] Suits are often brought in the High Court against States. Sometimes it is the residence of the plaintiff that forms the basis of jurisdiction, sometimes it is because the matter arises under the Constitution or involves its interpretation. The existence in the High Court of an original jurisdiction of this nature has made it easy, if the constitutional validity of a statute is impugned, to bring the question before that Court at once. A writ is issued and with it a pleading is delivered to which there is promptly a demurrer, or perhaps an agreed special case is stated for the opinion of the Full Court.

Marshall's principles of federal supremacy have had no application that has proved of more real importance in Australia than the invalidation of State laws where the ground is already taken or subsequently taken by federal legislation. Here Marshall's principles have now been carried into full effect by the decisions of the High Court of Australia. Yet there is no judgment of Marshall devoted to the essential question, when is it that a State law becomes inoperative in face of a law made by Congress, what is the nature of the incompatibility that will suffice, by what test or tests is it to be ascertained? These are matters that for a time vexed the High Court and were thought by some to place the paramountcy of federal law at hazard. It was on Marshall's principle that the judge who fought most valiantly for the true faith took his stand. The danger passed, the true faith was vin-

---

39. Section 78 of the Constitution of the Commonwealth; [63-64 VICT. Ch. 12, An Act to constitute the Commonwealth of Australia.]

40. Judiciary Act 1903-1955, Part IX (p. 2413 of Vol. III of the Commonwealth Statutes 1903-1950); Commonwealth v. New South Wales, 32 Commw.L.R. 200 (1923); Musgrave v. Commonwealth, 57 Commw.L.R. 514, 546-7 (1937); Werrin v. Commonwealth, 59 Commw.L.R. 150, 165-8 (1938); Harrison Moore in 17 JOURNAL OF COMPARATIVE LEGISLATION 163.

dicated and tests of inconsistency were established in Australia which would not be disowned in the United States. The trouble arose because under State law regulations of labor and employment operated upon matters with respect to which the Commonwealth Court of Arbitration found it necessary to make awards for the settlement of industrial disputes extending beyond one State. At first a majority of the judges of the High Court took the view that the Federal arbitral tribunal could not go outside the limits of State law within which the disputants might agree. From this Mr. Justice Isaacs vehemently dissented.

In Australia the matter does not depend entirely upon the general provision derived from the Constitution of the United States that the Constitution and all laws made by the Parliament of the Commonwealth under the Constitution shall be binding on the Court's judges and people of every State and of every part of the Commonwealth.[41] The Constitution of the Commonwealth of Australia adds a specific provision to deal with the inconsistency of State and federal statutes. It is section 109 and it provides that when a law of a State is inconsistent with a law of the Commonwealth the latter shall prevail and the former to the extent of the inconsistency shall be invalid. "This constitutional provision," said Mr. Justice Isaacs,[42] ". . . is essential to the very life of the Commonwealth; a decision in favor . . . of [State law] on this point [on a given case] destroys the supremacy of Federal law which alone has held the American Union intact, has preserved the character of the Canadian Dominion and can uphold the Australian Constitution. The supremacy of Federal law," he said, "in such a case has been steadily maintained by the American Courts from the time of Marshall C. J. in *Gibbons v. Ogden*[43] to the present day." A long passage is then taken from Marshall's judgment. It contains a simple if fundamental statement.

41. Section 5 of the covering clauses of the Commonwealth of Australia Constitution Act.

42. Federated Saw Millers etc. Association v. James Moore, 8 Commw. L.R. 465 at p. 530 (1909).

43. 9 Wheat. (U.S.) 1, 210 (1824).

> The nullity of any Act inconsistent with the Constitution is produced by the declaration that the Constitution is the supreme law. The appropriate application of that part of the clause which confers the same supremacy on laws and treaties is to such Acts of the State legislatures as do not transcend their powers, but, though enacted in the execution of acknowledged State powers, interfere with, or are contrary to the laws of Congress made in pursuance of the Constitution or some treaty made under the authority of the United States. In every such case, the Act of Congress, or the treaty, is supreme; and the law of the State, though enacted in the exercise of powers not controverted, must yield to it.

Today it all sounds to Australian ears just as evident and elementary as it sounds to Americans. But at first there seemed to be for some judges of the High Court a fascination in the idea that if you could obey one law without breaking the other and if there was no other flat contradiction between the two, there could be no inconsistency. It appeared possible that the specific Australian provision in section 109 instead of adding strength to the principle of supremacy might actually operate unexpectedly in a way which might weaken it. For a moment it looked as if the word "inconsistent" might receive a pedantic construction drawn rather from a verbal formalism than essential conceptions of federalism. In the end however the Court did not forget that it was a constitution they were expounding. Thus the Court now asks in such a matter whether the paramount legislature in Australia has dealt with a topic falling within a field of its power in a manner showing that it has undertaken to determine what the condition of the law shall be on the subject. If so the High Court holds that State law can have no valid operation upon the same topic.[44]

It would be possible to trace into many other developments of Australian constitutional law the influence of ideas which Marshall expressed with such mastery. You could for example show how the general conception of interstate com-

---

44. See Clyde Engineering Co. Ltd. v. Cowburn, 37 Commw.L.R. 466 (1926); McKay v. Hunt, 38 Commw.L.R. 308 (1926); Hume v. Palmer, 38 Commw.L.R. 441 (1926); *Ex parte McLean,* 43 Commw.L.R. 472 (1930); Victoria v. Commonwealth, 58 Commw.L.R. 618 (1937); Wenn v. A.G., 77 Commw.L.R. 84 (1948).

merce expressed in *Gibbons v. Ogden* has affected this or that judgment in which some elucidation has been offered of the provision native to the Australian Constitution which declares that trade commerce and intercourse among the States shall be absolutely free.[45] But enough has been said to show that Marshall's exposition of the basal concept of federalism as an instrument of national life carried persuasive force in a new country and in a new century and made some significant contribution towards determining the course of Australian constitutional development.

Distinguishable periods in the history of the interpretation of the American Constitution have been discerned. Marshall's judicial life has been assigned to a period of the dominance of the constitutional document when the tradition was fresh and often verifiable.[46] Much the same could be said of the period of Australian constitutional interpretation during which Marshall was most quoted in the High Court. Further the fact that Australia did not adopt the Bill of Rights or the Fourteenth Amendment made it possible to consider judicially the basal federal character of the Constitution in a light which was neither dimmed nor colored by the multitude of complexities to which the application of these famous provisions to modern life must give rise. It is a light more favorable to the acceptance of Marshall's simple modes of thought. Marshall did not admire Napoleon but he shared the view expressed in his maxim that to divide the interest of a nation is to injure all. Indeed there are others of the Emperor's sayings in which Marshall might have concurred. He might have answered Holmes' suggestion of outmoded simplicity by repeating Napoleon's words "From lawyers it is not easy to get simplicity." Marshall's life and work perhaps may serve to illustrate Napoleon's dictum that the power of thought appears to be an attribute of the will. It is because his will played such a part in his thought that force, clarity, and conviction are such conspicuous qualities of his judicial

45. Section 92.
46. Cf. Corwin, Twilight of the Supreme Court, p. 180.

reasoning. His judgments have that rarest of properties; when you read them they appear always to be right. It is a sufficient explanation of why they have carried so far in time and space.

The third discussion concerned the theme—"The Meaning of Due Process of Law." The Conference on Thursday afternoon had developed the necessity, in a constitutional order, that government provide to a wronged individual procedures for orderly recourse against government itself. And because this concept is closely related to the institution of separated powers, the second discussion, on Friday morning, concerned the survival of that institution and the practicability of maintaining our constitutional system generally in times of national stress. With this background the discussion of Friday afternoon turned to the means of discovering substantive justice. If government even in times of stress and danger stands ready to correct its own injustices, by what shall it measure justice? In the United States "due process of law" has come to be used as a synonym of justice itself; inquiry into the substance of due process was a logical next step for the Conference.

Accordingly, Judge William H. Hastie of the United States Court of Appeals, and Dean McGeorge Bundy of Harvard College, led the discussion of their papers, "Judicial Method in Due Process Inquiry," and "A Lay View of Due Process."

Judicial Method in Due Process Inquiry

WILLIAM H. HASTIE *

In the fifty-first of the Federalist papers James Madison wrote:

> If angels were to govern men, neither external nor internal controls in government would be necessary. In framing a government, which is to be administered by men over men, the great difficulty lies in this: You must first enable the government to control the governed, and in the next place, oblige it to control itself.

In the subsequent development of our constitutionalism, judicial power guided by flexible concepts broadly stated in an authoritative document became a dominant force in the business of obliging government to control itself. That method of control has found its sternest testing ground in the due process clause of the Fourteenth Amendment.

A very learned Justice of the present Supreme Court[1] has said that the due process clause of the Fourteenth Amendment is "the provision of the Bill of Rights which most plagues us, certainly me." A distinguished colleague[2] has even conceded that in such an uncharted area of constitutional decision judges act "not by authority of . . . [their] competence, but by force of . . . [their] commissions."

In such attitudes our contemporaries are poles removed from their 19th century predecessors who characteristically exhibited sublime faith in the ability of judges to discover and systematize solving concepts which would lead unerringly to the correct solutions of the most difficult constitutional problems. Yet modernity is always foreshadowed; rarely more

* For biographical note see page 344.

1. Mr. Justice Frankfurter, in the 1953 Ernst Freund Lecture at the University of Chicago Law School, *Some Observations on Supreme Court Litigation and Legal Education* 11.

2. Mr. Justice Jackson in W. Va. State Board of Education v. Barnette, 319 U. S. 624, 640 (1943).

oddly than by an obscure little nineteenth-century lady writing verses in the seclusion of her New England home:[3]

> Faith is a fine invention
> For gentlemen who see—
> But microscopes are prudent
> In an emergency!

In any event, it is an important fact that many judges today are losing the old faith in constitutional right reason, as they turn microscopes on themselves and their intellectual processes involved in the solution of Fourteenth Amendment problems. In the course of such inquiry it has been discovered that constitutional decision very often has less assured and definable groundings and more personal and subjective premises than heretofore had been supposed. As a result there is great concern to discover more objective bases and systematic methods of decision. Some have found this search so unrewarding that they have come to doubt whether it is desirable that federal judges have such authority to invalidate state action as is conferred by the due process clause.

Among judges Cardozo has been both pioneer and exemplar of judicial analysis of the way cases are decided. Recognizing the absence of precise authoritative guides and controls for judicature in a broad range of cases, notable among them due process cases, he found moorings and meaningful guides in the duty and habit of the judge "to exercise a discretion informed by tradition, methodized by analogy, disciplined by system and subordinated to 'the primordial necessity of order in the social life'."[4] Yet this does not tell much about how a judge will or should decide whether a state requirement that employers grant their employees vacations with pay, or the failure of a state to provide counsel for an accused person too poor to hire a lawyer, or any of countless other state acts, amounts to a denial of due process of law.

The trouble, says Judge Learned Hand, is that such problems often "demand the appraisal and balancing of hu-

---

3. The Complete Poems of Emily Dickinson 32 (1924).
4. Cardozo, The Nature of the Judicial Process 141 (1921).

man values which there are no scales to weigh." It is then a short step to Mr. Justice Jackson's already quoted concession that in these most difficult areas of constitutional decision judges act "by force of their commissions" rather than "by authority of their competence", and but little further to Judge Hand's own conclusion that it would be better to relieve the federal courts of the uncongenial task of ultimate enforcement of these "general principles" placed in the Constitution "to insure the just exercise of . . . [the] powers of government." In his matchless prose, Judge Hand states the matter this way:[5]

> . . . these stately admonitions refuse to subject themselves to analysis. They are precipitates of "old, unhappy, far-off things, and battles long ago", originally cast as universals to enlarge the scope of the victory, to give it authority, to reassure the very victors themselves that they have been champions in something more momentous than a passing struggle. Thrown large upon the screen of the future as eternal verities, they are emptied of the vital occasions which gave them birth, and become moral adjurations, the more imperious because inscrutable, but with only that content which each generation must pour into them anew in the light of its own experience. If an independent judiciary seeks to fill them from its own bosom, in the end it will cease to be independent.

So the question is raised by very wise men whether the business of monitoring the state's obligation to observe due process of law is an appropriate function for courts in general and the national courts in particular. More succinctly, is judicial process adapted to the ultimate determination of due process?

The answer each individual gives to this question is likely to depend largely upon his evaluation of the guides and correctives which are available to courts in this area and his opinion of judicial susceptibility to guidance and correction. Of course if judicial process in due process cases defies meaningful analysis, little more can be said. Accordingly, it is proposed in this paper to undertake a tentative statement of the

---

5. Hand, The Spirit of Liberty 180 (1953).

nature and source of some important guides and correctives which influence due process adjudication.

I

In beginning, it may be helpful to look for some acceptable generalization which provides a path of judicial approach to the responsibility which must be discharged when a litigant asks a court to find that state action[6] harms him in some way inconsistent with the due process clause. The first and most obvious fact is that the Constitutional text—"nor shall any State deprive any person of . . . liberty[7] . . . without due process of law"—states an authoritative standard of extreme generality but includes no rules to guide its application. In such circumstances the judge's entire training and experience in a profession which constantly administers standards as useful tools in the systematic regulation of conduct impel him to seek an understanding of the conception the standard embodies which will orient his effort to bring the facts of particular cases into intelligible relation with the standard.

Even this beginning is not easy here. In fact we have seen in our own times an important change in consensus as to the general idea reflected in the constitutional language.

It probably would have been agreed in the 1860's as readily as in the 1950's that the due process clause expresses the general idea that the effort to achieve justice is the legitimating principle of state impositions upon the individual,[8]

6. The evolution of the idea of state action in constitutional adjudication since Chief Justice Stone's analysis of the concept in United States v. Classic, 313 U. S. 299 (1941), is beyond the scope of this paper. But for a commentary on its importance, see PEKELIS, LAW AND SOCIAL ACTION 97-127 (Konvitz ed. 1950).

7. Because so much of the protection of "property" under the 14th Amendment has been in terms of "liberty," and because no special difficulties inhere in the application of the due process standard to the protection of "life", this discussion will ignore the words "life" and "property" in the constitutional text.

8. "This [due process of law] is an idea born out of the hearts of men. It has great capacity for development and growth, and yet a rather clear basic content. Perhaps the essential thought can be put by saying that due process

and accordingly, in a regime of judicial supremacy, confers upon the courts ultimate responsibility to decide whether any challenged state imposition is made intolerable by anything fundamental in the conception of justice.

But the idea of justice itself is evolutionary, as the development of thought in this very area shows. It was for a long time a postulate of American thinking about the legal order that the essence of justice was to be realized in the providing of a workable maximum of individual freedom in human community. Much has been written of the way in which such influences as the philosophy of the Enlightenment, the revolutionary origin of the United States and the pioneer and frontier character of our society in a continental vastness contributed to such thinking.

But, understanding this point of view, many of today's most observing and thoughtful men find it inadequate. They are impressed that among the 20th century's most notable social phenomena have been the emergence and persistence and variety of human demands that society make greater affirmative provision for the well-being of its members. They find yesterday's view of justice deficient in its failure to take sufficiently into account, as Pound puts it, that "Men wish to be free, but they want much besides." So, in informed thinking there is an observable trend away from the idea that justice consists of providing a workable maximum of individual freedom, and toward a more inclusive concept of reconciling and satisfying a great diversity of deserving but often conflicting human claims.[9] For the judge whose task is to decide due process controversies, this evolving conception of justice provides an intelligible and valuable frame of reference. It gives him no answers to particular Fourteenth

---

has some application wherever men feel a sense of injustice." GRISWOLD, THE FIFTH AMENDMENT TODAY 37 (1955).

"More than any other single clause in the Constitution, it [the due process clause] seems *on its face* to guarantee, so far as any provision can, both universal and personal justice. No doubt the principal reasons are that one synonym of 'due process' is 'just' process, and one popular connotation of 'law' is 'right and equity.' Graham, *Procedure to Substance—Extra-Judicial Rise of Due Process, 1830-1860,* 40 CALIF. L. REV. 483, 488 (1952).

9. Epitomized in POUND, JUSTICE ACCORDING TO LAW (1951). The words quoted in the preceding sentence appear at page 31.

Amendment cases. But it defines in a useful way what he is trying to accomplish through application of the constitutional standard. Such orientation is all-important for the entire course of systematic solution of diverse controversies.

Of course we cannot be sure whether the constitutional design is best described in terms of effort to achieve justice, or whether the reconciling of diverse human claims expresses the best the legal order can do in formulating a working conception of justice. But we do know that these ideas have been derived from the study and analysis of the course of systematic thinking about the legal order, examined and corrected in the light of the social experience of our times.

This is as scientific and trustworthy a way of finding a starting point as we know. Moreover, if such a starting point and its derivation are made explicit we can be confident that inadequacies in our present thinking will be revealed in the future by more skillful analysts and discerning observers even as we think we have discovered shortcomings in yesterday's reasoning. Thus, our search for an approach to due process problems is carried along in the main stream of man's continuing search for a more inclusive and rewarding order in the changing circumstances of human society. We will agree that it belongs there and will try to keep it there so long as we retain confidence in the constructive power of human intelligence to improve our way of life.

II

The selection of a starting point in such a way as has been outlined is calculated to bring the judge to grips with the major difficulties of the case he has to decide. This is notably true of the controversies and competing claims with which courts must deal in the so-called substantive due process field, where the only "process" challenged as less than due process "is the mandate of the [questioned] act itself."[10]

10. An old formulation of Professor Kales in his still rewarding essay, *"Due Process", the Inarticulate Major Premise and the Adamson Act,* 26 YALE L. J. 519, 548 (1917).

The asserted libery can be identified and the circumstances and effect of its curtailment examined. This process will require judgment, essentially conceptual, whether the particular liberty is important in our society; and judgment, essentially factual, of the impact of the challenged imposition upon individuals. Usually, it will disclose rather quickly whether a complainant's charge of injustice is substantial rather than frivolous.

On the other hand, it is characteristic of our stage of civilization that state-imposed regulations exhibit some perceptible design and tendency to advance interests of public concern, which may or may not include the protection of individual liberties in conflict with those the complainant asserts. Forces operating within the state itself will almost always prevent adoption of a patently whimsical or capricious regulation designed in restraint of liberty without anticipation of compensating public advantage. This will be the other side of the picture for the judge who has viewed his task as an effort to discover whether the state has made a tolerable reconciliation of substantial claims.

Appellate courts in their dealing with fact finding and related discretionary exercise of judgment, as reflected in decisions of administrative agencies, repeatedly apply technique appropriate for discovering and sustaining permissible conclusions which the reviewer himself would not have reached on the same record.[11] In due process cases the court of first instance itself starts with a comparable problem of judgment as to the existence of basis for the state's election to impose the questioned restraint. Of course a state legislative imposition is rarely supported by a record equivalent to that which a commerce commission or a labor relations board ordinarily makes. It is for this reason that ways of establishing the reasons for the restraint, whether by proof or judicial notice, or presumption in the absence of proof, may be decisive in due

---

11. For a recent analysis of this kind of judicial review, see Jaffe, *Judicial Review: "Substantial Evidence on the Whole Record"*, 64 HARV. L. REV. 1233 (1951).

process adjudication.[12] But for present purposes the point is merely that legislative restraints on liberty almost always seek public advantages, however discovered, which can rationally be pursued in that way. Analysis and evaluation may be aided by experience in judicial technique as developed and employed in the normal review of administrative decisions.

If this were the end of the matter the rarity of judicial proscription throughout the area of substantive due process would make the judicial role so unimportant as to merit little discussion. But the fact is that courts have persistently found some restraints on liberty so harmful that not merely some significant countervailing consideration, but only the clearest and most urgent public concerns on the other side, make them tolerable. It is this determination that certain intrusions upon liberty belong in a category of special and extreme objectionableness that gives trouble. It seems to be this which has led Judge Hand to say that we are dealing with "values which there are no scales to weigh." We must inquire, therefore, whether courts seem to be finding understandable and correctible ways of judging whether such extraordinary seriousness is to be attributed to particular invasions of liberty.

Among the most important ideas which come into play at this point are ethical notions of the worth and importance of the individual human being which cause us to believe that vindication of human personality and respect for human integrity are central in the design and responsibility of American government. For some the tenets of organized religion dictate this conclusion. Others are persuaded by humanistic thinking. There are various influences which create a philosophy of life in organized society. In totality they have created an American consensus which has meaning and utility

12. Twenty-five years after the term at which the same Court decided both cases, it is still instructive to compare O'Gorman & Young, Inc. v. Hartford Ins. Co., 282 U. S. 251 (1931), with Near v. Minnesota, 283 U. S. 697 (1931). More generally see Biklé, *Judicial Determination of Questions of Fact Affecting the Constitutional Validity of Legislative Action,* 38 Harv. L. Rev. 6 (1924).

for the judgment of due process problems. We do not hesitate to postulate the conception expressed by this contemporary formulation:[13]

> The well springs of our vitality . . . are ethical and spiritual. Our society in America is founded . . . upon a faith in man as an end in himself. . . . We conceive that the development and happiness of the individual is the goal and purpose of American life.

We repeatedly quote the words of Mr. Justice Brandeis in his *Olmstead* opinion,[14] never doubting general approbation of the idea he expresses:

> The makers of our Constitution undertook to secure conditions favorable to the pursuit of happiness. They recognized the significance of man's spiritual nature, of his feelings and of his intellect. They knew that only a part of the pain, pleasure and satisfactions of life are to be found in material things. They sought to protect Americans in their beliefs, their thoughts, their emotions and their sensations. They conferred, as against the Government, the right to be let alone—the most comprehensive of rights and the right most valued by civilized men.

This common understanding becomes important when the impact of governmental imposition is to restrain the individual in the expression of his thoughts or beliefs or to violate the integrity of his personality. It gives judges a basis for confidently asserting that such intrusion on liberty is of the gravest concern and is to be justified, if at all, only by overwhelming urgency rather than merely by substantial countervailing considerations.

At times it is suggested that such a view may be questionable because it places a greater value on personality than on property.[15] But that is characteristic of the ethics we profess and accept as the foundation of our polity. This does not mean that asceticism is an American ideal. It still permits recognition that the individual requires material provision for physical well-being and the meaningful exercise and de-

13. Lilienthal, This I Do Believe 17-18 (1949).
14. Olmstead v. United States, 277 U. S. 438, 478 (1928).
15. *E.g.,* Corwin, Liberty Against Government 154-161 (1948); Freund, On Understanding the Supreme Court 8-22 (1949).

velopment of personality. But it does recognize personality as the fundamental ethical concern, with property in a supporting role, albeit an essential one.

It is noteworthy that during the long controversy over the impact of the due process clause on economic regulations, no state legislation challenged or jeopardized the institution of private property. No questioned enactment seemed likely to pauperize the complainant or to deprive him of opportunity to earn a livelihood. Thus, although courts have differed in their toleration of particular economic restraints and requirements, they have not had occasion to evaluate the individual's interest in such material provision as can fairly be called essential to the support of personality.

The sum of the matter seems to be this. It is possible to state and support in intelligible fashion ethical ideas and consequent political conceptions believed to make state impositions on personality and individual integrity of the gravest concern in our society. And these ideas can be related in a useful and realistic way to many claims advanced in the name of human liberty. Very often this process will greatly facilitate rational determination whether a particular infringement of liberty is so grave a matter that its objectionableness becomes dominant among the competing considerations presented by the case at hand.

Another reason for placing certain encroachments on liberty in the most objectionable category was suggested by Chief Justice Stone's now familiar inquiry "whether legislation which restricts those political processes which can ordinarily be expected to bring about repeal of undesirable legislation is to be subjected to more exacting judicial scrutiny under the general prohibitions of the Fourteenth Amendment than are most other types of legislation."[16] Similar thinking seems to underlie Mr. Justice Frankfurter's equally familiar pronouncement that liberties which are "the indispensible conditions of an open against a closed society"

16. United States v. Carolene Products Co., 304 U. S. 144, 152, footnote 4 (1938).

generate an extraordinary "momentum of respect."[17]

Here, political circumstance is the basic datum: the organization of our society so that principal reliance for the avoidance and correction of injustice in state action is placed upon the force of manifest public opinion. The reasoned conclusion is that an infringement of liberty which impedes the expression of ideas is doubly bad. Its impact on personality is bad enough. But its obstruction of the normal course of development and assertion of the public will, our basic institutional safeguard against injustice, is even more serious.[18]

There is need that thoughtful men continue to state, explain and critically examine these and other reasons for attributing extraordinary seriousness to certain invasions of liberty. Professor Paul Freund, to whom we are indebted for some of our most helpful discussion of the judicial problem of evaluating interests in due process cases, has noted how little we are told by opinion writers whether their evaluation "is derived from the evidence of history regarding the relative social utility of different kinds of freedom, or is derived from convictions about the nature and duties of man, or from an analysis of representative government."[19] Certainly explanation of these evaluations is very desirable. This paper is token of the writer's belief that such aspects of the judicial process lend themselves, perhaps more than is generally acknowledged, to intelligible exposition. To the extent that such exposition reveals sense and system it will jus-

---

17. Kovacs v. Cooper, 336 U. S. 77, 95 (1949). One is the more confident of this meaning because of other statements of the same Justice, for example: "Where all the effective means of inducing political changes are left free from interference, education in the abandonment of foolish legislation is itself a training in liberty." See Minersville School District v. Gobitis, 310 U. S. 586, 600 (1940).

18. See the impressive statement and development of this thesis in MEIKLEJOHN, FREE SPEECH AND ITS RELATION TO SELF-GOVERNMENT (1948) *passim*. While some of Dr. Meiklejohn's legalism is controversial, it is hard to fault his basic position: "the highest insight which men have reached in their search for political freedom" tells them that "if men are to be their own rulers . . . no idea, no opinion, no doubt, no belief, no counterbelief, no relevant information, may be kept from them." At 88, 89.

19. FREUND, *op. cit supra* note 15, at 11-12. Compare Kales' urging that "the 'fundamental conditions upon which the existence of the social order rests' should not, . . . as far as counsel are concerned, continue to be 'the inarticulate major premise.' They should be discussed and arguments made as to whether such a fundamental condition is involved." See Kales, *supra* note 10, at 549.

tify confidence that what the courts are doing amounts to a reasonably satisfactory discharge of a difficult responsibility. Beyond that, in the intelligible revelation of underlying bases of evaluations lies our greatest assurance that informed advocacy and criticism can and will be so directed as constantly to improve the working of the judicial process.

III

In the field of procedural due process the judge is more at home. He is not required to weigh policy considerations of the kind which underlie substantive legislation. Rather he is deciding whether the devices and procedures adopted by the state and its functionaries in the authoritative settlement of controversies and the official administration of justice are tolerable in our society. In dispute come such matters as adequacy of notice and hearing, the propriety of inquisitorial methods of investigation and, in the general run of criminal cases, the relation of the total circumstances of conviction to the conception of fair trial.[20] The problem is literally whether "process of law" has been "due". Two characteristics of the due process problem as it normally emerges in this area deserve particular mention.

First, the questioned state action very often involves some rather evident or even admitted departure from the modes and processes which are generally accepted and approved in our system of legal administration.[21] The ultimate question is likely to be whether plainly aberrant procedure is too bad for toleration in our legal system.

When such a question must be decided, one normally important consideration loses force. Ordinarily, it is important

---

20. In whatever category the problem of the vague statute may fall analytically, the judicial task is of that kind with which this section is concerned. See, for example, Connally v. General Construction Co., 269 U. S. 385 (1926); Note, 62 HARV. L. REV. 77 (1948).

21. Of course in the unusual case where the normality of a challenged practice can be demonstrated this fact becomes the basis of an often persuasive argument that customary process is on that account due process, as in Betts v. Brady, 316 U. S. 455 (1942), and Wolf v. Colorado, 338 U. S. 25 (1949).

that judicial decision reveal such rationale as will facilitate prediction of the outcome of a considerable class of analogous cases. This makes for greater assurance in the conduct of business and personal affairs. But the case is different where, for example, public officers detain a suspect without authority and "grill" him, or normal opportunity to prepare and present a defense is willfully curtailed. In cases of this kind the responsible public officers know that they are in some degree mistreating the accused or imposing abnormal hardship upon him, whatever the answer to the due process question may be. The problem of prediction which arises in the crisis of action is how bad official conduct can become without serious risk of federal interdiction. It may be more desirable that the state officer realize that the whole adventure into impropriety is risky than that he be confident that he can proceed unchecked for an indicated distance on his aberrant course. Situations of this type most strongly support the extreme individualization of procedural due process adjudication as opposed to the view that the federal courts should use procedural due process decisions to set up for the guidance of the states defined and comprehensive categories of unconstitutional official behavior.[22]

Second, and for present purposes more important, the judge's entire training and experience in the area of law and his normally assigned role in our legal system familiarize him with problems of procedure and make him specially competent to decide them. Most of the due process cases[23] turn upon the objectionable tendency of particular methods and procedures to impede or distort the official effort to find and objectively judge the facts. Separately, or in addition, there may be a claim that the conduct of the state's representatives

22. The opinions of Justices Jackson, Clark and Frankfurter in Irvine v. California, 347 U. S. 128 (1954), place this disagreement in sharp focus. It is not clear whether they reflect a more basic difference in conception of the interrelation of state and federal roles in maintaining trustworthy and decent practices in the administration of state law.

23. Including those where the controversy goes to the way the trial tribunal has been constituted, or the influences to which it has been subjected, or the manner in which a confession has been obtained, or the opportunity and professional assistance afforded the accused to defend himself.

has been intolerably lacking in humanity or integrity.[24] Such questions are often very hard to decide. But to the extent that their solution is guided by history and experience, it is legal history and experience. If ethical notions become important they appear in the context of fair trial where the judge is professionally at home. He has no reason to defer to the legislature or the sheriff or the prosecutor in judging whether what has been done in the course of the administration of justice has met minimum "standards of civilization." However questioned procedures may be related to the practical problems of law enforcement, the judge's professional competence and his disinterest combine to qualify him preeminently for judgment whether there has been an intolerable sacrifice of decent and trustworthy modes on the altar of expediency.

Judges will differ among themselves whether particular improprieties constitute a denial of the essence of fair procedure.[25] The problem is not on this account any less the kind which seems best entrusted to the majority vote of a court of last resort. Yet, one influential factor may have greater harmonizing potentiality throughout this area than is generally recognized. That is the reaction of judges to the superimposition of national authority upon the conduct of state officers, even after that conduct has been reviewed by state courts of competent jurisdiction. Of course this problem of federalism is not peculiar to procedural due process. It merely stands out more clearly when unattended by the many

24. For a situation where the constitutional consequence of the misconduct of state officers had to be determined in the absence of any general tendency of such behavior to distort the fact finding process, see Rochin v. California, 342 U. S. 165 (1952).

25. At present disputation seems to center on the question whether, in a constitutional view, the seriousness of official behavior that is either outrageous in itself or dangerous in its tendency to distort the trial process, or both, is mitigated by the unlikelihood that harm has been done the accused in the case at hand. For citation and critical discussion of the cases, see Green, *The Bill of Rights, the Fourteenth Amendment and the Supreme Court,* 46 MICH. L. REV. 869 (1948); Garfinkel, *The Fourteenth Amendment and State Criminal Proceedings—"Ordered Liberty" or "Just Deserts,"* 41 CALIF. L. REV. 672 (1953); Perlman, *Due Process and the Admissibility of Evidence,* 64 HARV. L. REV. 1304 (1951). The most recent relevant decision of the Supreme Court is the unexplained announcement per curiam in Reeves v. Alabama, 348 U. S. 891 (1954), that the judgment of the state court, 260 Ala. 66, 68 So. 2d 14, is reversed.

other difficulties which plague substantive due process adjudication. It will be discussed as a consideration of major importance and harmonizing potentiality in all federal judgment of due process in state action.

This paper began with Madison's formulation of the eternal riddle of obliging government to control itself. The Fourteenth Amendment is just one lately added device in the search for a more complete answer to that riddle. Madison himself would have approved it, but in his times confidence in the adequacy of intrastate controls of state government was great enough to defeat his effort to have such a restraint upon the states incorporated in the original Bill of Rights.[26] It took a later skepticism of state self-control intensified by civil warfare to add the Fourteenth Amendment to the Constitution. However, there it now stands as a monumental source of federal judicial power.

Those who administer that power must do so in the light of some conception of the way in which the judicial power of the United States fits into the total enterprise of obliging the government of a State of the Union to control itself. That conception will supply a measure of the federal judge's willingness or reluctance to override questionable actions and decisions of state authorities. Recognizing his own great power under the due process clause, he will use it in accordance with some idea of the respect owed the domestic decisions of a state and some view of the sufficiency of popular will exercised through representative government, in turn controlled by the state's own courts, as a curb on governmental excesses and unfair impositions.

This does not mean that a judge who is unimpressed by the state's self-sufficiency or internal capacity to control its government will be disposed to invalidate any state-imposed restraint of which he disapproves. Nor does it mean that a judge who is convinced that federal interference with local affairs should be minimized will refuse to invalidate im-

26. The legislative history of this effort as reported in 1 ANNALS OF CONGRESS is summarized by Charles Warren in *The New "Liberty" under the Fourteenth Amendment,* 39 HARV. L. REV. 431, 433-5 (1926).

positions which to him clearly contravene the fundamentals of justice. But in that shadowland of judgment where the objectionable merges into the intolerable the judge's idea of the appropriate interrelation of state power and federal judicial power must influence his decision. The difficult cases are those that lie in that shadowland.

Supreme Court decisions today reflect very great respect for the role and competence of the states. The present Court, unlike its predecessors, is notably reluctant to interfere with much state action that the Justices strongly disapprove. The kind of self-restraint which once marked Holmes as a judge apart has now become normal in due process adjudication. Part of the proof is that for more than fifteen years the Supreme Court has consistently refused to employ the due process clause to invalidate novel and questionable state economic regulations.[27] In the procedural field, the Court demonstrates its strong conviction that unwarranted search and unlawful detainer are dangerous and unfair methods of obtaining evidence by prohibiting the use of such evidence in the national courts; yet it holds that the injustice is not so great as to make the same procedure in state courts intolerable under the due process clause.[28] Equally noteworthy is the contrast between the Court's view of the duty of the United States to assign counsel in criminal cases under the Sixth Amendment and analogous state duty under the Fourteenth Amendment.[29]

Mr. Justice Holmes indicated one basis of his judicial restraint when he questioned whether we can do much better than to accept the resultant of forces in democratic society. "What proximate test of excellence can be found," he asked

27. For a contrast indicative of this restraint, compare Day-Brite Lighting, Inc. v. Missouri, 342 U. S. 421 (1952), with Illinois Central Ry. v. Commonwealth, 305 Ky. 632, 204 S.W.2d 973 (1947). And see Williamson v. Lee Optical of Oklahoma, Inc., 348 U.S. 483 (1955). For a striking example of similar restraint in the administration of the equal protection clause, see Kotch v. Board of River Port Pilot Commissioners, 330 U.S. 552 (1947).

28. With Wolf v. Colorado, 338 U. S. 25 (1949), compare Weeks v. United States, 232 U. S. 383 (1914); with Gallegos v. Nebraska, 342 U. S. 55 (1951), compare McNabb v. United States, 318 U. S. 332 (1943).

29. With Johnson v. Zerbst, 304 U. S. 458 (1938), compare Betts v. Brady, 316 U. S. 455 (1942).

rhetorically, "except correspondence to the actual equilibrium of forces in the community . . .?"[30] At least one of his judicial disciples is said to be more concerned with assigning responsibility as between state and nation.[31] But the two ideas mingle inextricably in influencing due process adjudication. And they seem to have become more impelling in the minds of judges today than they were yesterday.

Such judicial behavior is neither idiosyncratic nor inscrutable. The self-restraint of Holmes and those who have come after him has groundings in the teachings of the nearly two hundred years of American experience with both democracy and federalism.

Our experience with the functioning of democracy through representative government has served progressively to allay early fear of popular will. It is to be remembered that one strongly supported view of the original Constitution pictures it as an expression of distrust more than confidence in democracy.[32] Certainly many men took seriously the predictions of extreme Federalists like Chancellor Kent and Senator Ames that the impact of popular will on our society would be catastrophic.[33] But such prophecies of doom have not been realized. In the stable and mature America of today our consensus is that the great experiment has worked well. Willingness to abide the results of a state's internal processes in doubtful cases is derived from that consensus.

We have also had the experience of that considerable period during which judges aggressively, almost eagerly, used the due process clause to strike down whatever state legislation to them seemed unwise and undesirable. There seems to be general agreement that this aggression did more

---

30. MONTESQUIEU, in COLLECTED LEGAL PAPERS 258 (1920).

31. See Jaffe, *The Judicial Universe of Mr. Justice Frankfurter*, 62 HARV. L. REV. 357 (1949); Braden, *The Search for Objectivity in Constitutional Law*, 57 YALE L. J. 571, 582-589 (1948).

32. BEARD, AN ECONOMIC INTERPRETATION OF THE CONSTITUTION OF THE UNITED STATES (1913) *passim*.

33. See excerpts collected in COMMAGER, LIVING IDEAS IN AMERICA 212, 215 (1951).

harm than good and, in contrast, that the judicial self-restraint of today is working better.[34]

Such seems to be the kind of experience which has created and is still developing in the minds of those who exercise federal judicial power, an attitude of deference to a state's own processes as responsible and effective means of curbing governmental excesses and unfair impositions. Should such deference, once very small, tend to become too great, new experience as better understood by wiser men must be relied upon to supply correctives.

Such decisional guides as have been suggested in this paper will not make certain the outcome of any hard case. Any useful function they may have lies in the ordering of the whole course of due process adjudication so that the constitutional restraint will better operate as a valuable added safeguard of individual liberty without clogging the normal functioning of representative government. We must persist in the effort to find and follow such guides so long as we assert the justiciability of the due process concept.

Along the way we will have frequent occasion to remember with Holmes that "to have doubted one's own first principles is the mark of a civilized man"[35] and with Aristotle that "it is the mark of an educated man to look for precision in each class of things just so far as the nature of the subject admits."[36] Certainly neither dogmatism nor exactitude can characterize intelligent handling of due process problems. Yet, it seems possible to believe both Holmes and Aristotle without ceasing to view the due process clause administered by the national courts in restraint of the states as a very worthwhile American contribution to the unending human enterprise of obliging government to control itself. This

---

34. It also seems worth mention, without hazarding opinion on its influence, that federal judges reading state reports must observe that state courts of last resort continue rather aggressively to invoke state constitutional provisions of the Fourteenth Amendment type in monitoring local economic and social regulations. See cases collected in Note, *State Views on Economic Due Process: 1937-1953,* 53 COLUM. L. REV. 827 (1953).

35. *Ideals and Doubts* in COLLECTED LEGAL PAPERS 307 (1920).

36. NICHOMACHEAN ETHICS 1094(b).

should not be too Federalist a thesis for an occasion on which we celebrate the two-hundredth anniversary of the birth of John Marshall.

COMMENT

JUDGE HASTIE*

In the foreword for the essays for this conference, Dean Griswold, speaking generally, has said that "our concern here is for the fundamental and widespread principle that government should strive to be just and should establish sound institutions for the correction of its own injustices." The overall position taken in my paper is that the due process clauses of our national Constitution authoritatively administered by our national courts, should be counted among the most worthwhile implementations of this stated principle. Certainly, conceptually the due process clauses of the Fifth and Fourteenth Amendments constitute a device calculated to have some substantial effect in preventing and correcting unjust impositions by government on the members of our society.

As to the Constitutional text itself, perhaps little more can be or need be said than that it is apt to indicate, wholly without specification, that unjust governmental action is to be avoided and corrected. In my paper I have said that the due process clause expresses the general idea that the effort to achieve justice is the legitimating principle of state impositions upon the individual, and accordingly, in a regime of judicial supremacy, confers upon the courts ultimate responsibility to decide whether any challenged state imposition is

* WILLIAM HENRY HASTIE, *Judge of the United States Court of Appeals for the Third Circuit.* Judge Hastie was born in Tennessee in 1904. He took degrees at Amherst and at Harvard Law School, including the S.J.D. in 1933. He engaged in the private practice of law between 1930 and 1933, was Assistant Solicitor of the Department of the Interior for four years, and thereafter a Judge of the United States District Court for the Virgin Islands. He has been Dean of the Howard University School of Law. He served as a civilian aide to the Secretary of War during World War II, and was thereafter Governor of the Virgin Islands. He was appointed to the United States Court of Appeals in 1949.

made intolerable by anything fundamental in the concept of justice. Now, some may find a bit more, some may find a bit less or something somewhat different in the short text itself. However, I believe what I have attempted to say in a sentence or two may well be a not too controversial starting point for discussion.

A different idea that seems worth leaving with you before the general discussion starts is this: the discussion of due process in the sense of fair procedure should, in my view, be rather distinct from the discussion of due process in the sense of tolerable legislative restraint. My paper treats them separately, discussing so-called substantive due process first and procedural due process second. But I would like now to start with a word about procedural due process, thus inverting the order of my paper.

The course of a litigated case is said by a complainant to reveal something intolerably unjust in the procedures used by officers and agencies of government in settling a controversy or in administering the criminal law. This is our classic procedural due process situation. I think there will be little dispute that this type of issue is appropriately resolved in final instance by some court. Whether it is alleged that evidence has been extorted from an individual, or that the state has not done what it should do in providing a person professional assistance in making his own defense, or it is said that the prosecuting authorities have acted dishonestly in presenting the matter to a court, it seems to me that in all such cases there will be little question but that this is the kind of problem that is appropriately assigned to some court for final decision.

But what court? That is one of the questions which disturbs us. Particularly, if the situation is one in which an officer of one of our forty-eight states is alleged in some way to have imposed upon an indivdual, why is it that the courts —the highest court, if you will—of that state, should not finally decide the justice or injustice of that imposition? The issue whether or not it is necessary or really valuable to have a residium of power in the national courts over such matters is one that greatly troubles us in this field.

I have indicated my belief that this residium of federal power does help us to settle such controversies better than we would in the absence of that power. A testing of that thesis is to be found in that body of cases since the middle 1930's, since *Brown v. Mississippi,* the first of the forced confession cases, in which the Supreme Court has been exercising this power, sparingly, but certainly more frequently than in the generations which went before. Has it been the net result of such intervention that state as well as federal officials, be they prosecutors, or sheriffs or jury commissioners or trial judges, have become more sensitive to injustice and more careful to protect the individual? My own observation is that the result has been greater care, a manifestation of greater sensitivity by local officials. If that is correct, then it seems to me that on balance the result of federal monitoring and supervision has been good.

Now, one or two observations about the substantive due process problem. Here the typical complaint of the private litigant against government is that some general legislation affects him unfairly. In this field, as distinguished from the one I mentioned originally, there is a very real question of governmental policy, of division of function, as to whether a judicial body should review or monitor the legislative decision. Our friends in other countries with legal institutions similar to ours, though they may not have a formal Constitutional due process clause, are reaching equivalent results of judicial control over procedural due process in other ways. But in the field of substantive due process they do not follow our scheme and we must recognize that they get along reasonably well without the monitoring by the courts. Yet again it has been my conclusion that as exercised by our courts this power has worked reasonably well.

One final thing that has disturbed me, that has been a good part of the burden of my paper is this: it is complained again and again that it doesn't seem possible to systematize the treatment of these due process problems, to present them in an orderly and explainable fashion so that lawyers can understand what courts are doing and why things are being done. It is suggested that it is impossible intelligently to criticize decisions because one cannot be sure what their basis is. One of the members of the Conference has said that we are dealing with values which there are no scales to measure. My suggestion is that we who are judges probably can explain, somewhat more and somewhat better than we usually do, what the values are that we throw into our intellectual scales and why we think one outweighs another. Certainly in this process we will utilize many materials from outside of the formal legal field. We will get much assistance from social disciplines other than law. And of course our legal scholars in the universities as well as our advocates at the Bar will supply most valuable correctives. So much for a very brief preliminary statement. Perhaps some of the matters that come up in discussion will themselves suggest the desirability of elaboration of what I have said.

MR. THURGOOD MARSHALL*

This afternoon for just a few minutes I want to throw two or three ideas in the hopper for the purpose of discussion; that is, to bring up certain practical matters, nothing of which is new but which I for one believe should be thrown out to be considered in the discussion.

In the first place, I find no disagreement with Judge Hastie's paper at all. And as a matter of fact, some of the matters that are in footnotes in the paper and some that are not covered there, should be brought out. Those are the real

---

* THURGOOD MARSHALL, *of the Bars of Maryland and of the Supreme Court of the United States.* Mr. Marshall was born in Baltimore in 1908. He took his undergraduate college work at Lincoln University, his LL.B. at Howard, and was admitted to the Maryland Bar in 1933. After private practice in Baltimore, Mr. Marshall devoted himself to the legal problems of the office of Counsel of the National Association for the Advancement of Colored People, becoming Chief Counsel of that organization prior to World War II. He has been counsel in a large number of leading cases in the Supreme Court of the United States involving principally problems of racial equality under the Constitution. He appeared for the successful plaintiffs in the school segregation cases, decided by the Supreme Court on May 17, 1954 and May 31, 1955. His most recent biography appears in the issue of *Time* of September 19, 1955.

practical matters that come about in the everyday trial of law suits. These practical matters, to my mind, give the necessary practical support to the thesis that runs throughout the paper. In the first place, we have the question of judicial self-restraint. And of course, at the very beginning, there is no argument with that. I believe everyone will agree that in this field of due process, at least, there should be judicial restraint. The only problem is how much or how little.

Let's start with that basis. In the first place, there is a definite need for certain minimum standards. In order to get to the minimum standards, we have, it seems to me, first to get to what is the general idea of due process. Well, it's a distillation of many theories, much practice, and considerable knowledge not only in the law courts, not only in the law books, not only from our common law tradition, but also from our general theories of fair method and fair trial, as well as ethics and possibly some religious scruples. These all go into the judges' minds on these cases. Of course, they cannot be spelled out in detail. And as a matter of fact it is very often a combination of all of these elements. But underlying all of this is the contrast between one side—the protection of the individual, personal rights—and the other—the actual belief and need of protection of society, whether it be the state or the federal government. Very often state action—either legislative, executive or judicial—is dictated by the belief that the end justifies the means. Ofttimes local mores and customs from long usage have completely beclouded the true meaning of clauses of the state and federal constitutions. And then constitutionally protected rights become small "niceties of the law" or "mere legal technicalities to free vicious criminals." There is this constant danger of these local mores and customs in one small community being combined with similar customs in other local communities, with the result, in the end, that the entire state law enforcement machinery is tainted with the belief that it is necessary, for the time being, to step on a little right here, or ignore a little personal right there. So we do need these minimum standards in the regular substantial due process cases involving legislation, executive rules, etc.

The same is true in criminal trials. We need fair and just trials. Everybody will agree on that. Where we have that we can all recognize it; and then everyone, from the individual layman up to the highest court in the land, will become shocked at any other sort of trial because it shocks the very decency of man as well as of the law. Well, there is no trouble with either of those cases. One good—the other bad. But it's that great big 99 44/100 per cent of cases that lie between those two—that's the group that I'd like to talk about for a minute. And I think all of us in reading or in actual practice have run across this throughout the procedural due process cases so far as criminal trials are concerned.

You look at the average criminal trial, and what do you have? Well, pick one where everybody is actually playing fair; where all the parties concerned are actually looking for justice; they all are looking for a fair and just trial. One group of advocates in that trial—the prosecuting attorneys—are constantly seeking evidence and testimony for the sole object of getting all the truth before the court, but in doing that they want all restraints taken off, withdrawn, so that they can get all the "evidence" they can find. On the other hand, there's the other group of advocates—the defense attorneys—also seeking justice and truth, and they are constantly seeking more restraints to protect the defendant from what they consider to be unlawful procedures. As a matter of fact, the defendants say—as I have heard some lawyers say and I have heard it argued in court—that they believe that a defendant legally arrested should be put in jail and allowed to remain there and not be required to talk to anybody under any circumstances, should be left completely alone. We have all heard prosecuting attorneys say that if they are prevented from talking to a defendant they would never be able to get a conviction in many instances. So there we have the two. On one hand, there is the defendant's counsel saying he wants as many safeguards as possible; on the other, the prosecuting attorney is saying he wants as much freedom as possible to get the facts before the court.

But the real evil in all of this is that in many communities and in many areas this practice one way or the other tends to become the accepted law of that community, unwritten if you please, and there is always the danger in these communities of what was just a mere practice, temporary in the first instance, perhaps tolerated in the belief that it could be pushed aside, coming up to the point where on one side one group of lawyers think it can be done, or to put it even more bluntly, that they think they can get away with it.

So to my mind, and I'm sure to the minds of many other advocates, there is a necessity for many safeguards, many lines of attack to protect us against this sort of injustice; for our courts of last resort, if you please, to work this out so that there will be assurance that these rights are not stepped upon.

There is also another conflict; this belief in "substantial justice," that in this particular trial, although some constitutional right was violated, anybody, absolutely anybody, can see that the man would have been convicted anyway. There is too much of the belief that regardless of what happened in the trial the jury can, for some reason I have never been able to understand, cut through and give this "substantial justice." The biggest danger to due process in a criminal trial is the theory of substantial justice. It's obviously impossible to set out detailed rules that you can question a defendant for one hour and fifteen minutes a day but after that it is a violation of due process. Or that you can question him in his cell but you can't question him in a police room. Or that you can question him in the police jail, but you can't take him out to another jail. Or that it is perfectly all right to obtain evidence if you only break open one door but if you break open two it is wrong. Obviously, that is not what, I believe, anybody would argue for.

On the other hand, there is the theory that this matter should be left entirely to the state courts—that once the state supreme court passes on it, that's it. In that area, the record will show, I think, that the Supreme Court, the United States Supreme Court, has already used the necessary restraints. If anybody is interested in figures, the number of petitions for certiorari applied for and the number granted will certainly convince you of that. So what do we suggest as a working basis in the everyday practice of the law in conjunction with Judge Hastie's paper?

It seems to me that there must be certain agreements at the outset. There are three points I would like to leave with you. One is that the only possible damper to hold down the possibility of temporary local customs and mores denying fundamental theories of due process that all of us agree on is to have ultimate review in the federal courts, meaning, of course, the United States Supreme Court. And that the only restraint on the right, this goes for substantive as well as procedural due process, is the restraint that the court itself exercises. And third,—and now we will have considerable discussion,—I for one would like to see less self-restraint than has been used.

PROFESSOR McCLOSKEY*

Judge Hastie's admirable paper raises questions on two broad fronts. In the first place, there is the question he himself propounds at the outset—whether courts are competent to make the complex and subtle evaluations that the latitudinarian view of due process involves. As Judge Hastie says, we cannot even begin to answer this question unless we can identify the guidelines that mark the path of due process adjudication. But even when these guidelines *have* been identified, the question remains, and the analysis of judgment

---

* ROBERT GREEN McCLOSKEY, *Associate Professor of Government, Harvard University.* Professor McCloskey was born in Wisconsin in 1916. He was graduated in 1939 from the University of Wisconsin with an Arts degree; and took his M.A. in 1942 at the University of Michigan. He was awarded another M.A. in Public Administration at Harvard in 1946 and took his Doctorate there in 1948. He joined the Harvard faculty in 1948, and is now an Associate Professor of Government. In 1944 and 1945 he served as Executive Assistant to the Governor of Michigan. He is the author of "American Conservatism" and of numerous articles in learned periodicals.

criteria has served, not to answer it, but to sharpen it. What reason is there to believe, for example, that courts are better equipped than legislatures to determine when a statute has unduly cribbed and confined the human personality? What reason is there to think that courts are better able than legislatures to balance the value of federalism against such values as the right of fair trial or of economic liberty?

The question is not answered by declaring that the courts will exercise their power in a spirit of respect for majority rule and will assert it only in "that shadowland of judgment where the objectionable merges into the intolerable". The issue is whether courts are especially competent to decide questions within that shadowland, or whether perhaps they are especially *ill* equipped for that venture by their training and their traditions. Nor is it an answer to say, with Justice Jackson, that courts act "by force of their commissions" rather than "by authority of their competence." As he well knew, the commissions are ambiguous, and nowhere more so than in the field of due process. The question of competence to hold them is an old one, but it is still very far from dead.

So that is one question that surely merits discussion. However, Judge Hastie's paper raises another issue, or range of issues, which we reach if we assume, for the sake of argument, the general competence of courts to assess justice under the due process clause. And that is the question of the adequacy of the "guides and correctives" that Judge Hastie has described. I would like to make some comments about that system of guidelines. I here assume, as I have said, that the courts should and will accept the broad responsibility Judge Hastie prescribes. But it may be that these footnotes will help explain why Judge Hand is doubtful about the judiciary's capacity to cope with that assignment.

In the first place then, I would suggest that the system of guidelines could be amplified by explicitly recognizing that the competence of courts in this field may be modified by considerations of degree. Even if we concede the courts' competence to enter the due process field, doesn't the question of more or less remain? Judge Hastie indicates the relevance of this degree-of-competence question when he points out that the judge is especially competent to decide issues in the field of procedural due process, because this question of fairness in arrest and trial is, after all, his cup of tea. I agree, and my suggestion is simply that this question of the degree of competence in particular fields be made a part of the overall rationale in due process questions. Granted that the judge is especially competent in the field of procedural due process, is not his superiority more doubtful when a free speech issue is raised? And is it not still more doubtful when the complex and specialized field of economic regulation is involved? Should not these variations in competence be reflected in a variable boldness of judicial veto? I suggest that they should, and that the rationale based on varying estimates of competence be explicitly incorporated in any system of guidelines in the field of due process.

Second, I should think that the courts, if they accept this assignment at all, are in duty bound to evaluate the public good sought by the statute that is challenged. And they are compelled, I think, to go a little beyond the time-honored inquiry into whether the legislature might reasonably have thought that the law would achieve a legitimate result. They cannot escape the question of whether the result is beneficent enough to warrant the concomitant deprival of liberty. At least, they cannot escape it if they are going to accept the basic responsibility to administer justice under the due process clause. The late Justice Jackson obviously felt that there was something outrageous about the law involved in the Day-Brite Lighting case, a law which required employers to pay their workers for the time they spent at the polls on election day. But he could not or did not put his finger on the distinction between that law and a minimum wage law that might require me to pay an employee more than he was worth. The difference, I suggest, is in the worthiness of the objects sought by the two laws, the one to provide a sort of voters' bonus, the other to maintain a minimum standard of health. Justice Jackson was prevented from taking judicial notice of that difference by his adherence to the ancient convention that the courts are unconcerned with a law's wisdom. I realize that a contrary view would fly in the face of a tradition that extends back to the great Chief Justice himself. But I cannot see how the courts can avoid that course, if they accept the assignment that is marked out for them. Unless indeed we adopt the wholly irrational position that the needfulness of a law is irrelevant to the question of justice.

Finally, I would suggest that, if encroachment on the human personality is to be a determining factor in due process calculations, the courts will have to recognize that economic liberty is still germane to the due process question. Nor is it enough, I think, to say that due process will protect the right to a minimum of material subsistence. The right to pursue the calling of one's choice is surely as important to some people as free speech is to professors. Mark Twain, with his dreams, would have felt that his personality was vitally inhibited if he had been prevented by a legalized system of nepotism from becoming a river boat pilot on the Mississippi. The Supreme Court cannot, I think, go on ignoring the issue of substantive due process in economic legislation, *if* it accepts even a reasonable facsimile of Judge Hastie's formulation.

These then are some amendments, or rather supplements, that I would propose to Judge Hastie's system of guidelines. I think each of them is unavoidably implied by the original premise that the courts should undertake to administer justice under the due process clause. They bring me back therefore to the point I raised at the beginning. Are the courts competent to handle this intricate and elusive multitude of problems? Are they equipped to balance such complex values as federalism, the integrity of the human personality, the right of fair trial? And, if I am right in my supplementary suggestions, are they equipped for a task which they have still further complicated by introducing variables in their approach to different fields, by evaluating the public good of legislation, by supervising the vast field of economic regulation? Anyone will agree, I think, that it is a tough assignment. Whether it is an impracticable one is the very nub of the matter that I have tried to raise.

PROFESSOR FREUND*

It is a special pleasure for me to follow in the wake of Judge Hastie. This is a position in which I found myself many years ago when we were both students in the Law School. At that time I came to have for Judge Hastie that special kind of ineradicable respect which is felt only by a second-year Law Review editor for a third-year Law Review editor.

Judge Hastie's paper, it seems to me, went right to the heart of the hard problem in judicial review of due process issues, or more generally judicial review of the large open-ended guarantees in the Bill of Rights—namely, what is to be the focus or the standard or the scale in which review is to take place, first in the area of economic regulation and second, in the area of civil liberties. Is there any intellectually honest case to be made for a double standard in this regard?

I shall try to present some considerations on both sides in that spirit of sweet reasonableness and equipoise which during this conference you have come to associate with the faculty of the Harvard Law School.

On the one side, the case is that the judiciary is ill adapted for the task in general; that the judiciary is inept and inapt to serve as a kind of censor over legislation of any kind,

---

* PAUL ABRAHAM FREUND, *Professor of Law, Harvard Law School.* Professor Freund was born in St. Louis in 1908. He was graduated in Arts from Washington University in 1928, took his LL.B. at Harvard in 1931 and his S.J.D. at Harvard in 1932. After serving as law secretary to Mr. Justice Brandeis he was admitted to the bars of the District of Columbia in 1935 and of the United States Supreme Court in 1938. He served in the Department of the Treasury, the Reconstruction Finance Corporation, and in the Department of Justice, office of the Solicitor-General, for a number of years. He became Lecturer in Law at the Harvard Law School in 1939 and was appointed Professor of Law in 1940. He is the author of "On Understanding the Supreme Court," is a co-editor of "Cases on Constitutional Law," and has published many articles in legal periodicals.

including measures which infringe on civil liberties. Almost every justice of the Supreme Court, over the generations, has had occasion to lament the fact that so grave and delicate a responsibility was intrusted to so incompetent a group as his colleagues. This unanimity of judgment is, I submit, the most impressive argument against the practice of judicial review in due process cases. And if the judges made a botch of things in the twenties when they were censors on the right, how can we expect them to do any better as censors on the left? For, if, as Holmes said, the Fourteenth Amendment does not enact Mr. Herbert Spencer's Social Statics, it should be equally true that it does not enact Mr. Justice So-and-so's Social Ecstatics. That completes my presentation of that side of the case. Having adequately covered it, I turn to some other considerations.

I take it that everyone would agree that it is a primary responsibility of the Court to help maintain the constitutional order. That means the basic processes and structure of our constitutional society. In the area of procedure in the narrow sense, that function is relatively clear. It has also become relatively clear in another area of process and structure, namely, the relation of the state to the central government in regard to a common national market.

I suggest for your thought that equally important to the maintenance of a constitutional order is a safeguarding of the freedom to believe, the freedom to think and the freedom to hear, as essentials of representative self-government. I am somewhat fortified in this suggestion by looking at the post-World War II constitutions in democratic states, such as India and Germany, which are striving for an enhanced rule of law, where the substance of our Bill of Rights provisions is spelled out in considerable detail, and subjected to the guarantee of judicial review. The wording is somewhat different, to be sure; they attempt to envisage some of the problems that we stumbled over, they reserve the right of reasonable legislation in the interest of public security, and so forth. But I should suppose that any judge, whether he be Ameri-

Chief Justice Earl Warren (left) and Professor A. James Casner.

Judge William H. Hastie.

Chief Justice Patrick Kerwin.

Professor Robert G. McCloskey comments on Judge Hastie's paper.

Professor Henry M. Hart, Jr., discusses the paper given by Father Snee.

Left to right: Gordon Huggins, Executive Director of the Harvard Foundation for Advanced Study and Research, and Deans Bundy and Griswold.

can or Indian or German, faced with the kind of problems that have arisen here under those constitutional provisions would find, as Holmes said, in a very different context, that once you strip off the lion's skin of language, you find the same old jackass of a legal problem underneath.

Let me be more concrete in the analogy to cases involving fundamentals of process and structure. Consider a typical case that we call an interstate commerce case, such as arose when the city of Madison, Wisconsin, attempted in the interest of public health to require all milk brought into the city to be pasteurized in the environs of the city. Considered as a domestic due process issue, the measure was reasonable enough. But it had to be considered in the light of some countervailing considerations, namely, the interest of out-of-state suppliers in bottling their milk for the Madison market. And on balance, the court said that although the scheme is rational enough as a health measure there are less drastic means, perhaps not quite so efficient, but there are alternative means available for reaching the health ends which are more compatible with the interests of the national market and the city will have to do better.

Now, I suggest a parallel between that and a rather simple civil liberties case, the handbill case of *Lovell v. Griffin,* where in order to prevent littering of the streets, a perfectly justifiable local end, the city penalized the distribution of handbills on the sidewalks. As applied to commercial handbills that is presumably valid enough, but as applied to handbills containing political or ideological messages, the ordinance was struck down, because the process of political flux required that a less drastic measure be taken in promoting the interest, a justifiable interest to be sure, of maintaining a clean city.

I suggest a similarity in these cases also in terms of the effect of judicial veto. In the old days, the most grievous use of the veto consisted in isolating certain areas of legislative control and making them immune to treatment. I mean particularly such matters as minimum wages and prices and hours of labor, so that you had certain islands in which legislative power was incompetent. I think the typical so-called civil liberties case today involves a rather different approach, one more like that in the commerce field. That is, the court says you can't do it this way, you have to do it in some less drastic way. You can't penalize all house-to-house religious solicitation by a general ordinance, but you could provide that a householder may post a warning notice and put the force of the state behind that warning through the processes of the law of civil and criminal trespass. And in the *Smith Act* case, if the court had held it unconstitutional, I dare say there were other ways in which Congress could have dealt with the menace of the Communist Party. It wouldn't follow, if that act punishing advocacy of violent overthrow had been held invalid, that Congress could not have dealt with the Party under a charge of conspiracy to overthrow the government, or to teach the arts of espionage and sabotage, or to disseminate and advocate ideas under the domination of a foreign power through the instrumentality of an oath-bound secret society.

Finally, I suggest, one should not be ashamed to say that an argument for the special function of the Court in this area derives from what is the essentially spiritual character of the individual, recognized in our constitutional system. This character is by no means antithetical to the interest of society. Quite the contrary; the one reinforces the other, as has been beautifully brought out in John Lord O'Brian's paper to be presented tomorrow.

In closing, having begun on a frivolous note, I beg your indulgence for the frivolities by becoming solemn. I should like to read a few sentences, not from a lawyer, but from a philosopher, a religious philosopher, from whose little book, *The Children of Light and the Children of Darkness,* I confess I have had more profit than from many books many times its size written by constitutional lawyers about "understanding the Supreme Court". I think that constitutional lawyers would do well to supplement their reading about the

Supreme Court by browsing in the works of such philosophers, and I only hasten to add that I would wish such philosophers would sharpen their own sense of philosophic problems by reading the opinions of the Supreme Court. At any rate, let me read what seems to me to be a beautifully expressed statement of the interrelation of the fulfillment of man's spiritual nature with the maintenance of a healthy, growing community, free from fetters on communication and on what Judge Wyzanski aptly calls political fraternity.

Professor Niebuhr says: "The man who searches after both meaning and fulfillment, beyond the ambiguous fulfillments and frustrations of history, exists in a height of spirit which no historical process can completely contain. This height is not irrelevant to the life of the community, because new richness and a higher possibility of justice come to the community from this height of awareness. But the height is destroyed by any community which seeks prematurely to cut off this pinnacle of individuality in the interest of the community's peace and order."

DISCUSSION

Frank Sander, of Washington, D. C., and the Massachusetts Bar: I wonder whether, in view of Mr. Marshall's eloquent plea for less judicial restraints, a theme which has run throughout this conference, both affirmatively and negatively, whether Judge Hastie would comment a little more on that—particularly in view of Professor Tunc's discussion of the French system?

Judge Hastie: I will comment only in saying that in the most recent case decided by our court involving that matter of judicial self-restraint, the dissenting members of our court felt that I, writing the majority opinion, used too much restraint. I suspect that by and large (of course, I can't speak for all judges) federal judges feel very intensely today the need to restrain themselves in passing judgment upon state action. Perhaps it is history, the observation of what happened, as

Professor Freund said, in the twenties when there was the opposite attitude. Maybe we are going too far and we'll see that we are and we'll swing back, but I do believe the federal judiciary is holding itself very tightly in check in monitoring state action.

Professor Kaplan: Is there another question or comment?

Judge Hastie: I'd like, if I may, to volunteer just one more observation on a question asked—I don't know whether it was rhetorical—in one of the comments, as to whether or not courts can do a better job than legislators in some of these difficult value judgments, particularly in the field of substantive due process. Perhaps it would be better for this to be said by somebody who is neither a member of a court nor a member of a legislature, but I'll say it anyhow.

Take a piece of legislation like the Smith Act. Read legislative debates, committee reports, arguments pro and con made in and to the legislature as an indication of the value judgments or the considerations that influence legislative action. Then read briefs and opinions of courts involving the same legislation to see the way courts are striving to weigh values in passing upon the propriety of the legislation. This process should shed some light upon the canons of judgment the legislatures use, as contrasted with the canons of judgment the courts use. I also repeat the suggestion already advanced that the materials courts receive and find useful and persuasive may include such materials as Professor Niebuhr and other philosophers contribute. In brief judges use all of the materials which those of us in the legal tradition see as going into the making of the legal order. To what extent are those things used in the exercise of legislative judgment? It seems to me these questions are worth considering.

Raymond Pace Alexander, of the Philadelphia Bar: Because of my great experience in the actual trial of cases, the remarks of Judge Hastie bring two questions to my mind which have often puzzled me; first, what part, if any, Judge Hastie, do public opinion and public clamor, whipped up ofttimes by the press out of all proportion to the issues involved, play in arriving at your and your associates' almost always calm and well-reasoned opinions? And secondly, on the question of judicial restraint, what part, in this process of judicial conferences and review, if any, does the atmosphere of the general community play?

I ask these questions particularly in view of two cases: one in which I was chief counsel for the National Association for the Advancement of Colored People (NAACP), the celebrated *Trenton Six* Case,[1] which lasted 124 days in Trenton, New Jersey—the longest murder trial in the history of our country and perhaps in the English-speaking world—and the other, the case of the *United States of America, ex rel. David Darcy, Appellant, vs. Handy, Warden of Bucks County Prison* (Pa.),[2] which was a 4-3 decision, denying a writ of habeas corpus to a prisoner sentenced to death, in which case you wrote the majority opinion and our distinguished Chief Judge (Biggs) was among the three minority Judges. Here you reviewed due process at length. This case is now on appeal to the Supreme Court of the United States.

Judge Hastie: Well, my answer would be, as little part as judges, being human beings, can let it play. How little that is, I don't know. We like to believe that it plays almost no part. That's certainly our goal. How near we come to achieving it I can't say.

[*A speaker from the floor*]: I would like to ask a question of Judge Hastie. In your paper, page 336, you were discussing substantive due process and you quoted Professor Freund; I'll read the essence of the quotation: "Professor Paul Freund . . . has noted how little we are told by opinion writers wheth-

1. State of New Jersey, Plaintiff-Respondent vs. Ralph Cooper, and Collis English, Appellants, et al., Defendants, Docket #877 (1952), on appeal from Superior Court, Mercer County, N. J.

2. United States, Ex rel., David Darcy vs. Handy, Warden, Bucks County, Pennsylvania et al., 224 F.(2d) 504 (3d Cir. 1955).

er their evaluation is derived from the evidence of history regarding the relative social utility of different kinds of freedom, or is derived from convictions about the nature and duties of man, or from an analysis of representative government." Will you please comment briefly on that?

Judge Hastie: Well, let me take a perhaps oversimplified situation. A case arises in which police officers seizing a suspect observe that he swallows something, which is believed to be a narcotic. They wish to recover that. They give him an emetic and he regurgitates. Now, how do we reach the conclusion that this method of getting evidence is intolerable in our society? What are the criteria that go into our value judgment? Is it that we have had some very terrible recent experiences with governments whose officers do not respect the integrity of the human personality? Is it something that has been instilled in us through humanistic thinking? Professor Freund, as I understand him, is saying that if we judges would get clear in our minds what makes us reach such a conclusion, and then articulate it in our opinions it would help. I hope I am doing justice to his thinking. The process of improving the administration of justice would be aided, if only in that scholars in the universities and lawyers who are advocates, could feel more confident that they were getting at the things that make us tick in their attempts at constructive criticism and advocacy. I think Professor Freund is dealing with that sort of thing, and I think it is very important.

A Lay View of Due Process

McGeorge Bundy*

What can a layman say to lawyers about a subject so near the heart of their calling as due process of law? Not all of those who understand something of the matter are at the bar, of course; we all know scholars, not themselves lawyers, whose work has illuminated the meaning of the law. But such men bring their own professional skills to the task, and I do not. The law has not been my professional study, even from afar.

In this situation I will make a virtue of necessity and begin from what I take to be the standard lay opinion of your profession. Here I find a double sentiment. First, we laymen want as little to do with the law as possible, and second, when we want its help, we want it very much indeed. I should like to suggest in this paper that both of these basic reactions are correct, and that they tell a good deal about the nature of due process of law.

Most of the time, for the ordinary citizen, the machinery of the law has the appearance that all machinery tends to have in the eyes of the untrained. It seems a powerful and incomprehensible affair, driven by invisible forces to an implacable end—a turning mass of procedures, prohibitions, and prosecutions, into which one cannot insert so much as one's little finger without running the risk of being gobbled up and kept churning for years, at one's own expense and without prospect of escape. Simple naked fear—that is what the law inspires in most of us most of the time—whether in the shape of a motorcycle cop, a threatened lawsuit, or the fine print on an income tax form. And even those who rise above fear tend to feel an emotion toward the law which I can best suggest by varying the metaphor. To you, by traditional rhetoric, the law is a stern mistress; to the rest of us she is capricious, costly, and somewhat alien. These are qualities

* For biographical note see page 382.

which may be attractive in one's own mistress, but never in the other man's, especially when she has great power.

Now in very large part what we laymen think, I beg you to observe, is true. The law is almost always expensive, often clumsy, not seldom unjust, and generally imperfect. Not only so, but necessarily so.

For brief illustration, let us take the matter of cost. Whether we think of criminal or civil law, we cannot think of modern legal process as cheap. When the Government prosecutes an individual, whether for simple robbery or for income tax evasion, costs to both sides must often exceed the real value of the issue for either party, even when we weigh in the supposed effect of "making an example". And the pattern is still more familiar in civil suits, so that there has developed an acceptable alternative for those who fear costs but confess nothing. A modest settlement, out of court, often is more nearly fair to all concerned than the best test in court could be, simply because of its inherent expense to all. So conscientious members of the bar spend much of their time persuading litigious or naive laymen that as a remedy for most of life's quarrels legal process as it is today can only be described as quite undue.

Yet the real point about costs, and the one which bears also upon all our lay complaints, is that in large measure it is *right* that law should be expensive. The notion of cheap justice is a mirage. If by some miracle our courts were to become as fast as baseball umpires, and as cheap as advice from Dorothy Dix, it seems certain that new swarms of litigants would soon clog the courthouses. And with overcrowding and delay new costs would begin. By a false economy our judges and our juries may be kept relatively cheap, but the law has never sought or found a way to make the lawyer a continuous benefactor of his clients.[1] As long as the courts are crowded, there will be delay, and as long as there is delay, there will be costs. The law's delays must be the litigant's

1. This is the principal difference between lawyers and college professors, but while misery loves company, the remedy for this difficulty is for us to gain from your example, and not for you to lose by ours.

dollars. It may even be true that justice will be cheaper in the end if first costs are reasonably high. Perhaps a threshold of expense must be part of due process, lest all of life's adjustments become legal.

But if costless justice is a mirage, may not the same be true of other things we think we ought to find in the law? Is it not possible that just as the law is necessarily expensive, so also it is necessarily cumbersome and even unjust? Let me tip my hand and say flatly that in my view the only thing that is wrong with the lay attitude toward the law is that the layman should be so surprised. The imperfections of the law, I believe, are not so much a ground for criticism as an index to its extraordinary importance in our society. And if all this seems merely speaking in riddles, there may be a clue in the second lay attitude which I have already mentioned. Why is it that so many of us, fearing and disliking the machinery of the law, nevertheless, on occasion, feel a most desperate and urgent need for its support? In the answer to this question I think we shall come near to the center of our problem.

The answer is not a hard one. The urgency with which men seek the help of the law, when they do seek it, arises from their sharp and intense awareness of the fact that only the law stands between them and something much worse. The thing which is worse than the law may be any one of a vast number of possible happenings—an unjust eviction, an open theft of one's property, or something still nearer and more terrible, like the kidnapping of a child. When these things happen, or are merely about to happen, the layman turns to the law.

I suggest, then, that legal process is best understood not as a source of pure and positive justice, but rather as an imperfect remedy for gross wrongs—not as the blind balance of the familiar image, but rather as a keel on the ship of society, which will not keep life even, but can perhaps prevent complete capsizal. Or perhaps we can think of the law not as something good in itself, but as an instrument which derives its value less from what it does than from what it prevents, like the sprinkler system which substitutes water for fire as a threat to property. On this construction our courts appear not as the source of fairness for all, but as the last refuge of the wronged. What one asks of them is not that they do justice but that they give some protection against grave injustice. Verdicts, in such a view, need not be right; they need only be, on the average, substantially less wrong than what would have happened without legal process.

I suggest, in short, that the fundamental function of the law is to prevent the natural unfairness of human society from becoming intolerable, to punish enough of the most wicked to keep crime a merely endemic disease, and to right enough of civil wrong to keep the scoundrels within bounds. On this view, I suggest further, we should excuse the law not only from the care of the minimal, but from all light work of any kind, asking only that it serve as a rough guardian against major incursions of barbarity. And if this be its function, its imperfections will surely appear in a different light, for life on the frontier has never been refined, and from the time of the Romans the costs of containment have never been low.

Like the Roman legions in barbaric territory, moreover, the law may justly claim that its value should not be finally judged by the quality of its own current contests. Behind the frontiers of the law, safely away from the firing line, a peaceful citizenry lives by rules of precedent that are the inheritance of earlier legal wars. The precedents of the common law have often been wrought out of suffering and a sense of wrong, and not only on the winning side. But when the issue has been settled, other men may guide their choices with some sense of certainty. Even when a current question is not clear (and how often such clarity is impossible because it is the facts and not the legal rules which are in doubt!), the mere existence of the legal process, with all its failings, is often a great force for peaceful settlement. A wise lawyer, persuading angry clients to the course of calm good sense, and negotiating for an advantageous agreement with the other man's counsel, necessarily relies upon the fact that if he has to, he can go to law. Clumsy and imperfect it may be, but its effects have weight far beyond any of its immediate proceedings.

Now let me admit at once, lest I be misunderstood that this limited but heavy view of the place of law among us does not exhaust the topic. This becomes apparent at once if we look at the contrast between the law as I have been describing it and the laws—constitutional, statutory, or administrative. Evidently there is something more than a purely negative avoidance of evil in the steadily multiplying variety of rules and regulations which affect every aspect of our social life. It is not easy to think of a traffic court or an O.P.A. or even a tax code as playing the ponderous role of a keel to the ship of state. The modern law is evidently an instrument not only of equilibrium but also of command and navigation.

All this is clear, but command and navigation are another part of the law, to be treated in another part of this conference. Some of what I have been saying may apply to this other realm, but I do not press the matter here. Our concern is with due process of law, and for due process, our limited and heavy view has immediate meaning.

Yet before leaving this question of the law as command and navigation, we must consider one point which is important not merely in itself, but for what it tells us of due process. For if there is to be due process, there must be process; if it is to be due process of law, there must be law, and it must operate. If the law of the land is to hold up, someone must have the power to uphold it. Underneath and within all that is implied by due process, as protection against gross injustice or outrage, there is implied a government. And there must be enough government. Ordered liberty—or the prevention of its opposite—implies effective authority. The kinds of authority that are needed must be as varied as societies themselves and sufficient to each one. All our rules and regulations, whether contrived by constitutional conventions, legislatures, or commissions, reflect in some measure a need for government. There are certainly too many of them, and some must be unwise, but unless lawmaking becomes quite divorced from reality, they will tend to reflect felt needs for government. In this measure they too, in all their multiplicity, detail, and frequent triviality, sustain the law as a bulwark against chaos.

That government itself, and strong government, is vital for the defense of society and all its fragmentary freedoms is the great hard truth that John Marshall wrote into American constitutional law. He did it over and over again, but never more powerfully than in sustaining the appeal of the bank officer McCulloch:

> The sword and the purse, all the external relations, and no inconsiderable portion of the industry of the nation, are entrusted to its government . . . A government, entrusted with such ample powers, on the due execution of which the happiness and prosperity of the nation so vitally depends, must also be entrusted with ample means for their execution. The power being given, it is the interest of the nation to facilitate its execution. It can never be their interest, and cannot be presumed to have been their intention, to clog and embarrass its execution by withholding the most appropriate means.[2]

This doctrine, right for government in general, is right in particular for the whole field of due process of law. Where law is not enforced, lynch law takes its place, and even when no such limit is reached, it is remarkable that the most distressing breaches of due process tend to occur in the backwash of resentment against a neglect or carelessness which permits crime to spread or civil danger to grow. There can be no justice where there is not strength to govern.

* * * *

I believe that the general view which I have been expressing has certain consequences for lawyers, but before I attempt to show what these consequences are, it may be useful to make it quite plain that one view not reinforced by this assessment is that of the cynic—the man who tends to see in all the majesty of the law, and especially in the opinions of judges, only the protective covering for a play of raw forces. On the surface, there is some similarity between the rather limited expectations I have outlined and the dim view that because the law is what the judges say it is, it is no better than

2. McCulloch v. Maryland, 17 U.S. (4 Wheat.) 316, 407 (1819).

a reflection of their personal, sectional, class, or intellectual biases. But fundamentally, I believe, the view I have suggested operates in just the reverse direction.

I think that precisely because at its best the law is so imperfect, precisely because it is so hard either to come near justice or to liberate government for genuine action, the role of the law and its professionals is of the highest intellectual and moral significance. To draw the opposite conclusion is to make the error that Tolstoy made about war and generals. He saw correctly that battles and campaigns are massively confused, and that many of the decisive forces are beyond the grip of any consciously purposeful human will. No reader of *War and Peace* can ever again believe in the neat chessboard battles that the generals—and even the historians—so often create after the event. But from this great insight Tolstoy drew the conclusion that generals are really unimportant, except in the measure that they are in or out of harmony with forces larger than they. The right conclusion, I think, was and is exactly opposite. Just because war is so massively unpredictable, and every battle in it so confused, the man who can in any measure translate his will into results must have the highest professional merit—and so the right conclusion from Tolstoy's insight is not that generalship is unimportant, but that it is rare, difficult, and greatly to be prized. This conclusion allows us to come to terms with the plain fact that military history is full of great captains, many of whom were self-evidently out of harmony with the "moving forces" of their time. We can admire their quality the more when we understand how much the best of them was enveloped in the fog of battle.

It is the same, I think, with judges and leaders at the bar. We do not lessen their stature if we make their task more difficult. The fact that the law at its best is imperfect must give us the greater regard for those whose best work is so little bad. And if in some degree the construction I am suggesting can illuminate the nature of the profession, it may even give us better reason to admire the really great men. Fashions in analysis are variable, but there is a peculiar durability in the really big men, and it will be something of a test of any view of due process whether it does well by Marshall and by Holmes.

This particular test our argument readily passes. For one of the things which is most striking about Marshall and Holmes, in quite separate ways, is the degree to which they saw themselves not as agents of truth, but rather as contenders against error—and this is precisely the distinction whose importance I am urging. For Marshall the errors were feebleness in Government, defiance of the national authority, and attempted invasion of the independent judiciary. For Holmes the error was sometimes in the attempt to make due process do too much, sometimes in mistrust of chartered rights or chartered government, and perhaps most of all in the human tendency to praise or dispraise, use or abuse the law without trying to know it fully, and its limits. Is it unfair to suggest that these two masters can be understood better by considering the things they fought against than by attempting to set forth in golden language the ideals for which they stood?

Let me generalize, indeed, and argue that one merit of the view I am suggesting is that it may liberate us from the prevalent compulsion to make demigods of our great judges, and also from the still less appetizing habit of general denigration. These are men, not heroes or devils. They are contending, as men must, with extraordinarily difficult problems of choice, in which their object must be to prevent the worst. They cannot do justice, in and of themselves; they can only help in the prevention of evil—and even in this they are limited by their obligation to preserve and interpret the law itself, which is not always just. It is to be expected that they will make errors, and it does them little honor to ignore that expectation in the case of special favorites. The man who praises any judge for perfection is a man who betrays an unbecoming certainty that he knows just what is right.

A controversial view of a familiar question may be tested not only against men but against settled ideas. I take it that most of us would agree upon the importance, in maintaining due process of law, of an independent judiciary. From time to time the principle has been called into question, but each time it has emerged from the challenge with reinforced standing, and the arguments raised against it are not remembered to the credit of their makers. In any event, it will take a bold man to question this particular principle at a celebration in honor of John Marshall, and I take as my text this statement from his very old age: "I have always thought, from my earliest youth till now, that the greatest scourge an angry Heaven ever inflicted upon an ungrateful and sinning people, was an ignorant, a corrupt, or a dependent Judiciary."[3]

Observe, first, that Marshall makes this point, too, in the negative. The first justification for an independent judiciary is the probable character of any other kind. But there is more to it than that, on the present view. Like the general in combat, the judge is surrounded by confusion, turmoil, and the likelihood of error. He is engaged, not in a great constructive work, but in a labor of prevention and avoidance. The odds are against him. Let us, in simple good sense, leave him alone. For the sake of the litigant, too, we need the independent judge. If he is not going to get self-evident and perfect justice—if, indeed, a measure of injustice is and must be his normal reward, let him at least have the comfort of knowing that his judge does not belong to someone else. And finally, the present argument gives more urgency than ever to the traditional opinion that judges should keep clear of political controversy. Like generals in the field, they are engaged in a steady struggle against the common enemy of wrong and evil; it can only spread disunion if they take up arms also in the political arena.

So I assert that my argument is sufficient to indicate that Marshall and Holmes were considerable judges, and that an independent judiciary is a good thing. That it leads to these conclusions is comforting, but not earthshaking. We have earned the right to go on, but we had better do so quickly.

---

3. 4 Beveridge, The Life of John Marshall 495 (1919).

* * * *

The law as we have pictured it carries a heavy burden of social responsibility. Not only is there the massive function of standing against disorder and grave injustice; there is also, as we have seen in passing, the job of providing paths for action through the tangled complexities of modern life. Is there not, as one immediate consequence of this vast role, a simple rule that no additional burden should be placed upon the law if it can possibly be avoided? American legislators, and the American citizenry, can do nothing better for the law, the judges, and the lawyers than to cease and desist from their painful passion for lawmaking. I suspect, although I cannot prove it, that the very people who complain most about the wickedness of judges and lawyers are frequently to be found among those who are most eager for more controls to meet their own preferences.

There are two particular forms of offensive overuse of law to which I would call your attention—one is Noseyparkerism, and the other is Barndooritis. Each of them is widespread, and each has attained the dignity of an adopted Constitutional Amendment. The Eighteenth Amendment, of course, is the classic case of Noseyparkerism, and I suggest that the Twenty-second Amendment, which restricts the length of service of the President, is an excellent illustration of Barndooritis. Noseyparkerism is essentially an effort to rewrite human nature, and especially private life, in the image of the self-appointed guardian of morals; Barndooritis is an effort to rewrite public history, and the reason for its name is, of course, that the horse has almost invariably escaped before the rewriting is accomplished. The law is an instrument of great power and usefulness, but it is needed on the frontiers of injustice and crime, and nothing is gained by trying to use its awkward strength against such elusive targets as the ordinary man's fondness for alcohol and Franklin Roosevelt's fondness for high office. While these are extreme instances, we all know that they do not stand alone. If the law is to do its own work, and hold the respect of the citizen, we should all forswear the bad habit of unloading our troubles into the legislative hopper.

There is a deeper sense, too, in which it is important that the field of service of the law should be limited. If it is correct to suggest that the broad purpose of the law—as distinct from the myriad specific provisions of the laws—is negative, then the role of the lawyer as adviser in other fields than his own should be a distinctly limited one. I am not talking about the individual who happens to be a lawyer and also has judgment and wisdom in human affairs. Such men are frequent, and perhaps more frequent among lawyers than elsewhere. My concern is with the idea which I often find among my friends at the bar, that the advice of lawyers, simply as such, has a special virtue in nearly all human situations. Mr. Charles Curtis, in his recent volume, *It's Your Law,* tells us of the distinguished lawyer who once remarked in his old age that he had been trying to think of an occasion in any man's life in which he would not be better off for the advice of a lawyer, and had not been able to think of one.[4] With this sentiment I find myself in cordial disagreement. It has two pernicious consequences; first, it shows precisely that overweening confidence which tends to break down the general trust of the layman in lawyers; second, and more serious, a view of this sort distracts the lawyer himself from his own central and difficult business. I leave aside, as a matter of negligible selfish preference, the fact that the rest of us feel our own small personal need for a sphere of action. The lawyer can often tell me what I must not do; he can often tell me what I am required to do; when he is very good at his business, he can do for the layman what Elihu Root is said to have done for William C. Whitney, he can tell him how to do what he wants to do.[5] But he cannot tell me two things—what I want to do, and what I ought to do, nor can he tell me, in whatever trade I find myself, how I shall learn what these things are. And both his function and the framework

4. CURTIS, IT'S YOUR LAW 37 (1954).

5. A somewhat defensive account of this notable story is to be found in 1 JESSUP, ELIHU ROOT 185 (1937).

of society are subtly distorted when his claim to give advice becomes too big.[6]

* * * *

Let us limit our concern, then, to those central activities which are peculiarly the province of the law. And in particular, now, let us consider the problem of due process. What is the meaning, for due process of law, of the general view I have set forth? What does it mean for due process to conceive of it not as a handsome device for ensuring justice, but as a blunt instrument for the prevention or avoidance of the most serious forms of unfairness?

In the first place, it means that we must come down quite firmly on the side of those who hold that due process of law is not likely to be defined by any additive series of specific rights or processes. In the general and interminable war against unfairness, it is most unlikely that any one set of weapons will always serve. Moreover, it must be steadily recollected that on the view we are urging, due process is only half of law; the rest is enforcement, and the two cannot survive separately. Thus the man who cares for due process must also care for the enforcement of the law, and he will not suppose that a steady accumulation of small hurdles can be placed in the way of the police officer without reducing the effectiveness of the general defense against unfairness. And by the

6. It may be that one exception to this general rule of limited concern and minimum lawmaking is to be found in the field of international law. It has seemed to me that such enterprises as the Nuremberg Trials were, on balance, highly desirable, in order to give concrete expression to sentiments strongly held among civilized men. But it would have to be granted that the law of Nuremberg pressed somewhat beyond the limits of what was clearly defined and expressly understood as enforceable law before 1945. There is nothing new in this difficulty; Sir Henry Maine pointed out long ago that international law bears the scars of its mixed ancestry, and remarked that in studying writers on international law, "the great difficulty is always to discover whether they are discussing law or morality—whether the state of international relations they describe is actual or ideal—whether they lay down that which is, or that which, in their opinion, ought to be." [MAINE, ANCIENT LAW 57 (Everyman Edition)]. Perhaps we should do better to speak not of international law, but of the organized processes of international morality. In that case, we might find the limitation for which I am contending in the application of unusually strict standards of proof and unusually heavy obligations of certainty before punishment is applied. In this manner we might rescue Nuremberg, because the most cursory examination of the records of that trial makes it plain that no conviction was obtained except upon evidence which would lead to a verdict of guilt by almost any standard of behavior, and many times over. But I shall not quarrel if the purists will not call it law. Perhaps it is better in this field to be moral.

same token, it must be urged from the present analysis that it is not wise to stretch the meaning of due process to include all that honorable judges think is wise or unwise legislation. If the law is to have the public support it needs for the hard work before it, we must count on the judges not to stretch the due process clause beyond the limits of plain necessity.

This is hard counsel, and we all know that it has been disregarded frequently. Due process, justices have said, requires the law to stand clear of the sixty-hour week in baker shops; due process, they have suggested, means that all the states must find twelve men to hear the story whenever more than twenty dollars is at issue; due process, they have urged, means that you not only have a right to counsel, but sometimes you have no right *not* to have him. To the layman this last view suggests that your profession has been learning from such other insistent trades as medicine and teaching; to the health officer and the truant officer, we are asked to add the compulsory advocate. Which is more like Big Brother I leave to another judge.[7]

It is in keeping with all of my remarks that I find it easier to tell by example what due process is not than to define what it is. It will not escape your notice that the cases at which I laugh are outside the limits of present law, since one of them has been long since overruled, and the other two are minority arguments which have not gained the favor of the Supreme Court as a whole. The prevailing view of due process is surely different—why do we not work from that? It is a good suggestion, but the task is beyond my skill—and beyond my presumption in the presence of a practicing judge. So I back off from the final question of judicial understanding, but I do take with me the comfort that more than one of our distinguished justices, of the past and present court, has himself backed off at the ultimate point of definition. Indeed, it may be that the dominant sentiment of the Supreme Court has been that the last test of due process is not in the

7. Lochner v. New York, 198 U.S. 45 (1904); Adamson v. California, 332 U.S. 46, 68 (1947) (Mr. Justice Black's dissent); Carter v. Illinois, 329 U.S. 173, 182 (1946) (Mr. Justice Murphy's dissent). In the two latter cases, I concede, justices might resist my interpretation of their views.

court itself, but in the governing feelings of the American people. Mr. Justice Holmes spoke of "fundamental principles as they have been understood by the traditions of our people and our law."[8] Mr. Justice Frankfurter, in our own time, has spoken of "those fundamental notions of fairness and justice in the determination of guilt or innocence which lie embedded in the feelings of the American people and are enshrined in the Due Process Clause of the Fourteenth Amendment."[9] So perhaps if we wish really to know what due process is we must ask ourselves. Here we all become citizens together, and the distinction upon which I have insisted between the layman and the lawyer will tend to disappear.

As I leave the judges to my betters, I will make one more explanation of what I do not mean. In the end, when their other weapons fail, our judges may have to ask themselves what is fair, or even what the layman feels to be fair, but of course not every case comes to this point. There is no substitute for learning in the law, or for a sense of judicial history; a judge must have the power and skill to understand and apply a vast amount that is well settled, and a vast amount more that leans heavily to one side or the other. Moreover, though I describe the law as a blunt instrument, thinking of its general social purpose and effect, I find no contradiction in the fact that much of the best work of lawyers and judges must be subtle and complex. This is as it must be — though no great judge, I suspect, indulges in complexity for its own sake. Now I really must not talk about judges any more.

* * * *

If I ask myself, as a layman, what I mean by due process of law, I know at once this much: That I mean something good. It may often be abused—and indeed I may abuse it myself—but I believe in it. And I know why; I believe in it as a shield for the private citizen against state authority.

So far, I think, I follow the best authorities. But I am a layman, and I do not follow them much further. I do not mean by due process nearly what the legal tradition of the

8. Lochner v. New York, 198 U.S. 45, 76 (1904) (dissenting opinion).
9. Haley v. Ohio, 332 U.S. 596, 607 (1948) (concurring opinion).

country seems to mean. I do not measure my sense of fairness by constitutions, statutes, or precedents—I am more direct. Take, for example, one of the greatest of the legal rules of a fair trial—that a man is presumed innocent until he is proven to be guilty beyond a reasonable doubt. I may well pay lip service to it, but I do not really believe it—not when the accused is the sort of obvious criminal type that experience has taught me to recognize. As layman, I am like the jurymen in James G. Cozzens' fine novel of the law:

> "Justice for all was a principle they understood and believed in; but by 'all' they did not perhaps really mean persons lowdown and no good. They meant that any accused person should be given a fair, open hearing, so that a man might explain, if he could, the appearances that seemed to be against him. If his reputation and presence were good, he was presumed to be innocent; if they were bad, he was presumed to be guilty. If the law presumed differently, the law presumed alone."[10]

It behooves us all to be careful on this point—for very few of us are any better than Mr. Cozzens' jury. We differ, of course, in our judgment as to what constitutes good reputation. To many, Alger Hiss was almost literally above suspicion; to many more, he was just the sort of man they had been wanting to catch up with for a very long time. And if you feel that you were virtuous in your assumption that Hiss was innocent, ask yourself how much you have been eager to believe against Whittaker Chambers—it is out of a lack of innocence that I ask.

In some measure, then, we believe in due process of law in spite of ourselves—or to put it another way, we believe in due process as a whole, and we extend the protection of that belief to cover doubts about specific elements in traditional legal forms. We do not really practice the presumption of innocence, but we agree that we should. Out of a general respect for the Bill of Rights, we put up with a number of its undesirable consequences. Freedom for the thought we hate

10. Cozzens, The Just and the Unjust 57 (1942).

is really a very hard rule, and as a matter of fact a lot of us do what we can, half-consciously, to see to it that the thoughts we hate are not expressed very often or loudly in our own area of influence—the professor who nominates his great academic opponent as a colleague is very rare indeed.

There is another trouble with the layman as protector of due process. Remember that we do not turn to the law, except *in extremis*. When the law turns to us, we are not likely to find it pleasant, and when we find ourselves so far in its toils that the protections of due process become personally important to us, we are quite likely to think that we had better make the utmost use of them. If in our view the law is unfairly pestering us, and if there is a technicality by which we can escape it, what could be a neater retribution? And so, as consumer, we try to take due process for a ride. Nothing is more natural, and nothing is more dangerous to the law as a whole.

Here again, of course, different men use different tricks, and the other man's misuse of legal process is likely to be a good deal more offensive than our own. Currently the principal offenders are those who brandish the Fifth Amendment—but there was a time when misuse of the law was more conspicuous among officers of speculative corporations and income tax dodgers. One man's due process is another man's strained technicality—and there is little doubt that the strain can be great enough to inspire a fairly violent reaction. A man who is in trouble with an angry public as well as with the law is not likely to be protected indefinitely when he stretches the technical protection of the laws and calls it due process.

For in the end the law is no better than we laymen make it. And if the law, due process and all, cannot satisfy our fundamental sense of what is fair and right, so much the worse for the law. That is why, when we put too much weight on due process, we become its enemies, and why also judges warn us off the twisted notion that courts will always protect us against ourselves.[11] They will, but only if we want them to. A man who is devoted to due process of law must find this a very strong argument against using its technical protections when such use is generally and deeply disapproved. It is remembered of Socrates that, scorning to flee the verdict of his countrymen, he died to keep the law of Athens, and it is remembered of Thoreau that to keep his conscience clear he bluntly broke the law. But in between, among those who have bent due process to their fears, the heroes are very few.

There arises here, however, in a new and sharper form, a question we have already touched upon. It is well enough to warn against the abuse of due process which comes from stretching its technicalities, but how shall I say which is a stretched technicality and which a basic right exercised in the way the lawmakers intended? Suppose you grant me that by its very nature a bill of rights will offer handholds for abuse, so that what safeguards the innocent will also give some comfort to the guilty? It still remains unclear in each case whether a given right is being misused. And surely I do not wish to claim that every procedural safeguard which may at any time be momentarily irritating to a majority must be discarded—or its use avoided—by the virtuous.

I can raise the question, but it has no answer. It is a fact that due process will be weakened if its protections are so used as to become widely unpopular; it is a fact that in any system such abuse is possible; but it is also a fact that popularity does not always measure what is fair. What we must hope is that the stresses inherent in these facts can be mitigated by civic virtue, clear communication, and a decent confidence in our own strength. It is civic virtue which accepts due process even when it seems unfair, or which scorns its use for technical advantage. It is clear communication which can help the layman—and the lawyer, too—to a better

11. The classic statement is Learned Hand's: "Liberty lies in the hearts of men and women; when it dies there, no constitution, no court can save it; no constitution, no law, no court can even do much to help it." THE SPIRIT OF LIBERTY 190 (Dilliard ed. 1953). This is splendid—but I share the doubts of C. P. Curtis about a following passage in which Judge Hand appears to say that courts are unnecessary while men prize liberty. See CURTIS, *op. cit. supra* note 4, at 154.

understanding of the great meaning of some parts of our tradition. So Dean Griswold helps us all when he insists upon the splendid origins of the privilege against self-incrimination—let us grant its annoyances but never forget the troubles we should have without it.[12] But above these, in maintaining due process of law, I should emphasize the importance of a certain self-respect and self-confidence among laymen. Nearly all the significant stains upon our record of due process can be laid to a sense of insecurity—a general panicky distress which suddenly puts safety far ahead of fairness. And most of the time—not always, I grant—the fear far outruns the reality. This is not an argument against fear—it is only an argument in favor of action through due process—and a warning that the very standard of legal fairness which has us laymen for its final arbiters has us also, in a different mood, for its most dangerous enemies.

* * * *

Let me press one step further. We are asked to be clear about due process, to give it the honor that a citizen should give his basic framework of law, and above all not to be too easily afraid. Are these commandments sufficient in themselves, deriving only from a reasoned interest in the avoidance of most grievous wrong? Does all this really turn, as I have claimed throughout, on the law as a negative instrument, a barrier only, and not a beacon? Grant me, for argument, that the law as I have described it is full of honor, skill, and service, and that due process, on this argument, deserves the cool and firm allegiance of all who care for civil decency and know how much unfairness and injustice are the normal habit of the human being. Is this, still, enough?

It is not enough, I believe, but I also believe that if we want more we must pass beyond the law. Beyond this point we come to those values in our life which do not analyze themselves in terms of any one profession or any one code,

---

12. I will confess to a lingering doubt that the privilege is quite as full of virtue as Dean Griswold suggests in THE FIFTH AMENDMENT TODAY (1955), and I certainly share his view that in the Rogers case (340 U.S. 367, 1951), judicial wisdom rested with the minority.

however great or noble. The law is for life, and not the other way round, and the final demands of justice are beyond the range of justices. Even the great concept of due process is fallible, in contest with a higher law—and in the end the law must be justified not merely by the heavy negatives I have been emphasizing, but also by the larger test of justice, or the good, or God. In the best of our law, I believe—and still more in the best of our lawyers—there is a strong connection to aspirations and standards whose power is independent. The war against evil which is the unending work of the law does, in the end, imply some reverence for what is good.

And that is why even if all I have said is right, even if the law in action is properly mistrusted and clearly full of danger, we still cannot rest content with any reckoning of due process which omits the strong and central role of simple fairness, exercised not simply against evil, but in and for itself. In helping to celebrate John Marshall's birthday we shall do well to think not only of the judge but of the man, and to remember with pride and gratitude that the great Chief Justice was a man of honor, courage, generosity, and love. There have been great lawyers whom we cannot much like, but it is a sound instinct which reserves the highest respect for those whose human character is high. To the layman, persisting in his daily fear of the law and also in his occasional but urgent need of its clumsy help, a man like Marshall must serve as a steady reminder that this negative and overstrained institution yet has about it all that is needed for the challenge and the ripening of human nobility. Perhaps the lawyer will forgive the layman for the claim that just here, where the profession transcends itself, both due process of law and its great defenders belong to all of us at once, as a reminder of the best that men can live by.

COMMENT

DEAN BUNDY*

I shall do best, I think, to take it for granted that those of you who felt any need to do so have read my paper. The only man to whom, if I were teaching in a class, I should wish to recommend a re-reading is, of course, Professor Hart.

In essence, my paper says, simply if not always politely, that law, and especially due process of law, is important not because it is ever very good, but because without it we should be in desperate condition. It assumes, more readily than many distinguished judges have done, that due process is unthinkable without able judges and zealous lawyers, for exactly the reason that it is so hard to get. It suggests, however, that in the end due process depends also on the fairness and good sense of laymen, and it comes out in favor of "civic virtue, clear communication, and a decent confidence in our own strength." It praises Marshall, Holmes, Sir Henry Maine, and justice. It is cool toward Dorothy Dix and definitely hostile to the Eighteenth Amendment. You will see that it is a harmless document, not worth repeating or even summarizing except that the summary may perhaps explain to you, first why I was somewhat startled at the remarks of Mr. Hart, second why I myself have felt a sense of incompleteness and dissatisfaction in considering the trifling distance which my paper moved. These conclusions, after all, have been expressed on higher authority than mine, and with greater felicity of expression, many of them in this very Con-

---

* McGeorge Bundy, *Dean of the faculty of Arts and Sciences, Harvard University.* Dean Bundy was born in 1919. He took his A.B. at Yale in 1940, served in the Army in World War II, in various grades from Private to Captain. He had been a Junior Fellow at Harvard in 1941, but his tenure was interrupted by his military service. Dean Bundy returned to Harvard as a Junior Fellow in 1946. Until 1948 his time was largely devoted to collaboration with Henry L. Stimson in the preparation of Mr. Stimson's biography, "On Active Service." He then edited "Pattern of Responsibility," a collection of papers of Dean Acheson; it was published in 1952. He became a member of the Harvard Department of Government in 1949; was appointed Associate Professor of Government, July 1, 1951; and Professor of Government in 1954. In 1953, he became Dean of the Faculty of Arts and Sciences of Harvard University.

ference, as you all know. And I've had the feeling that I stopped just as the going began to get rough. But let me save my own doubts and worries and begin with Mr. Hart.

His complaint is that we are all too negative. In my case, the specific charge is that I assume the law to be mere litigation; that I wrongly limit the field of effort of lawyers; and that in general I am simply another horrible example of the way in which lawyers have allowed themselves to be misunderstood.

I think I can deal very briefly with the second and third complaints. The third charge, is, of course, directed at you, not at me. That I say what I say, Mr. Hart says, is the fault of lawyers. Thus I need not answer it at all; but that he made it, I suggest, is proof that his second point is ill-taken, and that I am right in urging a certain restraint in the claims which lawyers assert. For since I believe that guilt is personal, I cannot admit that lawyers are responsible for my errors; and I find his attempt to blame you a confirmation of my passing assertion that many lawyers try to extend the field of the responsibility of their profession into areas which they should avoid.

The immediate answer to Mr. Hart's main complaint, that I limited the law to litigation, is a double one: first, I did not quite do so, and second, in so far as I did, I did it deliberately and explicitly, taking two pages to explain why I did so, and how much, how very much, this definition excluded. When I am not trespassing upon your patience to talk about subjects as slippery as due process, I am a student of American foreign affairs, and this is not a field in which it is easy to undervalue the importance of action by government under enabling legislation. The great questions of foreign affairs, which all turn around the central issue of survival in freedom, are hardest not in the analysis of what to do, hard as that is, but in the development of adequately based and supported authority to act. And so students of foreign affairs are seldom among those who think that *government* should be passive. When I assert in my paper that the fundamental function of the *law* is negative, I mean something very different, as I hope most of its readers may agree.

Now, these four words are, I think, near the root of my difficulty with Mr. Hart: *government* as against *law,* and *passive* as against *negative.* When Mr. Hart talks of the law, I suggest, he is really talking about all of government, and when he says some of us are negative, he is really saying that we may be passive in a time when all sorts of action, governmental action, are not only necessary but desirable. I believe this to be a reasonable suggestion because I can find no other way to explain the fact that I found much of his affirmation as palatable as did Father Snee.

But these four words cover some real issues, and the great service in Mr. Hart's skyrocket was not the sound of the explosion, but the flashes of light that came with it. I will insist, for my part, that it is a dangerous error to make the words law and government coextensive, and for two main reasons. First, no rational account of all that government is and must be can be written on the assumption that it is comprehended within the subject of law, if we assume that word to mean the sorts of things that lawyers and judges have as their special competence, and the sorts of things that law schools teach, even if we include a rival institution in New Haven. The legislative process is not just lawyers making law. We Americans would be clearer on this point if we were not often beguiled by the fact that so many members of Congress are also members of the bar. The point becomes clearer if we look at the United Kingdom. Consider the great legislative leaders there in the last 100 years, and ask yourselves how many of them were lawyers. Or in our own country, consider the Presidents who by their leadership have secured major legislation since 1900. The most significant, I should suggest, are the two Roosevelts, Wilson, and Truman. Two studied law but never practiced.* One practiced but gave it up after a year; and the fourth, Mr. Franklin Roosevelt,

* In my original remarks I said that one never even studied law, thinking of Mr. Truman: this was an error for which I apologize. He attended the Kansas City School of Law for two years, in 1923-25.

while he retained his membership at the bar and spoke of himself as a lawyer, will, I venture to suggest, not be considered by this gathering as a lawyer's lawyer.

Legislation is knowledge, purpose, politics, as well as law, and what is true of passing public laws is true also of their administration. I do not wish to slight the great works of lawyers in both fields, in craftsmanship, as Sir Raymond noted this morning, in council, and often as legislators and administrators. I mean only that when we think of government as an active art we must not leave it all to lawyers (and still less, of course, to political theorists or political scientists). After Burke, we must see it as a partnership of all art and all science, connecting purpose and action in relation to the aspirations and necessities of a society of individuals. I found myself, for one, in full and hearty agreement with Mr. Hart's own eloquent statement of the function of government in this sense. I particularly liked his reminder to us all that even government, larger in this sense than law, is a way of setting other forces free. No one who works in a university can be blind to the great freedom conferred, in Harvard's case, by the Constitution of the Commonwealth, just as no one can be blind to the danger of intervention in the freedom by unwise legislative or governmental action.

This government, however, I suggest—and here is my second reason for urging a separation between the two terms—always imperfect and often wrong as it is, is also always, at least by our intent and national conviction, government under law, and the existence of this more elevated place, above government, is the second great reason for avoiding a merger between the two terms. To any man of law, therefore, who wants all government for his business, the first answer is that he is greedy, but the second is, friend, go up higher.

Yet, of course, even if this is good advice, the problem of connection remains: government under law, but how? If the relationship is disconnected, relative position is unimportant, and we could as well speak of government beside law, or over law, or in another world from law. I had the feeling yesterday that Father Snee, coming down from natural law, and Professor Wechsler, working up toward norms from a sensitive appreciation of American legal process, were attacking this problem of connection, and I wish they could have had more time to chart a possible meeting, or perhaps to discover that they had passed each other in the night.

And here is where I am worried about my own paper, for between the layman's sense of fair play and the role of law there is much thick country. One tangled area that I might have tried to cut into is that battleground on which felt needs fight their way to legal membership in the settled behavior of the nation. Often in these battles, I think, the hasty insertion of law or legal process may do more harm than good, and I was deeply interested in the comment of the Master of the Rolls on rent tribunals, for if I understood him aright, he was talking to this point, at least in part.

I believe that this is also a part of our trouble in learning to deal with real problems of internal security. Is it not at least possible that much of the vicious folly of recent years has been protected, not prevented, by a feeling that the question is more procedural, more "legal" in some sense, than substantive? Have we not tried to deal with it by working on the process instead of bluntly asserting that in many fundamental premises it may be deeply wrong? I think I should have studied this kind of question. I think Mr. Justice Frankfurter said something relevant to this problem when he remarked on the danger inherent in the public notion that because a program appears, so far at least, to be constitutional, it is therefore right. I wonder also, however, given the reservoir of esteem and strength which our Supreme Court holds in the affections of the nation, whether it is really possible that judicial restraint through a long period of time should be the only guiding post in dealing with these problems.

But in finishing, let me go back to my paper's emphasis on the negative. I admit it, and I urge it on you. But what I am urging is not that government under law is, or can be, passive. I am urging, rather, that our virtue is not so certain, our society not so surely safe and free, that we should think of government and law only, or even primarily, as instruments of added blessing. We are the heirs of suffering, hope, and triumph, but the heritage is not entailed by any higher law unto the last generation. It is easy to lose, and in times past there have been many other groups of free men whose society has not survived. Ahead of us are dangers that can strangle speech with terror, and we heard some of them this morning. And the more so, as all speakers noted, if we do not look them in the eye. Even without the radiating gifts of science, our society is not free of disease and challenge. What we know that other men have done and are doing in this century, and what we know of ourselves, in honest self-appraisal, suggests that when we are measured against the dangers to freedom, we are all a little wanting. It will be a triumph for us, worthy to be measured up to our account in full equality with our predecessors of 200 years, if we can help to pass to our successors of that distance as much as has been left to us.

And set up against these dangers, as a great negative force against them, is the hard but central idea of due process of law. I will not assert that it is necessarily efficient, though I hope it may be. I will not assert that it can surely be defended or maintained, although I think it can. All that I assert is that doubts about its value, generated sometimes by efforts to understand it more closely than perhaps we can, are easily dissipated when we think of life without it. If this way of stating the matter is clearer or more useful than what I wrote in my paper, the credit must go to Mr. Hart. But if I have simply confused maters, I will not charge him with any guilt by association.

PROFESSOR CUSHMAN*

Dean Bundy is a wolf in sheep's clothing. I do not see

* ROBERT EUGENE CUSHMAN, *Professor of Government, Cornell University.* Professor Cushman was born in Ohio in 1889. He took his Arts degree at Oberlin in 1911 and his Ph.D. at Columbia in 1917. He has been a member of the faculties of the University of Illinois, and the University of Minnesota, and has been Professor of Government at Cornell since 1923. He has published a number of books on constitutional law and is a frequent contributor to periodicals on legal and constitutional subjects.

why he should be allowed to label himself as a layman. I was not here yesterday afternoon and cannot participate in Hart v. Bundy, or comment on it. Nor did I find in Dean Bundy's paper anything that I wanted to take issue with.

But since his paper suggests that laymen do have views about due process of law, I thought I might try something a little different, and present very briefly indeed the views which an observant layman might hold with respect to due process of law during the important periods in its evolution in our constitutional history, and the views which he might hold at the present time.

The first 100 years of due process of law in this country held little to stimulate the imagination of the layman. It was a dull story and seemed remote from his own concerns. The due process clause had been incorporated into the Fifth Amendment without any debate or public discussion. It was certainly not put there to quiet the fears of any body of irate citizens who asserted that they had been denied due process of law. During this long early period, due process, as everyone knows, was a requirement of fair procedure. It imposed limits, not upon what government might do, but upon how it might do it, and while not unimportant, it was a most undramatic guarantee of civil liberties.

Whether the framers of the Fourteenth Amendment intended the due process clause which it contained to have broader applications and meanings than these just described, I leave to the historians. The Supreme Court certainly did not at first give it such broader meanings. When urged to do so in the Slaughterhouse Cases, Mr. Justice Miller stated brusquely that there had been plenty of judicial interpretation of the due process clauses and that none of it gave due process any relevance to the validity of a statute passed by the government of Louisiana creating a slaughterhouse monopoly in the city of New Orleans. Thus due process remained a procedural limitation.

The second phase of due process history comprises the court's retreat from this rigid procedural interpretation, and

Dean McGeorge Bundy.

Chief Justice Centlivres.

Robert M. Benjamin, of the New York Bar, asks a question.

Professor Robert E. Cushman comments on Dean Bundy's paper.

Charles P. Curtis, Jr., comments on Dean Bundy's paper.

Left to right, front row: Professors Louis L. Jaffe, Robert Braucher, and Richard A. Field. Back row: Professor Donald T. Trautman, Mme. André Tunc, and Professor Abram J. Chayes.

the emergence of due process as a direct and effective limitation upon the police power of the states. That police power was beginning, in the '80's and '90's to be exercised to provide a wide range of legislative protections for the health and safety of laborers. This was a direct challenge to our American pioneer philosophy of individualism, and the courts of that period, under heavy and continued pressure from the bar, at last turned to the due process clause as a constitutional weapon with which to combat the onward march of the new social control.

They converted it into a drastic limitation upon the substance of state police legislation. This revolutionary change made due process something very real and very important to the layman. It affected directly his interests and his welfare. If the layman were a factory owner and employer, he viewed with profound approval the court decisions which struck down as violations of due process laws requiring him to pay his men regularly and in money, to abolish night work by women, to employ women and minors for reasonable hours, and to pay reasonable wages. To the working man, on the other hand, due process of law came to be the slogan by which the courts could nullify any legislative effort to improve the grim conditions under which he worked. The advance of social legislation, however, could not permanently be blocked by abstract legal principles, such as liberty of contract, which had been embodied in the legal concept of due process of law. New judges came to the bench—judges who were willing to listen to Louis D. Brandeis and later to Felix Frankfurter when they presented their compelling briefs setting out the social justification for the laws which sought to rescue the American working man from injustices which had come to shock the community conscience.

The judicial approach to due process in police power cases began to change, but it did not change completely over night. And the legislative minimum wage came finally to represent the last resort of the old individualism. As late as 1936 in the *Tipaldo* case, the Supreme Court held a New York minimum wage act void as a denial of due process of law. The layman was stunned by this decision, and I suppose this decision, as much as anything, motivated President Roosevelt's ill-fated court-packing proposal. In December of 1936, I took part in a very impressive and earnest conference in New York at which Judge Charles E. Clarke, then Dean of the Yale Law School, speaking for a substantial group, proposed, as a federal constitutional amendment, that "Due process of law shall have reference only to the procedure of executive, administrative, and judicial bodies charged with the execution and enforcement of the law." The tide had begun to turn, however. The *Tipaldo* case was reversed the following year, and it has been a very long time since any sharp controversy has arisen over the validity of state police legislation of this type.

The third phase in due process history came with the *Gitlow* case in 1925 in which the court began the process of expanding the meaning of the word liberty in the due process clause of the Fourteenth Amendment to include the freedom of speech, press, religion and assembly protected by the First Amendment. The layman probably did not comprehend at once the importance of this doctrine. What it did was to place the states of the union under federal judicial discipline in their management of these vitally important civil liberties, and the bulk of our constitutional law with respect to First Amendment rights has been built up in cases in which state action has been involved. Mr. Justice Cardozo observed that First Amendment rights are binding on the states through due process "because of the belief that neither liberty nor justice would exist if they were sacrificed". The effect of this new doctrine was to apply due process of law to a wholly new set of interests and values. The layman who had come to regard due process as a legal formula for protecting entrenched property interests against protective labor legislation, now began to see in due process of law, the effective protection of his most valued civil liberties. It not only protected his First Amendment rights against state invasion, but it also guaranteed him essential justice and fair play in many of his other dealings with government. In a paper written in 1933, Professor Felix Frankfurter referred to "the blessed versatility of due process" and the Supreme Court, over the ensuing years, has moved in the direction of making that a reality. The self-incrimination clause in the Fifth Amendment does not bind the states, but the Supreme Court has held that it denies due process to use against a man a confession of crime secured by force. It denies due process to punish a man for a crime so vaguely defined that he cannot reasonably know when he is committing it. It denies due process to bar from public employment persons who cannot swear that they have not belonged for a fixed period of years, to an allegedly subversive organization, without giving such persons an opportunity to show that such membership was innocent. It denies due process for the Attorney General to list as subversive organizations and groups without prior notice and hearings, and very recently, in the Court of Appeals in the District of Columbia, it has been held to deny due process to refuse a citizen a passport without providing an orderly and fair procedure for doing so. The list could be expanded at great length.

All this has sharply affected the layman's view of due process law. He has become increasingly due-process-of-law-conscious. He talks about due process of law, glibly, as he does about self- incrimination, with the same lack of accurate information about each. He has been told that due process of law means essential justice and fair play. He takes this at its face value. He does not understand why it does not mean justice and fair play in all situations, rather than in just some situations. Since he is a layman, he is not very familiar with the doctrine of the separation of powers, which leads the courts, no doubt very soundly, to refrain from imposing upon our badly behaved legislative investigating committees the more obvious requirements of procedural due process, and this disturbs him. Since he is a layman, he does not fully understand why due process does not guarantee to a federal employee accused of disloyalty or worse an explicit and accurate statement of the charges against him, and the right to know who has accused him. Since he is a layman, he does not understand why the Supreme Court, which has dramatically extended protections of due process in the past, should not extend them still further in the future to deal with new kinds of injustice.

I fully understand how annoying all this amateurish talk by laymen about due process of law can be to the experts who really know what due process of law means. I merely observe in closing that there are always more laymen than lawyers, that the history of human freedom in the last analysis, while spelled out in characters and decisions formulated by lawyers, has largely been shaped by the sustained and articulate demands of laymen for what they have come to regard as the principles and procedures without which justice and fair play are impossible.

MR. CURTIS*

When I was asked to comment on the Dean's paper—a paper on the law by a layman—my first thought, of course, was to see if I could detect in it some legal mistakes, some legal errors, other than the common error which lawyers so often observe in their discussion of the law with any layman—that the law itself is not without flaw, not without some fault, not completely perfect. That, of course, was obvious from the Dean's paper, but I could detect no other legal error. It may be that that was because I was not as good a critic as I should have been, because I agreed with everything that the Dean said.

I wonder if the only real fault to find with lawyers isn't

* CHARLES PELHAM CURTIS, *of the Boston Bar.* Mr. Curtis was born in 1891, attended the Ecole des Sciences Politiques at Paris, took his A.B. at Harvard College in 1914 and his LL.B. at the Harvard Law School in 1917. He served in the Navy in World War I, and has practiced law since 1919 in Boston. He has served his State in a number of public capacities, has been a lecturer in Government at Harvard, and is the author of several books including "Lions Under the Throne," written about the Supreme Court of the United States, in 1947. His most recent book is "The Oppenheimer Case," which appeared in August, 1955.

that lawyers are so thoroughly and successfully trained that they find it hard to look at the law from the outside in as well as from the inside out. I know they live in glass houses, but I think the glass has been polarized, or whatever they do to make it transparent in only one direction. It is true that the law does sometimes make mistakes. I think particularly constitutional law. I wonder if the Supreme Court may not itself sometimes wonder whether it acted prudently when it allowed itself to be persuaded to extend due process of law into fair play in fact.

I use the word prudently advisedly. We have heard a good deal of discussion of self-restraint and the degree of proper self-restraint. I suggest that what should be discussed, explored, is what lies behind self-restraint. Prudence, obviously; respect for the other organs of government, obviously. Beyond that, of course, we go into those intriguing questions which are raised by that excellent quotation from Paul Freund. I wonder, as I say, whether the Supreme Court has not had some qualms about its prudence. They, as they learned later, were engaging in a hazardous employment, an employment in which they were not covered by their usual insurance policy against liability for blame. Now I know that the Supreme Court is not eligible for what we in New England have learned to call extended coverage; that is, against criticism. But in this case, I think that they later found that they weren't covered by any insurance at all.

Holmes warned them about economics, and the dangers to them in some of Mr. Herbert Spencer's doctrines. Justice Stone repeated the warning in the *Tipaldo* case, that the Fourteenth Amendment has no more embedded in the Constitution our preference for some particular set of economic beliefs than it has adopted a system of theology which we may happen to approve.

But now Dean Bundy raises the question how far the courts should go in teaching us a code of morals. How far can they go, as lawyers? How far must they go, as human beings? That seems to me the particular and important and interesting issue that the Dean's paper has raised, at least with me.

Now I'd sooner the Court brought down further sections of a moral code from another Sinai than have it teach us orthodox economics or give us a creed from a new Nicea. I look with admiration and awe at the Court's undertaking to do away with the moral affliction of segregation, with, I quote from the Chief Justice's opinion, "deliberate speed". I go on and add, from Francis Thompson's *The Hound of Heaven,* "with majestic instancy". Of course, the Chief Justice refrained from adding that to his quotation. That is why I now undertake to add it, for it seems to me equally apt and appropriate.

I ascribe the quotation to the Chief Justice. I don't know how many of the Justices have read Francis Thompson, or were then reading *The Hound of Heaven;* there are only two people, one person, in the room who knows, and he won't tell us. Nor do I think it much matters, because I suspect in future that the phrase will be ascribed to the Supreme Court's opinion and no longer to Francis Thompson.

Lawyers can take credit for starting this difficult enterprise. Lawyers alone certainly cannot bring it to success. Lawyers alone cannot cure what so many of us for so long have regarded as a chronic affliction. It's a case which calls for nursing more than it does for doctoring. It's a layman's job; it's not a lawyer's; and if the laymen need advice, they need more than legal advice. They need also spiritual advice.

I've read, and I think you've read, a couple of weeks ago, what Bishop Sherrill told the convention in Honolulu, but I'll quote one sentence, two sentences.

"Are we to leave moral issues of nuclear warfare to groups of scientists, or the spiritual implications of the race problem to the courts?" he asked the delegates. "No. The Church, with an humble realization of the complexity of modern problems nevertheless has a responsibility to state great ethical and spiritual principles."

The Church may well be humble before this moral task. The Court, and its attendant lawyers may be even more humble, for the burden of our decencies rests on the backs of laymen. As the Dean truly and good naturedly told us, in the end the law is no better than the laymen make it. We lawyers know that this is true, at least in respect of due process. The Dean quotes high authority. These moral principles, these fundamental notions of fairness which are enshrined in the due process clause, they are those which "lie embedded in the feelings of the American people."

V

One feature of the Marshall Bicentennial Conference which troubled the faculty of the Harvard Law School was the difficulty of including its fifteen hundred students in sessions of the Conference in the Ames Courtroom, which has seats for only about six hundred and fifty people. To the end that the students might be invited to the session of Friday evening, September 23, it was held in the much larger Sanders Theatre, in Memorial Hall. Dean Griswold, presiding, said after his opening welcome:

"Before going on with the program of the evening, I want to introduce our distinguished judicial guests to those of you who have not been attending the previous sessions. We have Mr. Chief Justice Kerwin, the Chief Justice of Canada; Sir Owen Dixon, the Chief Justice of the High Court of the Commonwealth of Australia; Sir Raymond Evershed, the Master of the Rolls of England; and then we are honored to have with us tonight three members of the Supreme Court of the United States, Mr. Justice Harold Burton, of the Harvard Law School class of 1912; Mr. Justice Felix Frankfurter, of the Harvard Law School class of 1906; and finally, I want to introduce to you (and he has kindly consented to say a few words of greeting) a gentleman whom I cannot claim for the Harvard Law School, but whom we are glad to allow to the University of California Law School, the Chief Justice of the United States."

Chief Justice Warren spoke a few words of encouragement to the students of the Law School, and added:

"There are even greater challenges for the legal profession today than there were in Marshall's time. The great legal rights of Americans are never secure by themselves. Every generation must preserve its own freedoms. I remind you that in no generation has our liberty ever been safe unless some advocate was willing to stand up in court and fight for a client's rights. I know that you in the Law School are looking forward to doing this some day. There is as great a need for you now in such service as there ever was. We will welcome your help."

Dean Griswold next introduced Professor Tunc. As the students in the audience had not attended the previous gatherings of the Conference, Dean Griswold explained the connection between Dr. Tunc's earlier paper and this evening's address. In part he said:

"Mr. Tunc at the Conference yesterday afternoon told us of what may seem to an American lawyer the surprising degree of judicial control in modern France. He pointed out that while French administrative courts do not review the validity of parliamentary legislation, they vigilantly watch the administration of statutes and they offer effective remedies for abuse of legislatively granted powers.

"This evening in accordance with the custom which we who study Anglo-Saxon law share with our civil law friends, Professor Tunc turns back through the centuries to see what lessons the legal history of his country can give to peoples of our own day. He brings us insight into the thought of the Middle Ages on government under law. He shows us that the kings were admonished by the Church that they governed under a duty to govern justly, and not in defiance of established law; that the kings acknowledged this subjection; but that for lack of governmental institutions to secure the subject's immunities against wrongful government, these royal obligations were not translated into popular rights.

"Coming to a later date, Professor Tunc gives us a review of the contests between the Parlements and the crown —conflicts in some ways suggestive of Coke's England. But he draws for us a picture of separation of powers too effective to permit government to adapt itself to change in society. He shows this frustration ending in the violence of the French Revolution.

"From these examples we may well think, while our friend from France tells us the story that any government, if habituated to think in terms of law, tends in fact to become lawful even though its institutions do not so compel it; this reflexive effect is one justification for our deliberations tonight.

"But he also suggests, by his second example, that separation of powers must not extend to the point where government becomes incapable of governing, ceases to exist, and thus, with its own end brings an end to freedom. We are reminded that when the President of Harvard University confers our degrees he refers to the laws as 'those wise restraints which make men free'."

ADDRESS

The Royal Will and the Rule of Law

A SURVEY OF FRENCH CONSTITUTIONALISM UNDER THE ANCIEN REGIME

ANDRÉ TUNC

Rex non debet esse sub homine, sed sub Deo et sub lege quia lex facit regem. (The king should not be under man, but under God and law, because law made him king.)

Quod principi placuit legis habet vigorem. (What pleases the king has the force of law.)

The contrast between these two sentences has often been pointed out.

In the first, Bracton expressed a traditional principle, the very principle of government under law, rightly regarded as one of the bases of the whole common law, a principle which a justice of the Supreme Court of the United States was to deem it necessary, seven centuries later, to express again before the Military Tribunal of Nuremberg.

In the second, Ulpian set forth a principle of absolutism. From century to century, the principle was to be repeated in the common law world by the counselors of kings. Like any human being entrusted with power, most kings strove toward further power. The Ulpian rule permitted their jurisconsults to supply a justification for such increased power.

This rule, however, should not mislead us. Whatever may have been its real meaning and its legal value in the second century, in France it has never been more than a reasonable statement, in one sense, of public law, and, in its apparent meaning, a political slogan, a slogan which never prevailed over the contrary fundamental laws of the kingdom.

The meaning of the rule, as it was accepted by the most authoritative doctrine of ancient France, is very clearly explained, in the thirteenth century, by Beaumanoir in his

Livre de Jostice et de Plet. Beaumanoir considers the rule as a mere expression of the fact that the king is vested with the legislative power. This power, however, cannot be exercised arbitrarily, nor by the king alone. The king may, in Beaumanoir's view, legislate only "par raisonnable cause et pour le commun profit du Royaume" (for reasonable purpose and in the common interest of the kingdom). He may legislate only "à très grand conseil" (with the advice of many wise people). He must never do anything which would not be agreeable to God or would be *contra bonos mores.* Each of these three limitations on the royal power was repeated for centuries. Together, they formed one of the basic doctrines of public law of the Ancien Régime, a doctrine which was never rejected. Under this doctrine, when a serious decision must be made, the power of the king is only to call a large council of wise people. After due deliberation, he will choose the decision which "pleases" him. But the whole context indicates that the decision is not a despot's decision. It is the decision of a man entrusted with the duty to make the wisest possible decision "in the common interest of the people." If one solution must "please" him more than another, it must be for the sake of God and of the kingdom. He will choose what, after mature deliberation, appears good, wise, reasonable.

In this context must also be understood many sentences of the ancient writers and even the formula *Princeps est animata lex*: the king is the living law. After all, the same has been said of the English judge, and that does not imply that he exercises an arbitrary power. If a doubt still remains as to the meaning of the Ulpian formula for Beaumanoir and for the greatest ancient writers, it would be completely driven away by a sentence of Beaumanoir himself which is as striking as Bracton's: "Li prince n'est pas sus la loi, mès la loi est sus le prince; quar il li donèrent tiel privilege comme il avoient." (The king is not above the law, but the law above the king; for the laws give him his position.) Beaumanoir's statement is so close to Bracton's that both must certainly be regarded as expressions of an idea which was commonly accepted, in England and in France as well, unless Beaumanoir, who had traveled in England, had copied Bracton.

It is true that an impression of absolutism is also given by the enacting clause of the royal ordinances: "Car tel est notre plaisir," by the famous exclamation of Louis XIV: "L'Etat c'est moi," and by such institutions as the *lettres de cachet.*

Again, all these factors may be misleading. The enacting clause of the ordinances does not imply a power to make frivolous or capricious decisions: the word *plaisir* partakes of the qualified meaning of the word *placuit* in the Ulpian sentence, a meaning which has already been explained. There is very little evidence that Louis XIV had ever said: "L'Etat, c'est moi." The statement is reported for the first time in the middle of the eighteenth century by an obscure chronicler. Louis XIV, it is true, succeeded in being to a great extent— although not fully — an absolute monarch, but this was essentially due to his personal ability and prestige. His authority, like Queen Elizabeth's a century before, came from his personality, much more than from national institutions. After him, the Ancien Régime disappeared much more from want of leadership than by reason of excesses of power.

It appears, therefore, that we must eliminate certain preconceived ideas about the government of France during the Ancien Régime. We may keep an open mind in trying to observe (and that will be the purpose of this paper) whether the principle of government under law was a part of the French constitutional tradition and to what extent it was given a practical recognition. While there is little doubt on the first point, we shall see that, in practice, the supremacy of the law was often disregarded.

I

There may be little doubt, as I have just said, of the respect of the writers of the Ancien Régime for the idea of government under law.

As early as the end of the eighth or beginning of the ninth century, Smaragde, Abbé de Saint Mihiel, defines the king as the representative of God, entrusted with the duty of "facere justitiam et judicium." By a daring etymology, he explains the word *rex* by the duty of governing rightly: "Rex a recte regendo vocatur." When he comes to give the detailed duties of the king, he prohibits him from committing any abuse of his power and obliges him to render justice according to the law and without any consideration of the personalities of the parties.

One century later, Hincmar, Archbishop of Rheims, also very clearly placed the king under the law. He expressly writes that nobody, king included, may disregard the law. The principle applies not only to the king "as a man," but to the king "as a king." According to the view that he takes of the positive law, nothing can be changed or added to the customs without the consent of the people: "Lex consensu populi et constitutione regis fit." We will see this principle repeated by the Parlements and by the Etats Généraux of the people of France as long as France was a kingdom. The principle was not challenged by the kings themselves. Pepin, son of Charlemagne, will say, "Inasmuch as we shall observe law toward everybody, we wish everybody to observe it toward us." Charles the Bold will swear, "I shall keep law and justice"; and Louis the Stammerer, "I shall keep the customs and the laws of the nation." In modern terminology, it might be said that the power of the king was more executive or regulatory in nature than legislative, and this will remain a basic principle of the French monarchy, even under Louis XIV. And even when the king exercises his regulatory power, he cannot do it alone. Up to the thirteenth century, he cannot make any decision as a king without the advice *and the consent* of the "plaids", gatherings of the important lords, bishops and high civil servants, which will later become the Conseil du Roi. Of course, the king is not the beneficiary of a power, but the trustee of it: Hincmar always writes in terms of duty for the king, according to the divine law and to the customs.

No purpose would be served in quoting all the authors who, through the centuries, expressed the same ideas. We have seen how Beaumanoir, in the thirteenth century, faced with the reception of the Roman law and the principles, or at least the formula, of absolutism, succeeded in coating them with the traditional law of France.

Beginning with the thirteenth century, however, we find two schools of thought. Most of the authors, of the political authorities, and of the kings themselves, continued to express the principles of a limited monarchy. The idea is generally expressed and widely recognized that no important decisions may be made without the advice and sometimes the consent of the people represented either by the Etats Généraux or by the Parlements. Nevertheless, some legal counselors in the service of a king who, under special circumstances, wanted especially to impose his will, made arguments based on the Ulpian formula: *Quod principi placuit, legis habet vigorem, Princeps est animata lex* (the king is the living law); or even *Princeps legibus solutus est* (the king is not bound by the laws). This second current of thought was of secondary importance, expressed in pamphlets much more than in treatises. It had, however, an influence on serious writers, and it certainly helped the kings to make their powers stronger, a development which, even when desirable for the nation, was not free from dangers.

As for the authors favorable to a limited monarchy, they express many new ideas. Some explain the submission of the king to law as based on a contract by which the people, at the beginning of France, vested a certain power in the king (this is the idea of social compact which will gain popularity with J. J. Rousseau): the provisions of this contract could not be changed either by the people or by the king. Others explain the relationship of the king and the people by a comparison with the desirable relationship of the head and the rest of the body: the king's power must be limited exactly as the head must not receive all the blood and the strength of the body. Some place the king under God and under "the fundamental laws of the kingdom" (*les lois fondamentales du royaume*), which are the unwritten constitution of the kingdom, but permit him to change, subject to the limitations expressed by Beaumanoir or to similar limitations, the customs or normal laws of France. A contrast is thus made between "the laws of the kingdom" and the mere "laws of the king." Some prefer to say that the king must keep the good customs, and work toward the improvement of the bad ones. Claude de Seyssel, in the sixteenth century, makes another distinction and writes that there are three checks to the power of the king: religion, justice, which is represented by the Parlements, and "police," that is to say the established principles of the customs and normal laws of France. All of the authors subject any decision to be made by the King to the law of God, to reason, to justice, and to the common interest of the people. These, of course, are not in themselves effective checks on his possible absolutism. But the idea is generally expressed and wisely recognized that no important decision may be made without the advice and sometimes the consent of the people represented either by the Etats Généraux or by the Parlements. During the whole Ancien Régime this idea carried important political and sometimes legal consequences.

At the end of the sixteenth century, we find the same two trends in important political works. In the *Franco-Gallia,* published in 1573, François Hotman, on the basis of history, considers the government of France to be a diarchy: the king and the people are co-sovereign. Three years later, Jean Bodin, in *Les Six Livres de la République,* presented a quite different picture of the government. Bodin, while he insists on the duties of the kings, places few institutional checks on the exercise of their powers. But François Hotman, unconvinced by Bodin, adds to his work a last chapter in which he sums up the constitutional rules of the kingdom, the first rule being as follows: "The King is not permitted to decide on affairs which are of interest to the State without the consent of the people assembled" (*sine publici concilii auctoritate*).

More important than the opinions of legal writers may be the declaration of high officials. In 1586, Henry IV hears without protest a speech of the Chief Justice of the Parlement of Paris, Premier President de Harlay, in which we find an echo of Bracton's and Beaumanoir's formula as well as the distinction between laws of the king and laws of the kingdom: "Thus," said President de Harlay, "you must, if you wish to be regarded as a just and legitimate king, observe the laws of the State and of the kingdom. You could not disregard them without calling in question your own power and sovereignty. We have, Sire, two kinds of laws: some of them are orders of the king and they may be changed according to the circumstances; others are laws of the kingdom: they are sacred and it is according to them that you went on the royal throne." We find Henri IV himself saying on another occasion: "The first rule of the king is to observe all the rules." Those statements explain the testimony of Machiavelli in the first decades of the sixteenth century: "The kingdom of France is happy and quiet because the king is subject to an infinite number of laws which are the safeguard of the people."

The first half of the seventeenth century is an important political period. In England, it starts with the reign of James I, who, to his misfortune and that of his successor, tries to make a reality out of his conception of an absolute monarchy. The period ends with the trial of Charles I. In France also, it witnesses the success — at least the temporary success — of the traditional doctrine according to which sovereignty is shared between the king and the people. In 1648, the Parlement of Paris, in rebellion against the regent Anne d'Autriche, went as far as to make a "union decree," according to which the Parlement itself, the Chambre des comptes, the Cour des aides, and the Grand conseil, all of them called "sovereign courts," were united and were required to choose deputies to prepare the reform of the State. The regent tried to prevent the deputies from convening, then let them meet and discuss for a few days. The deputies wrote a kind of charter in twenty-seven articles, in which the Parlement and the other courts were again referred to as being "the sovereign courts." The regent accepted some of these articles, refused others, finally sent some of the deputies to jail. It was the beginning of a very difficult period of four years: the Fronde.

This was the atmosphere in which Louis XIV lived as a minor. When, at his majority, he undertook the exercise of power, he was fully aware of the danger of the doctrines of co-sovereignty. He had seen the kingdom divided against itself, imperiled by internal strife while the enemy was threatening it. He may have been authoritarian by nature. He was certainly led to a philosophy of authority by the experience of his young years. As early as 1661, he speaks of the courts "which pretend to be sovereign." In 1667, he forbids them to use the term of "sovereign" in speaking of themselves, and writes in his *Mémoires* that this is a "necessary humiliation for the gown which wanted to rank with the king." Notwithstanding his prestige, his approach to an absolute power, notwithstanding Versailles, *la cour, l'etiquette,* and a certain personal dissoluteness, Louis XIV must not be regarded as a despot. In the same year, 1667, in an ordinance, he states: "Let it be not said that the sovereign is not subjected to the laws of his State; the contrary proposition is a truth of natural law (*une vérité du droit des gens*); what brings perfect felicity to a kingdom is the fact that the king is obeyed by his subjects and that he himself obeys the law." That was the theory of Louis XIV.

And such was the prevailing doctrine of that time. Again, no institutional check is placed upon the power of the king, so that the traditional view according to which Louis XIV was an absolute monarch is not wrong. However, the king's duties toward God and toward the people are emphasized by everybody, himself included. The power of the king is absolute, but it must always be exercised for the sake of justice and to make the reign of God prevail on earth. If we read *Droit public,* the treatise of the greatest and the most intellectually powerful of the authors of the Ancien Régime, Jean Domat, we find, in a masterly exposition of "the power, the rights and the duties of those who have the sovereign government," the typical theory of the French absolute monarchy. A kind of introduction explains that "there cannot be any legitimate authority of a man upon others if it is not vested in him by the hand of God"; from that result the two following principles: First, the fuction of the king is "to assure the reign of justice, to which all his power must be devoted"; second, the power of the king must be "as absolute as must be the empire of justice, that is to say, the reign of God." From this basic conception of the function of the king, Domat derives the "rights" and the "duties" of the king. The modern reader will find that the so-called "rights" are only functions, none of them more unreasonable than the present functions of the Président de la République francaise. As far as the duties of the king are concerned, they are numerous: to recognize that power is entrusted by God and must be exercised on His behalf; to this end to study the rules of government under divine law; to use power only for justice; therefore, to strive to know at every moment what justice requires; to be ready to receive any complaint of grievance or injustice and take the necessary measures to correct injustices or abuses; to choose good secretaries and officials; not to make any decision without having considered all the factors and having heard all the persons interested in the decision. (The substance of some of these rules we may find in the Administrative Procedure Act of 1946!) The king is bound "to listen equally to those who complain and to those against whom complaint is made, and to give them as much as he can the free use of the means which can lead him to the truth, so that, having discovered it, he may order and have executed what will be right"; to protect religion and the laws of the Church; to be very considerate in granting the favors which may be deserved for merit; to be moderate in punishments and merciful whenever possible; to preserve the peace if possible, and preserve the kingdom; to impose taxation on the people only according to the needs of the State and the capacity of the people to bear it. Finally, Domat dispels a misunderstanding by explaining the dictum *Princeps legibus solutus*: "Although the power of the king seems to place him above the laws, since nobody can ask of him an account of what he has done, still he must observe the laws which concern him . . . his power does not free him from his own duties. On the contrary, his rank obliges him to prefer to his personal interests the common good of the State."

This, however, is only the exposition of one theory. Although this theory prevailed under Louis XIV, the earlier school of thought in favor of a limited monarchy or even of a diarchy could still find expression at the same moment and was never fought against by any kind of censorship. In the second half of the seventeenth century, Claude Joly was able to have printed and reprinted a *Recueil de maximes* in which he restated and emphasized all the traditional principles which led to a diarchical view of the government of France. He went even as far as to repeat that the king held his power from the people, who gave it to him by a contract, the provisions of which are the "fundamental laws of the kingdom." "It appears," he writes, "that no people ever agreed to submit purely and without reservation to the discretion of a king; the condition is always that the king would govern according to the provisions of the laws; the law is a synallagmatic contract, made of two factors equally important: the suggestion advanced either by the king or by the people, and the free acceptance by the other. The king, he expressly states, is "subject to the laws." No legislation is valid except when made after advice of the officials and with the consent of the Parlements. No taxation is valid except with the consent of the people. In the same manner, François de Launay, "royal professor of French law" teaches in the *Collège Royal* and publishes in 1688 "avec privilège du roi" the traditional doctrine of a limited monarchy, and expounds President de Harlay's famous speech of 1586, asserting that even the King is "sub Deo and sub lege." Finally, in an anonymous book written at the request of Louis XIV himself and approved by him, the *Traitè des droits de la Reine trés chrétienne sur divers Etats de la monarchie d'Espagne,* published in 1667, the idea is still expressed of a contract between the king and his descendants, on the one hand, and the subjects and their descendants, on the other hand, and the kings are said to be "fortunately unable (*dans la bienheureuse impuissance*) to destroy the laws of the state or to disregard, contrarily to public law, the particular customs of the provinces."

There is no need to give longer quotations. The concept of an absolute monarchy may have gradually emerged. It may have received a wider recognition during the sixteenth century and even more in the seventeenth, and it may have become a reality during the reign of Louis XIV. It was never imposed and it never supressed other schools of thought. Moreover, it was never the concept of a nation under the arbitrary will of a man. As the power increases, so do the duties. The concept of an absolute monarchy was the concept of a perfectly orderly society, entirely turned toward justice and truth. A beautiful conception it was. Too beautiful, as a matter of fact, too ambitious for human nature. Neither James I or Charles I, nor even Louis XIV, were worthy of the powers which would have been bestowed on them under this doctrine. Human defects must be recognized. No man in public office should be above checks and controls, as the Fathers of the American Constitution so wisely recognized.

If there were time to review the political thought of the eighteenth century, we would find a decreasing number of publications in favor of an absolute monarchy and many publications either against some form of absolutism or in favor of a limited monarchy, or even in favor of a republic. The Revolution, as it is well known, did not come from the people; it was prepared, although more or less involuntarily, by the philosophers — Montesquieu, Rousseau, Voltaire, Diderot, and many others—and the members of the Parlements.

We shall see this better if, having considered political theory, we now consider political life as it actually was in the kingdom of France. We may, for the purpose of this study, consider only political life during the last three centuries of the monarchy. In the earlier centuries, it was too clear that government was limited. The king, for centuries, had been little more than a baron among others. It took him centuries to unite the provinces which were to become France and to gain, over the other barons and lords, over the great officials of the palace and the people itself, the minimum of power which was necessary to be actually a government and to defend the national territories against their enemies. The last stage of the monarchy may be considered to start with the accession to the throne of François I, in 1515.

If, then, we consider this period, 1515-1789, we find a twofold picture. On one hand, the king appears to have too much power in small matters. There is no efficient check which protects the people against an abuse of power, either from the king himself or from one of his officers. On the other hand, the king had not succeeded, Louis XIV excepted, in gaining sufficient power to provide an efficient government. The Revolution in great part came from this contrast.

The first part of the picture is certainly the better known. The very life of the king may appear as an insult to the people, not only through modern democratic eyes, but, at certain times at least, through contemporary feelings. The king no longer lives in the Louvre, in the heart of Paris. More and more, in a time when the standard of living is still extremely low, he passes his time in Fontainebleau or Rambouillet, hunting or enjoying an ostentatious life in the pomp of "la Cour". Louis XIV permanently left Paris for Versailles. The private lives of the kings were not always above criticism. The wars they fought for reasons not understood by the people were highly unpopular:

"Et celà pour des altesses
Qui, vous a peine enterré,
Se feront des politesses
Pendant que vous pourrirez."

Another institution which was the subject of much dissatisfaction was the famous *lettre de cachet.* The king might, by a *lettre de cachet,* order the incarceration of any citizen in the Bastille or some other jail. No court was authorized to pass over the royal decision. The situation must be contrasted with that prevailing in England at the time, resulting from Section 39 of the Magna Carta, which was later to be developed in the Habeas Corpus Act. It is true that *lettres de cachet* were not very frequent and were used, usually, for cause thought reasonable in the light of the social order of the day; for instance, against an insane person, a dissolute son, an unworthy priest, a person suspected of crime, until judgment could be made, or an offender whom the authorities wanted not to try—perhaps for his own sake. However, the fact remains that they could be used arbitrarily and without justification, or without justification other than the *raison d'Etat.* The young Arouet, who was to become Voltaire, had been the object of a *lettre de cachet* after—I must confess—he had written a licentious pamphlet. *Lettres de cachet* were even used against protestants as such. Even if not very frequent, they were employed much too often, and much more often than the hated bills of attainder were in England. The popular dissatisfaction with them was such that it found its expression in the famous *prise de la Bastille* on July 14, 1789, and was such that the assault on the Bastille, though its main results were the murder of the governor and the freeing of a few inveterate offenders, became the symbol of the Revolution and was considered as its starting point. There was also a great dissatisfaction with the administration of justice, chiefly of criminal justice, although the king was not directly responsible for the matter. Voltaire pointed out in many pamphlets that people who were probably innocent had been put in jail and had suffered.

On the other hand, it appears that the kings did not succeed, Louis XIV excepted, in gaining the powers that they would have needed to introduce desirable reforms. The government, it is true, in the period we consider, was reasonably well organized. The king was surrounded by a certain number of Secretaries whose functions were reasonably defined, and he had the benefit of the advice of the Conseil du Roi, the new form of the very old *curia regis,* which was reorganized many times, but remained during the entire monarchy an important advisory body. The kings, however, found in their way two important institutions which at certain times were real obstacles to their government: the Etats Généraux and the Parlements.

The Etats Généraux were the most authoritative representation of the people. Their origin was very old. They had taken the place of the "plaids" or *placita* of the Carolingian period. They were really "the people" without the advice or consent of which the king, in the traditional view, could not make any important decision. Deputies to the Etats were elected in each county by each of the three classes or "orders" of the nation: clergy, nobility and "third estate". Each order within the territory of the country used to draft a bill of complaints, and its deputies had as a mission to discuss it with the other deputies of the same order so as to arrive at a national bill of complaints for the whole order. When the three bills were ready, the king, according to the custom, was to come to the Etats Généraux and listen to the speeches of the deputies presenting the complaints. He used to promise to study them and consider reforms. In turn, he used to ask the consent of the Etats Généraux on some matters. A few months or a few years later, an ordinance normally enacted some, though ordinarily few, of the desired reforms.

In fact, the Etats Généraux were losing their powers at the beginning of the period under consideration. They could convene only at the request of the king. They were not called between 1484 and 1560, that is to say, during a period of eighty years. In 1560 and in 1561, they were called by the Chancellor Michel de L'Hôpital on behalf of the king François II and the regent Catherine de Medicis, in the hope that they would proclaim and promote toleration between Catholics and members of the Reformed Church, and would consent to new taxation. The Chancellor succeeded in obtaining additional revenue; he did not succeed in preventing the unfortunate religious wars.

At the end of the sixteenth century, however, the Etats Généraux appeared again as a powerful institution. The Etats Généraux of 1576 asked to be considered as vested with the legislative power of the nation; they asked for the right to elect some members of the Conseil du Roi; they considered that the so-called "fundamental laws of the kingdom" could be changed only with the consent of each of the three orders of the Etats Généraux. In 1588, new Etats Généraux went further: they claimed to have the power to enact legislative measures which would not be, as the royal ordinances were, subject to the control of the Parlements. These measures could not have been changed by anybody but the Etats Généraux—not even by the king. Henri III, afraid of their pretensions, used political strategy to avoid answering them.

That was nearly the end of the Etats Généraux. Henri IV, taught by previous experience, was careful not to call them. Louis XIII called them in 1614, but the Etats Généraux were divided by tension between nobility and third estate. Louis XIV closed the place of their deliberation after a few months and ordered their dissolution. Between 1506 and 1626, the kings had often tried to replace the Etats Généraux by certain "Assemblées de notables," which clearly had only advisory power and which were composed of members chosen by the king. It was to one of these "Assemblées de notables" that Henri IV delivered his famous speech: "I convened you in order to receive your advice, and to follow it in order to place myself under your guardianship (*me mettre en tutelle entre vos mains*), a behavior which is rare among kings, greybeards and victorious warriors." It is true that Henri IV needed some additional revenue and that, when asked by an intimate about his speech, he added: "Of course, I said it. I meant: sword to the belt" . . .

If, however the Etats Généraux were the true representative of the people, the Parlements claimed this quality for themselves, and, in fact, were the great rival of the king during the last three centuries of the monarchy. At the beginning of the seventeenth century, Etienne Pasquier could write that they were the main restraint (*retenail*) of an absolute monarchy. Established in Paris and in the capital of each province (Normandy, Burgundy, Anjou, Champagne, etc.), the Parlements had many powers. They were the supreme courts of justice of the Ile de France and of the other provinces. They could also, during the sixteenth century, make regulatory decisions on behalf of the king. But their main political power was the power to refuse royal ordinances.

For many centuries, the king, having promulgated either ordinances or edicts in accordance with the substantive rules expressed by Beaumanoir, or simply orders (*lettres patentes*), used to send them to the Parlements. The Parlements had to be informed of them in order to apply them as courts of justice. They began, therefore, the habit of copying those ordinances and orders on a special register: this formality was called registration (*l'enregistrement*).

As far as orders—simple orders—were concerned, the Parlements had over them a certain power of control. It was a doctrine well established and always accepted by the kings during the whole Ancien Régime that the Parlements were under duty to refuse to register an order inconsistent with an existing ordinance; since the ordinances were a higher law (comparable to a statute with respect to an executive order) such an order could only have been "obtained by surprise" from the king, and it was their duty to call the inconsistency to his attention. Even after registration, any private person could still raise the question, which was then decided either by the Parlement or by the Conseil du Roi. This doctrine thus established a real process of judicial review of orders of the king.

As far as ordinances were concerned, on the contrary, the Parlements historically had no such power. During the course of the fifteenth and sixteenth centuries, however, they made the claim that they were the representatives of the people and therefore, according to the traditional view, had the power to control ordinances. On June 13, 1499, for instance, Jean le Maistre, Avocat Général du Roi au Parlement de Paris, in a speech addressed to Louis XII, stated that the Parlement was "the true Senate of the kingdom" and that "ordinances and edicts of the kings received their final form and their final authority only when published and registered by the Parlement." The control claimed was not simply a legal one: it was not only the control of the consistency of the ordinance with the "fundamental laws" of the kingdom. It was also a political one: it was a power of control of the wisdom of the ordinance. The Parlements therefore asserted it to be their power and their duty to give advice to the king, even when the king had already made a decision, even on ordinances already signed and sealed, and, if they could not approve an ordinance, to refuse its registration and to send it back to the king with advice as to how the ordinance should be amended; this was the right of remonstrance.

At the beginning, they did not claim any other power than an advisory one. The king, therefore, could make a final decision and order them to register the ordinance, either as it was or with amendments. Later on they claimed that ordinances were not valid without their consent; and they received at the beginning of the seventeenth century the approval of such an author as Guy Coquille, in his *Institution au droit des Français,* written in 1609. They refused, therefore, to obey these orders, either by simply disregarding them or by sending them back to the king with new advice (*itératives remonstrances*). Sometimes they did not dare to disregard repeated and unqualified orders of the king. But they used to proceed to the registration only "on the express order of the king," which implied that they had not given their consent, and therefore would not apply the order, or "temporarily and until the king repeals the ordinance," or even sometimes they made by themselves corrections to the royal ordinances.

If the king could not obtain from some Parlement the registration of an ordinance, he still had the possibility of going in person to the Parlement, and holding a *lit de justice*. According to the principle that "all justice comes from the king," the Parlements were without power as soon as the king was present in the room of their deliberations. Even then, however, some Parlements dared to register with the notation "on the express order of the king," which again implied that they had not given their consent. Moreover, the king could not go to Toulouse, Rennes, or Grenoble every time the Parlements were refusing a registration. Finally, although the popular feeling was usually unfavorable to the Parlements, which quite often opposed much-needed reforms such as a more equal tax system and fought for the conservation of privileges, it sometimes happened also that popular feeling backed the Parlements and the king did not dare to insist too much.

The political history of France during the seventeenth and eighteenth centuries is, to a great extent, as was England's during the seventeenth century, the history of the rivalry of the Parlements and the king.

Louis XIII, in 1641, decided to curb the powers of the Parlements. An ordinance provided that all royal ordinances registered should be strictly observed; it provided furthermore that certain acts only could be the subject of remonstrances, and that the decision of the king should be obeyed.

This ordinance was not long in force. Louis XIII died in 1642. Louis XIV being a minor, the Parlements fought back and recovered their powers. We have already seen some of the decisions which they made in 1648. They also decided that no tax or duty should be levied without their consent.

In 1667, Louis XIV promulgated new provisions comparable to the provisions of 1641, and made them even more severe a few years after. The Parlements were authorized to make remonstrances only after registration. The prestige of Louis XIV and the impression produced by his systematic appearance in Parlement at the beginning of his personal reign were such that the Parlements did not dare to object. This was the only period of absolute monarchy in French history.

It did not long survive after the death of Louis XIV, in 1715. The regent, having asked the Parlements to cancel provisions of Louis XIV's will restrictive of his powers, felt obliged to give them back the right to make remonstrances before registration. Three years afterward, the Parlements had already proved so unreasonable that the king came back to the provisions of 1667.

During all the eighteenth century, the conflict remained open between the Parlements and the king. The Parlements went so far as to refuse to pronounce judgments, and even to submit collective resignations. The king went so far as to prevent the Parlement of Paris from convening in Paris and to exile it to Pontoise, and to send to jail the most turbulent of its members. On January 15, 1771, the Parlement of Paris once more submitted a collective resignation. During the night of the 19th, on the order of Chancellor Maupeou, every member of the Parlement was asked by the police whether he maintained his resignation. Each of them gave a positive answer, each of them was delivered a *lettre de cachet;* was ordered to leave Paris without delay, and was informed that his office was confiscated. On January 23rd, the Conseil du Roi was vested with the powers of the Parlements until the latter could be reorganized. Chancellor Maupeou spent a great part of the year in that reorganization. In 1772, the reform was made and accepted by public opinion. In 1774, however, the death of the king once more destroyed the progress which had been made toward a more effective exercise of governmental power. Louis XVI took a purely legalistic view of the problem; he considered that the confiscation of the offices had been unjust, that, moreover, under the fundamental laws of the kingdom, the Parlements were companions of the king in his exercise of the power; he asked Maupeou, therefore, for his resignation and cancelled all the measures taken in 1771.

The Parlements (and we are approaching the end of the story) resumed their functions with the feeling that they had won and that they had to show it. Furthermore, they were afraid of the reforms, prepared previously by Maupeou and now by Turgot, for the improvement of the administration and the improvement of the economy of the kingdom. Their opposition became systematic. In 1788, Louis XVI was obliged to deprive the Parlements of the power of remonstrance and to give it again, under strict regulation, to a new "Cour plénière." Although he was backed by the people, the protestations of the Parlements were such that he considered it necessary to appeal again to new Etats Généraux which were called in 1789. The Etats Généraux dissolved the Parlements on November 3, 1789, but the Revolution had already started, the Revolution which was to sweep away Parlements, Etats Généraux, and kings, and to threaten the more or less absolute monarchies of Europe.

The lesson which emerges from this sketch is easy to state, even though hard to apply. A proper scheme of government must provide institutional checks against abuses of power. The reign of law must be permanently assured. Yet the government should have sufficient strength; the checks should never be used in an exclusively conservative spirit; avenues should be kept open for improvement, growth, response to popular feeling. The reign of law must be assured, but the law must be flexible. The Ancien Régime of France never achieved this scheme of government. The kings had excessive powers, yet the negative powers of the Parlements prevented them from introducing desirable reforms and answering popular desires. France was old before being mature.

But at least, centuries of struggles and trials had made the supremacy of law a part of the collective mind of France. The supremacy of law had been invoked at the same time by the kings and by the Parlements, although both sides, in their struggle against each other, had been inspired only part of the time by an ideal of justice, and too often by a spirit of pride or by the defense of vested interests. Each of the parties, in fact, had often disregarded the law. When their common disappearance opened the way to a new regime, it appeared in the perspective of history that the struggle between kings and Parlements had been the fight of the people of France for the reign of law. The Revolution at certain stages, and Napoleon, established governments more absolute than had ever been experienced. But liberty, which was the cry of the Revolution, remained cherished and worshiped, even when temporarily buffeted about through the revolutionary storms. When the political sky cleared up, liberty blossomed again, and there was a clearer understanding that freedom can be reconciled with a strong government, that liberty is assured as long as the government is responsive to popular desires, and, at the same time, with institutional devices securing continuous control, is itself placed under the law.*

---

* Professor Tunc prepared the following bibliography for his paper: Emile Chénon, *Histoire générale du droit français public et privé des origines à* 1815, (2 vols., 1925, 1929); Fr. Olivier Martin, *Histoire du droit française des origines à la Révolution* (1948); J. Declareuil, *Histoire générale du droit français des origines à 1789* (1925); A. Esmein, *Cours élémentaire d'histoire du droit français* (15e éd., 1925); Henri Regnault, *Manuel d'histoire du droit française* (5e ed., 1947); G. Lepointe, *Petit précis des sources de l'histoire du droit français* (2e éd., 1949); Auguste Dumas, *Manuel d'histoire du droit française* (mimeographed; without date); André Lemaire, *Les lois fondamentales de la monarchie française* (1907); Fr. Olivier Martin, *Les lois du roi* (1946, mimeographed), and *Les Parlements contre l'absolutisme traditionnel au XVIIIème siècle* (1950, mimeographed); Gaston Zeller, *Les institutions de la France au XVIème siècle* (1948): A. Aulard, *Les lettres de cachet* (1927); Marcel David, *La souveraineté et les limites juridiques du pouvoir monarchique du IXème au XVème siècle* (1954); Roger Bickart, *Les Parlements et la notion de souveraineté nationale au XVIIIème siècle* (1932); Pierre Jacomet, *Vicissitudes et chutes du Parlement de Paris* (1954).

The second address of the evening was presented by Chief Justice A. Van de S. Centlivres of the Appellate Division of the Supreme Court of the Union of South Africa. Introducing him Dean Griswold said:

"Chief Justice Centlivres within the past few years has had first-hand experience with problems of government under law. The measure of the man may be found in his judgments, but I will also pass on a story about him which I heard the other evening.

"He was a Rhodes Scholar from South Africa, and his room-mate at New College, Oxford, was a man who is now an American lawyer from Seattle. They have been fast friends ever since that time; the American lawyer visited South Africa several years ago; Chief Justice Centlivres was of course his host. The Chief Justice arranged for his American friend to call upon General Smuts, who was then the Prime Minister of South Africa. In due course he drove the American to the apartment where General Smuts was living; and he got out, and showed him to the door; then the Chief Justice returned to his car. The American asked, 'Aren't you coming along?' And the Chief Justice said, 'No. No member of the South African judiciary ever calls upon a member of the government, or upon a politician of the opposition.' And so the American went and made his call alone.

"A few days later, the Chief Justice arranged for the American to visit the South African Parliament, and again the American said, 'Aren't you coming along?' And again the Chief Justice said, 'No. No member of the South African judiciary ever attends the debates of Parliament; some question there discussed might come before him, and not having heard all of the debates, he might have a distorted view of the problems. So he simply stays away from the debates in Parliament.'

"This tradition—a tradition of the independence of the judiciary, of the separateness of the judiciary from the other branches of the government,—might well stand as an example in any country whose ideal is a government under law."

The Constitution of the Union of South Africa and the Rule of Law

A. VAN DE S. CENTLIVRES *

There is, perhaps, nothing more fascinating and instructive than to compare the various forms of government which the wit of man has devised. Those of us who are firmly convinced that the best form of government must be based on the democracy of the people had every reason for hoping, after the First World War, that the pattern of democratic government would spread throughout the world. We have been disappointed in those hopes and today we find that large portions of the world know nothing of the blessings of democracy and that those portions are in the grip of autocracies which set the State above the individual and which deny their citizens the fundamental rights of an independent judiciary, freedom of movement within and outside the limits of their own country, freedom of speech, freedom of the press, freedom of assembly, freedom of association, and freedom to elect representatives of their own choice. There are various forms of democratic government and tonight I propose to address you on the theme of the Constitution of the Union of South Africa and the rule of law as applied there. You will find that there is not much resemblance in detail between your Constitution and the Constitution of my country. In the limited time at my disposal I shall have to be se-

* HON. ALBERT VAN DE SANDT CENTLIVRES, *Chief Justice of South Africa.* Chief Justice Centlivres was born in 1887. He was graduated from South African College and from New College, Oxford. He was called to the Bar at the Middle Temple in London in 1910, and was admitted the next year as an Advocate of the Supreme Court of South Africa at Capetown. In 1914-1915 he was on active military service in Southwest Africa. Beside many other public services he became a judge of the Cape Provincial Division of the Supreme Court of South Africa in 1932, became a Judge of Appeal in 1939 and since 1950 has been Chief Justice of South Africa.

lective and much must be left unsaid and unexplained but I hope to be able to give you in broad outline some idea of the Constitution of the country which I have the honor to represent at this memorable celebration of the two-hundredth anniversary of the birth of that great Chief Justice, John Marshall, whose decisions on Constitutional law paved the way towards the United States becoming the mightiest nation in the world today.

In 1908 there were four Colonies in South Africa—the Colonies of the Cape of Good Hope, Natal, Transvaal, and Orange River. Each of these colonies was self-governing but subject to the over-riding authority of Great Britain and all their constitutions had as their pattern the constitution of Great Britain excepting, of course, the fact that their upper Houses of Parliament were not hereditary in their composition. The Legislatures of these four Colonies agreed to send delegates to a National Convention to consider whether some form of Union should be brought above between the four Colonies. This Convention was presided over by Sir Henry de Villiers who had been Chief Justice of the Colony of the Cape of Good Hope since 1873. It was largely due to his tactful and skillful piloting of the proceedings at the Convention that the delegates hammered out a draft constitution for a new political entity and submitted to all the four Colonial legislatures a draft bill to establish a union of the four Colonies. This bill was agreed to by three of those Legislatures; the fourth stipulated that the bill should be submitted to a referendum of the voters who elected that legislature. The referendum resulted in an overwhelming majority in favor of Union. Delegates were then selected to take the draft bill to England for the purpose of obtaining its enactment by the Parliament at Westminister, and that Parliament duly passed what is called the South Africa Act 1909—an Act which, though it is in law and in theory an Act of the British Parliament, was an Act which was drafted by South Africans in South Africa and agreed to by the four self-governing Colonies. The fact that it was possible to agree to unify South

Africa within the short space of about seven years after the conclusion of the Anglo-Boer war is a remarkable tribute to the statesmanship of those who were in control of the four South African Colonies, more especially when one takes into consideration the different political associations of those who became the architects of Union. All political parties were represented at the National Convention and all its members worked with a will to bring about union and such difference of opinion as emerged during the meetings of the Convention were, as a rule, not along party political lines. One of the first issues to be decided was whether the Union should be federal or unitary in character. The Convention had the advantage of being able to study various Constitutions, such as those of the United States, Canada, Australia, and Switzerland. It rejected a federal union. The existing Colonies were to become provinces, the legislatures of which were to have only those powers specifically mentioned in the Constitution and such further powers as might from time to time be conferred on them by the Parliament of the Union. Parliament was made, subject to certain limitations, supreme: it could by ordinary legislation diminish the powers of Provincial Councils and even abolish those Councils. I shall refer later to an Act of 1934 which purports to safeguard those Councils. Under the South Africa Act as originally enacted the Parliament of the Union was not a sovereign legislature, for certain specified bills had to be reserved for "the King's pleasure" which in practice meant the King acting by and with the advice of His Majesty's Ministers in the United Kingdom; even a Bill which had been assented to by the Governor-General could be disallowed by the King within a year of such assent. I am not aware of any case in which a Bill passed by the Union Parliament did not become law or was disallowed but the matter has now become academic as a result of the Statute of Westminster and the Status of the Union Act of 1934.

The Constitution furthermore provided that it could be amended by Parliament itself legislating in the same manner as it legislates in respect of other matters save that a special procedure was required for amending the section (137) guaranteeing equality of rights for the two official languages and the section (35) which prevented discrimination of voting rights in the Province of the Cape of Good Hope by a reason of a voter's race or color only. The special procedure required that any Bill amending those two sections should be passed by both Houses of Parliament sitting together and that it should be agreed to at its third reading by not less than two-thirds of the total number of members of both Houses. In 1936 the two Houses of the Union Parliament sitting in joint session, by Act Number 12 of that year, passed a Bill which was agreed to at its third reading by over two-thirds of the total number of members of both Houses and which removed native voters in the Province of the Cape of Good Hope from the common roll of voters, which up to that date had contained both white and non-white voters. Speaking broadly, by "native" is meant a member of an aboriginal race or tribe of Africa, as distinguished from colored persons who form a separate group. The natives so removed from the common roll were placed on a separate roll and were entitled to elect three members of the House of Assembly. By Section 44 of that Act it was provided that section 35 of the South Africa Act be amended by requiring the procedure therein prescribed to be followed in the case of a Bill (a) disqualifying a native who under the 1936 Act would be or might become capable of being registered in the Cape Native Voters' roll instituted under that Act, or (b) altering the number of representatives who in terms of that Act may be elected by natives registered in that roll.

Only in the two instances I have given are the Courts called on to express an opinion whether an Act which purports to have been passed bicamerally by the House of Assembly and the Senate has been validly passed. In considering any such case the approach by the Courts to the problem is strictly on legal grounds as the Court is not in any way concerned with the policy of the Act, the validity of which is attacked. In this connection I cannot do better than quote the remarks of Sir Owen Dixon when he took his seat as Chief Justice of Australia. He was dealing with the problems of federation but those remarks apply with equal force to the question which I am now discussing. Sir Owen said:

> Federalism means a demarcation of powers and this casts upon the Court the responsibility of deciding whether legislation is within the boundaries of allotted powers. Unfortunately that responsibility is very widely misunderstood, misunderstood by the popular use and misuse of terms which are not applicable, and it is not sufficiently recognized that the Court's sole function is to interpret a constitutional description of power and say whether a given measure falls on one side of a line consequently drawn or on the other, and that it has nothing to do with the merits or demerits of the measure.
>
> Such a function has led us all, I think, to believe that close adherence to legal reasoning is the only way to maintain the confidence of all parties in Federal conflicts. It may be that the Court is thought to be excessively legalistic. I should be sorry to think that it is anything else. There is no other safe guide to judicial decisions in great conflicts than a strict and complete legalism.

The Courts in South Africa adopt the same method of approach as Sir Owen Dixon. It has been held that the Courts are not the place where the merits or demerits of legislation enter into the question whether a particular enactment has or has not been passed conformably to the Constitution. The responsibility for enacting legislation rests fairly and squarely on the shoulders of the Legislature and not on the Courts and the sole question is whether the enactment is *intra* or *ultra vires* the Constitution.

A strict and complete legalism in the sense used by Sir Owen Dixon is unquestionably easier to adhere to in the case of the South African Courts than in the case of the Supreme Court of the United States. For there is nothing in the South African Constitution which in any way resembles some of the provisions of the Constitution of the United States which are cast in general terms and are, to a foreigner like myself, somewhat vague and ambiguous. The provisions which

I have in mind are the due process and commerce clauses. As regards the former, Mr. Justice Frankfurter observed recently that "due process as a concept is neither fixed nor finished"—a process which he also described as inherently living and therefore changing in its applicability. Small wonder then that, confronted with the obvious difficulty of interpreting the Constitution in given circumstances, Judge Learned Hand remarked as follows:

> I venture to believe that it is as important to a judge called upon to pass on a question of constitutional law, to have at least a bowing acquaintance with Acton and Maitland, with Thucydides, Gibbon, Carlyle, with Homer, Dante and Shakespeare and Milton, with Machiavelli, Montaigne and Rabelais, with Plato, Bacon, Hume and Kant, as with the books which have been specifically written on the subject. For in such matters everything turns upon the spirit in which he approaches the questions before him. The words he must construe are empty vessels into which he can pour nearly anything he will. Men . . . must be aware that there are before them more than verbal problems; more than final solutions cast in generalisations of universal applicability. They must be aware of the changing social tensions in every society which make it an organism; which demand new schemata of adaptation; which will disrupt it, if rigidly confined.

The approach suggested by Judge Learned Hand to constitutional problems is no doubt an approach dictated in part by the generality of some of the Constitutional guarantees and in part by the fact that the Constitution of the United States is what has been described as a rigid constitution, the amendment of which is a long and laborious operation. It may be that the greater the rigidity of the Constitution the greater the flexibility of interpretation should be. The views taken by society as to the scope of State activity change from time to time, and, according to Judge Learned Hand, regard must be had to such changes in interpreting a Constitution such as yours.

There is no consensus of judicial opinion as to the proper method of approaching the solution of constitutional questions. Chief Justice Marshall's famous dictum that "we must never forget that it is a *constitution* we are expounding" does not, speaking generally, seem to be favorably regarded by British Courts which draw little or no distinction between interpreting a constitution and interpreting, let us say, a statute dealing with dogs. For instance the Judicial Committee of the Privy Council in *Bank of Toronto v. Lambe* (12 A.C. 575 at p. 579 (P.C. 1887)) said that Courts of law must treat the provisions of the Canadian Constitution "by the same methods of construction and exposition which they apply to other statutes." On what may be regarded as two isolated occasions the Judicial Committee seems to have taken a wider view. I refer to the cases of *Edwards v. Attorney General for Canada* ([1930] A.C. 124 (P.C. 1929)) and *British Coal Corporation v. The King* ([1935] A.C. 500, 518 (P.C.)). In delivering the advice of the Judicial Committee in the latter case Viscount Sankey, Lord Chancellor of England, said: "In interpreting a constituent or organic statute such as the Act [the British North America Act] that construction most beneficial to the widest possible amplitude of its powers must be adopted."

The above general statement proved to be of no assistance to McGillivray J.A. in *Kazakewich v. Kazakewich* ([1937] 1 D.L.R. 548 at p. 567) where he said:

> It seems to me that none of the observations of Viscount Sankey can be said to provide legal justification for an attempt by Canadian Courts to mould and fashion the Canadian Constitution so as to make it conform, according to their views, to the requirements of present day social and economic conditions.

The difference in approach to constitutional questions may be explained by saying that some interpreters of a constitution regard as essential the strict letter of the Constitution while others pay more regard to what may be described as the spirit or object of the Constitution. I may illustrate what I mean by quoting from Dean Griswold's very valuable and informative brochure on *The Fifth Amendment Today.* As you know the Fifth Amendment provides, *inter alia,* that no person shall be compelled in any criminal case to be a witness against himself. Literally construed this provision only applies to criminal cases and not to civil cases or to any other proceedings of an investigating nature. But, as the learned Dean points out, "early courts saw that the protection of the amendment itself would be an empty gesture if it was literally applied. . . For this reason, courts long ago concluded that if the privilege is to be effective at all it must prevent compulsory self-incrimination in *any* proceedings. This is, indeed, a broad construction which has seemed to be required if the basic objective of that language is to be realized."

The judges in South Africa have, in comparison with the judges of the Supreme Court of your country, a comparatively easy task. As I have pointed out there are no such provisions in our Constitution in any way resembling the due process and commerce clauses. One of the main duties of the Courts in South Africa today is to interpret the language used by Parliament in a particular act and if their interpretation does not commend itself to Parliament there is nothing to prevent Parliament from immediately amending the Act and even making the amendment have retrospective effect to the date when the original enactment came into operation. The burden which the justices of your Supreme Court carry on their shoulders is, therefore, considerably greater than the burden carried by South African judges.

Under the South Africa Act a distinction is drawn between the functions of the Executive, Parliament, and the Judiciary. The Legislature enacts the laws and it is the duty of the Executive to administer those laws and of the Judiciary to interpret them. Who constitute the Executive? A person reading the South Africa Act with no knowledge of constitutional usages and conventions will obtain an entirely erroneous view as to who constitute the Executive. Section 8 of the Act provided that " the Executive Government of the Union is vested in the King and shall be administered by His Majesty in person or by a Governor-General as his representative." This section was replaced by Section 4 of the Status of the Union Act (69 of 1934) to which I shall refer later. Section 14 of the South Africa Act provides that the Governor-General may appoint officers to administer such departments of State of the Union as the Governor-General-in-Council may establish and that such officers shall hold office during the pleasure of the Governor-General. The concluding portion of this provision, with Section 8 in its original wording, creates the impression that the Governor-General is an autocrat who is solely responsible for the administration of the Union and who has unfettered discretion to dismiss any officer of State who incurs his displeasure. Although such an impression may be justified by the language used, the unwritten conventions and usages of the Constitution show that it is erroneous. In actual practice the Governor-General requests a person who commands a majority in the House of Assembly to form a cabinet. If that person succeeds in doing so, he becomes the Prime Minister of the Union. If a Prime Minister wishes to get rid of a member of his cabinet who refuses to resign he may conceivably advise the Governor-General to dismiss him but the practice in South Africa has been for the Prime Minister in such circumstances to hand in his own resignation whereupon the Governor-General requests him to form a new cabinet. As soon as the resignation of the Prime Minister is accepted by the Governor-General all the cabinet posts immediately become vacant and the Prime Minister can then form a new cabinet and exclude therefrom the member he wished to get rid of.

It is to be noted that the words "Prime Minister" and "cabinet" are not to be found in the South Africa Act. This illustrates how necessary it is in order to understand the working of that Act to have some knowledge of the usages and convention of the Constitution, which is in part written and in part unwritten.

Section 4 of the Status of the Union Act (69 of 1934) sets forth the position more accurately than Section 14 of the South Africa Act. Under that section the Executive Government of the Union in regard to any aspect of its domestic and external affairs is vested in the Queen, acting on the advice of Her Majesty's Ministers of State for the Union and may be administered by Her Majesty in person or by a Governor-General as her representative. As the chief representative of the State the Governor-General opens Parliament every year and delivers a speech from the throne. This speech is prepared by the cabinet and sets forth the Government's programme for the ensuing session of Parliament.

The real responsibility for administering the Government of the Union falls on the cabinet and not on the Governor-General. Proclamations issued under any law are signed by the Governor-General and must be countersigned by the Minister concerned who must bear the responsibility involved in such proclamation. Constitutionally the Governor-General cannot be held responsible for any act of the Executive but he may give advice to his Ministers. They are, however, free to reject that advice and act contrary to that advice. Even in the exercise of the few Royal prerogatives that are left, the Governor-General acts on the advice of his Ministers. For instance the prerogative of commuting a death sentence and of granting a free pardon are exercised by the Governor-General not personally but on the advice of his Ministers.

Professor Wheare in his valuable and instructive treatise on the Statute of Westminster and Dominion Status (5th edition, p. 126), says that "it was declared in 1926 [at the Imperial Conference held during that year] that the Governor-General of a Dominion held in all essential respects the same position in relation to the administration of public affairs as is held by His Majesty the King in Great Britain. Thus the Governor-General must act in accordance with the same rules as the King recognizes in his relations with his Ministers. No attempt was made to indicate what those rules were. The problems of discretion still remain unsolved."

As Professor Wheare indicates, there is a field in which the Governor-General has a discretion and in a note to the passage I have quoted he states that "the Governor-General of South Africa refused to grant a dissolution to General Hertzog in 1939 and this refusal aroused controversy." What happened was that General Hertzog as Prime Minister decided to submit to the vote of the House of Assembly the issue whether the Union of South Africa should, after Great Britain had declared war on Germany, also declare war on Germany. General Hertzog was defeated in the House of Assembly and then advised the Governor-General to dissolve Parliament. The Governor-General declined to do so and asked General Smuts to form a Government. As Professor Wheare says this action on the part of the Governor-General aroused controversy but it is generally thought that if General Hertzog, *before* submitting the issue of war or peace to the House of Assembly, had advised the Governor-General to dissolve Parliament in order to obtain the view of the electorate on that issue, the Governor-General would have been bound to give effect to that advice. The view taken by the Governor-General was that as General Smuts commanded a majority in the House of Assembly he was able to form a Government to carry on the administration of the country and that in these circumstances a dissolution of the House of Assembly was unnecessary. The controversy over the South African Governor-General's refusal in 1939 to accept General Hertzog's advice to dissolve the House of Assembly reminds one of the controversy that arose in Canada when Lord Byng declined to accept Mr. Mackenzie-King's advice to dissolve. In practice the occasions on which such advice is not acted on by the Governor-General are very rare. Except in a vague and undefined field, therefore, the Governor-General bears no responsibility in connection with the Union's affairs. I think that I have said enough about the position occupied by the Governor-General to show that he occupies a very different position from that occupied by your President upon whom your Constitution confers greater powers. Their method of appointment also differs: the Governor-General is appointed by Her Majesty the Queen on the advice of her South African Ministers; your President is elected. In respect of executive power his position corresponds rather to that of our Prime Minister than to that of our Governor-General. And yet your President and his cabinet occupy a very different position from that occupied by our Prime Minister. The President's tenure of office, unlike that of our Prime Minister, is not dependent upon a majority in either House of Congress. Under the South Africa Act no Minister of State can hold office for a longer period than three months unless he is or becomes a member of either House of Parliament. Consequently every member of the cabinet must be or become a member of Parliament and is responsible to Parliament for any administrative act which he performs. A Minister who is a member of one House has the right of audience but not vote in the other House. This is a very useful provision and it means that a Minister is subject to questioning in both Houses of Parliament.

The Executive cannot, as I have already indicated, function without the support of a majority in Parliament. Although in theory Parliament is independent of the Executive, in practice the Executive has an enormous influence on legislation—a far greater influence than the Executive of your country may have, as it may not always command a majority in Congress. The position is, I believe, the same in all the member-states of the British Commonwealth of Nations. Lord Justice Denning in *The Changing Law* makes the following remarks in regard to the relationship of the Executive and the Legislature in Great Britain: "There is no rigid separation between the legislative and executive powers; because the Ministers, who exercise the executive powers, also direct a great deal of the legislative power of Parliament." Indeed Lord Justice Denning goes so far as to suggest that "in practice sovereignty no longer rests with Parliament. It rests with the executive and in particular with the Cabinet."

The Government of the day arranges the agenda of Parliament and very little time is available to private members who may wish to introduce legislation. Practically all legislation is initiated by the Executive and in view of the fact that it has as its beck and call a majority of the members of Parliament it can successfully resist, if it wishes to do so, any amendment to the legislation which it introduces. But it seldom happens that any bill of any importance is passed without any amendment at all; the Minister in charge of a bill accepts some of the amendments that are moved, leaves some to the free vote of the members and intimates that he is unwilling to accept other amendments. When the last-mentioned course is adopted, the party whip cracks and each member of the Government party is required to vote against the amendment while each member of the official Opposition is required to vote for the amendment, if the amendment was moved on behalf of the Opposition. This may not be regarded as a satisfactory state of affairs because under this system it may well happen that desirable amendments are negatived. This is, however, the price that must be paid for the party system which has taken deep root in all the member-states of the British Commonwealth and which is, perhaps, an inevitable result of the requirement that the Executive must have a majority in the Legislature. An individual member of Parliament is free in theory to vote as he pleases but if he is a member of a party he is placed in a difficult position; he may vote according to his own views or vote with his party contrary to his own views. If he does the former he may disrupt his party and in these circumstances he may choose what he regards as the lesser of two evils and vote with his party.

There are rare occasions when a great principle is at stake and a member's inner conscience tells him that he cannot, without losing his self-respect, vote with his party. On such an occasion he will, if he is a man of honor, vote according to his own convictions and against his party in the full knowledge that he will probably be putting an end to his political career.

In the Constitution of your country there are provisions which safeguard the fundamental liberties of the individual.

There are no such safeguards in the Constitution of my country. Theoretically there are none, for the simple reason that Parliament is omnipotent. Our Parliament has as regards the matter I am now considering exactly the same powers as the British Parliament. Anson in his work on the *Law and Custom of the Constitution* puts the matter very clearly when he says:

> The legislative omnipotence of Parliament is, perhaps, the most conspicuous feature of our Constitution to anyone who seeks to compare the disposition of forces in different political societies. What is usually understood, elsewhere than in England, by a constitutional government, is a government the ordinary working of which is regulated by a written constitution, which cannot be altered by ordinary legislative procedure, which needs for its alteration some adnormal process for obtaining the expression of national consent.

Clement in his "Canadian Constitution" puts the position very vividly when he says: "*Magna Charta* may be interfered with; taxation imposed without regard to uniformity or equality; class legislation and laws discriminating against race may be enacted; one man's property may be taken from him and given to another without compensation; *ex post facto* legislation passed."

The observations of the Lord President in *MacCormick v. Lord Advocate* in 1953 (See Scots Law Times, Oct. 17, 1953, p. 255, at 262) that the British Parliament established by the Treaty of Union between England and Scotland does not have unlimited sovereignty in the matter of altering the provisions of the Treaty does not seem to affect the absolute sovereignty of the Parliament in other respects.

But the omnipotence of Parliament is in practice always subject to the electorate and if Parliament were to pass a law which unjustifiably curtails the liberty of electors they can express their views through the medium of the ballot box at the next general election and elect a Parliament that will undo the legislation of its predecessor. Subject to the two exceptions I have mentioned no Act by the Union Parliament and assented to by the Governor-General (such assent is always given as a matter of course) can be regarded as unconstitutional in the sense used by John Marshall. When it is said that a law passed by Congress is "unconstitutional" the meaning is, as I understand it, that the law is in conflict with the Constitution of the United States and therefore of no force or effect in so far as it is in conflict with that Constitution. The word "constitutionalism" has, perhaps, a wider import both in South Africa and in Great Britain that it has in the United States. As an illustration of the wider import I may quote from Professor Goodhart's "English Law and the Moral Law of England." This is what he says:

> I believe that whatever the theoretical power of the Queen in Parliament may be, there are certain general principles which are so firmly recognized as authoritative that they could not now be violated without causing a revolution. In those cases it seems to me to be correct to say that those principles are part of the British constitutional law. . .
>
> It is, I am convinced, inconceivable that any Parliament in Great Britain, would, during ordinary conditions of peace, regard itself as constitutionally capable of abolishing the writ of Habeas Corpus. It is therefore correct to say that it is a basic part of English constitutional law that no man is above the law.

Professor Goodhart takes much the same view as Dicey who suggests that an unconstitutional law is a law which is opposed to the spirit of the English Constitution (*Law of the Constitution,* 6th edition, p. 464).

I shall now take an example from the South African Constitution. Section 101 of the South Africa Act provides that the judges of the Supreme Court shall not be removed from office except by the Governor-General-in-Council on an address from both Houses of Parliament in the same session praying for such removal on the ground of misbehavior or incapacity. This section the Union Parliament is free to amend by a bare majority; it may, for instance, repeal the section and substitute another section providing that judges may be removed from office at the whim of the Executive. I am giving this simply as an example to illustrate the unlimited powers of the Union Parliament but I do not wish to suggest that any Government of the Union would use its parliamentary majority in order to abolish the independence of the judiciary—an independence which all countries which are entitled to call themselves civilized jealously safeguard as the only way of ensuring that justice is fairly and impartially administered as between man and man and as between the citizen and the State. It would be unconstitutional in its widest sense for the Union Parliament to destroy the independence of the judiciary; just as it would be unconstitutional in that sense for the Parliament at Westminster to abolish the writ of Habeas Corpus; yet an Act bringing about either of those results would be perfectly constitutional in its narrowest sense. So too would an Act making a radical alteration in the Constitution be unconstitutional in its widest sense, if it were passed without, as the politicians call it, a mandate from the people and yet such an Act would be valid. If, for instance, the Parliament of the United Kingdom had passed the Parliament Act of 1911, whereby the powers of the House of Lords were curtailed, without a prior general election to obtain the views of the electorate on the matter, such an Act would have been unassailable in the Courts. The appeal to the electorate in this instance may be regarded as one of the conventions of the Constitution and yet it is one of the conventions which is not always observed in practice. For instance the Parliament of the United Kingdom in the absence of a general election on that one point passed an Act in 1949 which, by an amendment of the Parliament Act of 1911, further curtailed the powers of the House of Lords by providing that the power of that House to delay the enactment of bills passed by the House of Commons be reduced from two years to one year. In short, the powers of the Parliament of the Union are as far-reaching as the powers of the Parliament of the United Kingdom and the Courts in the Union can question what purports to be an Act of Parliament only in the two cases I have mentioned.

I have thus far dealt with the powers of Parliament. A few words will suffice in regard to the powers of Provincial Councils. The Supreme Court of South Africa has the power of declaring a provincial ordinance unconstitutional and in this respect the function of that Court is similar to that of the Supreme Court of the United States, the Supreme Court of Canada, and the High Court of Australia but the consequences of such a declaration are not as far-reaching as in the case of the United States, Canada, and Australia, because Parliament is always at hand to enlarge, or restrict if it deems fit, the powers of Provincial Councils. In other words there is no difficulty in obtaining a speedy amendment of the Constitution in so far as the powers of Provincial Councils are concerned. A provincial ordinance may be *ultra vires* because the provincial council which passed it had no power to enact it or because it is in conflict with an Act of Parliament but an Act of Parliament can never be invalid on the ground that it is in conflict with a provincial ordinance or on the ground that Parliament has usurped the power of Provincial Councils. The legislative authority of such councils was clearly enunciated by Innes C.J. in *Middelburg Municipality v. Gertzen* ([1914] S.Ct. So. Af., App. Div., 544, 550):

> It was probably the intention of the framers of the [South Africa] Act that Parliament should be relieved of the labour of dealing with the matters enumerated in section 85, and that the task of making laws in regard to them should devolve in practice upon the Council alone. But Parliament has not parted with its powers; its authority over the whole domain of legislation remains unimpaired. It may repeal, directly or by implication, an ordinance passed by the Council, and it may by statute deal with any matter falling within the restricted authority of that body. In this respect the relation between Council and Parliament is very different from that which exists between the Provincial and the Dominion legislatures of Canada. The British North America Act enumerates certain subjects in relation to which the exclusive right of making laws was given to the Provincial legislatures. In regard to all other subjects, general powers of legislation were conferred upon the Dominion Parliament. The result of the creation of two bodies, dividing almost equally between them the field

> of legislative activity was an ever present danger of intrusion by the one upon the proper domain of the other. Hence the necessity for careful and rigid examination in each case in which the validity of a Canadian statute is challenged. Under the South Africa Act no question of legislative competition can arise. The power of Parliament is never in doubt; the enquiry in each instance can only be whether the subordinate legislature has exceeded the authority assigned to it. And hence, in deciding upon the validity of a Provincial Ordnance regard must be had to the terms in which the grant of jurisdiction over the relative subject matter has been expressed. . . Once it is clear that the legislative provisions which are challenged fall within the power conferred on [Provincial] Councils then we should not be justified in interfering with these merely because we may consider them unwise or impolitic. That is a matter for Parliament . . . to deal with, if necessary: courts of law are concerned with the validity, not with the wisdom or the policy of Provincial Ordinances.

After the above judicial announcement was made it was enacted by an Act passed in 1934 that Parliament shall not:

(a) alter the boundaries of any province, divide a province into two or more provinces or form a new province out of the provinces within the Union, except on the petition of the provincial council of every province whose boundaries are affected thereby; and

(b) abolish any provincial council or abridge the powers conferred on provincial councils except by petition to Parliament by the provincial council concerned.

The efficacy of the above Act has not been tested in the Courts.

Having dealt with our written Constitution, I shall now proceed to deal with the rule of law, which may be regarded as part of our unwritten constitution. As regards constitutional usages generally it may be stated that those usages are the same in broad outline as those of the United Kingdom. There are still a few of the Crown prerogatives left. Theoretically they are the prerogatives of Her Majesty the Queen but in practice they are exercised only by a Minister of State who is the representative of the Queen. In exercising such of the prerogatives as are still in existence a Minister is answerable to Parliament. Save for these prerogatives, the Executive can act only under the law as enacted by Parliament. Under the Crown Liabilities Act of 1910 the Executive can be sued on contract or for damages occasioned by the act of its servants; and in this respect it is in no different position from that of an ordinary citizen.

The rule that the Executive is not above but is subject to the law of the land is a rule which is common to Great Britain and to Holland from which two countries the bulk of the white population of South Africa is derived. Bracton's oft quoted "*quod Rex non debet esse sub homine sed sub Deo et lege*" is familiar to all of you—a quotation on which Coke relied in the seventeenth century in his dispute with King James I. The details of that dispute I need not enter upon, for they are well known to all lawyers. A similar dispute arose in the United Netherlands in 1581 when the States-General emphatically affirmed this rule in an Act which deposed Philip II of Spain. This Act of Abjuration is to be found in Volume I of the Groot Placaet-Boeck (pg. 26) and is significantly classified under the heading of *Fundamentele Wetten* (that is, Fundamental Laws). The preamble to that Act contains, *inter alia,* the affirmation of the following principle (in free translation; the original is in Dutch):

> Everybody knows that a Prince is appointed by God as head of his subjects in order to preserve and protect them from all wrongs, excessive burdens, and violence as a shepherd to guard his flock and that subjects have not been created by God for the benefit of the Prince, to obey him in everything he commands, whether divine or profane, right or wrong and to serve him as slaves, but the Prince is appointed for the welfare of his subjects (without whom there would be no Prince), to govern them justly and reasonably and to protect them and love them as a father protects and loves his children. And when he does not do this, but instead of protecting his subjects seeks to oppress them and deprive them of their ancient liberties and use them as slaves he must be regarded not as a Prince but as a tyrant. Then the estates of the land may depose him and elect another in his place.

William the Silent, Prince of Orange, succeeded Philip II of Spain as the supreme but constitutional executive authority of the United Netherlands and it is interesting to note that a little over a century after the passing of the Act of Abjuration of the States-General, England made the famous Declaration of Rights under which another William, also a Prince of Orange and a great-grandson of William the Silent, ascended the English throne.

I can, perhaps, best illustrate the rule of law as applied in my country by referring to various provisions in your Constitution and ascertaining to what extent the principles enshrined in those provisions are recognized in my own country. Article I, Section 9 of your Constitution provides, *inter alia,* that "the privilege of the writ of *habeas corpus* shall not be suspended, unless when in cases of rebellion or invasion the public safety may require it." No such guarantee is to be found in the Constitution of the Union of South Africa nor is the term *habeas corpus* in use among us. In Roman-Dutch law which jealously safeguarded the liberty of the individual the writ is known as the writ *de homine libero exhibendo* and as indicated by Chief Justice de Villiers in the case of *In re Willem Kok* (1879 Buch. (vol. 9) 45 at p. 64) the common law rights of personal liberty enjoyed by the inhabitants of South Africa are for practical purposes the same as those under the writ of *habeas corpus.* In 1895 Chief Justice de Villiers heard a case which caused a great deal of excitement in political circles. That was the case of *Sigcau v. The Queen* (12 Sup. Ct. Cape of G.H. 256 & 283). Sigcau was a native chief living in Pondoland. He was a source of irritation to the Government. Pondoland had recently been annexed to the Cape Colony and section 2 of the Pondoland Annexation Act of 1894 gave authority to the Governor of Cape Colony to add such laws as "he shall from time to time declare in force in such territories" to the existing laws, already proclaimed and in force in the territories annexed. Professing to act under this provision the Governor issued a proclamation which set aside the established law of Pondoland with respect to arrest, trial and conviction, and punishment, and condemned Sigcau untried and unheard to imprisonment, the place and duration of his captivity being left to the uncontrolled will of the Governor. This proclamation was countersigned by Cecil John Rhodes who was then Prime Minister and Minister of Native Affairs of Cape Colony. Under this proclamation Sigcau was arrested and kept in captivity. He applied to the Supreme Court for his release and his application was vigorously opposed by the Attorney-General. Chief Justice de Villiers in granting the application firmly upheld the independence of the judiciary and the duty of the judiciary to come to the assistance of those whose liberty was interfered with without justification in law. In two striking sentences he said: "The Civil Courts have but one duty to perform and that is to administer the law without fear or favor or prejudice, independent of the consequences that may ensue. . . With a full sense of responsibility resting on this Court I am of opinion that the Proclamation relied on has not the force of law and that the petitioner must be discharged from further custody." The Government appealed to the Privy Council which dismissed the appeal.

Coming now to your Bill of Rights which embodies the first ten amendments to your Constitution it may be stated generally that the provisions contained in the first nine amendments may be regarded as constitutional conventions applicable to the Union of South Africa, any one of which Parliament is, in law, entitled to infringe.

Under your due process of law provision which was embodied in the Fifth Amendment there can, I assume, be no violation of the maxim *audi alteram partem*. There are numerous judicial decisions in South Africa in which it has been held that, when a statute empowers a public official to give a decision prejudicially affecting the property or liberty of an individual, the individual has a right to be heard before action is taken against him, unless the statute expressly or by necessary implication indicates the contrary or unless (possibly) there are exceptional circumstance, such as a national emergency, which would justify the Court's not giving effect to the maxim. "Sacred though the maxim is held to be," said Chief Justice Stratford in *Sachs v. Minister of Justice* ([1934] Sup. Ct. So. Af. Ap. Div. 11 at p.38), "Parliament is free to violate it. In all cases where by judicial interpretation it has been invoked, this has been justified on the ground that the enactment impliedly incorporated it. When on the true interpretation of the Act the implication is excluded there is an end of the matter."

The right to be heard before you are deprived of your life, liberty, or property is a fundamental constitutional convention but, here again, there is nothing to prevent Parliament from infringing that convention.

There are other provisions in your Fifth Amendment which may be regarded as constitutional conventions in South Africa, namely; that no person shall "be subject for the same offence to be twice put in jeopardy of life or limb"; that no person "shall be compelled . . . to be a witness against himself . . . nor shall private property be taken for public use, without just compensation." Those principles are generally observed in South Africa but it is interesting to note that under the Insolvency Act of 1936 it is provided that a person interrogated at a meeting of creditors is not entitled to refuse to answer a question upon the ground that the answer would tend to incriminate him and that any evidence given by him is admissible in any proceedings against him. This you may regard as a drastic provision but it serves as an example of the unfettered power of the Parliament of the Union.

The Fifth Amendment also provides that "No person shall be held to answer for a capital, or otherwise infamous crime, unless on a presentment or indictment of a Grand Jury," excepting in certain specified cases. In South Africa we have no grand jury system but before an accused is tried before a Superior Court a preparatory examination is held before a magistrate and it is for the Attorney-General to decide whether the accused should be indicted before a Superior Court. Your Sixth Amendment carries the matter further and provides that "In all criminal prosecutions, the accused shall enjoy the right to a speedy and public trial, by an impartial jury. . ." So it may be said that the right of trial by jury is firmly established in your Constitution.

Lord Justice Atkin (as he was then), stated in 1922 that "trial by jury has been the bulwark of liberty." There is no doubt that this method of trial is highly prized both in your country and in England and yet there have not been wanting eminent critics of that method. Dicey in his *Law of the Constitution* (9th Ed. p. 394) says that "trial by jury is open to much criticism; a distinguished French thinker may be right in holding that this habit of submitting difficult problems of fact to the decision of twelve men of not more than average education will in the near future be considered an absurdity as patent as ordeal by battle." This prophesy has been proved to be incorrect, for trial by jury is still, and is likely to continue to be, regarded in Anglo-Saxon countries as the palladium of liberty. Stephen in his *History of the Criminal Law of England* (Vol. I, p. 566) says that trial by jury "is perhaps the most popular of all our institutions, and has certainly been made the subject of a kind and degree of eulogy which no institution can possibly deserve." Fulsome praise carries with it its own dangers and it is impossible to generalize on the subject. The great merit of the jury system is that it brings the ordinary man and woman into a close relationship with the administration of justice; it makes them feel that the people of the country are in-
in holding that this habit of submitting difficult problems of
the law of the land but no institution run by human beings can be perfect, for all human beings are fallible and a human agency like a jury may work well in a country with a homogeneous population but work badly in multi-racial countries or in countries where political passions run high. In South Africa serious inroads have been made into the jury system. Experience has shown that it was in the interests of justice that such inroads should be made. In 1917 the Union

Parliament passed the Criminal Procedure and Evidence Code which brought about important alterations in the system of criminal trials before Superior Courts. Under section 215 it is provided that the Minister of Justice may in cases of treason and sedition order a trial by a court consisting of two or three judges. This may appear to you to be a drastic provision but it is a provision which for practical purposes comes into operation only in times of revolutionary passion when in the view of Dicey (loc. cit. p. 395) "trial by jury cannot secure respect for justice." Another far-reaching inroad on the jury system was made in section 216 which conferred on an accused person the right of electing to be tried without a jury. This right was freely exercised. Cynics take the view that innocent men prefer to be tried without a jury. The trial judge may summon to his assistance one or two assessors and in murder and rape cases he *must* summon two assessors. When a judge sits with assessors the assessors have an equal say with the judge on the facts. Another change brought about by the 1917 Act was that the verdict of a jury need not be unanimous. A majority of 7 to 2 is sufficient for a conviction or an acquittal.

By subsequent legislation further inroads have been made into the jury system. The Minister of Justice is empowered to order trial before a judge and two assessors in cases where the complainant is a white person and the accused is a non-white person and vice versa and also where a knowledge of accounting is essential for the proper adjudication of the case. The power given to the Minister to order a trial without a jury in cases where the parties are not both whites marks a great advance in the administration of impartial justice. Experience in the past showed that where a non-white was charged with having committed a crime on a white he invariably elected to be tried without a jury; in the converse case the accused elected to be tried with a jury. In the latter type of case there could be no reasonable certainty that justice would be done and cases did occur where it was patent that a guilty person was acquitted. Last year there was a further amendment of the law. Prior to that amendment trial by jury was the usual or ordinary procedure: now such a trial is exceptional, for if an accused wishes to be tried by a jury he must specifically ask for such a trial within a stipulated period. If he makes no such request within the stipulated period he is tried without a jury.

Today quite 80 per cent of criminal trials before a Superior Court take place without a jury as most accused persons prefer to be so tried. This means, of course, that a greater burden is placed on the judges than was the position when trial took place before a jury. For a trial judge must give his findings on the facts and he cannot pass that burden on to a jury. There is one great advantage to an accused person if he is tried without a jury. A jury in finding an accused person guilty gives no reasons and although there is a right of appeal from a verdict of a jury if leave is granted that right is in practice of very little value, for if there is any evidence on which a jury can reasonably convict, the conviction cannot be upset on appeal unless there has been some irregularity in the proceedings or some fault in the summing up to the jury. But when an accused is tried by a judge with or without assessors the judge gives reasons when he convicts the accused. It is always dangerous to give reasons for those reasons may be unsound. The Court of Appeal knows from those reasons the inference drawn by the trial court from the evidence and which of the witnesses, whether for the State or the accused, are credible or not, and, while it is always reluctant to differ from a finding of fact by a trial court, it is at liberty to do so when it considers that the State has not proved the guilt of the accused beyond reasonable doubt. Having been intimately concerned in the administration of justice in South Africa for the past forty years I think that I am entitled to say that by trial and error we have succeeded in working out in South Africa a system of trying criminal cases in which, as far as is humanly possible, impartial justice is administered.

Now just a few words about trial by jury in civil cases.

Up to 1927 a party to civil proceedings in the Provinces of the Cape of Good Hope and Natal could demand a trial by jury in civil cases. Dicey says (loc. cit. p. 398) that "juries are often biassed against the Government." Dicey's view was clearly borne out by my experience at the Bar for sixteen years before trial by jury in civil cases was abolished. I cannot remember a single case in which a jury found a verdict for the Government. Juries seem to have gone on the principle that the Government can afford to pay. That principle certainly relieved them of the difficulty of ascertaining the facts before arriving at their verdict. They applied the same principle when public bodies or corporations were sued. No tears were shed in South Africa when trial by jury in civil cases was abolished.

Ladies and gentlemen, I have attempted in the short time at my disposal to give you in broad outline some idea of the Constitution of my own country, its unwritten conventions, and the rule of law as applied there. Let me in conclusion make a few general remarks. As long as the principle of government under law is faithfully observed by the Legislature, the Executive, and the Judiciary of any country, the liberty and dignity of the individual living in that country will be safe. A written constitution, even if it purports to enshrine that principle, is of little avail unless it is honored in the letter and the spirit. When a constitution is silent about the principle of government under law, the unwritten conventions must be relied on in order to uphold that principle, and this necessitates an enlightened electorate. These are the considerations why I regard this great Conference as being of prime importance to mankind; it will, I hope, focus the mind of the world upon what may be described as the essentials of true democracy. There are undoubtedly difficulties in this modern world of ours where the sphere of governmental activities seems to increase from day to day—an increase which often tends to result in the curtailment of the liberty of the individual—and it is the task of those who are competent to do so, to suggest ways and means of overcoming those difficulties. Today the issue lies between democracy and totalitarianism. That issue has to be faced with courage and determination, and in fighting totalitarianism of whatever kind care must be taken not to adopt the technique of the totalitarian—if such care is not taken, then the human values which we of the Western world cherish as the hallmark of true civilization will be destroyed.

VI

This session of the Conference was held in the Ames Courtroom in Austin Hall. Professor Arthur Sutherland* of the Harvard Law School was chairman. Again the proceeding consisted of two parts—an address by the Chief Justice of Canada, and a discussion of the papers written by Judge Charles Wyzanski, Jr., and Mr. John Lord O'Brian on the fourth theme of the conference, "The Value of Constitutionalism Today."

The members of the Conference first heard Chief Justice Patrick Kerwin, of Canada, present his address, "Constitutionalism in Canada."

* ARTHUR EUGENE SUTHERLAND, *Professor of Law, Harvard Law School.* Professor Sutherland was born in Rochester, New York in 1902, took his A.B. at Wesleyan in 1922 and his LL.B. at Harvard Law School in 1925. Between 1926 and 1941 he practiced law in the State of New York with interruptions for service as law Secretary to Justice Oliver Wendell Holmes, and as a member of the 1938 Constitutional Convention of his State. He served in the Army from 1941 to 1945 in various units including the First Infantry Division and the Fifth Army. He was appointed Professor of Law at Cornell in 1945; since 1950 he has been a Professor at Harvard Law School. He has been co-editor and co-author of books on public and private law subjects.

ADDRESS

Constitutionalism in Canada

PATRICK KERWIN *

It is a privilege and a pleasure to do honor to the memory of the great Chief Justice whose judgments are so often quoted not only in the United States, but in many other countries and not least in Canada. Throughout the length and breadth of Canada his opinions are from time to time referred to and particularly those dealing with the construction of the Constitution of the United States. He had a robust mind which, coupled with a felicity of expression, enabled him to put in trenchant terms the philosophy of the Constitution and to infuse its majestic outlines with a living spirit. The free peoples of the world are indebted to him and are happy to take part in a discussion of the general subject of this Conference.

It is apparent from a perusal of the papers published for the purposes of this gathering under the heading "Government under Law" that more than one meaning may be attached to the term "constitutionalism" even in the United States, and that when one goes beyond the confines of the Republic even greater variations may be found. As it was intimated that a discussion of The British North America Act, 1867, as amended, might be of some interest, that suggestion will be followed, although it must be immediately emphasized that it is only the *written* Constitution of Canada, and, as will subsequently appear, there are other matters to be considered in applying the term to that country.

* HON. PATRICK KERWIN, *Chief Justice of Canada.* Chief Justice Kerwin was born in 1889. He studied law at Osgoode Hall in Toronto, was called to the bar of Ontario in 1911, became King's Counsel in 1928, and became a Justice of the Supreme Court of Ontario in 1932. In 1935, he became a Justice of the Supreme Court of Canada, and in 1954 he became Chief Justice.

The Act was enacted by the Parliament of Great Britain and Ireland in 1867 following conferences at Charlottetown, in Prince Edward Island, Quebec City, and London, England, but it is impossible to understand what was accomplished thereby without a brief—and I emphasize the word brief — historical summary. Following the wars between France and England, the latter became the sovereign power over a great part of what is now Canada, although certain areas had been settled and not conquered. The Treaty of Paris of 1763 was followed by the Quebec Act of 1774 and then by the Constitutional Act of 1791, under which Upper Canada and Lower Canada were established. These two were united by the Act of Union of 1840 and became the Province of Canada, so that the title of the Act of 1867 is "An Act for the Union of Canada, Nova Scotia, and New Brunswick, and the Government thereof; and for Purposes connected therewith." Provision was made and steps subsequently taken for the admission and creation of other provinces so that at the present time there are ten in all. Nova Scotia and New Brunswick, as well as the others now forming part of Canada, had a long and eventful history as colonies or as parts of the old Northwest Territories. The old Province of Canada was re-subdivided to form two separate provinces under the names of Ontario and Quebec. So much for that history.

After the establishment of the United States of America its history and development and that of the colonies to the north proceeded along different lines. Many of the battles for representative and responsible government had been fought and won before 1867. While the War of 1812 had passed into history, the Union would, in the words of one of the recitals of The British North America Act, "conduce to the Welfare of the Provinces and promote the Interests of the British Empire." Conditions varied in the four provinces, particularly in Quebec where the overwhelming majority of the population were French and Roman Catholic, while in the other provinces the great majority were English-speaking and Protestant. In the former, the basis of the civil law was French, while in the latter, save as altered by statute, the English common law held full sway. In all of them the criminal law, save as varied by local enactments, was English.

At the conferences preceding the enactment of the Act considerable attention was directed to the Constitution of the United States but it was considered advisable to endow the legislatures of the provinces exclusively with power to make laws in relation to matters coming within certain enumerated classes of subjects, being, in general, local matters which solely affect a province (section 92) and to confer the residue of legislative authority upon the Parliament of the new entity, Canada (section 91), although in that section there is also an enumeration. Nowhere does the Act empower any court to declare an Act of Parliament, or of a legislature, *ultra vires.* However, the authority of the Privy Council in England had for years been exercised in deciding appeals from the colonial courts, in conjunction with a legislative and executive authority exerted by the disallowance of colonial legislation. The Privy Council treated as invalid and void ordinances and statutes of colonial legislatures when they exceeded the powers committed to them, or when they had neglected to observe a prohibition contained in the charter of government. In fact, the colonial courts themselves declined to give effect to legislation which had been enacted in contravention of some such restriction. Although considerably amplified, that would appear to be one of the bases of the argument of James Otis in the case of General Warrants, and it is considered by some that this practice of the Privy Council and of the colonial courts prepared the way for the ultimate adoption by the people of the United States of the principle and practice of the judicial review of legislation. In colonial days the superior authority was the Sovereign, either in Council or in Parliament, but after the Revolution that became in the new republic the sovereignty of the people.

Whatever the origin, the power was exercised during

Chief Justice Marshall's incumbency with respect to state and federal legislation. In Canada the courts have exercised a similar jurisdiction in connection with legislation of the Parliament of Canada and of the legislatures of the provinces. There is allotted to the latter by Head 14 of section 92 authority to make laws in relation to "The Administration of Justice in the Province, including the Constitution, Maintenance, and Organization of Provincial Courts, both of Civil and Criminal Jurisdiction, and including Procedure in Civil Matters in those Courts." By Head 27 of section 91 which is the one conferring powers upon Parliament, the latter is empowered to make laws in relation to "The Criminal Law, except the Constitution of Courts of Criminal Jurisdiction, but including the Procedure in Criminal Matters." And as a result, a criminal code has been enacted which holds sway over the whole of the Dominion, although the duty and the power of taking steps to see that the law is complied with—the criminal law—rests upon provincial officials. By another section (96), the Governor General, which means the representative of the Monarch acting on the advice of the Canadian Cabinet, is to appoint the judges of the Superior, District, and County courts in each province, except those of the Courts of Probate in Nova Scotia and New Brunswick. Magistrates, justices of the peace, and some others may be appointed by a province. Section 101 enacts as follows:

> The Parliament of Canada may, notwithstanding anything in this Act, from Time to Time, provide for the Constitution, Maintenance, and Organization of a general Court of Appeal for Canada, and for the Establishment of any other additional Courts for the better Administration of the Laws of Canada.

It was pursuant thereto that the Supreme Court of Canada was established in 1875.

Subject to what is later stated as to the Exchequer Court, the provincial courts, whether the members are appointed by Canada or the provinces, deal with federal and provincial matters alike and The Supreme Court Act provides for and regulates appeals from their decisions, so that the Supreme Court of Canada is a general court of appeal. At first appeals could be taken to the Judicial Committee of the Privy Council from the provincial Courts of Appeal and, by leave of the Committee, from the Supreme Court of Canada. Pursuant to the Imperial Statute of Westminster of 1931, enacted as a result of conferences among representatives of Great Britain and the Dominions, an amendment to The Supreme Court Act was passed by Parliament in 1933 abolishing appeals to the Privy Council in criminal cases and in 1935 this amendment was held valid by the Judicial Committee.[1] In December, 1949, another amendment was enacted abolishing appeals in civil cases from any court in Canada, which the courts, including the Judicial Committee, also upheld in 1940 and ultimately in 1947,[2] and, therefore, at the present time, The Supreme Court of Canada is the final court of appeal for the country, except as to civil matters commenced before that time—that is, 1949. It has a qualified original jurisdiction by which every member of the Court "except in matters arising out of any claim for extradition under any treaty, has concurrent jurisdiction with the courts or judges of the several provinces, to issue the writ of *habeas corpus ad subjiciendum,* for the purpose of an inquiry into the cause of commitment in any criminal case under any Act of the Parliament of Canada."[3]

The only other additional court for the better administration of the laws of Canada established by Parliament is the Exchequer Court, dealing with such matters as patents, trademarks, copyrights, revenue, and expropriations by, and claims against, Canada. It also has jurisdiction in admiralty cases. Appeals lie in most cases from the decisions of that court to the Supreme Court of Canada.

Now in all courts the question may be raised as to the validity of Canadian or provincial statutes and, in addition

1. British Coal Corporation v. The King, [1935] A.C. 500 (P.C.).
2. Reference Re An Act to Amend The Supreme Court Act (1940) S.C.R. 49; (1947) A.C. 127.
3. Supreme Court Act, R.S.C. 1952, c. 259, s. 57.

thereto, the Supreme Court Act from its very inception provided for the giving of advice by the Court upon certain questions that might be submitted to it by the Governor General in Council. What follows for a moment was really inserted at the suggestion of several friends of mine from the United States, who expressed some surprise, shall I say, at the inclusion of such a power, and some concern as to how it operated. This provision is now to be found in section 55 of the Supreme Court Act, and for the reasons I have given —it is not very long—I shall quote it.

> (1) Important questions of law or fact touching
> (a) the interpretation of the British North America Acts;
> (b) the constitutionality or interpretation of any Dominion or provincial legislation;
> (c) the appellate jurisdiction as to educational matters, by the British North America Act, 1867, or by any other Act or law vested in the Governor in Council;
> (d) the powers of the Parliament of Canada, or of the legislatures of the provinces, or of the respective governments thereof, whether or not the particular power in question has been or is proposed to be exercised; or
> (e) any other matter, whether or not in the opinion of the Court *ejusdem generis* with the foregoing enumerations, with reference to which the Governor in Council sees fit to submit any such question; may be referred by the Governor in Council to the Supreme Court for hearing and consideration; and any question touching any of the matters aforesaid, so referred by the Governor in Council, shall be conclusively deemed to be an important question.

Considerable discussion occurred before this was written in the Act, but it was acted upon in a number of cases and when the question was squarely raised it was held by the Judicial Committee of the Privy Council in 1912 in a case of the Attorney General of Ontario against the Attorney General of Canada that that provision was *intra vires* Parliament.[4]

I had written here, before I arrived at Harvard, that that system was adopted notwithstanding the fact that in the

---

4. A.G. of Ontario v. A.G. of Canada, [1912] A.C. 571 (P.C.).

United States it had been decided to confer no such power upon any court in your country. Since my arrival here, I take it that that statement must be qualified, certainly so far as Massachusetts, as I am informed, is concerned, because of certain powers that exist in this state. Difficulties sometimes arise, caused by the generality of the questions put, but, on the whole, the jurisdiction has not been used extensively and it has served the useful purpose of obtaining an authoritative pronouncement upon the legality of actual, or proposed, legislation, without putting a litigant to the trouble and expense of raising the issue and carrying it through several courts. For the same reason that I indicated a moment ago, I give you a recent example, in fact, so recent that the judgment has not yet been reported.[5] It is found in a dispute that had occurred as to the labor union which should represent the employees of a stevedoring company at Toronto whose operations consisted exclusively of services rendered in connection with the loading and unloading of ships, all of which were operated on regular schedules between ports in Canada and ports outside of Canada. Collective agreements had been entered into by the company and one union but another applied to the Ontario Labour Relations Board—a provincial one—for certification as the bargaining agent of the same employees and that Board decided that it had jurisdiction to hear the application and to deal with it on the merits. The first union applied to the Supreme Court of Ontario for an order quashing the decision, or, in the alternative, for an order prohibiting the Board from taking proceedings with respect to the application. The Attorney General of Ontario intervened and notified the Attorney General of Canada that in those proceedings the constitutional validity would be brought into question of an Act of the Parliament of Canada to provide for the investigation, conciliation, and settlement of industrial disputes. An order of reference by the Governor General in Council was made in order to settle the dispute

5. Reference Re Industrial Relations and Disputes Act, [1955] Sup. Ct. Can. 529.

and obtain the opinion of the Supreme Court of Canada as to the jurisdiction of Parliament to enact the statute. And the result was, instead of taking perhaps two years or more, the matter was decided in the course of, roughly, one year.

All of the provinces have enacted similar clauses authorizing references by the Lieutenant Governor in Council to the Provincial Court of Appeal. Coupled with those clauses is a provision that the opinion is to be considered a judgment, and, therefore, by virtue of a section of the Supreme Court Act of Canada an appeal may be taken to that Court from the Provincial Court of Appeal.[6]

Thus The British North America Act provides a division of legislative authority between Parliament and Legislature and the all-pervading jurisdiction of the courts warrants that neither may encroach upon the territory of the other with impunity. That is one example of constitutionalism, or government under law. That branch is important in a federation even if, as has been asserted by some writers in Canada, The British North America Act is a highly specialized kind of federalism.[7] It is indeed necessary in a country covering such a large area and following different traditions and possessing diversified economies. And while every decision of the courts has not met with unqualified approval from the bar and, shall I add, the commentators, that is merely an indication that any form of federalism and judicial supervision is subject to strain and stress.

Few amendments to the Act have been made altering the allocation of legislative jurisdiction. One, in 1940, was the insertion of Head 2(a) in section 91 conferring power upon Parliament to make laws in relation to unemployment insurance.[8] The date, 1940, is significant, following, as it did, the impact of the serious days that we experienced in Can-

---

6. Supreme Court Act, R.S.C. 1952, c. 259, s. 37.

7. Professor Scott, *The Special Nature of Canadian Federalism* (1943) 13 Can. Journal of Economics and Political Science 13, referred to by Hon. Mr. Justice Vincent C. Macdonald in *The Privy Council and the Canadian Constitution* (1951) 29 CAN. BAR REVIEW, 1021 at 1031.

8. U.K. Statutes of 1940, c. 36.

ada, as well as here, about 1939 and 1940. Another was in 1949 by the enactment of Head I reading a matter of several pages which I shall skip because I think I can state fairly or give you fairly a summary of it.

The object of this last amendment is to permit Canada to amend the Constitution—that is, Canada as distinct from the provinces—subject to qualifications, so far as relates to the powers of the nation as distinguished from those of the provinces. Exactly what will be done under it is a matter awaiting development. There is in it a reference to schools and language. The position of each of these subjects in the various provinces cannot be adequately covered on this occasion and it must suffice to state that the Act of 1867, and later Acts dealing with the admission or creation of other provinces, contain certain provisions relating to education; and that as to language, section 133 provides as follows:

> Either the English or the French language may be used by any Person in the Debates of the Houses of the Parliament of Canada and of the Houses of the Legislature of Quebec; and both those Languages shall be used in the respective Records and Journals of those Houses; and either of those Languages may be used by any Person or in any Pleading or Process in or issuing from any Court of Canada established under this Act, and in or from all or any of the Courts of Quebec.
>
> The Acts of the Parliament of Canada and of the Legislature of Quebec shall be printed and published in both those Languages.

I might mention shortly two other points. First, under section 95 of the Act concurrent powers of legislation respecting agriculture and immigration are vested in the provincial legislatures and in Parliament, but, in case of repugnancy, enactments of the latter prevail. Secondly, by section 125, "No lands or property belonging to Canada or any Province shall be liable to Taxation."

Now legislative jurisdiction being thus divided and the power of the courts to ensure its continuation being present, what is the position of the individual or corporation desirous of questioning any proceeding purportedly taken under *intra vires* enactments of Parliament or a legislature? In these days of delegated authority it is particularly important that the delegate should be restricted to the authority conferred upon him and jurisdiction exists by way of the well-known writs of *habeas corpus, certiorari, mandamus,* and *quo warranto* in a hierarchy of courts to determine the rights under such enactments. These methods are recognized and authorized by other statutory provisions of the proper legislative authorities. Thus, no man is made to suffer in body, in mind, or goods, except for a distinct breach of law established in a legal manner before the ordinary tribunals.

The legislative power in Canada is conferred upon the Houses of Parliament consisting of an elected House of Commons and a Senate whose members are appointed for life by the Government from the different sections of the country in a fixed proportion. In the provinces there is only a Legislative Assembly, save in Quebec, where there is a Legislative Council consisting of members appointed by the Lieutenant Governor in Council. Within the ambit of their respective powers the Parliament of Canada and the provincial legislatures are supreme.

The agitation as to the incorporation of a Bill of Rights in the Canadian Constitution led to an Order of Reference by the Senate in 1950 to a Special Committee of that body on Human Rights and Fundamental Freedoms. Witnesses were heard and briefs submitted to the Committee which reported to the Senate in favor of the inclusion of certain recommendations into the written Constitution. The difficulty was realized of meeting the wishes of the provinces in providing for such matters and that it would, therefore, be necessary for conferences to be held between representatives of Canada and of the provinces. The Committee's report was adopted by the Senate; later resolutions along similar lines have been introduced by private Members in the House of Commons, but without reaching a vote; and there the matter rests.

The contention against these endeavors is based upon

the effect in practice of the first recital in the British North America Act of 1867, which reads as follows:

> WHEREAS the Provinces of Canada, Nova Scotia and New Brunswick have expressed their Desire to be federally united into One Dominion under the Crown of the United Kingdom of Great Britain and Ireland, with a Constitution similar in Principle to that of the United Kingdom:—

Except for the radical differences between a federation and a unitary state like Great Britain, the Constitution of the United Kingdom applies not only to Canada but also to each of its ten provinces. Sir Ivor Jennings has pointed out that with the exception of the Instrument of Government which made Cromwell Lord Protector and established a new legislature, Britain has never had a written constitution, and that "If a Constitution consists of institutions and not of the paper that describes them the British Constitution had not been made but has grown—and there is no paper."[9] In his lectures delivered at the University of Toronto in 1921, under the Marfleet Foundation, Sir Robert Borden, who was the Prime Minister of Canada during the first Great War, pointed out that the great constitutional change in various provinces before confederation by which responsibility of the executive to the legislative body came to be established was not based upon any statutory provision but was consummated by the adoption of a recognized convention.[10] Since the date of his lectures, 1921, other constitutional changes have occurred but it must be noted that the Act itself provides that bills for appropriating any part of the public revenue or for imposing any tax or impost shall originate in the House of Commons[11] and that that House may not adopt or pass any vote, resolution, address, or bill, for the appropriation of any part of the public revenue or of any tax or impost to any purpose that has not been first recommended to it by message of the Governor General in the session in which such vote, resolu-

9. The Law and the Constitution, 3rd ed., pp. 7-8.
10. Borden, Canadian Constitutional Studies, 1922, pp. 45-46.
11. Section 53.

tion, address or bill is proposed.[12] This ensures that no bill which might be termed "a money Bill" may be introduced except by the Government.

In connection with the gradual evolution of the Canadian Constitution, it is interesting to notice that for various reasons some of Chief Justice Marshall's opinions on the written Constitution of the United States have been distinguished even in the Republic. His famous dictum, which has been referred to earlier in these proceedings, that "the power to tax involves the power to destroy"[13] was capped by Mr. Justice Holmes' epigram,[14] "The power to tax is not the power to destroy while this Court sits," and several decisions of the Supreme Court of the United States based upon the dictum were finally reversed by that Court in another well-known case of *Graves v. New York.*[15] In the meantime in 1939, in the case of *Abbott v. The City of St. John,*[16] the Supreme Court of Canada had held that subsection 2 of section 92 of The British North America Act giving provincial legislatures exclusive powers of legislation in respect to "direct taxation within the province," was not in conflict with subsection 8 of section 91 which provides that the Parliament of Canada shall have exclusive legislative authority over "the fixing of and providing for the salaries and allowances of civil and other officers of the Government of Canada," and, therefore, the legislature of a province had the right to impose income tax upon Canadian officials' salaries paid to them in the province. In a case of *Caron v. The King*[17] in 1922, it was decided by the Supreme Court of Canada that Parliament had the right to impose income taxes upon the salaries of provincial officials. This was affirmed by the Judicial Committee of the Privy Council[18] and followed in two

12. Section 54.
13. McCulloch v. Maryland, 4 Wheat. (U.S.) 316 at 431 (1819).
14. Pan-handle Oil Company v. Mississippi, 277 U.S. 218 at 223 (1927).
15. 306 U.S. 466 (1939).
16. 40 Can. Sup. Ct. 597 (1908).
17. 64 Can. Sup. Ct. 255 (1922).
18. Caron v. The King, [1924] A.C. 999 (P.C.).

other cases, the last of which is known as *Judges v. A.G. of Saskatchewan,* [19] and which decided that, shall I say, even judicial emoluments are not protected by any paramount principle making inapplicable to such income a tax imposed by a statute in terms wide enough to include it. Neither the independence, it was held, nor any other attribute of the judiciary could be affected by a general income tax which charged their official incomes on the same footing as the incomes of other citizens.

To turn to another field, it was pointed out in one of the opinions in *In re Storgoff*[20] a decision of the Supreme Court of Canada in 1945 that a statement by Chief Justice Marshall in a case of *Ex parte Bollman and Swartwout*[21] in 1807 could not, in the court's opinion, be justified in view of a more thorough investigation than had been possible in 1807. The statement of the great Chief Justice read:

> It has been demonstrated at the bar, that the question brought forward on a *habeas corpus,* is always distinct from that which is involved in the cause itself. The question whether the individual shall be imprisoned is always distinct from the question whether he shall be convicted or acquitted of the charge on which he is to be tried, and therefore these questions are separated, and may be decided in different courts.

The Supreme Court of Canada held that certain provisions in The British Columbia Court of Appeal Act granting a right to the Provincial Attorney General to appeal to the Provincial Court of Appeal from an order of a single judge in *habeas corpus* proceedings freeing an individual were inoperative, if the applicant for that writ be detained in custody by virtue of a conviction for a criminal offence under the Criminal Code of Canada. Leaving aside the use of the writ of habeas corpus to determine questions of nurture and education of infants, a more comprehensive research had in the opinion of the court shown that while the writ is one to enforce a

19. 53 T.L.R. 464 (1937).
20. [1945] Can. Sup. Ct. 526.
21. 4 Cranch (U.S.) 75 (1807).

right to personal liberty, that right may have been infringed by process in criminal, or civil proceedings, and that in the instant case it was merely a step in the proceedings under which the applicant was imprisoned.

The growth of the British and Canadian constitutions from the days of the absolute sovereigns disputing with the barons has continued to the present era of constitutional monarchy. Under this system the Government of the day executes the authority conferred upon it, but its very life depends upon its retention of the confidence of the legislative body. When it is apparent that this condition no longer exists, the question of who shall carry on the Government is finally determined by the electors at the poll. This close affinity between the wishes of the ultimate masters and the resulting enactments is what may be described as a government of opinion. The preservation of fundamental rights, except as they are covered by The British North America Act, as amended, depends upon an enlightened public opinion and a history which, while it has had its dark days, has gradually evolved a system in which it is taken for granted that an alert public will see that the legislators keep an even balance between the rights and duties of the individual. In truth the individual is the most important fact in the world in all enlightened systems and it must be the aim of the State to preserve his natural rights while at the same time ensuring that the rights of one do not interfere with those of another.

Some of the provisions of The British North America Act must be read in view of the similarity in principle of the Canadian Constitution to that of the United Kingdom. For instance, section 9: "The executive government and authority of and over Canada is hereby declared to continue and be vested in the Queen." But this means that, in a constitutional monarchy, while the Sovereign is the head of the state, constitutional usage now demands that the executive power be exercised by and with the advice of Her Majesty's advisers. Those constitute the Government for the time being in Canada or the Provinces, as the case may be. The Governor

General, for whose appointment provision is made, represents the Sovereign and a stranger to the Constitution might be pardoned for thinking that his powers as to assenting to bills is absolute, if attention were directed only to sections 55, 56, and 57 of the Act. Section 55 reads:

> Where a Bill passed by the Houses of the Parliament is presented to the Governor General for the Queen's Assent, he shall declare, according to his Discretion, but subject to the Provisions of this Act and to Her Majesty's Instructions, either that he assents thereto in the Queen's Name, or that he withholds the Queen's Assent, or that he reserves the Bill for the Signification of the Queen's Pleasure.

Section 56 provides for disallowance of any Act assented to by the Governor General within two years after receipt thereof by the Secretary of State in Britain and section 57 enacts that any bill reserved by the Governor General for the signification of the Queen's pleasure is not to have any force unless within two years from the day on which it is presented to him the Governor General signifies that it has received the assent of the Queen in Council.

The Letters Patent appointing the Governor General were formerly either accompanied, or succeeded, by instructions suitable to the constitutional practice that was then in vogue as expressed in the sections mentioned. While it was not suggested in 1867 that the Sovereign might appoint a Governor General without the advice of the Imperial Cabinet, it is now settled that the appointment is made by the Sovereign on the recommendation of the Canadian Government. The form of the Letters Patent has been altered to meet the new conditions and at the present time assent to the bills passed by parliament is given as a matter of course. There is no power of reservation by the Governor General or of disallowance by the British Government.

By another section (90), the provisions of the Act respecting the Parliament of Canada as to assent to bills, the disallowance of Acts and the signification of pleasure on bills reserved shall extend and apply to the legislatures of the

Provinces. While in provincial affairs the Lieutenant Governor of each province, who is appointed by the Canadian Government, represents the Sovereign, the Supreme Court of Canada has held in a Reference in 1938[22] that the power of the Dominion to disallow within two years bills passed by the legislative authority of a province is still a subsisting power and its exercise is not subject to any legal limitations or restrictions. Needless to say, the Court was not concerned with the constitutional exercise of that power.

From something that was said to me in another connection before I arrived here, it occurred to me that you might be interested in section 5 of The Canada Evidence Act.[23] The first subsection speaks for itself:

> No witness shall be excused from answering any question upon the ground that the answer to such question may tend to criminate him, or may tend to establish the liability to a civil proceeding at the instance of the Crown or of any person.

Subsection (2) which I must quote in full is in these words:

> Where with respect to any question a witness objects to answer upon the ground that his answer may tend to criminate him, or may tend to establish his liability to a civil proceeding at the instance of the Crown or of any person, and if but for this Act, or the Act of any provincial legislature, the witness would therefore have been excused from answering such question, then although the witness is by reason of this Act, or by reason of such provincial Act, compelled to answer, the answer so given shall not be used or receivable in evidence against him in any criminal trial, or other criminal proceeding against him thereafter taking place, other than a prosecution for perjury in the giving of such evidence.

As long ago as 1873 it was held in connection with a somewhat similar provision by the Judicial Committee of the Privy Council:[24]

> that the depositions on Oath of a Witness legally taken are evidence against him, should he be subsequently tried on a criminal

22. Reference Re Power to Disallow Acts passed by Provincial Legislatures [1938] Can. Sup. Ct. 71. An appeal to the Judicial Committee was abandoned.
23. R.S.C. 1952 c. 307.
24. Regina v. Coote 4 L.R., P.C. 599 at 607 (1873).

> charge, except so much of them as consist of answers to questions to which he has objected as tending to criminate him, but which he has been improperly compelled to answer. The exception depends upon the principle . . . but does not apply to answers given without objection, which are to be deemed voluntary.

In 1947 this decision was applied by the Supreme Court of Canada in a case arising under the Criminal Code[25] and it was held that, if a person testifying does not claim the exemption, the evidence so given may be later used against him and this notwithstanding the fact that he may not have known of his rights.

In all of the provinces the legislatures have enacted provisions presumably with the same object in mind, but in 1955 the Supreme Court of Canada decided,[26] with reference to the British Columbia statute: first, the legislature could legislate only with reference to proceedings over which it had legislative authority; second, since it had coupled with the obligation to answer a proviso that the answer could not be used against him in proceedings under the Criminal Code of Canada, the proviso could not be severed from the rest of the section and, therefore, the whole was *ultra vires,* and the witness was entitled to rely upon his common law right to refuse to answer on the ground that to the best of his belief his answers to particular questions would tend to criminate him. It should be observed that this case was decided upon the provisions of the particular British Columbia statute and without considering the terms of any other provincial enactment.

A word might be added as to the operation of the Constitution in time of crisis. On the outbreak of war in 1914, Parliament passed the War Measures Act,[27] by section 6 of which:

> The Governor-in-Council shall have power to do and authorize such acts and things and to make from time to time such orders and regulations, as he may by reason of the existence of real

---

25. Tass v. The King [1947] Can. Sup. Ct. 103 (1946).
26. Klein v. Bell [1955] 2 D.L.R. 513.
27. STATUTES OF CANADA, 1914, 2d. Sess. Ch. 2.

> or apprehended war, invasion or insurrection, deem necessary or advisable for the security, defence, peace, order and welfare of Canada;

and for greater certainty there follows an enumeration of powers. It was held by the Supreme Court of Canada[28] in a case in 1918 that certain Orders-in-Council passed under the authority of this Act were *intra vires.* By The War Measures Act, Parliament absorbed practically the whole legislative field of the provinces for the purposes of the conduct of the war, and, in 1923, the Judicial Committee of the Privy Council held in a case in Fort Frances[29] that, under sections 91 and 92 of the Act, Parliament had an implied power for the safety of the Dominion as a whole to deal with a sufficiently great emergency such as that arising from war, although in so doing it trenches upon property and civil rights in the provinces from which subjects it is excluded in normal circumstances. It was accordingly held that The War Measures Act and Orders-in-Council made thereunder during the war for controlling throughout Canada the supply of newsprint paper by manufacturers and its price, and also an Act of Parliament passed after the cessation of hostilities for continuing the control until the proclamation of peace with power to conclude matters then pending were *intra vires.* Finally, in the case of the Japanese Canadians in 1947[30] Orders-in-Council passed under the authority of The War Measures Act and continued in force by an Order-in-Council passed pursuant to a section called The National Emergency Transitional Powers Act of 1935, were *intra vires.* The judgment of the Privy Council states: "The Parliament of the Dominion in a sufficiently great emergency, such as that arising out of war, has power to deal adequately with that emergency for the safety of the Dominion as a whole."

These are some aspects of constitutionalism as under-

28. Re George Edwin Gray, 57 Can. Sup. Ct. 150 (1918).
29. Fort Frances Pulp & Power Company, Limited v. Manitoba Free Press Company, Limited [1923] A.C. 695 (P.C.).
30. Cooperative Committee on Japanese Canadians v. A.G. for Canada [1947] A.C. 87 (P.C. 1946).

stood in Canada in times of peace and of war. I take it for granted that from what you have heard you are aware that, of course, in accordance with Anglo-American jurisprudence, we rely upon the maxim, or the statement, as to the presumed innocence of anyone accused of a crime. These aspects do not appear in precisely the same form in all countries that profess the dignity of man and take steps to uphold it, but it is an indication of the pervasiveness of this ideal in all these countries that, as de Tocqueville pointed out more than one hundred years ago in his *Democracy in America*,

> [The individual] obeys society, not because he is inferior to those who conduct it or because he is less capable than any other of governing himself, but because he acknowledges the utility of an association with his fellow men and he knows that no such association can exist without a regulating force. He is a subject in all that concerns the duties of citizens to each other; he is free, and responsible to God alone, for all that concerns himself.[31]

In all these lands to which I have referred the hymn and prayer described by one of our Canadian poets, Bliss Carman, may be raised and proclaimed to all the world:

> Praise for faith in freedom
> Our fighting fathers' stay,
> Born of dreams and daring,
> Bred above dismay.
>
> Prayer for cloudless vision,
> And the valiant hand,
> That the right may triumph
> To the last demand.[32]

---

31. Vintage Edition, vol. 1, c. 5, p. 67.

32. "In the Day of Battle," reprinted from BLISS CARMAN'S POEMS by permission of Dodd, Mead & Company, New York, McClelland and Stewart Limited, Toronto, and the Bliss Carman Trust, University of New Brunswick.

The Conference next turned to a discussion of the papers written by Judge Wyanski and Mr. John Lord O'Brian on the theme—"The Value of Constitutionalism Today."

The preceding three sessions had treated of the necessity of remedial institutions; of constitutionalism in times of crisis; and of the formulation of standards of due process. This fourth discussion sought an evaluation of the general concept of limited government in today's world.

Constitutionalism: Limitation and Affirmation

CHARLES E. WYZANSKI, JR.*

When F. W. Maitland lectured on *The Constitutional History of England* he postponed until his concluding chapter his definition of constitutional law, and this apparent inversion of the normal order is a precedent peculiarly appropriate for our discussion of constitutionalism. For although the dictionaries trace the evolution of the term from its first appearance in English on the eve of the Glorious Revolution, and men can thus readily agree upon what it meant in a specific place at a particular past time, the interpretation of its precise current connotations has little objective warrant and reflects largely a subjective political philosophy. So this paper attempts to understand what modern constitutionalism is by considering why the doctrine is so widely acclaimed by the lay public, how far the praise accorded it is questioned by those of unusual insight and candor in the academic and legal professions, what are the basic elements found in virtually all states universally recognized as constitutional, and to what extent these elements serve not merely as limitations upon arbitrary power but also as the source of an affirmative creed of political values.

To the layman constitutionalism never stood in higher esteem than now. The cruelties of the Nazi and Soviet totalitarian regimes have given horrible illustrations of Lord Acton's aphorism that "all power tends to corrupt, and absolute power corrupts absolutely", and have focussed popular concern upon the need of some avowed limitations upon political authority. This concern finds its natural expression in a renewed declaration of faith in the Western doctrine of constitutionalism—a doctrine so historically conditioned as to be more resistant to perverted explanations than the older, more

---

* For biographical note see page 490.

abstract terms "liberty", "freedom", and "democracy". For constitutionalism draws its main tenets from a clearly marked line of intellectual development to which outstanding contributors were the Stoic founders of natural law, the religious teachers of the dignity of man and of his duty "to render unto Caesar that which is Caesar's and unto God that which is God's", the mediaeval contestants seeking to establish or maintain immunities, privileges and licenses, the Eighteenth Century philosophers with whose names we associate theories of "social contract" and "separation of powers", and the leaders of the English, and American (and, to a lesser degree, the French) Revolutions. With due allowance for chauvinistic exaggeration, one might almost say that the doctrine reached not perfection but maturity in Philadelphia in 1789. At any rate that particular embodiment of the principles of constitutionalism, as Lord Radcliffe reminded us in The Reith Lectures, "was one of the most important events in modern history."

The political conceptions of the Founding Fathers and the instruments they devised for their realization spread throughout the world, particularly in English-speaking countries, in Western Europe and, in form at least, in Latin America. And the pace of apparent if not real influence has been recently accelerated. Since the end of World War II the United States Constitution has been among the important influences shaping organic charters adopted in fifty different nations.

In this country loyalty to the Constitution has become what in *The American Dilemma* Gunnar Myrdal quite correctly described as part of "the American creed". All observers recognize the practical role the United States Constitution played in uniting under one symbol men of diverse racial, religious, and cultural backgrounds, and in facilitating the expansion of a small settlement of colonial peoples into first a continental and then a world power. Indeed the American Constitution is almost the classic case to prove Whitehead's proposition that "The art of free society consists first in the maintenance of the symbolic code" for "when we examine how a society bends its individual members to function in conformity with its needs, we discover that one important operative agency is our vast system of inherited symbolism."

Yet although conceding constitutionalism's record of practical accomplishment and its continued symbolic value, some of our most penetrating professional thinkers are disturbed lest we put too high our value of its present worth as compared with other possible approaches to the never ending attempt to accommodate the rival claims of authority and the individual.

For the moment we may lay aside criticisms founded on the failure of constitutionalism in ordinary times effectively to cover all its claimed area, and in extraordinary times fully to maintain all its asserted barriers. Such criticisms, no matter how well buttressed by facts, have only a secondary importance. No doctrine of politics or indeed of human behavior, no code, legal, moral, or religious, grasps all it seeks to reach, or commands perfect obedience under stress. And while it is important in assessing a doctrine of politics or law to know how far it is a rule adhered to in practice, the questions which the learned raise as to the value of constitutionalism probe much deeper. Their challenge is based not on a narrow statistical chart of constitutionalism's day to day performance of its promise, but on the broader analysis these critics make of the structure of modern society, the problem of power, and their view of the insignificance of legal institutions compared with popular habits in maintaining the standards of a society.

Of doubts as to constitutionalism's value today the most radical is the view that its assumptions reflect and its remedies are addressed to a world that no longer exists. Constitutionalism, according to this approach, presupposes an unplanned society where the economic and social as well as the political system is highly individualistic. It coincides with the existence of small-scale capitalism. It takes for granted that most men are either self-employed or employed by enterprises that are within the measure of their understanding. It assumes that men live in communities where they mingle freely with their neighbors, exchanging views with workers from varied occupations, and assessing not merely their character but their competence. Not only are the economic, social, and political dimensions comprehensible by the average man, but the conflicts of interest are at least obscured and minimized, if not eliminated, by the common life, the constant scope afforded for discussion and the exercise of reason, and the consensual selection of leaders intimately appraised. In such an atmosphere of apparent freedom, initiative, and enterprise, the state alone seems powerful and it alone is to be feared and checked.

Regardless of the accuracy of this Arcadian picture of the eighteenth century, it is, as we are reminded by E. H. Carr's lectures on *The New Society,* assuredly no portrait of our world. Whatever country may be our residence, we live in a mass democracy founded on a refined technology and administered by a managerial class controlling vast organizations. For prudential and pietistic reasons we may talk as though men retained a high degree of independence, were intimate enough with their neighbors and with the graver issues of the day to have a common understanding, and were accustomed to solve their differences by rationally selecting representatives who in turn choose the wisest policies for the nation. But as Schumpeter asks in his *History of Economic Analysis* (p. 429) is not this picture of the "freely voting rational citizen, conscious of his (long run) interests, and the representative who acts in obedience to them, the government that expresses these volitions . . . the perfect example of a fairy tale"?

Our society is one in which men work in highly specialized occupations, many of them located in a different community from where they live, so that they hardly know either community well. Their opinions are formed largely from their vocational associations and from what they derive from the strident and reiterated appeals of mass media of communication. The political world becomes a realm governed not by natural reason but by immediate pressures. And a large part of each man's concern is with utilizing these pressures to achieve new material advantages for himself and to hold in check the adverse forces. The state now emerges as the mechanism through which he and his associates in interest will gain victory, not agreement.

Under the view just stated constitutionalism sinks into a minor role in political theory. The vital issues revolve upon objects and techniques characterizing the struggle to acquire, not to restrain or mould, power. In this study of the clash of interests, constitutionalism represents a sub-topic,—the limits that the victor imposes upon himself not because he is required to do so, for by hypothesis he has command of the field, but because he is sentimentally attached to a tradition of moderation or because he is prudently planning precedents for a future day when another may conquer him. So regarded, constitutionalism becomes little more than acceptance of the Melian argument to the Athenians. It is adherence to the counsel of expediency attributed to Thucydides—"of all the manifestations of power, restraint impresses men most."

A kindred depreciatory view of the conventional laudation of constitutionalism comes from those who, without relying particularly on the changes in the economic and social background, assert that our political theory and hence our political life suffer from the historically false notion that power tends to be evil and should be curbed. No one has put the argument more persuasively than Lord Radcliffe in the slender but superb volume of lectures upon *The Problem of Power,* an as yet unacknowledged masterpiece of political science. Some quotations, taken out of order but not out of context, will summarize his theory. He recognizes that at least in all English-speaking countries there is a "wry native tradition that all men abuse power and are the worse for having it." (pp. 3-4) "One attitude is to be afraid of power . . . Mistrust is the dominant note . . . expressed by such constitutional devices as those of the American Constitution. Power is placed under restraint; it is deliberately shared out so that it cannot all be grasped in the same hand" (p. 100). But "power is good or evil according to the vision it serves" (p. 110). And in English life sources of that vision are not the rules of law but the traditions of the people and the insight of its noblest men. "Great words such as constitutional rights, liberty and the rule of law seem to change their meaning even while one looks at them." (p. 104). "There is a tradition of life in these [British] islands that both ennobles and restrains authority. Only it lives in the spirit, and has no special form to express it." (p. 107). "The best in us wants to be ruled by the best that others can reveal to us. The best is the real common wealth." (p. 108).

Whatever else may be said of these utterances of a Lord of Appeal in Ordinary they do not echo the hymns to constitutionalism regularly intoned at festival rites by laymen or by the run-of-the-calendar lawyers. Lord Radcliffe, it is true, does pay tribute to "the tradition that there are a citizen's rights standing between him and despotic power . . . rights . . . in the main, won in the courts of law." (p. 101). Yet he makes this deserved acknowledgement not because power is evil, or law is its antidote, but because legal tradition is part of our culture, our culture is part of our vision, and our problem of power is a problem of vision, "not the vision of governors alone, nor the vision of governed alone but a vision that is somehow common to them both, though not discerned with equal range of sight." (p. 110).

Not fundamentally different, although more specifically challenging to American lawyers and to judges, is the skeptical attitude toward constitutionalism and to the cognate subject of judicial review proclaimed by the most distinguished living judge of the United States Courts. Judge Learned Hand's addresses, collected in *The Spirit of Liberty,* reiterate the theme that constitutional prohibitions are not law and do not depend primarily upon institutions judicial or otherwise, but reflect "a mood, an attitude towards life, deep rooted in any enduring society." He concludes that "A society so riven that the spirit of moderation is gone, no court *can* save; that a society where that spirit flourishes no court *need* save."

There is nothing unusual in the first half of this last quotation. Not even the most optimistic supporter of constitutionalism has supposed that it could be saved if the only ones prepared to defend it were judges acting without support from the habits and prejudices of the people. But the second half should give us pause. The assertion is that the courts and, one might fairly add, the constitution as a legal instrument play so subsidiary a role that society would get along as well without them. We must not suppose that this extreme statement was made carelessly or merely provocatively. Judge Hand is giving utterance to a widely held positivist position that the Constitution and other forms of law are to be regarded primarily as historical compromises among competing interests, that they embody almost nothing in the way of durable principle and have little to contribute to modifying the moral climate of the community and that those who interpret them have only the subsidiary task of discerning the meaning of the compromisers. For judges to search for any more ultimate value or to furnish any more comprehensive guidance to society is to violate the basic postulates of democracy, to go beyond the jurisdiction granted to courts, and to assume a role for which men on the bench are not suited because of the limits of their background, their social and professional allegiances, and their incapacity to manage large issues within the forensic framework.

The foregoing contrast between the attitudes of the applauding unsophisticated layman and the critical informed professional is admittedly exaggerated. But the recital of these diverse opinions will remind us not to be too facile in attempting to determine what is the essence and value of constitutionalism.

Surely little turns on whether in a particular state the doctrines have been codified. It is true, as has already been said, that in the United States the codification of 1789 became a symbol of unity, its words making possible a much greater range of emotion and perception, helping people comprehend the incomprehensible, and fulfilling Tom Paine's boast that with us "the Law is King." But we must not be so provincial or naive as to regard this as of primary importance. One of the most constitutional of states, the United Kingdom, has no single record of its constitution; one of the least constitutional of states, the U.S.S.R., has a document dated 1936, not yet effective in altering the tone of the government.

What then is the root nature of constitutionalism?

Many would assert that its fundamental quality is "the division of power". This is assuredly a respectable view, supported, for example, by Professor C. J. Friedrich's *Constitutional Government and Democracy.* It quite rightly reminds us that constitutionalism has as its antonym "absolutism", or "tyranny", or in modern parlance, "totalitarianism." Also it summons to our recollection the mediaeval distinction between the King's *Gubernaculum* and his *Jurisdictio,* the attempts since the seventeenth century to keep separate legislative, executive, and judicial power, and the constantly expanding practice of federalism, so recently reviewed at the Columbia University Bicentennial Conference.

We may readily agree that structural arrangements restraining the concentration of power are essential to a constitutional state. But we should be quite provincial if we supposed that one particular pattern was clearly the best. In the United Kingdom we all know that the chief executive and legislative powers rest in the same hands—a Cabinet drawn from the Parliament; in France there is hardly any application of the federal principle. Can we say more than that the multiplication of centers of governmental power prevents one centralized authority from stifling growth, and allows more opportunity for new or different ideas to be given a chance for development and trial?

The separation of powers prevents one arbitrary will

from ruling a people. It gives time for the presentation of opposing considerations, and the strength to insist on them. It permits the development and trial of new ideas. It underlines our belief that, in politics as elsewhere in life, antinomies are eternal and polarity is of the essence of truth. It represents our confession that today we are all pluralists. And from these premises, it accepts as a counsel of prudence the principle that there should be legal limits not only to any particular organ of the state but to all organs of the state looked at collectively. It is for this reason that Professor C. H. McIlwain in *Constitutionalism Ancient and Modern* writes that "constitutionalism has one essential quality: it is a legal limitation on government; it is the antithesis of arbitrary rule; its opposite is despotic government, the government of will instead of law."

Does this mean that we should take as the core of constitutionalism the application of "the rule of law"—a phrase against which, let us not forget, we were warned by Lord Radcliffe, even though it seems closely akin to the over-all title of this conference, "Government Under Law." The idea of governors acting under the law was expressed as far back as Aristotle. Yet perhaps Professor McIlwain is right in saying that the Greek notion was that the state made the laws, while constitutionalism presumes that the law makes the state. At any rate, in Anglo-American legal history the most quoted statement of the principle comes from Bracton's *De Legibus et Consuetudinibus Angliae*—"the King ought to be under no man, but under God and the law, for the law makes the King." Yet Bracton meant that governments are under a fixed set of principles of divine origin, a view which only a minority of us would be prepared to support.

What then does the phrase mean to most of us? Not that there is a corpus of principles derived from a natural law or a theory of social justice which governs the substance of positive law. We know too well that there is no such corpus to settle the major questions of foreign affairs, of the rates of taxation, of the objects of expenditure, of the regulation of enterprise. Nor does the phrase imply that there is a definable corpus which regulates the due procedure of the government. The same types of matters are handled quite differently in different constitutional states: in one state by courts, and in another by executives; in one, after hearing, in another, summarily; in one by accusatory methods with severe limitations upon the prosecution, in another by investigatory methods founded upon full disclosure. Indeed all that one seems able to spell out of the rule of law concept, when looked at universally, is first, that the state recognizes a presumption that an individual has the right to have his person or property free from interference by any officer of the government unless that officer can justify his interference by reference to a general law, and second, that the state provides some machinery for the vindication of that right before an independent tribunal in all cases where a crime is charged, and sometimes in other cases involving serious interferences with persons or their property.

To go beyond this is to indulge in readily disproved fictions. The presumption that a person can be restrained only by general laws is overborne in time of crisis. Without leaving our own national boundaries, we know that in war the writ of habeas corpus has been explicitly suspended by the President and implicitly by the courts through failure to provide relief to citizens detained in guarded reservations on account of their color. Nay, no less a believer in constitutionalism than Justice Holmes expressed the Supreme Court's view that in a purely domestic situation a Governor could imprison a labor union official for two and a half months. "When it comes to a decision by the head of the State upon a matter involving its life, the ordinary rights of individuals must yield to what he deems the necessities of the moment." *Moyer* v. *Peabody,* 212 U. S. 78, 85 (1909).

Moreover, aside from penal, tax, and property matters, most regulatory laws although drafted in general terms in fact vest unreviewable discretion in officials. In most countries this is true of the admission and deportation of some or all aliens. It is often true of the appointment and dismissal of persons from the public service. And, in practice, close to unlimited discretion exists in the conferring of many financial benefits, grants of property, and license privileges.

Despite these and many other illustrations that will occur to any sophisticated person, it is not meaningless to assert that constitutionalism includes as a primary element the application of the rule of law to an ever-increasing area. The constitutional state has a progressive tendency to enlarge the jurisdiction of independent courts before which an individual can challenge the fairness of the procedure underlying official action. Once the rule of law is accepted as governing the main procedural impacts of the criminal law, its principles may, by the force of public opinion, be accepted as binding in additional fields where the state exercises coercive power. Such extensions have, in fact, almost always covered disciplinary actions in the armed forces, some aspects of the treatment of aliens, and the more drastic types of regulation of private economic action. The contest over the extension of the rule of law is even now being debated in connection with the dismissal of public servants, and interrogations conducted in administrative or legislative hearings.

As important as legal procedures are political procedures in maintaining a constitutional state. It may be conceded that the critics are correct in pointing out that we no longer live in a world governed by the individual rational voter or the type of independent representative depicted in Burke's November 3, 1774 Speech to the Electors of Bristol. But if it be true that political power now responds chiefly to organized pressures, it has become even more vital to emphasize that a constitutional state provides that there shall be orderly, regular processes of election of officers and amendment of the fundamental laws. Professor Lon Fuller's observations in *The Law in Quest of Itself* put the point admirably: "It is only in a democratic and constitutionally organized state that ideas have a chance to make their influence felt. By preserving a fluidity in the power structures of society, by making possible the liquidation of unsuccessful governments, democracy creates a field in which ideas may effectively compete with one another for the possession of men's minds." Conventional arrangements for terminating existing administration and installing successors with different ideas are essential to constitutionalism, in a monarchy as well as in a republic. For such conventions give significance to the principle that victory in the free state is founded not upon coercion, but persuasion. Thus paradoxically the merit of a constitutional regime rests upon its promotion of constant peaceful revolution. In this sense, there is much wisdom in the apparently extreme aphorism of Jefferson that "every constitution . . . naturally expires at the end of nineteen years."

Neither the division of power, the recognition of the rule of law, nor the maintenance of political machinery for making a government responsive to current conflicts of ideas and interests reaches what most laymen would regard as the most characteristic element of the doctrine of constitutionalism as it spread from nation to nation in the last two centuries. To the layman constitutionalism's emphasis upon freedom of movement, freedom of belief, freedom of communication, and freedom of association would seem the kernel of the doctrine. These freedoms are directly connected with the recognition that the individual is the ultimate seat of authority. They emphasize the principle that the end to be served by organized government is the cultivation of spiritual and creative values in the individual. They are the values guarded by rules of law and devices of politics.

There is abundant truth in this approach. But the difficulty is that we professionals know that no matter how hospitable to these freedoms a constitutional state may be, no one of them represents an absolute right. All liberties are the result of a social process. Charles Morgan gave us as his perceptive image of freedom the room which would not exist without the walls. We know that each day constitutional liberties are weighed against considerations of order, stability, security. Often we see that even in the most clearly constitutional state the balance is cast against the claims of freedom. Their practical place in the life of a particular people or in that people's state can only be portrayed casuistically, just as they can only be, in Jacques Maritain's words, "realized institutionally." How then can we say that upon such evanescent shadows rests the existence of a constitutional state?

Although no answer will be completely satisfactory, may it not be said that the vital distinction between a tyranny and a constitutional state is that the latter recognizes these freedoms as ends not means, promotes procedures to further these freedoms, and always gives these freedoms a high, perhaps a preferred, place in framing all policy decisions.

But it may now reasonably be asked, If the essentials of constitutionalism are as vague and vagrant as this paper suggests, does it not follow that Judge Hand was substantially correct—all depends upon the mood and habits of a people; courts amount to little; and the doctrines of constitutionalism constitute not law but the sort of myth which has as its chief worth the encouragement of a continuity of customary habits and a spirit of moderation?

Before we jump to embrace this self-depreciatory skeptical seer, let us ask ourselves why it is that no constitutional state seems ever to have existed without independent courts, and that those states that have reached the highest levels of constitutionalism have the deepest respect for courts. May it not be that, as this paper illustrates, constitutionalism cannot be either meaningfully defined in, or maintained by, abstract absolutes? It cannot even be preserved merely by the retention of the conventions of the past or the practice of reasonable compromise. What is required is the careful analysis of concrete issues arising in current controversies, the weighing of conflicting claims, the expression of preferences based upon practical reasoning. For these requirements courts are the best instrument so far devised. In performing these tasks their role far transcends the search for, or the formulation of, rules purportedly emanating from a written compact, or the statute book, or the common law. The courts, especially in constitutional cases, are teachers to the citizenry. In every country where there is an independent judiciary, not only in countries where courts have power to disregard statutes violative of the local constitution, the judges mould the people's view of durable principles of government.

Indeed the instruction given to the public by the judges is indispensable for the existence of a pervasive spirit of constitutionalism. For, as is pointed out in Professor Arthur H. Goodhart's Hamlyn Lectures on *English Law and the Moral Law* constitutional law does not rest on the ordinary type of Austinian sanctions. It rests upon the reverence people show and the obedience they give to rules which they regard as obligatory. And such reverence and obedience flows in no small part from an awareness of basic principles concretely illustrated in court decisions and constantly explained in opinions circulating among a wide audience.

We turn now to consider the oft-repeated contention that both in popular estimation and in legal character the chief role of constitutionalism is negative—a system for the division, limitation, and restraint of power to prevent its abuse—and that, being negative, the doctrine is, if not outworn, at least subordinate in a world where modern technology, military and economic conditions, and the prevailing desire to translate the claims of private interests into legal rights all contemplate not a less powerful but a more powerful state.

There are times in history when constitutionalism has appeared to be largely a negative doctrine. Emphasis on the negative was natural in a society where the barons sought to check the King, or the church sought to be free of the royal power. It was likewise natural in the succeeding period when bourgeois capitalists purported to operate in a laissez-faire economy and to wish state action confined to the suppression of force and fraud.

But constitutionalism has always been more than a prescription against Acton's disease. It is not addressed solely to curbing "the strong man's craving for power", nor does it entirely ignore "the poor man's craving for food." Constitutionalism has not so far departed from Cicero's "conception of a universal justice which ought to animate all human legislation and pervade all acts of human authority" to quote E. S. Corwin, *Liberty Against Government,* p. 169. Nor is it hostile to the deeper religious vision of what Professor Tillich in *The Protestant Era* (p. 157) calls "the principle of love" and what others might call the political principle of fraternity.

Neither analytically, nor historically, nor in the light of present day social and economic conditions is there any reason to take a view that constitutionalism implies exclusively Constitutional Limitations and never Constitutional Affirmations. If constitutionalism is defined, as I believe it should be, as the institutionalization of the principle that the state's goal is the increase in opportunities for the development of the individual as the seat of ultimate spiritual, political, and creative authority, and if the four essential means used by constitutionalism are first, a division of power upon pluralistic principles; second, an expanding rule of law, third, political devices allowing peaceful revolutions in the state's machinery responsive to alterations in the structure and power of interests and ideas in society, and fourth, continued emphasis upon practical measures for achieving the liberties of movement, belief, communication and association, then there is as much room for affirmative as for negative aspects of constitutionalism.

Indeed unbiased history would reveal that the object and means of constitutionalism have always required the active intervention and procedural assistance of the state. This is true of the writ of habeas corpus. It is illustrated by almost the whole of criminal procedure from the requirement that the defendant be informed of the charge to the guarantee that he will be able to compel the attendance of witnesses on his own behalf. This is equally true of the so-called private law of property, contracts, and torts where rights regarded by us as basic to a free society exist only as a result of remedies supplied by the state and its courts. It is often true of the right of association—for most business enterprises act under state charter and most trade unions could not have grown without state action preserving them from employer interference.

Nowhere indeed has the affirmative aspect of constitutionalism been more stressed than in the United States. John Marshall deserves to be remembered as much for *McCulloch* v. *Maryland* as for *Marbury* v. *Madison*. And though the two sides of his contribution have not always been equally emphasized, neither theme has for long been obscured, as we are reminded in Professor E. S. Corwin's paper on *The Constitution As Instrument And as Symbol,* delivered at the Harvard Tercentenary symposium on *Authority And The Individual.* Nor is this a purely parochial attitude. Witness the recent proposals at the United Nations for a Declaration of Essential Human Rights and the debates in every land when a written constitution is under consideration. Only those whose views reflect a particular economic creed or social bias regard constitutional liberty as being always a problem of freedom from state intervention and never a problem of freedom through state action. Lord Radcliffe speaks for many of our profession when he writes that "liberty looked upon as the right to find and to try to realize the best that is in oneself is not something to which power is necessarily hostile: more, such liberty may even need the active intervention of authority to make it possible" (pp. 106-107).

In estimating the value of constitutionalism today it therefore becomes relevant to ask how far we are concerned with affirmative procedures which encourage freedom of movement, which stimulate men in forming their own judgments, which enable them effectively to communicate their opinions, and which foster associations free of state domination.

In these directions no government has made many significant forward steps in recent years. Fear of foreign foes has caused sharp retreats. The tendency in new procedures has been to regard all else as subordinate to the physical security of the nation. The post-war generation has lacked the self-confidence and adventuresomeness proclaimed by the older belief that liberty is our best security.

But the quintessence of constitutionalism's virtue is that retreats from liberty make us not merely remorseful, but determined to establish better methods for safeguarding the interests of the individual as well as the state. On the local scene we observe the constant stream of proposals for establishing standards for legislative committees, for improving the methods of checking the loyalty of government employees, for moderating exclusionary immigration rules, for assuring free access to mass media of communication, and for more favorable treatment under the law of taxation and of business corporations for those who contribute to voluntary associations. Similar tendencies in other countries reveal that a chief virtue of constitutionalism is that it makes men believe that they are the masters of the state; it keeps fresh their hope that they may achieve freedom through the political order. Like Prometheus, constitutionalism does not merely defy whatever powers there may be, it brings an alphabet for the more specific formulation of our aspirations and a set of tools with which to build ladders to scale the ramparts of destiny.

Before concluding, let me confess how gravely troubled I am at the inadequacies of this presentation. Full well, I recognize how far it recites platitudes and reviews them sententiously, almost bathetically. To say something new, interesting, and true about any fundamental value system is a privilege granted only to genius. A pedestrian mind, unable to find new insights, and too immodest to be content with reciting ritual, may injure the cause he purports to serve. His cautious analysis of the record of performance, of qualified successes and apparent failures, drops to the lowest level of truth, and diverts men from contemplating the deeper meanings revealed to those who sense an indescribable yet ever influential climate of opinion. He fails to recognize the realities experienced by the "company of those who are continually conscious of the weight of all this unintelligible world." [Willey, *Eighteenth Century Background*, p. 244]. His narrow criticism overlooks what Wordsworth called "the vital power of social ties endeared by custom." His barren phrases, lacking the familiar accents of a simpler faith, never convey the beauty of the well-remembered creed.

Concerned to avoid the cant which characterizes so much worship of the constitution, we may forget that only through reverence can one build or maintain a system of immaterial values. Let us, the legatees of the Western heritage, not destroy by corrosive cynicism the structure through which we have realized our liberties. Let us forgive more readily the simple, sincere overstatement of constitutionalism's value than the subtle, timorous understatement. For faith has virtue in politics and in law as in religion and in personal relationships. It summons men to the performance of their best. It makes them conscious that citizenship in a constitutional state brings communion with a great tradition—the tradition that the state is a spiritual as well as a territorial, historical, and economic partnership and that its spiritual end is to nourish the dignity and creativity of individual men.

COMMENT

JUDGE WYZANSKI*

We have come here not only to honor the most gifted practical expositor of the Constitution, but, if I may borrow a phrase from the Master of the Rolls, we have come to consider constitutionalism not as a mere theme for discussion but as an article of a creed.

---

* CHARLES EDWARD WYZANSKI, JR., *Judge of the United States District Court for the District of Massachusetts.* Judge Wyzanski was born in Boston in 1906, and took degrees at Harvard College in 1927 and at Harvard Law School in 1930. Beside being law secretary for Judges Augustus Hand and Learned Hand, he has been Solicitor in the Department of Labor, Washington, has represented the United States at the sessions of the International Labor Organization at Geneva, and has been on the staff of the Solicitor General of the United States. He was appointed United States District Judge for the District of Massachusetts in 1941. He has filled faculty appointments at Harvard College and at Massachusetts Institute of Technology.

It would be shallow to pretend that we in this room come to this topic uncommitted. Those of the bench and of the bar, and, in this Commonwealth, even of the university community, have already sworn to uphold the Constitution. Yet it does not follow that we are less qualified on that account to deal with this subject and to search for the higher levels of its truth. For in political philosophy, as in religion, and in love itself, those who are already engaged and prepared to participate are the ones who most surely discern the profoundest truths.

And yet, we of our generation face a very special problem. I do not mean the concern and doubt which beset any practitioner when he looks at his own field. I do not even mean the kind of thoughts that were expressed by Bishop Butler a hundred years after the beheading of Charles I when he reminded us how in every age and in every clime, political practice departs from political profession. We come in our generation after an age of positivism. All of us have been schooled in a type of self-analysis which makes it particularly difficult for men of our time fully to appreciate creative insights. Yet, this is the struggle of our time.

Mr. Justice Frankfurter in referring to a recent book by Mr. Isaiah Berlin reminded us that in history the professional writers are dealing with this crisis. Professor Freund by invoking Niebuhr makes us think of another aspect of the problem.

Here today we are trying to consider both the affirmative and limiting aspects of our creed. We march somewhat warily for we have been early taught to take a skeptical look at any type of absolute.

You will recall the debate between Professor Hart and Dean Bundy. I do not intend to enter it. I warned Professor Hart that it was dangerous to speak before Dean Bundy. It is even more fatal to speak afterwards. But I think we saw that the problem of this Conference was perhaps somewhat too narrowly stated as "government under law," for it is also dealing with government *through* law, and that the problems are not easily separated into law, government, the philosophy to which the Master of the Rolls referred, and the preaching which Mr. Justice Frankfurter scorned. It seems to me that constitutionalism in reality as etymologically is a method of establishing a way of life. Therefore it includes both government and law. It includes the attitude of the legislator who makes the law as well as of the judge and lawyer called upon to interpret it.

Yet, how shall we define this constitutionalism? In my paper I have tried to select four of its aspects, and you will, I think, observe that perhaps the second is predominantly legal, and the third is predominantly political, but the first and the fourth are plainly mixed questions of law and politics. For I selected first, the division of power according to pluralistic principles; second, the rule of law; third, those political devices which assure that by amendment and by the sort of rotation in office to which Chief Justice Kerwin referred a few moments ago, we shall have a responsive government; and fourth, the gradual adoption of affirmative measures for increasing freedom of communication, freedom of movement and freedom of association.

There is no doubt that all of these are means toward a greater end both of government and of law, the use of organized activity as a *means* for the furtherance of the ultimate end, the spiritual and creative aspects of individual men.

In the short time now alloted to me, I shall not try to deal with each of these four aspects. But perhaps those of you who looked at this morning's *New York Times* would think I might well say something about the rule of law which one column in the *New York Times* reminded us is the slogan under which a South American government is preparing to depart from tyranny. Another column in the *Times* reminded us how much more difficult in practice it is to procure in Sumner, Mississippi, the rule of law, than it is to state it in theory. And the doubts with respect to theory are not easily reconciled, as Lord Radcliffe's little volume on *The Problem of Power* told us.

Yet I think we can spell from the rule of law at least two elements. There is a presumption, perhaps nothing more, that before an individual loses his liberty or his property, there must be some *general* justification for the officer who proposes to deprive him. And second, that if this interference with his person or property is so serious as to involve a *criminal* charge, then he is entitled to a trial before an independent tribunal. Even where no criminal charge is involved, the *tendency* of the rule of law is to allow independent tribunals to consider his complaint. The progress of constitutional law is the progress in the creation of a *right* of review.

In the early days, the problem was one to some extent of dealing with those who claimed a privilege to be exempt from the law. In our day the problem, strangely enough, comes back under the guise of the word "privilege" with a slightly different twist. Is it a mere privilege to hold a public office when a million people hold public office? Is it a mere privilege to travel from one country to another? Or, looked at philosophically, is there no difference between freedom of movement to get new ideas and to communicate them, and freedom of speech? These are the questions which are before the world today. And these questions are resolved in part by reference to an ever-present movement to expand the rule of law.

But we are told that we expect too much from the courts. And Judge Learned Hand, and if I understood him correctly, Mr. Justice Frankfurter, suggest to us that political virtue is habit. I suggest that Socrates was nearer right, and as extreme as it seems at first, "virtue is knowledge." And that universities and courts and like institutions engaged in spreading knowledge, in dealing *concretely* with cases, enhance political morality and do in fact preserve the state in its ultimate purpose.

It is common to say that courts have had an unfortunate effect upon our public philosophy, and that we in America suffer from an excess of constitutionalism, so that, as Professor Thayer suggested in the last generation, it has been a misfortune that so much of public controversy has been cast in constitutional terms. Is this really so? Or did not Judge Hastie give us the answer yesterday? Is it not true that in courts, at least at present, when, as Professor Freund told us, we are no longer taking an *absolute* view of constitutional questions, every consideration is debated and brought forward with greater skill, with more attention to detail, with wider intellectual resources, than is common in the legislatures? Is it not true that the legislators and the people at large have had their whole horizon *expanded* by the work of the courts?

But there remains another and greater doubt. We are told that law is nothing but a facade, that interests compete for power, and that all we have is a compromise—something which those on the bench are but to define and interpret without adding or subtracting. Law is and should be based upon a conflict of interests. It is a resolution of difference. But it is a resolution under a great tradition. In a constitutional state it summons to our recollection the ancient Greeks, the Stoics, the struggles of the church for recognition, the philosophy of the Middle Ages, the struggle to make immunity and license liberty. It reminds us of our whole history. And so we may say that the Constitution calls to mind constantly the history which helps us govern ourselves. It brings us an alphabet and a set of tools to scale the ramparts of destiny.

It tells us that law and constitutionalism are founded on more than compromise and social contract. They rest on reverence for restraint!

MR. SEYMOUR*

At the Player's Club in New York, we have a wonderful collection of death masks of the great people of the theater,

* WHITNEY NORTH SEYMOUR, *of the New York Bar.* Mr. Seymour was born in Chicago in 1901, took his Bachelor's degree at Wisconsin in 1920, and his LL.B. at Columbia in 1923. He was admitted to the New York Bar in 1924 and has practiced law in that city ever since, with interruptions for federal service as Assistant Solicitor-General of the United States and as Special Counsel

and there is one of Richard Sheridan. Some years ago, Mr. Oliver Herford, who was then one of our fine light poets, was showing a friend around the club, and he took him to this collection of death masks. His friend saw the one of Sheridan and said, "You know, I always thought he was a wit, but he looks rather dour." And Herford said, "Well, that's true, but you must remember that he wasn't at his best when that was done."

Now if Marshall had been born two or three years before he was, and if we had had to have this meeting two or three years ago, I'm not sure that all of us could have been as optimistic about the future of constitutionalism as we are. Judge Wyzanski's paper reflects that optimism, and we share it. It's a great treat to follow him. In New York—since I don't practice in his court, I think I can say this—in New York we regard him as in the very forefront of the federal judiciary and when he makes an occasional missionary trip to us, we are very grateful.

I was a little afraid the other day that Professor Hart would have taken care of all comments throughout the entire session, but yesterday when Dean Bundy spoke, as when one sees a deep-sea fish grab somebody and take him down, I saw Professor Hart disappear and I haven't seen him since. [DEAN GRISWOLD, *interjecting from the floor*: In his defense, I think I can say that he is now conducting a class.] All I can say is that I am sure he is still breathing hard.

I'm not in disagreement with anything Judge Wyzanski said either in his paper or in his fine summary. I'm grateful to him, as I think we all are, for reminding us as he does in his paper of some of those fine skeptical observations made by Judge Learned Hand. We've come to expect of Judge Hand both a mannered skepticism and a powerful affirmation, and so while he has written skeptically about liberty,

---

for the Comptroller of the Currency. Mr. Seymour has been a member of the faculties of Law at New York University and at Yale. He has been President of the Association of the Bar of the City of New York. His practice of law has included much activity both in the field of corporate enterprise and in that of civil liberties.

no judge and no lawyer in our history has ever written more powerfully in its support. I am also grateful, as I think we all are, for his reminding us of Lord Radcliffe's Reith Lectures which some of us have read as a result, and it brings home again what we were reminded of yesterday when the Master of the Rolls spoke and what we've been reminded of by the Commonwealth Chief Justices, that we can always look to the English trained judges for great presentations of our common problems.

Of course, as Judge Wyzanski said, constitutionalism depends primarily upon the judgments of an independent judiciary. They are the great teachers of constitutionalism. The problem, as we've also learned, is almost everywhere in the entire field to weigh competing values. Today, it is primarily weighing the competing values of security and liberty. When Robert Frost said, when interviewed on his eightieth birthday, that liberty was to feel easy in your harness, he may have put it about as well as it could be put, or a little more harshly than perhaps some of us would like to see it put. And the way the people respond to a great piece of teaching in this field is further confirmation of Judge Wyzanski's premise, the way the people responded to the decision in the *Steel Seizure* case, and the way they responded to the great opinions in the *Segregation* case, certainly shows that. And I can't help but say, when I remember that only two weeks ago he was sitting through our session in the Second Circuit Judicial Conference in Hartford, that certainly the bench and bar of this country are enormously indebted to him for his interest and his leadership.

What I want to say is in supplement to what Judge Wyzanski said. It seems to me that courts cannot be expected to assure government under law alone. There are too many pupils for too few teachers. It's impossible for judges to police the recesses adequately and to be sure that the students don't misbehave after school. There are too many juvenile delinquents at large, and therefore the teachers, the courts, must have the support, I submit, of an independent bar, which believes in and supports these essential liberties. Not only is such a bar necessary to renew the bench as a source of the judges and teachers of constitutionalism, but to provide adequate representation and presentation of the great issues.

I was interested as I sat here to notice that in the rafters of this room there is a representation of the first requirement of an independent bar—those lupine faces remind one that the first requirement is to keep the wolf from the door. As students sit here and observe those carvings, they will have inculcated in them the proposition that before there is time for other things, they must learn to keep those figures away from their front doors. Of course, there's no problem about an independent bar in most situations. But there is a problem where defendants are unpopular, their causes are unpopular, where there is a hue and cry, and it's in those cases that the obligation of the bar is peculiarly important. And I think we must frankly face the fact that it is not as easy as it should be in all the communities of this country to get competent representation of all kinds of defendants by people who fully believe in and support our system. It must be clear, and I think the bar and perhaps also the law schools and the judges, have failed to make it clear, that it is an essential part of government under law that a defendant charged with however odious a crime, be it murder, rape, income tax evasion, conspiracy to overthrow the government, or whatever it may be, is entitled to get competent representation, and ought not to be left to get representation only in the last extremities. I submit that the education of the public on this issue is a major problem, both for the bench and bar, and for the law schools. And we must get it out through the country, so that when a lawyer is interested in taking on such a case, and obviously the lawyer must have some choice in the matter, that he will be supported in the community and not pilloried as one who must be considered to support the defendant's views.

It was only a couple of years ago in New York that one of our leading lawyers who represented a defendant in an income tax evasion case, a defendant who was charged with relations with the underworld, was publicly attacked in one of our newspapers. When we had a dinner in New York last week with Sir Alfred Denning, who is one of the Master of the Rolls' colleagues in the Court of Appeal, we mentioned this episode, and he said, "In England, the editor of that paper would have been in jail almost immediately. We wouldn't have stood for that sort of thing." Our tradition of the freedom of the press is different, and we can't deal with this by putting people in jail, but we must, I submit, if government under law is to be upheld and courts are to be sustained, we must make it possible to have adequate representation without a lawyer being attacked for undertaking it. And that's an obligation which rests on all citizens, and on all lawyers, and on all judges, and on all law teachers.

I suggest that that is not alone enough. It isn't only in court, and in defense, that the lawyer can make a contribution, because the secret of the permeation of the bones of our people by the doctrine of due process, the doctrine of fair dealing, is to have it so clear that it won't be necessary to go to court with a lot of these issues. And so it's important that the lawyers in the legislatures and in the executive departments should always exercise their influence in favor of fair procedure and process, and also, that in their dealings with private groups, they should continually exercise that influence. The fact is, as we all know, that through voluntary organizations there is a great pressure in many communities against freedom—freedom in the libraries, freedom in the schools, and so on—and it's up to the lawyers as leaders in the community to do all they can to show how inimical to our system that kind of pressure is unless fair hearings are provided. It may be reasonable enough that people should raise questions as to whether certain books should be used in the schools, but if that question is to be raised, it ought to be raised with some kind of a hearing and some opportunity to have the other view expressed. I submit that when an undoubtedly good but somewhat over-zealous lady demanded that a library in Indiana remove Little Red Riding Hood because it was subversive, the least that the library board should have done was to have a hearing unless it was going to throw out the complaint at once.

Now I would not for a moment suggest that the bar has been supine about some of these obligations. I think the organized bar has been making very good progress, but the point is that it ought to make more. Take a few things that have been accomplished. It was the bar that led the opposition to the court-packing plan, supported by the public, supported as Mr. O'Brian says, by the moral sense of the public. But it was the bar that recognized that if it became the practice to seem to load the dice in our system, the people would lose their faith in an independent judiciary. And this was at a time when many members of the bar who opposed the scheme also opposed the new position which the court had taken on many issues. It was the bar, largely, that brought about reform in the administrative agencies. You remember that there was a great development of administrative tribunals, and when it was suggested that they ought to proceed fairly, there was an outcry that this was going to interfere with the genius of such institutions; but Congress adopted measures which have seemed to work very well. And that was a valuable contribution.

In the field of military justice, the bar, with the aid of Professor Morgan, prepared or urged the adoption of the new military code, and the creation of a civilian Court of Military Appeals, the chief judge of which was here yesterday. And that has been a contribution. I know there is debate about it, but it has improved an important area of justice with which people are concerned.

Last year the American Bar Association made recommendations for improvements in Congressional investigating procedures, and they have somewhat improved. The Association of the Bar of the City of New York is conducting a study of the Federal Loyalty-Security Program, in an effort to take a cool lawyers' view of that program. There's widespread recognition, which we all know about, of the need for legal aid and the speeding up of trials without losing their essential quality. It's clear that this too is a part of due process. As Judge Learned Hand said most aptly, justice cannot be rationed, and poor people must be assured of adequate representation. And all these things contribute, and the bar is busy on a great many fronts. All I say is that the bar must be more busy, and the right of representation must be fully defended and secured by the bar.

Now, I shall hurry on. I don't think I need to make the point that obviously there are many matters which legislatures deal with which cannot be handled by the courts—for example the improvement of legislative investigations. Obviously the courts are not in a very good position to step into investigations and try to regulate their fairness. There are many problems of maintaining the separation of powers which only Congress can deal with. Congress must, largely by its own self-restraint, deal with those matters with the aid of the influence of the bar and the opinion of the public, as Dean Bundy pointed out.

So with the executive department. There are many matters dealt with in the executive department which it's extremely difficult to have dealt with in the courts, including fairness in the treatment of employees. Those matters depend upon an informed opinion in the bar and among the citizens.

Now, I approach the end. I haven't said as much as I wanted to about Judge Wyzanski's fine paper. He does trouble me a little bit about one point. I agree, of course, that the doctrine of constitutionalism involves both the negative and the affirmative, and that in many ways courts are dealing with the affirmative when they are insisting upon fair procedures in criminal trials and so on. But there was once a school of thought, and I don't know whether Judge Wyzanski associates himself with it at all, that it was a part of the duty of government and a part of the function of sustaining the freedoms in the First Amendment to prop up the weak in the exercise of those freedoms beyond giving them an opportunity to exercise them. In other words, if there was a small group of people who never had been able to win any substantial support on their merits that somehow the government ought to support them so that they could have just about as good a chance as those who persuaded people more successfully. Now I'm sure he doesn't mean that, but I should be very troubled by any notion of carrying the affirmative support of these rights to that point. We all recognize that it's vital to keep the right of dissent and keep the non-conformists as an essential part of the leaven of American life. As an example, we should all think that our system must always give hospitality to the Henry Thoreaus. I must say I do remember that my wife and I were having tea with Justice Holmes one day and we got to talking about Thoreau and I'd always thought of him as a dissenter and a non-conformist, and he told me this story, which is the source of the only doubt about Thoreau I've ever had. Holmes said that a friend of his in Concord had once said. "You know, I've read everything Henry's ever written about those nuts and berries he used to eat, but I never found a word about the apple pies that he used to get at our back door."

Laying aside the apple pies, our system ought to work so that the Henry Thoreaus could live and work and write about the nuts and berries and also about civil disobedience. But if we ever tried to implement the civil liberties that we believe in defending by having the government go out of its way to support people so that they could write about the nuts and berries, I have a notion that the tendency would be to say to them, "Well, you'd better forget about that civil disobedience." So the bar should be the defender of freedom: it might not fare so well if it were left entirely to the government.

PROFESSOR HARTZ*

Judge Wyzanski's paper set off in my own mind a whole chain of reflections which I think, at least from my point of view, is one of the testimonies I would offer to its merits, and I want to develop one of them here. In the course of doing this, I will unfortunately be compelled to distort the argument of Judge Wyzanski, but it seems to me that in most cases the evidence of the real fertility of an insight is the amount of distortion it has to undergo in history.

The concept I would like to take is the basic concept in the paper—the concept of limitation and affirmation, and I would like to project it onto an international plane. If we do this, I think we'll see that there are stages in the history of nations when the quest for liberty concerns itself predominantly with the affirmation of power, and there are other stages when it is concerned predominantly with the limitation of power.

The high point in the stage of affirmation is surely at one of those revolutionary moments in history when the frustrations and oppressions of an old society become so intense that men yearn for some sharp and sovereign instrument which will clear it away, liberate them from it. The age of Cromwell in England was such an era. The French Revolution was surely another such era. Now after these upheavals, when the worst of the *ancien régime* is cleared away, men begin to tame these giants of power that they have created for their own liberation, and the age predominantly of limitation, the age when liberty is defined in terms of control of power, begins to set in. And the old revolutionary memories are in many ways buried, repudiated and forgotten.

England and America, and indeed it seems to me for the most part, this whole family which I have heard referred to as really constituting the focus of this conference, have

* Louis Hartz, *Professor of Government, Harvard University.* Professor Hartz was born in 1919 in Youngstown, Ohio; he took his B.S. at Harvard College in 1940, and his Ph.D. in 1946. He has been a member of the Harvard faculty since 1941, and is now Professor of Government. He is the author of "The Liberal Tradition in America" and many other publications.

for a long time been living in what might be described as predominantly the age of power limitation. And America, I would contend, almost from its outset, having fled from those struggles which I described in Europe, has lived with this perspective on power.

The question I want to raise is this: how are societies in different phases of this development, in different phases of this power-liberty cycle, to judge each other, and how are they to communicate with each other? The irony of the question is in part this: that these stages which I have described are never clear-cut. Both always go together. At times of revolutionary upheaval, the men who have fashioned sharp power instruments for their liberation never completely forget that these instruments also involve a potential threat to liberty. So they are forever coming to terms with their consciences on this score. In the affirmative moments, so to speak, they are forever struggling with the limitational side of their personalities, they are trying to suppress it, to rationalize it, and in some sense, the whole history of revolutionary thought can be interpreted in terms of this preoccupation.

An illustration of this problem, one that has always fascinated me, is a brief and neglected moment in the intellectual history of France on the eve of the revolution. There were a group of French thinkers, part of the larger group of French philosophers that flowered during this period, whom we know as the physiocrats. With other illuminated Frenchmen, these people believed in the concept of enlightened absolutism. They were fashioning an absolute sovereign for the purpose of liberation, for the purpose of liberty and equality, and yet they were more sensitive than their friends on this count. They began to worry, what if this absolute sovereign becomes a threat to liberty almost as serious as the *ancien régime* itself? What if this sovereign really gets out of hand? Then they would have erected an instrument for their liberation only to create in the end an instrument of oppression. So they solved this problem—some of them did, at any rate —by erecting a set of judges, and these judges would watch the absolute sovereign. Above the supreme power would be another supreme power—a judicial court which would make really sure that this sovereign would be concerned with liberation.

What happened to this effort? Well, these men were discredited on the ground that they were compromising liberty itself, liberty requiring an absolute sovereign for the task of social reconstruction. They repudiated the judicial idea, and it disappeared from the intellectual history of that age.

What are we to say of this particular effort? What are we to say of the anguish of the physiocrats on this particular count? Surely we cannot accuse these men of having simply made a logical mistake when they gave up judicial review, of having been misguided, of having been less lucid in their thinking than John Marshall in the case of *Marbury v. Madison.* When I used to study the decision in *Marbury v. Madison,* my impression was that John Marshall, on this count, was actually less lucid than the physiocrats with respect to the issue he confronted.

Surely we cannot accuse these men either of lacking an interest in the libertarian ideal, for it was their dedication to this ideal in the context of the French eighteenth century which produced their dilemma. We cannot even accuse them of making a wholly bad empirical judgment when they repudiated the doctrine of guardianship. The question of whether or not you would vote for the French revolution in the light of history is an open one, but my judgment is still that I would vote for it, if I had to. I trust that this is not too subversive a statement to make, but I think the atmosphere has cleared enough so that a man could actually vote for the French revolution, historically.

Which means that in empirical terms, too, we cannot wholly repudiate the decision that these men arrived at. So a real problem exists here: how two societies, looking at each other from different vantage points in this particular cycle of power and liberty, are to evaluate each other? And there is another problem. How are these societies to communicate with each other? The entire vocabulary of libertarian thought is absorbed into this very question of power. Liberty actually meant unlimited power for the physiocrats; equality was the end of that power and, as individual rights, was also its purpose. The whole vocabulary of liberal philosophy is absorbed into this distinction with respect to the power question. If you have a limitational perspective, you look at it in one way, but the words mean something entirely different if you are at a stage where you are concerned with the other perspective.

The fact is, that men who speak to one another across this division use the same words but they mean different things. They are in some sense brothers, they derive from a common cultural ancestry, they use the same language, but they are baffled by one another.

This is obviously a pressing question in our own time, because whole areas of the world have begun to experience developments of one kind or another with respect to this question, and no area of the world is isolated from any other any longer. The obviously decent solution to this question is through understanding. Battles between people who share the same values are the most violent battles, but they are also the most intolerable ones to observe. But the effort to solve the problem of evaluation and communication through the perspective of understanding is bound to meet with great cultural resistance, simply because every culture is provincial and its memory is short. A laborious enterprise in social, political and historical semantics is not the habit of cultures. It is not by such enterprises that cultures live; actually, they live by a series of affirmations, remarkably few in the end, and remarkably elementary.

Hence I suggest to you this, that there is almost by definition a tension that is going to take place between the individual who seeks to develop the perspective involved in understanding, and the pressure of the culture upon him. For the solution involved in that cultural pressure will usually be the solution of conflict. The social semanticist who worries about the meaning of words, whose historical memory is long rather than short, who is concerned with this cycle that I have described, may often find himself in a position which his society discovers to be embarassing, and a position which is not always for himself a wholly satisfactory one from the strategic point of view.

What then should his position be? Empirically, this question may be difficult. Ethically, however, it is not. The man who has seized a wider perspective than his own culture has simply not to give that perspective up. This is not an ethic derived from utility, although clearly there would be a good deal of utility in this position for the culture. It is not even an ethic derived from benevolence, although I am talking about cultural benevolence implicitly, am I not? I think it is an ethic derived from a principle higher than either of these which is surely one that requires no defense in this room, simply the historical truth.

The Value of Constitutionalism Today

JOHN LORD O'BRIAN*

I

It has been suggested that I speak to this topic from the practical viewpoint of a lawyer who has been actively engaged in his profession throughout the period in which the most serious interpretative changes have taken place in the Federal Constitution since Marshall's day. These comments will, therefore, in the large be confined to constitutionalism in the United States.

The scope of the title was defined by my invitation in these terms:—

> "Has Government limited by law worked? Have our people been able, by the exercise of foresight, to make rules for those who govern them, and by the exercise of self-restraint have they been able to abide by these rules, or have we paid only lip service to this ideal? Has this concept affected our people one way or another? Has constitutionalism taught us anything; or, on the contrary, do we take good ideals of constitutional government and use them for bad ends? And in what direction is all this moving?"

Reviewing the preceding topics on the agenda for this conference, it seems unnecessary to elaborate the historical origin and developments of our Constitution beyond reminding ourselves that among its most distinctive features were the restraints upon official authority, the relatively new experiment of federalism, the tripartite division of powers, and the implied supremacy of the judicial power. Needless to say, the Bill of Rights, and particularly the guarantees of the First Amendment, were a unique contribution. It is well to remind ourselves at the outset that the guarantees and procedures for the protection of the individual, so eloquently ar-

---

* For biographical note see page 533.

ticulated in the Bill of Rights, dealt with evils long experienced and long resented. Historically it is clear that these concepts embodied in the first ten amendments were, in reality, originally inspired by moral conviction and then became political in their direction and their consequences. Even now they depend for their effectiveness largely on "the developed conscience" of the individual.

Although under the pervasive influence of Madison, Wythe and their Southern associates the Constitution was formulated largely by Southern statesmen, the document reflects, as Dean Pound has said, the old Puritan distrust of authority. Until at least the Civil War there remained dominant in this Country the Puritan attitude — "He rebelled against control of his will by state or magistrate, yet he loved to lay down rules."[1]

The timeliness of our topic—the value of constitutionalism today—is undeniable. As our own Professor McIlwain has expressed it:—

> "Never in its long history has the principle of constitutionalism been so questioned as it is questioned today, never has the attack upon it been so determined or so threatening as it is just now. The world is trembling in the balance between the orderly procedure of law and the processes of force which seem so much more quick and effective. Never in recorded history, I believe, has the individual been in greater danger from government than now."[2]

Although this comment was written in 1940, it is equally impressive as of today.

Just what do we mean by this "principle of constitutionalism?" It is not an area which lends itself to dictionary analysis. Yet I feel that to all of us constitutionalism has one essential quality: It is a legal limitation on government, the antithesis of arbitrary rule and of a government of will instead of law.

---

1. POUND, THE SPIRIT OF THE COMMON LAW 56 and *passim* (1921).
2. MCILWAIN, CONSTITUTIONALISM ANCIENT AND MODERN 143 1 (1940). The same writer has emphasized that our modern tendency to identify all law with legislative enactment has contributed to the modification of old ideas respecting the law. We no longer think of either constitutional or private law as "custom binding because it extends backward to a time 'whereof the memory of man runneth not to the contrary'." *Id* at 23.

Perhaps no one has given a better summary of the tradition of constitutionalism than Cardozo:—

> "The great ideals of liberty and equality are preserved against the assaults of opportunism, the expediency of the passing hour, the erosion of small encroachments, the scorn and derision of those who have no patience with general principles, by enshrining them in constitutions, and consecrating to the task of their protection a body of defenders. By conscious or subconscious influence, the presence of this restraining power, aloof in the background, but none the less always in reserve, tends to stabilize and rationalize the legislative judgment, to infuse it with the glow of principle, to hold the standard aloft and visible for those who must run the race and keep the faith."[3]

The power implicit in this rich tradition has not been so much weakened as it has been re-directed. Nevertheless, all constitutionalism retains its essential quality. Despite changes wrought by interpretation, it still remains the one answer to Acton's apothegm that "Passion for power over others will never cease to threaten mankind." It is certainly unnecessary to remind this audience that the Constitution itself was the result of conflicting influences arising from differing convictions as to social and economic values, or that it represented a fixed attitude on certain values like that of property as well as that of individual freedom. This same conflict in the realm of values is the underlying reason why changing conditions and pressures in these same areas compel both the Congress and the courts to give more and more weight to sociological considerations. It was the fundamental moral aspect implicit in some of these social problems which originally brought about their close inter-relationship with the morality sanctioned by the common law. This was particularly true of the ideals of the essential dignity of the individual and of his so-called inalienable rights. Democracy was envisaged in religious or moral terms long before it assumed a political terminology. Furthermore, it seems to be generally agreed that it was the tradition of civil liberties

---

3. Cardozo, The Nature of the Judicial Process 92-93 (1921).

firmly rooted in and defended by the common law which inspired both the revolution of 1640 and the revolution of 1688.[4]

II

Before turning to the future of constitutionalism one must necessarily take account of its status today and of at least the more significant changes in interpretation which have definitely affected some of the more important of its original features. Any such forecast must also take account of the social forces which have compelled those changes and which are likely to continue to exert their pressures in the same direction. This is not the time or place to trace in detail the development of all these forces which have brought about the extensive changes. For us here today the important fact is that the changes have been made. The serious task is to appraise their effect upon pre-existing concepts and then to attempt a forecast of future developments affecting constitutionalism.

Although the process of new interpretation deliberately adapted to changed social conditions began early in this century, the most far-reaching of the changes, as we all know, have occurred within the last twenty years. They have come about chiefly from changed interpretation of the Commerce Clause, of the guarantees of Due Process, and of the power of taxation, particularly in relation to the General Welfare Clause. Broadly speaking, the three most important developments have been: First, the tremendous expansion of the executive power and the dispersal of that power through innumerable administrative agencies established by the Executive; secondly, the ultimate triumph of the Hamiltonian theory of a strong central government, and the extensive use

4. This statement may savor of over-simplification. But it does not seem pertinent to discuss here at length the concept of the relationship of property to power which, under the inspiration of Harrington and Locke, became a vital feature of the great Whig tradition.

of the taxing power for social ends and to promote projects conceived to be legitimately within the field of the General Welfare Clause, and thirdly, the altered conception of "liberty" and "property" in the Due Process Clause, as a result of which that clause is no longer an obstacle to the initiation of social projects and the advancement of particular social interests.

It seems unnecessary at the moment to discuss the broadening of Federal constitutional power in promulgating policies in the various fields of Reclamation and other similar aspects of Federal power. As another outstanding result of these changes has come the great expansion of the regulatory power of the central government and its infiltration into the daily affairs of the private citizen. And the broad reach of increased regulatory power, as will be seen, still has implications not yet fully developed. On the other hand, it is clear that the original conception of the Constitution as a limitation upon the power of the Government has been definitely altered. As has been said, the old Constitution was one of restraints: now it is one of powers. Simple and convincing illustrations of this will be found in the Wagner Act cases, those dealing with agricultural reforms and the validation of the Social Security Act, including old age benefits, unemployment relief, etc. It seems unnecessary to present here a complete catalogue, for the change in interpretation in the particulars above mentioned should be sufficient illustration of the striking developments in basic constitutional interpretation.

The decision of Chief Justice Hughes in the *Jones & Laughlin*[5] case is the landmark most conspicuously altering old concepts. In this opinion the Court reapproved its earlier decisions upholding the right of employees to organize; but went further by upholding the new statutory provision restraining the employer from interfering with the exercise of that right. The ruling was based primarily on economic and social conditions. Its special significance lies in the recogni-

5. NLRB v. Jones & Laughlin Steel Corp., 301 U.S. 1 (1937).

tion given by the Court to the necessity for protecting the individual wage-earner in his unequal struggle with the employer. Replying to the company's argument that it was being deprived of "liberty" by this statutory provision, the Court declared, in effect, that the rights conferred were fundamental to the "liberty" of the employee and that interference with them was a proper subject for condemnation by competent legislative authority. Thus the Court held, by indirection, that the judicial power extends to the protection of the interests of particular social groups. In the same category is the decision that in the Due Process Clause the word "property" does not forbid the use by Government of public funds for the immediate benefit of private persons in the realization of an ulterior public end, and that the word "liberty" includes fundamental rights so broadening the previous concepts that it lent "positive constitutional sanction to projects of social reform—it is not solely a constitutional barrier."[6] Obviously, as will be seen, the more striking of these changes in interpretation were the outcome of the exigent demands during the great depression and emergencies presented by the second world war.[7]

The importance attached to these changes by various commentators differs greatly. Professor Laski, sympathetically accepting them all, thought that the Constitution represented a clear effort to protect a certain view of property from invasion by the demands of the multitude. That such

---

6. Cf. Corwin, Constitutional Revolution, Ltd. 78, 79.

7. The results as compiled by one critic are:—
   1. The attribution to Congress of a legislative power of indefinite scope.
   2. The attribution to the President of the power and duty to stimulate constantly the positive exercise of this indefinite power for enlarged social projects.
   3. The right of Congress to delegate its powers *ad libitum* to the President for the achievement of such enlarged social objectives (qualified by the right to withdraw such powers through a Concurrent Resolution).
   4. The attribution to the President of a broad prerogative in the meeting of emergencies defined by himself and in the creation of executive agencies to assist him, and
   5. An aggressively expanded replacement of the judicial process by the administrative process in the enforcement of the law, sometimes even in the enforcement of constitutional law.

   Corwin, Total War and the Constitution 179 (1947).

an attitude should so long have gone unquestioned was due, he thought, first to the skill with which, behind the formal facade, the actual working of the Constitution has been adapted ceaselessly to new needs, and secondly, to the fact that America has genuinely been the land of opportunity for the comparatively humble man.[8]

A different view is that today "for the first time in our history there is, following a great war, no peacetime Constitution to which we may expect to return in any wholesale way, inasmuch as the Constitution of peacetime and the Constitution of wartime have become, thanks to the New Deal, very much the same Constitution."[9] Under Marshall's conception the Supreme Court was the supreme judicial organ. Professor Corwin, after emphasizing that dual federalism was the contribution of the Court under Taney, declares that today not only dual federalism but federalism in any sense has escaped effective control through judicial review. That is, that it is now beyond the power of the Court—if it so desired—to check the continued centralization of power in the hands of the National Government.[11]

Over against views like these, Professor Carl Becker declared that although the original Constitution viewed Government as a "friendly enemy" and embodied the Puritan view that political power was inherently dangerous, nevertheless "in its structure and operation the American system of federated governments is substantially what the Founding Fathers made it." [12]

There is not much to be gained after all from studying these conflicting views because there are too many imponderables involved to warrant any certainty of conclusion. Moreover, regardless of which of these views one takes, there can be no denying that there have been extensive permanent changes affecting the property and also the liberty of the individual in the area of economics. Perhaps this has been

8. See D. W. Brogan, Government of the People, 7 (1943 ed.)
9. Corwin, Total War and the Constitution, 172 (1947).
11. *Id.* at 173-74
12. C. L. Becker, Freedom and Responsibility, 26 (1945).

seen most clearly by our economists. In particular, Professor Schumpeter has made the point in striking terms:—

> "[u]nder modern conditions—to an extent undreamed of by nineteenth-century socialists—it is possible to extract from the bourgeois stratum, by taxation and wage policies, the bulk of what in Marxist terminology is called Surplus Value . . . To an extent which is not generally appreciated, the New Deal was able to expropriate the upper income brackets even before the war. One indication will have to suffice, one that shows no more than the effects of the increase in the (personal) Income and Surtax and these only *up to 1936* . . . irrespective of the war, a tremendous transfer of wealth has actually been effected, a transfer that quantitatively is comparable with that effected by Lenin. The present distribution of disposable incomes compares well with the one actually prevailing in Russia. . . . "[13]

The extensive changes which have occurred in the past few decades suggest a fundamental question for which a fully satisfactory answer has not yet been found. Why is it that with such far-reaching changes enacted—and validated—and concentrated in so short a period, most of them have been so readily acquiesced in by the public and have become permanent features of the national economy, and, more important, have established new principles of American political philosophy? Was this due to indifference, to impatience with constitutional restraints, or to unthinking neglect of principle?

Many answers are offered. The first is suggested by Laski's comment. Due to the widespread change in the nature of property from the tangible and substantial to the intangible and invisible, a large proportion of those whose property consisted of shareholdings in corporate enterprises did not at first feel directly or even realize the impact upon them of the policies of the Administrations of the past twenty years. A more plausible answer lies in the excuse of necessity

---

13. SCHUMPETER, CAPITALISM, SOCIALISM, AND DEMOCRACY, 382 (2d. ed. 1947).

Of course the power to impose such taxes was conferred by the Sixteenth Amendment to the Constitution: but it is fair to say that no responsible statesman at that time advocated or perhaps even contemplated the use of this power to promote social ends apart from the ordinary fiscal needs of government.

stemming from dire emergency. Thus, a multitude of restraints were imposed during the great depression and, more importantly, during World War II when there was the general feeling that patriotism required acquiescence. Another explanation is closely related, namely, that these emergency measures were first advanced as temporary. When reforms such as the farm supports and the drastically higher brackets in income taxes were established, they were professed to be temporary measures. Still another factor lies in the incredible complexity of the national economy and the bewildering number of administrative agencies and officials set up to deal, as it was thought, temporarily, with emergency conditions.

It is often overlooked that there was nothing sudden or abrupt in adopting many of the changes. Many years earlier, for example, President Wilson had envisioned the Welfare State. He had also stated his conviction that the separation of powers had broken down and advised that "we think less of 'checks and balances' and more of coordinated power." He had also "early arrived at the conclusion that fear of government was illogical in a Democracy and that there was nothing immoral or illegal in a welfare state."[14]

The recent changes in constitutional interpretation have been confined to the field of economics. But after all the extent of these changes during the decade 1935 to 1945 has been no greater than the effect of Marshall's interpretations defining the extent of Federal and State power. Of course in his amazing contribution to the development of the central government Marshall was under no such pressure or social demands as was the Court in the mid-1930's. Furthermore, he was resisting the growth of the power of the States rather than amplifying Federal power.

In this same connection it should be noted that many of the most sweeping of the changes were effected not by direct Congressional legislation but through powers delegated by Congress to the Executive or, in some instances, through simple assertion of executive power. For example, the Presi-

14. COMMAGER, THE AMERICAN MIND 324 (1950).

dent, during the war, undertook by an Executive Order issued to one of his administrative subordinates to establish a maximum for personal incomes at $25,000. The allegation of war necessity was the excuse for the action of the President by Executive Order perpetrating one of the greatest invasions of personal liberty in our history when he directed the removal of some 80,000 citizens of Japanese origin and provided for their imprisonment in detention camps.[15] Incidentally, the losses to these unfortunate persons in property as well as liberty have never been computed. (This order was later confirmed by Congress in the Act of March 21, 1942.)[16] However we may theorize that "economics and politics are not separate from ethics and morality" the events of the last twenty years give depressing evidence that, regardless of the feelings of the general public, many of those in authority were indifferent to such considerations.

Fair-minded citizens must admit that as the result of many of these changes, and in particular the operations of countless administrative agencies, there has come about a definite curtailment of the judicial power of review and that in the broad field of activity of these agencies the original theory of the separation of powers, and of checks and balances, has become largely mythical. Although certain important safeguards have been provided by the Administrative Procedure Act, it is important to remember that the attitude of reviewing courts towards findings of fact have greatly restricted review by the judiciary.[17] Of this, more later. Furthermore, beyond its own estimate of national needs, there is now no restraint or check upon the spending power of Congress other than that of Presidential veto. There are and there can be no standards for and no restraints upon the character of social projects established by Congress or by the Executive beyond the power of public opinion.

---

15. See Hirabayashi v. United States, 320 U.S. 81 (1943); Korematsu v. United States, 323 U.S. 214 (1944); *Ex parte* Endo, 323 U.S. 283 (1944).

16. 56 STAT. 173.

17. There is another view, skeptical as to whether the courts should undertake to deal with incommensurable values. See L. HAND, THE SPIRIT OF LIBERTY, 177-78 (1952).

Professor Arthur E. Sutherland (right) greets Chief Justice Kerwin.

Professor Louis Hartz comments on the paper given by Judge Wyzanski.

Thurgood Marshall discusses Judge Hastie's paper.

John Lord O'Brian.

Left to right: Master of the Rolls Sir Raymond Evershed, Associate Dean David F. Cavers, Associate Justice Felix Frankfurter, Dean Erwin N. Griswold, and Chief Justice Earl Warren.

Mrs. Erwin Griswold and Chief Justice Stanley E. Qua at the dinner which concluded the conference.

From the standpoint of political science the most serious result lies in the fact that in certain broad fields of governmental activity, because of the lack of standards or controls, irresponsibility has been substituted for the original constitutional concept of responsibility by the Government to the citizens. Whether this is due to the complexity of social conditions or of government administration, the fact is undeniable that all of these changes combined have seriously impaired this most fundamental concept. As has been repeatedly pointed out, "the true safeguards of liberty against arbitrary government are the ancient legal limitation and the modern political responsibility." But, if the power which is being exercised is not concentrated and obvious to all, there can be neither the fixing nor the enforcement of this responsibility. To quote Professor McIlwain again:

> "The one thing in our political machinery which, more than any other, has fostered the growth of 'pressure groups', with all their attendant corruption, is the inability to fix responsibility . . . Our government has become to an alarming extent a mere process of 'passing the buck,' and that means shifting the responsibility for acts which could not be defended for one moment if responsibility for them could ever be fixed.
>
> For this dissipation of governmental power with its consequent irresponsibility I can find no good precedents in the constitutional history of the past . . . Unlike the legal limitations in our bill of rights, it is not the matured result of centuries of trial and error."[18]

This is particularly true of the recent expansion of the regulatory power conferring upon administrative officials jurisdiction to deal with the rights of individuals in the field of ideas and, more particularly, the guarantees of the First Amendment and the other assurances of the Bill of Rights. The very readiness with which the public has accepted the great changes both in economic theory and in constitutional law gives rise to anxiety as to their possible attitude with respect to the protections guaranteed in the Bill of Rights. As regulation followed regulation in the field of economics during the past two decades the public mind undeniably became

18. McIlwain, Constitutionalism Ancient and Modern 146 (1940).

habituated to acquiescence without serious remonstrance. Whether this was due to thoughtless complacency or to recognition of the critical necessities, as already pointed out, the most surprising development was the readiness of acquiescence and the smoothness with which the new policies took effect. No one can deny that many of these changes were intended to be and have proven to be far-reaching measures of social change. But that they should all have been put into effect and accepted with such celerity and complacency and without serious difficulty presents in itself a problem of justifiable anxiety for the future.

As already intimated, this thought becomes doubly menacing now that the regulatory powers have become active in the fields so directly concerned with our basic personal freedoms. This grave danger is presented by the larger aspects of the so-called programs to ensure loyalty and security. In carrying out these programs which were promulgated by Executive Order the citizen, for the first time in our history, has been subjected to inquisitions relating not only to his acts but his private convictions, his aspirations and his attitude toward government. To be sure, these inquiries were originally confined to determining fitness for government employment; they have now, however, been extended to large regions of private employment. Up to now the citizens involved have been refused the protection of the concept of Due Process—by invoking the cliche that no man has a right to employment by the Government. The courts with unaccustomed sophistry have asserted that hearings in proceedings of this character are not trials, that they have no substantial effect upon the liberty or property rights of the individual concerned, and that therefore he is not entitled to the protection of due process.[19] Yet there has been powerful protest against this doctrine and there is still ground for hoping that the courts will recognize the sanctity of reputa-

19. Bailey v. Richardson, 86 U.S.App.D.C. 248, 182 F. 2d 46 (1950) *aff'd per curiam by equally divided court,* 341 U.S. 918 (1951). Compare, also, the views embodied in the separate opinions in Dennis v. United States, 341 U.S. 494 (1951), Joint Anti-Fascist Refugee Committee v. McGrath, 341 U.S. 123 (1951), and Adler v. Board of Educ., 342 U.S. 485 (1952).

tion as well as the ancient right of privacy and reassert a man's right to procedural due process. In one of his last addresses, Mr. Justice Jackson said:

> "We believe it a duty to champion all fundamental rights under the law, but we recognize a special trust and competence to safeguard every man's right to fair trial, on which every other right is dependent.
>
> "We cannot approve any use of official powers or position to prejudice, injure or condemn a person in liberty, property *or good name,* which does not inform him of the source and substance of the charge and give a timely and open-minded hearing as to its truth,—safeguards without which no judgment can have a sound foundation."[20]

If the American people ever permit themselves to become reconciled to this type of regulation in the field of ideas, then indeed the First Amendment will become a declaration devoid of substance. Nevertheless the declarations of policy and the conduct of administrative procedures in this field by the officials of the present Administration, like those of the last Administration, all operate in the direction of making this danger daily more and more real. Unfortunately, in some quarters we find the idea that because it is constitutional for the Federal Government to regulate stocks and bonds or to set acreage limitations for crops, it is also perfectly proper for government agencies to ride rough shod over personal liberties.

III

What about the future? It is a platitude to say that one of the tragic facts of man's existence is his inability to grasp the full significance of passing events and his lack of competency to forecast the future. A. J. P. Taylor in his recent book makes the surprising assertion that on the eve of World War I no one foresaw or had any realization of the tremendous social upheaval which that war would entail. The view was

---

20. Address to American Bar Association, November 2, 1953.

that the war could be fitted into the existing framework of civilization: it was expected to interrupt the even tenor of civilian life only while it lasted. As in the past, there would be a war, certain international adjustments would result, and the world would go on. The prevalent attitude was exemplified by Sir Edward Grey who told the House of Commons that "if we are engaged in the war, we shall suffer but little more than we shall suffer if we stand aside", and meant by "suffering" only the interruption of trade.[21]

Nor can it be said that the extent of chaos which has followed World War II was adequately foreseen by even the best-informed statesman. Moreover, despite the number of newspaper columns devoted to commentary on the significance of events today—whether they be a shake-up in Moscow or the fate of Germany—I fear that at best only part of the picture can be drawn.

With these thoughts in mind it is only with great diffidence that one may undertake to appraise the influence of conflicting social forces, the power of tradition, the sense of individual responsibility, and then to conjecture as to the future of constitutional government. Nor is it surprising that there should be a wide area of conflict of opinion as to the significance of events in this so-called "Age of Anxiety". One extreme view is that the conception of a constitution of rights, featured especially by an elaboration of checks and balances, "is not only on the way out—it *is* out."[22] Also that "judicial review has contributed to the survival of the Constitution largely by displacing it, for most of the Court's excursions in the constitutional field nowadays the amended document of 1787 has become little more than a point of reference."[23]

By contrast, others assert that despite all the changes the essential features of the Constitution have not been seri-

---

21. A. J. P. Taylor, The Struggle for Mastery of Europe 1848-1919, at 529-30 (1954).

22. Corwin, Total War and the Constitution 180 (1947).

23. Another and similar estimate was that of Carl Becker who prophesied that the Constitutions of the future would be codes shaped by experimental and pragmatic rather than by an absolute conception of rights. See C. L. Becker, New Liberties for Old 95 (1941).

ously altered because there still remain in the Bill of Rights the essence of the procedures devised for the protection of the individual. There still remain, also, the specified restraints upon the executive and legislative branches, and in the minds of the people there can be no doubt that up to now both these branches of government have pretty generally retained their old faith in the supremacy of law. These observers also emphasize that no basic alterations have been made with the acquiescence or approval of the courts; and that as of today, if these or other changes were embodied in Constitutional Amendments, they would be adopted.

A new approach must be found for solving this problem. It seems to me that in the existing state of constitutionalism adequate methods have not yet been found to make public opinion sufficiently effective. Some of the disintegrating factors have already been outlined. Such constructive measures are urgently required; for the very complexity of administration baffles the citizen, impairs his sense of responsibility, and discourages him because of his own lack of expertise in dealing with the exercise of governmental functions.[24] In appraising the future of constitutionalism it is no less important to realize that the forces which have brought about the present degree of social and economic reform will continue increasingly active. More and more their tendency will be to minimize the individual, diminish his power and, in general, lessen his importance in contrast with what is thought to be the general welfare of the generality of citizens. The growth of centralized power in the different industries from steel to entertainment, and even in the larger labor unions, everywhere tends to the requirement of conformity and acquiescence on the part of the individual. The same pressure is more conspicuous in the field of education where interference by political forces or by intolerant trustees is so

24. "Conceding the necessity [for this uncanalized discretionary power] . . . nevertheless, we are confronted by the uncomfortable fact that the experience of history has not yet shown us how constitutional democratic institutions can be preserved in the presence and under the control of ever increasing administrative discretion." E. B. Stason in his introduction to CORWIN, TOTAL WAR AND THE CONSTITUTION viii (1947).

frequent and so disruptive. As Doctor Oppenheimer, Vannevar Bush and many other eminent physicists have repeatedly warned us, all the operations of technology, to say nothing of the revolutionary discoveries in physics, tend inevitably to dwarf the individual.[25] Other powerful forces such as the present processes of mass education and the use of mass media of communication all are making mediocrity an accepted standard and are operating in the direction of reducing the intrinsic importance of the individual.[26]

During the depression and the war, as has been stated, many measures were justified on the basis of emergency and temporary need. But the older law of human psychology has re-taught us the lesson that governmental powers, once exercised, can rarely be denied. The same is true of governmental benefits—once conferred, they can rarely be withdrawn. There is no better illustration of this than the history of the farm support programs. For this reason if for no other we must accept as permanent the changes that have already been made. And it may be said in passing, as already indicated, that one of the gravest doubts as to the future is embodied in the question of whether the public today have an adequate understanding of the origin, the meaning, or the value of restraints in Government and whether the individual has a corresponding sense of personal responsibility for preserving the constitutional guarantees.

In a recent address the late Justice Jackson thus epitomized the problem which confronts the nation:—

> "It seems to me that these traditional freedoms are less in danger of any sudden overthrow than of being gradually bartered or

25. "The modern industrial revolution is bound to devalue the human brain, at least in its simpler and more routine decisions. Of course, just as the skilled carpenter, the skilled mechanic, the skilled dressmaker have in some degree survived the First Industrial Revolution, so the skilled scientist and the skilled administrator may survive the Second. However, taking the Second Revolution as accomplished, the average human being of mediocre attainments or less has nothing to sell that it is worth anyone's money to buy." N. WIENER, quoted in the Saturday Review of Literature, Jan. 22, 1955, p. 13.

26. Compare Lippman's comment on "the fact, so disconcerting an experience in this century that the enfranchised masses have not, surprisingly enough, been those who have most strongly defended the institutions of freedom." W. LIPPMANN, THE PUBLIC PHILOSOPHY 40 (1955).

traded for something else on which the people place a higher current value. In this anxiety-ridden time, many are ready to exchange some of their liberties for a real or fancied increase in security against external foes, internal betrayers or criminals. Others are eager to bargain away local controls for a federal subsidy. Many will give up individual rights for promise of collective advantages. The real question posed by the Fascist and Communist movements, which together have captivated a large part of the world's population, is whether, today, liberty is regarded by the masses of men as their most precious possession. Certainly in the minds of many foreign peoples our type of individual liberty has been outvalued by promises of social welfare and economic security, which they want too passionately to be critical of the price. If this indifference to traditional values should spread to us, it would be the greatest threat to our own liberties."[27]

Here is a statement that goes to the heart of the matter. How is the danger of apathy to be overcome? This is the question that gave pause to Bryce, to Acton, to Godkin and countless other observers, in weighing the future of Democracy—and of constitutionalism as well. And the problem was never more acute than it is today.

This diagnosis suggests implications more profound than appear on the surface, for it reveals that any forecast of the future must rest on the value to be attached to imponderables. While, of course, the reasons for and the importance of the changes in the last twenty years must be the starting point for any estimate of the future, the first question that arises from their consideration is whether they did in fact really embody a "social revolution" and a destructive alteration of constitutional principle? After all, should not the word be evolution instead of revolution? Already, in the lengthening perspective of recent experiences, it is becoming apparent to fair-minded critics that the social and economic pressures which compelled these changes had been building up for at least a generation and that some of them at least were long overdue. Is it not still too early to appraise the influence of these changes upon the mind of the people?

27. Jackson, *The Task of Maintaining Our Liberties: The Role of the Judiciary,* 39 A.B.A.J. 961, 963 (1953).

These questions can be answered only in terms of conjecture. It is at least clear that the public are satisfied with the changes, all of which they conceive to have been made in their interest. It is perhaps not too much to assert that the American social order is on a firmer popular basis than it was in the last generation. One outstanding proof of this is evident in the greatly changed relationships between labor and management. In her recent book, Miss Barbara Ward emphasized the extent to which the new trends have developed most widely and successfully in the United States.

> "Nothing illustrates more starkly the force of myths than the way in which men of the Left in Europe have ignored the transformation that has come about in American industrial society. . . . —the transformation of labor-management relations, the growth of bonus, production and profit-sharing schemes, the experiments in industrial self-government and even private collective ownership,—all these are thoroughly unknown outside America. Yet added together they amount to something close to a revolution."[28]

The same might be said of the success of the farm programs. The question of whether the price paid for these satisfactions is too high lies outside the scope of this discussion. What we are referring to is the present degree of satisfaction and the likelihood that further efforts at economic and social reform and perhaps further extensions of executive and legislative power will continue to develop.

For what remains to be said the fundamental premise, in the last analysis, is that constitutionalism and desire for stability are synonymous. All men, consciously or unconsciously, recognize a hierarchy of values, some more fundamental than others. It is the desire for stability in the social order that induces men to treat certain values as supreme and to protect them by enshrining them in a written document which cannot be readily changed. Accepting, arguendo, this premise, what are the stabilizing forces which will probably operate against further drastic change in constitutional

---

28. B. Ward, Faith and Freedom 220 (1954).

developments? First and most important of these elements making for stability is, of course, the power of tradition, the fact that the American people are thoroughly indoctrinated with respect for constitutionalism. They are law-abiding people.

But in weighing the power of this tradition the history of its origin must be studied and taught afresh in every generation. As has been recently said by Judge Learned Hand:—

> ([M]ake no mistake, the battle is not won; nor will it ever be won. Each generation must decide how far it will seek refuge in eternal and immutable verities rather than grope its way through the tangle of human passions and human credulity. . . . [29]

The assertion that the sense of personal responsibility is the chief guarantee of stability in our Government embodies a real truth. But it is equally important to note that the American conception of that responsibility is moral conviction. Historically the origin and influence of this conception has a long and well-documented record. Lord Lindsay of Balliol quotes Dollinger, Acton's teacher, as saying that "Cromwell was the first among the mighty men of the world to set up one special religious principle, and to enforce it so far as in him lay: . . . the principle of liberty of conscience and the repudiation of religious coercion."[30] Under his powerful leadership this element was transformed into a definite political principle and, as Dollinger adds, "The Constitution of the United States has been built up upon Cromwell's doctrine.[31] The oft cited alliance between the Puritan and the common law lawyer was a natural alliance and it has long been recognized by historians as a powerful factor in developing the distinctive policy both of England and of the United States.

Yet commentators seem all too prone to ignore the ethical content of the Federal Constitution, and particularly of the Bill of Rights. For the fundamental sense of right and wrong which has been in evidence in politics and also in law

---

29. New York Times Magazine, Aug. 9, 1953, p. 8, col. 2.
30. A. D. Lindsay, The Essentials of Democracy 76 (1929).
31. *Ibid.*

ever since the days of the Puritan Commonwealth still remains as the controlling principle embodied in the Bill of Rights.

Acton declared that the political discovery of the seventeenth century was that religious liberty is the generating principle of civil liberty. Throughout his writings the word "conscience" is continually emphasized as the most important human attribute in maintaining the traditional power of freedom. Cardozo expresses something of the same thought in his declaration that a judge is under a duty, within the limits of his power of innovation, to maintain a relation between law and morals, "between the precepts of jurisprudence and those of reason and good conscience."[32] Whether this conviction of right and wrong, of what is fair between man and man, be treated as of sacred origin or as the result of life experience is something not immediately involved in this discussion. The important fact is that this innate quality is characteristic of the free citizen and that throughout our history this has been an all-important factor. This element was the "higher law" to which Otis appealed in the Revolution and Seward in the crisis of the Civil War. This is the element which Elihu Root thought determined the quality of public morality over and above all considerations of law and social theory. It is the quality that Hughes had in mind in declaring that "in the forum of conscience, duty to a moral power higher than the State has always been maintained."[33]

The effect of this conscience, or whatever it may be called, connotes today, as it has for generations, the fundamental necessity for self-restraint and self-discipline as necessary supports for the doctrine of legal restraints upon Government. Whatever the name given to this influence it has always expressed the close relationship between law and moral experience and it has a long history of unwavering faith in the dynamic power innate in the concept of indivi-

---

32. Cardozo, The Nature of the Judicial Process 133-34 (1921).
33. United States v. Macintosh, 283 U.S. 605, 633 (1931) (dissenting opinion).

dual freedom. While political scientists and the school of positivists seem consciously to avoid the words "conscience," "religion," etc., it is none the less true that this regard of the citizen for moral quality is one of the most profoundly significant as well as pervasive influences in shaping public opinion. The Court Reorganization Bill of 1937, for example, was defeated not because of legalistic considerations; but because the masses of the people, once they understood the problem, were overwhelmingly antagonistic to the proposed change in the structure of the Court: it violated their ideas of fair play. If and when the realization is brought home to them of the unfair character of hearings by many administrative officials, they will show the same resentment. The recent overthrow of a Senatorial demagogue was not entirely due to the solicitude of Senators for the honor of their body. It was due to the ground swell of moral protest coming from the masses of the people. They were primarily inspired not by emotion, but by moral conviction. It was the "public conscience" that rebelled. As already indicated the immediate and widespread approval of the Supreme Court's decision on seizure of the Steel Plants in 1952 was due to the same sense of moral resentment.

In relation to public affairs, and particularly to the original Constitution, this moral attitude is unquestionably one of the great stabilizing forces in American society. Nor can its origin or power be explained away by attributing it solely to early struggles on "the moving frontier", the inevitable growth of neighborliness, the necessity of inter-dependence, or similar reasons. Confirmation for this statement may, I think, be readily found in the views of the late Professor Whitehead. He thought that the Americans had developed into a separate and distinctive race,—a race dominated by good will and an unprecedented willingness to cooperate in good causes. In fact, he believed that no other race in the history of mankind had ever shown such innate qualities of tolerance and cooperation.[34]

---

34. DIALOGUES OF ALFRED NORTH WHITEHEAD 134 157, 316 and *passim* Price ed. (1954).

The incalculable unifying effect of the social forces embodied in community cooperation is the greatest of these stabilizing factors, and these factors have a very definite relation to law observance as well as to the continued maintenance of faith in "Constitutionalism". It is not only important that there are some eighteen hundred Community Chests supported by annual campaigns through the voluntary efforts of hundreds of thousands of citizens, nor that history affords no similar record of voluntary efforts unselfishly put forth for a common purpose. The really important fact is that these organized efforts can be maintained in no other nation except America. Undoubtedly this is the kind of phenomenon that led Professor Whitehead to the conviction that the American social system is, on the whole, the best that has ever existed. This unifying effort of common purpose operating in all parts of the nation and in all types of communities is something wholly new in the world. No appraisement of ideas, philosophical, political or social, can be made without taking into account these forces promoting common morality everywhere latent in the American polity. The most common demonstration of the power of this web of good will is in the way in which the old test of what is fair between man and man dominates every aspect of American life. Once a political question takes on moral aspects in the minds of the general public, there is but one answer to the problem.

And it is this imponderable factor above all which will protect the future of constitutionalism. The principles that provide this pervasive stability are the same principles that men recognize as morally inspired and which in the past they have sought to protect and preserve by enshrining them in constitutions. Professor Edman was right in saying that throughout the nineteenth century constitutionalism was a religion in America. It represented the elemental moralities, —powers above and more sacred than the law. And as long as this all-pervasive condition of common purpose and cooperative effort continues, Americans will seek to protect the values which they deem of most importance by enshrining them in constitutional declarations.

Certain general observations suggest themselves. In one sense the most important is that historically our constitutional development has been one of oscillations. During the recent war there was, perhaps naturally, a vast expansion of executive power. Today, on the contrary, we seem to be in an era of attempted expansion of power on the part of Congress. Examples of this are the recent attempts to interfere with the decisions of the Executive in the field of foreign policy, of which the advocacy of the Bricker Amendment is only one example. Then, too, it may be fairly said that the Congress has been literally running wild with trials and investigations and, disgracefully enough, playing fast and loose with old doctrines of fair play. We have already commented on the changing attitude on the part of the general public and the reviving of a sense of moral resentment after the war. Perhaps we have not realized sufficiently that in the early 1930's Congress was not legislating in the ordinary sense of the term with reference to the so-called New Deal program, "[r]ather, it had responded to the demands of the executive branch for power to meet an emergency."[35] This observation suggests another pertinent thought. In the light of the character of issues, both domestic and foreign, now under debate in the Congress it seems clear beyond doubt that the Congress will act with a great degree of deliberateness in enacting any further drastic legislation in the economic field or in extending perceptibly the powers of the Executive.

There are other uncertainties in such a forecast. The most outstanding example of this is the extraordinary popularity of the Court decision in the *Steel Seizure*[36] case. Similarly, as Professor Freund has recently shown, the constitutional principle of federalism which twenty years ago was thought to be hopelessly neglected has now been re-asserted and the separate States with fresh interest are successfully establishing policies which must inevitably slow down the

---

35. 2 PUSEY, CHARLES EVANS HUGHES 731 (1951).
36. Youngstown Sheet & Tube Co. v. Sawyer, 343 U.S. 579 (1952).

tendency to centralization in the National Government.[37]

All this corroborates the familiar assertion that constitutional history is usually the record of a series of oscillations. The attitude of the public in the *Steel Seizure* case and the re-development of federalism are, to say the least, not symptoms of disregard of the original constitutional principles. As a calculated risk one may venture the observation that the last national election clearly established that the popular will favored the middle way and was not sympathetic with radical change.

And recurring to the topic of oscillation in the exercise of power, it must be said that the rulings of the Supreme Court have not been entirely consistent. While that Court has shown the greatest sensitiveness and concern in dealing with State legislation and in protecting the liberties of the citizen under the Fourteenth Amendment, it has not exhibited quite the same degree of concern in dealing with issues of this character resulting from the activities of the Federal Government. Perhaps this is due to the reluctance of the Court to interfere with the Executive and with Congress in what are said to be the areas of national defense. The failure of the Court to do justice in *Bailey v. Richardson*[38] and in the *War Bride* case[39] illustrates this point.

In disposing of the issue of the refusal by Jehovah's Witnesses to register for military service, the Court during wartime evaded decision by resorting to the theory that the plaintiff had not exhausted his remedies.[40] It was not until after hostilities had ceased that the basic issues were answered. Similarly, it is not without significance that the Court during the war refused to protect the citizens of Japanese origin against a grave invasion of their rights both to liberty and to property.[41] The same Court, after the war, declared invalid the im-

37. P. Freund, *Federalism in America,* in PERSPECTIVES U.S.A. No. 10, at 5(1955).

38. *Supra* note 19.

39. Knauff v. Shaughnessy, 338 U.S. 537 (1950).

40. Falbo v. United States, 320 U. S. 549, 554 (1944).

41. Cases cited note 15 *supra.*

position of Military Government upon the Hawaiian Islands.[42] This same phenomenon occurred in and after the Civil War and, to some degree, in and after the first world war. It is mentioned here not by way of criticism but as proof that even our highest Court in crises shows some of the signs of the same oscillation which is characteristic of the other branches of Government.

In the area of administrative process the Court has been fairly vigilant on the issue of division of powers. While the decisions are few in number, the *Lovett* case[43] and also the *Humphrey*[44] case present clear demonstrations of this sensitiveness. Outside the fields occupied by the administrative agencies, recent history seems to show that the doctrine of separation of powers has much greater vitality than it was credited with twenty years ago. In the field of administrative agencies much improvement must be made. The early attitude of the judiciary was unmistakably jealous of the increasing creation of administrative agencies, and it would seem that Congress, in attempting to protect them, has taken too much power away from the judiciary. Any practicing lawyer familiar with the procedures in many of these agencies will cordially endorse this statement. In this field, no less than in that embraced in the field of individual rights, matters of procedure are of the first importance.

These observations suggest that perhaps we are too sensitive and over-critical about changes in fields not affecting the liberties of the individual. There is certainly evident a slowing down at this moment in the process of socialization or other radical changes in the field of economics. In short, there is apparent in this area no immediate threat to the existing status of constitutionalism. The changes of interpretation in the field of economics made in the last twenty years demonstrate at least that the constitutional framework is sufficiently rugged to meet great emergencies.

42. Duncan v. Kahanamoku, 327 U.S. 304 (1946).
43. United States v. Lovett, 328 U.S. 303 (1946).
44. Humphrey's Executor v. United States, 295 U.S. 602 (1935).

In the field of civil liberties, however, the trend is quite the other way and, as has already been indicated, the threat to individual freedom is immediate and menacing. Even more portentous is the fact that invasions of individual freedom in this field during this generation show historically a clear and consistent trend inimical to all previous concepts of freedom. The worst evil is, of course, the refusal to ensure a fair trial to persons seeking employment either in the Government or in certain areas of private industry. Congress could change this if it were not living in an atmosphere of all-pervasive fear. But here above everywhere else the judiciary could, if it chose, find adequate reason for outlawing the alien procedures which are becoming fixtures in the administrative process. In *Rochin v. California*,[45] an unlawful invasion of personal liberty by state action, Mr. Justice Frankfurter, speaking for the Court, declared that due process of law under the Fourteenth Amendment is a summarized constitutional guarantee of respect for those personal immunities which, as Mr. Justice Cardozo twice wrote for the Court, are "so rooted in the tradition and conscience of our people as to be ranked as fundamental."[46] We can only hope that when the issue of fair hearing comes squarely before the Court it will use these same standards in protecting the individual who has been accused in administrative proceedings of subversive practices, leanings or associations.

These views are not those of a legal philosopher: they embody only the observations and experience of one who has been actively engaged in practice during the past generation. After all, and despite all the changes, the daily life and habits of the citizen have not changed—except perhaps in an increased sense of well being. His respect for law and government has not changed, nor is there any indication that he has lost his reverence for constitutional government. Above all, and despite threatened curtailments of his liberty, his sense of fair play remains unaltered. That moral conviction must

45. 342 U.S. 165 (1952).
46. *Id.* at 169.

be his shield and buckler. And although those threats are menacing at the moment, perhaps we can derive hope from the increasing frequency with which members of the Supreme Court in these latter years have been referring to "standards of fair play". And we may also derive some confidence and encouragement from Cardozo's observation:—

> "Ever in the making, as law develops through the centuries, is this new faith which silently and steadily effaces our mistakes and eccentricities. I sometimes think that we worry ourselves overmuch about the enduring consequences of our errors. They may work a little confusion for a time. In the end, they will be modified or corrected or their teachings ignored. The future takes care of such things."[47]

COMMENT

MR. JOHN LORD O'BRIAN*

When I was invited to come to this conference, I promptly declined, with the explanation that I was neither a legal philosopher nor a legal scholar, not a graduate even of the Harvard Law School, but simply what my friend Judge Wyzanski genially calls a "run of the calendar" lawyer. To my regret (and perhaps to yours eventually), the Dean wrote back that he knew all that, but he thought it would be wise to have an old trial lawyer as a foil, perhaps. I couldn't think of the answer to that, so I accepted.

Our friend Learned Hand said the other day that one advantage of old age—he was talking of men of my vintage —was that it gives you time to reflect on the values and sort out those which, after all, have proven to be most worth while. That idea is my excuse for admitting that this paper

47. CARDOZO, THE NATURE OF THE JUDICIAL PROCESS 179 (1921).

* JOHN LORD O'BRIAN, *of the Washington, D. C. Bar.* Mr. O'Brian was born in Buffalo, New York, in 1874. He took his A.B. at Harvard College in 1896 and his LL.B. at the University of Buffalo in 1898. He has practiced law in Buffalo and in Washington. He has served in the legislature of his State, and assisted in the drafting of his State constitution. He has held many different legal offices in the federal government. He has served Harvard as a member of the Board of Overseers and as President of the Alumni Association. His Godkin Lectures, delivered at Harvard in 1955, were published under the title, "National Security and Individual Freedom."

of mine deals largely with the imponderables, because that is the world in which at present I am living. If you disagree with my views, as many of you will, I am sure, you can comfort yourselves perhaps in a degree by the fact that you are listening to one of the last of the Victorians, and perhaps the last one that you will ever hear.

For when I came to the law—in the last century—I accepted gladly the definition that "the law is the witness and the external deposit of our moral life: its history is the history of the moral development of the race." It may surprise some of you, in view of a different interpretation later given by the same individual, to know that that was the definition given by Mr. Justice Holmes in 1897. I don't know whether in later years he would have quite put it that way; I think not. But perhaps he was corrupted or seduced on this occasion by the fact that he was addressing what Dean Bundy would say is a singularly moral community. He was speaking at a Yale Commencement.

In what I've written in this volume, of course the overtones throughout are, I frankly admit, those of one who believes that the Constitution and Bill of Rights embody certain concepts of conscience which were originally inspired by moral conviction and later adopted into the common law and given a political direction. I shall not pursue that particularly because no one has contributed more to enlighten us on that fact than Dean Pound in his earlier essays. While I never had the privilege of being a student under him, I'd like to assure him today, as he has been assured many times, that all of us look to him with gratitude as our greatest scholar and exponent of American law.

The first part of my paper deals with the origin of certain guarantees of the Bill of Rights as moral convictions in the time of the Puritan ascendency under the Commonwealth. Speaking, though, of the present value of constitutionalism, I summarize very briefly now my own view in this way: I accept Judge Wyzanski's definition that constitutionalism as of today is "the institutionalization of the principle that the state's goal is the increase in opportunities for the development of the individual as the seat of ultimate spiritual and creative authority." And may I say right here that I especially appreciated the privilege of listening to his very thoughtful address. I think you share in my sense of misfortune that I should be placed on the same program with him this morning. For me his was not only a very profound statement but a very moving one, and if you will forgive me, may I say also that it was in that ennobling vein which we have come to associate with his utterances, and which in reality reflects the personality of the Judge himself.

I accept for the purpose of this discussion—although as a life-long Republican I accept it with a hard swallow at the moment—I accept the fact that we are living in a service state. I also accept the great changes that have been made in the interpretation of the Constitution of late years. I realize that I'm living in a welfare state, I realize perhaps more than some others the extent to which new responsibilities and new obligations will be placed upon the citizen by this revolutionary change which has taken place. But immediately there arise in my mind certain questions. And one concrete question comes from the fact that you and I believe that the stability of this country and its continued existence as a nation depend upon the sense of responsibility and the conscience of the individual citizen. And we view with something like alarm the fact that all economic tendencies at the moment are in the direction of dwarfing his sense of significance. I am not sure but that a good many of the statutory changes tend to produce the same disastrous effect.

The second concrete problem that arises with some of us is what is to be done about review in the field of the administrative agencies. The diffusion of executive power through a vast number of agencies is bound to increase the initial steps towards socialization, if I may use that subversive word. Many of us believe that this tendency will continue—there will be more agencies, there will be more administrative officials — and the great unsolved problem I think in government today, the greatest one affecting the liberties of the citizen, is what is to be done about providing adequate review for the findings of these agencies. As Professor Corwin, whom I quoted in my paper, said: "Historical experience has not shown us how democratic institutions can be preserved in the pressures and under the controls of administrative discretion." And this danger takes on very serious proportions, I think you will admit, now that the regulatory power of government has been extended to encroach upon the field of freedom formerly thought to be protected by the First Amendment.

Few people realize—few lawyers, I find, realize—that for the first time in our history we have empowered administrative officials—and that means subordinate administrative officials— to deal with the ideas of men and hold inquisitions into their beliefs, their associations, and their aspirations. But passing that for the moment, you will admit, I think, that in the administrative agencies the so-called doctrine of separation of powers has really become a myth in actual practice. The standards of competency for appointment to administrative agencies is a subject that would take a paper in itself. I pass that.

As of today the citizens of this country are content with the changes. They may not grasp the full significance of some of them, but with that infinite patience which characterizes our citizens the changes have been accepted. The people are satisfied and their sense of well-being has been increased.

Now, what about the future of constitutionalism, the other topic assigned to me for discussion? That depends, I think, upon what the stabilizing influences are in the minds of the people. The American citizen lives by faith. While he cannot quote the Constitution verbatim, he believes in his own way, as was said yesterday by, I think Professor Cushman, he believes that the Constitution of the United States will protect him in all lawful activities because unconsciously he equates it with his own sense of right and wrong. This is a fundamental belief of his, and the emphasis of right and wrong in his mind comes from a long, long inheritance. As Vannevar Bush said the other day in an address to his fellow scientists, the urge to help one's fellow man does not derive from knowledge of the physical sciences. It is these imponderables that I am speaking of, which are difficult to define and which may seem out of place in a legal discussion; but which are nevertheless the imponderables that determine the course of history in this country.

I lay special emphasis on one feature of American life which is significant and the significance of which I think escapes most foreign critics—even so gifted a critic as D. W. Brogan. I refer to the effect of the vast number of voluntary associations in this country, in communities extending throughout the entire United States where people annually band themselves together to pursue and support good causes. Did it ever occur to you that the so-called Community Chest is an institution unique and peculiar to this country, and that it probably could not be maintained in any other country, unless in our neighboring country, Chief Justice Kerwin's nation? Think of the drives that we complain about. Think of the incredible number of activities where citizens band themselves together, temporarily, perhaps, for a particular purpose. That is a phenomenon that, I think I may fairly say, is peculiar to America, and it is a phenomenon that has had a very definite effect upon the body politic. The moral attitude evinced by these organizations, the pervasive sense of moral values which they implement, I venture to think, is the controlling influence in the public opinion in America today. The reason why I think that constitutionalism will continue to have validity for an indefinite period is that there are these intangible evidences of faith on the part of the individual—the element of conscience which contributes to the mutual confidence that is the only real foundation for the continuation of this nation.

And no appraisement, I said in this paper, no appraisement of progress in this country in the field of ideas can be made fairly without taking into consideration this fundamental fact. What astonished Professor Whitehead was the amazing extent of will to cooperate in this country. It is this all-pervasive exercise of will for a common purpose which is one of the great imponderable influences. I think even our social scientists up to now have not realized the power resulting from this spirit.

We have listened to enlightening discussions on due process; but the common man thinks that due process of law is equivalent to a conscientious determination of what is right, and that he will be protected in that. If he had heard our discussions, he might have had some doubt about that; but fortunately he doesn't know any better, and he expects that the government will be a bulwark of protection for all his rights.

Having said that, and having said that we all agree that the Constitution now has become an affirmative instrument with which social ideas are to be put into practice, it is a little chilling to discover that there is one area today where injustice does continue and where practices that are unjust are held to be beyond the reach of the courts. This significant fact suggests also that perhaps the idea of the Constitution as a limitation upon official power is not yet quite obsolete. I refer, of course, to the procedures which characterize the so-called loyalty and security programs. This is the most controversial subject one could discuss and I have no intention of getting into the controversy. I call attention to its existence, however, as one that presents grave dangers. Let me say at once that those of us who are disturbed about these problems fully realize the extraordinary character of the dangers that surround us, and the difficulties that we have in meeting foreign infiltration and corrosive ideas. We fully agree that this country must protect itself by some sort of security program, but when it comes to hearings, conducted by subordinate administrative officials, when it comes to attributing ideas to people through guilt by association, when it comes to refusing a brilliant young lieutenant a commission because of his mother's former views, the situation is not only grotesque: it is wicked. Beyond this I am not going to enter that discussion, though I hope there may be some discussion from the floor about it. Here is a field of patent injustices where you do not need any discussion of the refinements of due process of law, or any subtle approach supported by citations of law. Here is an evil that is bold and barefaced. What is the use of our talking about presumptions of innocence and the other presumptions we've been discussing, when this situation can go unremedied? What is it that I am saying? Well, I am saying that this is an area into which the courts must extend their powers. Repeatedly they have told us that the concept of due process is not a fixed concept; it is the most majestic concept in our law; that it can't be defined and perhaps it will have to be extended. And in my opinion it is peculiarly their obligation to deal with problems of fair hearings.

The American test of right and wrong is the test of fair play—what is fair between man and man. The public, once they become aroused to the facts of a situation like this, will not rest until something is done, either by the legislature or the courts, to correct it. In that regard, I place myself gladly in accord with the view of Mr. Justice Jackson in one of his public addresses, in which, among other things, he said: "We cannot approve any use of official powers or position to prejudice, injure or condemn a person's liberty, property or good name, which does not inform him of the substance and source of the charge, give him a timely and open-minded hearing as to its truth, safeguards without which no judgement can have a sound foundation."

You see, I was brought up in an atmosphere pervaded by Victorian concepts of law. In carrying out those concepts many think that the Victorians failed pretty miserably; but they did have the idea that standards of justice were to be measured by the needs of the individual—not of the state.

Some years ago, in an exchange of correspondence with my friend the late Elihu Root, we were discussing with each other the qualifications of a candidate for a vacancy on our great court, and he made this remark: "I should hope that a man would be found who was fully conscious of the moral quality of honor that underlies all Anglo-American jurisprudence." And in my view on this subject I take my stand in accord with that ideal. I am not a pessimist. This particular evil that I refer to will be corrected, as I point out in my paper. Whenever the American public gets the idea that a public issue involves a question of honor, of right and wrong—a moral question—there's never but one answer. That was true in the Court Packing episode, that was true of the enthusiasm which the decision in the *Steel Plant Seizure Case* aroused. You have seen similar instances of it everywhere about you. In other words, in approaching the Constitution, what I'm really saying is that no canon of interpretation in this day can omit the element of moral conviction. And I might quote somebody who said it more wisely, in saying that "there can be no health in a democracy where there is no acceptance of the supremacy of law, where the law is not interpreted in terms of the highest moral insights regarding man's nature." And incidentally I fully agree with the remark made by Dean Bundy yesterday that we cannot rest content with any reckoning of due process which omits a strong and central role of simple fairness.

Gentlemen, you may not agree with these views. I can only say that they are the views of one who, with advancing years, has grown more and more sensitive to the injustices that he has encountered in the field of the law. As some wise man said a while ago—and this is my own apologia—we progress as a race only as we consciously increase the intensity of our sense of injustice. This, then, is my faith. I personally have all confidence in the continued existence of constitutionalism in this country, because of my faith in the irresistible moral power exerted by the conscience, the sense of fair play, and the sense of decency which I believe to be inherent in the average American.

Mr. O'Brian spoke without oratorical display, but his quiet words had an obvious and profound effect on the audience which filled the Ames Courtroom. When he came to his conclusion, by a common impulse the assembly stood and applauded long beyond the time required only for a generous salute to an old friend. The reminder of an intimate connection between moral power and human freedom had deeply moved the Conference.

MR. BIRNBAUM*

Mr. O'Brian mentioned the difficulty of following Judge Wyzanski. Need I mention the difficulty of following Mr. O'Brian?

I think we are here because the law is not a learned profession—it is a learning profession. We have come here to learn, in the company of this distinguished group, what government under law means. As I studied the papers and listened to the discussions, I have been more and more impressed not only with the differences in the answers that have been given, but even more with the differences in the problems which have been selected for discussion under the aegis of this one basic subject.

Many philosophers have been quoted here and I would like to refer, if I may, to the modern Machiavelli, Pareto, who wrote four volumes filled with what I think may charitably be described in large part as intellectual rubbish. However, he did urge one thing that I believe is at least a keynote for our thought; we spend our lives in the hope, some profitably, some unprofitably, of approaching truth.

In the field of constitutional law, it seems to me that above all we must realize that all absolutes are not absolutely true. A constitution, at least our constitution, consists in large parts of thou shalts and thou shalt nots, and if I may, without offense, draw my first illustration from holy scriptures, let me compare the Sixth Commandment, thou shalt

* HAROLD FISCH BIRNBAUM, *of the Los Angeles Bar.* Mr. Birnbaum was born in 1901. He graduated from the University of Colorado in 1920, and took his LL.B. at the Harvard Law School in 1923. He practices law in New York and in Los Angeles, specializing in financial legal problems, and in the reform of law in this field. He has served the United States on the legal staff of the Shipping Board, and as a Special Assistant to the United States Attorney for the Southern District of New York. He is the author of "Secured Transactions Under the Uniform Commercial Code," published in 1954, and of many periodical articles. Mr. Birnbaum has combined with his practice of law in financial fields an acute and continuing interest in problems of civil liberties.

not kill, and the Ninth Commandment, thou shalt not bear false witness. We know that killing may be excusable in self-defense, it may be justifiable to prevent the commission of a crime, it may be mandatory at the order of the state, and yet it is expressed in the same absolute terms of the Ninth Commandment, thou shalt not bear false witness against thy neighbor, to which, so far as I know, there are no exceptions. Perjury is not justified in self-defense, or in the prevention of crime; and perjury at the behest of the government is among the most reprehensible things which we can conceive.

Therefore I approach the problem of government under law as I think Mr. O'Brian has done, with the desire to test once more the axioms and postulates on which we were brought up, to see whether rules which were accepted as true in 1920 or 1900, or even in 1789, are entitled to equal acceptance today. In fact, as I was reminded by the terms of my invitation to speak here, some of these axioms are themselves topics which I think deserve the concentrated attention of the members of this conference as we continue at our homes to reflect upon what we have learned during our assemblage. I mean that we must re-examine again and again, in calmer days, the conclusions that were reached in time of crisis, bearing in mind the function of government. I should like, with deference, to attempt a new definition of government (at least one I have not heard before) derived from the President's oath of office. Just as the President swears to preserve, protect and defend the Constitution, so it seems to me that the function of government is to preserve, protect and defend the nation, and the individuals who make it up.

First among the matters to be re-examined, I would list the issue of free speech. At least before the techniques of propaganda developed as we have witnessed in totalitarian regimes, most of us believed in free speech as one of the absolute marks of free society. We recognized that there is no absolute privilege to utter libel or to cry fire in a crowded theater, but so far as ideas were concerned, we subscribed to the views of Voltaire that we must defend the right to urge views that we hate, as well as those which we believe in. I suggest that this view of free speech should be re-examined, not only as it was involved in *Dennis v. United States,* 341 U.S. 494 (1951), but also as it was involved in the cases involving *Terminiello,* 337 U.S. 1 (1949) and *Beauharnais,* 343 U.S. 250 (1952). Have we set the right limits on freedom to preach the doctrines of Communism, and are we equally right in regard to preaching religious and racial bigotry? Is it true that a free government must allow freedom to attack its principles up to the point where there is a clear and present danger that the attack will succeed? How far must we keep in mind the warning of Mr. Justice Jackson, that we can keep our eyes on the stars and stumble into the well?

A second question for re-examination is guilt by association. I mean all forms of nonpersonal guilt. Let me illustrate by referring to the internment camps which our country established, on American soil, for persons of Japanese ancestry, citizens and noncitizens alike. I am far from saying that the decision made under the stress of war to intern them was wrong; perhaps it was right by every pragmatic standard; but that again is a decision which I think is relevant for reconsideration by a conference like this.

Next is the question which was left unanswered by the Supreme Court in the *Peters* case, 349 U.S. 331 (1955). When a man is accused of wrongdoing, does he have an absolute right to know who accuses him, and what the evidence is? Is it possible that the disclosure of these facts might jeopardize effective counter-espionage, and might endanger the safety of the country? If so, what are we going to do about it? Must we choose between letting the ten guilty men escape and letting one innocent man suffer?

Again, when Paul Robeson is denied a passport to Russia, we accept the decision, some of us, with more or less equanimity. But suppose Fermi, to whom we owe so much, had applied for a passport to Russia, or Albert Einstein? You all remember that Major General Dean, writing about the episode of his captivity, said that his one hope was for strength that he would not reveal military secrets under torture. This led me to wonder: Suppose a retired general of the Strategic Air Command applies for a passport. May a free government say to him, "Of course we trust your loyalty, but we must restrict your civic liberty merely because of what you know"?

I don't pretend to have the answer to these questions, and I cite them only as illustration of the broad issue which is posed by this conference: What is the place of constitutionalism in government, if the function of government is to protect, preserve and defend the nation?

Mr. O'Brian has pointed to the environment of constitutionalism in the United States, the spirit of tolerance and good will, the desire to work together, combined with a love and a reverence for fair play. Second, he has traced for us the way in which our constitutional doctrines change by oscillation, like a pendulum. Third, he has warned us that the greatest current danger is the fact that we have accepted or acquiesced in the regulation and control of commerce and business, which leads to the danger that we will equally acquiesce in the control and regulation of individual liberties.

I venture to express one final thought of my own. A generation ago, the cardinal rule for constitutional lawyers was the Latin motto, *insta principiis,* beware of beginnings! Don't allow the slightest invasion of the constitutional principle, because once it has started, you can never stop. Once you have started down the road, you must follow it to its end, even though you perceive that the end leads over the precipice. This, I respectfully submit, is not so, for history has shown that we can put on the brakes and stop.

We have realized, I think, that the greatest freedom is the freedom of choice. I illustrate it by reminding you that over ten years ago governmental officials regulated what goods could be manufactured, the prices at which they could be sold, the salaries and wages which could be paid, and whether you were even free to quit your job if in the judgment of government officials you were engaged in an essential industry. These were surely the beginnings of socialism, the beginnings of the impairment of liberty. But it required no revolution—not even a new election—for us to reverse this trend.

The greatest freedom is freedom from the tyranny of absolutes, the freedom to make a new and different choice when a new and different choice seems wiser and better. In our never-ending search for truth, we know that we can bar polygamy, or perhaps require innoculation in time of an epidemic, and yet that this is no precedent for proscribing the free exercise of any religion or of all religions. We know that we can make it illegal to use the fighting words which incite disorder and riots, and that this is no precedent for censoring an appeal to reason. Our courts can create the doctrine of a federal common law, or separate but equal education facilities, and the courts can overrule these doctrines sometimes after a century of acceptance, when they conclude that it is wiser to go in the opposite direction.

We have confidence that we can recognize, before it is too late, when a difference in degree has become a difference in kind. As Chief Justice Kerwin mentioned this morning, the gloss of Holmes on Marshall is that the power to tax is not the power to destroy as long as the Supreme Court sits. In my judgment, in the field of government, this is the triumph of constitutionalism.

PROFESSOR BEER*

I think it is appropriate that these last words should be words of criticism of government under law, constitutionalism, the rule of law, the supremacy of law, and in general, what Mr. Justice Frankfurter calls the spirit of law. He spoke in praise not only of the spirit of law, but also of imaginative insight, not too much burdened by the demands for

* SAMUEL HUTCHISON BEER, *Professor of Government, Harvard Unversity.* Professor Beer was born in 1911 in Ohio. He took a B.A. at Michigan in 1932, and, as a Rhodes Scholar, a B.A. at Oxford in 1935. He was awarded the Ph.D. by Harvard in 1943. He was a Captain of Anti-Aircraft Artillery in World War II. He has been a member of the Harvard faculty since 1946; he became Professor of Government in 1953, and is now Chairman of the Department of Government. He is the author of "The City of Reason," and of numerous periodical publications in the field of government.

uniformity. I take these two to be antithetical, and wish to strike a blow against the spirit of law and in favor of imaginative insight. After all, my colleague, Professor Hartz, has spoken in praise of revolution; I don't see why I shouldn't try to raise three cheers for Charles the First.

I'm a little surprised to find myself in this particular situation, and I don't find it an easy task, but I do find it an inevitable one, after being inundated by the praise of constitutionalism and the spirit of law generally which we find in the papers printed last May and in this conference. I think it must make you wonder whether such popularity can be deserved. Unanimity is always a little fishy. I mean this seriously. How can you assess the value of constitutionalism if you don't seriously compare it with its opposite, and that's what I want to try to suggest to you. For I think there is something to be said for the opposite, namely for unconstitutionalism, or, if you like, for personalism. (I won't say despotism; that would prejudice my case even more, although it might be technically more accurate.)

With Mr. O'Brian I agree—we favor both the supremacy of law and moral insight. But these two things continually run against one another. Any judge must know that very well, whether he admits it or not.

Let us begin from common sense. Is there any other social activity which we think ought to be under a government of laws, not men, which we think ought to be run as strictly as possible according to the rule of law? Take the family, for instance. Did those of you who are parents ever satisfactorily frame a rule which defined when your little boy ought or ought not to fight, or when your teen-age daughter had to get in after her date? I mean a real rule, a clear, comprehensive rule — without any bogus escape clauses, such as "reasonableness," or some such phrase—which covered all the cases which did arise or were likely to arise. I don't have to say any more than that to remind you of those many occasions when the rule did not cover the case, or the even more painful time when the rule, logically and strictly speaking, did cover the case, but when it would have been unjust and impracticable and contrary to the interests and common purposes of the family for you to enforce it. What you did then, I suggest, was to follow the demands of moral insight and justice, depart from the rule, and make a judgment based upon the unique and special circumstances of that particular case. It is not only the family that provides illustrations. Take business, for example. What kind of success would an entrepreneur have if he ran his business according to the book? Or what chance would a general have of winning his battles if he fought them strictly according to the manual?

In any social activity there is an element of science in the large sense of the word: domestic science (if that's the right word) in the home; economic science, political science, legal science, military science. But if you are going to achieve the purpose which you set out to achieve, there is also another element—an element of, let us say, art—through which the wisdom appropriate to a unique situation may be found. This means that it is through this art that decision and action are adapted to new and possibly unique circumstances.

Whether you are speaking of the moral science or the social sciences—those sciences which are descriptive or those which are imperative—there is this same general situation. On the one hand you have the repetitive and recurring situations which are essentially alike and which can be dealt with by rules, by law. On the other hand, continually and perhaps all the time, there are unique situations which must be dealt with by acts of evaluation and judgment which are not logically derived from the rules and may, indeed, even be in conflict with them.

Now if this is true of other social activities, why shouldn't it also be true of government in general, and in particular of that part of government which is constituted by the administration of justice? Why, at any rate, in the administration of justice, should we try to eliminate the element of art, of personal judgment, of imaginative insight, and insist instead upon the spirit of the law? Why should we make an ideal of the spirit of law, when the spirit seems—from a common sense point of view—so hostile to the task which we have before us? For in government, also, "the differences of men and actions, and the endless irregular movements of human things, do not admit of any universal and simple rule; and no art, whatsoever, can lay down a rule which will last for all time."

These, of course, are the words in which Plato argued this point. From that reasoning, he went on to propose his state governed by the philosopher kings, who would be free of legal restraint and who—I am quoting Professor McIlwain's summary—by their wisdom, would achieve justice by giving every man his due, not the due of some average man who never existed or can exist. Now, of course, Plato, like any sensible man, was of two minds on this question—this whole great and ancient question whether it is better to be governed by the best man, or the best laws. And similarly, what I would propose is that what we ought to have, and indeed, what it seems to me we actually do have in our political and judicial systems, is a mixture of the rule of law and the rule of men. We have constitutionalism and we also have personalism, meaning by this the existence of wide opportunities for judgments which do not follow strictly from the existing rules, but which serve justice by considering the exceptional circumstances. Off hand, I would think the most striking example is the power of pardon which we normally find possessed by the executive. When you get into the work of a parole commission, you see even more this opportunity to make some kind of more subtle adjustment of punishment and treatment to the circumstances of the criminal and the crime.

Now I say we have both things — constitutionalism and personalism—not one under the other, but each on a plane with the other, each, we hope, offsetting and guarding against the vices of the other. The vices of personal discretion or personalism are so well known, so often mentioned, that I do not need to speak of them. I suppose the principal one is the danger that the prejudice and passions of the judge or the administrator or the official will lead to injustice in his decisions. But note: if that is the characteristic vice of personal discretion, its virtue also is that it opens up the opportunity for the moral sensitivity of the judge or the official to achieve that greater justice required by the special circumstances which always or almost always are present. Furthermore in addition to its virtues, which are well known, the rule of law has also its less-often mentioned vice. This vice is the one that Plato emphasized and it appears precisely when the law is impartially and impersonally administered. Indeed, what excites our anger and despair is to see this passionless, impersonal machine imposing the crude generalities of law upon this infinitely various, complex, shifting, changing, human material of society where each individual is not a case under a general rule, no matter how complicated you make the rule, but an individual.

I suppose it is a function of the legislature to bring this personal element into government. Yet the legislature, too, must work by means of general rules; hence, continually we see this great impersonal machine created in large part by statute doing injustice, or preventing a greater justice. To some extent this is offset by the fortunate provision of opportunity at every level for personal discretion—whether it is that of a policeman who happens to be able to make a distinction between things which are legally the same but morally different, or a judge, or a jury, or a governmental official, and so on.

What is the bearing of this on constitutional law? I suppose the root of the trouble is that law is not an adequate means of expressing justice and it is precisely because we are concerned with justice that we must be dissatisfied with law. This is true of justice in general or of those particular expressions of justice which we might call the national purpose and which we try to embody in constitutional law.

Hence, the vice of the rule of law also applies to constitutional law, as we may see from the story which was rehearsed by Professor Cushman yesterday. You have a constitutional code—Mr. O'Brian's code, for example—which, in its time, was just, gradually and fortunately giving way to a new code—Judge Wyzanski's, and Father Snee's. This, I say, is fortunate, and the very vagueness of our Constitution is the source of this good fortune, since it enables the court to use its wisdom and its moral and imaginative insight in order to make a needed adaptation. It is this element of personalism which enables us to tolerate the degree of constitutionalism which our law imposes upon us. Such adaptation should not be an effort to take one supposedly permanent code and put in its place a new code which will really be permanent. For in time this new code will and must also change. And it is not because we do not believe in justice, but precisely because we do believe in justice—I am not afraid to say eternal justice—that this continual readaptation must take place.

I have a word or two of conclusion. If there is anything in what I say, it follows, first, that in fact our system of government, including our administration of justice, is a mixture of constitutionalism and personalism and that both are needed and both are good. Secondly, it follows that we should not make an ideal of the rule of law without regard to the ideal of discretion or personal wisdom also, and that we should not feel too great uneasiness when we are unable to achieve a complete regularization of the judicial process. Thirdly, I suggest that instead of the opportunities for personal discretion simply being swept under the rug as a rather shameful and exceptional thing, the virtues of both personalism and constitutionalism should be admitted and the proper relation between them should be made an explicit subject of study. And finally—perhaps this really doesn't need to be said—it follows that the education of future judges and of government officials should be not only a legal education, but also a liberal education.

VII

A heavy rain during most of Saturday discouraged all but a few members of the Conference from making the planned visit to Lexington Green and to the Concord battlefield. But Vice-Dean and Mrs. Hall invited everyone to come to tea at their house in Concord; wood fires made the afternoon cheerful despite the rain outside; and so passed one of the pleasantest hours of the three days.

On Saturday evening the Conference assembled in Memorial Hall for its final gathering, the Marshall Bicentennial Dinner. The Great Hall, built in honor of Harvard men who had died in the War of 1861-65, was full of warm memories. On one wall was the framed standard of the 20th Massachusetts Infantry, under which Oliver Wendell Holmes, Jr., and his classmates of 1861 had gone forth to war. Behind the speaker's table hung the flags of the many nations represented in the membership of the Conference. An orchestra of strings played chamber music heard in the United States in the time of Chief Justice Marshall.

After dinner, Dean Griswold called the meeting to order and referred at the outset to the fact that this gathering occurred on the ninety-fourth birthday of Professor Emeritus Samuel Williston, who had been the teacher of many of those gathered in the audience. Dean Griswold had called on Mr. Williston during the afternoon and had taken him the greetings of the Conference.

DEAN GRISWOLD

Arthur Sutherland has had his research team hard at work on the matter, and they have ascertained that Chief Justice Marshall was born on September 24, 1755, at 9:16 P.M., Eastern Daylight Saving Time. And so we are at this moment entering upon the third century of the Marshall era.

It is truly appropriate that we should have had this gathering in honor of the great Chief Justice who did so much through his life and work to develop the ideas and standards of government under law in this country. It is appropriate, too, that we should have at this celebration, which, in essence, is a peculiarly American occasion, distinguished visitors from many parts of the world, whose flags stand on the platform above you. For we are all engaged in the common task of trying to achieve this ideal of government under law. Throughout the world, mankind is striving to achieve government under law. In the course of time, many of the principles have been learned, but the application of those principles must often be learned anew by each generation.

One of the principles which has been developed in this quest is that of the separation of powers, which, like any good principle, is not an absolute. It's appropriate for this conference, I think, to refer to the fact that the principle of the separation of powers has never been stated more clearly than in the Constitution of our Commonwealth of Massachusetts. And I would like to read Article Thirty of that Constitution, with particular reference to its closing phrase:

> In the government of this Commonwealth, the legislative department shall never exercise the executive and judicial powers or either of them. The executive shall never exercise the legislative and judicial powers or either of them. The judicial shall never exercise the legislative and executive powers or either of them, to the end it may be a government of laws and not of men.

We have, here at this conference, truly a galaxy of Chief

Justices, but we have one who has been seen by the Conference for the first time this evening, one who is very close to the hearts of all of us. One of the functions of a chief justice is to hold court, and Chief Justice Qua has been holding court this week, this being the week which is appointed by law for the Supreme Judicial Court to sit in the western counties of the state. Chief Justice Qua is going to give a word of greeting from the bench and bar of Massachusetts to our distinguished guests, and to the Conference. And before calling him to the rostrum, I would like merely to observe the well-known fact, that the court over which he presides has a much longer history, a much longer continuous history than that over which Chief Justice Warren presides.

CHIEF JUSTICE QUA*

When I learned a moment ago of the exact minute of John Marshall's debut into this vale of tears, I looked at my watch instinctively, and I saw that either John Marshall was one minute too soon, or my watch was one minute too fast, and when I get home I'm going to fix that, because I want to be synchronized with John Marshall, and I want to stay that way as long as I can.

I regret very much that I have not been able to attend the meetings of this conference, all of which I should like to have attended, but my legislature, whose commands we have to obey, a long time ago said that we should go to Pittsfield and Springfield and some other places this last week, and so we shall go that way. My sixteenth or twentieth successor in office will be going there at the same time, because those things don't change in this Commonwealth.

Now everybody who lives hereabouts knows that Boston is the hub of the universe. And everybody knows that Harvard is the hub of Boston. And everybody knows that the

* STANLEY E. QUA, *Chief Justice of the Supreme Judicial Court of Massachusetts.* Chief Justice Qua was born in Lowell, Massachusetts, in 1880. After finishing his education at Dartmouth College and the Harvard Law School he began practice at the Massachusetts Bar in 1904. He became a Judge of the Superior Court in 1921 and was appointed to the Supreme Judicial Court of the Commonwealth in 1934. Since 1947 he has been Chief Justice.

Law School is the hub of Harvard. Of course, I have heard it said that some people, somewhere, a few people, possibly do not recognize these three great postulates, but they'll come to see them in time. And I know, from what I have seen here tonight, that they are all true, because we have here with us so many distinguished men who have come to the hub of the universe and the hub of Boston and the hub of Harvard from all parts of the earth,—even from such remote corners as England. And I won't name all the others, but you've seen these gentlemen here, and they come because they realize the three propositions that I stated at the outset.

And all I have to say, really, is that we are glad they are here, and we welcome them most sincerely, and we hope they will come again, and I wish to extend to them the heartiest welcome and good wishes on behalf of the Commonwealth of Massachusetts, its judiciary and its bar.

Dean Griswold then introduced the first of the principal speakers of the evening, President Pusey of Harvard University.

ADDRESS

Justice, the University, and the Professions

NATHAN MARSH PUSEY

There are many unexpected things that have happened to me in the two years that I have been the President of Harvard College; not the least of them is eating a meal in this room. I had heard a rumor that people once did that, long, long ago, and this evening I've been hearing about the behavior of certain undergraduates who once dined here. I've also been told that many of them are here tonight, and I would just like to commend those people for the remarkable restraint they have shown in their behavior.

The subject under consideration here has been government under law. The discussion quite properly was not narrowly confined, but frequently encompassed a variety of problems and considerations sometimes perhaps only distantly related to the theme. Yet never has the conversation moved far from the question of justice in the affairs of men, and the responsibility implicit in law, and imposed on all who work with the law, to endeavor to serve this end. Perhaps, therefore, the more inclusive theme has been justice. If so, the talk we have been having is only one more chapter in a discussion that has been going on for a very long time.

Without going back to a more distant antiquity, we can find a proximate beginning of this conversation near the very headwaters of western literature in an indignant cry made long ago by a peasant farmer against what he called the "crooked judgments" of certain "gift-devouring princes". Thus early in our western tradition, we meet an appeal from horrendous fact to moral law with a refusal to concur in a situation simply because it *is*, or to bow without protest before obvious injustice simply because of the strength of the party committing it. Ever since, although force has never abated her insistence, there have always been some ready to stand with Hesiod, unwilling like him to accept as wisdom the hawk's statement to the nightingale that "he is a fool who tries to withstand the stronger." If there is any one thing deeply rooted in western civilization it is this tradition of moral protest against the unjust and inconsiderate use of strength.

Another example will underscore the early origin of this enduring concern for justice. You will remember reading of that afternoon more than two thousand years ago when he who has long been a symbol in the west of the thinking man, and so of the use of reason and analysis in human affairs, was stopped as he was hurrying away from the Peiraeus to make his way back to his own city. He had gone down to the harbor town earlier in the day to participate in a religious observance. His duty, done he wanted to go home, but was overtaken, and then persuaded—persuaded, not forced, despite a playful threat of force—to remain for dinner and to see a torch race in the evening. Scarcely had he arrived at the home of Cephalus, however, when he found himself involved in a discussion that has never since ceased to intrigue and instruct our western world. Called upon to explain what justice is, and its power among men, he embarked upon a discussion that must have lasted for hours even if only a small part of what is recorded was actually said.

It is a tribute to the importance of the subject that the discussion of that evening is still going on. Socrates went a long way round in trying to demolish the heretical view, stated as forcibly then perhaps as it has ever been stated, that the word justice is an excessively high abstraction virtually devoid of meaning, having almost no correspondence with any actuality. Socrates wanted to show both that justice *is,* and that it is to be chosen. But in the end, you will recall, he could do no more perhaps than affirm that there is a pattern of it laid up in heaven for the guidance of him who wants it.

At the end of that very long evening Socrates could do no more than assert that justice exists and has a place in the affairs of men. Perhaps at the end of our three days of discussion we have done no better. But if this is true, it is also true that we have done no less. For there have been few speeches made here during the past few days that have failed to make appeal to moral principle. Implicit in virtually everything said has been a conviction that in most human affairs there is a right as well as a wrong way. The late Mr. Justice Jackson maintained in the Godkin lectures he was to have given here last spring that the safety of the juridical order depends in the last analysis upon an informed and committed citizenry—both informed and committed, but no less committed than informed. If this be true, then from the evidence given here, it is clear there is still much of this kind of preservative for free institutions in our country and in the West. We are not yet ready to tailor our values to accord with men and events.

Through the discussion of these days there has repeatedly shone an allegiance to a large number of political and moral principles. Basic to the whole discussion has been the tenet that government exists for the sake of the individual, and that there is a limit to what government can do to him. It seems to have been pretty generally agreed that human affairs must be guided by a sense of decency and fair play, that personality is more to be regarded than property, that men are morally obligated to try to be reasonable and be guided by reason. There have been repeated references to "fundamental notions of fairness and justice" and to "the precepts of reason and good conscience". We have been reminded again and again of the worth and importance of the individual, and we have been told, correctly, that this was a religious insight before it became a political aim. There seems to have been an almost universal recognition that thought we have only very imperfect scales to weigh values, as one said, of this kind in specific situations, the values themselves and, back of them, the agelong concern for justice, are not to be gainsaid. From words spoken here, it would appear rather that we are still committed with Socrates to the view that the word justice can have meaning, that it stands for something independent of force, that it is desirable for men, and that both law and government exist to foster its realization.

The fourth century before Christ and the last century were not the only times in history when analysis laid bare the hypocrisy that can inevitably be found beneath many human pretensions to virtue and thus cast doubt upon virtue itself. For almost a century some of the more searching currents in the thinking of the western world worked to make it increasingly difficult to keep a grasp on principle. This produced in an important segment of the population, including large numbers of those within the universities and in the professions, a deep aversion to discussion of moral principles —an aversion strengthened by the too ready habit of indiscriminating individuals to appeal without conviction to principle or to seem to understand without ever getting near the root of a matter. The efficacy of principle is brought into question by many less amiable than the old Scottish preacher whose practice was to extricate himself from treacherous discussion with his parishioners with this statement: "It may not be right, and it may not be just, but it is the will of God." If only the will of God could be so certainly known!

If the debilitating prejudice against admitting considerations of principle is now abating, a reason is not far to seek. There have always been some to maintain that the world of knowledge owes little to events. Yet, surely it is the events of our century that have been forcing this particular change in intellectual convention. It is the wars and inventions of this century, the acts of inhumanity it has seen, and the cynical misuse of elements in our civilized tradition which have been quickening fresh interest in the nature and authority of principles long voiced only by rote whose existence was all too recently either denied or casually and indifferently taken for granted.

In a recent conversation, the Principal of the University

of Aberdeen told me happily about a statement of a former teacher of his—obviously a more perceptive Scot than the preacher just quoted—to the effect that "a long look in the dark is worth any number of your penny candles."

We have been having such a long look in the dark at the acts of violence within and among the nations of our time, that lines are again beginning to be drawn distinctly between those for whom, as another has said, "all law is 'what the Sovereign commands' and those who recognize some kind of superior 'Law' that is binding because it is *intrinsically right* and *reasonable*."

This surely is gain. But have we then only to rejoice? Quite clearly the justification for this and similar conferences is not simply to reaffirm allegiance to principle in the abstract, and to moral order, welcome as this is as a refreshing change. It is rather to suggest a responsibility again and always to inquire how principles work in particular instances and how they are constantly both to be used and defended. Our proper concern is not justice in the abstract, but the work-a-day practice of justice. The purpose of such a meeting as this then is to give us a fresh view of the goal and encourage us to go to work. And there is need for new effort.

For it is not only people in the universities and professions who have been showing a reawakened interest in our moral and political tradition. Many from various parts of society have in recent years been increasingly ready to make professions of principle and eager to come forward to protect and defend what they take to be our best tradition. A few have done this for transparently dishonest reasons, not because they know or care about the tradition, but because they find it a useful tool. But the great majority clearly have acted in good faith. They *do* care about the country and its traditions. They want to serve and protect their heritage. Many of these are apt to do so in a crude, uninformed, therefore finally destructive fashion. You can cite your own examples. A moral resurgence may be evident in their acts, but it is more to the point that the great majority of them give added testimony that moral intent must ever be shored up with a vast amount of understanding and knowledge if good rather than harm is to result. Our moral convictions may antecede examination, discussion, and debate, but is it also true that it is only as they are raised from obscurantism by examination, discussion, and debate that they rightly and safely become operative in human affairs.

Recently there has been an extraordinary amount of vociferous talk calculated to return our attention to the central truths of our political inheritance. But in too many instances have not these efforts been so ill-informed that the tradition carelessly held up by well-meaning people for enforced admiration could not fail to present itself to many as a miserable caricature of the real thing? And the end is not yet. There was a peculiarly unpleasant instance only a few days ago. I refer to what must have seemed to many an incredibly misguided attack on the Fund for the Republic and its much maligned president.

This Fund, as you know, was set up in order that there be an institution among us to devote single-minded attention to our political inheritance and especially the preservation of our liberties. Several of the trustees of this Fund are here tonight. Their program was launched with this statement: "Basic to human welfare is general acceptance of the dignity of man. This rests on the conviction that man is endowed with certain unalienable rights and must be regarded as an end in himself, not as a cog in the mechanism of society or a mere means to some social end." There is more in the same vein. As a statement by which they were to be guided, it had been laid down as early as 1950 that "The Foundation [will] support activities directed toward the elimination of restrictions on freedom of thought, inquiry, and expression in the United States, and the development of policies and procedures best adapted to protect these rights in the face of persistent international tension." The record should show to any fair-minded observer that in more than two years of operation the Fund has hewed to this aim.

And yet what happens? Its efforts are denounced in the public press as un-American by the leader of another group which is also professedly seeking to serve the country's best interest. *Sunt lacrimae rerum.* It would of course be foolhardy in view of evidence repeatedly brought forth—most recently, for example, in the findings of the Australian Royal Commission on Espionage—to close our eyes to the very real danger of Communist espionage. But does not this kind of unwarranted attack from the inside prove also that we are under urgent necessity to be saved from ill-informed, unqualified protectors, and does it not establish beyond cavil the need for the Fund's effort?

There are other examples of the same kind of misguided zeal where violence is done to such central articles in our tradition as respect for evidence and fair play. The several instances when attempts have been made to eradicate all mention of the United Nations from the curricula of public schools belong in this category. For surely obscurantism is not an article in the American creed. And there are other sadly familiar efforts motivated by a runaway desire to achieve security.

The chief trouble with most assertions of principle is that they lead very quickly to self-righteousness. Our feelings get involved, then out the window goes reason. We are right, and the other fellow a fool or a hypocrite. Unfortunately sometimes he is! The final judgment in these matters, of course, has to be left to the Lord. But meanwhile it is necessary to remember that it is the peculiar mission of the university, and of all professions which have their nurturing roots within the university, to believe in principle, yes,— but also to have the skill, the knowledge, and the will to work for increased understanding and the resolution of conflict. We cannot—we must not—plead indifference or retire from the field simply because the matter is difficult and feelings run high.

It is of course true that in virtually any issue of moment, different people will see the path of principle leading in different directions. This is as unfortunate as it appears to be inevitable, and it makes the matter of determining exactly what principle says in a particular instance most difficult. But it does not destroy the validity of principle or the necessity for new effort. There is a responsibility upon the members of a profession to keep on trying.

It has been said of tradition in literature that it does not consist "in preserving a form or set of forms, but in keeping alive an interest in the solution of contemporary problems in contemporary terms or materials." If in this statement the phrase "contemporary terms" be understood to include the grand precepts of the juridical order we have inherited, then surely the same can also be said of government and law.

It is because of this that certain recent examples of activity in the great tradition, where knowledge and devotion to principle have worked together, can bring encouragement to us all. Not every case has been abandoned to the ignorantly insistent. Here in our own community, for example, Professor Sutherland and his colleagues have worked quietly to throw light on the activity of the Communists in America by making available a digest of the principal judicial and administrative hearings in which the Communist party has been involved. Professor Stouffer has produced his book *Communism, Conformity and Civil Liberties.* In volume after volume the real thing as it operates in Russia has been studied and explained to the American public by various people on the staff of the Russian Research Center. Above all perhaps should be cited the example of the Dean of the Harvard Law School who with his colleagues, in the difficult matter of the use of the Fifth Amendment, in a time of such emotional tension that reason has been all but stifled in parlor, office, and club, sought conscientiously and courageously to bring information to bear. The dictate of prudence in times such as those through which we have come is to say nothing. Painfully difficult on the other hand is the exercise of professional responsibility. Under its compulsion one is bid not to seek refuge in silence and thus avoid censure, but to stand for principle, to work for understanding, and while avoiding self-righteousness, to strive to help people to rational judgment in a difficult situation in full awareness of as broad a range of relevancies as possible. In the eyes of this university, the professional conduct of the Dean and his colleagues has been of a very high order. Knowledge, commitment, courage—all three make part of the professional life, and all three must be involved in our efforts.

A perceptive literary critic said recently that, "The problem of the modern literary artist . . . is . . . to find ways of handling knowledge in a context of value." I have been trying to suggest that this is also the problem that confronts teachers and lawyers. Conditions for its favorable solution may be better now than they have been for a long time. There seems indeed to be freshening interest in considerations of value and new hope in the possibility of their solution. Technical knowledge adequate for new endeavor is abundantly at hand, and there will be more of it. It is to be hoped, therefore, that we have come to a time when we can move forward in a new creative effort to understand and practice what is best in our tradition, and in doing so sacrifice nothing either in our devotion to reason or in our debt to faith.

Our meeting was called to honor John Marshall. I have been told he was a very conservative kind of fellow; and yet surely he was no reactionary. He said in a letter to Charles Mercer in 1827 that the best that can be done for the mass of the people is to educate them. This responsibility lies especially on us in the universities and in the professions in the matter of civil liberties, in the proper sphere of government, and all the rest. In the same letter he went on to say, "But as our country fills up how shall we escape the evils which have followed a dense population." This is the great problem that now lies before us.

This meeting called to honor John Marshall should have had the attendant result of reminding us of the requirements of mind and heart and will necessary if we are to continue to move along toward the more perfect justice for which man has been seeking at least since the time of Hesiod.

The tradition in which we work and which we are called

to serve is primarily and inalienably intellectual and experimental. But it is also moral. It envisages a mind working with dedication and direction. It is to be hoped that our meeting will have served to call us all to renewed confidence in this faith.

After President Pusey had concluded his address, Dean Griswold introduced the Chief Justice of the United States.

CHIEF JUSTICE WARREN*

The first thing I want to do is to inform the Chief Justice of Massachusetts that I am thoroughly aware that I am here talking at the hub of the hub of the hub of the universe. I would have him know, also, that I have been acquainted with that fact for a long period of time. When I was a boy in California, we had a very distinguished visitor from Boston in San Francisco—it was a lady, a rather elderly lady. She had lived in Boston all her life, as had her ancestors since the Pilgrims landed. She was finally prevailed upon to go to California, to San Francisco, and when she arrived there, everyone wanted to be very kind to her and show her the city in the best light possible, so they put her in a very fine apartment overlooking the Golden Gate. She was there about a month, and apparently had a delightful time; and when she was about to leave, someone said, "Well, Mrs. So-and-so, how do you like California and San Francisco?" "Well," she said, "it's a very nice state. San Francisco seems to be a very nice city; the climate's been fine; the people have been very nice to me; but you know, I just can't get used to being 3000 miles away from the ocean!"

---

* EARL WARREN, *Chief Justice of the United States.* Chief Justice Warren was born in California in 1891, took degrees at the University of California in 1912 and 1914 and was admitted to the California Bar in the latter year. He practiced law in San Francisco and Oakland, and, beside other public service, he became Attorney General of his state in 1939, and served as Governor of California from 1943 to 1953. He was appointed Chief Justice of the United States in 1953. He was Chairman of the United States John Marshall Bicentennial Commission created by the Congress in 1954.

Now this has been such a wonderful experience for me, that I've been wondering this afternoon if we couldn't repeat it every year. I think it's the precise time of year that it should be held—on Marshall's birthday. And I think there should be a requirement of law that the Chief Justice and all of his associates should attend every year. And I'll tell you what my theory is. I suppose this university, like all the universities in the country, calls its football team back to the university about two weeks before it calls the students back, before the football season opens. They bring them back to drill them once more in the fundamentals of the game, and when the coach gets them there, he doesn't teach them a lot of new, fancy plays the first couple of weeks. He teaches them the fundamentals of blocking and tackling, no matter whether they are freshmen or are seniors who have played football since infancy; no matter whether they have blocked and tackled thousands of times, that is what he drills them in. And I think that our court, on the same theory, should come back here two weeks before the October term and do some work in the fundamentals of our business; because what blocking and tackling is to football, constitutionalism and obedience to law are to our system of justice.

This has truly been a great Conference, and on behalf of the United States Bicentennial John Marshall Commission, I want to thank President Pusey, Dean Griswold, and the members of the Faculty of the Harvard Law School for the spirit of this observance. I have been stimulated by it, as I'm sure all of you have been. My only regret is that at this particular time, everything appropriate to be said has been said, and has been said so well as to defy embellishment.

Without reflecting in the slightest on the other splendid messages that have been brought to this Conference, I want to say that there have been two times, prior to this moment, when I thought the Conference could be properly closed. One of those was this morning, at the conclusion of the address by Mr. John Lord O'Brian. No more fitting benediction could be given to a conference of this kind than his address. And then, again, I think it should have ended just before I stood up. To have ended it on the thoughtful and scholarly note of President Pusey would have been an ideal conclusion.

So I come to this final gathering faced with a fearful dilemma. My only choice is to grab either the horn of repetition or the horn of irrelevance. But, it seems, that has been more or less my lot through life. You know, at school, invariably, we youngsters were called on alphabetically to recite, and when the teacher reached the W's, there was rarely anything left to be said. This difficulty followed me into politics, too, and I recall very well that the first time I ran for public office, I encountered it in a very aggravated form. There were a great many candidates for county office in the county in which I was running, and in order to stimulate interest, we all used to travel together, and we would have five or six meetings every evening—school house here, public center there, and so forth—but we would all go to all of them, and we would all speak. In order to be perfectly fair, they used to have us speak alphabetically. You know, nobody went to these meetings except the candidates and three or four retainers of each one of the candidates—that was the audience—and as the speaker would finish, he'd leave, he'd take his retainers with him and go to the next meeting. Well, I rarely had many people to talk to, but one night it got down to a situation where there was just one fellow left in the room. Not to be ungrateful, I gave him the full treatment; I just gave him my speech as I would have given it if there had been a full auditorium, and when I finished, I stepped down, and I said, "Well, my friend, I'm very grateful to you; you've been very kind to show me the courtesy to stay here and hear me." He said, "You're quite welcome, but really, I'm not entitled to any thanks. My name is Young, and I'm the next speaker!"

For me it has been a particularly thrilling experience to hear the addresses of our distinguished visitors from all parts of the globe. My brother Chief Justices, the Master of the

Rolls, Professor Tunc, and all who have come from afar, have done great honor to our country as well as to your great University. After hearing them, and visiting with them, I marvel, not at the difference of approach that we all have to the problems of government under the law, nor at the diversity of opinion concerning them, but I marvel, rather, at how much we have in common in this regard, and at how understanding men in all parts of the world become when they dedicate themselves to the rule of law.

The twin spirits of contention and ill-will that encompass but divide the world today have been entirely absent from this gathering. On the contrary, there has been a personification here of the words of Alexander Pope in his essay "On Man," where he says:

> For forms of government let fools contest.
> What ere is best administered, is best.
> For modes of faith let graceless zealots fight.
> His can't be wrong, whose life is in the right.

No nation has a monopoly on freedom. No people has a copyright on law. We all learn from each other, and from those who have preceded us throughout civilization. I like to believe that in America at least we want to live in that spirit. In the courtroom of our Supreme Court at Washington, we have written in stone our acknowledgment of indebtedness to those of all lands who have contributed to government under law as we understand it. On the frieze of the south wall of our courtroom are carved the likenesses of the law-givers who lived before Christ — Menes, Hammurabi, Moses, Solomon, Lycurgus, Solon, Draco, Confucius, and Octavius. On the north wall are those who lived after Christ —Justinian, Mohammed, Charlemagne, King John, St. Louis, Hugo Grotius, Blackstone, John Marshall, and Napoleon. Only one of those whose images appear on the frieze of our courtroom is American—John Marshall alone. And we show our respect, our honor, and our indebtedness to all of these law-givers of the world without regard to race or religion or country. Over the entrance to the Supreme

Court building itself, where the world may see it at all times, is the inscription, "Equal justice under law." That is our profession of faith. It is our goal. We do not claim we have achieved it, but we are constantly reaching for it, as many other nations have done since before recorded history.

At the dawn of our civilization, which was ushered in by the deliverance of Israel out of bondage, we find these people in a federation and living under a constitution, the covenant they had made with their God. Their tribes were federated, their communities integrated, yet they governed themselves without any central authority, without any king, without any executive of any kind, without any legislature, without any courts, or without any hierarchy. They governed themselves merely by adherence to their basic covenant, and for hundreds of years, thus governing themselves, they avoided both anarchy and subjugation by the despotisms of various kinds that surrounded them. And even after they chose a king, some hundred years later, he too lived under the covenant his people had made with their God. Five hundred years before Christ, there were hundreds of commonwealths in the Mediterranean basin with republican forms of government, many of them in form resembled Rome. But of these only Rome survived for any great length of time, and in doing so, Rome made its greatest contribution to our civilization—the contribution of law.

A thousand years ago, little Iceland had a constitution and the elements of an independent judiciary; and although it was marooned up there in the frozen north, by-passed by the commerce of the world, it has continuously had a constitution and an independent judiciary during all of those one thousand years.

In the fourteenth century, several monarchies in Europe had constitutional similarities to England, and gave promise of like development. One by one, they succumbed to some form of despotism, until at the end of the eighteenth century, England alone retained a government capable of securing both public order and freedom of the individual. Through the ages, nations striving for freedom have had their ups and downs, and this age in which we are living is no exception.

But every struggle that is made for government under law anywhere in the world, contributes to the sum total of the force of law everywhere. We in America believe that the independence of our judiciary is a major factor in our government of laws. We point to our separation of powers, to judicial review as we know it, and to other features of our institutions that make that independence possible.

Our nations put their faith in their adaptations of the parliamentary system. The fact is, those nations that are free today are so, not merely because of the forms of government they have, but because, and only because, their people are determined to be free. How they acquired this spirit of freedom and how they established the virility and independence of their institutions depends upon their experience with both freedom and despotism. Some of these experiences have been written into constitutions. Others have been written only in the hearts of people, but they are nonetheless indelibly written.

I doubt if anything in modern times has done more to preserve an independent judiciary than the action of the Supreme Court of Norway when it was face-to-face with the Hitler despotism in the late war. When Germany occupied Norway, Hitler wanted the Norwegian institutions to be continued during the occupation, because he knew the people were a law-abiding people, and he felt that if they could be led to believe that they were living under their own institutions, they would be more tractable under the occupation. He pleaded with the Supreme Court to remain in office. The Chief Justice, after consulting with his government in exile, agreed, providing the court could administer and guarantee the protection of Norwegian law. Hitler glibly consented, but proceeded immediately to undercut the court. When that became obvious, the entire court, realizing their action probably would bring about their deaths or incarceration in prison camps that were often worse than death, resigned in a body, violently protesting against the oppression of their people. Immediately thereafter, the clergy followed the same example, then they were followed by the teachers, by the university professors, by the students, and other governmental bodies—all of them rose in protest. Resistance groups sprang up all over the country. Sabotage replaced order, and for the remainder of the war, Norway became a total liability to its oppressor. And I am sure that nothing in the long history of that country has done more to preserve the independence of its judiciary than the indomitable spirit shown by Chief Justice Paul Berg and his Supreme Court.

I also suppose that one of the greatest foundation stones in the judicial independence in England was the day when Lord Coke, told by his king that his court must confirm to the king the prerogative to dispense with laws in certain cases or be dismissed, said this: "For my place, I care little. I am old and worn out in the service of the crown. But I am mortified to find that Your Majesty thinks me capable of giving a judgment which none but an ignorant or a dishonest man can give." "I am determined," said the king, "to have twelve judges who will all be of my mind in this matter." "Your Majesty," he said, "may find twelve judges of your mind, but hardly twelve lawyers." He thus forfeited his position as Chief Justice.

It is said that some of the other judges of that court recanted and prostrated themselves before the king. Their names are not known.

In this state of Massachusetts, some time after the Revolutionary War, in 1787, when the people were greatly harassed by their debts and by the judgments of the courts, you will recall, Shays' Rebellion took place in this state. And during the course of it, a great mob formed at a courthouse, for the purpose of preventing the Chief Justice and his court from entering and opening the session. Chief Justice William Cushing, later of the Supreme Court of the United States, decided that court must open, and he, with his court behind him, marched in to that mob. The mob fell back sullenly, but continually, with the Chief Justice advancing, bayonets pressing against his breast all the time, until he reached the courthouse. The court walked in, took the bench, and opened court in the accustomed manner.

It is said that this incident had much to do with the ratification of the Constitution by the state of Massachusetts. Who knows how much it may have had to do with John Marshall's opinion in *Marbury v. Madison* and his other opinions establishing the independence of the courts? Of this I think we can be sure: remembrance of that experience has done much to inspire and fortify the long line of able judges in this state, as well as to inspire a great bar, both of which have contributed greatly to the development of our country. And so it is in all free lands. Human experiences, courage, sacrifice, travail, are the backbone of the will to be free.

And it will not change, at least, until that day Kipling was thinking about when he wrote:

> When Earth's last picture is painted, and the tubes are twisted and dried,
> When the oldest colors have faded, and the youngest critic has died,
> We shall rest, and, faith, we shall need it—lie down for an aeon or two,
> Till the Master of All Good Workmen shall set us to work anew!
>
> And those that were good shall be happy: they shall sit in a golden chair;
> They shall splash at a ten-league canvas with brushes of comets' hair;
> They shall find real saints to draw from—Magdalene, Peter, and Paul;
> They shall work for an age at a sitting and never be tired at all!
>
> And only the Master shall praise us, and only the Master shall blame;
> And no one shall work for money, and no one shall work for fame;
> But each for the joy of the working, and each, in his separate star

Shall draw the Thing as he sees It for the God of Things as they are!*

That day is not to be for us. While through the ages human nature has cried out for freedom and justice, the same human nature has always denied those things to others. None of us can afford to be too proud of our handiwork as we daily see its shortcomings passing in review before us. But we can all strive for equal justice under law; we can honor the people in every land who work for the same end. Occasionally we can meet, as we have met here, to learn that we share common weaknesses and frustrations, to encourage each other to find common strengths, and to cherish common hopes. So doing we will find, as we have in these three days, that despite all differences of form, we aspire together to one ideal of justice.

When the Chief Justice of the United States had come to the end of his address, Dean Griswold spoke the thanks of the University "to all those who have come to give us their thoughts and learning and wisdom; and to all of those who have come as members of the Conference to take part in these great meetings." He asked the people to rise, and the National Anthem closed the Conference on Government Under Law.

---

* From: THE SEVEN SEAS, by Rudyard Kipling. Reprinted by permission of Mrs. George Bambridge and Doubleday & Company, Inc.; Methuen Co., Ltd.; and the Macmillan Company of Canada.

INDEX